W9-BAL-903

BUILDING LITERACY
IN THE CONTENT AREAS

Thomas G. Gunning

Central Connecticut State University
Adjunct Professor

Southern Connecticut State University
Emeritus

Boston | New York | San Francisco
Mexico City | Montreal | Toronto | London | Madrid | Munich | Paris
Hong Kong | Singapore | Tokyo | Cape Town | Sydney

Series Editor: Aurora Martínez-Ramos
Editorial Assistant: Beth Slater
Development Editor: Alicia Reilly
Senior Marketing Manager: Elizabeth Fogarty
Editorial-Production Manager: Elaine Ober
Editorial-Production Services: Helane M. Prottas
Photo Research: Helane M. Prottas/Posh Pictures
Interior Design: Carol Somberg
Cover Coordinator: Linda Knowles
Composition and Prepress Buyer: Linda Cox
Manufacturing Buyer: Megan Cochran
Electronic Composition: Dayle Silverman/Silver Graphics

For related titles and support materials, visit our
online catalog at www.ablongman.com.

    Between the time Website information is gathered and then published, it is not unusual for
some sites to have closed. Also, the transcription of URLs can result in unintended typographical errors. The publisher would appreciate notification where these errors occur so that they
may be corrected in subsequent editions.

Library of Congress Cataloging-in-Publication Data

Gunning, Thomas G.
   Building literacy in the content areas/Thomas G. Gunning.
      p. cm.
   Includes bibliographical references and index.
   ISBN 0-205-31958-0 (alk. paper)—ISBN 0-205-36822-0
   1. Content area reading. 2. Language arts. I. Title.

LB1050.455 .G86 2003
372.47'6--dc21

2002074426

Printed in the United States of America
10 9 8 7 6 5 4 3   RRD-IN

Photo credits begin on page 490 which constitutes a continuation of the copyright page.

*To Andrew Thomas Pizzuto,
the newest member of the family*

BRIEF CONTENTS

SPECIAL FEATURES

EXEMPLARY TEACHING

CONTENTS

vi

6 COLLABORATIVE AND COOPERATIVE APPROACHES FOR LEARNING 188

7 STUDY SKILLS AND STRATEGIES 216

8 WRITING TO LEARN *262*

9 TEACHING CONTENT AREA LITERACY TO DIVERSE LEARNERS *296*

10　READING AND WRITING IN LANGUAGE ARTS AND SOCIAL STUDIES　326

11　READING AND WRITING IN SCIENCE AND MATH　340

12　USING TECHNOLOGY, TRADE BOOKS, AND PERIODICALS IN THE CONTENT AREAS　360

13 *EVALUATING PROGRESS IN THE CONTENT AREAS* 384

14 CREATING AN EFFECTIVE CONTENT AREA PROGRAM 420

PREFACE

GOALS OF THIS TEXT

Building Literacy in the Content Areas presents techniques, strategies, approaches, and materials that will enable you to build the skills students need to become literate in the content areas so that they can successfully read and write about content topics. You will learn how to analyze content area materials in terms of their text characteristics and the demands that these characteristics make upon the reader. You will then learn how to use this information to plan appropriate instruction. Throughout *Building Literacy in the Content Areas*, you will be asked to look at a variety of content area texts in terms of organization, vocabulary, and concepts covered and to assess what level of background knowledge, reading competence, and thinking skills students need to comprehend the texts. You will then be shown teaching techniques and student strategies that best enable students to learn from particular kinds of texts.

Building Literacy in the Content Areas covers all grade levels, so you will find instructional suggestions for students in grades 1 through 12.

Given the current focus on standards and high-stakes tests, this textbook emphasizes setting clear objectives for your students that are grounded in accepted content area standards and conducting ongoing assessment that makes sure your students are making steady progress toward meeting those standards. Higher-order thinking skills, integrating content areas, using multiple sources, and considering multicultural perspectives are other important topics in this textbook.

IMPORTANT FEATURES OF THIS TEXT

Because this is a text on teaching reading and writing in the content areas, techniques and strategies used to learn in the content areas have been incorporated into the text so that you can experience as well as read about them. In the following pages you will get a snapshot of all the main features of this text.

Each chapter starts with a graphic organizer of the main topics you will learn about in the chapter. Before reading each chapter you will be asked to complete an **Anticipation**

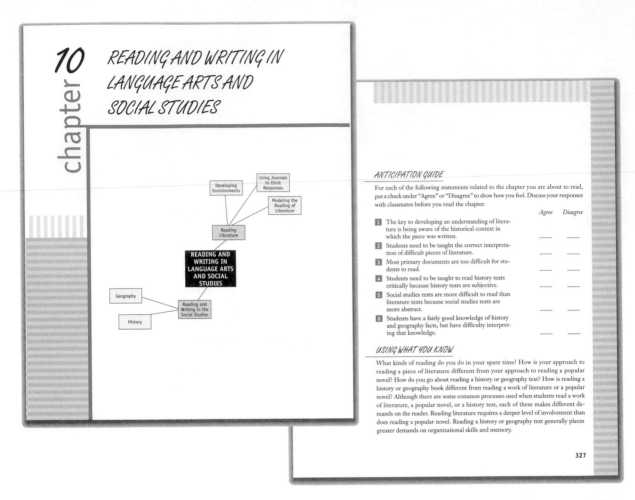

10 chapter

READING AND WRITING IN LANGUAGE ARTS AND SOCIAL STUDIES

Using Journals to Elicit Responses

Developing Envisionments

Modeling the Reading of Literature

Reading Literature

READING AND WRITING IN LANGUAGE ARTS AND SOCIAL STUDIES

Geography

History

Reading and Writing in the Social Studies

ANTICIPATION GUIDE

For each of the following statements related to the chapter you are about to read, put a check under "Agree" or "Disagree" to show how you feel. Discuss your responses with classmates before you read the chapter.

	Agree	Disagree
1 The key to developing an understanding of literature is being aware of the historical context in which the piece was written.	___	___
2 Students need to be taught the correct interpretation of difficult pieces of literature.	___	___
3 Most primary documents are too difficult for students to read.	___	___
4 Students need to be taught to read history texts critically because history texts are subjective.	___	___
5 Social studies texts are more difficult to read than literature texts because social studies texts are more abstract.	___	___
6 Students have a fairly good knowledge of history and geography facts, but have difficulty interpreting that knowledge.	___	___

USING WHAT YOU KNOW

What kinds of reading do you do in your spare time? How is your approach to reading a piece of literature different from your approach to reading a popular novel? How do you go about reading a history or geography text? How is reading a history or geography book different from reading a work of literature or a popular novel? Although there are some common processes used when students read a work of literature, a popular novel, or a history text, each of these makes different demands on the reader. Reading literature requires a deeper level of involvement than does reading a popular novel. Reading a history or geography text generally places greater demands on organizational skills and memory.

327

Guide and to activate your knowledge by answering the questions under **Using What You Know.**

You will also be asked to check your reading periodically through **Checkup** questions posed throughout the text and to reflect on your reading after finishing each chapter. You will find motivating and insightful questions in the **Reflection** boxes at the end of each chapter. These are strategies that you will also be teaching your students.

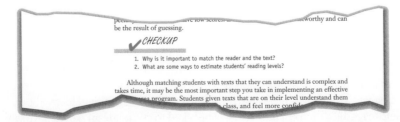

peer... ...ave low scores... ...eworthy and can be the result of guessing.

✓ CHECKUP

1. Why is it important to match the reader and the text?
2. What are some ways to estimate students' reading levels?

Although matching students with texts that they can understand is complex and takes time, it may be the most important step you take in implementing an effective ...ea program. Students given texts that are on their level understand them ... class, and feel more confid...

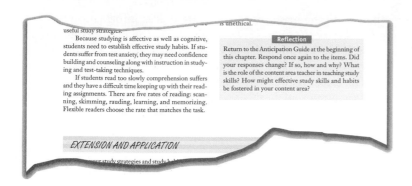

This text carefully considers the nature of student readers. Given the current inclusion movement, this textbook emphasizes instruction that includes *all students*. It suggests how to plan programs and make modifications so that you can provide for struggling learners as well as for achieving students. Approximately 25 percent to 40 percent of today's students have difficulty coping with their content area texts. Rich and extensive marginal annotations for **Struggling Readers** offer strategies, techniques, and materials especially appropriate for students who are struggling to learn.

For English language learners, stress will be placed on learning academic language and the key technical vocabulary of each major subject matter area. Additional information on how to adapt instruction for ELL students can be found in the **English Language Learners** marginal annotations throughout the text.

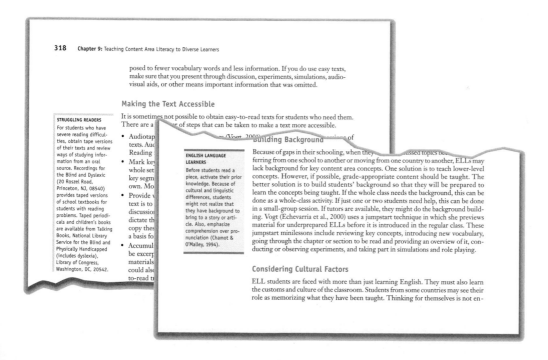

Although textbooks are the main source of content area information for most students, *Building Literacy in the Content Areas* advocates the use of trade books, periodicals, and technology. A **graded list of trade books** appears in Appendix A. It includes many easy-to-read books that can be used if the content area textbook is too difficult.

In addition there are numerous Web sites devoted to the content areas. There are also tools available on the Internet or as software that foster learning. These plus other technological advances and the reading and writing skills needed to get the most benefit from them are discussed within the chapters as well as in the **Using Technology** annotations.

APPENDIX A
GRADED LISTING OF CONTENT AREA TRADE BOOKS

First-Grade Books

Easy First
Morris, Ann. *Tools.* Lothrop, Lee & Shepard, 1992, 32 pp.
Noll, Sally. *Surprise!* Greenwillow, 1997, 24 pp.
Perkins, Al. *The Ear Book.* Random House, 1968, 28 pp.
Siddals, Mary McKenna. *Tell Me a Season.* Houghton Mifflin, 1997, 26 pp.

Middle First
Barton, Byron. *Bones, Bones, Dinosaur Bones.* Crowell, 1990, 30 pp.
Brown, Craig. *In the Spring.* Greenwillow, 1994, 24 pp.
Donnelly, Liza. *Dinosaur Days.* Scholastic, 1987, 30 pp.
Miller, Margaret. *My Five Senses.* Simon & Schuster, 1994, 22 pp.
Morris, Ann. *Work.* Lothrop, Lee & Shepard, 1998, 29 pp.

Ending First
Arnosky, Jim. *Come Out, Muskrats.* Lothrop, Lee & Shepard, 1989, 22 pp.
Barton, Byron. *Dinosaurs, Dinosaurs.* Crowell, 1989, 36 pp.
Greene, Carol. *Truck Drivers Deliver Goods.* The Child's World, 1999, 32 pp.

Demuth, Patrick. *Johnny Appleseed.* Grossett & Dunlap, 1996, 32 pp.
Jordan, Helene J. *How a Seed Grows.* HarperCollins, 1960, 1992, 30 pp.
Ling, Mary. *See How They Grow, Butterfly.* Dorling Kindersley, 1992, 21 pp.
Penner, Lucille. *Dinosaur Babies.* Random House, 1991, 32 pp.
Rotner, Shelley, & Kreisler, Ken. *Nature Spy.* Simon & Schuster, 1992, 26 pp.

Second
Arnosky, Jim. *Otters Under Water.* Putnam, 1992, 24 pp.
Arnosky, Jim. *Every Autumn Comes the Bear.* Putnam, 1993, 28 pp.
Branley, Franklyn M. *Day Light, Night Light.* HarperCollins, 1998, 32 pp.
Brenner, Barbara. *Wagon Wheels.* HarperCollins, 1978, 64 pp.
Chermayeff, Ivan. *Fishy Facts.* Harcourt Brace, 1994, 29 pp.
Demuth, Patricia Brennan. *Achoo! Grossett & Dunlap, 1997, 30 pp.
Fowler, Allan. *Frogs and Toads and Tadpoles, Too.* Children's Press, 1992, 32 pp.
Hopkins, Lee Bennett (Ed.). *Surprises.* HarperCollins, 1986, 64 pp.
Hopkins, Lee Bennett, *Good*

Pocahontas. Random House, 1994, 48 pp.
Rabe, Tish. *On Beyond Bugs! All about Insects.* Random, 1999, 44 pp.
Ryden, Hope. *Joey, the Story of a Baby Kangaroo.* Tamborine, 1994, 38 pp.
Wallace, Karen. *Duckling Days.* Dorling Kindersley, 1999, 32 pp.
Zoehfeld, Kathleen Weidner. *What Lives in a Shell?* HarperCollins, 1994, 26 pp.

Third-Grade Books

Easy Reading Level: Grade 2 (Interest Level: Grade 3)
Dorros, Arthur. *Ant Cities.* HarperCollins, 1987, 32 pp.
Hopkins, L. B. (Ed.) *Questions: Poems of Wonder.* HarperCollins, 1992, 64 pp.
Lundell, Margo. *A Girl Named Helen Keller.* Scholastic, 1995, 48 pp.
Penner, Lucille Recht. *Sitting Bull.* Grossett & Dunlap, 1995, 48 pp.
Dr. Seuss. *The Cat's Quizzer.* Random House, 1976, 62 pp.
Smith, Christine. *How to Draw Cartoons.* Gareth Stevens, 1997, 24 pp.

Average Reading Level: Grade 3

Carefully chosen Web sites can be used to amplify information contained in texts.

information; understanding complex work systems; and working with a variety of technologies. These are the skills of the information age.

✓ CHECKUP

1. What role is technology, and especially the Internet, playing in content area instruction?

TEACHING STUDENTS HOW TO USE THE INTERNET MORE EFFECTIVELY

The Internet has been described as the greatest library in the world, but one in which all the books have been tossed onto the floor. The information is there but it can be hard to find and overwhelming. Typing in key words such as *Martin Luther King* or *diabetes* can turn up thousands of sites. Mixed in with excellent sites are sites of limited value or sites that are too advanced for students.

Although most students may be familiar with the Web, they may not understand how to conduct an efficient search. An efficient search starts with a careful delineation of the topic and the questions that the student hopes to answer and then a determination of whether the information is relevant and reliable. The topic might be assigned or selected. Whether assigned or selected, the student writer must formulate a thesis statement or question to be answered. With novice writers, a key skill is narrowing the topic so that it has reasonable limits. A student interested in the development of the automobile, for instance, might limit her topic to concept or prototype cars. On reflection, she might decide to focus on current concept cars as a

Because today's students have so much more to learn, this textbook presents study skills in detail. It includes explanations of some of the study aids that accompany electronic encyclopedias and other references. Moreover, it highlights writing to learn.

Above all else, *Building Literacy in the Content Areas* is designed to be a practical guide to helping today's students use reading and writing to learn content area subjects. There are numerous step-by-step sample **Lessons** covering a wide range of key topics such as, comprehension, vocabulary, and writing skills, to help students apply these techniques into the classroom.

Exemplary Teaching features in all chapters bring teaching techniques to life with real accounts of effective teaching practices garnered from memoirs of gifted teachers, newspaper accounts, or the author's own observations.

---

88   **Chapter 3:** Building Content Area Vocabulary

LESSON 3.7   Morphemic Elements Lesson

Because they appear first in a word and ge[...]
prefixes are the easiest of the morphemic e[...]
anti- might be introduced.

Step 1: Construct the Meaning of the Prefi[...]

Place the following words on the board: *anti[...]
constitution, antigun, antismoking, antifreeze.* Sor[...]
from a chapter on the Civil War, which stude[...]
meanings of these words. Note how *anti-* ch[...]
precedes. Encourage students to construct a [...]
to see that *anti-* is a prefix. Discuss, too, th[...]
prefixes. Explain to students how knowing t[...]
them figure out unknown words. Show them [...]
that contain prefixes and how they would us[...]
out the words and determine their meanings[...]

Step 2: Guided Practice

Have students complete practice exercises sim[...]

Fill in the blanks with these words containi[...]
antiunion, antifreeze, antismoking.

1. When winter comes, you will need to put[...]
2. One town passed an _____ law that fo[...]
   town.
3. The _____ demonstrators gathered outside [...]
   that the United States planned to send sol[...]
4. The owner of the factory was _____ be[...]
   telling him how to treat his workers.
5. Because they were against the new road, t[...]

Step 3: Application

Have students read the selection about the C[...]
containing the prefix *anti-.* You can also hav[...]
anti- in other reading that they do.

Step 4: Extension

Present the prefix *pro-* and have students c[...]
prefixes. Using words containing the prefix *p*[...]
that they may be in favor of: *proschool, procan*[...]
the prefix *anti-,* they can make a list of things t[...]

---

336   **Chapter 10:** Reading and Writing in Language Arts and Social Studies

EXEMPLARY TEACHING

READING PRIMARY SOURCES

Zev was a typical high school history student. When asked to read and discuss an actual letter in which ex-slaves pleaded to be allowed to retain land that had been given to them but was now about to be taken back, Zev expressed reluctance. He saw history as facts carved in stone, not something that could be imagined or thought about or interpreted: "You can't just read into a document like it's some kind of story that ends any way you want it to" (Holt, 1995, p.41). Zev's teacher was complementing the course textbook with primary sources. Zev read the letter and other primary sources. The letter was an eye-opener. Zev had believed that the slaves were illiterate. Yet the letter was an eloquent plea. Zev shifted his thinking. He began to see the freedpeople in a new light. He changed his view of the problem facing the freedpeople. Illiteracy was not their problem.

Their problem was getting the people in power to listen to them. Zev imagined how the three signers of the letter must have felt. He imagined them sitting around a table drafting and redrafting the letter until it said exactly what they wanted it to say.

Zev then made a connection between the letter writers and more current figures in the Civil Rights Movement. He related their breaking of the literacy barrier to barriers broken by Malcolm X, Martin Luther King, and others. Thinking of the letter writers, Zev was also better able to reflect on one of the overall messages of the unit, which was the concept of *freedom:* Is freedom just freedom from slavery, or is it also the freedom to develop one's abilities and quality of life to the fullest? Zev had learned that to do history is to "pursue an idea, to fit it out with facts, to test it, and to ask what it means" (Holt, 1995, p. 48).

not only ask what the documents have to tell them, they must also ask whether the documents can be trusted. Context is also needed. Interpretation requires knowledge of the times and the circumstances under which the document was produced and also information about the person or group who created the document. One of the goals of using primary documents is to help students become more analytical readers of history. Realizing how history is created, they will be better able to read with a critical eye.

History becomes more understandable if students learn to see similarities in events and draw conclusions about these similarities. In order to learn to form generalizations about historical events, students should ask such questions as these:

• What was the long-term significance of these events?
• What impact did these events have on people living then? Living today?
• What can we who are living today learn from the past?
• And taken together—as a whole—what do these events tell us about the way the world of people works? (Hennings, 1993, p. 368)

Students might create organizers that show how generalizations they have formed are supported, as in the sample organizer shown in Figure 10.1.

Comprehending history also requires understanding historical figures in the context of the times in which they lived. When reading about famous people, students should ask themselves the following questions in order to develop their own hypotheses about historical cause-and-effect relationships.

348   Chapter 11: Reading and Writing in Science and Math

> The **meridian** is the line that bisects the sky by running from the due north point on the horizon up to the zenith and then down to the due south point on the horizon. (Schaff, 1998, p. 7)

Meridian is boldfaced, so it must be important. This word bisects. I've never seen it before. But bi means two, as in bicycle for two wheels and binomial for two numbers. So I think it means divides something in two. And that's what the drawing shows, the sky divided into an eastern part and a western part.

If you don't know where due north and due south are at the place where you're now standing, just look back toward the setting sun. And once you know which way west is, you can figure where north and south are and where the meridian runs. (Schaff, 1998, p. 7)

Let's see. The sentence says, "And once you know which way west is, you can figure where north and south are and where the meridian runs." But I can't. I'll look at the illustration. It shows a man looking west toward where the sun is setting. Well, I do know that the sun rises in the east and sets in the west. But how does that help me figure out which way north is? Let's see; the drawing shows that north is to the right of the man as he stands facing west. Now I get it. But how will I remember that north is to the right and south is to the left when you are facing west? Hey, they call lefthanders southpaws, so I'll just remember it that way. South is to your left when you're facing west.

But why is the meridian, dividing the sky into eastern and western halves, more important than a line dividing the sky into northern and southern halves?. (Schaff, 1998, p. 7)

That's a good question. I wonder why.

The answer is that the sun and almost all heavenly objects—the moon, planets, and most stars—appear to ascend in the eastern half of the sky and descend in the western half of the sky. (Schaff, 1998, p. 7)

Ah ha! Now I get it.

Discuss with the class strategies that you used as you read. Talk over, for instance, how you monitored for reading as you read, how you used an illustration to help you, and how you responded to the author in an interactive way. When the author asked questions, you attempted to answer them.

After modeling the process of thinking your way through a difficult segment of text, provide students with opportunities to do the same. You can have them work in pairs and take turns thinking out loud as they read to a partner. Discuss any difficulties that they may have encountered as they read. Discuss strategies that they use. In their journals, they can reflect on reading strategies that they used as well as on the content that they read. As their reading requires the use of specialized strategies, demonstrate with think-alouds and provide guided practice. For instance, you might

Passages from Books, from textbooks to tradebooks, appear in most chapters to help students see what kinds of reading pupils are expected to do.

ORGANIZATION OF THIS TEXT

The first chapter of *Building Literacy in the Content Areas* explores the nature of content area literacy and discusses basic principles of content area instruction. The second chapter analyzes the kinds of texts that students will be required to read in the content areas and presents ways of assessing the texts and matching readers with texts at the appropriate level. Chapter 3 discusses learning content area vocabulary. Chapters 4, 5, and 6 explore techniques for fostering comprehension. Chapter 7 examines study skills and habits. Chapter 8 discusses writing to learn in the content areas. Chapter 9 considers ways to help all students learn, placing special emphasis on helping those who are struggling. Chapters 10 and 11 highlight techniques that can be used in specific content areas. Chapter 12 highlights the use of trade books, periodicals, and technology. Chapter 13 presents suggestions for evaluating students' progress and looks at assessment issues. Chapter 14 sums up the text and looks at ways to organize and improve literacy instruction in the content areas.

Building Literacy in the Content Areas provides extensive coverage of a variety of key assessment measures and instructional techniques. Particular emphasis has been placed on assisting struggling readers. The text is designed to help you develop the kinds of literacy skills and strategies that will enable all of your students to learn your content more fully and more efficiently.

SUPPLEMENTS FOR STUDENTS AND INSTRUCTORS

Instructor's Manual with Test Bank: For each chapter, the instructor's manual features a series of Learner Objectives, a Chapter Overview, suggestions for Before, After, and During Reading, a list of suggested Teaching Activities, and suggestions for Assessment. The Test Bank contains an assortment of multiple-choice, short essay, and long essay questions for each chapter. This supplement has been written completely by the text author, Tom Gunning.

"TestGen EQ" Computerized Test Bank The printed Test Bank is also available electronically through our computerized testing system, TestGen EQ. The fully networkable test generating software is now available on a multi-platform CD-ROM. The user-friendly interface enables instructors to view, edit, and add questions, transfer questions to tests, and print tests. Search and sort features allow instructors to locate questions quickly and arrange them in a preferred order.

Companion Web Site (http://www.ablongman.com/gunningcontent) Designed for students reading the text, the web site includes the following features:

- *Chapter Overview:* This section previews the chapter's contents and explains the significance of the chapter in terms of understanding literacy instruction.
- *Online Study Guide:* In addition to general suggestions for studying the text, the online study guide previews key concepts; provides focus questions and core questions for students to keep in mind as they read the chapter; and offers suggestions for using a graphic organizer to help students organize and remember material. It includes 10 multiple-choice questions for each chapter.
- *Update:* This section provides updated information and research on key topics covered in the text. Updates appear monthly.
- *Discussion Corner:* This is a Listserv in which the author will post questions concerning key issues and readers will respond and carry on discussions. Students may, for example, discuss how a suggested teaching technique worked for them.
- *Links:* This key section provides links to other relevant and useful web sites.

Allyn and Bacon offers an array of student and instructor supplements on the overall topic of literacy. All are available with this textbook and include:

Allyn & Bacon Digital Media Archive for Literacy: This CD-ROM offers still images, video clips, audio clips, weblinks, and assorted lecture resources that can be incorporated into multimedia presentations in the classroom.

Professionals in Action: Literacy Video: This 90-minute video consists of 10- to 20-minute segments. The first four segments provide narrative along with actual classroom teaching footage. The final segments present, in a question-and-answer format, discussions by leading experts in the field of literacy. Segments include: Phonemic Awareness, Teaching Phonics, Helping Students Become Strategic Readers, Organizing for Teaching with Literature, and Discussions of Literacy and Brain Research with experts.

Allyn & Bacon Literacy Video Library: Three videos that address core topics covered in the classroom: reading strategies; developing literacy in multiple intelligences classrooms; developing phonemic awareness. and much more. Videos features renowned reading scholars — Richard Allington, Dorothy Strickland, and Evelyn English.

VideoWorkshop Teaching Guide for Reading (with CD-ROM): VideoWorkshop is a total teaching and learning system containing 50–60 minutes of video footage illustrating textbook concepts. The Instructor's Teaching Guide contains a multitude of ideas, teaching suggestions, and answers to integrate VideoWorkshop into courses. A correlation guide helps you relate the materials to your text. (The VideoWorkshop program is available for FREE when packaged with an A&B textbook. Special package ISBN required from your representative).

VideoWorkshop Student Learning Guide for Reading (with CD-ROM)
This package contains all the materials students need to get started: CD-ROM containing specially selected video clips and a tear-out page workbook with Learning Objectives, Weblinks, Observation Questions, Next Step Questions, and a multiple-choice quiz. (Not sold separately. Available only when packaged with an A&B textbook. Special package ISBN required from your representative)

Allyn & Bacon PowerPoint™ Presentation for Content Area Reading: Available on the web at http://www.ablongman.com/ppt. This PowerPoint™ presentation includes approximately 100 slides that cover a range of content area reading topics: assessment, vocabulary concepts, literature in the content areas, language diversity and culture, study skills, and content literacy and the reading process, among others.

LiveText: LiveText is a set of online tools for developing, sharing, and evaluating lesson plans, portfolios and projects. (Not sold separately. Available only when packaged with an A&B textbook. Special package ISBN required from your representative.)

CourseCompass™ Content for Content Area Reading: CourseCompass™, powered by Blackboard™, is the most flexible online course management system on the market today. By using this powerful suite of online tools in conjunction with Allyn & Bacon's preloaded textbook and testing content, you can create an online presence for your course in under 30 minutes. You can find course objectives, lecture outlines, quizzes, essay activities, tests, and a glossary of key terms in content area reading that you can adapt for your course. In addition, you will find weblinks providing access to a wealth of resources in the field of reading. Log on at http://www.coursecompass.com and find out how you can get the most out of this dynamic teaching resource.

Research Navigator Database for Education (Access Code Required) Order access to Research Navigator for your students!: Available at http://www.ablongman.com/reasearchnavigator, this free research database, searchable by keyword, gives you immediate access to hundreds of scholarly journals and other popular publications. Students will also receive access to the New York Times database, where they will find previously published articles. Ask your local representative for details. (Not sold separately. Available only when packaged with an A&B textbook. Special package ISBN required from your representative)

iSearch: Education
This resource guide for the Internet covers the basics of using the Internet, conducting Web searches, and critically evaluating and documenting Internet sources. It also contains Internet activities and URLs specific to the discipline of education. (Not sold separately. Available only when packaged with an A&B textbook. Special package ISBN required from your representative)

Allyn & Bacon LiteracyZone SuperSite (Access code required)
(http://www.ablongman.com/literacy) A website with a wealth of information for pre-service and in-service teachers —whether you want to gain new insights, pick up practical information, or simply connect with one another! It includes State Standard Correlations; Teaching Resources; Ready-to-Use Lesson Plans and Activities for All Grade Levels; Subject-specific weblinks for further research and discovery; information on A&B professional titles to help you in your teaching career; Up-to-date "In the News" features, a Discussion Forum, and much more.

ACKNOWLEDGMENTS

My thanks to Aurora Martínez-Ramos and Virginia Lanigan of Allyn and Bacon, who provided many helpful suggestions as well as support and encouragement, and to Alicia Reilly, Development Editor, who suggested a number of key features. I am also grateful to Beth Slater, editorial assistant at Allyn and Bacon, for her gracious, competent assistance.

The following reviewers provided helpful insights. I appreciate the time they took to detail specific suggestions for clarifying and improving the text.

Rebecca S. Anderson, University of Memphis
Sheila Baldwin, Monmouth University
Mickey L. Bogart, Kansas State University
Karen Mayo, Stephen F. Austin Sate University
Anne Crout Shelley, University of South Carolina, Spartanburg
Randy M. Wood, Baylor University

READING AND WRITING IN THE CONTENT AREAS: AN INTRODUCTION

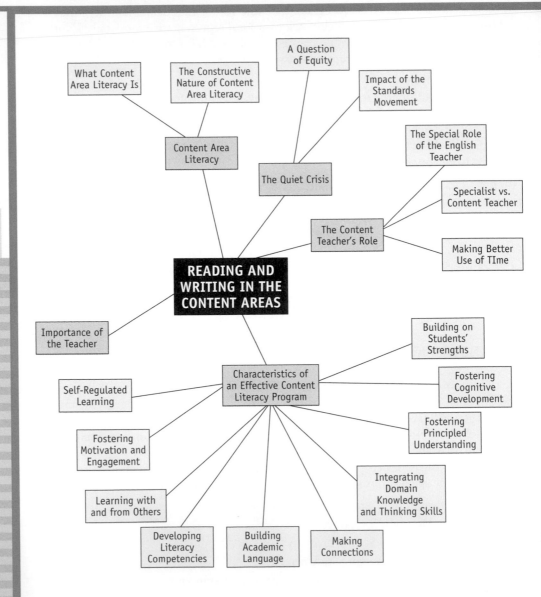

What Content Area Literacy Is

The Constructive Nature of Content Area Literacy

A Question of Equity

Impact of the Standards Movement

The Special Role of the English Teacher

Specialist vs. Content Teacher

Content Area Literacy

The Quiet Crisis

The Content Teacher's Role

Making Better Use of TIme

READING AND WRITING IN THE CONTENT AREAS

Importance of the Teacher

Building on Students' Strengths

Fostering Cognitive Development

Characteristics of an Effective Content Literacy Program

Self-Regulated Learning

Fostering Principled Understanding

Fostering Motivation and Engagement

Integrating Domain Knowledge and Thinking Skills

Learning with and from Others

Developing Literacy Competencies

Building Academic Language

Making Connections

ANTICIPATION GUIDE

Before reading this chapter, complete the anticipation guide below. It will help to activate your prior knowledge so that you can interact more fully with the chapter. It is designed to probe your attitudes and beliefs about important and sometimes controversial topics and issues. Often, there are no right or wrong answers; the statements will alert you to your attitudes about literacy instruction in the content areas and also raise key issues. The anticipation guide will work best if you discuss responses with classmates before reading the text. At the end of the chapter, respond to the anticipation guide again to see whether your answers have changed in light of what you have read.

For each of the following statements related to the chapter you are about to read, put a check under "Agree" or "Disagree" to show how you feel. Discuss your responses with classmates before you read the chapter.

		Agree	*Disagree*
1	Because the content area teachers' main responsibility is to cover the key concepts set down in the school district's curriculum guide, they do not have the time to spend teaching content area reading and writing skills.	____	____
2	Students who have adequate general reading and writing skills should have no difficulty with reading and writing in the content areas.	____	____
3	Content area teachers have the right to expect that the majority of students coming to them will have the basic reading and writing skills needed to learn content area material.	____	____
4	Students who have difficulty reading their content area texts should be presented subject matter through lectures, discussions, hands-on activities, and audio visual aids.	____	____
5	The reading specialist is the best person to teach content area reading and writing skills.	____	____

USING WHAT YOU KNOW

As you can see from the chapter organizer, this chapter discusses the nature of content area reading and the factors that enhance literacy skills in the content areas. It also discusses the quiet crisis: the fact that 25 to 40 percent of today's students have difficulty coping with their textbooks (Schoenbach, Greenleaf, Cziko, & Hurwitz, 1999; Snow, Burns, & Griffin, 1998). Before reading this chapter, reflect on your knowledge of reading in science, history, and other content areas. What steps did your teachers take to help you learn the reading and writing skills that were a part of the content area they taught? Do you use any special learning strategies to comprehend what you read in the content areas? If so, what are they? How well do they work for you? Do you have any problems reading and writing in the content areas? How might you improve your comprehension and retention of the material? How might you help students improve their reading and writing in the content areas?

CONTENT AREA LITERACY

Although apparently reading on grade level, Jeremy, a middle school student, is struggling with his science and social studies texts. In the elementary school, students have limited experience with **expository text.** Mostly, they read narrative fiction or expository text written in narrative style. As a result, Jeremy is neither experienced nor skilled in reading content area texts. As an observer in Jeremy's class explained,

■ **Expository text** is designed to explain. Other main types of text are descriptive, narrative, and persuasive.

■ **Inconsiderate text** is text that is difficult for the reader to understand because it has not been written with the reader in mind.

> Jeremy had encountered text that, for him, was **inconsiderate.** The paragraph from which he read was fifteen sentences long. There were no characters. There was no bold print to draw the reader's attention to important ideas. The subheading "Lexington and Concord" referred to towns that weren't mentioned until the fourth and fifth sentences. Words such as *forestall* and *tactic* weren't defined contextually in the passage. It was a far cry from Beverly Cleary's *Dear Mr. Henshaw,* which Jeremey had recently read: "It wasn't inappropriate for Jeremy to read that text; we all have to tackle inconsiderate text. But Jeremy needed some specific instruction to help him pay attention strategically, to focus on the most important ideas" (Keene & Zimmermann, 1997, pp. 87–88).

When asked what was important in the article he had read about the Revolutionary War, Jeremy was at a loss. Further discussion revealed that his comprehension of the article was inadequate to the point of being almost nonexistent. He was able to recite a few minor details, but he was unable to explain the significance or overall meaning of the article. Jeremy wasn't alone. Many of the other students in his class were also unable to cope with content area texts. As the observer commented, "Many were so disconnected from the meaning of the text, especially expository text, that they were often unaware of the essence of what they were reading" (Keene &

Zimmermann, 1997, p. 82). Encouragingly, when Jeremy and the other students were carefully taught strategies that included reading to determine the most important information in text, they made substantial progress.

There is a belief that students learn to read and then read to learn. Actually, the two are reciprocal processes. As students improve their reading, they are better able to learn from their reading. As they learn through reading, they naturally acquire added knowledge and vocabulary and apply their skills to a greater variety of materials. As they learn through their reading, students develop more advanced reading skills.

Although students may acquire basic **decoding** and comprehension skills in their language arts classes, they don't learn all the skills that they will need to read in the content areas. Each subject matter area requires unique skills. For instance, in geography students must learn to read a variety of kinds of maps. In history, students read political maps and time charts. In science, students must be able to read and understand formulas in subjects such as chemistry, biology, and physics. The teacher's responsibility is twofold: to teach skills unique to the subject matter and to teach students how to use reading and writing to learn subject matter content (Parker, 2001). The teacher must also help students learn the structure of the discipline, the ways in which knowledge is presented and acquired in the discipline, and the key concepts and vocabulary of the discipline.

■ **Decoding** is using phonics or other word analysis skills to translate print into speech.

To get a sense of what content area literacy involves, read each of the following excerpts from content area books. Which excerpt did you find easiest? Which did you find most difficult? What background knowledge and skills are required to read each of these?

The Cell Divides

Thousands of events take place during the cell cycle, but two of these events are so important that they are used as landmarks to define everything else. One of the events is **cell division.** Cell division is the process in which the cell divides into two independent cells called daughter cells. In eukaryotic cells, this process is called **mitosis.** The period of time when mitosis takes place is the M phase of the cell cycle.

The Cell Copies Its Chromosomes

The other major event in the cell cycle is the copying of the chromosomes that contain the cell's genetic information. When the cell copies this information, it synthesizes, or makes, a duplicate set of DNA molecules. As a result, this part of the cell cycle is called the S phase.

Because most cells do not begin DNA synthesis right after cell division, there is a time gap between the end of one M phase and the beginning of an S phase. This time gap is called the G1 phase. A similar gap, the G2 phase, occurs between the end of the S phase and the beginning of the M phase. (Miller & Levine, 1998, p. 102)

How Did the Supreme Court React to Reforms?

Roosevelt and his New Deal programs ran into problems with the Supreme Court. Most of the members of the Supreme Court believed some of the New Deal legislation was unconstitutional.

The Supreme Court declared the National Recovery Act and the Agricultural Adjustment Act unconstitutional. This declaration angered President Roosevelt. He believed that the "nine old men" on the Supreme Court stood in the way of progress. Six of the justices, who had been appointed for life, were over seventy years of age. Roosevelt decided to appoint a new justice for every justice over the age of seventy.

The six new justices, Roosevelt thought, would assure that New Deal laws would not be **overturned** by the Supreme Court. Roosevelt's decision was not well accepted. Members of Congress **denounced** it as political "court-packing." Many Americans also rejected the plan. (King & Napp, 1998, p. 502)

The Sentimentality of William Tavener, by Willa Cather

One spring night Hester sat in a rocking chair by the sitting room window, darning socks. She rocked violently and sent her long needle vigorously back and forth over her gourd, and it took only a very casual glance to see that she was wrought up over something. William sat on the other side of the table reading his farm paper. If he had noticed his wife's agitation, his calm, clean-shaven face betrayed no sign of concern. He must have noticed the sarcastic turn of her remarks at the supper table, and he must have noticed the moody silence of the older boys as they ate. When supper was but half over little Billy, the youngest, had suddenly pushed back his plate and slipped away from the table, manfully trying to swallow a sob. But William Tavener never heeded ominous forecasts in the domestic horizon, and he never looked for a storm until it broke. (Cather 1990, pp. 353–354)

Although all of these excerpts require basic reading skills, including a good general vocabulary and the overall ability to construct meaning from print, each content area has its own organization and language. The first excerpt, which is drawn from a tenth-grade biology text, has an overall main idea–detail organization, but its second paragraph has a sequence structure. To comprehend the passage, students must grasp the overall main idea of the two major events in cell division and also the sequence of cell division. The passage contains a number of specialized science words: *cell division, eukaryotic, mitosis, chromosomes, DNA molecules.* In addition, there are a number of general vocabulary words that would be important for an understanding of the excerpt: *cycle, landmarks, genetic, duplicate, synthesizes,* and *gap.* The passage assumes knowledge of concepts such as *cell, eukaryotic, chromosomes,* and *DNA molecules.* Coverage of material is cumulative. If students fail to grasp key concepts, they will have difficulty with passages that build on those concepts.

The second excerpt has an overall sequential narrative structure. It is telling the story of Roosevelt's attempt to "pack" the Supreme Court. However, it also has a cause–effect substructure that explains why Roosevelt appointed new justices and why many rejected his strategy. In addition to such technical terms as *New Deal, legislation,* and *unconstitutional,* its readers need to know the general vocabulary words *declaration, denounced,* and *rejected.* Needed background knowledge includes information about the Supreme Court, the New Deal, and the National Recovery and Agricultural Adjustment acts. The vocabulary in science tends to have specific, concrete meanings. In history and the social studies, many terms refer to highly abstract concepts. The word *liberal,* for instance, does not lend itself to easy explanation.

The third excerpt is from a short story by Willa Cather. It portrays a conflict between a husband and wife and has a narrative structure. The story contains such potentially unknown words as *vigorously, agitation, heeded, ominous,* and *domestic.* The story also contains figurative language such as "never heeded ominous forecasts in the domestic horizon, and he never looked for a storm until it broke." Needed background knowledge involves understanding family dynamics and what life was like during the late 1800s.

What Content Area Literacy Is

All three of the excerpts above require a fairly sophisticated vocabulary and well-developed comprehension skills. However, each also makes its own unique demands. Each has its own background requirements. As learning researchers Bransford, Brown, and Cocking (2001) conclude,

> Different domains of knowledge, such as science, mathematics, and history, have different organizing properties. It follows, therefore, that to have an in-depth grasp of an area requires knowledge about both the content of the subject and the broader structural organization of the subject (pp. 237–238).

The first excerpt requires a background in knowledge of cells, the second background in the Great Depression, the third background in personal relationships, literary techniques, and the ability to empathize with characters. Having overall competency in reading is not enough. A successful reading of these excerpts also requires strategies and understandings specific to each subject matter. These are strategies and understandings best taught by the subject matter teacher. The theme of this text is that an important element of teaching in the content area is helping students acquire skills and understanding they need to learn a particular body of content.

Content literacy is the "ability to use reading and writing for the acquisition of new content in a given discipline. Such ability includes three principal cognitive components: general literacy skills, content-specific literacy skills (such as map reading in the social studies), and prior knowledge of content" (McKenna & Robinson, 1990, p. 184). We are not all equally literate in each content area.

■ **Content literacy** is the ability to use reading and writing to acquire information in a subject area.

 CHECKUP

1. What does content area literacy involve?

The Constructive Nature of Content Area Literacy

At one time, reading was seen as a relatively passive process of acquiring the author's message. Reading was thought to be akin to transferring data to a student in much the same way that data is transferred from one computer to another. However, reading is now viewed as a constructive process. The reader doesn't simply get the author's meaning. Rather, the reader uses his personal background of experience to construct meaning based on information provided by the author. Reading is said to be a **transaction.** The reader is changed by the text and at the same time the text is changed by the reader, with both coming together in a dynamic transaction (Rosenblatt, 1994). The meaning does not reside in the text or in the reader but in a transaction between the two.

■ ***Transaction*** refers to the relationship between the reader and the text in which the text is conditioned by the reader and the reader is conditioned by the text.

Readers actively seek meaning and interpret text in the light of their own background of experience. Use your experience to interpret the following passage. What do you think it might be about?

> Every Saturday night four good friends get together. When Jerry, Mike, and Pat arrived, Karen was sitting in her living room writing some notes. She quickly gathered up the cards and stood up to greet her friends at the door. They followed her into the living room but as usual they couldn't agree on exactly what to play. Jerry eventually took a stand and set things up. Finally, they were eager to play. Karen's recorder filled the room with soft and pleasant music. Early in the evening, Mike noticed Pat's hand and the many diamonds. As the night progressed the tempo of play increased. Finally, a lull in the activities occurred. Taking advantage of this, Jerry pondered the arrangement in front of him. Mike interrupted Jerry's reverie and said, "Let's hear the score." They listened carefully and commented on their performance. When the comments were all heard, exhausted but happy, Karen's friends went home. (Anderson, Reynolds, Schallert, & Goetz, 1977, p. 372)

The text was given to a group of music students and a group of physical education students. The text is deliberately ambiguous so that it could be about a card game or a quartet practicing their music. The music students tended to interpret the selection as being about a practice session; physical education students were more likely to see it as an account of a card game. Most of the students failed to see that the passage was open to interpretation. Only 20 percent saw two possible interpretations. The researchers concluded that readers construct meaning in terms of their background knowledge and experience.

Conceptualizing the reader as being an active participant has a number of implications for teaching in the content area. It is important that the teacher be aware of the knowledge that students bring to the content area. Sometimes, the bacground information is sketchy or even erroneous. For instance, based on their experience with numbers, students may believe that ¼ is more than ½ because 4 is greater than 2. In order to teach students how to deal with fractions, the teacher must help students overcome this misconception. Ongoing assessment of students' knowledge is also essential. Unless teachers have some grasp of students' current levels of understanding, they will have difficulty helping them construct coherent concepts. For instance, realizing that students believe that seasons change because the earth is closer or farther from the sun, the science teacher can discuss and demonstrate the varying angles of the earth as it orbits the sun and explain how the angle of the sun determines the amount of heat that reaches the earth.

 **CHECKUP**

1. Why is reading called a constructive process?
2. What implications does this have for instruction?

THE QUIET CRISIS

There is a quiet crisis in content area reading. Thousands of middle and high school students are unable to cope with their academic texts (Schoenbach et al., 1999). National tests known as the National Assessment of Educational Progress have been administered in each of the major content areas and in reading over a period of three decades. Surprisingly, the results are similar from content area to content area. Most students have a basic knowledge of the content areas, whether it be science, geography, or history. However, in each content area, students have difficulty with tasks that require them to interpret or apply what they have learned. Students do best when they are required simply to recite basic facts or perform basic operations. Although specific percentages vary from subject to subject, about 30 percent of students have such severe difficulty comprehending each content area that they have not achieved even a basic level of competence (Campbell, Hombro, & Mazzeo, 1999). As might be expected, a disproportionate number of students who are poor or members of minority groups fall into this category. The National Research Council (Snow, Burns, & Griffin, 1998) concluded, "The educational careers of 25 to 40 percent of American children are imperiled because they do not read well enough, quickly enough, or easily enough to ensure comprehension in their content courses in middle and secondary school" (p. 98).

Content area teachers focus on presenting their subject matter. Seeing that some students are getting little from their texts, they teach around the texts. They paraphrase or summarize the text or use other methods, such as labs, simulations, or audiovisual aids, to convey the content. As one history teacher explained, "Because you can't rely on students to read, I feel like I'm constantly summarizing the history textbook so kids don't miss the main points. I wish I didn't have to assume that role as much, but I find I do" (Schoenbach et al., 1999, p. 8). The teacher becomes an enabler. Perceiving that they don't have to read the texts, the students stop reading assigned material. As a result, students fail to learn crucial reading skills. As they progress through the

USING TECHNOLOGY

Nation's Report Card
http://nces.ed.gov/
nationsreportcard/
Contains detailed information about students' performance in specific content areas.

*E*ach subject matter requires its own set of unique literacy skills.

grades, the gap between the difficulty level of the text and their ability to handle it increases.

Most of the students affected by the quiet crisis do possess solid basic reading skills. Although advanced vocabulary may pose problems, they have mastered basic decoding skills. They also have acceptable comprehension. What they are not prepared to deal with are the complex ideas and language structures embedded in their academic texts.

The blame for the quiet crisis has been placed, in part, on the quality of today's texts. They have been described as dull, poorly written, biased, stuffed with facts, inaccurate, and irrelevant. While content area texts could undoubtedly be improved, most do a decent job of presenting an overview of complex subject matter. Based on their work with reluctant and underprepared readers, Schoenbach, Greenleaf, Cziko, and Hurwitz, (1999) have concluded that it is the responsibility of content area teachers to help students work through texts that are challenging and that students may see as boring but that present key academic concepts. Helping underprepared readers is also a matter of equity.

A Question of Equity

One of the biggest changes in content area instruction has been the emphasis on equity. For instance, in math and science in past years, there was a push to make sure that the best students were provided with a rigorous background. Although the number of students taking advanced science courses has increased, approximately 30 percent of today's high school students take only general science courses; they do not take separate courses in biology, chemistry, or physics (Nelson, 1999). While emphasis in the past was on preparing students for science careers, the emphasis today is on providing all students with a basic education in science, math, and technology so that all are scientifically and technologically literate. To meet this challenging goal, teachers will need to be prepared to teach a wider variety of students and to gear instruction to meet a greater diversity of backgrounds, abilities, and learning styles. A lack of equity is one of the factors that has fueled the standards movement.

 *CHECKUP*

1. What is the quiet crisis?
2. Why is solving the crisis a matter of equity?

Impact of the Standards Movement

■ **Standards** are statements of what students should know or be able to do.

After the failure of the New Math in the 1980s, the National Council of Teachers of Mathematics sponsored the development of new **standards** (MCREL, 2001). The organization hoped that these standards would raise teachers' expectations and students' achievement. The idea behind standards is to improve the quality of instruction. Clearly stated objectives should lead to improved instruction, especially if assessment is closely tied to the standards and if there are adequate instructional resources for helping students meet standards. As Wixson and Dutro (1998) note, "A standards-based view of reform holds that once broad agreement on what is to be taught and learned has been achieved, everything else in the education system can be redirected toward reaching higher standards."

Published in 1989 and most recently revised in 2000, the math standards were widely adopted and led to changes ranging from the revision of textbooks to the way students were taught. Scores on national tests began to rise (MCREL, 2001; National Council of Teachers of Mathematics, 2000). Urged on by the federal government and content area organizations, each major discipline began creating standards. (Spurred by the text *A Nation at Risk* [1983], which called for reconsideration and reform of the U.S. education system, science educators had already begun construction of new standards). When writing standards, organizations try to reach a broad consensus about what students should know and be able to do; the resulting standards should be equitable but also foster excellence. Curriculum, textbooks, teacher training, and tests would then be aligned with the standards. "The object was not to create high hurdles for students, but to demystify what was to be learned and to help all students reach higher levels of learning" (Ravitch, 1993, p. 769).

At the same time that national standards were being created, states were being urged by the federal government to develop curriculum frameworks. Although typically based on national standards, state curriculum frameworks are usually more specific and more detailed (Ravitch, 1993). State assessments and textbook adoptions are frequently based on state curriculum frameworks. State curriculum frameworks also function as a guide for local school districts. In a sense, national standards are filtered through state frameworks.

Goals for all major content areas now exist in lists of standards. In the preface to their standards, the International Reading Association and National Council of Teachers of English explained that the "standards would address the literacy needs of today and tomorrow, articulate a shared vision of what the nation's literacy teachers expect of their students, and promote high educational expectations for all students and bridge the documented disparities that exist in educational opportunities" (International Reading Association and National Council of Teachers of English, 1996, p. 4). The National Council of Social Studies (NCSS) also saw their standards as providing guidance for teachers:

> These social studies standards provide criteria for making decisions as curriculum planners and teachers address such issues as why teach social studies, what to include in the curriculum, how to teach it well to all students, and how to assess whether or not students are able to apply what they have learned" (NCSS, 2000).

More specifically the standards would help classroom teachers:

- provide outcome goals for units and courses;
- evaluate current practices; and
- glean ideas for instruction and assessment. (NCSS, 1994)

Standards are nothing new. They are just a more formal embodiment of what good teachers have always done. As Hill noted (2002), "Good teachers have standards in mind when they set their lessons up, where the idea of a 'standard' repre-

USING TECHNOLOGY

Developing Educational Standards
http://edstandards.org/standards.html
Provides information about curriculum frameworks and standards and provides links to each state so you can examine your state's standards.

sents a specific idea of what the teacher expects a student to recall, replicate, manipulate, understand, or demonstrate at some point down the road—and of how the teacher will know how close a student has come to meeting that standard."

In many states, expectations for student performance are up, test scores are on the rise, the curriculum is being revised to reflect higher standards, and teachers are being provided with additional materials and professional development. In addition, more attention is being paid to underachieving schools and students. In New York City, for instance, $31 million has been set aside to add Saturday classes for students struggling in math and science and another $175 million for summer school for struggling students (Zhao, 2001). Massachusetts allocated $85 million to set up programs to foster academic achievement for struggling learners in the ninth grade (Education Week on the Web, 2001).

However, despite these encouraging developments, there are problems within the standards movement. Standards vary from state to state and range in quality and specificity. Tests are not always aligned with standards. Tests may assess some standards but not others, and many are of the multiple choice variety that fails to assess higher-level thinking. In addition, professional development and allocation of resources are lacking. States and thousands of local districts have established standards or frameworks, but they have not always allocated the resources and professional development needed to meet those standards (Education Week on the Web, 2001).

The major problem seems to be not so much with the standards as with the devices used to assess whether students have met the standards. In essence, the tests become the standards. Pressured to cover an ever-increasing amount of content and to prepare students for high-stakes tests, teachers may resort to an overemphasis on lecturing and other highly directive approaches and fail to teach students how to learn. In highly teacher-directed classes, students tend to be passive. In addition, there tends to be a narrowing of the curriculum. Overly concerned with having students score high on the test, educators focus on teaching to the test and neglect important areas that are not assessed. In addition to restricting what students are learning, this takes the fun out of teaching and learning. For instance, in preparing for writing tests, teachers might spend an inordinate amount of time having students practice writing to prompts rather than providing them with a well-rounded program of expository and creative writing. Writing to prompts day after day can cause students to lose interest in writing.

Some educators have opposed the standards movement and the accompanying high-stakes tests as being unnecessary and, worse, as forcing a one-size-fits-all mentality. Speaking of secondary programs, Sturtevant, Ivey, and Anders (2000) commented,

> Developing effective adolescent literacy programs is challenging, especially in the current political climate that requires middle and high school students in many states to pass high-stakes tests that emphasize content coverage over depth and inquiry. Theory-based practices, such as curricula that emphasize choice, the use of multiple sources, and process writing, may be avoided by teachers and school leaders in favor of more expedient measures that are thought to help young people pass tests. (p. 10)

In her study of schools that had exceptional achievement despite having large numbers of at-risk students, Langer (1999) found that higher-performing schools seem to focus on students' learning, using the tests as an additional device for noting whether the skills and knowledge that are tested are being learned within the context of improved instruction. The more typical schools seem to focus on raising test scores, rather than on students' learning, as the primary goal (Langer, 1999). As one teacher in a high-performing school explained, "Standards, as much as they're a kind of pain . . . when we have these meetings and align the standards and all that stuff, it has helped me. . . . My curriculum is strong. But once I started really looking at the standards I realized I didn't have a lot of writing activities, and so it kind of helped me to conceptualize that a little better and forced me to incorporate that" (Langer, 1999).

Although controversial and undoubtedly incorporating a number of drawbacks, the standards movement is now well established. Perhaps the best plan is to take advantage of its positive aspects, as Langer's exemplary teachers are doing, and work to ameliorate or eliminate its negative features.

 **CHECKUP**

1. What is the standards movement?
2. How does it affect content area instruction?

THE CONTENT TEACHER'S ROLE

One English teacher sent the following e-mail query to a language arts specialist:

> I encountered a question at a job interview for a high school position that totally caught me off guard. The question was "How would you teach reading?" To be honest, teaching reading never occurred to me.
>
> As an English teacher, I take it for granted that my students know how to read, especially in regular high school English classes. Am I wrong to assume this? We are so pressured to teach what the state and district requires in a short amount of time. How do we stop to teach students how to read? (NCTE, 2001, p. 10)

*C*ontent teachers teach content and the literacy processes involved in learning that content.

Content literacy does not require content teachers to instruct students in basic reading skills such as decoding or getting the main idea or in such basic writing skills as composing a sentence or a paragraph. It does require that the science teacher teach word forms such as *hydro*, *derma*, and *endo* that are common in science. It also requires that the science teacher show students how to read science texts critically and with a sense of inquiry and to compose lab reports. For the history teacher, it means teaching students to read maps and charts of various kinds, to compare sources of information about historical events, and to draw conclusions based on primary sources. These are skills needed for an understanding of science and history,

and they are best taught in the context of exploring these subject matter areas. In other words, content area teachers are expected only to teach those literacy skills needed to read and write about their subject matter area. Content area teachers are asked to teach both the content of their subject and the processes involved in learning that content. After all, who is better equipped to teach students how to learn subject matter than someone who has firsthand experience learning it? To explain the thinking processes necessary to learn a subject, one must possess those processes.

The Special Role of the English Teacher

Because of the nature of their subject, English teachers should be prepared to teach comprehension and study skills and some advanced word recognition skills such as using the dictionary, using context, or using knowledge of roots, prefixes, and suffixes. These skills do not need to be taught separately; they can be taught as part of the language arts curriculum. Because of their expertise in language arts, English teachers have a greater responsibility for instruction in reading and writing than do other content area teachers.

While it is true that good students might pick up learning strategies on their own or may have learned them in earlier grades, it is also true that, for the most part, poorly prepared students do not have an adequate grasp of strategies. Even if they have been taught them, they might not be able to apply them. When one realizes that about 25 to 40 percent of students fall into this category, the importance of teaching students how to learn becomes more apparent.

Bereiter and Scardamalia (1987) caution that content area teachers risk the danger of becoming knowledge tellers if they simply dispense information and don't guide students in ways of understanding, organizing, and retaining that knowledge. Students might simply accumulate knowledge without relating it to what they know or organizing it within their own knowledge of the world. Superficially learned, this knowledge is all too readily forgotten because it was never integrated into students' existing core of knowledge. Learning strategies, such as summarizing important information, that help students process information so it is more fully understood and more deeply processed, will be explained in this text.

Specialist vs. Content Teacher

One solution to teaching literacy in the content areas is to have the reading specialist or English teacher instruct the students in key strategies. This approach has some merit. The reading teacher or English teacher has specialized expertise in this area, and the content area teacher would not lose valuable instructional time. However, if this approach is used, the content area teachers should work carefully with the specialist so that they understand the strategies and are able to help students apply them to each particular content area. Although there are general strategies that apply across content areas, they may need to be modified to fit a particular content area. In addition, transfer is a problem: Students taught strategies in one context may not apply them to another context; they need to be reminded to apply strategies that they have been taught. In addition, learning to use a strategy takes a considerable amount of time. The content area teacher must reinforce the strategies that the specialist has introduced and help students when they are having difficulty applying them.

Making Better Use of Time

Pressured by an ever-increasing amount of content to cover—more scientific discoveries are being made each day; history is happening at this very moment—and faced with high-stakes tests, content area teachers may believe that they can't take time out to teach literacy skills. However, in addition to being an integral part of the content areas, content area literacy skills should actually save time: If they possess the necessary skills, students should be able to learn more of the content on their own and should also benefit more from the teacher's guidance. In one chemistry class, a resource teacher who was helping new teachers noted that the teacher had to explain all the material that students were supposed to have read the previous night (Patton, 1993). The selection had been on using moles in measurement. Wondering why the students hadn't understood the material better, the resource teacher asked students how they had gone about reading the chapter. The students had failed to use any strategies and had merely focused on solving the problems in the chapter. Because the students did not have or had not applied strategies, the class was bogged down with the explanation of routine procedures rather than going on to a higher-level application. The teacher spent virtually the entire period explaining what the students should have been able to learn through their reading. Time spent on strategies for reading the chemistry text would have saved valuable instructional time.

 *CHECKUP*

1. What is the content area teacher's role in the teaching of literacy?
2. Why might the language arts teacher have a special role?

CHARACTERISTICS OF AN EFFECTIVE CONTENT AREA LITERACY PROGRAM

An effective content area literacy program has a number of components. They include building on students' strengths, fostering cognitive development, fostering principled understanding, integrating domain knowledge and thinking skills, making connections, building academic language, developing literacy competencies, learning with and from others, and fostering motivation and engagement.

Building on Students' Strengths

Building on basic reading and writing skills, content area reading and writing require content knowledge and vocabulary and whatever specialized skills are needed to read and write about content (McKenna & Robinson, 1995). The key word here may be *building*. Learning to read and write in the content areas builds on skills that students already possess. As Herber and Herber (1993) comment:

> Teachers manifest a positive approach to instruction when their teaching is designed to capitalize on students' strengths rather than to compensate for students' weaknesses. In a context that focuses constructively on students' strengths, teachers can eventually help students deal with their weaknesses. In a context that focuses on means to compensate for students' weaknesses, teachers find it difficult to get around to building on their strengths. (p. 23)

Among the strengths students bring to the content areas are background of relevant knowledge, ability to reason, understanding of language, and ability to communicate with others (Herber & Herber, 1993). Students frequently have a wealth of knowledge and experience to bring to the content areas. This is especially true of the sciences. Students have experienced weather of all types; have observed animals, plants, and the stars; and have directly experienced many of the laws of physics. As Gallas (1994) notes, although every child observes and thinks about the world, they may not realize that their thoughts may contain the contents of science: "Somehow for them science is something mysterious and vague, and their life has nothing to do with science" (p. 72). Because it is concrete and personal, students' everyday knowledge has a power that school-type knowledge may lack (Alexander & Jetton, 2000). Although this knowledge may be unorganized and fragmented, and some of it may also be erroneous, it can provide an excellent starting point. And if the students' knowledge is erroneous, encountering this knowledge is a first step toward correcting or clarifying it.

One approach that builds on what students know is progressive formalization (Reeuwijk, 1995). Instruction begins with the informal ideas that students bring to school and uses these ideas as a foundation for building formal academic knowledge. In one program, middle school students studying algebra use their own words, drawings, or diagrams to describe the procedures that they use to solve problems. Later, students create their own symbol systems. Ultimately, students use conventional symbols to solve algebra problems. Building on students' knowledge fosters a depth of understanding.

Fostering Cognitive Development

More than ever, learning in the content area demands higher-order thinking skills:

> Doing mathematics involves solving problems, abstracting, inventing, proving. . . . Doing history involves the construction and evaluation of historical documents. . . . Doing science includes such activities as testing theories through experimentation and observation. . . . Society envisions graduates of school systems who can identify and solve problems and make contributions to society throughout their lifetime. . . . (Bransford et al., 2001, pp. 132–133)

■ **Literal comprehension** involves understanding stated information but does not include interpretation.

As noted earlier, the vast majority of students can answer questions of a **literal** nature, but in every content area students have difficulty answering questions that require a depth of thinking. For instance, in a national geography assessment, most students were able to answer the following factual question: Where is the world's largest tropical rain forest? But only a small percentage were able to answer the application question: Support the conclusion that tropical rain forests promote wide species variation (Hawkins, Stancavage, Mitchell, Goodman, & Lazer, 1998). Although in the history assessment most students were able to note that a political cartoon was addressing the issue of civil rights, only a very small percentage could explain that the cartoon was pointing out the gap between the passage of civil rights legislation and actual change (Hawkins et al., 1998). Therefore, a key element in developing content literacy is building thinking skills, especially those that involve interpreting and applying principles and concepts.

An effective program emphasizes developing students' thinking. Instead of simply acquiring information, students should be learning to evaluate that information and to apply it when appropriate. Developing thinking skills might also entail learning to think like an historian, a scientist, or a mathematician. In traditional science experiments, students learn the procedures for conducting experiments. The experiments have predetermined results and are designed to illustrate scientific principles and to acquaint students with procedures for conducting experiments. Current emphasis is on having students plan and conduct their own experiments much as a scientist would. In literature study, emphasis is also on a depth of learning and understanding. For example, after studying the major themes of *Invisible Man* (Ellison, 1952), a teacher led her class in a discussion of their own ethnicities (Langer, 1999).

Fostering Principled Understanding

Besieged by information, today's students may find it more difficult to determine which information is important or relevant. Students may also have difficulty judging the accuracy and reliability of information. Ironically, students' attention is all too often drawn to information that is trivial. Students, especially those who are less knowledgeable, need instruction that helps them "separate the message from the noise that surrounds it" (Alexander & Jetton, 2000).

With so much knowledge available now, it is essential that students have some way of organizing it. Unfortunately, much of the information that students take in is fragmented and so is not related to core concepts (Gelman & Greeno, 1989.) Knowledge needs to be organized around key concepts and principles so that students attain a principled understanding. In addition to helping students see the relevance of information, a principled understanding also helps them see how information relates to key concepts.

Students should study topics that are generative. Generative topics are central to both the subject area students are studying and to the topics which students and teacher find interesting (Perkins, 2001). Broad, overarching themes as well as specific understandings should be developed. For instance, an overall understanding of the Westward Movement might be that possession of land has had a major impact on our nation. Herber and Herber (1993) recommend creating an **organizing idea.** The organizing idea specifies the conceptual focus of the lesson and unites the content of reading with the processes of reading. Organizing ideas can be created for

■ An **organizing idea** is a "declarative statement that identifies a targeted relationship among details or among concepts" (Herber & Herber, 1993, pp. 20–21). The organizing idea identifies the conceptual focus of a lesson or piece of information, such as a textbook chapter or presentation.

lessons as well as for units. Organizing ideas for units would be more abstract and more inclusive than those for individual lessons. In addition to giving focus to a lesson or unit, the organizing idea can be used to help students relate their prior knowledge to content area information. An organizing idea for lessons on the rise of labor unions might be "In unity there is strength."

Students need an in-depth understanding of key concepts. A basic goal of learning is that students should be able to transfer knowledge and skill to other topics in the domain, to other domains, and to the world outside school. Before knowledge or skills can be transferred, they must be mastered. Information that is thoroughly understood is far more likely to be transferred than information that has simply been memorized or skimmed (Bransford et al., 2001).

Integrating Domain Knowledge and Thinking Skills

■ A **domain** is a specific field or area of knowledge.

Although developing thinking skills and building **domain** knowledge are often treated as separate categories, they are complementary. Without a degree of content knowledge, students are unable to engage in some types of higher-order thinking skills (Penner, 2000). Fostering content knowledge can also promote cognitive development. As they acquire knowledge, students are better able to see patterns and induce generalizations. Novices in a content area become experts by acquiring extensive knowledge. The knowledge they acquire affects how they organize and interpret that knowledge and how they reason and solve problems (Bransford et al., 2001).

Making Connections

Making connections fosters learning and retention. We understand new ideas better when we can connect them to familiar concepts. The concept of representative democracy becomes more understandable when students relate it to selecting a class representative for the student government. Understanding is also enhanced when connections are made between concepts learned at different times. United States democracy becomes more understandable when compared with democracy in ancient Greece and the parliamentary form of government in Canada and the United Kingdom. The concept is further enhanced when connections are made across subject matter areas. Students studying democracy in history class will more fully understand the concept if they make connections with the novel *Johnny Tremain*. In one study of a secondary school that had high performance despite having a large number of at-risk learners, the researchers found that the teachers were constantly making connections among knowledge, skills, and ideas across lessons, classes, and grades as well as across in-school and out-of-school applications (Langer, 1999). For instance, at Springfield High School, English teacher Suzanna Rotundi helps her students make connections with other works, with tests, and with life when she presents *Invisible Man*, by Ralph Ellison:

> My primary goal is to provide them with what I consider a challenging piece of literature that will give them an excellent resource for the AP exam. It fits in well with the works we have studied in that it explores the inner consciousness and makes use of a recurring image/symbol that has been the key to several other literary works . . . that of blindness. It allows them to explore the way a symbol can convey meaning in several literary works.

. . . The ramifications in terms of social psychology with the concept of invisibility apply to so many different life experiences. I try to open the students' appreciation of how this work relates to their own world and it introduces them to the question of identity and how the daily interactions are crucial to identity formation. . . . (Langer, 1999)

Descriptions of content curricula typically list key objectives, all of which may be important in themselves. However, the individual objectives may not be seen as being part of a larger network of knowledge. "Stress on isolated parts can train students in a series of routines without educating them to understand an overall picture that will ensure the development of integrated knowledge structures and information about conditions of applicability" (Bransford et al., 2001, p. 139).

 **CHECKUP**

1. How can higher-level thinking skills be fostered within the content areas?

Building Academic Language

The hallmark of a content area is the language used to express its major concepts. In addition to a specialized vocabulary, each content area also employs syntactic and rhetorical structures to convey information. Compare the vocabulary and syntactic and rhetorical structures used in the excerpts presented in the beginning of the chapter. The excerpts include technical vocabulary as well as high-level general vocabulary, formal use of language, and a highly structured organization.

Apart from the specialized language of the discipline, content areas also use a formal English that may be more complex and abstract than the language students are used to. Even the language of the classroom lecture may pose problems for some students. This is especially true for **English language learners,** who may have a relatively good grasp of conversational English but may not be familiar with expressions such as *categorize the following*, *analyze*, *compare*, and other terms typically used as part of the language of instruction.

Developing Literacy Competencies

An essential element in learning content concepts is acquiring and implementing the strategies that make learning possible. For science, this means learning how to read and write science text. On a deeper level, it might mean learning how to think like a scientist. For history, it means learning to read and write historical accounts. On a more advanced level, it involves drawing and evaluating conclusions based on historical data. For instance, when writing about social studies issues such as the fairness of the death penalty or the role of the electoral college, the teacher can walk students throughout the steps of locating descriptive accounts and opinion pieces and help them distinguish between the two. The teacher can also discuss ways in which the material might be handled. The class might even do a cooperative piece on the role of the electoral college or death penalty so that students can better understand how to implement needed reading and writing strategies. The teacher and the class can create a set of guidelines, or a **rubric,** for writing the piece. In successful con-

■ **Academic language** is the formal language of instruction used in classrooms and texts.

■ **English language learners** are not native speakers of English, but they are acquiring English.

■ A **rubric** is a description of the traits or characteristics of standards used to judge a process or product.

■ *Metacognitive* refers to the quality of being aware of one's thinking processes.

tent area programs, teachers break down new or difficult tasks and provide students with step-by-step guidance. The guidance is **metacognitive:** Students are not just given a list of cookbook-type directions; they also learn the reason for the procedures and when and where these procedures are best applied. In this way, students take cognitive control of the strategies so they can adapt them to fit their own working styles. For instance, at Hudson Middle School, teacher Cathy Starr encouraged her students to reflect on their research efforts by asking themselves such questions as: Did you spend the time trying to find the information? Did you keep going until you had learned enough to write your report? (Langer, 1999).

Initially, students might follow the teacher's lead as the teacher models strategies and coaches students in their use. Ultimately, students are responsible for adapting strategies to fit their own styles and needs and applying these strategies independently.

 CHECKUP

1. How can academic language and literacy competencies be developed?

Learning with and from Others

■ *Scaffolding* refers to the support and guidance provided by an adult or more knowledgeble peer that helps a student function on a higher level.

Much of what we learn, we learn through discussion with others or through **scaffolding** offered by adults and more knowledgeable peers. In a cooperative or collaborative learning group, students organize and test out their learning when they present their ideas and their views. Through listening to others, they add to their own understanding and learn to view ideas from multiple perspectives and gain not just information but also insight into other ways of thinking. Students can both seek clarification for their ideas and help others to understand content area concepts better.

Learning is fostered when students have a sense of being part of a supportive learning community. "Learning seems to be enhanced by social norms that value the search for understanding and allow students (and teachers) the freedom to make mistakes in order to learn" (Bransford et al., 2001, p. 145). In some classes, students may not respond because they fear making mistakes or, conversely, they may not want to be perceived as being bright. Grading practices also have an impact on the classroom community. Highly competitive classes discourage cooperation. Culture also has an impact on the classroom community. According to their culture, Inuit students are expected to learn by listening and observing; therefore, they are hesitant to speak out in class (Crago, 1992). In Japan, students learn from the errors of others. Teachers regularly ask students who have made errors to share their thinking with the rest of the class. Japanese teachers have created a classroom community in which students expect to help their classmates by discussing errors (Hatano & Inagaki, 1996).

Fosterering Motivation and Engagement

Students' motivation depends, in large part, on their goals. A major goal for some students might be passing tests or pleasing teachers and parents. Others may have a genuine interest in the subject. Some, while not genuinely interested in the subject, may see that it provides information worth knowing. Goals, of course, can be overlapping. Students can have a genuine interest in a subject and also be concerned about doing well on tests. In his chemistry text, Dickson (1995) motivates readers by making connections between chemistry and their everyday lives. He quotes and discusses a number of familiar statements that use chemical terms:

> I'm on a low-sodium diet.
> Watch your calories.
> This is iodized salt.
> Chlorofluorocarbons contribute to the destruction of the ozone layer. (p. 3)

He also motivates students by taking extra pains to make the subject understandable and readable. And he shows how chemistry can be applied both to their understanding of other science courses and to their functioning in everyday life.

Students whose learning goals are external are more anxious learners. They are concerned with pleasing teachers and parents and measure progress in terms of how well they do in comparison with others. They tend to be more passive, more reliant on the teachers. They may not use as many strategies, and their learning may lack depth. In contrast, learners who are intrinsically motivated tend to be less anxious and more confident. Since they enjoy learning for its own sake, their learning has more depth. In addition to being more confident, they persist in the face of challenge (Nichols, Jones, & Hancock, 2000).

Goals should be specific and attainable. Students may have long-term goals, such as learning basic algebra so that they can take more advanced courses, but they should also have goals that are short-term and immediate, such as being able to solve at least 80 percent of the problems at the end of the chapter or being able to use a microscope to examine slides. Having set goals, students are now in a position to **monitor** their learning to see if they are reaching their goals. If they aren't reaching their goals, they are then in position to take corrective action. Setting and achieving learning goals fosters both autonomy and a sense of **self-efficacy.** Setting and monitoring goals can also lead to more effective learning. For instance, a student who rereads a chapter in an attempt to increase her understanding of how to solve simultaneous equations may find that simply rereading does not work. However, when she studies the sample equations and works on some practice problems, she begins to understand the procedure. Setting and monitoring her goals has helped her to adopt strategies that enable her to reach her goal.

> ■ To **monitor** means to be aware of or to check one's cognitive processes.
> ■ **Self-efficacy** is a belief in oneself as a learner.

How a subject is presented can have an impact on goals. Downplaying grades, presenting interesting topics, planning discussions and hands-on activities, and highlighting ways in which topics in the content areas apply to students' lives fosters deeper interest and involvement in learning. On the other hand, negative comments, competitive practices, emphasis on grades, threats of failure, homogeneous grouping, negative attitudes towards underperforming students, and having little choice or control over one's learning may undermine students' motivation (Conley, 1997).

Knowledge about a subject and being interested in the subject are interrelated. The more students know about a subject, the greater their interest. The greater their knowledge and interest, the fuller their comprehension is likely to be (Conley, 1997). However, as students grow older, their interest in academic subjects may decline, especially if they are struggling with the subject. What's more, **intrinsic motivation,** which is a powerful force in performance, decreases while **extrinsic motivation,**

> ■ **Intrinsic motivation** is a natural internal desire, such as curiosity or interest, that leads individuals to engage in an activity.
> ■ **Extrinsic motivation** is an external reward, such as praise, group approval, or money, that leads individuals to engage in an activity.

EXEMPLARY TEACHING

CORI

Using a framework known as CORI (Concept Oriented Reading Instruction) with fifth-grade students in a Title 1 program, Guthrie, Bennett, Rice, and McGough (1996) established a teaching unit that builds intrinsic motivation. CORI has four major elements:

Observing and personalizing. To initiate a unit of study, students observed some material phenomena. This could be crickets, the life cycle of caterpillars, or the phases of the moon. Students' observations were discussed and they noted what they knew about the topic and what they wanted to learn. Topics of interest and questions to be answered were listed. Observations were recorded.

Searching and retrieving. Through brainstorming sources of information, students learned where to go to get information to answer their questions and to search for subtopics related to their general area of interest. Students learned how to locate appropriate trade books, make appropriate scientific observations, use globes, and find other sources of information. In addition to discussion, direct instruction was used to show students how to use the table of contents and index to locate relevant information.

Comprehending and integrating. Students learned how to identify important ideas and how to take notes to summarize what they had read and to synthesize information. They also learned how to combine information from several sources, including both informational and fiction books and real-life sources. Technical vocabulary was also developed. During this and other stages, peer interaction was encouraged.

Communicating to others. Students learned to use the process approach to compose a report. Typical reporting activities included sketching, labeling, and describing cricket parts; inventing an insect; creating habitat posters; creating fictional pieces based on facts they had researched; and creating other types of reports (Grant, Guthrie, Bennett, Rice, & McGough, 1994).

As a result of combining strategy instruction with elements such as building on students' choices, the CORI program produced students who were intrinsically motivated. Students read more, understood what they read better, and were better able to transfer both their knowledge and strategies to solve new problems. Perhaps most important of all, they were better able to engage in higher-level thinking. Based on their observations of students, the project planners note that the students were excited: "They want to learn. [They] have powerful reasons for reading and writing that are vital motivations . . . for learning. Without these motivations, the difficult work of cognitive learning does not occur rapidly, if it occurs at all" (Guthrie & Wigfield, 1997, p. 3). Indeed, Guthrie and associates (1996) found that students who experience an increase in motivation are also more likely to use higher-level cognitive strategies. These students are involved in engaged reading. Engaged reading is a combination of intrinsic motivation and use of cognitive strategies that results in deep conceptual learning from text. Engagement is fostered when students pose questions that they want answered, when students see the value of topics they are studying, when students are given some choices in such matters as material being used and assignments to be completed, and when they have the opportunity to work with others and share what they have learned (Guthrie et al., 1996).

a much weaker element, increases. If students are struggling, their confidence in their ability as learners also declines, as does their expectancy for success (Guthrie, Alao, & Rinehart, 1997). Struggling learners are left with a diminished sense of competence. It diminishes further by the time the student reaches the middle school and high school environments, which are more competitive and place a greater emphasis on performance and grades. To make matters worse, all too often teachers emphasize the performance of top students.

Self-Regulated Learning

Motivation is metacognitive. Students are aware of what the teacher expects, how to meet these expectations, and what to do if problems arise (Conley, 1997). In other words, students' learning is self-regulated. In self-regulated learning, students take control of their learning. They set goals, create plans to meet those goals, and implement the plans and monitor their progress. They can assess their performance by noting whether the science experiments yield the hypothesized results or whether the answers to the math problems make sense logically. They are also reflective. By reflecting on their progress, they are able to see which strategies are working and which need revising.

Because self-regulated learning is metacognitve, students reflect on their learning. Because they reflect on what they know, students are aware of when they understand and when they need more information or information needs clarifying. They also know what they need to do if what they are reading doesn't make sense and what kinds of study techniques work best for them. With these kinds of awareness, they are able to take charge of their learning.

 *CHECKUP*

1. What are the characteristics of motivation?
2. What role does motivation play in learning?
3, What are the characteristics of an effective content area literacy program?
4. Which of the characteristics are most crucial?

IMPORTANCE OF THE TEACHER

Of all the elements needed to create an effective content area program, the teacher is the one that is far and above the most important. Shadowing Landy, a highly successful chemistry teacher, for a period of two years, researcher Elizabeth Moje (1996) discovered that Landy taught students learning strategies because she cared about them. She wanted them to be successful and so taught them a host of reading and writing strategies so that they would be better able to learn the principles of chemistry. Seeing chemistry as being a highly organized, precise body of knowledge, she taught students strategies that would help them organize information in a precise way. The students perceived the strategies that they were taught and were required to use as evidence that Landy cared about them and was trying to help them. One of the reasons they had faith in the strategies and persisted in their use was because of the positive relationship they had with Landy.

In addition to teaching them highly effective strategies for reading and retaining information from the text, she also taught students how to talk about chemistry in a precise and objective fashion. By asking students not only to make observations but also to critique observations, she taught students how to think like scientists. In addition to learning the meanings of technical terms, she also had students use these terms so that they were able to incorporate them in their speaking and writing in meaningful ways. To make abstract concepts concrete, she often made analogies between a key concept and some outside activity in which students were engaged. In addition to helping students understand concepts, she was showing an interest in them and building relationships with them. This relationship was a key factor in her success with students. In explaining her approach to teaching, Landy stated:

> When I started teaching I taught very traditionally. I taught my subject. I taught all the facts. But I've learned over the years that I don't teach subjects, I teach students, and so I've geared my teaching toward helping them learn how to learn. (Moje, 1996, p. 186)

Commenting on Landy's effectiveness, Lew, a struggling learner, noted that SQ3R, a study system, helped him cope with his chemistry text:

> SQ3R helps because she has you put the main topics in question form. So throughout your notetaking you should be able to answer the question, so it will give you a better understanding for what you read about. (Moje, 1996, p. 187)

But he also attributed his relative success as a student to Landy's caring attitude:

> She never puts someone down. She keeps them focused and makes them want to do the work more and more and more. . . . That's why I like this class so much even though I'm not an A student in there. She's positive so she keeps me into it so I'll keep trying harder. I'd be flunking chemistry if I didn't have a positive teacher. You need something to keep you going. (Moje, 1996, p. 187)

Effective content area teachers, like Landy, have a quality known as teacher efficacy. Teacher efficacy is the belief that teachers can have a positive influence on students. Teachers with high efficacy stress learning for the sake of learning, use praise rather than criticism, accept students as they are, and have a deep and abiding belief in students' ability to learn. They also use their time effectively and persevere with struggling learners (Eggen & Kauchak, 2001). They teach appropriate strategies and expect learning to require sustained effort (Eisenberger, Conti-D'Antonio, & Bertrando, 2000). Other characteristics that lead to increased learning include the following:

- Students engage in higher-order thinking by synthesizing and explaining information and reaching their own conclusions about the topics they study.
- Teachers introduce students to established branches of learning—accepted facts, concepts, and theories—with enough depth that students develop a complex understanding of the subject matter, including alternative explanations for different phenomena.
- Students interact with the teacher and each other to expand their understanding of existing branches of learning.
- Classroom learning has value beyond the classroom, enabling students to make connections between what they learn and their lives outside school. (Newmann & Wehlege, 2000).

The best instruction is the result of a combination of content and teaching knowledge. Content knowledge is necessary for good teaching, but it is not sufficient. Experts are not automatically good teachers. However, even the most gifted teachers need a solid grounding in content. Although there are general principles for effective instruction, some aspects of teaching are content specific. Good teachers know which concepts in their domain are difficult to understand and have devised ways to foster students' understanding of these concepts. Teachers who are able to instruct effectively in more than one discipline are able to do so because they have expertise and experience in more than one discipline (Bransford et al., 2001).

 *CHECKUP*

1. What are the characteristics of an effective content area teacher?

SUMMARY

Content area literacy is the ability to use reading and writing to acquire new knowledge in a content area. Although general reading and writing skills are needed, each discipline also has its own specific literacy demands. Unfortunately, about 25 to 40 percent of students have difficulty reading their content area texts. The content area teacher's role is to teach to all students those reading and writing skills needed to learn a particular subject. Although the reading specialist or English teacher may help, the content area teacher is in the best position to teach content-specific literacy skills. Elements of an effective literacy program require fostering cognitive development, recognizing and using the sociocognitive nature of learning, making connections, building academic language, developing literacy competencies, and fostering motivation and engagement. Equity and the impact of the somewhat controversial standards move-

ment are also factors that will influence effective content area programs. When all is said and done, the most important factor in an effective content area program is the teacher. An effective subject matter teacher focuses on students' needs and integrates content and strategies so that students will learn.

Reflection

Return to the Anticipation Guide at the beginning of this chapter. Respond once again to the items. Did your responses change? If so, how and why? What do you think should be the role of content area teachers in fostering literacy in their content areas? What should be the role of content area teachers in helping struggling learners?

EXTENSION AND APPLICATION

1. Read Elizabeth Moje's account of Landy, an exceptionally effective content area teacher who, because she cared deeply about her students, taught strategies that she believed would help them learn. This account can be found in Moje, E. (1996). "I teach students, not subjects": Teacher-student relationships as contexts for secondary literacy. *Reading Research Quarterly, 31,* 172–195.

2. What do you think the role of the content area teacher in your discipline should be? Write a brief reflection on this topic.

3. Analyze a current textbook in your subject matter area. What skills and strategies would students need to apply to read it?

chapter 2

THE NATURE AND ASSESSMENT OF CONTENT AREA TEXTS

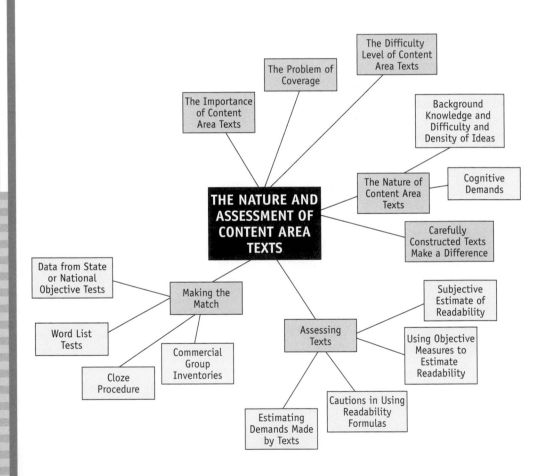

THE NATURE AND ASSESSMENT OF CONTENT AREA TEXTS

The Problem of Coverage

The Difficulty Level of Content Area Texts

The Importance of Content Area Texts

Background Knowledge and Difficulty and Density of Ideas

The Nature of Content Area Texts

Cognitive Demands

Carefully Constructed Texts Make a Difference

Data from State or National Objective Tests

Making the Match

Word List Tests

Commercial Group Inventories

Cloze Procedure

Assessing Texts

Subjective Estimate of Readability

Using Objective Measures to Estimate Readability

Cautions in Using Readability Formulas

Estimating Demands Made by Texts

ANTICIPATION GUIDE

Read each of the following statements. Put a check under "Agree" or "Disagree" to show how you feel about each one. If possible, discuss your responses with classmates.

		Agree	Disagree
1	Students make the most progress when their texts are on the easy side.	____	____
2	Low-achieving readers should read regular texts and not watered-down versions.	____	____
3	By and large, most texts are written on the grade level for which they were intended.	____	____
4	Content area teachers are too reliant on their textbooks.	____	____
5	Students should be able to handle texts that are on grade level.	____	____

USING WHAT YOU KNOW

This chapter contains the single most powerful procedure for improving reading in the content areas. As simple as it is effective, the procedure consists of matching students with materials that they can read.

Have you ever had the experience of having to read a text that was simply too difficult? How did you feel about it? What did you do to try to cope with the situation? Unfortunately, 25 to 40 percent of today's students are being asked to read content area books that are far too difficult for them (Schoenbach, Greenleaf, Cziko, & Hurwitz, 1999). This problem can be avoided by carefully selecting books and other materials that students can handle. This chapter explores the nature of content area texts, looks at ways of assessing their difficulty levels, and then discusses techniques that can be used to make sure that students are given materials that they can read.

THE IMPORTANCE OF CONTENT AREA TEXTS

The textbook has been described as the predominate tool in content area instruction (Alvermann & Moore, 1991) and as the "core of the curriculum in many schools" (Duffy et al., 1989, p. 436). In one survey, from 55 percent to nearly 80 percent of high school students reported using their English, math, science, or social studies texts from three to five times a week (Lester & Cheek, 1997–1998). When asked about their texts, students replied that they liked those texts best that were interesting and had information that they could relate to. Students disliked texts that were boring or hard to understand. Almost 50 percent of the students chose literature texts as their favorite. Math and social studies texts were rated as the least favorite texts. Student suggestions for improving texts included using of more graphics and up-to-date illustrations, featuring interesting topics, and creating texts that are easier to understand. A significant number felt that texts should not use "big" words that "nobody understands" (p. 289).

THE PROBLEM OF COVERAGE

Although a major tool in content area instruction, today's texts are so packed with facts that the reader may lose sight of the overall point of a section or chapter. Indeed, many texts jump from topic to topic without fully developing any one idea. Compared to math and science texts used in other countries, U.S. texts cover more topics but covered them in less depth. Breadth rather than depth is definitely emphasized. The typical U.S. science text covers between fifty-three and sixty-seven topics. In Germany, the range of topics covered is nine to sixteen, and in Japan, texts cover between eight to seventeen topics (National Science Boards, 2001). As might be expected, key topics were given less coverage in U.S. texts. The five most emphasized topics in U.S. fourth-grade science texts accounted for 25 percent of the total textbook space, compared to the international average of 70 percent to 75 percent. In eighth grade, the five most emphasized topics in U.S. general science texts accounted for 50 percent of textbook space, compared to 60 percent internationally (Science and Engineering Indicators, 2001).

Textbooks are expensive to produce. Textbook publishers include topics that will appeal to the widest possible audience so as to generate maximum sales; this translates into the fact that most texts conform to the content standards set by the largest states. Content standards that are overly inclusive lead to textbooks that cover too many topics. Moreover, pressured by high-stakes tests geared to state standards, teachers feel compelled to cover the text, even though it covers an excessive number of topics.

THE DIFFICULTY LEVEL OF CONTENT AREA TEXTS

Many, if not most, content area texts are written above the grade level for which they are intended; Conard (1990) suggested that 57 percent of the best-selling content area textbooks are above the grade level for which they were written. Social studies texts were one or two years above the designated grade level, while science texts were two or three years above grade level. On the seventh-grade level, for example, the average social studies textbook is written for grade 8 or 9 and the average science textbook for grade 9 or 10. Of course, this is not true of all textbooks. The difficulty of textbooks written for a particular grade level varies widely. However, in many instances the text is too difficult for as many as half the students in the class (Singer & Donlan, 1989). In his landmark study of **readability,** Bormuth (1971), who assessed both the difficulty of texts and the reading levels of students using them, found that the readability level of the materials he was assessing were often above the reading levels of the students using them.

■ **Readability** is the difficulty level of a selection.

Comprehension suffers when texts are too difficult. When high school students reading below their grade level were given material on their instructional level, their comprehension was adequate. However, when these same below-level readers were given material on their grade level but above their reading level, comprehension plummeted, and a number of students simply gave up (Kletzien, 1991). As one frustrated student commented, "I have no idea what this is talking about; I am just trying to remember anything that I can about Africa" (p. 82).

Texts can be too difficult, even for students reading on grade level. Some middle-grade students who possessed at least grade-level reading ability had difficulty with a long poem and an excerpt from a primary-source diary that was included in their text (Afflerbach & VanSledright, 2001). Although the text was on grade level, the adjunct materials were apparently on a higher level. Students experienced difficulty with the condensed language of the poem and the archaic language of the diary. Students also had difficulty integrating information from the main body of the text with the supplementary readings. However, targeted teaching might have been sufficient to help them overcome their difficulties.

 CHECKUP

1. What role do textbooks play in the teaching of content area subjects?
2. Why is it important that textbooks be at the appropriate level?

THE NATURE OF CONTENT AREA TEXTS

Containing new concepts and technical vocabulary, content area texts are generally more difficult to read than the fiction pieces that make up a large part of the reading students do during their early years of schooling. Moreover, being less complex in vocabulary, sentence structure, and overall organization, narrative texts do not provide adequate preparation for reading expository material (Stotsky, 1984). As it becomes more advanced, expository text also diverges more substantially from oral language and so requires more advanced text processing skills. Read and compare the following presentations.

Presentation One

As the devastation wrought by the drought and grasshopper infestations worsened, crops failed and cattle and other farm animals sickened and died. As a result farm income fell drastically.

Presentation Two

In the summer of 1931 there was no rain. The dry weather was bad for the crops, but it was good for the grasshoppers. Hordes of grasshoppers began attacking the crops. They hungrily ate plant after plant. Later more grasshoppers appeared. They ate much of what was left. The crops failed. The grass and the feed corn that the cattle ate dried up. The cattle grew sick and died. Farmers made very little money that year. (Press, 1999, p. 37)

The ideas are the same, but the expression of them is very different. The first is a written explanation. The second is an oral presentation. The oral presentation requires more clauses and more words to say basically the same thing as the written presentation. However, with its step-by-step explanation, the oral presentation is easier to understand. The written passage is more condensed, more complex, and has a greater lexical density (Unsworth, 1999). Lexical density is the proportion of content words per clause. Speech has an average of two content words per clause. Written text has a lexical density of four to six content words but may be higher (Halliday, 1994).

This greater density is achieved through a process of turning action verbs into nouns. The nouns are more abstract than the verbs they replace. The concrete idea of drought ruining crops is turned into the more abstract concept of *devastation*. Hordes of grasshoppers attacking crops becomes the more abstract term *infestation*. *Farm income* replaces the idea of farmers making money. This nominalization of the language, while more abstract, makes it easier for authors to build complex ideas. However, the more the language is nominalized, the further it departs from everyday language and the more challenge it offers to readers. Readers must learn to comprehend the language of informational text. In addition to learning the technical vocabulary of a content area, they must learn the grammar of the content area. As Unsworth (1999) notes, "For many students this does not occur spontaneously. It will need carefully scaffolded experience with written texts and explicit teaching of knowledge about language" (p. 514).

Vocabulary may also need to be scaffolded. As texts become more advanced, the nature of the vocabulary changes. Up until about grade 4, most of the vocabulary is familiar. Texts are written in a straightforward style that is characteristic of oral language. However, from grade 4 onward, there is an increasing proportion of technical or literary vocabulary and general vocabulary words that may not be familiar to the reader (Chall, Bissex, Conard, & Harris-Sharples, 1996).

Complex expository language is not the only element that causes content area text to be more difficult. As students progress through the grades, the expository texts they encounter grow in difficulty along three other dimensions: background knowledge required, density and difficulty of ideas, and cognitive demands.

Background Knowledge and Difficulty and Density of Ideas

As texts move up in grade level, they present a greater number of ideas and the ideas become more complex and abstract. The texts also require a greater amount of background knowledge. Note the density of ideas in the following passage and the background that a reader would need to fully comprehend it.

> The fifties may have been marred by racism and the threat of nuclear annihilation, but many Americans floated through those years on a cloud of prosperity and family values. An emphasis on marriage, children, and family life prevailed throughout the decade. The thirties had been the era of the Great Depression, when couples could not afford children and lived in crowded shacks, flats, or dilapidated apartments. The forties were war years, when women worked while husbands, fathers, brothers, and boyfriends marched off to battle. Many returned with serious injuries; some never returned at all. By the fifties, Americans had had enough of deprivation and anguish. (Kallen, 1999, p. 52)

Cognitive Demands —skills ; complexity of Ideas

Having a greater density and complexity of ideas, more advanced texts require higher-level reasoning skills. Students may be called upon to analyze a situation, infer causes, compare or contrast solutions, draw conclusions, apply a proposed solution, and evaluate the credibility of information. Note the cognitive skills required to read the following passages. Readers are called upon to compare and contrast Jefferson with Washington and Adams and to predict how Jefferson's beliefs might affect his presidency and the new nation.

> Thomas Jefferson, the victor in the fierce contest between the Republicans and the Federalists, was quite a different sort of person from the presidents before him, Washington and Adams. Those two Federalists believed in government by an elite of mostly "well born" men who had proved themselves by becoming wealthy. They adopted some of the manners of the British aristocracy, dressing in elegant clothes and holding formal parties at which leading figures from law, business, and government mingled. Thomas Jefferson was a Republican who believed that the strength of the country lay in the vast majority of Americans who owned their own farms. Such people had no bosses over them: in those days, before the secret ballot, they could vote as they wished,

not how a landlord or employer told them to vote. Jefferson had faith that they would elect the most talented and virtuous men available. (Collier & Collier, 1999, p. 18)

All content area texts are not equally difficult. History texts may be a bit easier than science texts because they tell a story and may be written in narrative style. Moreover, within each content area, the demands change as the material becomes more complex. Beginning science texts, for instance, are written in narrative style; more advanced texts are written in a technical, expository fashion. Each content area text makes its own unique demands on the reader. Knowing the demands made by a particular subject matter text, teachers are in a better position to help students comprehend material in that area. Following is a overview of the major texts in the subject matter areas and the demands made upon readers.

■ Science

Science texts at the elementary level tend to be descriptive/explanatory/technical. They describe scientific phenomena, such as what insects look like or how far away the sun is, and explain processes, such as how caterpillars develop into butterflies and how the earth revolves around the sun. At the primary level, an attempt is made to explain concepts in terms of the readers' background of everyday experience. Technical terms are generally explained within the text. In grades 4 and beyond, the texts continue to build on the readers' background of everyday experience but, increasingly, the texts allude to concepts that have not been taught in school. Note how a science text develops the concept of *convection currents:*

> Air begins to move when the sun heats the land and warms the air above. Molecules in the air move faster when they are heated and the air starts to expand. It becomes less dense than the surrounding air. At the same time, cooler, heavier air is drawn in below to replace the rising air. This circulation of air is called convection current. (Morgan, 1996, p. 10)

Reading science requires being able to follow the chain of reasoning used to explain processes that result in phenomena such as convection currents. Each link in the process must be understood and connected to the next link. Then, when readers encounter the name of the process in future reading, they must remember the process that this name describes.

As students move up through the grades, concepts become more complex and abstract. A greater number of technical terms are introduced. The reader must be able to deal with a large number of details and engage in some abstract reasoning—for instance, the type of reasoning needed to understand the relationship between the angle of the sun and the temperature on earth. On the high school level, the student must be able to deal with theoretical ideas. This is especially true in the physical sciences. Life sciences texts (biology, health, ecology) tend to be more descriptive and technical, whereas the physical sciences (physics, astronomy) tend to be more abstract and theoretical. Life sciences texts also tend to be more explicit. Being more abstract and more theoretical, the physical sciences require a greater number of inferences (Chall et al., 1996). Physics texts are usually harder to read and more demanding cognitively than biology texts.

■ Social Studies

Social studies texts may be narrative or expository. Narrative texts present events in storylike fashion. Expository texts discuss events in terms of causes and effects and issues involved; more analysis and evaluation is required for reading expository texts. Texts at the lowest levels tend to be narrative. Events are explained in concrete fashion in terms of the readers' experiences. Events are described but not analyzed. Vocabulary is generally defined in context. Beginning with grade level 3, writing style becomes more formal and concepts become more abstract. More prior knowledge is also required. At levels 5 and beyond, ideas and vocabulary are denser, with many new words not explained in context. More demands are made on the students' background of experience and reasoning. Readers, especially at the high school level, are involved in interpreting and evaluating events and ideas (Chall et al., 1996).

Although not as technical a subject as science, history can be very abstract, especially in the upper grades. In the early grades, history is presented as a story that involves people and their actions. In later years, history becomes more analytical. Notice the difference between the first passage below, excerpted from a fifth-grade history text, and the second passage, excerpted from a tenth-grade text.

📖 Passage from Fifth-Grade Text

The Committees of Correspondence called for action. They felt that the Intolerable Acts were simply—well—intolerable! On September 5, 1774, representatives from 12 colonies met in Philadelphia. Among the representatives were Samuel Adams, Patrick Henry, and George Washington.

These men wrote down their complaints and sent the list off to the king, asking for help. They also agreed to meet again in May 1775. (Garcia, Gelo, Greenow, Kracht, & White, 1997a, p. 170)

Passage from Tenth-Grade Text

The First Continental Congress meets in Philadelphia. Colonial leaders immediately answered Massachusetts' call for a meeting. In September 1774 delegates from every colony except Georgia met in Philadelphia to form what became known as the First Continental Congress. (The term "Continentals" was often used to refer to the colonists in North America.)

A heavy burden rested on the shoulders of these delegates, most of whom still regarded themselves as loyal British subjects. In only 11 years the world they had known had vanished. In 1763 they had been proud British citizens, celebrating one of Great Britain's greatest military victories. Now, in 1774, they were meeting to find ways of resisting what many of them felt was British tyranny.

◼ Literature

Reading popular fiction, readers must grasp only the surface meaning of a work. Reading literature requires going beyond the surface meaning and to experience the emotional depth of the work. Reading literature also requires a greater intensity of involvement as the reader identifies with complex characters and situations. At higher levels, knowledge of literary conventions and literary language are required, as is the exercise of aesthetic judgment. Compare your reading of the following two selections:

Passage from *Sweet Valley High: Winter Carnival*

It was four o'clock on a rainy Tuesday afternoon, and Elizabeth Wakefield was looking down at her sopping shoes with a rueful smile on her face. It figured that she missed the bus on one of the few rainy days that they had had all winter. And it also figured that her twin sister, Jessica, would have taken the Fiat that they shared to run an errand for the cheerleading squad. Elizabeth sighed. There were still four blocks to go before she got home, and at this rate she could practically swim. (William, 1986, p. 1)

Passage from *The Witch of Blackbird Pond*

It took nine days for the *Dolphin* to make the forty-three mile voyage from Saybrook to Wethersfield. As though the ship were bewitched, from the moment they left Saybrook, everything went wrong. With the narrowing of the river the fresh sea breeze dropped behind, and by sunset it died away altogether. The sails sagged limp and soundless, and the *Dolphin* rolled sickeningly in midstream. On one or two evenings a temporary breeze raised their hopes and sent the ship ahead a few miles, only to die away again. In the morning Kit could scarcely tell that they had moved. The dense brown forest on either side never seemed to vary, and ahead there was only a new bend in the river to tantalize her. (Speare, 1958, pp. 14–15)

In addition to a greater richness and originality of language, *The Witch of Blackbird Pond* has a more complex plot and more lifelike characters. It has the power to transport readers to another time and place. It enables them to see the world through the eyes of another person and to experience a wide range of deep emotions. Although readers may enjoy *Sweet Valley High*, they will not have the depth of experience that may be evoked by *The Witch of Blackbird Pond*.

 **✔ CHECKUP**

1. What demands do content area textbooks make on the reader?
2. How do texts from different content areas make different demands?

CAREFULLY CONSTRUCTED TEXTS MAKE A DIFFERENCE

In their study of history texts, Beck, McKeown, Sinatra, and Loxterman (1991) found a number of deficiencies that made textbooks difficult to understand. As Armbruster (1996) points out, considerate texts "say a lot about a few ideas rather than a little about many ideas. . . . By sacrificing depth for breadth, textbooks often fail to explain concepts and clarify the relationships among ideas in a way that matches the topic knowledge of the intended audience" (p. 55). Beck and her colleagues (1991) revised a segment of a history text by clarifying confusing elements, elaborating and explaining key events, making connections explicit, and explaining why the groups acted the way they did so readers can understand their motivation. They explained key terms, such as *intolerable*, that are necessary for an understanding of the piece but which would probably be unfamiliar. They also broke up sentences so that they would be less dense. In addition, they filled in background information that students might lack but that would be important for an understanding of the passage. In making these revisions, they doubled the length of the text. However, comprehension of the revised passage was dramatically better: Students recalled 25 percent more information and were able to answer nearly twice as many comprehension questions. In other words, having a reader-friendly text enabled students to learn 25 percent more of the subject matter.

A text is reader friendly when authors go out of their way to make their writing as clear and understandable as possible, when they carefully consider their readers as they write. Reader-friendly texts use headings to announce main ideas, define words in context, and give plenty of examples. Notice how the author of a popular book on weather, excerpted below, uses questions, examples, and analogies to make a difficult concept meaningful. Note, too, that the author does not assume background knowledge that the reader may not possess. He begins by explaining the states of water, an understanding of which is necessary in order to grasp the concept of *humidity*.

Moisture and Humidity

In all my years of teaching and talking about the weather, I have never encountered a concept more difficult to grasp than humidity. If you make it through the next few pages, the rest of the book will be a breeze. [This alerts the reader to read slowly and carefully because a difficult concept is being explained.]

Let's start off by recognizing that water can exist in three different states: solid, liquid, and vapor. All states consist of the molecule H_2O; the only difference concerns the spacing of the molecules. The following figure depicts these different states. As a solid, the water molecules are closest together. As a vapor, the molecules are farthest apart. So, the whole story here hinges on what makes these molecules drift apart, or come together. Any guesses? [The question prompts readers to become active and to predict why molecules drift apart, or come together, something that proficient readers do.]

How about temperature? Think of the molecules as popcorn in a popper. When the heat is first turned on, the kernels are just sitting there, solidly, on the bottom of the popper. But then, as heat is added and the temperature increases, the kernels start popping, and the popped corn starts moving around. Like popcorn, water vapor molecules are bouncing around, thanks to heat in the atmosphere. The water molecules are far enough apart that the vapor is invisible. The vapor itself comes from the water that is evaporated from the earth's surface, including oceans and lakes. [The use of analogy makes an abstract concept concrete. It also invites the reader to visualize the process, which is an excellent aid to comprehension and retention.]

In subsequent passages, the author uses illustrations, examples, and the analogy of a glass that overflows if too much water is poured in it to explain humidity. Part of what makes the text understandable is that the author took his time and gave a detailed, step-by-step explanation. Some science texts provide a highly condensed version of this process that omits the helpful examples and analogies that make a difficult concept understandable.

 *CHECKUP*

1. What are some of the characteristics of a carefully constructed text?
2. In what ways does a carefully constructed text help the reader?

ASSESSING TEXTS

Because texts are a key element in most content area classes and can make a significant difference in students' learning, they should be carefully assessed. It is essential that students be able to read their texts. Although today's texts, with their many charts, diagrams, color photos, and sidebars, are more attractive, they are more complex. In the past, captions and illustrations generally supported or even repeated information in the main body of the text. Today, many of the graphic features present additional information. The reader needs to decide whether the additional information is essential and, if so, to integrate it with information from the main body of the text (Walpole, 1998–1999).

When assessing the demands made by content area texts, factor in the author's style and reading aids that the author includes. Text features that hinder comprehension include: difficult or unfamiliar language, ambiguous or distant references, failure to provide information that will enable the reader to activate appropriate background knowledge, lack of clear connections between ideas or events, inclusion of irrelevant material, and a high density of ideas.

The difficulty level of material is also influenced by the organization of a text. A text that is well organized and well written is easier to understand. Elaboration, or developing ideas fully, makes a text easier to comprehend (Coleman, 1971), as does repeating key ideas (Kintsch, Kozminisky, Streby, McKoon, & Keenan, 1975). Using comprehension aids also lowers the difficulty level of a text. An introductory overview, headings, and questions placed before and after the text and interspersed within the text can aid comprehension (Zakaluk & Samuels, 1988). Explicitly stating instructional objectives can also foster understanding (Anderson, 1980). Charts, tables, maps, photos, drawings, phonetic respellings of difficult words, defining words in context, and a glossary are other features that aid the reader. Interest is also a factor in estimating the difficulty level of a text. Students may put forth extra effort to overcome difficulties if they have a strong interest in the text. Table 2.1 contains a number of subjective factors that may be considered when assessing texts.

Subjective Estimate of Readability

Fostering literacy in the content areas requires being aware of the complexities of the texts that students will be reading and the demands that these texts will make on students. A good starting point is to estimate the overall difficulty level of the text.

*T*eachers can use one of a number of Web sites to check the readability level of texts.

TABLE 2.1

SUBJECTIVE READABILITY INDEX

Text Factors

Content	Low				High
Familiarity of concepts	1	2	3	4	5
Concreteness of concepts	1	2	3	4	5
Style					
Clarity of writing	1	2	3	4	5
Elaboration of key concepts	1	2	3	4	5
Ease of vocabulary	1	2	3	4	5
Simplicity of sentences	1	2	3	4	5
Use of anecdotes	1	2	3	4	5
Relates text to students' background	1	2	3	4	5
Organization					
Use of heads, subheads	1	2	3	4	5
Focus on major ideas	1	2	3	4	5
Logical flow of ideas	1	2	3	4	5
Exclusion of irrelevant material	1	2	3	4	5
Features That Enhance Comprehension					
Chapter overview	1	2	3	4	5
Summary	1	2	3	4	5
Questions	1	2	3	4	5
Graphics	1	2	3	4	5
Phonemic respellings	1	2	3	4	5
Definitions provided in text	1	2	3	4	5
Glossary	1	2	3	4	5

Total
(The higher the total, the easier the text)

Reader Factors					
Background of knowledge	1	2	3	4	5
Vocabulary	1	2	3	4	5
Overall reading ability	1	2	3	4	5
Interest	1	2	3	4	5
Motivation	1	2	3	4	5
Study/work habits	1	2	3	4	5

Total
(The higher the number, the better the reader)

From *Assessing and Correcting Reading and Writing Difficulties* (p. 471) by T. Gunning, 2002. Boston: Allyn & Bacon. Reprinted by permission.

This can be done subjectively or objectively or by using a combination of objective and subjective methods. The quickest and perhaps most widely used technique for estimating text difficulty is teacher judgment. Unfortunately, teacher judgment can be wide of the mark. In one study, teacher's judgment differed by as much as six years from estimates yielded by a readability formula (Jorgenson, 1975). However, teacher judgment can be greatly improved if teachers use guidelines and anchor passages to help them estimate difficulty levels (Carver, 1975–1976; Singer, 1975). Listed in Figure 2.1 are science anchor passages arranged in order of difficulty. Passages are provided for grades 2, 4, 6, 8, 10, and 12. Accompanying each text selection is a brief description of the language, background, idea density, and cognitive level of the passage. Using the passages and descriptions as a guide, assess the difficulty level of the two passages in Figure 2.1. When assessing the difficulty of a passage, locate the passage in Figure 2.1 that seems most like the passage you are assessing. If the passage seems to be between two of the scaling passages, place it between the two—if it seems harder than passage 8 but easier than passage 10, place it at level 9. If in doubt, err on the conservative side. If you can't decide between two levels, choose the higher level. It is better to give students a passage that is a little on the easy side than one that is too difficult. After estimating the difficulty level of the passage, note the skills and knowledge that the average student in that grade would have to bring to the passage to read it successfully. Consider the subjective factors noted in Table 2.1. If you are estimating the difficulty level of a textbook, examine three or four sample passages of about 100 words each and average the results of your estimates.

The passages in Figure 2.1 can be used to estimate the readability of science passages or passages in other subject matter areas, but they provide most valid results when used with science passages. A better instrument is the *Qualitative Assessment of Text Difficulty* (Chall et al., 1996). Based on research that indicates that different types of text require different kinds of background and different types of strategies, the *Qualitative Assessment of Text Difficulty* has six scales: one for popular fiction, one for literature, one for biographical and narrative history, one for expository history, one for the biological sciences, and one for the physical sciences. Most of the scales contain nine levels and range in difficulty from grade 1 through college. To estimate the difficulty level of a text, the user chooses the most appropriate scale and then selects 100-word samples and compares them with the scaled passages. Using the scales, teachers' judgments were within one year of the quantitative readabilities of texts nearly 100 percent of the time (Chall et al., 1996).

Using Objective Measures to Estimate Readability

Along with subjective measures of readability, you may use an objective formula. **Readability formulas** have a long history of use for checking the difficulty level of texts. Although there are many factors involved in determining the difficulty level of a text, the two factors that have the highest correlation with text difficulty are sentence complexity and difficulty of vocabulary. Sentence or syntactic complexity is typically assessed through sentence length. Although some short sentences are harder than some long sentences, the longer the sentence, the more difficult it tends to be, on

■ **Readability formulas** are objective measurements of the difficulty level of reading material. They generally consist of some measure of the average sentence length and the proportion of hard words in a selection.

FIGURE 2.1

Science Anchor Passages

Grade 2

Sentences are relatively short and the vocabulary is fairly simple. Concepts are concrete and familiar. All the words used are words that are in most second-graders' listening vocabulary.

> What are some ways you can keep your body healthy? You can eat healthful foods. These kinds of foods help your body grow strong. You can also exercise. This will make your muscles and bones stronger.
>
> Getting enough sleep helps keep you healthy, too. When you sleep, your body gets the rest it needs.
>
> What are some things that are not good for your body? Too many cookies, candies, or potato chips are not good for you. (Badders et al., 1999a, E 30–31)

Grade 4

Sentences are somewhat longer. Vocabulary is somewhat more advanced and includes words such as *reminders, ideas, disease,* and *regular* that are likely in fourth-graders' listening vocabulary but that some fourth-graders might find difficult to decode. Concepts are concrete and include *disease* and *germs,* which have probably been introduced in school.

> Don't forget to wash your hands! Eat all your vegetables. You'd better clean that cut. It's late; go to sleep! Have you ever heard these reminders? They're all good things for you to do because each can help your body fight disease.
>
> The best way to help your body fight disease is to keep your body healthy. You can do this by eating well, getting regular exercise, and getting enough sleep. These things will help your body stay strong so that it can fight germs. Keeping your body clean will also help keep germs from entering your body. (Badders et al., 1999b, F 54)

Grade 6

Sentences are a bit longer and vocabulary is becoming more advanced and more diverse and includes words such as *diet, grains, benefits,*

sparingly, and *flexible.* Concepts are becoming more abstract, and there is more school-type content to be grasped.

> Perhaps one of the most important steps in building healthful habits is to learn to eat in a healthful way. If the food you eat isn't healthful or if you eat too much or too little, then your body won't be as healthy as it can be.
>
> Meats and milk products should make up less of your diet than grains, fruits, and vegetables. And some of the foods that many people like best, including sugary and fatty foods, should be eaten sparingly. Some fat is needed in the diet. But generally people take in too much fat, causing them to gain weight. To cut down on fat in your diet, choose lean meats and avoid fatty food.
>
> Generally there is only one way to maintain proper weight—have a healthful diet and get regular exercise. Exercise has other benefits—it promotes a healthy heart, good lungs, strong muscles, a flexible body, and a feeling of well being. (Badders et al., 1999c, G59–60)

Grade 8

Sentences are longer and more complex. Vocabulary is definitely more advanced and includes technical words such as *pathogen, circulatory, respiratory,* and *resistance.* Concepts are becoming more abstract, and density of concepts has increased.

> One way to stay healthy is to avoid contact with pathogens. If someone has an infectious disease, avoid close contact. Wash your hands before handling food and eating. Prepare and store food properly and do not eat food that has spoiled. What are some other ways you can avoid contact with pathogens? Another way to protect yourself against disease is to practice good health habits. Good health habits promote your resistance, or ability, to fight pathogens. Studies show that healthful practices begun at an early age make it more likely that you

average. This is also true of words. Although some short words are hard and some long words are relatively easy, the longer the word or the more syllables it has, the more difficult it is, on average. Word length and number of syllables are frequently used as measures of vocabulary difficulty. However, some formulas determine difficulty level by calculating the proportion of words not on a list of easy or high-frequency words or the frequency with which the words appear in print.

FIGURE 2.1

Science Anchor Passages *(continued)*

will be a healthy adult. What kind of practices help you stay healthy? First, be sure to get regular exercise. Your heart and blood vessels are strengthened by exercise. Exercise also relieves stress. Stress often lowers your resistance to infection. Second, get enough sleep. Most teenagers require seven to eight hours of sleep each night. Too little sleep can lower your resistance to pathogens. Third, eat a nutritious diet. Start off each day with breakfast. Many teenagers skip breakfast, but your growing body needs three meals a day. . . . It's also important to eat fewer fatty foods, like butter, and fewer foods high in cholesterol, like eggs. These foods contribute to heart and circulatory diseases. Fourth, avoid tobacco and alcohol. By not smoking, you're protecting your body from respiratory disease. By not drinking alcohol, you are protecting your body from many diseases of the heart, stomach, and liver. Fifth, have regular medical checkups. (Warner et al., 1991, p. 477)

Grade 10

Syntax and vocabulary have become advanced. Concept density is high and vocabulary has become abstract and technical. Readers need a fairly good background in biology in order to comprehend this passage fully.

Although the body is able to manufacture many of the molecules it needs, it must still obtain the materials for this from the food it takes in. The classes of nutrients that are part of any healthy diet are water, carbohydrates, fats, proteins, vitamins, and minerals.

Water

Water is the most important of all nutrients. Water is needed by every cell in our body, and it makes up the bulk of blood, lymph, and other body fluids. Water dissolves food taken into the digestive system. Water in the form of sweat cools the body. Water is lost

from the body as vapor in every breath we exhale and as the primary component of urine. If enough water—at least a liter a day—is not taken in to replace what is lost, dehydration can result. This leads to problems with the circulatory, respiratory, and nervous systems. Drinking plenty of pure water is one of the best things you can do to help keep your body healthy. (Miller & Levine, 1998, p. 852)

Grade 12–adult

Sentences are generally long and complicated, and vocabulary is advanced. There is a high proportion of relatively difficult words. Concept density is high, and considerable background knowledge is required.

The health and fitness benefits of physical activity cannot be overstated: Exercise is essential for maintaining cardiovascular fitness, muscle strength, stamina, balance, and joint flexibility. Strength-developing exercise improves overall musculoskeletal health, and stretching maintains flexibility. Physical activity also increases energy level, improves mood, and diminishes anxiety and stress. Exercise can be beneficial in avoiding weight gain and in helping replace fat with muscle.

Moderate exercise performed consistently can prevent or control heart disease and diabetes. Higher levels of physical activity are linked with increased levels of high density lipoprotein (HDL), the "good" cholesterol in the blood. If you are a smoker, increasing your level of physical activity may motivate you to cut down on your smoking. Women who exercise may lessen the debilitating effects of osteoporosis, or avoid the disease altogether. Physical activity is also one of the best means we have of ensuring that we age well and enjoy life more fully. Exercise can even increase life expectancy. (Klag, 1999, p. 33)

■ Syllable Formulas

Because of its ease of use, the Fry Readability Graph is one of the most popular readability formulas. The Fry Graph, shown in Figure 2.2, measures sentence length and number of syllables in a word. Appearing in a number of popular word processing programs, including Microsoft Word, the Flesch-Kincaid formula is also widely used. It, too, measures sentence length and number of syllables and correlates very

FIGURE 2.2

Fry Graph for Estimating Readability

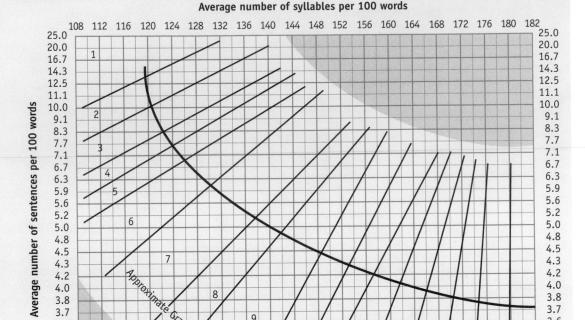

Average number of syllables per 100 words

Expanded Directions for Working Readability Graph

1. Randomly select three (3) sample passages and count out exactly 100 words each, beginning with the beginning of a sentence. Do count proper nouns, initializations, and numerals.

2. Count the number of sentences in the 100 words, estimating length of the fraction of the last sentence to the nearest one-tenth.

3. Count the total number of syllables in the 100-word passage. If you don't have a hand counter available, an easy way is to simply put a mark above every syllable over one in each word, then when you get to the end of the passage, count the number of marks and add 100. Small calculators can also be used by pushing numeral 1, then the + sign for each word or syllable when counting.

4. Enter graph with *average* sentence length and *average* number of syllables; plot dot where the two lines intersect. Area where dot is plotted will give you the approximate grade level.

5. If a great deal of variability is found in syllable count or sentence count, putting more samples into the average is desirable.

6. A word is defined as a group of symbols with space on either side; thus, *Joe, IRA, 1945,* and *&* are each one word.

7. A syllable is defined as a phonetic syllable. Generally, there are as many syllables as vowel sounds. For example, *stopped* is one syllable and *wanted* is two syllables. When counting syllables for numerals and initializations, count one syllable for each symbol. For example, *1945* is four syllables, *IRA* is three syllables, and *&* is one syllable.

Fry's Readability Graph: Clarifications, Validity, and Extension to Level 17 by E. Fry, 1977, *Journal of Reading, 21,* p. 249.

highly with the Fry Graph (Fusaro, 1988). In Word, it can be found in Tools: Spelling and Grammar. (You may have to use the Preferences [Options in PCs] menu to activate it. To avoid checking grammar, uncheck all grammar items under Settings.) After spelling and grammar have been checked, click on NO when you get the message: Word finished checking the selection. Do you want to continue checking the remainder of the document?

■ Word List Formulas

A number of readability formulas use proportion of words not appearing on a word list of familiar words instead of number of syllables as a measure of vocabulary difficulty. One of the most carefully validated of the word list formulas is the New Dale-Chall Readability Formula (Chall & Dale, 1995). The New Dale-Chall can be used to estimate the difficulty level of material from grade 1 through grade 16, but it is most valid for materials in the grade 3 to grade 12 range. The New Dale-Chall's estimate of difficulty is based on average sentence length and number of words not found on the Revised Dale List, a compilation of 3,000 words known by most fourth-graders. Recognizing that interest and background knowledge are important factors in readability, the New Dale-Chall features two worksheets, one for assessing reading characteristics, including probable interest of the reader in the topic to be read, and a second for assessing cognitive-structural aspects of the text. Complementing the New Dale-Chall is the Primary Readability Index (Gunning, 2002), which assesses readability levels up to grade 4.

How do the major formulas compare? Figure 2.3 shows three passages from a middle school earth science text (Exline, Pasachoff, Simons, Vogel, & Wellnitz, 2001) that were analyzed using the New Dale-Chall, the Fry Graph, and the Flesch-Kincaid. Note the calculations. The words that are in boldface are those that are not on the Dale List of Known Words and so are counted as being hard words according to the New Dale-Chall formula. Vocabulary difficulty for the Fry Graph is measured by counting the number of syllables per 100 words. The numbers above the words represent the number of syllables minus one in the word. Because each word has at least one syllable, the count is started at 100. Then a notation is made for each word that has two or more syllables. Subtract one syllable because you have already counted one syllable for each word, so if a word has two syllables, put a 1 over it; if it has three, put a 2 over it, and so forth. See Figure 2.2 for more detailed directions. Calculations for the Flesch-Kincaid are not shown. Only the results of the Flesch-Kincaid are shown because this formula was calculated by the word processing program being used.

What do you notice about the results shown in Table 2.2? For one thing, the difficulty level of the samples varies. Passages in the same text often range in difficulty. Books may become harder because the vocabulary and ideas in them are cumulative. Although a book may be relatively easy on average, it may have some rather difficult passages. Note also that different formulas give different results. The Dale-Chall estimates that the book is written on a sixth-grade level. The other two estimate the difficulty level as being grade 7. Because the samples varied in difficulty, with one being particulary low, it would be helpful to analyze additional samples.

FIGURE 2.3

Comparison of Passages Analyzed by Dale-Chall, Fry Graph, and Flesch-Kincaid

When waves hit a steep, rocky coast, they strike the area again and again. Think of an ax striking the trunk of a tree. The cut gets bigger and deeper with each strike of the **blade.** Finally the tree falls. In a **similar** way, ocean waves **erode** the base of the land along a steep coast. Where the rock is softer, the waves **erode** the land faster. Over time the waves may **erode** a hollow area in the rock called a sea cave.

Eventually, waves may **erode** the base of a cliff so much that the rock above **collapses.** The result is a wave-cut cliff. (Exline et al., 2001, p. 276)

Number of sentences 8.2, 130 syllables
Dale-Chall 4, Flesch-Kincaid 4.2, Fry 5

Coral animals are tiny **relatives** of jellyfish that live together in **vast** numbers. Most **coral** animals are the size of your fingernail or even smaller. Each one looks like a small sack with a mouth surrounded by **tentacles.** These animals use their **tentacles** to capture and eat **microscopic** creatures that float by. They produce **skeletons** that grow together to form a **structure** called a **coral reef.**

Coral reefs form only in the warm, **shallow** water of **tropical** oceans. **Coral** animals cannot grow in cold water or water low in salt. **Reefs** are most **abundant** around islands and along the eastern shores of continents. (Exline et al., 2001, p. 88)

Number of sentences 7.8, 156 syllables
Dale-Chall 7–8, Flesch-Kincaid 7.9, Fry 9

During the **California** Gold Rush of 1849, thousands of people headed west to find gold in the California hills. Some found gold, but most found **disappointment.** Perhaps the most **disappointed** of all were the ones who found **pyrite,** or "fool's gold." All three **minerals** in Figure 4 look like gold, yet only one is the real thing.

Because there are so many different kinds of **minerals,** telling them apart can be a **challenge.** The color of a **mineral** alone often **provides** too little **information** to make an **identification.** Each **mineral** has its own **specific** properties that can be used to identify it. (Exline et al, 2001, p. 49)

Number of sentences 6.9, 157 syllables
Dale-Chall 5–6, Flesch-Kincaid 8.9, Fry 9

Using the sample science anchor passages as a guide, what would you estimate the readability to be?

■ Formulas That Require Computers

Three widely used formulas are so complex that they require computers: the Degrees of Reading Power (DRP), the Lexile Scale, and ATOS. The Degrees of Reading Power

TABLE 2.2

COMPARISON OF READABILITY ESTIMATES YIELDED BY DIFFERENT MANUAL FORMULAS

	Fry	Flesch-Kincaid	New Dale-Chall
Sample 1	5	4.2	4
Sample 2	9	7.9	7–8
Sample 3	9	8.9	5–6
Avg. Readability	7.7	7.0	6

measures sentence length, number of words not on the Dale List, and average number of letters per word (Touchstone Applied Science Associates, 1994). Most readability formulas report their estimates in grade equivalent scores—for instance, 5.2, 9.7, 7–8. However, the Degrees of Reading Power reports its levels in DRP Units. Table 2.3 translates DRP units into grade equivalent scores. These translations are approximations. Compilations of readability levels expressed in DRP units for content area textbooks can be found on the Web site http://www.tasaliteracy.com. DRP readabilities for trade books are available on a piece of easy-to-use software titled *BookLink*.

The Lexile Scale is a two-factor formula that consists of a measurement of sentence length and word frequency. Because of the word frequency factor, calculating a lexile score without the aid of a computerized program is impractical. A software program, the Lexile Analyzer, is available from MetaMetrics. However, nearly 30,000 lexile scores are available on line at http://www.lexile.com/.

USING TECHNOLOGY

TASA Literacy
http://www.tasaliteracy.com
Contains compilations of readability levels expressed in DRP units for content area textbooks. DRP readabilities for trade books are available on a piece of easy-to-use software: *BookLink*.

USING TECHNOLOGY

Lexile
http://www.lexile.com/
More than 30,000 lexile scores are available.

TABLE 2.3

DRP AND LEXILE SCORES

Grade Equivalent	DRP Score	Lexile Score
PP	34–36	200–250
P	37–39	250–300
1	40–43	300–400
2	44–47	400–500
3	48–49	500–700
4	50–51	700–800
5	52–53	800–900
6	54–55	900–1000
7	56–57	1000–1100
8	58–59	1000–1100
9–10	60–64	1100–1200
11–12	65–68	1200–1300

ATOS (Advantage-TASA Open Standard) uses number of words per sentence, characters per word, and average grade level of words to analyze the entire text to estimate the readability of a book. The estimate is expressed as a grade-level equivalent. ATOS scores for more than 40,000 trade books are available from Renaissance Learning, the creators of Accelerated Reading, at their Web site http://www.renlearn.com. Click on Quizzes, and enter the title of the book for which you would like to have an ATOS score. If an ATOS score is not available, contact Renaissance Learning. The organization has ATOS scores for a number of books for which it does not have quizzes. The organization will also do a readability analysis of texts for which it does not have scores.

Table 2.4 presents a comparison of readabilities yielded by the Lexile, ATOS, and DRP. There is a fair amount of agreement between the ATOS and DRP. These two formulas yield readability estimates within one grade of each other 85 percent of the time. The ATOS and Lexile also agree within one level 85 percent of the time. However, the Lexile and DRP are in agreement within one level just 55 percent of

TABLE 2.4

COMPARISON OF READABILITY ESTIMATES YIELDED BY DIFFERENT COMPUTER FORMULAS

	Lexile	ATOS	DRP
Across Five Aprils	1000 (7–8)	6.6	59 (8)
Animal Farm	1130 (9–10)	7.3	60 (9–10)
Banner in the Sky	680 (3)	5.1	51 (4)
Brian's Winter	1140 (9–10)	5.9	54 (6)
Call It Courage	830 (5)	6.2	55 (6)
The Call of the Wild	1140 (9–10)	8.0	62 (9–10)
Catcher in the Rye	790 (4)	4.7	49 (3)
The Chocolate War	790 (4)	5.4	56 (7)
The Fighting Ground	580 (3)	4.2	50 (4)
Flowers for Algernon	910 (6)	5.8	55 (6)
Go Tell It on the Mountain	1030 (7–8)	6.5	59 (8)
The Great Gatsby	1205 (11–12)	7.3	61 (9–10)
Hiroshima	1190 (9–10)	8.4	64 (9–10)
Let the Circle Be Unbroken	850 (5)	5.7	53 (5)
Lord of the Flies	770 (4)	5.0	58 (8)
The Outsiders	820 (5)	5.3	51 (4)
The Pearl	1010 (7)	7.1	58 (8)
The Scarlet Letter	1420 (12+)	11.7	67 (11–12)
A Separate Peace	1110 (9–10)	6.9	59 (8)
Where the Lilies Bloom	920 (6)	5.2	53 (5)

Numbers in parentheses are approximate grade level equivalents of lexile and DRP scores.

the time. They agree within two levels 90 percent of the time. The ATOS tends to yield levels that are lower than the Lexile and the DRP. Of the three formulas, the DRP is the most conservative; it tends to yield higher levels than the other two. A formula that yields higher levels is better for students in some ways. There is less chance that it will underestimate the difficulty level of a book, so there is less chance that students will be mistakenly given a book that is harder than the readability formula suggests.

All three formulas function as screening devices. They indicate the approximate average levels of books. However, they occasionally disagree by as much as three or four years. This points up the limitations of readability formulas and the need for the teacher to complement the objective data yielded by the formula with subjective judgment about the difficulty level and suitability of materials for students.

Cautions in Using Readability Formulas

Readability formulas provide a useful objective estimate of the difficulty level of text. However, they must be properly used and carefully interpreted. Most formulas require that the user sample at least three or four passages because passages within a text often vary in difficulty. Different formulas also yield different levels. Note the levels in Tables 2.2 and 2.4.

Even the best of formulas is only a mechanical measure that fails to consider key factors such as complexity and density of ideas, author's style, and background required to read a selection. On the other hand, subjective judgment is prone to error. The most effective way to assess readability is to combine an objective measure with subjective judgment. In one study in which the researcher used both an objective measure of readability and subjective judgment, he changed readability estimates approximately one time out of four on the basis of subjective judgment (Gunning, 1999).

Estimating Demands Made by Texts

Although it is helpful to know the overall readability of a text, it is also important to know what demands it will place on students in the following areas: language complexity, including vocabulary and sentence structure; background knowledge, including general background knowledge and subject specific knowledge; density and difficulty of ideas; and reasoning skills required to read the text. In other words, as you look over a text, ask yourself the question What does the reader need to bring to text in order to be able to understand it? The answer will help you select texts that are on the appropriate level. It will also aid you in providing instruction that will help students better understand their texts.

 CHECKUP

1. How should the difficulty level of a textbook be assessed?
2. Why is it important to use both subjective and objective factors?

MAKING THE MATCH

Knowing the difficulty level of a passage is only half the equation. Now you need to know what difficulty level of material your students can handle. To do this, you need to find out what their overall reading level is. It is also helpful if you have information about their language ability, background knowledge, reasoning skills, and ability to read text typically used in your content area.

If your class is fairly typical, you will find a wide range of abilities among your students. To estimate the range of reading levels in a heterogeneously grouped class, multiply the average chronological age by $\frac{2}{3}$. Thus, if the average age of your tenth-graders is fifteen, then there may be a span of ten reading levels ($\frac{2}{3} \times 15 = 10$) ranging from grade 5 through grade 15.

There are numerous ways to obtain students' instructional levels. The most valid approach is to administer an **informal reading inventory.** In an informal reading inventory, students are asked to read a series of passages that gradually increase in difficulty. The idea is to locate the highest reading level at which the student can read both with and without some assistance by the teacher. A list of commercial inventories that have passages that range from first through eighth or twelfth grade is presented in Table 2.5. Unfortunately, administering an informal reading inventory is fairly time-consuming and so may not be practical unless you are in a self-contained class or teach small groups of students. It also requires training. However, if you have the training and the time, this is an excellent way to get valid levels and also to get to know your students and their reading abilities better.

The next best method for obtaining placement levels is to administer a group reading inventory. To administer a group inventory, select a typical passage from a

■ The **informal reading inventory** is a placement test that consists of a series of word lists and selections that grow increasingly difficult. The objective of the test is to find the highest levels at which students can read on their own independently and with help.

TABLE 2.5

COMMERCIAL READING INVENTORIES

Name	Authors	Grades
Analytic Reading Inventory	Woods & Moe	1–8
Bader Reading and Language Inventory	Bader	1–12 & adult
Basic Reading Inventory	Johns	1–8
Classroom Reading Inventory	Silvaroli & Wheelock	1–8
Ekwall/Shanker Reading Inventory	Shanker & Ekwall	1–12
English–Espanol Reading Inventory for the Classroom	Flynt & Cooter	1–12
Informal Reading–Thinking Inventory	Manzo, Manzo, & McKenna	1–11
Informal Reading Inventory	Burns & Roe	1–12
Qualitative Reading Inventory III	Leslie & Caldwell	1–12
READ: Reading Evaluation Adult Diagnosis	Colvin & Root	Adult
Reading Inventory for the Classroom	Flynt & Cooter	1–12
Stieglitz Informal Reading Inventory	Stieglitz	1–8

content area text that is of average difficulty. Pick a passage that is about 200 to 300 words long. Create a series of eight to ten questions, as in Figure 2.4. Most questions should be on a literal level. However, ask two or three questions that require students to make inferences, summarize information, or identify main ideas. The questions may require **constructed responses,** in which students have to compose answers, or they may be multiple choice. Constructed response questions provide more insight into the students' reasoning processes and writing abilities. Although more time-consuming to compose, multiple choice questions are easier to correct. Explain the purpose of the inventory and briefly introduce the passage. Ask a topic-related question that will lead into the setting of a purpose for reading the selection but will also provide an opportunity for you to assess students' background knowledge.

■ A **constructed response** is one in which the reader must compose an answer in writing or orally. An essay is a constructed response.

Once a purpose has been set, note what students do as they read. Note especially signs that they are having difficulty with the text. This might include puzzled expressions, lip movement, frowning, or asking about difficult vocabulary. After they have finished reading the selection, students respond to the questions that you have provided. When all have finished, discuss the selection, starting with the purpose question. During the discussion, note the adequacy of students' comprehension and also their ability to go back over the passage to find verifying information and read this aloud to the class.

After scoring students' responses and considering your observations of their work, note how many were able to handle the text. The criterion is 70 percent to 75 percent comprehension. For students for whom the text seems too difficult, try an easier-level text. For those for whom the text was not challenging enough, try a more difficult text. You might also retest low-scoring students with an individual in-

---

FIGURE 2.4

Sample Group Reading Inventory

Read "Progress and Reason" and "Two Views of the Social Contract" on pp. 446 and 447. Then answer the questions below.

1. What contribution did Lavoisier and Priestly make?
2. What did Jenner discover?
3. What are natural laws?
4. What did Enlightenment thinkers believe they could do?
5. Why do you think this period was given the name Enlightenment?
6. What did Hobbes believe people were like?
7. What kind of government did Hobbes believe was necessary?
8. What did Locke believe people were like?
9. What kind of government did Locke believe was best?
10. Whose ideas, Hobbes's or Locke's, were most influential in shaping the government of the United States? Explain your choice.

formal reading inventory or simply have them read portions of the text aloud. At this point, you want to see whether low comprehension scores are due to poor decoding skills. If lack of decoding skills is the major problem, students will need a text written in simpler language. If decoding is not a problem—if low scores are due to inadequate comprehension—students may need added preparation before reading, more background building, or instruction in effective comprehension strategies.

Once you have collected and examined all the data, decide on the text(s) that best fits students' needs. Make adjustments for those for whom the text is too difficult or too easy.

Commercial Group Inventories

Some national tests, such as the Degrees of Reading Power, are designed to yield an instructional level. However, the results of the DRP test are reported in DRP units. Not understanding the significance of the units, some teachers fail to make use of this information. Table 2.3 gives the DRP units for average students in grades 1 through 12. The Metropolitan Achievement Tests, one of the few sets of norm-referenced standardized tests designed to provide placement information, also provide instructional levels. The Scholastic Reading Inventory, which yields scores in lexile units, and STAR, a computerized placement test published by Accelerated Reading, also provide estimated reading levels. Estimated reading levels should be verified by noting how well students handle their text.

A quick but efficient way to obtain an estimate of students' reading level is to administer the Reading-Level Indicator (AGS). The Indicator is a brief test that contains forty multiple choice items, consisting of twenty vocabulary items (sample shown below) and twenty sentence comprehension items (sample shown below). The Indicator yields estimated instructional and independent reading levels. Tests come in two forms so that they may be used for pre- and post-test assessment. The Indicator can be used with students in the upper elementary grades through college.

Example for Vocabulary: **Example for Sentence Comprehension:**

Ex. Slice the apple.   Ex. Where have you _____ all this time?

_x_a. cut   ___a. left

___b. polish   ___b. seen

___c. sling   ___c. put

___d. deliver   _x_d. been

___e. bake   ___e. done

(American Guidance Service, 2002)

The Reading-Level Indicator has a companion version in Spanish. Giving both versions of the test will help you to determine the comparative literacy abilities of students in English and Spanish. You may find that a Spanish-speaking student who obtains a low score on the English version has a high level of reading ability in Spanish. Such a student will become a good reader in English once his knowledge of English improves. A Spanish-speaking student who scores low in both languages will need intensive instruction in reading. Some caution needs to be exercised in interpreting scores. The Spanish version is a translation of the English version. The difficulty of the items in Spanish may not be the same as the difficulty level in English.

Cloze Procedure

Instead of creating questions for a group reading inventory, you can use a fill-in-the-blank device know as cloze. Short for *closure*, **cloze** is a procedure in which students read selections from which words have been deleted. A sample cloze passage is presented in Figure 2.5. In classic cloze, every fifth word is deleted from a 250-word passage, so that there are a total of 50 missing words (see Figure 2.5). The first and last sentences are left intact, and no proper nouns or numbers are removed. Students use their background knowledge, language ability, and reading ability to predict in

■ **Cloze** is a procedure in which the reader demonstrates comprehension by supplying missing words. *Cloze* is short for *closure*, which is the tendency to fill in missing or incomplete information.

> ### FIGURE 2.5
>
> ### Sample Cloze Passage
>
> **Standard time.** Americans loved speed. And railroads made it _____ for them to race _____ the continent faster than _____ before. The trains that _____ from city to city _____ strange new problems. One _____ which had not been _____ till then was that _____ town had its own _____ set to its own _____ time. The astronomers said _____ it was "noon" when _____ saw the sun reach _____ zenith—the highest point _____ the heavens. Since the _____ was constantly in motion, _____ since the sun rose _____ when you were more _____ the east, then whether _____ was yet noon obviously _____ on *where* you were.
>
> _____ what this meant for _____ railroad! The Pennsylvania Railroad _____ to use Philadelphia time _____ its eastern lines. But _____ was five minutes earlier _____ New York time and five _____ later than Baltimore time. _____ Indiana there were 23 _____ local times. In Illinois _____ were 27, and in Wisconsin 38.
>
> _____ railroads used the local _____ for their arrival in _____ station. In between cities _____ was the greatest confusion. _____ for speeding trains a _____ minutes could make the _____ between a clear track _____ a fatal collision.
>
> Finally _____ was suggested that instead _____ "sun time" they should _____ a new kind of "_____ time"—which would be "_____ time."
>
> For the United States _____ a whole, you could _____ off on a map _____ few conspicuous time belts—_____and down the whole _____. You would only need four—_____ time, central time, mountain _____, and Pacific time—each several hundred miles wide. Standard time would be exactly the same for all places within each zone. (Boorstin & Kelley, 2002, p. 415)
>
> Answers:
> possible, across, ever, sped, brought, trouble, noticed, every, clocks, particular, that, you, its, in, earth, and, sooner, to, it, depended, Imagine, a, tried, on, that, than, minutes, In, different, there, Most, time, each, there, Yet, few, difference, and, it, of, use, railroad, standard, as, mark, a, up, country, eastern, time

TABLE 2.6

SCORING CLOZE

Level	Percentage
Independent	> 57
Instructional	44–57
Frustration	< 44

order to supply missing words. Passages are scored according to how many words students are able to replace. Exact replacements are required; otherwise, scoring becomes too subjective. However, standards are more lenient than are those of traditional tests. The instructional level is 44 percent to 57 percent. See Table 2.6.

Some students may be dismayed by the unfamiliar format, so give a few practice passages before using cloze as a placement device. Cloze works best when the passages are close to the students' actual reading levels. On easy passages, students tend to supply synonyms rather than exact replacement, even though their comprehension of the passage may be quite good. The substitutions, of course, are counted as errors and may lead to an underestimation of the students' reading ability (Smith, W. L., 1978). Vocabulary also plays a major role in students' performance. If the replacement word is not a familiar one, students will not be able to supply it. Had they been reading an intact passage they may have been able to infer the meaning of the unfamiliar word and so maintained comprehension.

Before administering a cloze test, the teacher explains the nature of cloze, gives tips for completing the exercise, and models the process of completing a cloze activity. Tips may include:

ENGLISH LANGUAGE LEARNERS

Because they have a more limited English vocabulary, English language learners find cloze especially difficult.

- Read the whole exercise first.
- Use all the clues given in a passage.
- Read past the blank to the end of the sentence. Sometimes the best clues come after a blank.
- If necessary, read a sentence or two ahead to get additional clues.
- Spell as best you can. You lose no points for misspelled words.
- Do your best, but do not worry if you cannot correctly complete each blank. Most readers will be able to fill in fewer than half the blanks correctly.
- After you have filled in as many blanks as you can, reread the selection. Make any changes you think are necessary. (Gunning, 2003)

Students are also given some practice sessions so that they become familiar with the format. A versatile procedure, cloze is also used to foster comprehension and assess the readability of texts.

Word List Tests

One time-saving way to get a quick estimate of students' instructional levels is to administer a word list test. In a word list test, students read a series of words that gradually increase in difficulty. There is a close correlation between the ability to pronounce words in isolation and overall reading (Manzo & Manzo, 1993), so the results of the word list test can be used to estimate students' instructional reading levels. Of course, requiring as they do only the ability to pronounce words, these tests neglect comprehension and may provide misleading levels for students who are superior decoders but poor comprehenders or vice versa. Two widely used word list tests are the Wide Range Achievement Test (WRAT) and the Slosson Oral Reading Test (SORT). In a comparison of commercial and teacher-made informal reading inventories with the reading subtest of the WRAT, which requires only the pronouncing of isolated words, the WRAT yielded estimates that were one to two grade levels above the estimates yielded by the inventories (Bristow, Pikulski, & Pelosi, 1983). The Slosson Oral Reading Test, which also seems to overestimate students' reading levels by a year or two, presents twenty words at each grade level from beginning reading (preprimer) through grade 12.

■ Word Reading Survey

One informal word list test that is quick and easy to use is the Word Reading Survey, which is based on the San Diego Quick Assessment created by LePay and Ross (1969). The Word Reading Survey consists of a series of graded words that range from beginning first grade through high school (see Figure 2.6). To administer the test, type the words on cards or present them in lists. Start at the beginning and continue to test until the student gets half the words on a level wrong. As the student reads, record his responses. This will provide insights into the students' word recognition needs. The students' estimated reading level is the highest level at which the student can read seven or eight words out of ten. Note that this estimate is based only on the students' ability to pronounce printed words. Neither the ability to read words in context nor comprehension is assessed. Verify the estimated level by having the student read a passage at that level or observe the student's performance as he reads materials on his estimated reading level. Make adjustments as necessary.

Data from State or National Objective Tests

Data from state or national objective tests may also be used to indicate students' instructional levels. These tests yield **grade level equivalents, stanines, percentile ranks,** and **normal curve equivalents.** The grade equivalent scores are some-

■ A **grade level equivalent** indicates the score that the average student at that grade level achieved.
■ A **stanine** is a point on a nine-point scale, with 5 being average.
■ A **percentile rank** is the point on a scale of 1 to 99 that shows what percentage of students obtained an equal or lower score. A percentile rank of 75 means that 75 percent of those who took the test received an equal or lower score.
■ A **normal curve equivalent** is the rank on a scale of 1 through 99 that a score is equal to.

FIGURE 2.6

Word Reading Survey

1	2	3	4	5	6	7	8	9–12
I	please	branch	reason	escaped	absence	continuously	calculator	administrative
the	never	middle	distant	business	instinct	application	agriculture	spontaneous
we	hour	stronger	lonesome	continue	responsible	incredible	prohibited	molecule
go	climb	picture	silent	obedient	evaporate	maximum	legislation	ritual
hat	field	hunger	wrecked	entrance	convenience	environmental	translucent	recipient
help	spend	several	decided	applause	commercial	accumulate	astronomical	conscientious
coat	side	empty	certainly	government	necessary	geographical	optimistic	infectious
are	believe	since	favorite	celebration	recognition	triangular	narrate	beneficiary
how	happen	impossible	realized	microscope	vertical	pollutant	persuasive	affiliation
work	suddenly	straight	solution	navigate	starvation	currency	obnoxious	paralysis

times interpreted as instructional reading levels, but they are not. A grade equivalent of 9.2 means that the test taker got the same number of items correct as the average ninth-grader in the norm group that took the test in October (the second month of the school year). It doesn't necessarily mean that the student can read ninth-grade material—the student might have made some good guesses. However, it does provide a reasonable estimate of what the student's reading level might be. If possible, use an individual inventory to check the students' levels, especially if they had very low scores.

If the test does not provide a grade equivalent score, giving only a stanine, percentile rank, and normal curve equivalent score, use these to get an estimate of the student's instructional level. A stanine of 5 and a percentile rank or normal curve equivalent of 50

Teachers assess the ability of students to handle texts by administering a group reading inventory.

are average, which suggests that the student is probably reading on grade level. A stanine of 4 and a percentile rank between 35 and 50 suggest that the student is probably reading a year or two below grade level. Lower stanines, percentile ranks, and normal curve equivalents indicate more serious underachievement. Stanines above 5 and percentile ranks and normal curve equivalents above 50 suggest above-average achievement.

Students' estimated levels should be verified with a group or individual reading inventory or by observing students' performance as they read their texts. This is especially true if students have low scores. Low scores are very untrustworthy and can be the result of guessing.

CHECKUP

1. Why is it important to match the reader and the text?
2. What are some ways to estimate students' reading levels?

Although matching students with texts that they can understand is complex and takes time, it may be the most important step you take in implementing an effective content area program. Students given texts that are on their level understand them better, work harder, behave better in class, and feel more confident about themselves as learners (R. Anderson, 1990; Gambrell, Wilson, & Gantt 1981).

Because most texts are written on or above grade level, matching below-level readers with materials they can handle poses a problem. Suggestions for making texts more accessible and locating appropriate materials for below-level readers are explored in Chapter 9.

SUMMARY

The core of instruction in many content area classes, textbooks tend to be difficult and may be too hard for as many as three or four out of ten students. Complex expository language, background knowledge required, density and difficulty of ideas, and increasing cognitive demands are the major factors that cause content area texts to be difficult. Although each content area makes its own set of demands on the reader, texts in all areas become more complex and demanding as students move up through the grades. The difficulty of texts can be assessed in a number of ways: objective formulas, comparison with benchmark books or passages, and use of checklists. There are three formulas that can be applied only with the aid of a computer: the DRP, Lexile Scale, and ATOS. Readability estimates of hundreds of content area texts are available on the Web, as are readability estimates of thousands of trade books. Because formulas measure only mechanical elements, the best procedure for assessing the difficulty level of a text is to use both objective and subjective measures.

To match students with texts, it is necessary to know students' reading levels. Students should be given text in which they know at least 95 percent of the words and understand 70 percent to 75 percent of what they read. Although individual informal reading inventories generally provide the most valid estimate of students' reading levels, group inventories and cloze tests can be used for that purpose. Most norm-referenced group tests do not yield reading levels; they simply tell how students did when compared with the norm group that took the test. However, the DRP and Metropolitan Reading Tests yield estimated levels, as do the Scholastic Reading Inventory, which yields scores in lexile units, and STAR, a computerized test published by Accelerated Reading. Word list tests and the Reading-Level Indicator can also be used to estimate reading level. Estimated reading levels should be verified by noting how well students handle their texts.

Reflection

Return to the Anticipation Guide at the beginning of this chapter. Respond once again to the items. Did your responses change? If so, how and why? What is the responsibility of the content area teacher in terms of matching readers and texts?

EXTENSION AND APPLICATION

1. Examine three textbooks in your content area. What demands do the texts seem to be making on readers? What helpful aids do the textbooks contain?
2. Using one of the formulas mentioned in the chapter, assess the readability of a content area text. Use the benchmark passages to verify the estimated readability level.
3. Construct and administer a group reading inventory to a content area class or use one of the group inventories or placement tests listed. What is the range of reading levels in the group? What seem to be the group's strengths and weaknesses?

chapter 3

BUILDING CONTENT AREA VOCABULARY

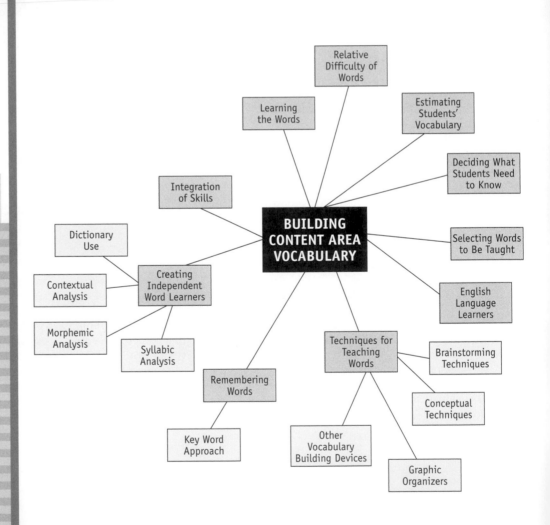

ANTICIPATION GUIDE

Read each of the following statements. Put a check under "Agree" or "Disagree" to show how you feel about each one. If possible, discuss your responses with classmates.

		Agree	Disagree
1	Most content area texts present too many new words.	____	____
2	It is better to teach a few keys words in depth than to try to introduce all the new words contained in a content area text.	____	____
3	If a content area text contains more new words than students can handle, the teacher should obtain an easier text.	____	____
4	Part of the content teacher's responsibility is to teach students skills for learning new words.	____	____
5	The primary tool for learning new words is the dictionary.	____	____

USING WHAT YOU KNOW

What made reading in the content areas difficult for you? For many students, the sheer number of technical terms to be learned is a challenge. How did you respond to the challenge of learning large numbers of difficult terms? What strategies did you use? How effective were the strategies? What strategies would you teach your students?

LEARNING THE WORDS

One of the chief barriers to learning in the content areas is that posed by the technical vocabulary that each employs. For instance, a section on the brain in a high school biology text contained fifteen technical terms on a single page. Each discipline has a specialized vocabulary used to label major concepts. The key to understanding the discipline is to grasp the discipline's vocabulary. In neuroscience, this would mean, in part, knowing the terms for the anatomy of the brain. However, what makes learning technical vocabulary especially challenging is that it usually isn't enough to learn a single technical word; it is often necessary to learn a cluster of terms (Nelson-Herber, 1986). For instance, it would be difficult to read even the most basic description of the brain without knowledge of such terms as *cerebral cortex, convoluted, hemispheres, corpus callosum, frontal, temporal,* and *parietal lobes, cerebrum, cerebellum, limbic system,* and *brain stem.*

One decision that the content area teacher needs to make is which technical terms the students should learn in order to be able to understand and discuss a concept. Current texts are overloaded with technical terms. One popular biology text includes 120 cell-related technical terms in its description of cells. In contrast, *Designs for Science Literacy* recommends just 11 technical terms (American Association for the Advancement of Science, 2001). Prestigious science reform groups fear that students see science as mainly a matter of memorizing technical vocabulary and often substitute memorization for genuine understanding. They recommend fostering understanding and then introducing technical vocabulary:

> Once students can understand that cells get energy from food and use the energy to put together complex proteins, their knowing such terms as "oxidation," "respiration," "mitochondrion," and "ribosome" can be helpful, but learning the words without the basic notion is empty. . . . Although Project 2061 recommends minimizing unnecessary technical terms, it is committed to expanding students' useful scientific vocabulary. The correct use of technical vocabulary is to be applauded once they understand the meanings. (American Association for the Advancement of Science, 2001, pp. 18–19)

In addition to the essential technical vocabulary required by the subject being studied, students should also have a solid general vocabulary. The section on the brain included the following general vocabulary words: *processes, routed, coordinates, efficiently, primary, automatic, response,* and *stimulus.*

Terms that need special attention in the content areas include the following:

Technical terms: Words, terms, and expressions that are peculiar to a particular content area and that are not typically found in general reading: *meridian, temperate*

Figurative terms: *pork barrel, cold war, domino theory*

Words with multiple meanings: Often, these are words that have a general meaning but also have a particular, sometimes carefully defined, meaning in the content areas: *force, mass, work, energy, cabinet, bill*

Words easily confused with other words: *longitude* for *latitude, executive* for *execution, principal* for *principle*
Acronyms: *OPEC, NATO, WHO* (Parker, 2001).
Terms written as formulas: H_2O, NaCl, CO_2

RELATIVE DIFFICULTY OF WORDS

Some words are relatively easy to learn. Concrete nouns that label physical objects, such as *kiosk* or *ibu*, are easier to learn than labels for complex processes, such as *oxidation* or *photosynthesis*, or abstract concepts, such as *ecology* or *democracy*. There is also a question of depth of knowledge. For instance, a reader needs to have a working knowledge of *molecules, carbon dioxide, photosynthesis*, and *food webs* in order to understand the following passage:

> Plants take in **inorganic** (IN or GAN ik) compounds, such as carbon dioxide and water. Inorganic compounds contain no carbon at all or just one carbon atom per molecule. Only small amounts of chemical energy are present in inorganic compounds.
>
> During photosynthesis, plants build larger, carbon-containing **organic** (or GAN ik) compounds. Using light energy, they link together many carbon atoms to make sugars. Both energy and matter are stored in organic compounds. A plant uses sugars as a source of energy as we learned in section 1.5. Or the plant can use the sugar molecules to make other molecules needed to build its body. To do this, a plant rearranges the atoms in the sugar molecules and adds new atoms. Thus sugars are a food. A **food** is an organic substance that an organism can break down to get energy for growth, maintenance, and repair. Food is also matter that can be used to build the structure of the body.
>
> An animal eats a plant, using it as a food. In this way both energy and matter are passed from one organism to another in a food web. However, unlike the flow of energy in a food web, the flow of matter is not one-way. Matter cycles within a community. Plants use carbon dioxide, water, and other substances in photosynthesis. These are the same substances that are given off by organisms when they use the food. (Milani et al., 1987, pp. 18–19)

ENGLISH LANGUAGE LEARNERS

In the sciences, many of the technical terms have cognates in a number of languages. That is, they have the same origin and so have similar appearances. This is especially true of the Romance languages, Spanish, Italian, French, Romanian, and Portuguese. For instance, technical terms in Spanish for a description of an atom include: *atomo, molecula, electron, neutron.*

✔ CHECKUP

1. What is involved in learning vocabulary in a content area?

ESTIMATING STUDENTS' VOCABULARY

The most important prerequisite for building vocabulary is having an estimate of the students' knowledge of words. Having an estimate of students' word knowledge allows the teacher to better select words to be taught and word learning techniques to be employed. It isn't just the number of words known. There is also the question of the degree of knowledge. Some words we know very well; others we know only vaguely. There also are some words for which we have everyday knowledge but lack a technical understanding. This is especially true of scientific words. For instance, students understand *machine*, *power*, *motion*, *work*, and *weight* when used in everyday language but may not know them when used in physical science.

Dale and O'Rourke (1971) described four stages of word knowledge:

(1) I never saw it before.
(2) I've heard of it, but I don't know what it means.
(3) I recognize it in context—it has something to do with . . .
(4) I know it. (p. 3)

Stahl (1986) describes three degrees of word knowledge: definitional, contextual, and generative. Definitional knowledge means that the student can tell what a word means. A *shelter* is "something that covers or protects us from the weather." Contextual knowledge, however, requires understanding the "core concept the word represents and how that concept is changed in different contexts" (p. 663). The student would understand the meanings of the word *shelter* in the expressions, "food and shelter," "sought shelter from the storm," and "a shelter for the homeless."

There are some words that are restricted to our receptive vocabularies. We grasp them when we hear them spoken or meet them in print, but we don't know them well enough to use them in our own speaking or writing. Generative knowledge is required before words become part of our expressive, or speaking and writing, vocabularies. Combining levels of knowledge and degrees of knowledge, Graves (1987) created six learning tasks for acquiring new words.

Task 1: Learning to read known words. This entails learning the printed forms of words that are in one's listening vocabulary. Novice readers face this task as they use phonics to sound out words. However, older students, especially those who are struggling readers or who are still learning English, also face this same task when they use phonics, syllabication, or a dictionary pronunciation guide to recognize words in print that they know when they hear them. Frequently, these are words such as *polymers*, *trough*, and *queque* whose pronunciations are difficult to predict from their spellings.

Task 2: Learning new meanings for known words. In science, there are a number of common terms that take on a specialized meaning. A student who knows *kingdom* and *family* would still need to learn the technical meanings of these words when used as part of a classification of animals.

Task 3: Learning new words that represent known concepts. Since the concept is already known, this simply entails learning a new label. A student learns that *humerus* is the technical name for the upper arm bone. This is a relatively easy task.

STRUGGLING READERS

Some very bright students are afflicted with a reading difficulty: they quickly grasp concepts presented orally but have difficulty when they have to get information from printed text because they are unable to read long or complex words even though they know their meanings and would recognize them if they heard them.

Task 4: Learning new words that represent new concepts. The difficulty of this task depends on the complexity of the concepts to be learned. Concepts such as *introvert, extravert, democracy, republic,* and *dictatorship* are abstract and complex.

Task 5: Clarifying and enriching the meanings of known words. Our understanding of recently acquired words may be general and vague until we have more experience with them. Words such as *focus, magnification, low-power, high-power, stage,* and *slide* take on more meaning for someone who has read and talked about a compound microscope and then uses it. Having partial knowledge of a word or tying it to one particular context limits students' understanding of the word; when they encounter it in their reading, they may misinterpret its meaning. For instance, one student thought that the word *ancestors* meant "relatives that he didn't see very often" (Curtis & Longo, 1999). This limited understanding of the word won't help him much when he encounters it in a history text. Students need to meet new words in many contexts.

Task 6: Moving words from receptive to expressive vocabulary. Because we have time to plan and revise what we say, our writing vocabularies should be richer and more varied than our speaking vocabularies. Writing is also a good place to start using new words, but students should also be encouraged to use newly learned words in their speaking. Planning opportunities to talk and write about newly learned concepts provides students with the opportunity and expertise needed to move words into their expressive vocabularies.

 CHECKUP

1. What are the different levels on which words are known?
2. On what level should words be known in order for this knowledge to have an effect on students' comprehension?

DECIDING WHAT STUDENTS NEED TO KNOW

Before introducing vocabulary, decide what students need to know. Sometimes, this may be simply a matter of learning the graphic form of a word. For instance, students may be familiar from classroom discussions with rocks called *gneiss,* dense rock occurring in layers, but may not recognize the word in print because of its *gn* spelling of /n/. With words of this type, simply teach students that the *gn* in *gneiss* is pronounced like the *gn* in *gnat* or *gnarled.* For many technical words, it will be necessary to develop conceptual knowledge. Words such as *symbiosis, anarchy,* and *latitude* and *longitude* require extensive teaching. Unfortunately, students are often familiar with labels but not the concepts behind them. This is especially true of abstract terms such as *republic* and *executive branch* and technical terms such as *digital* and *bytes.* Teaching vocabulary also involves clarifying and deepening students' understanding of known words and helping students use new words in their speaking and their writing. See Table 3.1 for a list of states of word knowledge and recommended instruction for each state.

ENGLISH LANGUAGE LEARNERS

When working with ELLs, determine whether an unknown word represents an unknown concept or is simply a new English label for a concept already known. A major vocabulary task for ELLs is learning the English equivalents for words they know in their native language.

STRUGGLING READERS

If a text contains an overwhelming number of words that pose problems for students, it may be too difficult. See Chapter 9 for suggestions for handling difficult texts.

> **TABLE 3.1**
>
> ## STATES OF WORD KNOWLEDGE
>
> | State | Instruction |
> | --- | --- |
> | 1. Knows word when hears it but does not recognize printed form. | Teach printed form. |
> | 2. Knows word's oral and written form but does not use it. | Promote generative knowledge. Give examples of its use. Clarify word. Encourage its use in a "safe" environment. |
> | 3. Knows the concept but not the label. | Teach the label and relate it to the concept. |
> | 4. Has partial knowledge of the word. May have definitional but not contextual knowledge. | Develop fuller meaning of the word. Examine the word in several contexts. |
> | 5. Recognizes the label but has no real conceptual knowledge of the concept: *republic.* Or the word may have a familiar everyday meaning but an unknown technical meaning: *energy, motion.* | Develop the concept. |
> | 6. Both the concept and the label are unknown. | Develop the concept and the label. |
>
> In addition, there are some words for which a student has partial knowledge. Students know that a colonel is someone who is in the armed services, but may not realize that *colonel* designates a rank just below general. Or students may know a word but not use it because they are unsure of its meaning or pronunciation or both.

Adapted from: "Vocabulary Knowledge and Comprehension: A Comprehension-Process View of Complex Literacy Relationships," by M. R. Ruddell. In R. B. Ruddell, M. R. Ruddell, & H. Singer (Eds.), *Theoretical Models and Processess of Reading* (4th ed.) (pp. 414–417). Newark, DE: International Reading Association, 1994.

From *Assessing and Correcting Reading and Writing Difficulties* by T. Gunning, 2002. Boston: Allyn & Bacon. Reprinted by permission.

SELECTING WORDS TO BE TAUGHT

A high school biology text lists more than 600 terms in its glossary. A middle school American history text lists nearly 300 terms. A two-page section in a text may contain more than a dozen potentially difficult terms. The number of new words in a content area can be overwhelming. Teachers need to select carefully words to be taught because our ability to learn new words is limited.

ENGLISH LANGUAGE LEARNERS

Self-Study Quizzes for ESL Students offers a variety of self-checking quizzes on common words, idioms, homonyms, and slang expressions. Also includes games and crossword puzzles.
http://www.aitech.ac.jp/~iteslj/quizzes/lb/ho1.html

Students should be presented with only seven or eight new words at one time. In order to decide which words to introduce, the teacher needs to ask, "What do I want my students to learn?" Two or three key concepts should be listed. The teacher should then go through the selection to be learned and select the words necessary for an understanding of the key concepts. The teacher should also consider the overall importance of the words. Are these words that are important for a basic understanding of the content area? Are these words that the student will meet again and again? If so, these are words that students might learn on their own. Also note whether the words are explained in context or in the margins.

In addition to technical vocabulary, there may also be some general words that students may not know but that are essential to an understanding of the passage. This is especially true if you are working with ELL students or below-level readers. If there are a large number of general words that pose problems for students, you may want to seek an easier text or take other measures to make the text more accessible. (See Chapter 9 for suggestions for making difficult texts more accessible.)

Listed below are key concepts for a selection on the Marshall Plan and the words the teacher selected as most needed for an understanding of the essential concepts:

- The United States gave billions of dollars to countries in Western Europe to help them rebuild after World War II.
- Because of the aid given to them, countries in Western Europe became strong enough to stand up against communism.

economies	starvation	resources	communism
poverty	prosperity	restored	

In order to select words that your students should know, you need to have a sense of their level of vocabulary development. You may be overestimating or underestimating students' knowledge of words. Observe the level of vocabulary that your students use in class discussions and in their writing. Conduct brainstorming sessions in which students volunteer associations for a particular word. For instance, you put a key word such as *ecology* on the board and students tell what words come to mind when they hear the word *ecology*. Note the breadth and depth of responses.

Before teaching a unit, make a list of potentially difficult words and distribute it to students. Have students place a check next to words that they know or use the four-point scale described earlier in the chapter: (1) I never saw it before, (2) I've heard of it, but I don't know what it means, (3) I recognize it in context—it has something to do with . . . , (4) I know it. Dale and O'Rourke (1971) found this to be a useful way to assess students' vocabulary. You might also occasionally ask students to make a list of unknown words encountered while reading a selection. If students list a great many unfamiliar words, you may want to seek out an easier book.

In many instances, you will have a lengthy list of possible words to teach. To pare that list down to a reasonable number, you may decide to focus on just a few high-priority words and teach these to a conceptual level of knowledge. Other, less important or less frequently appearing words might be taught to a definitional level.

The good news about vocabulary development is that even minimal instruction helps. Being given a definition of the word *biome*, a student later meets the word in her text and hears the word used in a discussion. With each encounter, the student's knowledge of the word increases. In time, the student's definitional knowledge becomes contextual.

However, although minimal instruction and casual contact with words helps build vocabulary, contextual knowledge is required before comprehension is fostered; definitional knowledge is not adequate. In addition to contextual knowledge, students must also have rapid access to word meanings and a network of meaningful connections (Beck & McKeown, 1983). Students reading the passage about the brain cited earlier in this chapter need to know the contextual meanings of the technical words. They also need to know how these words are interrelated, and they should know the words well enough so that they don't have to stop in the middle of their reading to try to remember what a key term means. If they have been given only a fleeting introduction to the words, they may have forgotten them or may take a little time to recall the words, either of which will interfere with comprehension.

To make your program of vocabulary development more effective, survey the text and make a tentative list of key words that will need to be introduced during an upcoming unit, semester, or school year. Note which words are most likely to pose problems, which words are most essential, and which are repeated. Focus instructional efforts on words that are essential and repeated. Also look for commonalties and relationships among words so that knowledge of one word reinforces understanding of other words. For instance, when introducing the word *devaluation*, stress the prefix and suffix because they will help students with the words *deregulation* and *desegregation*, which they will encounter later in their U.S. history texts. Introduce words such as *conservative* and *liberal* at the same time because looking at opposites helps to clarify both words. Also stress these words because they will appear in a number of chapters and are in common use today.

CHECKUP

1. How should words be chosen for instruction in the content areas?
2. What steps can be taken if there are an overwhelming number of words that are unknown to students?

ENGLISH LANGUAGE LEARNERS

Although virtually all students struggle with the task of learning content vocabulary, the task is far more difficult for English language learners. Whereas estimates of the English word knowledge of native speakers of English range from 10,000 to 100,000 words, estimates of the English vocabulary of English language learners range from 5,000 to 7,000 words (Johnson & Steele, 1996). A crucial factor in learning English vocabulary will be the number of words that students know in their native language. If this number is large, learning vocabulary in English should be a somewhat easier task. In many instances, they will be learning English labels for concepts and words known in their native language. This is a far easier task than learning new concepts and labels for those concepts.

While reading, many English language learners may hesitate over nearly every word. This, of course, slows down their reading process so much that comprehension is nearly impossible. English language learners need to learn that they don't have to know every word and should focus their efforts on crucial terms, which are those words that readers must know in order to be able to comprehend a passage. One way of helping students select crucial words is to explain and model the process and to provide an activity in which students are given a copy of a passage and asked to underline unknown words that are essential to an understanding of the passage. In a textbook, these might be words that have been highlighted in some way. These words are discussed and context, morphemic analysis, and glossary/dictionary skills

USING TECHNOLGY

The Way Things Work (Dorling Kindersley), a CD-ROM program, uses explanations, labeled illustrations, and animations to show how dozens of technical devices work. Excellent for building background and vocabulary.

are used to derive meanings for the words. Students might also seek out and identify cognates, words that are similar in both languages.

In one study, older English language learners found the dictionary to be a useful tool. Since many words were unknown, the dictionary provided a tool that these students could use to derive the meanings of unfamiliar words (Gonzalez, 1999). Although a number of the words they looked up were content-specific words such as *ecological* and *demographic*, many were general terms, such as *deny* and *fierce*. A number of the words were those that frequently appear in formal prose but are seldom heard in speech: *assertion*, *aftermath*, *cited*. Although they sometimes had difficulty deriving an understandable definition and were sometimes hindered by inflected forms, the students saw the dictionary as an indispensable tool and were able to derive appropriate definitions about 80 percent of the time. Fortunately, there are a number of techniques that can be employed to make word learning easier and more efficient for all learners, especially if the techniques are geared to the students' level of knowledge.

> **ENGLISH LANGUAGE LEARNERS**
> Obtain dictionaries designed for English language learners. These contain more illustrations and simplified definitions.

 ## CHECKUP

1. What special challenge does vocabulary pose for English language learners?

TECHNIQUES FOR TEACHING WORDS

One of the best ways to foster comprehension of complex content area reading is to make sure that students have a working knowledge of key words before they begin to read. Although today's texts frequently define technical words in context, learning a new word while reading takes the focus off the reader's major purpose, which is to construct meaning. Students are better able to construct meaning if they don't have to devote time and mental energy to figuring out what a difficult word means; they can instead devote their full attention to comprehending the passage. Instruction should be conceptual so that students have a sufficient grasp of the key words so that they don't have to pause and think about them as they are reading. A variety of techniques can be used to achieve this aim.

Brainstorming Techniques

One widely used approach that helps students organize new concepts and their labels and also activates prior knowledge is brainstorming. In **brainstorming**, students are asked to tell what comes to mind when they hear a certain term or phrase. Through their sharing, students learn from each other and build background knowledge for the whole class. In addition to activating and building background knowledge, brainstorming techniques provide the teacher with an opportunity to assess students' background knowledge. For example, unsure of how much students know about Congress, the teacher has the class brainstorm that topic. As a result of the brainstorming session, the teacher can determine the depth and accuracy of students' topic and vocabulary knowledge and plan instruction accordingly. During or after

> ■ **Brainstorming** is a process in which members of a group attempt to accomplish a task by submitting ideas spontaneously.

brainstorming, the teacher fills in gaps in students' knowledge, clarifies confusions, and corrects misconceptions. Although highly effective, brainstorming techniques don't work very well unless students have some knowledge of the topic.

List-Group-Label

■ **List-group-label** is a group brainstorming technique in which students tell what they know about a topic and organize that information.

In one of its simplest forms, brainstorming can be presented through a **list-group-label** framework (Taba, 1965). The topic to be brainstormed is written on the board and students are invited to tell what the topic makes them think about. Writing *light* on the board, for example, you would invite students to tell what comes to mind when they think of this word. All responses are listed, even those that don't seem to have any connection to the topic. After responses have been listed, the class—working together—categorizes the words into groups of three or more (a word may be placed in more than one group). Words that don't seem to fit anywhere else might be placed in a separate group. After all items have been classified, they are given category labels. As they group the words and label them, students explain why certain words should be placed together and why their category name is appropriate. Assistance is provided with categorizing if needed. For younger or poorer students, you might model the process of categorizing and labeling. As students supply responses, assess the depth and accuracy of students' knowledge of the topic.

As a member of the brainstorming group, you may volunteer words during the brainstorming portion of the procedure. For instance, if students didn't include *waves* or *spectrum*, you could add those to the list. Limit the number of brainstormed items to about twenty-five so the list doesn't become too cumbersome (Tierney & Readence, 2000).

Semantic Mapping

What is your concept of DNA? One way of gauging your concept of DNA is to list all the words that come to mind when you think about the word. Here are some responses compiled from three high school students.

Respondent A: *cells, nucleus, protein, amino acids, double helix, life, code, traits*

Respondent B: *heredity, traits, eyes, hair, sex, nucleus, chromosomes, threads, chains*

Respondent C: *biology, body, genes, dominant, recessive, characteristics, hair, eyes, Watson, criminals, unique, fingerprints*

If you analyze the responses, you can see that they vary from respondent to respondent. If you look closely at responses, you can see that the responses are not discrete items but are related in some way. As Lapp, Flood, and Hoffman (1996) note,

> Information and ideas seem to be connected with each other, even interdependent, in a web or network arrangement. When we recall one thing, several associated ideas always seem to come along with it. . . . (p. 292)
>
> Because our ideas are webbed in networks, new ideas are linked to old ideas. In fact, new information cannot be added to our mental storehouse unless it can be linked to old information. Existing information serves as hooks on which to hang or associate new information. Prior knowledge provides a structure into which we can link new information. (p. 295)

Creating added links improves retention and broadens understanding. Part of helping students learn is helping them see relationships and so forge links among ideas. Compartmentalized items of knowledge, such as isolated facts or lists of unrelated words, are harder to retrieve because there are fewer links to them.

Vocabulary words are best learned within a network of associations. One way of establishing relationships among concepts is through **semantic mapping,** which is based on the list-group-label technique. Semantic mapping combines brainstorming and graphically organizing information. After brainstorming, categorizing, and labeling, the class uses circles or rectangles and lines to show their relationships. More free flowing than outlines and easier to construct, semantic maps are popular with students. The steps in semantic mapping include: announcing the topic, brainstorming, grouping and labeling, creating a map, discussing and revising the map, and extending the map. Semantic maps are also flexible. Items can be added to them during or after reading or even during subsequent lessons. Here is how a fifth-grade class created a map for the planets in preparation for reading the section in their science text on the planets.

■ A **semantic map** is a graphic organizer that uses lines and circles to organize information according to categories.

Semantic Mapping Lesson

LESSON
3.1

Step 1: Announcing the Topic and Inviting Brainstorming Responses

The teacher wrote the word *planets* on the board and asked the class to tell what comes to mind when they think of the word *planets*. Students responded with the following words: *the sun, far away, appear in sky, moving bodies, Earth, moons, Mars, Jupiter, Neputune, Pluto, Mercury, Venus.* No one mentioned what the planets did, so the teacher asked what they did. One student volunteered that that they orbited the sun. The words *orbit sun* were added. The teacher explained that there are nine planets, but they had listed only seven. No one could think of the names of the other two, so the teacher added *Saturn* and *Uranus*.

Step 2: Grouping and Labeling Responses

Students discussed ways of grouping the words and possible titles for word groups. They constructed a preliminary map.

Step 3: Discussing and Revising the Map

The class discussed the map. One student stated that Earth turned on its axis and thought that the other planets did, too. The phrase "turn on its axis" was added.

Step 4: Using the Map

The semantic map was displayed so that students could use it as a reference as they read. After students read and discussed the selection, the map was reviewed and students were invited to add additional elements. As students read, they learned that some planets were near and some were far and that the near planets were called inner planets and the far planets were called outer planets.

They learned that the planets were made up of rock, liquid, and gas and have one or more moons. All of this information was added to their maps. A completed map is shown in Figure 3.1.

In addition to being a prereading vocabulary development technique, semantic maps can also be used as a way of summarizing the content of a selection or as a prewriting activity. However, in order to be of optimum value, students should participate in the creation of maps. If teachers create maps, they are the ones who sift the information and so students don't have the opportunity to organize and process the terms. According to research by Berkowitz (1986), students' performance doesn't show much improvement unless they have a hand in creating maps.

Conceptual Techniques

■ Concept Maps

■ A **concept map** is a graphic device that uses lines and circles to organize information according to categories but also uses words and phrases to show interrelationships among concepts.

Semantic maps are an excellent device for visually representing information. Through the use of lines, semantic maps show that concepts are related. However, they fail to say how the concepts are related. **Concept maps,** which are popular in the sciences, use brief phrases to show how concepts are related. The brief phrases link concepts and thereby produce statements that show what the student understands about the concepts. For instance, a concept might include: *energy, matter, food, living things, animals, plants, nonliving things.* A concept map shows how these items are related. The

FIGURE 3.1

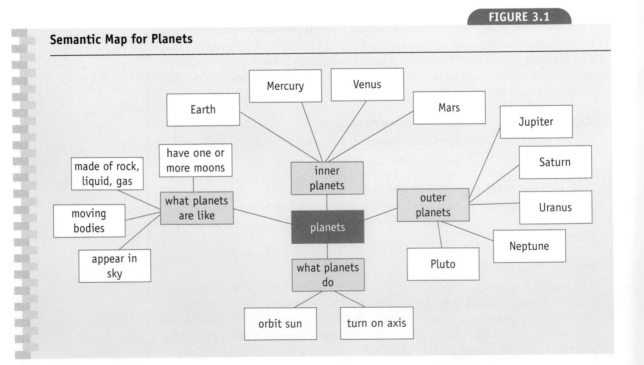

Semantic Map for Planets

map is hierarchical, so that the most general or superordinate concept is placed at the top of the page and subordinate or more specific items placed lower. Coordinate concepts are placed on the same level. So how, you might ask, is a concept map different from an outline or notetaking? For one thing, concept maps are more visual. For another, concept maps better show how ideas are related. In an outline, you can see how subtopic A is related to main topic I, but the outline won't show that subtopic A is also related to main topic II. Concept maps show crosslinkages as well as linear ones (Warner et al., 1991).

Concept maps, when created cooperatively, can be used to activate students' background. Some students may be intimidated by the technical vocabulary of science. Concept maps can become a reassuring element by demonstrating to students how much they already know and helping them link the known to the new.

Concept maps can serve several functions. They can be used as an advanced organizer at the beginning of a unit, as a reference during the unit, and as a running summary if they are added to as the unit progresses. Concept maps are also an excellent device for reviewing a topic and for studying. They can also be used as an assessment device if the teacher uses them to gauge the extent to which the student is able to show interrelationships among the concept's key elements.

General steps for creating concept maps include:

- Identify the most important ideas or key terms. Write them in a list. Each concept should consist of a single word or brief phrase of no more than three words.

- Place each concept on a separate piece of paper. They will be easier to manipulate.

- On a table or desk top, arrange the concepts in order from the most general to the most specific. Equal concepts are placed on the same line. Examples are highly specific and so go at the bottom.

- Copy your concepts onto a piece of paper. Put the concepts in boxes or circles. Write the most general ideas at the top of the page. Write the subordinate or supporting ideas underneath the most general ideas. Continue until all the key ideas have been included.

- Connect the ideas with lines. Write a word or brief phrase on the line to describe the relationship between the two items joined by the line. Write only linking words, such as *is, are, can be, has, such as, for example.*

- Check your map. Make sure that each concept, except the first and last, is linked to a concept above and below it. Make sure that linking words and not concept words are placed on the linkage lines.

Consider the map as tentative. Make changes as necessary. And don't be concerned if your map is different from maps drawn by others. There are different ways of drawing concept maps. As long as you have included the most important ideas and their relationships, your concept map is correct (Miller & Levine, 1998).

Creating Concept Maps.   Learning how to create a concept map takes time and guidance. Initially, teacher and students create concept maps together. As students gain more experience constructing maps, they begin to create their own. The map in the sample lesson was created after students read a section on tissues in their tenth-grade biology text.

Creating a Concept Map Lesson

Step 1: Introducing Concept Mapping

Explain what a concept map is and discuss its benefits. Show a concept map.

Step 2: Explaining the Construction of a Concept Map

Show how a concept map is created. Create a sample list of linkage words.

Step 3: Listing Concepts

After students have read a brief selection that lends itself to concept mapping, cooperatively list the key terms or concepts from the selection. For instance, after reading about body tissues, the class listed the following terms: *body tissues, muscle, can contract, nerve, messages, brain, epithelial, outside of body, body cavities, mouth, digestive tube, connective, bone, cartilage, fat, skeleton.*

Step 4: Arranging Concepts

Have the class cooperatively arrange concepts from most general to most specific, as in Figure 3.2.

Step 5: Adding Linkages

After key words have been put in place, have the class add linkages that show relationships among the concepts.

Step 6: Checking the Map

Have the class check the map to make sure that all the key concepts have been included and that linkages are correctly stated.

Step 7: Using the Map

Students can now use the concept map to review materials and to study for upcoming quizzes. As they acquire more information about tissues, they add it to the map.

■ **Frayer Model of Conceptual Development**

■ A **graphic organizer** is a diagram used to show the interrelationship among words or ideas.
■ The **Frayer model** is a graphic that organizes concepts hierarchically.

Students may be surprised to learn that snails, giant clams, and octopuses belong to the same phylum because these creatures seem so different. A **graphic organizer** that will help them see how these creatures are related and also how they fit into the animal kingdom is the Frayer model. The **Frayer model** develops concepts through discovering relevant attributes, considering irrelevant attributes, and noting examples and nonexamples (Peters, 1979). The concept is also organized into a hierarchy so students can see superordinate, coordinate, and subordinate categories. This allows them to see how the concept fits within an overall conceptual scheme. Seeing all these re-

FIGURE 3.2

Concept Map

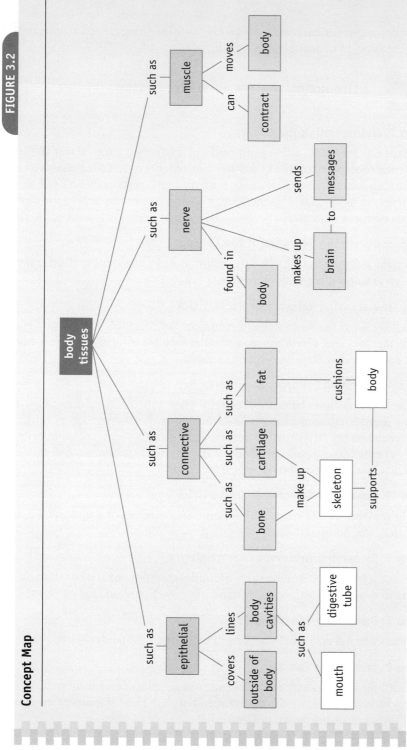

lationships, students learn concepts better because they have more semantic cues. Here is how the concept of *mollusks* might be taught.

Introducing the Frayer Model Lesson

Step 1: Brainstorming the Concept

In order to involve students and find out what they know about the topic, write the topic word on the board and ask students to tell what comes to mind when they hear the word *mollusks*. List students' responses on the board. If students are unfamiliar with the term, mention some members of the phylum: snails, clams, octopuses.

Step 2: Discussing Examples of the Concept

From the information listed on the board, note examples of mollusks. If there are few examples, list additional ones.

Step 3: Discussing Relevant Characteristics

Talk over what mollusks have in common; for instance, they have a similar body that includes a foot, gut, and mantle; they are invertebrates, soft-bodied, and cold-blooded; they usually have a shell.

Step 4: Arranging Concepts in a Hierarchy

Show where mollusks fall in the hierarchy. Show superordinate categories. Then show coordinate categories. Mollusks belong in the same group as cnidarians, platyhelminthes (flatworms), nematodes (round worms), echinoderms, annelids (segmented worms) arthropods and chordates. Discuss subordinate categories: bivalves, gastropods, and cephalopods.

Step 5: Discussing Common Characteristics

Help students decide what the relevant characteristics of a mollusk are, mantle, foot, soft body, and shell.

Step 6: Discussing Irrelevant Characteristics

Discuss irrelevant characteristics of mollusks: color, size, what they eat, climate in which they are found, whether they are found on land or in water.

Step 7: Discussing Nonexamples

Discuss why a fish, a whale, a worm, a toad, or a salamander is not a mollusk.

Step 8: Testing the Concept

Provide the students with examples and nonexamples of creatures and have them tell whether they are mollusks or not and explain their responses. An example of Frayer's model is shown in Figure 3.3.

Frayer Model

FIGURE 3.3

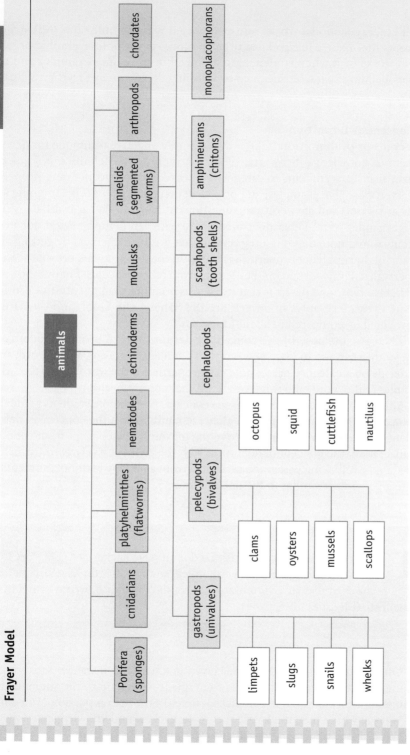

The Frayer model works best when used with complex but well structured concepts that have a hierarchical organization. As with other graphic organizers, it also works best when students are involved in providing examples and nonexamples, defining characteristics, and establishing the hierarchy (Tierney & Readence, 2000).

■ Concept of Definition

■ The **concept of definition** is a graphic organizer used to define a word.

The **concept of definition** (CD) is also a highly effective technique for developing conceptual knowledge (Schwartz, 1988). The concept of definition is a graphic organizer that leads students to categorize a word, provide its defining properties or characteristics, give examples, and provide a comparison concept. In doing so, students are asking and answering the questions What is it? What is it like? What are some examples of it? What does it compare with? In defining *desert*, for instance, students would note that it is a region and that it is characterized by getting very little rainfall. In supplying properties, it is important that students provide at least one property that defines or sets off the concept from other concepts. For instance, a defining characteristic of a desert is that it receives no more than twenty-five centimeters of rain a year. Examples of deserts are the Sahara, the Gobi, and the Mojave. A desert could be compared to a rain forest.

The basic purpose of the concept of definition is to provide students with a strategy they can use to learn new words. When encountering a new word, students can decide on a category name, note the properties of the word or concept, think of examples of the word, and think of a word that contrasts with it.

Although the teacher introduces the concept of definition, students gradually take responsibility for applying it. Once they are familiar with the concept of definition, students can use it to help them derive the meaning of a concept from context. For instance, using the concept of definition with the concept *invertebrates*, which is discussed in the following paragraph excerpted from a biology textbook, students would create an organizer similar to the one in Figure 3.4.

Invertebrates are animals that do not have backbones. They are much simpler creatures than vertebrates, animals that do have backbones. Some examples of invertebrates are sponges, jellyfish, worms, insects, and shellfish. (Bledsoe, 1994, p. 64)

Often only partial information is given in a text. For instance, a text might talk about energy but give no examples of energy. It is then up to the students to fill in the missing information or to complete as much of the map as possible. You might discuss ways in which they might use their own background knowledge or other references in order to obtain additional information about a concept.

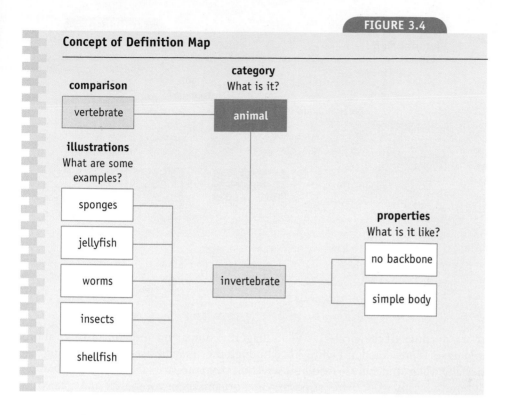

FIGURE 3.4

Concept of Definition Map

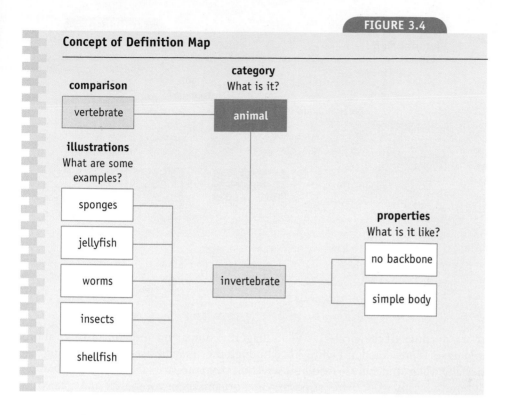

Graphic Organizers

In addition to semantic maps and concept maps, graphic organizers include charts, diagrams, and other visual devices that help students establish and display relationships among words. Graphic organizers seem to work especially well with students who might have difficulty seeing relationships when they are expressed only verbally.

Inspiration (Inspiration Software) or similar software can be used to create graphic organizers.

■ Pictorial Maps

As graphic displays, maps can include illustrations as well as words. They can also be visual or a combination of verbal and visual items. The words in semantic maps, for example, can be illustrated with drawings, or drawings can be used instead of words. This works especially well when working with concrete items. Figure 3.5 shows a pictorial map of two-dimensional and three-dimensional shapes.

■ Venn Diagram

The **Venn diagram,** which was originally used in math by John Venn (Electronic Journal of Combinatorics, 2001) to show logical relationships among sets, fosters the comparison and contrast of semantic features. In a Venn diagram, concepts are compared and contrasted. Features shared by the concepts are placed within the overlapping circles. Characteristics belonging to only one concept are placed in the

■ A **Venn diagram** is a graphic organizer that uses overlapping circles to show relationships between words or other items.

FIGURE 3.5

Pictorial Map

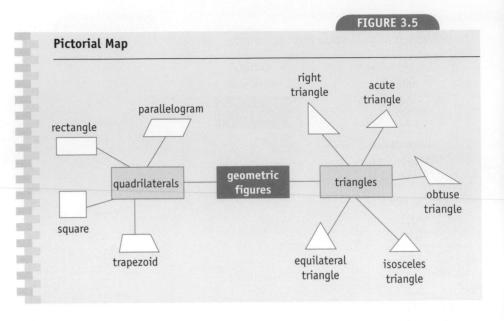

outer portions of the circles. A Venn diagram comparing and contrasting rabbits and hares is presented in Figure 3.6. Although they may be used before reading, especially when students are reading a selection that compares and contrasts, Venn diagrams typically work better as postreading organizers of vocabulary and concepts.

FIGURE 3.6

Venn Diagram

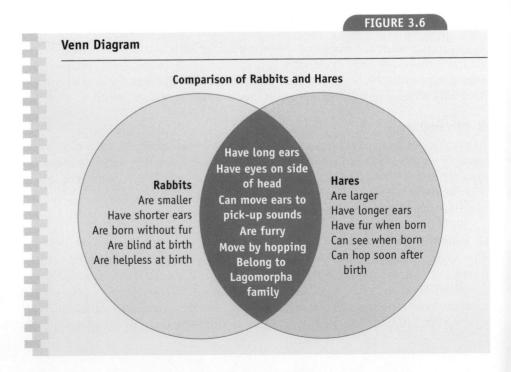

Comparison of Rabbits and Hares

*S*tudents can use *Inspiration* and other software to create graphic organizers.

■ Semantic Feature Analysis

In **semantic feature analysis** (SFA), students compare items in a category to see which features they share (Johnson & Pearson, 1984). Through having students examine the main features of words, SFA activates prior knowledge and helps students explore and organize relationships among words. By highlighting similarities and differences among words, SFA helps students see how words are related and note shades of meaning. SFA works best with words that have features that are either present (+) or absent (–). However, SFA can be adapted to include a graduated scale: A = always, S = sometimes, or N = Never, for instance. The steps for teaching SFA are described in Lesson 3.4.

■ A **semantic feature analysis** is a graphic organizer that uses a grid to compare a series of words or other items on a number of characteristics.

LESSON 3.4   Semantic Feature Analysis Lesson

Step 1: Choosing a Category

Select a topic or category: for instance, *insects, government officials, trees, minerals.* Tell students what the category is and ask them to give examples. In preparation for reading a textbook section on energy, present the category *sources of energy.* Ask students to name sources of energy. Provide prompts if necessary.

Step 2: Creating a Grid

Place an outline of a grid on the board or on an overhead transparency. List *sources of energy* in a column on the left. Encourage students to suggest features or characteristics that at least one of the sources possesses. These are listed in a row at the top of the grid. Not all features have to be identified at this point. Some may be added later.

Step 3: Determining Feature Possession

Put a plus (+) in the block if a particular source of energy possesses the feature being considered or a minus (–) if it doesn't. The plus need not signal that the source always possesses the feature; it can mean that it usually does. If the group is not sure whether the source of energy does or does not possess a particular feature, put a question mark in the box. Discuss items, especially those that students are unsure of.

Step 4: Discussion of the Grid

Discuss the grid with the class. If it is missing some words or features important to the overall concept, add them. After the grid has been completed, discuss its overall significance. This provides students with the opportunity to clarify concepts. Have the class note major similarities and differences among the sources of energy. Encourage the group to sum up the ways in which sources of energy are the same and the ways in which they are different. Note, too, that the SFA does not allow for making fine distinctions. For instance, both oil and coal are noted as creating pollution. However, oil generally burns cleaner than coal and hard coal is a cleaner fuel than soft coal.

Step 5: Extension

After students have read the section on sources of energy, discuss it, and extend the grid to include sources of energy or features described in the text but not listed on the grid or to change responses. The class may also want to list additional features of energy sources. The completed SFA grid is displayed in Figure 3.7.

Other Vocabulary Building Devices

■ Possible Sentences

Possible sentences, one of the simplest vocabulary building techniques, may also be one of the most effective. It taps prior knowledge, arouses students' curiosity and interests, elicits predictions, fosters discussion, and helps students detect relationships among known and unknown words. Because it challenges students to predict how words will be used in a selection, possible sentences is also highly motivating.

As with many of the other vocabulary techniques, the first step in possible sentences is to determine the major concepts that you want students to learn and then to list the key vocabulary needed to learn those concepts (Moore & Moore, 1986; Moore, Readence, & Richelman, 1989). List six to eight potentially difficult words (Stahl & Kapinus, 1991). Then choose a like number of words that are needed to understand the key concepts but are also familiar to students. Having familiar words available helps students make connections between the known and unknown. After recording the words on the board, invite students to read them and tell what the difficult ones mean, but supply help as needed. Briefly discuss the words. Explain that they have been taken from a selection that students will be reading. Invite

FIGURE 3.7

Semantic Feature Analysis

Sources of Energy	renewable	nonpolluting	cheap	can be used anywhere	safe	widely used
biomass	+	-	+	+	+	-
coal	-	-	+	+	+	+
geothermal	+	+	?	-	+	-
natural gas	-	-	+	+	+	+
nuclear	-	-	-	+	-	?
oil	-	-	+	+	+	+
sun	+	+	-	-	+	-
water	+	+	-	-	+	-
wind	+	+	-	-	+	-

students to think about the words and predict what the selection might be about. Then ask students to compose sentences using the words. Each sentence should contain at least two of the words from the list. Explain to students that the sentences should be like the ones that appear in the selection from which they were taken. Model the creation of one such sentence, explaining as you compose the statement why you think it might be like one in the selection. Then invite students to create possible sentences. Explain that words from the list may be used in more than one sentence. Students may compose their sentences individually, in pairs, or in small groups.

After students have composed their sentences, write them on the board and discuss them briefly. Students then read the selection to see how accurate their sentences are in terms of the selection's content. After students have completed their reading, discuss the accuracy of their sentences. Encourage them to use the text as a reference to clarify confusions, resolve controversies, and provide proof for assertions. Revise sentences that are inaccurate. Students may also expand sentences to include new information acquired from the selection. After discussing the sentences, encourage students to compose additional sentences using the words if their sentences do not incorporate the key concepts in the selection. Supply guidance as needed. Record the revised and additional sentences on the board. Students may copy these sentences into their notebooks so that they have a record of key concepts contained in the selection. A possible sentences exercise completed by a group of sixth-grade students is presented below. The exercise was written in preparation for reading about the Ukrainian poet Taras Shevchenko.

Key Words for Section on Taras Shevchenko

Ukraine	Russia	freedom	serf
hero	poet	arrested	Siberia
czar	ruled	criticized	estate

Students' Sentences

The Ukraine was once part of Russia.

Russia was ruled by a czar.

Taras Shevchenko was a serf.

Serfs worked on rich people's estates.

Serfs dreamed of freedom.

Serfs who ran away were arrested and sent to Siberia.

Poets wrote about the serfs who were heroes because they ran away.

Anyone who criticized the czar was sent to Siberia.

STRUGGLING READERS

By exposing them to the thoughts of others and having their thinking clarified, think-pair-share helps students develop concepts and vocabulary.

Adaptations of Possible Sentences.   In an adaptation of possible sentences, Jensen and Duffelmeyer (1996) incorporated think-pair-share. In think-pair-share, students think on their own about an issue or question raised in class, pair up with another student to discuss possible resolutions or answers, and then meet with another pair of students to share responses. After sharing in groups of four, one person from each group reports to the whole class. In this adaptation of think-pair-share, students were given two minutes to individually consider and match the key words, five minutes to share their responses with a partner, and five minutes to create possible sentences in groups of four. The class then met as a whole group and had ten minutes to share their possible sentences and write them on the board. According to Jensen and Duffelmeyer, the inclusion of think-pair-share resulted in richer discussions and improved sentences and so increased the effectiveness of the technique.

■ Predict-O-Grams

A technique that is similar to possible sentences but designed to be used with fiction, predict-o-gram challenges students to group words according to the likelihood that they will tell about characters, plot, setting, or other parts of a narrative (Blachowicz, 1986). Both known words and words likely to be unfamiliar are chosen and recorded on the board. Key words from the story are selected and each major story category is represented: characters, setting, problem, action, resolution. After listing the words on the board, the teacher invites students to read them and discusses their meanings and pronunciations if these are unknown. The teacher then invites students to classify the words according to how they believe the words will be used in the story —describing the setting, characters, problem, action, or resolution. In addition to building vocabulary, this activity helps build students' awareness of the structure of a narrative and fosters making predictions. After the words have been classified, the teacher invites students to use the categorized words to predict the story's setting, characters, problem, action, and resolution. Students then read the story to assess their predictions. Words for a predict-o-gram are listed below. They are drawn from Langston Hughes's classic short story "Thank You, M'am."

Predict-O-Gram for "Thank You, M'am"

boy	large woman	pocketbook	suede shoes
street	furnished room	hungry	cake
ten dollars	thank you	kicked	

■ Word Sorts

Word sort is a categorization device that can be used to manipulate words. It can be especially useful for grouping technical terms (Tonjes, 1991). The words are placed on slips of paper or 3 x 5 cards and the sort can be open or closed. In a closed sort, students are given the category name. In an open sort, they must compose a category name. An open sort forces students to see relationships and state what those relationships are. An open sort taken from a health text is shown below. If you prefer a closed sort, provide the category labels: Diseases Caused by Viruses, Diseases Caused by Bacteria.

diabetes	scarlet fever	tuberculosis
rabies	measles	mumps
chicken pox	flu	cold

■ **Word sort** is a categorization device used to help students discover common elements in words and make discoveries about words.

■ Vocabulary Self-Collection Strategy (VSS)

A simple but powerful technique, vocabulary self-collection strategy (VSS) has the potential to turn passive students into active seekers of word knowledge whose interest in words is so piqued that they begin a lifelong habit of seeking out and learning the meanings of new words (Haggard, 1982; Ruddell, 1995). A versatile technique, VSS can be used to acquire general or content-specific vocabulary or a combination of the two. The heart of the technique is self-selection of words. Each student chooses one word to learn. The word should be one that the student feels is important enough for the whole class to learn. The teacher also chooses a word. Students record the sentence in which they found the word if it is in a text or describe the context in which they heard it if it is from a lecture, conversation, TV show, movie, song, or other source. Students also tell what they think the word means in the context in which it is found. And they briefly explain why they think the class should learn the word.

Words are discussed and defined in context. Dictionaries and glossaries may be checked to make sure that the correct pronunciation and definition have been obtained. The discussion offers many opportunities for modeling the use of context clues and the dictionary and refining students' use of these tools. The teacher adds a word. And the final class list is reviewed. Students choose words primarily because they seem important, useful, or interesting (Ruddell, 1995).

Aware that they are responsible for selecting a word for the whole class to study, students begin noticing words as possible candidates for selection. In time, this

STRUGGLING READERS

Not having read much in the past, struggling readers often have a limited vocabulary. The vocabulary self-collection strategy is an excellent device for helping build their awareness of new words, which aids vocabulary acquisition.

word consciousness can lead to a greater interest in words and the building of vocabulary.

Students find the experience of choosing words very motivating. As one middle-school student explained, "I think that we should keep picking our own words because then we will want to study them more efficiently. If we get something handed or picked out by a teacher, we don't want to study something we don't like" (Shearer, 1999). Another student explained how the activity had changed his attitude toward learning new words:

> Now I often catch myself and when I listen to music or listen to someone talk, I listen to the words they say and I find myself asking what the words mean. I try to make sure I understand what it means. I find that doing this helps me understand big words when I read them in a book or a textbook or even in a magazine. . . . (Shearer, 1999)

Unlike other vocabulary learning techniques, VSS is initiated after the text is read because it is believed that students won't know which words are important until then. Here are the steps in the VSS procedure.

Vocabulary Self-Collection Strategy Lesson

Step 1: Selection of Words

Students select a word they would like to study. When announcing their choice, they read the word as it is used in context, tell what they think the word means, and explain why they think the word is important to know. The selection process is usually conducted in small groups of two to five, with each group nominating one word. Some eight to ten words are nominated and five to six are selected for the final list. The teacher may also nominate a word.

Step 2: Discussion of Words

Words are listed on the board and the class discusses their meanings as derived from context. If necessary, students check meanings with a dictionary. They record words selected in vocabulary notebooks or study sheets.

Step 3: Extension

Students practice and apply words in a variety of activities.

■ Vocabulary Squares

Vocabulary learning is enhanced when students can construct a personal connection to a word being learned. Applying this principle, Eeds and Cockrum (1985) devised an activity in which students used vocabulary squares to record personal experiences. In the first box of the four-box square, students write the target word. The teacher uses the word in a sentence and then asks questions to help students relate the word to their personal experiences. For the word *irate*, the teacher might ask, "Is there something that makes you angry?" After several students have responded with appropriate examples, the teacher notes that these are examples of things that make people irate. In box two, students briefly note something that makes them irate. After a discussion, students note, in box three, things that do not make them irate. In box four, students write a definition of the word.

Adapting the technique, Hopkins (Hopkins & Bean, 1998–1999) had students create a visual association with the word. He further adapted the technique by using it with affixes and roots. In box one, students wrote the word element and its meaning; in box two, they wrote a word that used the element; in box three, they wrote a definition of the word containing the element; and in box four, they drew a picture of the item named. For the prefix *tri–*, students wrote "tri—three" in the first box. In the second box, they wrote "trilobite." In the third box they wrote, "An extinct three-lobed marine arthropod of the Paleozoic Era." In box four, they drew a picture of a trilobite.

■ Affective Words

William Funk, the famous lexicographer, listed these as the ten most beautiful words: *chimes, dawn, golden, hush, lullaby, luminous, melody, mist, murmuring, tranquil* (Tonjes, 1991). Discuss with your students the affective side of words, the power of words to evoke strong feelings and images. They can compile a list of most beautiful words, favorite words, most frightening words, noisiest words, and so on.

Words can be ranked to show differences in power, size, or intensity (Nagy, 1988). For instance, the following words can be ranked in terms of intensity: *cold, chilly, freezing, cool, frigid, nippy, wintry.* Judgments will be somewhat subjective, but ranking words introduces students to synonyms and provides an excellent opportunity to discuss specificity in word choice. To convey the concept of connotations of words, you can ask students whether they would rather be:

determined	or	stubborn
nosy	or	curious
clever	or	sly
cheap	or	frugal
carefree	or	irresponsible

Discuss students' choices. Discuss the images and feelings that the words evoke and the importance of word choice. Talk over, too, how through our choice of words, we can make a person, place, or thing look favorable or unfavorable.

■ Word Origins

Knowing the history, or **etymology,** of a word can foster an understanding of the word and also make the word more memorable. As a bonus, the etymologies of some words are miniature history lessons. For instance, knowing the origin of *boycott*, which is derived from the name of an English land manager in Ireland in 1880, helps to explain what the word means and also provides information about land ownership in Ireland.

Knowing the history of a scientific term can sometimes help students understand the importance of the concept named. For instance, *radon* was named after ra-

■ **Etymology** is the history of the origin and development of words.

dium because it is a radioactive gas produced when radium decays. It is found in areas having radium- and uranium-bearing rocks.

Studying the history or origin of words can prevent confusion of terms. Math students often confuse the words *radius* and *diameter*. Math expert Rheta Rubenstein (2000) recalls hearing middle school students ask, "Is the diameter the short one or the long one?" (p. 493). Knowing the origins of these words would help students discriminate between the two. *Radius* comes from the same root as *ray*. If students picture the rays of the sun moving out from the sun, they can picture the radius of a circle starting at the center and radiating from there. *Diameter* comes from roots that mean "measure" and "through." The diameter of a circle is a measure through its center (Rubenstein, 2000). For a history of math words, see *The Words of Mathematics* (Schwartzman, 1994). For general word histories, see the Reading List below.

To extend students' learning and to drive home the meaning of *radius*, you can talk about radio waves, radiant heat, or radial tires. If the approach is interdisciplinary, the biology teacher can talk about the radius, a bone in the forearm, and the chemistry teacher can talk about radium. The language arts teacher can have students create a **web,** similar to the one in Figure 3.8, that shows some of the uses of the root. In explaining *diameter*, a similar process can be initiated. Students can explore other words that contain *dia: diagonal, diabetes, diametric, diabolic,* and *diagnosis.*

■ A **web** is another name for a semantic map, especially a simplified one.

Reading List: Word Histories

Ayto, J. (1993). *Dictionary of word origins.* New York: Arcade.

Ayto, J. (1999). *Twentieth century words.* New York: Oxford.

Barnhart, D. K., & Metcalf, A. A. (1999). *America in so many words: Words that have shaped America.* Boston: Houghton Mifflin.

Editorial Staff (1995). *The Merriam-Webster new book of word histories.* Springfield, MA: Merriam-Webster.

Ehrlich, E. (2000). *What's in a name? How proper names became everyday words.* New York: Owl Books.

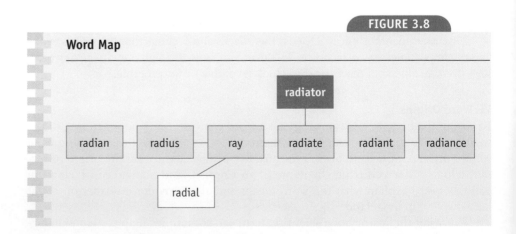

FIGURE 3.8

Word Map

radiator

radian — radius — ray — radiate — radiant — radiance

radial

Graham-Barber, L. (1992). *Doodle Dandy: The complete book of Independence Day words.*
    New York: Avon.

Hendrickson, R. (2000). *The Facts on File encyclopedia of word and phrase origins.* New
    York: Facts on File.

Klausner, J. (1990). *Talk about English: How words travel and change.* New York:
    HarperCollins.

REMEMBERING WORDS

Students may understand new vocabulary words once they have been presented, but
they often forget them. There are a number of techniques, known as mnemonic devices, that aid memory. One of the most carefully researched of these techniques is the
key word approach.

■ The **key word approach**
is a strategy in which students create images to
help them associate a
meaning with a new word.

Key Word Approach

In the key word approach, students create an image that forges a link between the
new word and its meaning. The key word is a term that both serves as a key to the
meaning of the target word and evokes an image that calls to mind the word and
its meaning. If possible, the key word embodies a portion of the target word. For
instance, in one study, the key word for *angler* was *angel.* The mnemonic image
showed an angel sitting on a cloud fishing. Two angels on a higher cloud have the
following conversation:

> Angel 1: That ANGEL down there sure knows how to catch a lot of fish.
> Angel 2: That's because he's an expert ANGLER. (Levin et al., 1984, p. 8)

The key word method works best if students create their own images. Creating
a key word and an image involves thinking about the target word and the kind of image
that might be used to depict it. This process, especially the creation of an image,
leads to a better understanding of the word because the student has to think of images that would appropriately portray the word. Younger students and some low-
achieving learners may need help creating mnemonic images. However, involve the
students as much as possible in the process. Here is how the words *embargo, blockade,
deserters,* and *impress* might be presented through the key word approach.

Key Word Approach Lesson

LESSON
3.6

Step 1: Introducing the Approach

Discuss with students difficulties they may have had remembering the meanings of new words. Explain that you will be showing them a special way to

learn new words. Inform them that this method works well because they will be creating images in their minds to help them make a link between the new words and their meanings.

Step 2: Explaining the Technique

Using a word that they are having difficulty with or need to learn, show how the technique works. Selecting the word *embargo*, for instance, explain that you are going to create a key word and a picture to help you remember the word *embargo*. Inform the class that you are going to use the word part *em* because it is the first part of *embargo*. Then explain that you are going to create a picture in your mind that uses the word part *em* and shows the meaning of *embargo*. You picture a giant with an *m* on his shirt. He is pulling down a large bar in front of a ship's harbor and he is saying, "This is an em bar go. No ships go in. No ships go out!" A huge sign that says "Embargo" is nearby.

Step 3: Presenting New Words

Present the words *blockade*, *deserters*, and *impress*. Discuss the meanings of each and some possible key words and interactive images: The king of England, putting up blocks around the coast of the United States, is saying, "I'll blockade these Americans." The captain of a ship is calling out to sailors fleeing the ships, "There will be no dessert for deserters." He is holding up a large cake. Two very muscular British sailors are grabbing an American sailor and saying, "I've got 'im. I've got 'im. 'Im's impressed!"

Step 4: Guided Practice

Provide practice in the use of the technique. For instance, you say the word *blockade* and have the class tell what the key word is and describe the interactive image. Students then tell what the word means. Also say the key word *block* and have students supply the target word, the interactive image, and the target word's meaning. Continue until students have a firm grasp of the technique.

Step 5: Application

Encourage students to use the technique on their own, if they are able to create their key words and interactive images without assistance. Periodically, review the technique and encourage students to use it.

How effective is the key word strategy? In an experiment with 100 sixth-graders, students who used the key word approach learned almost twice as many words as students who used a contextual approach in which they composed sentences using new words (Jones, Levin, Levin, & Beitzel, 2000). When students worked in pairs, the technique was even more effective than when they studied alone. Although students creating sentences were just as actively involved as the students using the key word technique, "they were not similarly engaged in producing essential retrieval links between the vocabulary items and the meanings to bolster subsequent memory and application" (p. 261).

 **CHECKUP**

1. What techniques can be used to teach and reinforce vocabulary?
2. Which of these techniques would seem to be most effective for your content area? Why?

CREATING INDEPENDENT WORD LEARNERS

Realistically, a systematic program of vocabulary development might cover only 400 or so words in a year's time. However, at the same time that students are learning these new words, they should also be learning strategies and habits that will foster independent word learning. As Curtis and Longo (1999) note, "They see the importance of a wider vocabulary, and become motivated to increase their vocabularies on their own" (p. 37). Because you cannot possibly teach students all the words they need to know, help them use tools that will make them independent word learners. These include syllabic analysis, morphemic analysis, contextual analysis, and dictionary/glossary use.

Syllabic Analysis

Students who have struggled with reading in the past may have mastered single-syllable words but may experience difficulty reading multisyllabic words, especially those that have three or more syllables. While it is not the responsibility of the content area teacher to provide basic instruction in analyzing multisyllabic words, you can help students with the multisyllabic words that appear frequently in your discipline and that they need to know in order to read the text. This need not be a time-consuming activity. As you discuss new vocabulary, place it on the board and highlight the syllables in the words. Have students read the words so that when they encounter them in print, they don't become stumbling blocks. For instance, when studying meteors, you might show the syllabication of the following words: *me-te-or, at-mos-phere, par-ti-cle, sil-i-cate, al-ti-tude,* and *lu-mi-nous.* Also discuss the meanings of the words if they are unknown.

Morphemic Analysis

Although not the longest word in the world, *pneumonoultramicroscopicsilicovolcanocon-iosis* is the longest word in at least one unabridged dictionary (Flexner & Hauck, 1994). Although it looks impenetrable, you may be able to derive its meaning if you break it down morpheme by morpheme. A **morpheme** is the smallest unit of meaning. It may be a word, a prefix, a suffix, or a root. The word *fear* has a single morpheme; however, *fearfulness* has three: *fear-ful-ness. Television* has three morphemes: *tele-vis-ion.*

pneumono means "lung"
ultra means "very"

■ A **morpheme** is the smallest unit of meaning. The word *nervously* has three morphemes: *nerv(e)-ous-ly.*

microscopic means "small"

silico means "white powder"

volcano means "volcano"

coni means "cone shaped"

osis means "disorder of"

How did you do? The *Random House Dictionary* (Flexner & Hauck, 1994) defines *pneumonoultramicroscopicsilicovolcanoconiosis* as "a lung disease caused by silica dust." If it serves no other purpose, *pneumonoultramicroscopicsilicovolcanoconiosis* demonstrates the power of **morphemic analysis.** According to Nagy and Anderson (1984), about 60 percent of the new words a reader meets contain morphemic units that provide clear, useable clues to the word's meaning. Another 10 percent give helpful but incomplete clues. This is especially true of words in the sciences, many of which have been formed by combining two or more morphemes: for example, *carbohydrates, conductor, electomagnetic, hologram,* and *metalloids.*

> ■ **Morphemic analysis** is the examination of a word in order to locate and derive the meanings of the morphemes.

■ Teaching Morphemic Elements

How might a knowledge of word parts help students better understand the following excerpt from a description of mollusks?

> The majority of mollusks are marine animals, but some live in fresh water, and a few live on dry land. They include clams, mussels, and oysters (bivalves), snails and slugs (gastropods), and cuttlefish, squids, and octopuses (cephalopods). (Brimblecombe, Gallannaugh, & Thompson, 1999, p. 495)

The *bi* should alert students that clams, mussels, and oysters have two valves. Knowing *gastro* and *pod* would help students realize that the locomotion of snails and slugs is close to their stomachs. Knowing *cephalo* and *pod* would help students realize that the means of locomotion for cuttlefish, squids, and octopuses is in the vicinity of their heads. Morphemic analysis, the study of meaningful word parts, such as roots, prefixes, and suffixes, can help students recognize hundreds of content area words.

Morphemic elements should be taught inductively and should build on what students know. For instance, students should use their knowledge of *thermometer* and *Thermos* to derive the meaning of *thermoplastic* and *thermal.* By noting the use of *therm* in all four words, the students should be able to derive a meaning for the morphemic form *therm.* Also using their knowledge of the words *geography* and *geology,* students may be able to derive the meaning of *geothermal.* Encountering the word *geothermal,* students can relate it to *geography* and *thermometer.* Morphemic analysis also aids memory. If students can't remember what *geothermal* means, they can use their knowledge of the combining forms *geo* and *thermal* to help them recall it. Morphemics is also generative: knowing *geo* can help students learn and remember such words as: *geology, geologic, geothermal, geophysical, geomagnetism, geophysics,* and *geopolitics.* Knowing *therm* will help students learn such words as *ectothermal, endothermal, endothermic, exothermic, hypothermia, isotherm, thermal, thermochemical,* and *thermodynamic.*

Making Connections. When introducing morphemic elements or new words, make connections whenever possible. For instance, a textbook section on cells introduces the following words: *chromosomes, lysomes,* and *ribosomes.* If students are led to see the common element in the words, they will understand them better, remember them longer, and, even if they forget their meanings, be able to use morphemic units to decode them. Lead them to see that *somes* means "bodies"; *chromosomes, lysosomes,* and *ribosomes* are "small bodies that perform functions in a cell." You might also discuss the meanings of the morphemic forms *chromo* (color), *lyso* (decomposition of), and *ribo* (sugary substance).

In addition to making connections between morphemic elements being taught, make connections between morphemic elements and students' current reading needs. In a geometry unit focusing on angles, introduce the morphemic forms that students will encounter: *polygon, heptagon, hexagon, octagon, pentagon, quadrilateral,* and *triangle.* Lead students to see the meaning of *gon* (angle) and the meaning of the other morphemic elements. Have students do an illustrated web of the words. Also discuss some everyday uses of the morphemic forms. What would the building called the Pentagon look like? How many sides would it have? How many events are there in the pentathlon? As an extension, you might study other morphemic elements that indicate number (for instance, *mono-, uni-, bi-, di-,* and *dec-*) or spend additional time with *poly,* since this is a frequently occurring morphemic unit and easy to understand.

Before assigning students a selection, scan it to see if any of the potentially difficult words contain morphemic elements that might be taught. And when teaching difficult words, be sure to include an explanation of morphemic forms or, better yet, help students note and build on morphemic forms that they already know. The key to teaching morphemic units is to build students' awareness of these elements in words so that when they encounter a difficult word, they see if they can figure out its meaning by analyzing it morphemically.

Often, a variety of techniques can be used to help students comprehend and recall technical words. As they read a section on cells in a sixth-grade science text, students must learn the following terms: *cell membrane, cell wall, chloroplasts, chromosomes, cytoplasm, mitochondria, nucleus,* and *vacuole.* One of the best ways to help students understand and remember these words is by using a diagram to show where each is found, what each looks like, and what each does. Morphemic analysis can also be used as an aid to understanding and remembering the terms. For instance, students learn that *cytoplasm* is formed from terms that mean cell (*cyto*) and the watery part of blood (*plasma*); *vacuole* is formed from the word *vacuum,* meaning "empty spaces," and the word part *ole,* meaning "small." Morphemic analysis can also be used to teach students how to predict the meaning of other unfamiliar words. For example, students might be asked, "If *cyt* means 'cell,' what do the following words mean?"

cytology　　　　cytochemistry　　　　cytoanalyzer　　　　cytotoxin

Morphemic Elements Lesson

Because they appear first in a word and generally have concrete meanings, prefixes are the easiest of the morphemic elements. Here is how the prefix *anti-* might be introduced.

Step 1: Construct the Meaning of the Prefix

Place the following words on the board: *antislavery, antiwar, anti-Lincoln, anti-constitution, antigun, antismoking, antifreeze.* Some of these words have been drawn from a chapter on the Civil War, which students are about to read. Discuss the meanings of these words. Note how *anti-* changes the meaning of the word it precedes. Encourage students to construct a definition of *anti-.* Lead students to see that *anti-* is a prefix. Discuss, too, the purpose and value of knowing prefixes. Explain to students how knowing the meanings of prefixes will help them figure out unknown words. Show them how you would syllabicate words that contain prefixes and how you would use knowledge of prefixes to sound out the words and determine their meanings.

Step 2: Guided Practice

Have students complete practice exercises similar to the following:

Fill in the blanks with these words containing prefixes: *antihighway, antiwar, antiunion, antifreeze, antismoking.*

1. When winter comes, you will need to put _____ in your car's radiator.
2. One town passed an _____ law that forbids smoking anywhere in the town.
3. The _____ demonstrators gathered outside the White House when they heard that the United States planned to send soldiers into battle.
4. The owner of the factory was _____ because he didn't want any group telling him how to treat his workers.
5. Because they were against the new road, the citizens set up an _____ group.

Step 3: Application

Have students read the selection about the Civil War that includes the words containing the prefix *anti-.* You can also have students note words containing *anti-* in other reading that they do.

Step 4: Extension

Present the prefix *pro-* and have students contrast the meanings of the two prefixes. Using words containing the prefix *pro-,* they can make a list of things that they may be in favor of: *proschool, procandy, proholidays, proallowance.* Using the prefix *anti-,* they can make a list of things that they may be against: *antigangs, antidrugs, antigerms, antisuspension.* Students can also take note of these prefixes in science: *antibiotic, antibacterial.*

Step 5: Assessment and Reteaching

Through observation, note whether students are able to use their knowledge of affixes to help them pronounce and figure out the meanings of unfamiliar words. Review common affixes from time to time. Discuss affixes that appear in selections that students are reading. Focus on elements that will appear over and over again. A list of roots, prefixes, and suffixes frequently found in content area materials is found in Appendix B.

Fortunately, many textbook authors include morphemic clues to help students understand technical terms, as in this excerpt from a fourth-grade science text:

Sometimes scientists talk about nimbostratus or cumulonimbus clouds. *Nimbus* is a Latin word that means "rain." When you see *nimbus* or *nimbo-* in a cloud name, you know the cloud is a rain cloud.

Clouds are also grouped by height above the ground. Some clouds are close to the ground, some are high in the sky, and some are in between. Clouds that form high in the sky have the prefix *cirro-* in front of their family name. Clouds that form at a medium height have the prefix *alto-* in front of their family name. (Badders et al., 1999a, p. E 57)

Highlight and discuss this feature so students take advantage of it. If the text fails to present useful morphemic clues, provide them to students.

■ Morphemic Analysis and Spanish-Speaking Students

If students know prefixes, suffixes, and roots in Spanish, they can transfer this knowledge to English. A number of elements are identical in both languages or altered slightly. For instance, the prefixes *ab, ante, anti, contra, inter, post, pro, re, sub,* and *super* are the same in both languages (Thonis, 1983). The suffixes *al, or, ar, able, ion* (except for the accent) are also the same. The suffix *tion* is slightly different in Spanish. It is spelled *cion* but may also be spelled *sion* or *xion.* The suffix *ismo* is similar to the suffix *ism* in English. Hundreds of roots, such as *libro,* are also identical or similar. One strategy Spanish speakers can use is to seek out familiar morphemes.

 **CHECKUP**

1. What are the key elements in the effective teaching of morphemic analysis strategies?

Contextual Analysis

Because content area reading is usually loaded with technical terms, writers often deliberately supply **context clues** for the reader. Note the technical terms in the following excerpt from a trade book on the oceans and the pains the author takes to explain them. Even such nontechnical terms as *pierce*, *steep*, and *incline*, which may pose problems for some readers, are surrounded by contextual clues.

■ **Context clues** are bits of information in the surrounding text that may help to derive the meaning of an unknown word. Context clues include appositives, restatement of the word's meaning, comparative or contrasting statements, and other items that might provide clues to the word's meaning.

> The ocean bed, or floor, is like a huge basin. In it there are channels, or trenches, that are deeper than the rest of the floor. Long lines of mountains and volcanoes rise from the ocean bottom, sometimes piercing the surface of the water to form islands. At the edges of the ocean, a steep incline called the continental slope separates the ocean bed from the more shallow seabed around the continents. The area nearest to the land is the continental shelf, where the water is not more than 650 feet deep. (Sauvain, 1996, p. 6)

Experienced writers want their readers to understand what they have to say and so intuitively remove obstacles to comprehension, such as hard words. Notice how science writer Seymour Simon (1998) explains in context the key words *optical* and *illusion*.

> Now look at the figure below. Which line is longer, AB or BC? Measure each line with your ruler. Surprised? Both lines are exactly the same length.
>
> You have been looking at two optical, or visual, illusions. An optical illusion is something you see that is not exactly what is really there. One line seems to be longer than another even though both are actually the same length. (p. 6)

Not only does Simon provide definitions in context of *optical* and *illusion*, he also gives an example.

■ Processing Context Clues

What context clues might students use to derive the meaning of the boldfaced word in the excerpt below?

To understand why these hundred or so people made that desperate voyage, we have to know something about the situation in England in their day. It was a country in **turmoil.** For one thing, after the long and stable reign of Elizabeth I, there came a time of much quarreling among factions in government. In particular, the Parliaments of the seventeenth century were attempting to take power away from the kings, and the kings of course resisted. In time there would be open warfare between king and Parliament.

For another, England, like much of Europe, was in the midst of the long-term, but profoundly important, switch from a farming economy to "capitalism"—the system of trade and manufacturing in which most Americans, Europeans, and others elsewhere today live and work. (Collier & Collier, 1998, p. 14)

Using context clues is a three-step process (Sternberg & Powell, 1983):

1. *Selective encoding.* Students separate relevant from irrelevant information. They focus on information that will help them construct a meaning for an unknown word.
2. *Selective combination.* Students combine clues into a possible but tentative definition.
3. *Selective comparison.* Students use their background knowledge to help derive the meaning of an unfamiliar word.

Here is how the three steps can be put to use to figure out the meaning of *turmoil* from the passage above:

1. *Selective encoding.* What information in the sentence containing the unknown word will help me figure out what this word means? Is there any information in earlier sentences that will help? Is there any information in later sentences that will help?

    Helpful clues include information about quarreling between the king and Parliament and the switch from a farming economy to one of trade and manufacturing.

2. *Selective combination.* When I think about all the information given about this unknown word, what does the word seem to mean?

    When readers put all relevant clues together, they will see that *turmoil* seems to mean that there is some disturbance because so many changes are taking place.

3. *Selective comparison.* What do I know that will help me figure out the meaning of this word?

    Using past experience, readers may realize that if the king and Parliament were arguing and the way people made their living was changing, there was a great deal of disturbance. It would be like having Congress trying to get rid of the president and at the same time having thousands of people change jobs. Life would not be calm or quiet.

Once readers have used context to construct a tentative meaning for the unknown word, they should try substituting the tentative meaning for the word. If the meaning does not fit the sense of the sentence, they should revise their substitution, use the dictionary, or get help.

■ Types of Context Clues

Here, in approximate order of difficulty, are eight main types of context clues. They have been drawn from a variety of content area materials.

1. *Explicit explanation or definition.* The easiest clue to use is a definition in context. For instance, the following passage gives an excellent definition of *asteroids:*

The solar system is made up of the Sun and objects circling it. In the solar system, there are 9 planets and more than 60 moons. Thousands of small, rocky lumps called **asteroids** also circle the Sun. (Nicolson, 1998, p. 14)

2. *Appositives.* Definitions are sometimes supplied in the form of an appositive immediately following the difficult word:

Oxides—the metal combined with oxygen—are important ore minerals. (Dixon, 1992, p. 27)

3. *Synonyms.* Often, a synonym for a difficult word will appear shortly after the unfamiliar word. In the following sentence, *odor* provides a synonym for *aroma.*

The sweet **aroma** of mince pies and pumpkin bread, floating from open bakery windows, contrasted sharply with the strong odors of oysters and cod hawked by fishmongers across the street. (Litwin, 1999, pp. 9–10)

4. *Function indicators.* Context sometimes provides clues to meaning because it gives the purpose or function of the difficult word (Sternberg, 1987). In the sentence below, the reader gets a clue to the meaning of *foragers* in a sentence that tells what a forager does.

We all have different jobs to do. Soldiers guard our nest, workers keep things neat and clean, and **foragers** look for food. (Parker, 1999, p. 12)

5. *Examples.* The examples—rain, snow, sleet, and hail—in the following passage would give the reader a sense of the meaning of *precipitation:*

Eventually the drops are too big to stay in the air, and they begin to fall as rain, snow, sleet, or hail. If you were to analyze the pH of this **precipitation,** you might discover readings as low as 2.0. (Badders et al., 1999c, p. C. 84)

6. *Comparison–contrast.* By contrasting the unknown word *ascend* with the known word *descend* in the following passage, readers can gain an understanding of the unknown word. Understanding that *descend* means to "come down," the reader can reason that *ascend* means to "go up."

The answer is that the sun and almost all heavenly objects—the moon, planets, and most stars—appear to **ascend** in the eastern half of the sky and **descend** in the western half of the sky. (Schaaf, 1998, p. 52)

7. *Classification.* By noting similarities in items, some of which are known, readers can guess what an unknown word means. In the following sentence, they know from the word *town* and the earlier mention of Canada that places are being talked about; based on this conclusion, they can infer that

province, the unknown word, is also a place. Because the sentence says that the town is in the province, they could infer that a province is larger than a town.

Gordie was born on March 31, 1928, in the town of Floral, in the **province** of Saskatchewan. (Neff, 1990, p. 48)

8. *Experience.* A main clue to the meaning of an unfamiliar word is students' background of experience. In the following passage, readers can use their own experience of being treated unfairly or being denied an opportunity to imagine how Abigail Adams feels; this will enable them to make an informed guess as to what the unfamiliar word *indignantly* means.

Abigail had always regretted her lack of schooling and was embarrassed by her peculiar spelling and punctuation, which she called pointing. And Abigail resented how most families neglected their daughters' education. "Every assistance and advantage . . . is afforded to the Sons," she commented **indignantly.** (St. George, 2001, p. 5)

A combination of clues can sometimes be used. In the following example, a republican form of government is contrasted with government by a king. The word *republic* is also defined in context.

Kings ruled Rome until 510 B.C. when the citizens expelled the last king, Tarquin the Proud. Rome then became a **republic** governed by officials who were elected by the people. (Roberts, 1997, p. 10)

Context clues and morphemic analysis can often be integrated. For instance, students might use their knowledge of the root word *photo*, meaning "light," and context to derive the meaning of *photic* in the following sentence.

USING TECHNOLGY

Vocabulary Drill for Kids
http://www.edu4kids.com/lang1/
Presents words in context. Students select from three options the one they think is the correct response.

As we have already established, the part of the sea where sunlight penetrates is called the **photic** zone. (Massa, 1998, p. 20)

Notice in the sentence below how the meaning of *di-* is suggested and how the meaning of *cotyledons* is provided.

The hibiscus is a **dicotyledon.** Its seedlings have two seed leaves, or cotyledons, and its leaves are broad with a central midrib and branched veins. (Smith, 1996, p. 39)

Generating possible definitions from context requires some thought. Students may have to consider several possible meanings before arriving at one that seems suitable. Here is how Angela, a middle school student, arrived at a tentative meaning for the word *qualms*, which was contained in a selection she was reading. First, the selection:

I had a few qualms at first about how Caroline and Julia would get along together. Julia was so different from all of our school friends that I felt sort of awkward with her myself. (Duncan, 1977, p. 55)

Now Angela's reasoning:

> *Researcher:* Talk to me. What do you think?
> *Angela:* That maybe there are questions of how they are going to get together.
> *Researcher:* What do you mean by questions?
> *Angela:* Like are they going to get together or are they not. Like she's thinking in her head how is she like going to get along with her friend.
> *Researcher:* So what does that tell you about the word *qualms*?
> *Angela:* That she might be thinking in her head.
> *Researcher:* What else can you tell me? (long pause before Angela responds)
> *Angela:* Ideas.
> *Researcher:* Keep talking.
> Angela: Maybe like an uneasy feeling. (Harmon, 1998a, p. 586)

Because of the complexity involved in using context clues, instruction is required. Sternberg and Powell (1983) conducted an experiment in which one group was given instruction and practice in using context clues, a second group was given practice, and a third group was given neither instruction nor practice. Only the group given both instruction and practice improved, but its improvement was substantial. One of the best ways to help students learn to use context clues is to model the process. Explain in concrete detail your reasoning processes as you work out a tentative meaning for an unfamiliar word. Because reasoning processes vary, also encourage students to discuss examples of when they were able to derive the meaning of an unfamiliar word. Also provide guided practice. During guided practice, ask such questions as What are the context clues here? What are the clues in the sentence telling us? Are there any clues in the sentences before the hard-word sentence? Are there any clues in the sentences after the hard-word sentence? When you put all the clues together, what does the word seem to mean? Another approach to try is previewing words in context.

■ Preview in Context

Provide opportunities for students to use their word learning skills. One quick and easy way to do this is to have students preview words in context:

1. Select a few key words likely to pose problems.
2. Have students try to use context and other clues to derive the meanings of the words.
3. Through discussion, help students compose tentative meanings for the words.
4. Check the derived meanings with those provided by the glossary or a dictionary.

 *CHECKUP*

1. What is involved in using context clues?
2. How might context clues be taught?

Dictionary Use

The dictionary or glossary is the word analysis strategy of last resort. Looking up a word interferes with the flow of reading and so can hinder comprehension. In most

*S*tudents use the dictionary as a functional word learning tool.

instances, students should use contextual or word analysis clues and, if they don't work, wait until after the section has been read to look up unknown words. However, if the word is central to the meaning of the section and context clues don't work, it should be looked up immediately.

Most content area textbooks and **trade books** contain glossaries. Glossaries are easier to use than dictionaries largely because they typically only present the definition of the word that fits the way it was used in the text. However, there may be some general words that the student doesn't know, and some technical words may not be included in the glossary, so general-use dictionaries should be available. If your discipline has its own dictionary, that should be available too: These specialized dictionaries are the tools of the discipline.

Students sometimes need conceptual information about a term, information that goes beyond the dictionary or glossary's definition. It is helpful to have on hand an encyclopedia for your subject area if one exists or a general encyclopedia if one doesn't. Fortunately, encyclopedias and dictionaries on CD-ROM are relatively inexpensive and widely available. They are also available on the Web.

When introducing the textbook, spend some time talking about the glossary. In many texts, words defined in the glossary are boldfaced in the text the first time they are used. Note, too, illustrations, sample sentences, phonetic respellings, and other aids provided in the glossary. Instruction in glossary and dictionary use should be functional. When students have difficulty with a word, have them look it up in the glossary or dictionary. Discuss the meaning they obtained and make sure it is appropriate for the context of the word they were looking up. Also make sure that the definition is understandable.

The key to turning students into skilled dictionary users is helping them discover the value of the dictionary. One way of doing this is by discussing the information that can be found in the dictionary. Students may be surprised to find out that in addition to providing definitions and spellings for words, dictionaries provide information on grammar and usage, weights and measurements, and spellings

■ **Tradebooks** are books written to be sold to the general public or collected in libraries, as opposed to textbooks, which are designed to be sold to schools.

USING TECHNOLGY

Merriam–Webster
http://www.m-w.com/
Presents a number of vocabulary building exercises. The site also provides pronunciations for words.

of geographical locations. In addition, some dictionaries provide a history of the language and common words found in other languages. A second way of turning students into dictionary users is by providing guided opportunities to use the dictionary in a functional fashion: to find the meaning of a difficult term in the text, to check the spelling of the name of a famous person, to check the pronunciation of a town or city. If students feel comfortable with the dictionary, chances are they will use it.

Because there are many general as well as technical terms that they may not know, English language learners should find the dictionary especially valuable. Dictionary usage is critical for ELL students. As they encounter unknown words in their reading, they have very little choice but to consult the dictionary. One problem is that the definitions often contain unfamiliar words. As one ELL student put it, "I find word in dictionary. But meaning I do not understand. I have to find other meaning [in dictionary] to explain this word" (Gonzalez, 1999, p. 269). Despite difficulty they experienced using the dictionary, ELL students in one study were able to determine correct definitions about 80 percent of the time (Gonzalez, 1999).

■ Contextual Redefinition

Contextual redefinition is an excellent technique for reviewing and integrating dictionary usage with other word analysis strategies. Contextual redefinition aids students in the use of context clues by contrasting definitions derived for words in isolation with definitions derived for words in context (Tierney & Readence, 2000). It also provides reinforcement for dictionary skills. An easy-to-implement but effective technique, it consists of four steps: (1) choosing hard words, (2) presenting words in isolation, (3) presenting words in context, and (4) checking derived meanings against those provided by a dictionary.

LESSON 3.8   Contextual Redefinition Lesson

Step 1: Selecting Hard Words

Choose words that are important to an understanding of the selection and that may be difficult for students.

Step 2: Presenting Words in Isolation

List potentially unfamiliar words on the chalkboard or on a transparency. Invite volunteers to pronounce them. Give help if it is needed and ask the volunteers to define the words. Because the words are presented in isolation, students rely on morphemic analysis clues to define them. Ask students to give reasons for their definitions. Because they lack context clues and the aid of the dictionary, their definitions may be off the mark. For instance, unless students spot the combining form *mon(o)* and the root *arch*, they might define *monarch* as "my bridge" or "one arch." Encourage students to agree on one meaning for each word.

Step 3: Presenting Words in Context

Then present the words in context. Ideally, this would be the context in which the words are used in the selection to be read. However, if the context is not adequate, compose your own sentence.

Using the context, students make their best guesses about the meaning of each word. They can do this alone, in pairs, or in small groups. After they have attempted to derive the meaning of a word from context, ask them to explain why they composed a particular definition. This gives them an opportunity to learn from each other as they share their reasoning processes. Ask the group again to agree on the best guess as to the target word's meaning.

Step 4: Checking the Meaning in the Dictionary

Students look up the word in the dictionary and discuss possible definitions with the group. The group chooses the most appropriate definition.

Contextual redefinition provides practice in three interrelated word identification skills: morphemic analysis, contextual analysis, and dictionary usage. In deriving the meaning of *monarch*, students can use their knowledge of the combining form *mono* and the root *arch*, the context clue, and the dictionary definition to arrive at an understanding of *monarch*.

 **CHECKUP**

1. How might dictionary skills be taught?
2. What are the skills students need in order to become independent word learners?
3. How might you integrate the teaching of these skills with the teaching of your subject matter?

INTEGRATION OF SKILLS

Although word analysis strategies have been presented separately, students should be encouraged to integrate their use. They may try context first, and if that doesn't work, they may try morphemic analysis, and, if all else fails, they may use the dictionary or glossary or seek help from a parent, a teacher, or a classmate. Or they may use partial clues from two or more sources of information. The strategies that students use depends on the nature of the word, the text, and students' ability and command of strategies. Struggling learners may use ineffective strategies. For instance, one struggling reader in the middle school used primarily a phonic or pronunciation strategy, and if that didn't work she would ask for help or skip the word (Harmon, 1998a). When prompted, she was partially successful with using context, but she did not use context on her own.

USING TECHNOLGY

Acquire a CD-ROM or other electronic dictionary for student use. Electronic dictionaries make it possible to locate words faster and are motivational. An electronic dictionary may also read the word and its definition. This is a help for students whose reading skills are limited.

EXEMPLARY TEACHING

Realizing that vocabulary is a key element in comprehension, tenth-grade English teacher Chris Sloan dutifully taught his students key vocabulary before they read a selection. However, students' comprehension failed to improve, and he wasn't even sure that the students' vocabularies were improving. After discussing his difficulty with two researchers, he devised a new approach to teaching vocabulary.

His revised approach embodied several facets. He taught students how to identify key vocabulary words—those that were especially important to an understanding of the selection—and he taught them strategies for learning unknown words. He also made sure that they learned the words in the context of the selection. As they read the selection, students underlined what they believed were the key words, used context to predict the words' meanings, and checked their predictions by looking the words up in the dictionary. The next day, students discussed the key words they had chosen as they discussed the selection they had read. Key words were related to the selection's characters, plot, or theme. For instance, they discussed the fact that Lemas, a character in the selection they were reading, was a **cynical** man who sought **vengeance.** His **cynicism** was related to his **profession** and his **motto,** "Trust no one." Through the discussion, the students deepened their knowledge of the selection and also developed their vocabulary. Their increased vocabulary knowledge was impacting their comprehension and vice versa. (Dole, Sloan, & Trathen, 1995)

Students may not realize that their texts offer a variety of word learning aids, so you should review these with them. Words may be boldfaced and defined in context. The text may have a glossary in the back or define words in the margins.

As with so many other areas, instruction in word analysis has to be affective to be effective. Instruction in word analysis strategies must include sessions in which the teacher assesses students' work in group or individual think-alouds to see what strategies students use and also what their attitudes are. Feelings of inadequacy and an unwillingness to try must be addressed. "Listening to learners voice what they know and how they use what they know about word learning seems a necessary part of vocabulary instruction" (Harmon, 1998a, p. 592).

 CHECKUP

1. What are the key elements in a program of vocabulary development?

SUMMARY

One of the chief barriers to learning in the content areas is that posed by the technical vocabulary that each employs. An effective program of vocabulary development features in-depth understanding, multiple exposures, active involvement, seeing relationships among words, and acquiring strategies for developing new vocabulary. Techniques for teaching words include conceptual teaching of key words and brainstorming techniques, such as the list-group-label and semantic mapping approaches. Graphic techniques include the Frayer model, concept definition, semantic mapping, pictorial maps and webs, semantic feature analysis, and the Venn diagram. Other vocabulary teaching techniques are possible sentences, predict-o-grams, word sorts, simulation, vocabulary self-selection strategy, and contextual redefinition. Strategies for remembering words should focus on building understanding and the key word method. Vocabulary instruction should also include instruction in morphemic and structural analysis and dictionary use so that students can learn words on their own.

Reflection

Return to the Anticipation Guide at the beginning of this chapter. Respond once again to the items. Did your responses change? If so, how and why? How do you now feel about the number of words presented in content area texts in your field? What is your responsibility as the content area teacher for helping students learn those words? What steps might you take to help students learn content words?

EXTENSION AND APPLICATION

1. Examine the technical terms in a text from your content area. Survey several chapters. How many new words are introduced per chapter? What kinds of strategies do the words lend themselves to? What kinds of morphemic elements might you introduce that would help students learn some of the new words? How helpful would contextual strategies be? What word learning aids do the chapters incorporate? Are words boldfaced and explained in context? Is there a glossary? Are illustrations used to help explain words?

2. Try out three of the graphic organizers described in the chapter. Try out each one for at least a week with words that you are trying to learn. What are the strengths and weaknesses of each of the organizers? Which was easiest to use? Which seems most effective?

3. Use the key word technique to learn five new words. Test yourself a day later and then a week later. How did the technique work? Try out the technique with a group of students and assess its effectiveness.

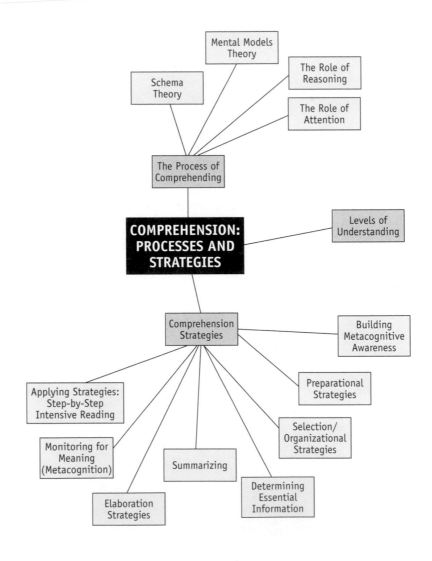

chapter 4

COMPREHENSION: PROCESSES AND STRATEGIES

ANTICIPATION GUIDE

For each of the following statements related to the chapter you are about to read, put a check under "Agree" or "Disagree" to show how you feel. Discuss your responses with classmates before you read the chapter.

		Agree	*Disagree*
1	Reading comprehension is primarily a matter of grasping the author's message.	____	____
2	The key to comprehension is having solid knowledge about the topic being explained.	____	____
3	Comprehension is more difficult to teach than vocabulary.	____	____
4	Implementing effective reading strategies is the best way to improve comprehension.	____	____
5	If given proper instruction in the use of strategies, poor readers can do as well as average readers.	____	____
6	Comprehension strategies that are effective in history can be used in the sciences and vice versa.	____	____

USING WHAT YOU KNOW

This chapter is the most important in the book. The essence of reading is comprehension. This chapter explores the nature of comprehension and looks at a series of strategies for fostering comprehension. The key idea in this chapter is that comprehension is an active, constructive process that can be fostered by the effective use of strategies. What do you know about comprehension? What strategies do you use as you try to understand what you read? Do you use the same strategies in all content areas? Do you read a history text the same way you read a science or math text?

THE PROCESS OF COMPREHENDING

What is comprehension? How do readers understand text? To gain some insight into the process of comprehension, read the following paragraph, which has been divided into a series of sentences. Stop after reading each sentence and ask yourself: What did the sentence say? How did I go about comprehending it? What does this paragraph seem to be about?

- To scientists living 150 years ago, they looked like pieces of a giant jigsaw puzzle.
- The edges in several of the pieces would fit neatly into the indentations of other pieces.
- Could it all have been one giant piece?
- If so, what caused it to break up?
- From this and observations that rocks and fossils in South America were similar to those found in Africa, the theory of continental drift was born.
- According to that theory, the Earth's crust was once one solid piece but broke apart into huge plates that move ever so slowly but have caused many changes in the Earth's surface. (Sattler, 1995)

At what point did you realize that the passage is about plate tectonics theory? If you are or were a geology major, you may have conjectured after reading the first sentence that this selection was talking about early inquiries concerning the shapes of the continents. Or perhaps you didn't catch on right away, but the third sentence, which talks about the unnamed object being all one piece, provided a clue that led you to suspect what the passage was about. If your knowledge of geology is minimal, you may not have understood what the passage was talking about until the last sentence.

Schema Theory

Comprehending is a process of constructing meaning. What we take away from a text depends on what we bring to it. We bring our reasoning processes and our background of knowledge to our construction of meaning, so the more we know about a topic before we come to a text, the deeper and more complete our comprehension of that text. According to **schema** theory, our background knowledge is packaged in abstract units known as schemata (Rumelhart, 1984). A schema is the organized knowledge one has about people, places, things, and ideas. A schema might be broad—our schema for the chemical elements for instance—or it might be narrow—our schema for oxygen. To understand a sentence or passage, it is necessary to activate the proper schema. To understand the passage in the previous section, you must activate your continental drift schema. And if you did not have a schema for a continental drift theory, you would need to build one. If you lacked a schema for continents, you could not build a schema for continental drift theory; you would have to build a schema for continents first.

When introducing a new topic, we often assume that students know nothing about it. However, students have knowledge of a surprising number of topics, although

■ A **schema** is a unit of organized knowledge. (The plural of *schema* is *schemata*.)

the information is sometimes poorly formed, sketchy, or even erroneous. We should first determine what students know about a topic so we can build on that knowledge. If the knowledge is erroneous, we must correct misconceptions because these misconceptions may well interfere with students' learning. For instance, when Mrs. Garcia introduced circles to her tenth-grade geometry class, she asked them to jot down everything they know about circles on a sheet of paper. Looking over their papers, Mrs. Garcia noted that there was a wide range of knowledge about circles and that several students had formed misconceptions about circles. Mrs. Garcia spent some time working with students whose knowledge of circles was so erroneous or incomplete that they might have had difficulty with the unit (Silver, Kilpatrick, & Schlesinger, 1990).

Mental Models Theory

Comprehension can also be thought of as the construction of a mental model or representation. Schema theory provides a good description of what happens when the students are reading about ideas, events, or processes for which they have some background knowledge. But what happens when readers are dealing with new information, as happens when readers who have never have heard of continental drift or even continents read about plate tectonics? The **mental models,** or representations, theory is a more inclusive theory of comprehension because it can handle both schema-based and new ideas (McNamara, Miller, & Bransford, 1991).

> ■ The **mental models** theory views comprehension as a "process of building and maintaining a model of situations and events described in text" (McNamara, Miller, & Bransford, 1991, p. 491). Schema theory describes how familiar situations are understood. Mental models theory describes how new situations are comprehended.

Comprehension requires that readers create a mental model, or representation, of textual information and its interpretation (van den Broek & Kremer, 2000). For expository text, the mental model reflects the organization of the content. The mental model for an article on simple machines might include a mental representation of the physical parts of the machines, the steps in the operation of the machines, relationships among the parts of the machines, and the ways in which people might use the machines.

 **CHECKUP**

1. What are the two major but related theories of comprehension?
2. What implications do these theories have for instruction in the content areas?

The Role of Reasoning

There is more to comprehending than activating schemata. As students read, they make two connections: one between pieces of information already read and one between information being read and background knowledge. Reasoning is also an essential component. Comprehension relies heavily on the reader's ability to use background knowledge to make inferences. Students who have a richer background and can make more connections between what they know and what they are reading have better comprehension and retention. For instance, in the continental drift example, readers might use their background knowledge of fossils to infer that the same animals once lived in both Africa and South America and so Africa and South

America might have been connected at one time. They might also connect information about continental drift with the study of volcanoes and earthquakes in geology and of the extinction of dinosaurs in biology.

Comprehension can be thought of as a network of ideas connected largely by referential and causal/logical relationships. Good readers use higher-level thought processes to establish relationships and store information in network form so that the concept of continental drift, for instance, has a number of connections in their schemata.

The Role of Attention

Attention is also a factor in comprehension. Making connections is hindered if the student is not reading actively and purposely. "Successful comprehension depends in part on readers' ability to allocate their limited attention efficiently and effectively to the most relevant pieces of information within the text and within memory" (van den Broek & Kremer, 2000, p. 7).

Another critical factor is the kind of comprehension readers demand before moving on to the next sentence. Good readers typically want to make referential and causal/logical relationships between the current and previously read sentences, whereas poor readers may have much lower performance standards and so are satisfied just with understanding each individual sentence; they fail to make connections between sentences. Standards of performance also depend on the goal for reading, the context in which the reading is being conducted, motivation, interest, skill of the reader, and other factors. Because they have higher standards of performance, good readers are more effective at monitoring comprehension and stepping in when there is a need to take corrective action. They are more aware of occasions when the text is not making sense and better able to take steps to gain an understanding of the text. Besides being better at monitoring their reading and demanding a higher level of comprehension, good readers are also better at seeking out essential information and making predictions.

One way to help students, especially below-level readers, improve their comprehension is to use causal questioning. In causal questioning, students are asked why and how questions to help them make inferences. These questions can be asked during discussions or can be added to the text at locations where comprehension is likely to falter. This may be at points where important cause–effect relationships are being established, where a reference is being made to a fact or event covered earlier in the text that the reader may have forgotten, or where the syntax is especially difficult (van den Broek & Kremer, 2000). Marginal notes known as glosses, which are covered in the next chapter, can be used for this purpose. Ultimately, students need to have a command of effective strategies that they can use to foster their comprehension.

STRUGGLING READERS

Strategy instruction is highly effective. One group of middle school students, who were poor comprehenders but good decoders, improved so much after strategy instruction that they were accused of cheating (Pearson, 1986). Other groups have transformed their D's to B's and even A's after strategy instruction. In other studies, poor readers began operating on the same level as average readers (Hansen & Pearson, 1982).

 **CHECKUP**

1. What roles do reasoning and attention play in comprehension?

LEVELS OF UNDERSTANDING

Comprehension consists of three levels of understanding: surface structure, textbase, and mental representation (Kintsch, 1994). The surface structure is composed of the exact words of the written piece. The **textbase** is the propositions or ideas conveyed by the surface structure. As students read, they transform text into propositions. **Propositions** are statements of information. Readers combine, delete, and integrate propositions to form a **macrostructure.** The macrostructure, which is a running summary of the text, may be composed of the statement of a cause and three or four effects or a main idea and three or four details.

The **mental representation** is a deeper level of understanding. The mental representation combines the reader's background knowledge with information from the text. For instance, when reading a section about exercise in a health text, a student operating on the surface structure level may answer an end-of-chapter question by going back to the text and copying the sentence that contains the same words as the question. The question may ask, "What is aerobic exercise?" To answer the question, the student copies the sentence that tells what aerobic exercise is, but does not really understand what the sentence says. The student would be unable to explain his answer or put it in his own words. A student reading on the proposition level might find out that aerobic exercises build up muscle endurance and resistance exercises build up strength and bulk. But lacking adequate background knowledge about the muscular system, the student cannot infer why this is so and is therefore unable to construct a mental model or representation. The student who lacks representational knowledge can recite the information that he has read but cannot explain it or draw conclusions about causes, because he doesn't understand it well enough (Kintsch, 1994).

A student who has knowledge of the muscular system can create a representational model by combining information from the text with background information from biology class and infer that aerobic exercises increase the efficiency of the flow of blood to the muscles, so the muscles don't get tired as quickly. Resistance exercises cause the white fibers in the muscles to grow in size and add more contractile proteins. Given representational knowledge, the student will be able to explain the effect of the two different kinds of exercise and will also be able to apply this knowledge by planning a program of exercise designed to meet personal goals of increased endurance or strength or both.

Had the text reviewed the operation of the muscular system, the reader might have had sufficient background knowledge to infer why one type of exercise builds endurance and the other strength. Or the teacher could have built the necessary background. Because comprehension is a combination of reader, text, and context, a well-written, well-planned text and building of essential background can fill in the gaps when students' background is inadequate.

■ The **textbase** includes the statements or ideas conveyed by the surface structure.
■ **Propositions** are statements of information.
■ The **macrostructure** is a running summary of the text.
■ The **mental representation** is the understanding that the reader creates. It combines the reader's background knowledge with information from the text.

 **CHECKUP**

1. What are the three levels of understanding text?

COMPREHENSION STRATEGIES

Read the following excerpt from a review text designed to assist elementary and middle school students with their science homework. Then complete the quiz that follows without looking back.

> Sound travels about 1,100 feet (335 meters) per second or 740 miles per hour. It travels a little faster on hot days than cold days. Sound travels four times faster in water and even faster still through solids than through the air.
>
> Sound doesn't travel nearly as fast as light. Take a close look at the marching bands the next time you see a parade. The marching band members closest to the drummers are slightly out of step from the band members farthest away from the drummers. This is because the faraway members hear the drumbeats a tiny bit later. (Zeman & Kelly, 1994, p. 118)

1. How fast does sound travel?
2. On which day would a call for help most likely be heard sooner? Why?
   a. December 1   b. July 1   c. October 1   d. March 1
3. In a parade, which member of a marching band would most likely be out of step?
   a. The band leader.   b. The buglers up front.   c. The trumpet players in the middle.   d. The bass drummer, who is last. Explain your choice.
4. Why does sound travel faster in water than on land?

After completing the quiz, check your answers. Then answer the following questions:

- Before reading the excerpt, what did you do? What were you thinking?
- As you read the excerpt, what thoughts were going through your mind? Did you do anything as you were reading?
- After you read the article, what did you do? What were you thinking?

■ A **strategy** is a deliberate, planned activity or procedure designed to achieve a certain goal.

Reading the excerpt and answering the questions was designed to help you experience what strategies are. The quiz was included because readers usually employ more strategies when they know they are going to be tested. **Strategies** are the deliberate, planned procedures designed to achieve a goal. Examples of comprehension strategies include previewing, predicting, summarizing, inferring, asking oneself questions, making images, and rereading.

How strategic a reader are you? Have you summarized main ideas? Have you questioned any of the statements made in this chapter? Have you made connections between an idea in the text and your personal experiences? Have you thought of times when you could recite from text but didn't really understand what you had read? Have you wondered what strategies you use? If you have done any of these things or involved yourself with the reading in any other way, these are signs that you are a strategic reader.

Building Metacognitive Awareness

Applying strategies requires being aware of one's thinking. Teachers model the processes they use when reading content area material so that students will gain insight into the thinking involved. Teachers use a device called a **think-aloud.** As they show students how they create visual images when reading about the composition of meteors, they reveal what is going on in their minds, what they see in their mind's eye, as they read the text. As they become more aware of their thought processes, students are better able to use cognitively based strategies to understand their content area texts more fully. Being aware of one's thinking is known as **metacognition** and is the foundation of comprehension instruction.

In order to understand metacognition and cognitive strategies, you must become aware of the strategies you use as you read and the thinking processes in which you engage. With practice, our use of strategies becomes relatively automatic. Stop your reading from time to time and think about the mental tools you are using to comprehend what you are reading. Do this especially when you are reading difficult material. Strategies tend to become more conscious when the material is difficult because we have to take deliberate steps to comprehend it. One technique that a group of highly successful staff developers and classroom teachers used was to try out each strategy on their own reading before teaching it. The result was that the staff developers and teachers improved their own comprehension:

> We test the strategies on our reading. We became more conscious of our own thinking processes as readers. We realized that we could concentrate simultaneously on the text and our ways of thinking about it. What seems most extraordinary, however, was that by thinking about our own thinking—by being metacognitive (literally, to think about one's thinking)—we could actually deepen and enhance our comprehension of the text. (Keene & Zimmermann, 1997, p. 21)

Careful metacognitive instruction is especially important for struggling learners because they are often the very students who lack insight into their thinking processes and do not possesses a repertoire of strategies; if they do possess the strategies, they often do not know when and where to use them.

 **CHECKUP**

1. What is metacognition?
2. Why is it an important element in comprehension?

Only a relatively small number of comprehension strategies have been found to be effective. These effective comprehension strategies are those used in preparing, organizing, elaborating, rehearsing, and monitoring (metacognition). There are also affective strategies (Weinstein & Mayer, 1986) in which motivation and interest play a role in the construction of meaning. Strategies are organized according to the thinking processes involved in their operation. Although strategies are presented in separate categories, there is some overlapping. See Table 4.1 for a list of strategies.

■ A **think-aloud** is a procedure in which a person describes her thought processes while engaged in reading, writing, or another cognitive activity.
■ **Metacognition** or metacognitive awareness means being conscious of one's mental processes.

Preparational Strategies

Preparational strategies are those that students use to prepare themselves to read a selection. Preparational strategies include previewing a piece before reading it, establishing goals and setting a purpose for reading, activating prior knowledge, and predicting what a selection might be about. Which of these strategies did you use as you read the excerpt on the speed of sound? Did you preview the title? Did you activate prior knowledge by thinking what you knew about the speed of sound? Did you have a purpose for reading? A purpose is the question that the reader wants to have answered or information that the reader is seeking. Did you set a goal? The goal is the outcome that the reader is seeking. Your goal may have been to do well on the quiz that followed.

■ Previewing

Having a general idea of what they are about to read provides readers with an overview of the selection and helps them organize their thoughts as they read. It also helps them activate prior knowledge. Students have two kinds of knowledge: subject knowledge and personal knowledge. For instance, if students are preparing to read about a balanced diet, they may have studied this topic previously and may have some knowledge of the food pyramid. They also have personal knowledge that they have picked up from parents, the media, or friends. Chances are they have been told that they should eat fruits and vegetable and shouldn't eat too much fast food. By bringing this knowledge to the fore, students are preparing themselves to get more out of their reading.

■ A **preview** is a quick survey of a selection in order to get an overview of its content.

A **preview** is a fast survey of a selection. Students read titles and headings, an introductory paragraph or blurb, if there is one, and the summary paragraph, if there is one. They might also glance at illustrations. As they preview, students infer or predict what the selection will be about. Previewing turns passive readers into active ones and is especially helpful when students encounter difficult text. Previewing should be brief and should take no more than three to five minutes. If a text is being read section by section, the readers can also briefly preview each section before reading it. This doesn't mean that the preview of the whole section or chapter should

TABLE 4.1			
COMPREHENSION STRATEGIES			
Preparational	Organizational	Elaboration	Metacognitive
Activating prior knowledge	Comprehending main ideas	Making inferences	Checking
Previewing	Determining important details	Imaging	Regulating
Predicting	Organizing details	Generating questions	Repairing
Setting purpose and goals	Summarizing	Evaluating	

be skipped. A preview of the whole helps the student see how each of the sections is related to the whole and how the sections are related to each other.

To introduce previewing, model the process. Show students how you preview. Think aloud so they can gain some insight into the process. Conduct some group previews with the class. After students have caught onto the idea of previewing, have them preview under your guidance. Discuss their previews. Also use naturally occurring opportunities to reinforce the concept of previewing. When students get a new textbook, preview it with them so they get an overview of it. Also encourage group or individual previews when starting a new chapter. As part of the preparation for reading a section, ask questions that require a preview. For instance, ask students to tell what they think the selection might be about. Give them a few minutes to preview. As you discuss their predictions, have them tell what led them to make their predictions. Have them explain what there was in the title, the heading, illustrations, introduction, or summary that led to their predictions. Provide opportunities for them to preview independently.

Most important of all, explain and demonstrate the value of previews. Also discuss when and where previews might be used. Have students compare the results of reading a section after a preview and reading a section without a preview. You might give them a brief no-grade quiz so they can see that reading with a preview results in improved performance. A good preview can function as a framework for constructing a mental representation of the selection.

◼ Activating Prior Knowledge

During the preview or during another step if there is not a preview, the teacher guides students in the activation of prior knowledge. This could be done by asking students what they know about a particular topic or asking a series of leading questions. Activating prior knowledge is a crucial step. Students comprehend by connecting new information with what they know. However, if they don't realize that they have information to bring to bear on a particular topic, they may not make the necessary connections. This failure to realize that one does have knowledge about a topic is more likely to happen when topics are presented in formal, academic, or technical language. For instance, the concept *supply and demand* may seem totally new, but students may have had experience collecting baseball cards and may know from that experience that rare cards are worth more, or they may have paid scalpers' prices for concerts or sporting events that were sold out. They may have bought athletic shoes on sale and realized that the manufacturer made too many or that they are no longer popular so the price has been reduced. The concept will be more understandable if students can build on their knowledge base.

In some instances, students' prior knowledge is erroneous. Students may confuse the Civil War with World War I. They may confuse countries with continents. Students frequently have mistaken notions about science. For instance, students may believe that plants feel pain and that seeds are dead. They may believe that only mammals are animals. They may believe that the moon can be seen only at night and doesn't move (Baker & Piburn, 1997). Unless they are able to confront and modify their erroneous beliefs, students may not construct an accurate representation of the material they are reading. For more information about changing erroneous concepts, see Chapter 11.

By probing students' prior knowledge, teachers can clarify incomplete or erroneous concepts, judge how much instruction is necessary and which topics need the most emphasis, and select the most appropriate activities and materials. Part of tapping into students' prior knowledge is using activities and materials that are culturally relevant to students. For instance, when discussing nutrition, use as examples the foods that students are most familiar with.

■ Predicting

> ■ A **prediction strategy** is a deliberate attempt to foretell the content of a segment of text.

Did you make predictions before you read the selection about the speed of sound? Predicting facilitates the activation of prior knowledge. Using a **prediction strategy,** a reader makes an educated guess about the course of events in a narrative or the kind of information that will be contained in an informational selection. Effective predictions are based on the thoughtful consideration of what we know. Predictions often determine purpose in reading. Students may read the selection to compare their predictions with the events or information contained in the selection.

■ Setting Purpose and Goals

> ■ The **goal** for reading is the outcome the reader is seeking: to gain information, to prepare for a test, to upgrade a computer, to relax, etc.

All too often students' **goal** for reading a text is to fulfill an assignment. Their goal is to start at the beginning of the assignment and read to the end. They may reach their goal of reading the assigned section but they may come away knowing little more than they did when they started. They may even have as their goal answering the questions at the end of the chapter. This, too, can result in failure to derive any benefit from the reading. As noted earlier, one strategy that struggling readers use when reading difficult text is to match the words in the questions with the same words in the text and to simply copy the sentence in which these words appeared. Struggling readers may have picked up the idea that the goal of reading is to pronounce the words and may not have as the goal the construction of meaning. The overall goal of all readers, whether struggling or adept, should be to construct meaning. A subsidiary goal might be to learn valuable or interesting information or, perhaps, to prepare for an upcoming test or to set up an experiment or assemble a piece of equipment.

> ■ The **purpose** for reading is the question that the reader wants to answer or the information the reader is seeking.

Students' **purpose** for reading consists of the specific question or questions that they are seeking to answer. Purposes are often set by the teacher but may be established by the students. For instance, students might create questions based on their preview and read to answer those questions. The purpose for reading might grow out of activating prior knowledge. Your activation of prior knowledge in preparation for reading an article about acid rain may cause you to realize that you know that acid rain is formed from chemicals from factories and cars. But you aren't sure what chemicals they are or how they are formed. Your purpose (question to be answered) in reading might then be to find out what the chemicals in acid rain are and how they are formed.

Chances are students have been taught to preview, predict, set goals, and activate prior knowledge in previous grades. These strategies are widely used. However, they may not realize that these strategies can be applied to your content area, may not be sure how to apply strategies to your content area, or may not see the value of

doing so. Provide guidance and encouragement in the use of these and other strategies. Ultimately, students are expected to apply these strategies on their own.

 *CHECKUP*

1. What are the key preparational strategies?
2. How do they function together?

Selection/Organizational Strategies

Of all the strategies, those that help students organize information are the most crucial. Without some way of organizing information, students would be lost in a sea of
details. Information is not stored in isolated fashion; our concepts are stored in networks. We can understand and retain new information better if we relate it to already existing concepts. In fact, we probably won't comprehend it or retain it if is
not connected to our existing framework of knowledge. In the content areas, one
organizational strategy is to use the structure of the text as a framework for comprehending and storing information.

What makes the following excerpt from a U.S. history text easy to understand?

> Why were the Americans able, finally, to beat what had been consid-
> ered the mightiest army in the world, supported by a great navy? For
> one, there was General Howe's slowness to take action at the beginning. Had
> he pushed hard at Washington in that first terrible winter, he might well have
> destroyed the American army and captured Washington. Instead, he let
> Washington drive him out of New Jersey at Trenton, and for the British a
> great opportunity was lost. For another, the general situation was ultimately
> favorable to the Americans.
>
> The British might beat the Americans as they did on Long Island, at
> Brandywine, and many other places; but Washington was always able some-
> how to find more men, more equipment, more courage. The British were al-
> ways squeezing a balloon that would pop up at another place. Finally, the help
> of the French was critical. Loans of money, beginning even before the Battle
> of Saratoga in 1777, and materiel gave the Americans a chance. And French
> aid after Saratoga entirely changed the odds. Without de Grasse's fleet to bot-
> tle up the British at Yorktown, Cornwallis would have been eventually rescued
> by British ships, and gone on fighting. (Collier & Collier, 1998, p. 83)

The text is well organized. The main idea is clearly stated in the first sentence,
so the reader has a good sense of the content of the passage. Better yet, the main
idea is stated in the form of a question so that all the reader needs to do is to read to
answer the question. And the use of *why* signals the reader that the author will be
supplying reasons or causes. The causes of America's victory are clearly stated. And

there is no extraneous information to distract the reader's attention. The causes are also highlighted by the use of signal words: *for one, for another,* and *finally.*

When reading, students need to activate two kinds of schema: prior knowledge and text structure. The content of a text cannot be separated from the way that content is expressed. Teachers are "well advised to model for students how to figure out what the author's general framework or structure is and allow students to practice finding it on their own" (Pearson & Camperell, 1994, p. 463). The better organized the text, the more apparent the structure of the piece and the higher the likelihood the reader will understand and learn from the text.

Effective readers make use of the structure of the text to help them better understand and retain what they read. Being able to use a text's structure aids the reader in three ways. It focuses attention on key ideas, it helps show how ideas are related, and it provides a framework to aid retention of information (Slater & Graves, 1989).

■ Types of Text Structure

There are two major types of text structure: hierarchical and coordinate (Simonsen, 1996). A hierarchical text structure features a main idea and subordinate details organization. The two main types of hierarchical structure are the list and the journalist structures. One advantage of list structures is that they develop one idea at a time. Readers can focus on one concept before proceeding to the next one. A disadvantage is that the list may fail to show how one main idea is related to another. Coordinate structures, on the other hand, show relationships among ideas. Coordinate structures include comparison/contrast, cause/effect, problem/solution, time sequence, and steps in a process (Armbruster & Anderson, 1981; Meyer & Rice, 1984; Simonsen, 1996).

■ Hierarchical Structures

List Structure. Most textbooks follow a list structure (Simonsen, 1996). The chapter title and introduction state the overall topic or theme. Each section of the chapter then announces its main idea in a heading or implies its main idea and develops it. Comprehending a list structure involves being aware of what a main idea is, being able to recognize the main idea in a paragraph or section, and being able to connect the essential details to the main idea. Note the list structure in the following two paragraphs.

The hydrogen atom is the simplest atom that can possibly exist. Its most common isotope is composed of a single proton and an electron. If you take away either of these parts, you no longer have an atom at all.

The hydrogen atom is the most abundant in the cosmos. There is relatively little hydrogen gas in the earth's atmosphere, but there are plenty of hydrogen atoms showing up in hydrogen compounds—ordinary water, for instance. Then consider that every molecule of water in all the seas, lakes, and streams includes two hydrogen atoms. (Heiserman, 1992, p. 82)

Journalist Structure. In a journalist structure, the main ideas are provided in the first paragraph or two. The remaining paragraphs expand on the main ideas.

New York this week became the first state to ban driving while using a hand-held cell phone. In a ceremony at a Manhattan park on Thursday, New York Governor George Pataki signed the bill into law that made driving while using a cell phone illegal.

Beginning November 1, drivers throughout the state will be fined up to $500 each time they are caught using a cell phone without speakerphones. Exceptions will be made for 911 calls. Drivers using cell phones were four times more likely to have an accident. Since 1999, dozens of localities have banned driving while using a cell phone, but New York is the first state to do so.

"This new law will make our roads safer and save lives," said Governor Pataki. "Too many families have suffered the tragedy of seeing a loved one injured— sometimes fatally—in an accident caused by someone who was driving and was using a cell phone." (Groff-Palmero, 2001)

■ Coordinate Text Structures

Coordinate text structures offer more guidance to the reader by highlighting relationships (Pearson & Camperell, 1994). Comparison/contrast structures highlight similarities and differences. Cause/effect passages signal cause–effect relationships. Problem/solution pieces highlight possible solutions to problems. Sequential passages signal key events or the steps in a process.

Comparison/Contrast. Comparison/contrast structures have two forms: block and alternating (Simonsen, 1996). In the block form, all of the characteristics of the first item are presented. Then the comparative or contrasting characteristics of the second item are presented. The advantage of the block structure is that the reader can focus on one item at a time. The disadvantage is that readers may fail to see similarities and differences. Here is an example of the block structure.

Imagine that you are a typical student in Ontario, Canada. English is your first language at home and in school, and you study British history in your classes. Perhaps you come home to tea in the afternoon.

In contrast, imagine that you live in Quebec, Canada's only predominantly French-speaking province. Your classes are probably taught in French. You might eat croissants for breakfast and toutiere, or pork pie, for lunch. Indeed as a Quebecois, your life might be quite different from that of a student living only a few hundred miles away in the province of Ontario. (Sager & Helgren, 1997, p. 178)

In the alternating format, the items are compared or contrasted by the first characteristic, the second characteristic, the third, and so forth. This is a more effective organization when there are a number of characteristics involved because the readers would have difficulty remembering those in the first block by the time they get to the second block. Here is an example of the alternating format.

> Ulysses S. Grant was the exact opposite of Robert E. Lee. Where Lee was quiet and gentlemanly, Grant was rough and unpolished. Lee won several battles for the South by brilliant maneuvering. Grant won battles for the North by hammering away at his enemy without mercy. (King, 1996)

Signal words and terms for comparison/contrast structures include the following:

although	similar	on the one hand	however
but	different	on the other hand	different from

Cause/Effect.   Either the cause or effect is presented first and then the effects or causes are presented. Causes or effects may also be implied. Readers may have to reason that a cause or effect is being stated, as in the first two sentences in the selection that follows. Although the word *effect* is used in the selection, the word *cause* is not.

> The working-class family underwent tremendous strain during hard times. Traditional roles of the father as provider and the mother as the homemaker became blurred as the entire family was forced to seek work to keep food on the table. The effect of a father's unemployment on the entire family was evident: "Bewilderment, hesitation, apathy, loss of self-confidence were the commonest marks of protracted unemployment. A man no longer cared how he looked. Unkempt hair and swarthy stubble, shoulders a-droop, and a dragging walk." In many instances the idle man just got in the way, hanging around home because there was no place else to go. Tempers grew short and tension between husband and wife resulted in quarreling. The family would lose touch with friends, especially those who were still working. (Nishi, 1998, pp. 30–31)

Signal words for cause/effect structures include the following:

because	therefore	thus	why
cause	since	for this reason	
effect	as a result	consequently	

Problem/Solution. In this structure, a problem is described and then a solution is explored.

> The moment you step out of the house and are on the road you can actually see the air getting polluted; a cloud of smoke from the exhaust of a bus, car, or a scooter; smoke billowing from a factory chimney, fly-ash generated by thermal power plants, and speeding cars causing dust to rise from the roads. Natural phenomena such as the eruption of a volcano and even someone smoking a cigarette can also cause air pollution. . . .
>
> The task of cleaning up air pollution, though difficult, is not believed to be impossible. The shift to less polluting forms of power generation, such as solar energy, wind energy, geothermal, tidal, and other forms of renewable energy in place of fossil fuel can be used for controlling pollution. (Edugreen, 2001)

Sequential. There are two types of sequential structures: time sequence and explanation/process. In the first type, the time sequence paragraph structure, the writer uses dates or other time-clue words to indicate the order in which events took place. In the second type, the explanation/process structure, one action leads to or causes the next action. Graphic organizers, such as time lines, work well with time order passages. Flow charts or process diagrams work well with process structures.

Time Sequence. In a time sequence paragraph, the order of events is the key element.

> In 1928 Roosevelt was elected governor of New York in a very close election. When the stock market crashed the following year, the nation plunged into the Great Depression. FDR responded with a groundbreaking system of relief for the vast number of unemployed workers in New York. His popularity soared and he won reelection to the governorship in 1930. He began to be mentioned as a possible candidate for presidency. (Moss & Wilson, 1998, p. 11)

Signal words for time sequence text structures include the following:

after	first	and then
today	next	finally
afterward	second	earlier
tomorrow	then	later
before	third	dates

Explanation/Process. This structure explains a process, such as how sleet forms, cells divide, or a digital camera works. Notice that it, too, follows a sequence, but the sequence consists of the steps of a process, with one step leading to or causing the next, rather than a simple time order.

> Snow begins in the same way as most rain. Snow crystals start to grow in the upper levels of towering cumulus clouds. Water freezes directly onto the cold crystals. Finally, the crystals grow heavy enough to start falling. If the air is cold all the way down, they reach the ground as snow. If the crystals melt on the way down and refreeze as they pass through cold air, the frozen raindrops are called sleet. (Simon, 1993, np)

Often, passages combine several organizational patterns, as in the following excerpt which combines time sequence and list structure.

> Babylon began as a small town in central Mesopotamia, on the banks of the Euphrates. In 1894 B.C. it was captured by an Amorite chief called Sumuabum. Babylon became the capital of his kingdom, and he became the first king in a long line of rulers. One of the descendants of Sumuabum was a king called Hammurabi. Hammurabi became king of Babylon in 1792 B.C. He established Babylon as the greatest city in the Middle East. Hammurabi also conquered neighboring cities in north and south Mesopotamia, and Babylon became the capital of a new Mesopotamian empire. One of Hammurabi's most important acts was to draw up a set of laws that everyone in his empire had to follow. (Malam, 1999, p. 21)

Structure can be signaled in a number of ways. Titles and subheadings often indicate structure—for instance: Causes of the Great Depression, How Hail Is Formed, Solutions to the Acid Rain Problem. Introductions and summaries may also alert the reader to the type of structure they will encounter. Graphic organizers also signal structure. A time line indicates sequence, a flow chart process, a matrix comparison and contrast (Armbruster, 1996). Still another way of detecting text structure is by noting signal words or phrases, such as *first, then, because, however,* and *on the other hand.* Signal words are often used within running text.

■ Teaching Expository Text Structure

Text patterns should be introduced one at a time. Start off with well-organized, single paragraphs that reflect the structure being taught. Signal words used in that structure should be presented. To provide practice in the recognition of signal words, use a cut-up paragraph or article and have students recreate the piece by using signal words and the sense of the piece as guides. For instance, students can use dates to help them rearrange a chronologically organized piece. Or they can use the signal words *first*, *second*, *next*, and *last* to arrange sentences or paragraphs explaining a step-by-step process. Gradually, work up to longer selections. Whole articles and chapters often use several text structures, and students should be aware of that. However, in many cases a particular structure dominates.

Point out and discuss the usefulness of key text structures in your subject matter area. Before students read a chapter, have them examine the title and headings to help determine the structure of the chapter. Before preparing students to read a selection, analyze it for content and structure. Create questions and activities that reflect the structure of the text as well as the content. For example, a biographical sketch of Thomas Jefferson would use a time sequence structure. You can instruct students to note key events and their dates to help keep them in order. As a postreading activity, have students create or complete graphic organizers that incorporate the structure of the text. For the biographical sketch of Jefferson, have them fill out a time line. After they read how rust forms or steel is made, have them create a process diagram. After they have read a section comparing and contrasting the Senate and the House of Representatives, have them create a Venn diagram.

Using Questions to Make Connections. Carefully planned questions can help readers establish relationships among ideas in a text. If the text has a cause/effect relationship, you can ask "why" questions that focus on that relationship. Questions can be posed in such a way that they seek out causes or effects. If students are reading a selection that uses a compare/contrast pattern to discuss how insects differ from arachnids, ask questions such as How do insects and arachnids differ? How are they the same?

Not only can questions help students see relationships among ideas in text (internal relationships), but also they can help students relate ideas in the text to their own backgrounds (external relationships). Here are some questions (adapted from Muth, 1987) that might be asked to help students who have read a selection about air pollution make internal cause–effect connections:

- What causes air pollution?
- What are some effects of air pollution?
- What are some of the most polluted areas? What are the main causes of pollution in those areas?

These questions focus on external connections:

- How does air pollution affect you and your family?
- How do you and your family contribute to air pollution?
- What can be done to lessen air pollution? Why would these steps work?

These questions require students to establish internal or external cause–effect relationships. Questions can also be created that foster establishing relationships in comparison/contrast, problem/solution, or other kinds of patterns. Once students have grasped the concept, encourage them to create their own connection questions.

ENGLISH LANGUAGE LEARNERS

Students who are still learning English can transfer their ability to use text structure in their native language to English. However, students must be proficient readers in their native language and fairly proficient in reading English (Hague, 1987). A lack of proficiency in English "short circuits" the transfer process.

Use graphic organizers to make full use of text structure. Process diagrams can be used to show the key steps in scientific and historical processes. They can be as simple as one showing how sonar works or as complex as one showing photosynthesis. Note the process diagram for lightning in Figure 4.3 on p. 142. If students are artistically inclined they might draw the actual objects involved in the process. Venn diagrams are excellent devices for comparing and contrasting technical concepts and terms. Note how the Venn diagram in Figure 3.6 on p. 74 highlights the similarities and differences between rabbits and hares.

Text patterns have a double value. They provide readers with a framework for organizing information as they read and so aid comprehension and retention. Text patterns can also be used to help students organize and present their ideas as they write.

1. How might text structure be used to help students better understand content area material?

Determining Essential Information

Condensed because they are attempting to provide a survey of broad topics, such as American history, physical science, or biology, today's texts are crowded with information. Retaining all that information would be overwhelming, if not impossible. A key strategy for today's students is the ability to determine the relative importance of information. Obviously, they can't learn all the facts, so they need to decide which ones are most important to learn. Determining relative importance of information starts with an identification of the main idea or the topic. Generally, the key ideas in a text are signaled by the chapter title, headings, an introductory paragraph, and main idea sentences. Determining the key ideas in a chapter starts with a preview of the chapter. Based on the preview, the reader can hypothesize what the main idea is. Having a sense of the overall main idea of the chapter, the reader is then able to structure the supporting details around the main idea. For instance, in a trade book on the War for Independence, *The American Revolution: How We Fought the War of Independence* (Dolan, 1995), a chapter title is "The Roots of Revolution." Subheads include New Angers, A Massacre, A Tea Party, and Intolerable Acts. From these, the reader can correctly assume that the chapter will tell about the causes and events that led up to the Revolutionary War and will make note of these as he reads. Seeing that the chapter has a cause and effect structure, the students might take advantage of this as they read. Because this is a trade book and the author has more space to tell his story than would the author of a textbook, the author is able to explain each cause in a fair amount of detail. In order to make the reading manageable, the reader must focus on the important data, which means deciding which facts to stress and which to disregard.

Although often more interesting to read because they contain fascinating facts, it may be more difficult to determine essential details in trade books and newspaper and magazine articles. Because they go into great detail, there are more details to sift through. As Harvey (1998) notes, "The most important ideas in well-written nonfiction are often deeply embedded in rich detail" (p. 83). In addition, students may mistake interesting details for important details. Fascinated by the fact that roaches can make themselves as thin as a dime, one middle schooler felt that this was an essential detail in an article about roaches. Although it perhaps was one of the most interesting facts about roaches, it was not one of the most essential (Harvey, 1998). To overcome this tendency, Harvey listed information about jellyfish that she had found interesting in one column and then discussed with students which of the interesting bits of information were essential. After an extended discussion, students were able to narrow down their choices to four key facts.

 *CHECKUP*

1. Why is determining essential information an essential strategy?
2. How might this strategy be taught?

Summarizing

Summarizing is a complex skill. Students often have difficulty deciding which information should be included in a summary and which should be left out. Although complex, summarizing is probably the most valuable comprehension strategy. As they read, students should be summarizing key ideas. The reader should stop after each section and summarize or recite what he has learned from the section. That is the purpose of the checkup questions in this text.

Summarizing serves several purposes. It lets the reader know whether or not he has grasped the information. If he can't summarize, then he must reread. It also gives him the opportunity to organize the information and fix it in his mind before he goes on to the next section. The summary could be oral or written. Oral summaries are easier and faster to compose. During discussions, encourage students to summarize sections of a chapter or the highlights of a discussion. To model oral summarizing, provide a summary of key content at the end of each class or ask students, "What are the main things we learned today?" Also call attention to end-of-chapter summaries. Recognizing the value of summaries, some authors also provide several interim summaries within a chapter. Prepare students for creating written summaries by having them compose oral summaries.

◼ Written Summaries

Until about the time they enter middle school, students tend to simply record what they have read word for word when they are called upon to summarize. They will need guidance in condensing information and putting it in their own words. When asking students to compose written summaries, model and provide practice with the process. Begin with brief, well-organized segments of text. Also distinguish between reader-based and writer-based summaries. Writer-based summaries are composed as a study aid for the benefit of the student reading the selection and writing the summary. These may be somewhat longer and informal. Reader-based summaries are more condensed and more polished because they are designed to be read by others. Because they require additional writing skills, reader-based summaries are more difficult to create. Research-based steps for creating summaries are listed below (Brown & Day, 1983; Rinehart, Stahl, & Erickson, 1986).

1. Selecting or constructing the overall (main) idea
2. Selecting important information that supports the main idea
3. Deleting information that is not important or is repeated
4. Combining and condensing information
5. Polishing the summary

Instruction given to students might include the following:

1. Use the title, heading, and first sentence to get a sense of what the main idea and important details might be.
2. Read the selection and note which details explain or describe the main idea.
3. Write down the main ideas and key supporting details in your own words.
4. Shorten the summary. Get rid of unimportant details. Combine details if you can. Get rid of unnecessary words. Show students how to paraphrase essential ideas, condensing as they do so. This involves explaining how to combine and collapse details into a more general statement. For instance, the sentences "Finally, the help of the French was critical. Loans of money, beginning even before the Battle of Saratoga in 1777, and materiel gave the Americans a chance" could be condensed to "The French helped with money and materiel."
5. Read the summary. Make sure that it contains the main ideas and most important details. Make sure that it makes sense and is smoothly written. Polish it if it needs it.

STRUGGLING READERS
Frame summaries are especially helpful to struggling readers.

To ease students into composing summaries, you might provide frame summaries that cover content in the text or in a class discussion. A sample frame summary is provided in Figure 4.1. In addition to preparing students to write their own summaries, frame summaries help them review content.

When introducing summaries, explain how they help readers organize and remember key information and are also a writing skill. Model the process of writing a summary, making known your thinking process by telling what's going on in your mind as you do so. Explain how you go about determining the main idea and how you decide which details to include. Also show how you condense ideas and put them in

FIGURE 4.1

Frame Summary

The amount that you pay for a car is only part of the cost of owning and driving a car. Before you can drive the car, you must _____ .

You will also need to pay for _____ .

And you will need to pay for _____ .

And you may have to buy _____ .

Still another cost is depreciation. Owning a car can cost more than you think.

your own words. Explain to students that when they put ideas in their own words, they own the ideas.

As a group, have the class summarize some key but brief paragraphs from their texts. Also provide guided practice for the individual construction of summaries. After students have learned to summarize brief selections—you may want to start off with short sections of text that contain just two or three paragraphs—lead them into the construction of longer segments.

Graphic Organizers as Summaries. For some students and for some topics, a visual summary may work better than a purely verbal one. Students can compose a map or other verbal organizer instead of creating a summary. One type of visual summary that is used to provide an overview of a chapter is the idea map (Berkowitz, 1986). To create an idea map, students write the title or heading of the chapter or section they are reading in the center of an 8½ × 11 sheet of paper, which has been placed horizontally. They use subheadings or skim the text to locate major topics, which are then numbered and placed in blocks arranged clockwise around the title. This gives them an overview of the section or chapter. After reading each section, students fill in the appropriate block with the most important details. Details are condensed, as illustrated in Figure 4.2. Providing limited space, the blocks lend themselves to brevity.

> **ENGLISH LANGUAGE LEARNERS**
> Because they rely less on language, graphic organizers are somewhat easier than traditional summaries for ELLs to compose.

FIGURE 4.2

Idea Map

4. Asteroids, Meteors, Comets

Asteroids—Rocky objects found between Mars and Jupiter

Meteors—Rocky objects from space that burn up as they enter the atmosphere

Meteorites—Rocky objects from space that pass through the atmosphere and fall to Earth

1. Planets in the Solar System

Biggest bodies in solar system.
Orbit the sun.

The Solar System

3. The Outer Planets

Jupiter—Largest planet, has 16 moons

Saturn—Surrounded by rings made of ice and dust

Uranus—Made up of ice and liquid hydrogen surrounding a solid core

Neptune—Has large blue spot

Pluto—May be an escaped moon of Neptune

2. The Inner Planets

Mercury—Closest to sun

Venus—Gases trap sun's heat

Earth—Contains water, oxygen, nitrogen, and carbon dioxide, which are necessary for life

Mars—Red planet. Has a trace of oxygen and water vapor

Graphic organizers can also be used to summarize. Because they don't require writing a paragraph, graphic organizers are easier to compose. Even so, graphic organizers do an excellent job of highlighting important information and showing relationships among ideas. They can be created as an end product or as a preparation for composing a written summary. In addition to idea maps, graphic organizers that might be used to create summaries include semantic maps and Venn diagrams, which were introduced in Chapter 3. Maps and Venn diagrams are easy to use and might be applied by students who are struggling with summarizing.

Integrating the use of related strategies can result in more effective summaries, especially if practice is provided. Combining instruction in several strategies, Weisberg and Balajthy (1990) taught secondary students reading on a fifth-grade level to identify main ideas, construct graphic organizers, and write summaries. Students who were trained in the three procedures were compared with a control group and a third group of students who received both training and practice. Both the training and training-plus-practice groups demonstrated significantly better comprehension than the control group, but the training-plus-practice group did the best. Weisberg and Balajthy concluded that modeling, guided practice, and immediate feedback were key elements in the program.

 CHECKUP

1. Why is summarizing a difficult strategy to master?
2. How might summarizing be taught?

Elaboration Strategies

■ **Elaboration** is the additional processing of text by the reader that may result in improved comprehension and recall. Elaboration involves building connections between one's background knowledge and the text or integrating these two sources through manipulating or transforming information.

Using **elaboration** strategies, the reader adds to, transforms, judges, or applies information from text in some way. Through elaboration, the reader may draw an inference, create a mental image, or evaluate the material that was read. Think about your own reading. What elaborations do you construct as you read? Did you use elaboration strategies as you read the excerpt on the speed of sound? Did you visualize sound traveling through water or sound traveling on a hot day as opposed to a cold day? Did you make any inferences about why sound travels faster on a hot day? If you had done any of these things, your comprehension would have been enhanced. Involving a higher level of comprehension and a deeper level of processing and also the creation and strengthening of bonds between networks, elaboration typically improves comprehension by 50 percent (Linden & Wittrock, 1981). What elaborations might students use to comprehend the following paragraph?

By the 1890s, Pullman stockholders were receiving an 8 percent annual dividend. Land that Pullman had paid $800,000 for was now worth $5 million. However, the return on his investment on that land, mostly rents from workers, only brought Pullman 4.5 percent. He was miffed over that, though his rents were 25 percent higher than comparable ones in Chicago. In 1893 he slashed wages 25 percent, and the company's dividends went up. (Rents stayed the same.) In the model town children went without shoes, homes without heat. (Hakim, 1994, p. 70)

You might infer that Pullman and the stockholders were greedy and uncaring. You might also infer that Pullman had made a huge profit on his investment. You may visualize Pullman at his desk with a very angry look on his face as he examines a balance sheet stating that he was receiving 4.5 percent on his rents. You might visualize a dingy company town composed of poorly constructed workers' houses with children running about barefoot, although it is a cold day. You might conclude that Pullman cared more about shareholders than workers. You might question why Pullman didn't treat his workers better. You might evaluate the passage by noting that the author has included only details that make Pullman look bad. You might wonder whether he had any good characteristics. Elaborations, especially visualizations, may vary from reader to reader, because each of us brings a different background of experience to our reading.

■ Making Inferences

Read the following excerpt about the Ukraine. What can you infer from the paragraph?

It is still quite common in Ukraine to see farm families riding along country roads in horse-drawn carts. They bring their fresh produce and meat to the cities, where they sell them in shops and outdoor stalls. (Clay, 1997, p. 22)

The paragraph suggests that farming is important in the Ukraine. It also suggests that there are many small family farmers. And it suggests that the people of the Ukraine are poor and may not be technologically advanced because they use horse-drawn carts rather than trucks or cars. In addition, the paragraph suggests that the farms are close to the cities. Otherwise, a trip by horsecart would take too long. The paragraph also suggests that supermarkets may not be common in the Ukraine.

    As you can see, much of the information that a reader derives from text is the result of constructing inferences. As you can also see, inferencing depends heavily on background knowledge. Some inferences are based primarily on the text. For instance, we can infer that there are many family farms in the Ukraine and they raise both produce and animals because the text states that it is common to see farm families going to market and they bring their produce and meat to sell. For many inferences, the reader uses background knowledge *and* information from the text to make inferences. For instance, our background knowledge tells us that horses and carts

STRUGGLING READERS

Because they are primarily asked low-level questions, struggling readers may have difficulty with inferential questioning because they have limited experience with it. However, with prompting and instruction, they often show substantial improvement.

*T*he teacher models strategies such as going back over the text to verify conclusions.

are cheaper than cars or trucks, so when we read that horse-drawn carts are common, we infer that the people are too poor to buy cars or trucks.

Of all the elaboration strategies, making inferences is probably the most important. Struggling to get the literal meaning of a content area piece, students may not make inferences or draw conclusions. Making an inference requires going beyond the page and bringing one's own experience and judgment to bear on a piece that one is reading. Some students may not realize that they can construct their own meanings and may even be confused when asked questions for which there is not a definitely stated answer in the text. However, elaborated responses incorporate the kinds of higher-order thinking skills that content area standards are asking for and also the kinds of skills in which students do poorly on national assessments (Donahue et al., 1999).

Two essential elements in making inferences are being asked questions that require making inferences and having the kinds of discussions that involve higher-level thinking skills. Both of these are incorporated in the sample lesson on making inferences.

LESSON 4.1   Making Inferences Lesson

Step 1: Explaining the Strategy

Explain what is entailed in making inferences and give examples. Explain why making inferences is important, and when and how this strategy is used. Encourage students to give examples of times when they have made inferences. For instance, have them tell how they infer a person's mood.

Step 2: Modeling the Process

Model the process of making inferences with a brief piece of text drawn from students' content area text. As you do so, explain how and why you make inferences. Think out loud. For instance, after reading the segment presented below about the Pullman strike, explain that the text states that, although highly profitable, the Pullman company cut wages for the fifth time.

> That summer, the highly profitable Pullman Company cut workers' wages for the fifth time. Pullman made railroad sleeping cars in a town near Chicago. When the company cut wages, it didn't cut the fees it charged workers for rent, heat, and lights, or to use the company church. The workers were angry; they went on strike. Soon the strike spread to 50,000 workers, throughout the railroad industry. The governor of Illinois said he could handle the situation. But Grover Cleveland's attorney general didn't agree. (The attorney general had been a railroad lawyer.) He insisted that the government take action against the workers

and their union. Federal troops were sent to Illinois, which led to violence, deaths, and arrests. (Hakim, 1994, p. 70)

In your think-aloud, you might make statements similar to the following: "That makes me think that the company is greedy and doesn't care about its workers. And here the text states that even though the company cut wages, it didn't lower rents or other expenses that the workers had to pay. That adds proof to my inference that the company cared more about making money than it did about its workers. Here it says that the workers went on strike and the strike soon spread. That tells me that the Pullman workers aren't the only ones who are fed up; other railroad workers are also unhappy. They are so unhappy that they are desperate. After all, these are poor people. By going on strike, they are giving up their pay and risking their jobs. You would have to be desperate to do such a thing." You should model the process with several other sections, so students see that a variety of inferences can be drawn.

Step 3: Locating Evidence for an Inference

Ask students to take part in the inferencing process. Ask an inferential question about a brief paragraph or excerpt and then answer it. The students supply supporting evidence for the inference from the selection itself and from their background knowledge. Discuss the reasoning processes involved in making the inference. Stress the need to substantiate inferences with details from the story. For instance, state that the attorney general favored business. Students should then locate evidence for this inference.

Step 4: Drawing an Inference

Ask students to read a segment of text and draw an inference. Provide the evidence. As an alternative, supply the evidence and have the students draw an inference based on it. Either way, a discussion of reasoning processes follows. For instance, based on their reading of the following excerpt, you might ask, "What kind of a person was Mother Jones?" Note that making inferences requires a command of background knowledge. The significance of Mother Jones's comment about Patrick Henry, Thomas Jefferson, and John Adams will be lost if the readers don't know how each of the men contributed to fundamental freedoms.

> The police said Mother Jones was a public nuisance. They arrested her. When the judge asked her who gave her a permit to speak on the streets, she said, "Patrick Henry, Thomas Jefferson, and John Adams!" Mother Jones was sent to jail—more than once. In jail she spoke of George Washington as a "gentleman agitator" who fought the powerful English establishment. Each time Mother Jones got out of jail she went straight back to speaking out for workers. (Hakim, 1994, pp. 105–106)

Step 5: Integrating the Process

Ask the inferential question. The students make the inference and locate support. In time, turn total responsibility for making inferences over to students.

Students create their own inferential questions and then supply the answers and evidence.

Step 6: Application

The students apply the process to texts and trade books.

Step 7: Assessment

Observe students as they make inferences in texts and trade books. Note how well they can do the following:

____ Make an inference based on two or more pieces of information in the text.

____ Make an inference based on information in the text and their own background of knowledge.

____ Find support for an inference.

____ Make increasingly sophisticated inferences.

Step 8: Reviewing the Strategy

In subsequent lessons, review and extend the strategy. To review the strategy, ask the following kinds of questions.

- What strategy are we learning to use?
- How does this strategy help us? (It helps us to read between the lines, to fill in details that the author has hinted at but not directly stated.)
- When do we use this strategy? (When we have to put together two or more pieces of information in a text and make an inference or conclusion. When the author has hinted at but not directly stated information.)
- How do we use this strategy?
  1. As I read, I think, "What is the author suggesting here?"
  2. I put together pieces of information from the text or pieces of information from the text with what I already know.
  3. I make an inference or come to a conclusion. (Gunning, 2003; Scott, 1998)

■ Imaging

Which is larger, a rabbit or a squirrel? How did you decide? Chances are you imagined a typical rabbit and a typical squirrel, mentally put the two together, and then decided on the basis of this visual comparison which one was larger (Moyer, 1973). In other words, you used a nonverbal process known as **imaging** to reason your way to the answer to the question. Imaging is a powerful cognitive tool for understanding, reasoning, and remembering. According to Paivio's **dual coding** hypothesis (1971), words that refer to concrete objects can be encoded in memory twice. The word *rabbit*, for instance, can be encoded verbally just as any other word can. But it can also be encoded visually. It can be encoded as a mental picture of a rabbit. Because it can be encoded as a word or picture, it can be retrieved from memory either ver-

■ **Imaging** is creating sensory representations of items in text.
■ **Dual coding** is the concept that text can be processed verbally and nonverbally. Nonverbal coding focuses on imaging.

bally or visually, so theoretically it is twice as memorable. Indeed, in one research study, participants who encoded words visually remembered twice as many words as those who encoded the words just verbally. (Schnorr & Atkinson, 1969)

Creating images has a host of benefits. It fosters increased comprehension and retention. Mental pictures provide a framework for organizing and remembering information and also lead students into deeper, more extensive processing (Gambrell, Kapinus, & Wilson, 1987). Creating images also serves as a metacognitive check on comprehension. As they attempt to create images, readers may find that they are unable to supply some details and so realize that they need to go back to the selection. Imaging is an active, generative process.

Imaging is frequently used in the study of literature. Being able to create images of setting and main characters and the characters' actions adds to our enjoyment of a selection as well as our understanding of it. However, imaging can also be used to picture historical scenes or scientific processes. For instance, a reader might use imaging to help him understand and recall the structure of an animal cell. Visualizing can assist in the comprehension of descriptions such as those found in the following paragraph. If the text is accompanied by illustrations, these should be used along with the text to create a visualization.

> Cumulus clouds are puffy white clouds with a flat base. They look a little like pieces of cotton drifting along in the sky. They are sometimes called cauliflower clouds because of their shape. Cumulus clouds are formed by rising currents of warm air called thermals. (McKeever & Foote, 1998, p. 260)

Visualizing can also be used to help the reader understand processes such as those described in the following paragraph. For visualizing a process, the reader might want to create a series of mental images.

> The human eye is a tough ball filled with fluid sitting in a bony socket. The cornea is the transparent protective surface of the eye. It also focuses light. The iris controls the amount of light passing through the pupil. It closes up the pupil in bright light and opens it wide in dim light. The lens helps focus light on the retina, which contains a layer of light-sensitive cells. These send signals via the optic nerve to the brain, where they are interpreted to build up our view of the world. (McKeever & Foote, 1998, p. 204)

ENGLISH LANGUAGE LEARNERS

Encourage students to draw pictures of concepts or topics along with using words to describe or talk about them. This provides ELLs who might have difficulty expressing their ideas through words alone with another medium for conveying their ideas.

Recitations or summaries can be visual as well as verbal. After reading a section in which she has visualized, the reader can see if she can recite by picturing the whole image or series of images or by making a quick sketch of the image(s). Or the reader might combine the visual and the verbal. In addition to taking verbal notes, the reader might include drawings of key elements. Translating verbal descriptions into pictorial ones is an excellent way to learn difficult material and retain it.

Because it relies more on mental pictures than on words, imaging can be an especially useful strategy for students who are still learning English. However, its use needs to be explained and encouraged. Imaging is used infrequently. Many students, especially those who are not efficient learners, may fail to create images spontaneously as they read (Harris & Sipay, 1990). However, imaging is easy to use and has a powerful payoff (Gambrel & Bales, 1986; Sadowski & Paivio, 1994). When presenting imaging, stress the fact that it is seldom used but highly effective. Also, lead students to see that it works with passages that lend themselves to imagery. One way of encouraging the use of imagery is to give students the opportunity to respond by making sketches or diagrams. This works especially well for English language learners. It allows them to show what they know without being limited by their lack of facility with English.

As with other strategies, imaging should be taught formally, although you should also incorporate informal imagery instruction and application where feasible. If students are learning concrete terms such as *circuit, geyser, glacier,* or *meteorite,* have them learn verbal definitions and also images of the words. As students are reading, provide guide questions that ask them to create images of a process, person, or scene. After students have read a selection, ask them questions that require imaging: When the soldiers landed on the beaches of Normandy, what did they see? What did they hear? If you were near the epicenter of an earthquake, what would you see, what might you hear, and what would you feel?

USING TECHNOLOGY

Encourage students who are helped by imaging to use one of the many Web sites that do an especially good job of depicting events and processes, such as American Memory from the Library of Congress (http://memory.loc.gov/ ammem/amhome.html) or the Franklin Institute Online (http://sln.fi.edu/).

USING TECHNOLOGY

CD-ROM and online encyclopedias have film clips and audiotapes to add additional input for many of their entries.

LESSON 4.2 Imaging Lesson

Step 1: Introducing Imaging

Explain what imaging is. Do a think-aloud as you read a passage and create an image. Tell what you see, hear, and feel. Explain, however, that imaging is individualized and that their images may differ from yours. Also explain the benefits of imaging. Tell them that students in experiments learned twice as much when they created pictures of words in their minds. Tell them that when they create images, they process words twice, once as a word and the second time as a picture or other image.

Step 2: Focusing

Encourage students to relax and clear their minds of distractions. Have students close their eyes and listen to a brief, concrete passage, forming pictures in their minds as they do so. Invite students to draw pictures of their images. This fixes the images so that when the class discusses them, individual students don't forget what their original images looked like (Maria, 1990).

Step 3: Discussing

Discuss students' images, but remind them that images may vary. Also stress that the quality of the artwork is not important. It's the thought behind the drawing that counts. Prompt students to elaborate on their images.

Step 4: Guided Practice

Encourage students to create images of text as they read. Discuss the images students have created. If necessary, prompt students to elaborate on their images. Also discuss when and where the use of imaging is helpful.

Step 5: Review and Application

Review and reinforce imaging. Suggest its use where it might be especially appropriate: imaging scenes, characters, or events in fiction; events or scenes in history; places in geography; and processes in science. Encourage students to use drawings, even if they consist mainly of stick figures. Also encourage the creation of charts, diagrams, geographical and semantic maps, and visuals to display and organize information. Also call attention to visuals included in their texts, especially those that foster a better understanding of the text.

■ Analogies

Encourage students to pay particular attention to analogies. Many analogies lend themselves to imaging and often clarify a concept in a way that literal descriptions can't. For instance, the analogy of a dried sponge is used to provide a concrete explanation of the effect of drought on soil. The analogy helps students understand an unfamiliar concept by comparing it to a familiar experience. Chapter 5 contains additional information about the effectiveness of analogies.

■ Generating Questions

Students spend much of their time answering other people's questions. One of the most powerful comprehension strategies is to ask one's own questions and, of course, to answer them. Question generation transforms the reader from passive observer to active participant. Through asking questions, students set their own purposes for reading. As Ciardello (1998) explains, "Self-questioning is among the most potent cognitive strategies for stimulating content learning, because question generation prompts learners to search for answers that they themselves want to know" (p. 211). Through answering their questions, they process the information they have just read and begin to make it their own. They also can determine whether or not their comprehension is adequate. If they can't answer their own questions, they can then take steps to clarify confusions or acquire information that they couldn't recall. In fact, self-questioning is said to be the most effective way to monitor comprehension (Rosenshine, Meister, & Chapman, 1996).

Question generation also involves activating schema. When reading narratives, students can use their knowledge of story structure to ask such questions as: What is the setting? Who are the main characters? What is the story problem? (Singer & Donlan, 1989). For informational text, they ask such general questions as: What is the author trying to say? What will I learn from this article? Or the student can ask more specific questions by using the title and heading to create questions. One way of getting students to ask their own questions is to ask them questions whose answers are questions. For instance, before students read an article, you might ask, "What questions does the title raise? What questions do you have about this topic? What questions would you like to have answered?" As students read, encourage them to ask questions about the subheads or to turn the subheads into questions.

Self-questions can be created on a variety of levels. Attempting to construct literal comprehension as she reads a selection about acids and bases, the reader might ask herself, "What is the author saying about bases and acids? What are the steps for determining acidity?" Or, operating on an elaborative level in which the reader draws inferences, makes judgments, makes comparisons, or thinks of examples or applications of the materials, she might ask, "What are some other examples of acids and bases? How might people use knowledge of acids and bases to test their swimming pools and add chemicals?" (Wood et al., 1999). Elaborative self-questioning is especially effective for comprehension because it builds connections between new knowledge and students' prior knowledge.

Asking good questions is a difficult skill. Many students lack the ability to ask higher-level questions (Van der Meij & Dillon, 1994). Generating questions works best when students have been given instruction. Instruction in question generation should include the following elements (Davey & McBride, 1986).

- *Overview and rationale.* Discuss how and why creating questions improves comprehension and helps students check the accuracy of their reading. Explain that if students can't answer questions that they have created, they must reread the passage. Explain, too, that creating questions helps students remember what they have read and that generating questions may alert them to questions that may be asked on upcoming tests.

- *Creating questions.* Ask students to create questions about what they think are the most important ideas in a selection. After students become accustomed to creating questions, explore differences between explicit- and implicit-level questions. Explicit questions are those that can be answered by citing a word or phrase from the text. More advanced explicit questions require the reader to put together two or more pieces of information from the text. Implicit questions are those that require the reader to make inferences or draw conclusions based on information from the text. Some questions require readers only to make a judgment or to express an opinion. Known as "on my own" questions, they do not require using information from the selection. Show students how to write questions on an explicit level and on an implicit level. Provide students with some possible question words and some model questions.

- *Determining essential information.* Show students ways to determine essential information in a selection and to compose questions that request that information. Require them to provide the answers to any questions that they compose.

- *Checking questions.* Supply students with four monitoring questions to respond to as they compose questions:

  - How well did I identify important information?
  - How well did I link information together?
  - How well can I answer my questions?
  - Do I use good signal words? (Davey & McBride, 1986, p. 258)

- *Practice and application.* Give students ample guided practice identifying important information, generating questions, and responding to the monitoring questions. Students do best with question generation when given specific, concrete prompts to use. Being provided with *who, what, where,* and other words that signal questions is effective, as is being provided with generic questions, such as How are ____ and ____ alike? What conclusions can you draw about ____?

In pairs, small cooperative groups, or as part of whole-class activities, students ask their questions. Each student can choose one question to ask. It is the responsibility of the student asking the question to judge whether or not the question has been answered fully. The inquiring student can ask for more details or for clarification and may call on more than one student. Each student should have the opportunity to ask at least one question.

 CHECKUP

1. What are the key elaboration strategies?
2. When and under what circumstances is each of these strategies most effective?

■ Categorizing Questions

Questions should be asked on a variety of cognitive levels. One way of categorizing questions is to examine the kinds of thinking processes involved in answering them. An arrangement of skills from least demanding to those that require the highest mental powers is known as a taxonomy. One taxonomy that is widely used in content area reading divides comprehension tasks into three categories: literal, interpretive, and applied (Herber & Herber, 1993). Literal comprehension involves apprehending the basic meaning of the text. Interpretive comprehension consists of making inferences by putting together several pieces of information from the text or combining information from the text with background knowledge. Applied comprehension involves making use of the information in the text in some way. The following taxonomy, or levels of questions, is based on Weinstein and Mayer's (1986) system, which has also been used to classify the comprehension strategies presented in this text. However, the first level, comprehending, is drawn from Bloom's (1957) taxonomy.

Comprehending. Students understand text on a literal level. They can tell when and where important events took place and who was involved. They can also list the effects of an event or cause. This level also includes having students put information in their own words. Comprehending (literal) questions often include the following question words: *who, what, where, when, how, how many, how much.*

Organizing. Students select important details from the selection and construct relationships among them. This involves identifying or constructing main ideas, classifying, summarizing, and noting sequence and similarities and differences.

Organizing questions: How are _____ alike? How are _____ different? What is the main idea? How would you summarize? In what order did the events occur? What happened first? What happened next?

Elaborating. Elaborating entails making connections between information from the text and prior knowledge and includes a variety of activities: making inferences and predictions, creating images and analogies, and evaluating or judging.

Elaborating questions: What can you conclude? What picture does this bring to mind? What kind of a person is _____? How do you know? What do you predict will happen next?

Metacognitive (Monitoring). Metacognitive questions involve reflecting on thought processes. Students pose questions about words that they didn't understand or passages that are confusing or any elements that need clarifying. Asking questions of this type helps students become more aware of the quality of their comprehension and steps that they might take to repair comprehension.

Monitoring questions: Were there any confusing parts? Were there any words or expressions that were unfamiliar?

Listed below are examples of each type of question. They are drawn from *Profiles in American History: Civil Rights Movement to the Present* (Moss & Wilson, 1998).

Comprehending

When was Nixon president? Why did he resign from office?

Organizing

Who were the important people in Nixon's growing-up years? In what ways did these people influence him? What were some of his accomplishments? How might you sum up his presidency? What personal characteristic did he and Robert Kennedy share?

Elaborating

What was Nixon's emotional life like when he was growing up? Why do you think he worked so hard to succeed? What kind of a campaigner was he? What kinds of techniques did he use to win elections? What are some examples of name calling that he used in his elections? Do you think the authors presented a fair description of Nixon and his presidency? Why or why not?

Metacognitive

Were there any parts of the chapter that confused you? Did you run into any words whose meanings you didn't know? If so, what did you do? What does the word *impeach* mean? What did you do to try to get an understanding of the kind of person that Nixon was? What did you do to try to understand and remember the highlights of Nixon's presidency?

One way to foster question generation among students is to invite them to submit questions for quizzes and tests and to use the best of these. Students might also

ENGLISH LANGUAGE LEARNERS

Because it may be more difficult for them to formulate their responses in English, allow ELLs more time to respond and supply prompts as needed. Focus on the content of their responses rather than on the form.

create questions for review in preparation for a test. Anticipating the kinds of questions that a teacher might ask is a valuable study skill. Students can also make up questions and quiz each other.

■ Question–Answer Relationships

Used to answering explicit questions, some students may not realize that some questions require them to use their background knowledge and reasoning ability in order to answer. They need to be taught Question-Answer-Relationships (QARs). QARs are activities in which they identify the sources of information needed to answer questions (Raphael, 1984, 1986). In one study, secondary students had the most difficulty with the implicit questions that required combining information from text with background knowledge or required the reader to make a judgment based primarily on background knowledge (Schoenbach et al., 1999). When students were taught QARs and given training and practice in finding the source of answers, comprehension improved, especially for text-implicit questions.

 *CHECKUP*

1. What are the main kinds of questions?
2. What are some techniques for helping students answer questions on a variety of levels?

Monitoring for Meaning (Metacognition)

Do you sometimes look up from your reading and realize that you just read a whole paragraph or a whole page and you don't have the slightest idea what you read? Do you sometimes read a headline and realize that you misinterpreted it? You have what is known as metacognition. Metacognition or monitoring means that we are aware of our thinking processes, including our reading.

An essential element in our cognitive processing is the executive controller (Ashcraft, 1994). The executive controller is goal oriented. When we have as our goal comprehension, and comprehension fails because we stopped paying attention or we misinterpret a word, the executive controller makes us aware of that. Metacognitive awareness operates in terms of the goal that we set. A key feature of metacognitive awareness for a student is knowing what she is expected to be able to do as a result of reading a selection. If her goal is to pronounce each word correctly in a passage and not worry about comprehension, she won't be notified if comprehension fails. Of course, awareness of misread passages is only a first step. The next step is to use strategies to repair a failed reading. This might include rereading the passage or looking up an unfamiliar word or using a map or diagram.

Metacognition, then, is the key to comprehension in the content areas. It involves setting a goal of constructing meaning, assessing whether that goal is being met, and taking appropriate steps to remedy the situation if the goal is not being met. Metacognition is a conscious process, and it can be learned. Indeed, the heart of any successful program of improved learning is metacognition.

Unfortunately, some students lack adequate metacognitve awareness or don't make use of it. Take the case of Benjamin. Picking up his biology text, Benjamin, a tenth-

STRUGGLING READERS
Ironically, struggling readers are often given less time than able readers to respond to questions. Provide added time and prompts.

grader, read the assigned section on DNA. After twenty minutes, he had completed the reading and began filling in the answers on the study guide sheet that the teacher had provided. Benjamin hadn't fully understood the section, but he had a strategy for answering the questions. Searching through the text, he found a series of words that were the same as those contained in the question. These words were usually contained in the first part of a sentence. Benjamin then copied the words from the second part of the statement onto the blank space on the guide sheet. Benjamin was not aware that his comprehension was not adequate, so he took no steps to improve his comprehension. He didn't reread or use any of the illustrations or look up unfamiliar terms in the glossary. Benjamin is lacking metacognitve awareness. The four key areas in metacognition are: (1) knowing oneself as a learner, (2) regulating, (3) checking, and (4) repairing (Baker & Brown, 1984; Garner, 1994).

■ Knowing Oneself as a Learner

The student knows what her background is and has a realistic picture of herself as a learner. She may realize that she is a fast, global reader but can slow down when she has to. She knows that she finds reading literature and history texts easier than reading science. Her background in science and math are poor, and she is less interested in these subjects than she is in history. She knows that she has to read the science and math texts very carefully. Concerned about her reading, she made an appointment with the school's reading consultant to get some help. The reading consultant gave her some good tips. One was to survey the text and to read one section at a time. The consultant also pointed out that the text had many helpful visuals, and sometimes a diagram provided clarification for a confusing passage. The consultant then demonstrated how she read difficult passages, such as the one from a math text that she is reading as part of a graduate course in methods of teaching math.

> *Math is not my best subject. I better slow down and read this carefully. Maybe I'll have to read this explanation twice.*

■ Regulating

Regulating is a metacognitive process in which the reader guides his reading processes.

In **regulating,** the student assesses her performance in terms of her goals. She is aware of the structure of the text and how this might be used to aid comprehension. The student also knows what she will be expected to do as a result of reading this selection: explain a process, discuss a selection in a small discussion group, set up an experiment, or write a response on an essay test. She surveys the material, gets a sense of organization, establishes a purpose for reading by creating questions to be answered, and selects from available strategies the ones that seem to be most appropriate.

> *I really would like to be able to find out the height of trees and buildings. This article tells how to make a measuring instrument, but I can skip that part. The teacher has some that she'll let us use. I'll just read the part that tells how the instrument works.*

■ Checking

The student assesses her performance. She is aware when comprehension falters because the text is dense or contains a complicated idea that she failed to grasp or an unknown term that is key to an understanding of the passage. At the sentence level, she is aware if the sentence she is reading didn't make sense. Or she may realize that she was daydreaming and so was not paying attention to what she was reading and must reread. On a more global level, she may realize that although she just finished reading about a procedure, she does not really understand how it works and so rereads or looks at the diagram in the text. At the end of a section, she may test her understanding by summarizing what she has read or asking herself questions about what she has read. **Checking** also involves noting whether the focus is on important, relevant information and engaging in self-questioning, summarizing, or visualizing to determine whether goals are being achieved (Baker & Brown, 1984). Here is how the consultant demonstrates checking in her think-aloud.

■ **Checking** is a metacognitive process in which the reader assesses the adequacy of her performance.

> *Let's see. This heading says, "Finding the Angle." I know how to measure angles. We measured them in class. So you must have to measure angles to find out how tall something is. I don't know how that works. But this will probably tell me.*
>
> *This tells me that you use an instrument called a theodolite to measure angles. I'm not sure how to say that word, but it doesn't matter. What does matter is that the article tells me how the theodolite works.*

■ Repairing

When comprehension is inadequate, students take corrective fix-up measures. In **repairing** comprehension, a student might reread a passage, look up a difficult word, or study an illustration to help create meaning.

> *I'm not getting this explanation of how the theodolite works. It says you can calculate the height by finding out the angle to the top of the object and the distance to the object from where you are standing. Maybe the illustration will help. I see you line up the flat edge of the theodolite with the top of the tree and then the plumb line swings away from the center and marks the angle. The angle is 25 degrees. The distance is 1,000 feet. I think I'm getting it now.*

■ Causes of Inadequate Comprehension

Failure to comprehend can be caused by any one of a number of factors or an interaction of factors (Collins & Smith, 1980):

- Key technical terms may be unknown or may be known but used in an unfamiliar way.
- Concepts are unfamiliar.
- Syntax is confusing.
- Figurative language is misunderstood.
- Paragraph organization is difficult to follow.
- Pronouns and antecedent relationships are unclear.
- Relationships among paragraphs and sections are not established.
- The reader becomes lost in details. Key ideas are misinterpreted.
- The reader has inadequate prior knowledge, or a conflict exists between that knowledge and the text.
- The reader reads the passage in rapid narrative style instead of careful, analytic fashion.

STRUGGLING READERS
Struggling readers may set fairly low goals and be satisfied with a shallow understanding. Adept readers, on the other hand, tend to set more demanding goals. A key element in instruction is to help students set adequate goals.

Inadequate monitoring for meaning may also be caused by poor comprehension strategies and material that has too many difficult words and concepts. When the reading material is too difficult, poor readers are unable to make full use of the strategies they do possess. If the text isn't making much sense because too many of the words are unknown, students may not comprehend the text well enough to see that there are inconsistencies.

■ **Repairing** is taking steps to correct faulty comprehension.

■ Repair Strategies

Repair strategies (Baker & Brown, 1984; Harris & Sipay, 1990) include the following:

- Keep reading to see if the passage becomes clearer.
- Go back to an earlier section if the problem is caused by a piece of information that was introduced earlier that you did not understand or have forgotten.
- Rereading the sentence or paragraph may clear up a confusing point or provide context for a difficult word.
- Reading to the end of the page or section might provide clarification.
- Reread the preceding section.
- If there are specific details that you cannot remember, skim back through the material to find them.
- The text may be difficult or require closer reading, so you may have to slow down, adjusting your rate of reading.
- Consulting a map, diagram, photo, chart, sample problem, or illustration might provide clarification of a puzzling passage.
- Using a glossary or dictionary will provide meaning for an unknown word.
- Consulting an encyclopedia or similar reference might clarify a confusing concept.
- Reading an easier book on the same topic might provide needed background.
- Use the **lookback** strategy. If you have gotten the gist of a passage but forgotten a fact or two, use a lookback to repair your comprehension. In a lookback, you skim over a passage to locate the forgotten fact. If, however, you fail to get the gist of the passage, a total rereading is required.

■ **Lookback** is a strategy that involves skimming back over a selection that has already been read in order to obtain information that was missed, forgotten, or misunderstood.

■ Teaching Metacognition

In one highly successful program for underachieving ninth-graders, metacognition was the centerpiece of instruction (Schoenbach et al., 1999). After being introduced to the concept of thinking about thinking, students were asked to respond to such questions as:

> How do you know when your understanding is breaking down? Can you point to certain places in text where you tend to "Lose it"? How do you get back on track when you begin to notice that you are not "getting it"? (p. 58)

The students spent much of their time talking about how they learned. These conversations helped them to become more aware of reading processes in particular and learning processes in general. Once they were aware of the processes they used, they were in a better position to take control of them, to shed habits that hindered their learning, and to foster strategies that enhanced their learning. In addition to discussion, students also reflected on their reading and thinking processes in learning logs. Students were required to read for twenty minutes each evening and to write a reflection in their learning logs. Instead of talking about plot or characters or ideas, students reflected on the ways in which they read their books. During discussions of their reading, students were encouraged to talk about the processes that they used when they read. They were especially encouraged to talk over puzzling passages and other obstacles to comprehension and how they dealt with them. In fact, they were given extra credit for being explicit about where they got lost in text and when they got lost.

To build metacognitive awareness, make it a part of every strategy that you teach. Whenever a strategy is introduced, do a think-aloud so that students get a look at your thinking. Also discuss how, when, and where strategies should be implemented and signs that a strategy isn't working and another strategy should be tried. During discussions, include process as well as content questions: How did you happen to draw that conclusion? How did you figure out the meaning of that difficult word? What study strategies did you use? Encourage students to mark confusing passages with Post-it notes. This will give you insights into the kinds of difficulties they are having with a text and also provide opportunities to discuss fix-up strategies they might use.

After a new strategy has been introduced, have students discuss how they are doing with it. Also have students discuss occasions when strategies have been especially effective.

Metacognitive Strategies Lesson

Step 1: Describing the Strategy

Explain the strategy in detail. Describe and demonstrate or model the strategy so that students know exactly how the strategy works. For instance, in teaching a monitoring strategy, explain that after you have read a paragraph, you pause and ask, "Did that make sense?" If not, you reread or take some other action.

Step 2: Explaining Why the Strategy Is Important

Explain and model why the strategy is a valuable one. Students may not realize that even you have difficulty with comprehension at times and, so, need to be aware of whether or not your reading makes sense. Also note that the advantage of checking your reading periodically is that it makes it possible for you to clear up puzzling parts and helps you to remember the material longer.

Step 3: Demonstrating the Strategy

Using modeling or another technique, show how you would use the strategy. Placing a brief selection on the board or an overhead, show how you pause at the end of a paragraph and ask, "Does this make sense?" Choose a tricky paragraph, one that you misread the first time, and show students how you stopped when the piece stopped making sense. Also discuss the steps you might take to repair the comprehension gap.

Step 4: Explaining When and Where to Use the Strategy

When teaching a strategy, be sure to note when and where it is to be used. For instance, when teaching repair strategies, note when it's appropriate to reread

---

STRUGGLING READERS

Provide struggling readers with extra instruction in metacognition. Struggling readers are less likely to detect lapses in comprehension and, when they do detect them, are less able to repair them. However, when instructed, struggling readers can and do learn to become effective monitors (Palincsar, Winn, David, Synder, & Stevens, 1993).

ENGLISH LANGUAGE LEARNERS

One of the strengths that bilingual students bring to reading is a more fully developed sense of metacognition. Learning a second language often entails viewing language as an object of study. Being more metacognitively aware, they are quick to pick up difficulties with understanding text. Bilingual learners often use knowledge of their home language to help them comprehend text in English. For instance, they may use English and their native language to activate background knowledge or they may translate a difficult passage into their native language so they can understand it or explain it better (Jiménez, 1997).

the sentence or the paragraph and when it might be a good idea to read ahead because the next sentence or paragraph explains the word or idea with which you were having difficulty.

Step 5: Explaining How and Why to Evaluate a Strategy

Explain how to evaluate a strategy and why that's important. For instance, explain that you need to see whether rereading a sentence works, because if it doesn't, you will need to use another strategy.

Steps 6 & 7: Guided Practice and Application

As part of instruction in metacognitive strategies, students need opportunities to try out strategies with guidance and feedback from you so they can clarify misunderstandings, make necessary adjustments, and get the feel of the strategy. Be sure to affirm students' successful efforts with specific praise: "I like the way you reread that sentence when you saw that it didn't make sense," or "I like the way you used the diagram to help you understand the paragraph." They also need ample opportunity to apply the strategy to a variety of texts in a variety of situations so that the strategies become automatic and they can see which strategies work best in which situations.

CHECKUP

1. What are the key elements of metacognition?
2. How might metacognition be developed?

Applying Strategies: Step-by-Step Intensive Reading

One procedure students will need to learn is to adjust the intensity of their reading to the nature of the text. When text is very difficult, as it so often is in content area reading, students may need to read in intensive, step-by-step fashion and integrate several strategies. One of the best ways to teach students how to read difficult text is to model the process. Here is how you might model the process of reading a section from a text on astronomy.

Explain to students that stories, biographies, and expository texts told in narrative form and text that is dealing with ideas that are familiar to us can be read with relative speed and ease. However, explanatory text that is describing a concept that is unfamiliar and complex needs to be read very deliberately and, if it's difficult enough, needs to be read step by step. Moreover, the reader must fully grasp the first step before going to the second and must understand the second step and integrate the first before going on to the third.

Students who are used to reading fiction or simple expository text with relative ease may not realize that much of their reading in the content areas will require an intensive reading. This might mean reading a selection paragraph by paragraph or even sentence by sentence. Demonstrate this kind of reading by selecting a dense

EXEMPLARY TEACHING

CLARIFYING CONFUSING CONCEPTS

Noting that her middle school class of English language learners was having difficulty reading Jane Yolen's (1992) *Encounter*, a fictionalized account of Columbus's arrival in the New World told from the native people's point of view, Carol put a key portion of the text on a transparency and gave students duplicated copies of the segments. As she read the segments, students raised their hands when an unknown word or confusing passage appeared (Harvey, 1998). When students asked about the word *landfall*, Carol asked if anyone knew what the word meant. One student believed that it might mean a place where the land falls off. But on rereading the text with that meaning in mind, he noted that it didn't make sense. A second student thought that it might mean a

place where ships land. She explained that if one reread the sentence while keeping that meaning in mind, the text made sense. Pointing to the word on her transparency, Carol explained that the student had made very good use of context and that rereading a sentence containing an unknown word was an excellent way to try to find out what the word might mean. After arriving at a possible definition, it was a good idea to see whether that meaning fit the sense of the sentence and the selection.

As she read and students noted other problems, Carol discussed and demonstrated other fix-up strategies that might be used to repair comprehension. Later, students tried their hands at applying the strategies independently.

passage and telling students you are going to show how you might go about reading it. Explain not only what is going on in your mind but why you adopt a particular strategy such as imaging or questioning or relating a new idea to a known one.

(Reading the heading, The Turning Earth)

This must be explaining how the Earth turns. I remember the teacher using a basketball to show us how the Earth turns on its axis. That must be what this section is about. I never really understood what he was telling us. This section will probably be tough. I better read it carefully.

(Teacher reads the first sentence.)

During a sunset, the Sun is essentially standing still while the Earth to the west of us is being turned upward, the land west of us rising up into a "hill" miles high (and soon miles higher) to block our view of the Sun. (Schaaf, 1998, p. 20)

I did not get all that. I better reread the sentence. This sentence has a couple of ideas in it. I'll focus on the beginning idea first. It says the sun is standing still during a sunset. I've heard that before but it never made any sense to me. When I look at the sunset, the sun seems to be setting in the west. But now it says that the sun is essentially standing still while the Earth to the west of us is being turned upward. Let's see if I get this. I know that the Earth rotates. I remember the teacher showing us a basketball and making it

The teacher provides assistance as students apply newly learned strategies.

spin slowly around his finger to show how Earth rotates. So what's happening is that the Earth to the west of us—that's the direction in which the sun is setting—it is turning upward. I can picture that. The sun is basically still. But the Earth is moving and the part I'm on is moving away from the sun, so it will soon be dark.

Now I understand the second part of the sentence. If the Earth is moving upward and away from the sun, the land west of us will form a big hill and block our view of the sun. I think I'm getting it.

(Teacher reads the next sentence.)

When we see what we call a sunset, what we are really watching is an earthrise—or at least part of the Earth heaving up to the west of us. (Schaff, 1998, p. 20)

This helps me understand the whole thing better. The sunset is not really a sunset. It's an earthrise. So that's what confused me. When people talked about sunsets and sunrises, I thought that the sun was moving. But the sun is just sort of sitting there. I'll remember this idea if I think of what's happening as an earthrise instead of as a sunset. Now I think I can picture this whole process in my mind.

STRUGGLING READERS

Struggling readers may believe that achieving students read effortlessly. Modeling the process of intensive reading helps them to understand that reading difficult text is hard work and that even the best readers encounter passages that are puzzling and so require careful application of a variety of strategies.

As you think aloud, you should also explain why you use certain strategies. You might explain that when a sentence contains several ideas, as in the first sentence, you might read just a portion, especially if the second part of the sentence builds on the first part. You might also explain that visualizing the sun standing still as the Earth moves helps you to understand the process.

You might also explain the importance of activating schemata and deciding how a piece is going to be read before beginning to read it. You should emphasize the importance of monitoring for meaning. For instance, after reading the first sentence, you were aware that you didn't fully understand it, so you reread it.

Because students may not realize that some kinds of text demand a great deal of effort from the reader, you should emphasize the active, effortful, planful nature of intensive reading of dense text. You should stress, too, that a number of strategies are used and the kinds of strategies used depend on the nature of the text and the reader's background. Focus throughout is on taking steps to make the reading as meaningful as possible. For instance, reading this passage at twilight and watching the sun as it sets would be an excellent way to make key concepts more understandable. As a way of retaining this information, the reader might also draw a labeled diagram of the movement of the Earth and the setting of the sun.

Demonstrate how being an active reader fosters understanding and retention and, if the material is particularly technical, helps the reader to maintain interest and attention. Some other strategies that might help students construct meaning from difficult text are connecting new information with background knowledge, using graphic organizers, applying knowledge, reading out loud, and paraphrasing.

■ Connecting New Information with Background Knowledge

Encourage students to connect new information with their background knowledge. For instance, after reading the following passage, students might reflect on practical applications. They might note that tires are more likely to fail in very warm weather and after being driven for long periods of time. They might also explain why a basketball or football might be slightly larger on a warm day and slightly smaller on a cold day.

When gases are heated, the gas molecules move faster and farther apart, causing the gas to expand. In a closed container the molecules strike the walls of their container with greater force. For this reason, tire manufactures recommend that tire pressure be checked only when the tires are cool. If you checked tire pressure in tires when they are hot, the pressure would appear too high and you would let out some air. Then when the tires cooled, they would be underinflated. (Cuevas & Lamb, 1994, p. 50)

■ Using Graphic Organizers

After modeling the strategy, encourage students to use a graphic organizer to help comprehend and remember the steps in a complex explanation. Note Figure 4.3, a process diagram used to summarize the steps of the formation of lightning described in the following passage. Students should read the explanation once to get an overview and then go back and put it into steps. By putting it into steps, they are breaking the process down into more understandable chunks, and they are also very carefully reviewing the process. It is also a way of monitoring for meaning. If they have difficulty putting the process into steps, they don't fully understand it and so should take actions to fix up their comprehension.

The most familiar lightning strokes are the negative flashes from cloud to ground. They start near the base of a cloud as an invisible discharge called the stepped leader, which moves downward in discrete, microsecond steps about 50 m (165 ft) long. It is believed to be initiated by a small discharge near the cloud base, releasing free electrons that move toward the ground. When the negatively charged stepped leader approaches to within 100 m (330 ft) or less of the ground, a leader moves up from the ground—especially from objects such as buildings and trees—to meet it.

Once the leaders have made contact, the visible lightning stroke, called the return stroke, propagates upward from the ground along the path of the stepped leader. Several subsequent strokes can occur along the original main channel in less than a second. These strokes continue until the charge center in the lower part of the cloud is eliminated. The explosive heating and expansion of air along the leader path produces a shock wave that is heard as thunder. (Grolier, 1997)

FIGURE 4.3

Process Diagram of the Creation of Lightning

| Stepped leader may be triggered by small discharge near base of cloud. | Stepped leader carries negative charges from a cloud toward ground. | Stepped leader moves downward. | When stepped leader gets close, upwards moving positive charges shoot up from tall objects. | Upward leader and stepped leader meet and form route between Earth and cloud. | Leaders make contact. Lightning flashes as return stroke moves upward from ground. | Strokes continue until charge in cloud is eliminated. |

Reading Out Loud

When you read a difficult passage, chances are you slow down considerably. You might even read the passage out loud or subvocally. The harder material gets, the more even the best of readers tend to subvocalize. Through vocalizing, we can "listen" to what we are reading, which can aid concentration. As one high schooler commented, "Reading out loud to myself helps me focus and remember important things. The reading seems more like a story that way. I also remember better if I reread the hard parts and then tell myself what I've read when I finish" (Harvey, 1998, p. 80).

Paraphrasing

When material is extremely dense and complex, one strategy students might use is to paraphrase it. This means carefully examining each phrase and translating it into language that the reader can understand. Notice how the reader paraphrased the following excerpt. The paraphrase need not be written. It can be oral, or the reader might just think of a paraphrase without saying it aloud.

Bernoulli's principle law stating that the pressure of a fluid varies inversely with speed, an increase in speed producing a decrease in pressure and vice versa (such as a drop in hydraulic pressure as the fluid speeds up flowing through a constriction in a pipe) and vice versa. The principle also explains the pressure differences on each surface of an aerofoil, which gives lift to the wing of an aircraft. (Brimblecombe, Gallannaugh, & Thompson, 1998, p. 85)

Speed causes the pressure of a fluid to change. Increasing the speed of the flow makes the pressure decrease. Pressure increases when the speed of the flow is decreased. When fluid is pushed through a narrow pipe, the fluid speeds up and the pressure in the pipe drops. This principle ex-

plains what keeps planes up. Because air flows more swiftly over the top of a wing than the underside, there is less pressure and the airplane is given lift.

 CHECKUP

1. What are some strategies that students might use when the text is especially difficult to understand?

SUMMARY

Comprehending is a process of using our background of knowledge and reasoning processes to construct meaning. According to schema theory, our background knowledge is packaged in abstract units known as schemata. According to a mental models theory, comprehension requires that readers create a mental model, or representation, of textual information and its interpretation.

Comprehension strategies include preparational, organizational, elaboration, and monitoring. Preparational strategies prepare students for the reading of a selection and include: previewing, setting goals and purpose for reading, activating prior knowledge, and predicting. Organizational strategies consist of selecting main ideas and relevant details and constructing relationships among them and include paraphrasing, summarizing, and using the structure of a text. Elaboration strategies consist of constructing relationships between prior knowledge and knowledge obtained from print and include drawing inferences, generating questions, creating analogies, visualizing, and evaluating, or reading critically.

Although strategies have been presented one by one, they are applied in integrated fashion. In reading even a brief selection, students might use three or four strategies or more. One of the best ways to teach students how to read difficult text is to model the process. When students are reading difficult text, it is important that they read it in step-by-step, intensive fashion. Some strategies that they can use to make dense text more understandable include connecting new information with background knowledge, using graphic organizers, applying knowledge, reading out loud, and paraphrasing.

Reflection

Return to the Anticipation Guide at the beginning of this chapter. Respond once again to the items. Did your responses change? If so, how and why? What is your view of comprehension? What role might strategies play in the development of comprehension? What role might content knowledge play?

EXTENSION AND APPLICATION

1. The next time you are reading difficult text, stop and note the strategies that you use to make the text more comprehensible.
2. Try using one or more of the strategies suggested in this chapter that you have not used. Try it over a period of several weeks. How did your use of the strategy change over that time? How effective was the strategy?

3. Which of the strategies discussed in this chapter would be most effective in the content area that you teach? Plan a direct instruction lesson for teaching one of these strategies. In your lesson, be sure to discuss what you are thinking about as you apply the strategy. If possible, teach it and evaluate its effectiveness.

chapter 5

READING TO LEARN CONTENT

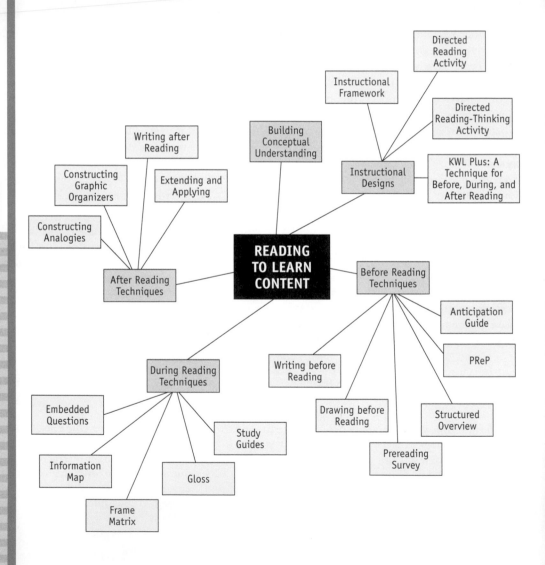

Read each of the following statements. Put a check under "Agree" or "Disagree" to show how you feel about each one. If possible, discuss your responses with classmates.

Agree   *Disagree*

1. Questions asked after a selection is read help comprehension more than questions asked before the selection is read.   ____   ____

2. Preparation for the reading of a difficult selection is more effective than explanation after the selection has been read.   ____   ____

3. Most students depend more on memory of key concepts than on true understanding.   ____   ____

4. The more direct instruction students are given, the more they learn.   ____   ____

5. Using a few teaching techniques works best because this builds a sense of familiarity and continuity.   ____   ____

USING WHAT YOU KNOW

Chapter 4 focused on the cognitive processes and strategies involved in comprehension. This chapter builds on the information presented in that chapter and presents a number of instructional frameworks or packages for delivering instruction. The lessons discussed attempt to blend the teaching of content and process. Think back on your secondary school days and also your elementary school experiences. What steps did your teachers take to help you use reading and writing skills and strategies to foster the learning of content? What techniques seemed to be especially effective? What else might have been done to foster your ability to use literacy skills and strategies to increase your learning?

BUILDING CONCEPTUAL UNDERSTANDING

In their study of middle school students who were reading about events leading up to the Revolutionary War, McKeown, Beck, and Sandora (1996) found that many of the students didn't really engage with the text. They seemed to be reading the text in the same way that they might read a popular novel.

> Students took what they could get in one swift pass through the words on a page, and then formed them into a shallow representation of the text. This kind of cursory use of the text suggests that students resist digging in and grappling with unfamiliar or difficult content. (p. 101)

■ **Conceptual understanding** is a depth of understanding such that students are able to go beyond the surface structure and textbase to create a mental model of the text by which they grasp underlying principles and so understand why an event happened or why a process works the way it does. Having conceptual knowledge means that they can apply this knowledge.

The students were failing to read for **conceptual understanding.** Putting little into their reading, the students got little out of it. Just as conceptual understanding is an essential element in the learning of the technical vocabulary of content area subjects, it is also a key factor in the comprehension of content area text. Conceptual understanding doesn't happen automatically. It must be carefully built. Teachers help build conceptual understanding when they plan activities that lead students to construct a deeper understanding of the text.

The first step entails deciding what conceptual understandings are important for the student to acquire. The next step is to plan activities that will foster an understanding of these key concepts. Traditional activities, such as answering factual questions at the end of the chapter, lead students to locate and remember the information requested. However, conceptual understanding requires integrating new information with one's background of knowledge and constructing generalizations about the information. Questions or activities must involve this integration, or conceptual understanding will not occur.

Developing conceptual understanding takes time. Through interacting with their text, the teacher, and peers, students see similarities and differences in ideas, note other viewpoints, and clarify their thinking, all of which leads to a deeper understanding. A text that is simply read in order to answer questions at the end is undigested. The information might be retained in memory, but it has not been used to form new understandings. For instance, students who read about the industrial revolution may be able to cite causes and effects of the industrial revolution, but they may not grasp the implications of what they have read or make connections between what they have read and their own experiences or other texts they have read. As Roehler (1996) explains, "Students learn to provide answers to questions. They do not necessarily construct the larger conceptual understandings associated with the content and how these relate to their lives" (p. 145). However, if, through discussion with the teacher and with each other, students compare the causes and effects of the industrial revolution with changes they have seen or read about in today's workplace, they can begin to relate what happened then to what is happening now. The teacher might have them construct charts, such as the one in Figure 5.1, in which they list causes of the industrial revolution and effects, both positive and negative, and compare these with causes of today's information revolution and effects, negative and positive.

The teacher's role is to ask the kinds of questions that lead students to see how these events are both similar and different and to guide their thinking so that it goes

FIGURE 5.1

Comparison of Industrial and Information Revolutions

	Industrial Revolution	**Information Revolution**
Causes		
Positive Effects		
Negative Effects		

beyond the factual information and allows them to make generalizations about changes in the workplace and, perhaps, even to make predictions for the future. In this way, instruction becomes a

> process of intentionally orchestrating the classroom environment so that students are helped to construct the concepts specified by the curriculum. . . . [T]he teacher develops lessons that provide the support students need to learn and the challenge students need to internalize the knowledge. (Roehler, 1996, p. 144)

How the teacher defines the learning task determines what students learn. Simply answering end-of-the-chapter questions lead to low-level learning. Questions and activities that involve drawing conclusions and evaluating what one has read and relating it to previously learned topics lead to conceptual understanding. Once the learning task has been set, understanding is fostered by the nature and number of interactions. Classroom discussions that lead to generalizations and hypotheses as opposed to mere recitation of facts lead to conceptual understanding.

For the teacher, building conceptual understanding is purposeful. In light of the students' background knowledge and the key concepts of the topic, the teacher plans reading, discussion, and other activities that build necessary background and guide the students in a thoughtful processing of the text, integration of new and previously learned information, and the construction of conceptual understanding. The teacher emphasizes understanding of information rather than the acquisition of information. The teacher gears instruction to the students' current level of competence and guides their thinking to higher levels of understanding.

The teacher also builds metacognitive awareness. As students become more aware of their learning processes, they can demand a deeper level of understanding. They also become aware of what it takes to achieve a depth of understanding. They realize that skimming through the text will generally result in a shallow grasp of key concepts. They come to know that thinking about what they have read; carrying on dialogue with the author; talking with classmates, friends, or family about what they have read; and similar activities lead to a fuller, deeper understanding.

STRUGGLING READERS

Struggling readers may be satisfied with a lower level of understanding of the text and so may benefit from prompts that help them to analyze and compare. Discussions that help them relate new understandings to their own lives and to past learnings should prove especially helpful.

Since the textbook is often the major source of information, the teacher should read the textbook the way a student might and imagine what kinds of understandings the student might construct (Roehler, 1996). If reading the text would lead to a surface understanding, the teacher must supplement the text or provide activities that lead to conceptual understanding.

 **CHECKUP**

1. What is conceptual understanding?
2. What steps might be taken to foster conceptual understanding?

There are numerous techniques that can be used to foster conceptual understanding. Some of these are used before reading, some during reading, some after reading, and some during all phases of reading. Before-reading techniques include the anticipation guide, PReP, survey technique, structured overview, and Frayer model. During-reading techniques feature frame questions and study guides, including glosses. After-reading techniques include reflecting, graphic post-organizers, applying, and extending. A technique that encompasses before, during, and after reading is KWL Plus. Teaching plans that foster comprehension before, during, and after reading include the instructional framework, the directed reading activity, and the directed reading-thinking activity. Collaborative techniques that incorporate several highly successful comprehension strategies are ReQuest, Reciprocal Teaching, Questioning the Author, Reading Seminar, and Cognitive Strategy Instruction. Collaborative techniques are explored in the next chapter.

INSTRUCTIONAL DESIGNS

How should content area reading lessons be structured so as to develop conceptual understanding? The structure of the lessons is determined by a number of factors. These include learning objectives or standards, students' background knowledge and reading ability, the nature of the material to be learned, and students' motivation and ability to work independently. Formats range from being teacher directed to collaborative to student directed. Some offer heavy support; others provide gentle guidance. Regardless of format used, the lesson should prepare students to read, should offer guidance as they read, and should help them summarize and organize what they have read, relate it to what they already know, and apply it. The instructional framework provides a flexible structure for designing lessons.

Instructional Framework

■ The **instructional framework** is a structure used to teach reading. It is composed of three main elements: preparation, guidance, and independence.

The **instructional framework** blends activities that foster the learning of content with activities that help students use content-related reading and writing processes (Herber & Herber, 1993). The instructional framework is composed of three main elements: preparation, guidance, and independence.

■ Preparation

Preparation includes all those activities designed to foster increased comprehension of the material to be read. This entails making connections between what is known and what is new, building vocabulary, establishing a conceptual context so that students can see how key ideas are organized, activating and building background, establishing a purpose for reading, and motivating the reading. As part of the preparation, the teacher might review previous lessons and show how the upcoming topic is related to what the class has studied in the past. For instance, when embarking on a study of the Revolutionary War, it would be most helpful to briefly review the French and Indian War and discuss how that conflict helped set the scene for the Revolutionary War.

■ Guidance

Preparation flows into guidance. Guidance is designed to show students how to use reading, writing, and reasoning skills to learn content material. It includes direct instruction in strategies, such as imaging, evaluating, summarizing, or drawing conclusions. As part of the preparation, the teacher could discuss with students how the text might be read. If this is a text with a strong bias, students might want to evaluate as they read. If the author is describing Pickett's charge at the Battle of Gettysburg, students might want to create images in their minds as they read so they can visualize the horror of the battle and hear the sounds of war.

Modeling is an essential part of direct instruction. Guidance also involves providing clear directions and using cooperative grouping. Guidance includes monitoring students' efforts and providing feedback.

■ Independence

Independence consists of applying content knowledge and the processes used to acquire content knowledge. Initially, students are taught how to apply content knowledge and skills and are guided by the teacher. Over time, they gradually begin to apply content skills and knowledge independently.

Using the instructional framework, you can design your own instruction. Or you can use or adapt one of the many lesson structures that enjoy widespread use in content area instruction. These include the DRA (directed reading activity), the DR-TA (directed reading-thinking activity), and KWL Plus, which are described in this chapter, and ReQuest, Reciprocal Teaching, Questioning the Author, and Reading Seminar, which are highlighted in the next chapter.

Directed Reading Activity

A flexible procedure, the **directed reading activity** (DRA) has five steps: preparation for reading, silent reading, discussion, rereading, and follow-up.

Preparation.   Through discussion, demonstration, use of audiovisual aids, and/or simulations, students are given guidance in the following areas:

- *Experiential Background/Concepts.* Students often have some background in a subject but may not realize it. Preparation includes activating students' background

■ The **directed reading activity** is a traditional five-step lesson plan designed to assist students in the reading of a selection.

and building new background if necessary. If students have erroneous concepts, these must be confronted and clarified, which may be more difficult than simply building new concepts. If students are about to read a piece about solar cells but have no experience with the subject, the teacher might demonstrate the workings of a solar calculator. Concepts or ideas crucial to understanding the selection are also developed: basic concepts of electricity, the flow of electrons, and semiconductors. Chances are that students have some understanding of electricity, so the teacher would activate that background and build on it.

- *Critical Vocabulary*. Vocabulary necessary for understanding the selection is presented. For an article about volcanoes, the words *lava, magma, crater, crust,* and *plates* are presented. Care is taken to show how these words are related to each other.

- *Reading Strategies*. Students have to know how a selection is to be read. Most selections require a mix of preparational, organizational, and elaboration strategies. However, some strategies work better than others with certain kinds of materials. A primary source in history, for example, requires evaluation. A science piece might require students to visualize a process. At times, the format might be unfamiliar. For example, before reading a weather map, students should be taught the symbols that the map uses. Because teaching a strategy is time-consuming, it would be best if the needed strategy were taught beforehand, if it is an unfamiliar one, and then briefly reviewed during the preparatory discussion.

- *Purpose for Reading*. The purpose for reading is the question or questions to be answered and usually embraces the overall significance of the selection. The purpose, which may be established by the teacher or the class, may grow out of the preparatory discussion. Students discussing hurricanes may want to know why they occur mostly in late summer and that would become the purpose for reading. On other occasions, the teacher might set the reading purpose.

- *Interest*. Last but not least, the teacher tries to create interest in the selection. To do this for an article about nutrition, the teacher may toss out the idea that proper nutrition can improve school and athletic performance.

The key elements in the preparation step have been described separately, but in actual practice they are merged. For instance, background concepts and the vocabulary used to label them are presented at the same time. The purpose for reading flows from the overall discussion, and throughout the discussion, the teacher tries to create an interest in the selection. Reading strategies might become a part of the purpose. As part of preparation for reading a selection about dinosaurs, the teacher might state, "As you read the selection, notice the possible causes for the disappearance of the dinosaurs (purpose). Think about the evidence given for each theory and judge on the basis of the evidence which theory makes most sense (strategy)."

Silent Reading.   The first reading is usually silent. Silent reading is faster than oral reading and promotes comprehension. For instance, students are more aware of their level of understanding and might reread a confusing sentence when reading silently but would not do so when reading orally. Oral reading places the focus on pronouncing the words correctly. Sometimes, teachers allow oral reading because the text is too difficult for students. A better solution would be to obtain a text on the appropriate level or use a technique such as Questioning the Author or Reading Seminar. During the silent reading, students should monitor their comprehension to check whether they adequately understand what they are reading and, if necessary, take appropriate steps to correct the difficulties. The teacher should note these monitoring and repair strategies. Charts or diagrams created in preparation for reading the selection should be kept on display, as should any vocabulary words that were placed on the chalkboard. These items can then be used as a reference as students read the text. The purpose for reading should be displayed so that students are reminded of the key question they are attempting to answer as they read.

Reading might be done in class or for homework. If the text is difficult or has a large number of concepts, you might want to have students read a segment and discuss it before going on to the next segment. This is especially helpful if the information is cumulative, if segment b builds on segment a.

Discussion.   The discussion flows from the purpose for reading. Students read a selection for a specific purpose; the discussion begins with the purpose question. If the students read about the effects of the Great Depression on farmers, the purpose question is What effect did the Depression have on farm life? During the discussion, concepts are clarified and expanded, background is built, and relationships between known and unknown, new and old are reinforced. The teacher also evaluates students' performance, noting whether they were able to comprehend the main concepts in the chapter. Were they able to reconstruct the suffering that farmers endured? Although the discussion is partly evaluative, it should not be regarded as an oral quiz. Its main purpose is to build understanding, not test it (see Chapter 6). Questioning techniques, such as probes, prompts, and wait time should be used. Part of the discussion might also be devoted to asking students to describe their use of strategies, with a focus on the strategy being emphasized.

Rereading.   In most lessons, rereading blends in naturally with the discussion. As part of the discussion, students may reread to correct misinformation, to obtain additional data, to enhance appreciation, or to deepen understanding. During the discussion, students might indicate that they believe that only the farmers in the Dust Bowl suffered (a mistaken notion). Students can then be directed to locate and read aloud passages that describe how farmers in other sections of the country were affected by the Depression. In other situations, students might dramatize a literary piece that has a substantial amount of dialogue or reread a selection to gain a deeper appreciation of the author's style. A separate reading is generally undertaken for a new purpose, although it may be for a purpose that grows out of the discussion. Rereading is not a necessary step. Some selections are not worth reading a second time, or students may have grasped the essence in the first reading.

In the rereading stage, oral reading should not be overemphasized. Unless a selection is being dramatized, it is generally a poor practice to have students reread an entire selection orally. Oral rereading should be for specific purposes: to clarify a misconception, to substantiate a conclusion, or to supply an answer to a question.

STRUGGLING READERS
Believing that this will help struggling readers cope with a text that is difficult to read, teachers sometimes have students take turns reading the text out loud. This is a poor practice that embarrasses the struggling readers and bores the proficient ones. See Chapter 9 for suggestions for handling this problem.

Follow-Up.   Follow-up, or extension, activities offer opportunities to delve more deeply into a topic, to apply knowledge, or, for controversial topics, to consult another source. Students who have read a general article on recycling might want to read more about that topic, contact recycling groups, find out what their town is doing about recycling, or start a recycling project for the class. Every lesson need not have a follow-up.

■ Preparing a Directed Reading Activity

Creating a DRA starts with an analysis of the selection to be read. After reading the selection, the teacher decides what she wants the students to learn from it. Content analysis of fiction may result in statements about plot, theme, character, setting, or author's style. For nonfiction, the statements concern the main principles, ideas, concepts, rules, or whatever the students are expected to learn. After analyzing the selection, the teacher chooses three to five ideas or story elements that she feels are most important. The piece may be loaded with concepts; however, more than three to five cannot be handled in any depth at one time. Even if an accompanying teacher's guide lists important concepts or provides key story events, the teacher should still complete a content analysis. That way, the teacher, not the textbook author, decides what is important for the class to learn. For example, for a section on the Civil War entitled "Gettysburg," the teacher composes the following major learnings. These will provide the focus for prereading and postreading activities and strategies for prereading, during reading, and postreading.

- A series of bad decisions by Lee led to defeat at Gettysburg.
- Gettysburg was a costly, deadly battle for both sides.
- Gettysburg was the turning point of the Civil War.

After selecting these key ideas, the teacher lists vocabulary necessary to understand them. As a rule of thumb, no more than seven or eight vocabulary words should be chosen, and five or six would probably be more effective. An excessive number of difficult words may be a sign that the selection is too difficult. From the list of difficult words, those most essential to an understanding of the selection are chosen. For example, the following words are chosen as most essential to understanding the three learnings listed for the section on the Battle of Gettysburg, and as being ones that students are likely to find difficult: *overconfident, strategic value, frontal attack, direct assault, maneuver, concentrated his forces.* Examining these words also gives the teacher a sense of what prior knowledge or schema the passage requires.

Once the major understandings and difficult vocabulary words have been chosen, the teacher looks over the selection to decide what major cognitive and reading strategies are necessary to understand it. For this selection, visualizing and using the map of the battlefield would be helpful strategies. Comprehension of the battle itself should be improved if students visualize the fighting that took place and the number of soldiers involved and the number killed. However, students should also read to find the causes of the South's defeat and the effects.

Building background and vocabulary, activating schema, piquing interest, setting purposes, and giving guidance in reading and cognitive strategies are all done in the preparatory segment of the lesson. Generally, this takes the form of a discus-

STRUGGLING READERS

Because it provides maximum guidance, the directed reading activity is especially effective with struggling readers.

sion. Key vocabulary words are written on the board. When discussing each word, the teacher points to it on the board so that students become familiar with it in print. Here is a sample DRA for a text segment on Gettysburg.

Directed Reading Activity

Step 1: Preparation

Have you ever played on a team that was overconfident? What happened? We have just read about Confederate victories at Second Bull Run and Chancellorsville. How do you think General Lee was feeling? Do you think he might have been overconfident? Lee decided to invade Gettysburg, but the North concluded that it had **strategic value** because so many roads led to Gettysburg. If you controlled Gettysburg, you could keep Southern soldiers from using those roads. Northern troops were sent to Gettysburg, and the two sides met almost by accident. No one had planned to have a battle there. But soon thousands of soldiers had gathered. Being **overconfident,** Lee decided on a **frontal attack.** What do you think a **frontal attack** might be? Instead of **maneuvering** around the enemy soldiers, you order a **direct assault.** You attack them directly. You try to go through the main parts of their lines. You try to hit a weak spot, but you may attack a place where an enemy commander has **concentrated his forces,** which means that he has gathered most of his soldiers at a certain place.

Read the section on the Battle of Gettysburg, from pages 63 to 69. Find out who won the battle and why and what effects this had on the war. As you read, try to picture the battles. Try to imagine what their battlefields looked like and what they sounded like. The map on page 67 shows the main places where the battle was fought.

Step 2: Silent Reading of Selection

Students read silently individually, or they may read in small cooperative groups.

Step 3: Discussion

The teacher begins the discussion with the purpose questions: Who won the battle? Why did the North win? What were the effects of the battle on the war? Why did Lee invade Pennsylvania? What mistakes did he make? What might have happened had he listened to Longstreet? How many men were lost at Gettysburg on both sides? (Figures are easily forgotten. This is a good point to model the strategy of looking back over a selection and skimming to find this fact.) How do you think Lee felt about the loss? As you read about the battles, what pictures came to mind? What sounds did you imagine?

Step 4: Rereading

Although rereading is listed as a separate step, it often occurs spontaneously during the discussion of the selection. For instance, during the discussion, students went back to the selection to obtain facts that they didn't recall and also to clarify and expand responses. Because student's basic understanding of the selection was adequate, there was no need for a total rereading, only some lookbacks.

Step 5: Follow-Up

This step, too, is optional. Some possible follow-ups might include reading Crane's *The Red Badge of Courage* or viewing a video on the Battle of Gettysburg.

Directed Reading–Thinking Activity

■ The **directed reading-thinking activity** (DR-TA) is an adaptation of the directed reading activity in which readers use preview and prediction strategies to set their own purposes for reading.

The DRA is primarily a teacher-directed lesson. The DR-TA **(directed reading-thinking activity)** has been designed to get students more involved. In a DR-TA, the teacher leads them to establish purposes for reading and to decide when these purposes have been fulfilled. Because it involves making predictions based on what students know, the DR-TA works best when students have background knowledge to bring to the selection. If students are lacking in background, the DRA is a better choice.

By nature, we have a tendency to look ahead, to predict what will happen. Stauffer (1969, 1970), the creator of the DR-TA, based the approach on our tendency to predict and hypothesize. Predicting and hypothesizing activate our background knowledge. They also pique students' curiosity and cause them to become more active readers. As they discuss their predictions and listen to the predictions of others, students' back-

EXEMPLARY TEACHING

USING AN ADAPTED DRA

Using an adaptation of the DRA know as SRE (Scaffolded Reading Experience), Rothenberg, a high school language arts teacher, helped her class of underachieving students read and appreciate *Macbeth* (Rothenberg & Watts, 1997). Prereading instruction focused on building a concept of literary tragedy and conveying a sense of the setting of *Macbeth*, Scotland in the eleventh century. To help students activate their prior knowledge, elements of *Macbeth* were compared to elements of contemporary works. There was also a minilesson on the structure of a play as literature. Students were shown how to use visualization, a strategy taught earlier in the year, to help them get a better sense of the play's action. Preparatory discussions and teacher-posed questions were used to guide each day's reading of the play. Students also dramatized the play. In addition, students kept a journal of their reactions to the play and their reflections.

As a follow-up activity, pairs of students responded to a statement in an account of Richard Nixon's death in which the former president was referred to as a "Shakespearean hero of tragic proportion." Students also viewed a film version of *Macbeth* and noted ways in which the movie version altered or affirmed their overall impression of the play.

Rothenberg successfully combined reading and literary instruction. With the careful scaffolding afforded by the structure of her instructional framework, she made the text accessible to these below-level readers. Building upon their enthusiasm, she encouraged students to create personal interpretations of the play. She also helped students relate the work to their lives and current events. She made the play come alive. Students both understood and appreciated the play.

ground is built. The DR-TA has the same five steps that the DRA has, but they are implemented differently.

Directed Reading-Thinking Activity

Step 1: Preparation

In this step, the teacher determines students' background, activates prior knowledge, and builds background and vocabulary as necessary. The major difference is that the teacher leads students to predict what the selection will be about. Their predictions are based on a survey of the selection. The teacher directs students to examine the title of the selection to be read, headings and subheads, illustrations, and the introductory paragraph, if there is one. Based on this survey, which should take no longer than a few minutes, the teacher asks the class what they think the selection will tell or what information it will present. The teacher also asks students to justify their predictions with why-do-you-think-so questions. This leads students to think more deeply about the selection and to make better use of the survey. Students' predictions are recorded on the chalkboard. As predictions are being discussed and recorded, the teacher can assess students' background. If background is very limited—if students have very little to say about the topic—the teacher can build background. The teacher can also highlight key vocabulary and concepts. Not every student need offer a prediction; however, every student should either have her or his own prediction or endorse one that has been recorded. After all the student predictions have been recorded, ask if anyone has a prediction not recorded. Record additional predictions. Then ask students to show by raising their hands which prediction they favor: How many favor the first prediction, the second, etc.? Students are then given a purpose for reading: to assess their predictions.

If the selection is lengthy or complex, it can be broken up into sections. For informational text, students can make a prediction based on the subhead and then read and discuss the section covered by the subhead before moving on. For a story or selection without a subhead, the teacher can note logical stopping places where old predictions can be discussed and new ones can be made. Breaking a selection up in this way makes it easier to read. Students grasp one section before moving on to the next.

Step 2: Silent Reading

Students read silently until they are able to evaluate their predictions; this might mean a single page, several pages, or a whole chapter. Students are encouraged to modify their initial predictions if they find information that runs counter to them.

Step 3: Discussion

This stage is almost identical to Step 3 of the DRA, except that it begins with the consideration of the class's predictions. If students' predictions turned out to be accurate, they can discuss information that supports them. They might also read passages that justify their predictions. If there is a disagreement about the adequacy of a prediction, students can read passages to support their positions. If students' predictions turn out not to be accurate and they changed them as they read, they can tell how and why they modified their predictions. During the discussion, emphasis should be placed on the reasoning processes involved and on students' willingness to alter predictions in the light of new information rather than on the rightness or wrongness of predictions.

Step 4: Rereading

This is the same as Step 4 of the DRA.

Step 5: Follow-Up

This is the same as Step 5 of the DRA.

Here is how a DR-TA might be used with the classic short story by James Thurber, "The Secret Life of Walter Mitty." The teacher might provide the following pre-reading guidance: "Read the title. What do you think the phrase a secret life means? What do you think this story might be about? What makes you think that? Does anyone have a different prediction? Read to the top of page 391. See how your predictions come out."

Students read to the top of the page and discover that Walter Mitty has been dreaming that he was the courageous commander of a hydroplane. The students discuss their predictions in light of what they have just read. The important point isn't whether the predictions are accurate but whether they were able to make reasonable predictions and whether making predictions helped to activate their background and made them more active and more productive readers. As they discuss their predictions and Walter Mitty's actions, students will undoubtedly note that he is a dreamer. As they predict, read, and discuss additional sections, they will probably discover that he is downtrodden and browbeaten. As part of the discussion, they might note the influence of movies and reading on his daydreams. They might also discuss times when they have escaped into daydreams. This could be a possible writing topic.

The DR-TA is designed to be used with both fiction and nonfiction, but probably works better with fiction. One advantage of using the DR-TA with informational text is that you can divide the piece into brief sections and also that you are getting students to think about what the selection is trying to explain to them. Here is a script recounting a segment of a DR-TA lesson with a seventh grade class reading a segment of a trade book on plate tectonics, *Our Patchwork Planet* (Sattler, 1995). Note in the segment how the teacher is accepting of predictions but prompts students to explain the reasoning behind their predictions. Although the discussions are student-centered, the teacher does step in to make sure that students grasp key concepts and vocabulary. The teacher wants to make sure that students know what a continent is and where the continents are located, since this is crucial to an understanding of the selection. The teacher prompts the students to use context to derive the meaning of *marine*. Through the discussion, the teacher also makes sure that the students have gotten the gist of the section and are ready to move on to the next section. Using a prediction strategy fosters comprehension because students will be unable to make reasonable predictions if they don't have a basic grasp of what they have read so far.

■ DR-TA Lesson

Teacher: Read the title. What do you think this section will be about? What do you think we will find out?

Student 1: The title is "Unlocking Earth's Mysteries."

Teacher: What are some of Earth's mysteries?

Student 2: How deserts were formed.

Teacher: Why do you think that?

Student 2: The photograph on the page shows a desert.

(Teacher writes this and other predictions on the board.)

Teacher: Does anyone have a different prediction?

Student 3: I think it might tell why Antarctica is covered with ice. The picture shows sheets of ice in Antarctica.

Student 4: I think it will tell why some parts of the world are hot and some are cold.

Student 5: I predict that the section will tell how the Earth has changed because one of the pictures shows a fossil.

Teacher: Excellent predictions. Read page 5 and see how your predictions play out.

(Students read page 5 silently.)

Teacher: How did your predictions play out? Which one of the predictions comes closest to stating what the text described?

Student 5: The last prediction, the one about how the Earth has changed.

Teacher: How about the other predictions? Could they also be right?

Student 5: Yes. The rest of the article will probably tell how mountains and deserts were formed, but I'm not so sure it will tell why part of Earth is cold and part hot.

Teacher: What made scientists believe that Earth had changed?

Student 6: They found fossils of plants and plant-eating dinosaurs in Antarctica.

Student 3: They found that a glacier had once been in the middle of the Sahara Desert.

Student 5: They found animal fossils at the top of the Himalayan Mountains.

Teacher: That is something because the Himalayas are the tallest mountains in the world. But what was extra strange about finding animals at the top of the Himalayas? What kind of animals did they find?

Student 5: It says they were marine animals.

Teacher: What kind of animals are marine animals? Read the second paragraph and see if you can figure from context what marine animals are.

Student 5: (Reading from text) "Nor could marine animals swim to the top of the world's highest mountain—not if continents had always been where they are today." (p. 5)

Teacher: So what do you think marine animals are?

Student 5: Sea animals. Like fish. Because they could swim.

Teacher: Very good. Marine animals are sea animals, so finding sea animals at the top of the world's tallest mountain would be a surprise. By the way, the sentence mentions continents. What are continents and how many are there?

Student 7: Continents are big chunks of land. I believe there are seven: North America, South America, Africa, Asia, Europe, Arctic, and Antarctica.

Teacher: There is one more. It's the smallest continent.

Student 7: Oh yeah. Australia.

Teacher: Good. The Arctic isn't really a continent and some geographers say that Europe and Asia form one big continent known as Eurasia. (The teacher points to continents on a world map.) What do you predict the next section will tell us?

(Students make predictions and read the next section. They continue in this fashion until they have read the entire text.)

 **CHECKUP**

1. What are the steps in the instructional framework, DRA, and DR-TA?
2. What are the advantages and disadvantages of each technique?

KWL Plus: A Technique for Before, During, and After Reading

■ **KWL Plus** (Know, Want to Know, and Learn) is a technique designed to help readers build and organize background and seek out and reflect on key elements in a reading selection.

KWL Plus was created as researcher Donna Ogle and a number of classroom teachers sought a device to "build active personal reading of expository text" (Ogle, 1989, p. 206). KWL Plus (What I **K**now, What I **W**ant to Know, And What I **L**earned, **Plus** What I Still Want to Find Out) activates students' background knowledge, has them think about what they want to know or need to know, and, then, after reading, has them tell what they learned and what they would still like to find out. The before-reading stage of KWL is composed of four steps: brainstorming, categorizing, anticipating or predicting, and questioning. Brainstorming begins when the teacher asks the class what they know about a topic. If students are about to read a selection about acid rain, for example, the teacher writes the words *acid rain* on the board and asks students what they know about acid rain. Responses are written on the board and discussed. The group brainstorming activates prior knowledge so that students become more aware of what they know and they also learn from others. If a disagreement occurs about a piece of information or if students seem unsure of a fact, these situations can be used to create what-we-want-to-know questions. After brainstorming, students record their personal knowledge of acid rain in the first column of a KWL worksheet. One of the advantages of having a group brainstorming session first and writing responses on the chalkboard is that it helps students with the spelling of technical terms. In tryouts, some students were reluctant to write down what they knew if they were unsure of the spellings of some of the content words.

In one version of KWL, students filled in two what-I-know columns on their KWL worksheets. The first column told what they knew about the topic before previewing; the second told what they knew after previewing (Richardson & Morgan, 1997).

After writing what they know about acid rain, students categorize their knowledge. Brainstormed items already written on the board are grouped into categories. Students then label the items already recorded in the what-we-know column with letters that name the categories, as shown in Figure 5.2: c = causes, e = effects, and m = measures taken to reduce acid rain. Students also predict what categories of information the author might provide. This helps them anticipate the content of the text and organize the information as they read it. The teacher models the process of predicting categories by asking, "What kinds of information do you think this article will give us about acid rain?" and telling what he is thinking about as he tries to figure out possible categories of information. Students then volunteer their predictions. Possible categories of information are recorded at the bottom of the KWL worksheet. The KWL approach can be simplified by omitting the category phase.

After deciding on possible categories of information, the students compose questions. The class discusses what they want to know about acid rain. Questions are written on the chalkboard. The class records these questions in the second column of the worksheet. Each student might also compose and record her personal questions. The questions might be the same as or different from those created by the group or a combination of group and personal questions.

Using their questions as a guide, the class reads the text. After reading, students record their responses and then discuss what they learned. Information is organized, misconceptions are clarified, and emerging concepts are developed more fully. After the discussion, students enter what they learned as a group and personally in the third column. Based on this information, they cross out any misconceptions that they entered in the first column. If students still have unanswered questions or if new questions have cropped up, they can create a fourth column entitled What We Still Want to Find Out and enter their unanswered questions (Sippola, 1995). You might also discuss with the class how they might go about finding the answers to the questions they still have. If the information that students have is important and if they need to retain it for a test or future units of study, you might also have them create a semantic map incorporating the information they have learned and also compose a summary based on the map (Ogle, 1996). The ultimate purpose of KWL is to lead students to ask KWL questions automatically as they read. A completed KWL worksheet is presented in Figure 5.2.

■ Adaptations of KWL

In one version of KWL known as Six-Step Topical Guide, students divide what they know into two categories: what I know definitely and what I think I know. They then read to verify their knowledge. After reading and discussing their reading, they note which of the items they listed are accurate, which are inaccurate, and which

STRUGGLING READERS

KWL was specifically designed for secondary students who were having difficulty understanding their textbooks. KWL builds on what students know and makes them active participants.

FIGURE 5.2

KWL Plus Chart

Name: _____ Date: _____

Topic: *ACID RAIN* _____

What We Know	What We Want to Know	What We Learned	What We Still Want to Know
C Acid rain is caused by dirty air. C Cars, trucks, and buses are the main causes of dirty air. C Factories also cause dirty air. E Acid rain harms forests. E Acid rain harms streams and lakes. E Acid rain kills fish. M Using tall smoke stacks helps cut down on acid rain.	How does acid rain form?	Burning coal, oil, and gasoline create sulfur dioxide and oxides of nitrogen. Acid rain forms when sulfur dioxide and oxides of nitrogen combine with water, oxygen, and oxides. Plants that make electricity give off 70% of the sulfur dioxide and 30% of the oxides of nitrogen. Cars also give off these pollutants.	Is acid rain getting better or worse? Where is acid rain the worst? Do other countries have an acid rain problem? If so, what are they doing about it?
	Is acid rain getting better or worse? Does acid rain do any damage besides harming forests and streams and lakes?	 Acid rain damages buildings and statues.	
	Does acid rain harm people?	Acid rain causes tiny particles of dirt to float in the air. These particles worsen lung diseases such as asthma and bronchitis.	
	Where is acid rain the worst?	Tall smoke stacks carry particles higher into the air. The particles are carried by the winds to distant places.	
	What is being done to lessen acid rain?	Cars and power plants are reducing their emissions.	

they are unsure of. They then record questions that they still have and possible sources for answers to these questions (Egan, 1999).

One problem with KWL is that students might neglect to pose questions about vital areas. In one adaptation of KWL, the teacher adds focus questions. These might be key questions that grow out of the objectives for the unit being studied, or they may be modifications of questions posed at the end of the chapter (Huffman, 1998). For each question, students tell what they know, what they want to know, and what they learned.

A flexible technique, KWL has been used in surprising ways. One teacher used KWL as an introduction to the reading of a Shakespeare play. Students were asked two questions: What do you know about Shakespeare, *Macbeth*, and literary tragedy? And what do you want to know? Students' responses were used to assess students' background knowledge and also techniques and activities that might be used to help them read *Macbeth* with understanding and appreciation (Rothenberg & Watts, 1997).

CHECKUP

1. What are the steps in KWL Plus and its adaptation?
2. What are the main benefits of using KWL?

BEFORE-READING TECHNIQUES

Before-reading teaching techniques provide an overview of the selection to be read, activate prior knowledge, build background and vocabulary, set goals, and construct strategies for reading and reasoning. Before-reading techniques feature the anticipation guide, PReP, the structured overview, the pre-reading survey, and drawing and writing before reading.

Anticipation Guide

At this point, you are in a position to judge the effectiveness of the anticipation guide. An anticipation guide appears at the beginning of each chapter of this text. An **anticipation guide** consists of a list of three to six controversial or debatable statements. Students respond to the statements by indicating whether or not they agree with them. The statements are carefully worded so as to challenge students to think over what they know and also to arouse their curiosity and interest. An anticipation guide gets students involved in thinking about a topic before they read about it. In addition to activating their prior knowledge, it may also highlight erroneous concepts that they may have about a topic. Anticipation guides, by bringing erroneous beliefs out into the open, make these easier to deal with. However, the anticipation guide only works if the students have some knowledge of the topic. Otherwise, they have nothing to think about or discuss. Steps for creating and using an anticipation guide are outlined below (Head & Readence, 1986).

■ An **anticipation guide** is an instructional technique designed to activate and have students reflect on background knowledge.

Anticipation Guide Lesson

Step 1: Identifying Major Concepts

List two or three major ideas that you wish students to learn.

Step 2: Determining Students' Background

Considering students' general knowledge and beliefs about the content of the selection to be read, what misunderstandings might they have about the topic? List these. Also consider the attitudes and values of the community. Students in an area that has coal mines or oil wells might have different opinions about using fossil fuels than students who live in a community that is attempting to use alternative sources of energy.

Step 3: Creating the Guide

Compose three to six statements that incorporate the major concepts that you listed in Step 1. Compose statements about ideas or events about which students may have misconceptions or doubts. Do not compose statements about areas in which students have no knowledge because they won't be able to say whether they agree or disagree. The most effective statements are those for which the students have enough information that they can respond but not so much that they won't be gaining new knowledge as they read. Avoid writing statements that are really true–false items and that don't require students to evaluate their knowledge, beliefs, and opinions (Head & Readence, 1986; Readence, Moore, & Rickelman, 2000). Opinion statements work better than factual statements. Settle on the statements that best fit the nature of the material to be read and students' goals for reading the material. Statements can be listed in order of coverage in the text, in an order that is most conducive to discussion, or from least to most important.

Step 4: Introducing the Guide

Explain the guide. It may be placed on the board or overhead or duplicated and distributed to students. Read the directions and the statements orally and ask students to respond to each statement by checking "Agree" or "Disagree." Students may work independently, in pairs, or in small groups. Small groups may be most effective in getting students to reflect on the topic and confront misconceptions.

Step 5: Discussing Responses

Discuss each statement. Students raise their hands to indicate whether they agree or disagree. Discuss students' reasons. Elicit at least one agree and one disagree statement for each item so students consider both sides of an issue. The discussion should help students open their minds as they assess these beliefs in relationship to the beliefs of others. The discussion should also motivate students to want to read so they can better evaluate their beliefs.

Step 6: Reading of Text

Summarize students' responses, highlighting areas of controversy or doubt. Then have students read the selection. As they read, they should consider their responses and those of others in light of the information presented in the text.

Step 7: Discussion of Text

Students again respond to the statements. Based on what they have read they can change their responses. Discuss the statements and students' responses once more. Emphasize changes in responses students may have made and the reasons for those changes.

Instead of using Agree and Disagree categories, you can have columns labeled as Author and Me in which the student checks statements with which he agrees and statements with which the author agrees. Another possibility is to have an Anticipation column, in which the student checks statements with which he agrees before reading the text, and a Reaction column, in which the student checks statements with which he agrees as a result of reading the text.

■ Extended Anticipation Guide

The extended anticipation guide adds a second part in which readers indicate whether or not they have found support in the text for their responses (Duffelmeyer, Baum, & Merkley, 1987). If they have not found support, they rewrite in their own words information from the text that conflicts with their beliefs. Because the extended anticipation guide requires the student to paraphrase information that conflicts with a misconception, it should be more effective in motivating students to revise erroneous information.

PReP

When presenting a new topic, it is important to have a sense of what students know about the topic. They may have limited or erroneous knowledge about the Spanish-American War, Reconstruction, the French Revolution, DNA, or cell division. A technique that combines assessment with the development of background knowledge and that also helps students activate prior knowledge is the **Pre-Reading Plan (PReP).** PReP is a three-step assessment–instructional procedure that helps the teacher determine what students know about a particular topic, how that information might be organized, and what kind of language the students use to describe or explain that knowledge. The teacher can then assess how much background and vocabulary might need to be developed before the students would be able to understand the text (Langer, 1981). For students who know a great deal about a topic, PReP can be used to help them organize and clarify their knowledge. For students who didn't realize how much they know, PReP can help them access their background knowledge. PReP can also help build knowledge for those whose background is limited or erroneous (Tierney & Readence, 2000). Here are the three steps in applying PReP.

■ The **Pre-Reading Plan** (PReP) is an instructional technique designed to help the teacher build background knowledge.

PReP Lesson

Step 1: Initial Associations with the Concept

Using a key word, phrase, or illustration from the text to be read as a prompt, say, "Tell me anything that comes to mind when you hear the words *United Nations.*" Students' responses are listed on the board.

Step 2: Reflections on Initial Associations

In order to assess students' associations with the key word or phrase, point to each student's response and ask a question about it. If one of the responses is the word *peace*, for instance, you might ask, "What makes you think of *peace?*" Students become aware of their network of associations and their own thinking as well as the associations and reasoning of the other students. They can consider, alter, accept, or reject ideas and associations as they become aware of their changing conceptions.

Step 3: Reformulation of Knowledge

To give students a chance to express associations that have been modified by the discussion, you might ask, "Based on what we have talked about, do you have any new ideas about the United Nations? Have you changed any of your ideas as a result of our discussion?" Since they have had a chance to think about their ideas, they usually are more refined at this point. The extent and depth of students' prior knowledge is reflected in their level of response during PReP. To determine the extent and quality of the students' prior knowledge, analyze their responses. Using the criteria supplied by Langer, outlined below, determine whether students seem to have much, some, or little knowledge:

STRUGGLING READERS

Because it provides an assessment of students' prior knowledge and a means for building background, PReP is an excellent device for use with students whose background is weak.

A. Much knowledge
Responses include superordinate concepts, definitions, analogies, or linking of the concept with another concept. The United Nations is like a world congress. Police force for the world. Organization devoted to peace of the world.

B. Some knowledge
Responses include examples, attributes, or defining characteristics. Gives food to hungry people. Place where countries talk over problems. Works for peace.

C. Little knowledge
Responses include low-level associations, such as words that sound like the stimulus word, or associations that aren't quite relevant. United. All together. Nations. Countries. Lots of people. It's in New York. Our class went there once.

During the PReP discussion, build concepts. Talk about why the United Nations was started and what it has done to promote peace. You might also lead students to see that the United Nations performs a number of humanitarian, research, and regulatory or advisory functions in addition to keeping the peace. Depending on the types of responses, students may need no instruction, a little, or extensive background building. Through building on what students know and using their concepts and language, you will be better able to give them the kind of preparation they need for reading a selection.

Structured Overview

In order to study how students read content materials, Barron (1969) took on the role of a student in a high school biology class, a subject in which he had little background. Overwhelmed by a long list of unfamiliar technical terms, he wondered how he would cope with all the new words. The solution was not long in coming:

> Later that evening, as I attempted to read the chapters associated with the unit, a simple fact began to dawn on me. *All the vocabulary words were related in some way.* I started to arrange the words in a diagram to depict relationships, occasionally adding terms from the two preceding units. Gradually, much of the content with which I had been struggling became clear. (pp. 172–173)

Out of this experience was born the structured overview. A **structured overview** builds on what students already know. It shows how new words in a selection that students are about to read or a unit that they are about to study are related to words that are familiar to them. For instance, students can better understand the word *mollusks* when they realize that the category includes *clams, snails, scallops, oysters,* and *octopuses.* The original structured overview was very much teacher directed and followed a series of six steps, as outlined below.

■ **A structured overview** is a graphic organizer in which the key concepts and vocabulary of a topic or unit of study are displayed. The structured overview is designed to help students relate new words and concepts to known words and concepts.

LESSON 5.5   Teaching a Structured Overview

Step 1: Selecting Key Concepts

Read over the selection or unit to be read and select two to four concepts or ideas that you wish to emphasize. In introducing a unit on diet, the teacher decided that she wanted to stress the following ideas:

- Macronutrients, micronutrients, water, and fiber are needed to keep our bodies healthy.
- Macronutrients include carbohydrates, proteins, and fats.
- Micronutrients include vitamins and minerals.

Step 2: Selecting Related Vocabulary

Analyze the vocabulary in the selection and choose words that you feel would be needed to understand the key ideas.

Step 3: Arranging Words

Arrange the words so that you show relationships. You might place words on cards so that they are easier to organize. Or you might use a piece of software, such as *Inspiration* (Inspiration Software), that is designed for the construction of graphic organizers.

Step 4: Inserting Known Words

Add words that the students already know so that they can relate new words to known words.

Step 5: Checking the Overview

Look over the overview. Are relationships clearly shown? Is the overview easy to understand? A completed overview is shown in Figure 5.3.

Step 6: Introducing the Overview

Place the overview on an overhead projector, chart paper, or the board. Point to the word *diet* and tell students that they will be reading about foods and other substances that we need to stay healthy. Ask them what they can tell about diet by examining the overview. Discuss the fact that in addition to food, the body needs water and fiber. Talk over the three main kinds of macronutrients and two main kinds of micronutrients and examples of each. Also discuss fibers. Clarify any concepts that seem confusing. Make any changes to the overview that seem necessary.

Keep the overview in a prominent place so that as students read about foods, they can refer to the overview. As students learn more about diet, encourage them to add to the overview. You may want to add sections that contain key words that give specific examples of sources of macronutrients and micronutrients.

■ Revised Structured Overview

The original structured overview is teacher directed and works well with students who have little background to bring to a topic. In the revised structured overview, students are more actively involved. Barron (1979) found that when students played a role in constructing an overview, they learned more. He also found that the structured overview worked well when it was used to organize information after the students had read the target sections.

The revised overview begins with brainstorming (Estes & Vaughn, 1985). Place the key concept on the board and discuss it. A concept such as *diet* would probably not work well for a prereading structured overview because students may have little background to bring to the concept. However, you might use a more familiar concept, such as *food*. As the students respond, probe and supply prompts, asking such questions as: What are the main kinds of foods that you need? What are some examples of fats? Proteins? What do you need besides food to stay healthy?

After listing on the board what students know, you can add some of your own items, especially if key concepts were omitted. You and the class would then group items that go together and devise a title or category name for them. The items

FIGURE 5.3

Structured Overview

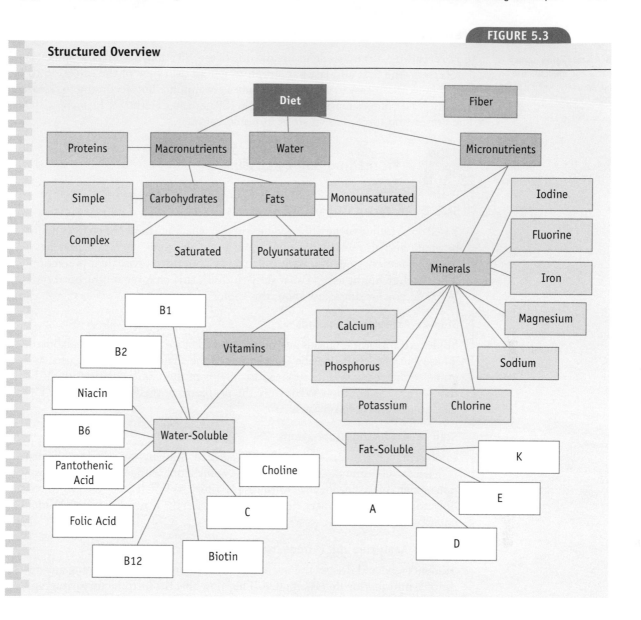

would then be arranged in a structured overview. Again, at this point, you should feel free to add important concepts or vocabulary that have not been mentioned. You should also review the overview and tie it in with the students' purpose for reading the selection. The students might use the overview to predict what the selection will be about. Students could also add to the overview after they have read the selection.

Prereading Survey

■ A **prereading survey** is a strategy students use to get an overview of a selection.

In a **prereading survey,** students use the title of the selection, headings, graphics, and, if necessary, the first and last paragraph to get an overview of the selection to be read. The survey is easy to use and takes only a few minutes but, according to research, it can increase comprehension by as much as 100 percent (Tierney & Readence, 2000). The prereading survey has six steps, as noted below.

LESSON 5.6

Prereading Survey Lesson

Step 1: Analyzing Title and Illustrations

Based on a reading of the title, students predict what they think the chapter might be about and also note what they know about the topic. If the chapter has a main illustration, students examine that and elaborate or revise their prediction. The teacher might ask: "What do you think this chapter might be about? What do you already know about this topic?"

Step 2: Analyzing Subheads

Students transform subheads into questions, which are placed on the chalkboard. These questions help provide an overview of the chapter and are also used as a guide to the reading. The subhead Problems of the Confederation might be turned into the question What were the problems of the Confederation? The questions are written on the board.

Step 3: Analyzing Illustrations

Photos, drawings, maps, and graphs are analyzed. Students are asked to tell what added information about the chapter these items supply. Students are asked questions about a map showing the Northwest Territory: Why is it called the Northwest Territory? Which country held land to the north of the territory? Which country held land to the west?

Step 4: Analyzing the Introductory Paragraph

Students read and discuss the introduction and summary, again noting any additional information that is supplied. They note that the introductory paragraph states that the United States had gained its independence and had formed a government, but never before had a democratic form of government ever included so many people scattered over such a wide area.

Step 5: Analyzing the Concluding Paragraph

Reading the summary can provide another highlight of the main ideas of the chapter and provide additional preparation for reading the chapter.

Step 6: Writing the Main Idea Statement

Based on their survey, students compose a statement that they believe encompasses the main idea of the chapter. The teacher briefly reviews the main idea statement and questions. The students then read to have each of the questions listed on the board answered. The main idea statement might be The United States was governing itself under the Articles of Confederation, but there were some problems. Questions include:

What were the Articles of Confederation?

What was the problem with the Northwest Territory?

What was the Land Ordinance of 1785?

What was the Northwest Ordinance?

What were some of the Confederation's problems?

What was Shays's Rebellion?

Drawing before Reading

Most prereading activities involve some sort of verbal interchange. One way of having students activate prior knowledge is to ask them to draw what they know about a topic. This works especially well with English language learners. Working first with an adult class and then with primary-level pupils, McConnell (1992–1993) used drawings as a way of having students convey and refine their concepts of a rain forest and the greenhouse effect. When students seemed unable to convey in words their concepts of a rain forest, McConnell asked them to draw their impressions of it. Other students were asked to sketch their concepts of the greenhouse effect. The results were startling. Students' concepts varied widely, as did their perspectives. Some focused on the causes of the greenhouse effect; others on the effects; still others depicted what the greenhouse effect meant to them personally. The students shared their drawings in a small group and noted similarities and differences. Later, the class as a whole discussed the drawings.

> **ENGLISH LANGUAGE LEARNERS**
> Drawing is a good way for ELLs to show what they know.

After the class discussed the features of the drawings and the teacher listed them on the board, she and the class created a semantic map of the topic. Students then read an article about rain forests. After discussing the article, students revised their drawings in light of what they had learned. Because they had learned so much, some students created entirely new drawings.

As a final step, students discussed changes in their drawings and the differences between before and after depictions. Students frequently justified or clarified their changes by reading pertinent passages from the text. Students also sought out other books on rain forests for additional information about the topic to help them with their drawings.

Using drawings as a springboard and integrating them with discussion and reading of the text, the students activated schemata, set a purpose for reading, and created a framework for organizing new knowledge. As McConnell (1992–1993) noted, drawings provide "a visible and explicit record of learning which can be reflected upon, altered, and developed" (p. 269). In addition to helping students explore prior knowledge and develop purposes for reading, drawings also fostered comprehension and language use and helped clarify concepts that are easily misunderstood. And they did all this in a novel, interesting way.

Writing before Reading

Instead of being asked to tell what they know about a topic, students can be asked to write what comes to mind when they think of of it. Free writing is a kind of written brainstorm. Students are asked to write whatever they want for a period of about three to five minutes about Canada, solar power, or a similar topic. One advantage of free writing is that it is nonthreatening. It also gives students a little think time because they have a few minutes to respond, as opposed to the immediate response usually required in a prereading discussion. And it allows everyone to participate.

 ✔ *CHECKUP*

1. What are some effective before-reading techniques?
2. How might each technique be taught?

DURING-READING TECHNIQUES

During reading, strategic readers construct meaning. Using chapter organization and the structure of the text as a framework, they seek out main ideas or themes and supporting details. Distinguishing between relevant and irrelevant details, they seek essential information. As they read, they integrate information from text with prior knowledge, make inferences, and make judgments about what they read. They may create images of processes or events described in the text. Strategic readers also regulate their rate of reading and monitor their understanding of the passage. They may reread or seek clarification if their comprehension breaks down. During-reading instructional techniques include guides and glosses, teacher-created devices designed to foster comprehension; frame matrices; information maps; and adjunct or embedded questions.

Study Guides

■ A **study guide** is a device that contains questions and/or suggestions designed to help students better comprehend text.

Study guides that foster higher-level thinking can be useful in developing conceptual understanding. However, the guides need to be complemented by discussions that help students construct and reconstruct their understandings. Study guides, or reading guides, as they are sometimes called, are instructional aids designed to help students during as well as after reading. They serve a dual function. They lead students to essential content and they provide guidance in the use of effective reading strategies. Study guides range in complexity from very simple guides designed to help students master basic facts to guides that require higher levels of thinking and application. Guides can include fill-in-the-blank, true–false, or matching items. Or they can feature graphic organizers or questions designed to help students reflect on what they have learned. The most effective guides foster conceptual understanding and reflection. Procedures for creating a study guide are outlinedon the nest page:

1. Analyze the selection to be read. Note the major concepts or principles that you think students should learn. Make a note of the sections that students must read to grasp these concepts.
2. Consider elements of the text that may pose problems for students, such as complex concepts, technical vocabulary, figurative language, confusing explanations, or poor organization.
3. Determine the dominant organizational patterns of the chapter, such as comparison/contrast, sequential, process/explanation, or other (see Chapter 4 for a description of patterns). Note that more than one pattern may be used.
4. Determine strategies that students can use to grasp key concepts.
5. Construct a study guide that leads students to essential content, helps them overcome possible obstacles to comprehension, and guides them in the use of effective strategies. Also make the study guide as interesting as you can. Pose intriguing questions. Include items that challenge the reader. Where appropriate, include gamelike activities, such as crossword puzzles.

■ Pattern Guides

Determining the dominant pattern in a section of text promotes both comprehension and retention (Herber, 1970). For example, if readers realize that the author is using a comparison/contrast pattern to describe the status of the North and the South during the Civil War, they can mentally sort the information into the proper categories. If readers know that a piece has a process/sequential organization, they can mentally keep track of the main steps.

Pattern guides come in varied formats. A pattern guide may include a partially completed outline in which just the main ideas are included and the reader is asked

Study guides help students focus on important information.

to supply supporting details. Or it may involve matching causes and effects or a compare/contrast pattern (Estes & Vaughn, 1985). The sample cause–effect pattern guide in Figure 5.4 helps students not only obtain essential information from the section but also organize that information so they can note both positive and negative effects.

■ Concept Guides

Concept guides focus on one or more key concepts. Through questions or other activities, they help students see how the concepts were formed. A sample concept guide is presented in Figure 5.5.

■ Levels of Thinking Guide

Levels of thinking guides are designed to foster comprehension at three levels: literal (comprehending, organizing), interpretive (elaborating), and applied (elaborating) (Herber & Herber, 1993). To construct a levels of thinking guide, create questions or activities that incorporate understanding and organizing essential information, drawing conclusions, evaluating, and/or applying.

After students complete the guides, they meet in groups of four or five and discuss their responses. The emphasis is on explaining and supporting responses.

FIGURE 5.4

Pattern Guide

Chapter 18: Prosperity and Change

In this section of the text, the authors use a cause–effect pattern to explain that automobiles had both positive and negative effects on life in the United States. Read a Changing Way of Life, page 420. List some of the positive effects:

1. _____
2. _____
3. _____
4. _____

Read Automobiles Brought Problems, page 421. List some of the negative effects.

1. _____
2. _____
3. _____
4. _____

For Discussion

Based on a consideration of positive and negative effects, what would you conclude about the overall effect of the automobile on the way people lived? _____

_____

FIGURE 5.5

Concept Study Guide

Our Patchwork Planet by Helen Roney Sattler

Read "Unlocking Earth's Mysteries."

Creating and testing hypotheses. Through observations and careful thought, scientists create hypotheses. They then use experiments or observations to test their hypotheses.

1. What observations led scientist to believe that the Earth had changed?

   a. _____

   b. _____

   c. _____

2. What observation led scientists to believe that Africa and South America had once been part of the same continent?

   _____

   Look at a map that shows the continents of Africa and South America. Do you agree with this observation? Why or why not?

   _____

3. How did scientists test the hypothesis that South America and Africa had once been part of the same continent?

   a. _____

   b. _____

4. What conclusion did scientists draw about the cause of the changes in the Earth? _____

Where possible, students should be prepared to refer to the text to support their responses. After small groups have completed their discussions, the class meets as a whole. A representative from each group summarizes his or her group's discussion. Students may also ask questions at this point. The teacher sums up the group's response and clarifies any confusing points.

Three-level guides can be composed of statements rather than questions. Students check statements with which they agree or that seem accurate. These guides are more thought-provoking than traditional guides because students must think about and reject statements with which they disagree or which seem inaccurate and provide support for statements that are correct or with which they agree. Responding becomes a more active process.

Three-level guides apply the processes of QAR (Question-Answer Relationships). Literal statements are constructed so that justification can be found in a single place. Although also literal, integration statements involve using information from two or more places in the text. Interpretative statements require that the student put together information from the text with information from her own background of experience. Application statements require students to apply the information in some way. A sample three-level thinking guide is shown in Figure 5.6.

■ Selective and Process Reading Guides

Knowing what is valuable information and what is not is an important skill. Some students believe that everything is important and may become overwhelmed when they try to learn every detail. A selective reading guide can be used to highlight the most essential information in a chapter.

Process guides focus on strategies that students can use to understand and retain content. A process guide tells students how a selection should be processed and provides suggestions for strategy use. Process guides are especially helpful to students who lack strategies or aren't sure which strategies to use. They can tell students when students can skim and when they need to read carefully, when questioning

---

FIGURE 5.6

Three-Level Guide

Read "Oscar de la Renta," pages 208–213 of *Latino Biographies*.

A. Literal: Using the dates below, make a time line of the key events in Oscar de la Renta's life. Most of the key events are given a definite date. However, you sometimes have to put two pieces of information together to get a date. For instance, the story does not tell what year Oscar de la Renta left the Dominican Republic, but it does say that he was 18 when he left, and it gives the year of his birth, so you can put the two pieces of information together and this tells you about when he left.

1932 | about 1950 | 1963 | 1964 | 1966 | 1967 | 1982 | 1983 | 1985 | 1989

B. Interpretive: The answers to the following questions are not directly stated, but they are implied. Use information from the story and think about what you have read to answer the questions.

1. What do you think would have happened to Oscar if his mother hadn't arranged for him to leave home?

   _____

2. Why did Oscar de la Renta give up painting?

   _____

3. What makes you think that Oscar de la Renta is a kind man?

   _____

4. What makes you think that Oscar de la Renta is very rich?

   _____

C. Applied: Read the following statements. Think about the events in Oscar de la Renta's life and the kind of person he was. Put this information together with what you know and believe from your own experience. Then, based on what you read and your own experience, put a check mark next to each statement you agree with. Be prepared to discuss with members in your group the statements that you checked.

_____ 1. Money can't buy happiness.

_____ 2. Helping others is more important than making money or becoming famous.

_____ 3. Enjoying your work is more important than making a lot of money.

_____ 4. People need people.

_____ 5. By helping others we help ourselves.

is a helpful strategy, and when summarizing can foster learning. A sample process-ing guide is shown in Figure 5.7.

Gloss

Glosses are study guides in which the teacher writes explanatory notes to students (Singer & Donlan, 1989). The glosses, which are written in the margins, can explore difficult vocabulary, explain confusing passages, highlight key ideas, or help students relate new information to what they already know.

■ A **gloss** is a study guide in which the teacher writes explanatory notes to stu-dents to provide them with added guidance as they read.

Process Guide

Chapter 4: Private Sector Decisions: Consumers and Businesses

Putting ideas into your own words and thinking how they apply to your life make them easier to understand. This also helps you to remember important ideas. Read the following sections. After reading each section, answer the questions **in your own words.** Read a section and answer the questions before going on to the next section. The ideas build on each other. Understanding the first section will make the second section that much easier to under-stand. And unless you understand the first two sections, you will have difficulty understanding the third section.

Private Ownership—Private Benefit, pages 52–53

1. What are private goods?

_____

2. What are some private goods that you own?

_____

3. What are public goods? What are some public goods that you use?

_____

4. How do private goods differ from public goods?

_____

5. Are most goods in the U.S. public or private? Explain.

_____

Private Sector—Private Choice, pages 53–54

The key idea in this section is the economic principle that "Individuals will choose the alternative that produces the maximum benefit or the minimum private cost to them."

6. How would you put this in your own words?

_____

7. Give three examples of ways in which you have used this principle.

_____

_____

Efficiency and Individual Choice, pages 54–55

8. This section applies the principle that we make choices based on maximum benefit or minimum cost. Describe a time when you made a choice based on maximum benefit or minimum cost.

_____

9. What is efficiency? How does efficiency fit in with the principle of making choices based on maximum benefit or minimum cost?

_____

10. What happens to businesses that are not efficient? Describe a business that failed because it was not efficient.

_____

_____

FIGURE 5.8

Megalopolis

 MEGALOPOLIS

FOCUS

- *What are the major cities of Megalopolis? What characteristics make each city important?*

- *What challenges do the cities of Megalopolis face?*

REGION The ongoing commercial and industrial growth of the Atlantic seaboard has led to the development of a continuous urban corridor. This corridor, called Megalopolis, was named by a French geographer in the 1960s. Gradually, the five major nodal cities of the Northeastern United States—Boston, New York, Philadelphia, Baltimore, and Washington, D.C.—spread toward each other. (See the map on page 121.) Excluding Washington, D.C., the original growth was due to the cities' good port sites, which linked the nation's interior to world trade routes.

The boundaries of Megalopolis continue to change and expand. Expansion has been most rapid as new highways allow commuters easy access to the cities. Subways, high-speed rails, and airline shuttles offer commuters an alternative to the automobile. In fact, this nodal region is connected by some of the densest railroad and interstate highway networks in the nation. The region has some of the world's busiest seaports and most crowded airports, as well.

From *World Geography Today,* Revised Edition, Pupil's Edition. Copyright © 1997 by Holt Rinehart and Winston. Reprinted by permission of the publisher.

Imagine you are a tenth-grader reading the passage in Figure 5.8. What difficulties might you encounter as you attempt to understand the passage?

Now read the passage again, this time with the aid of the gloss shown in Figure 5.9. How does the gloss help? Are there items not glossed that could use explanatory notes? Chances are there are a number of annotations that could be added, but glossing should be used sparingly. Use no more than two or three glosses per page. Otherwise, the glosses become burdensome and students are overwhelmed (Stewart & Cross, 1993).

The gloss may define hard words, explain a key concept, paraphrase a difficult passage, tap prior knowledge, point out a key point, suggest a strategy for reading the passage, or note a helpful visual. Various kinds of questions might be included: those that help a student relate new information to old, those that help a student use a key comprehension strategy, or those that help a student set a purpose for reading (Richgels & Hansen, 1984).

Illustrations as well as text can be glossed. A gloss can be used to provide information to students for whom the text is simply so overwhelming that they can't read it, no matter how much assistance you provide. You can use glosses to direct them to maps, charts, and illustrations so that they can make some use of the text. Your gloss might also contain a summary of the most essential information written in easy-to-understand language.

To create a gloss, first examine the text and decide what you want the students to get out of reading the text. List two or three key concepts. Then note any elements in the text that will hinder students' understanding of the key concepts. Create a gloss that helps students cope with these difficult elements. The gloss may be written in the margin of the text and then photocopied and distributed to students. Or you can line up a sheet of paper next to the text and write your gloss notes next to the target text. Make copies and distribute them to students.

Frame Matrix

Each discipline has its own way of looking at reality and its own tools of investigation. Each discipline also has its own questions. Science asks such questions as What

Gloss for Megalopolis, p. 127.

Mega means "very large" and polis means "city." Megalopolis is the name given to a row of five large cities that stretch from Washington, D.C., to Boston, Massachusetts. Find Megalopolis on the map on page 121.

 MEGALOPOLIS

As you read, keep these focus questions in mind:

FOCUS

- *What are the major cities of Megalopolis? What characteristics make each city important?*

- *What challenges do the cities of Megalopolis face?*

Megalopolis is said to be a corridor because it has heavily traveled highways, rail, and air routes.

A nodal city is one that is at the center of growth.

REGION The ongoing commercial and industrial growth of the Atlantic seaboard has led to the development of a continuous urban corridor. This corridor, called Megalopolis, was named by a French geographer in the 1960s. Gradually, the five major nodal cities of the Northeastern United States—Boston, New York, Philadelphia, Baltimore, and Washington, D.C.—spread toward each other. (See the map on page 121.) Excluding Washington, D.C., the original growth was due to the cities' good port sites, which linked the nation's interior to world trade routes.

What key to growth is being described in this paragraph?

The boundaries of Megalopolis continue to change and expand. Expansion has been most rapid as new highways allow commuters easy access to the cities. Subways, high-speed rails, and airline shuttles offer commuters an alternative to the automobile. In fact, this nodal region is connected by some of the densest railroad and interstate highway networks in the nation. The region has some of the world's busiest seaports and most crowded airports, as well.

From *World Geography Today,* Revised Edition, Pupil's Edition. Copyright © 1997 by Holt Rinehart and Winston. Reprinted by permission of the publisher.

is it? How might it be classified? What are its parts or systems? How do its parts or systems operate? What laws or regularities does it follow? The social studies ask such questions as What happened? When did it happen? What were its causes? What were its effects? What conclusions can be drawn? Math is concerned with questions of measurement and quantifiable relationships. Knowing the questions that a discipline asks helps us to determine the categories of information that it provides. By determining categories of information, we are organizing the information presented.

Learning the content of a subject matter is easier if students know the kinds of questions to ask. The questions help determine what information is most important and how that information is organized. Texts that answer implied or explicit content area questions are known as **frames** (Armbruster & Anderson, 1981). One device designed to take advantage of frame organization is the frame matrix.

A simple but effective device, the **frame matrix** has two intersecting parts: a frame, which highlights essential categories of information, and the matrix, which allows the comparison of two or more elements in terms of the frames or categories (see Figure 5.10). A frame for countries might include *location, area, population, natural resources, economy*, and *government*. The matrix would be the countries being compared: United States, Canada, India, China, Russia. A history frame, reflecting the content area's concern with causes and effects, might detail the major causes of the Revolutionary War. A student who knows what questions are important in history would know to ask, "What were the causes of the Revolutionary War? What were the effects?" The student could also take advantage of the cause–effect pattern in the writing to better understand the material, to see cause–effect relationships, and to organize the material for study purposes.

To construct a frame matrix, create the essential categories of information for a topic. Then note how each category might be subdivided. If you are familiar with a topic, you might set up a tentative frame and then verify it by checking the text that students are about to read (Armbruster, 1996). You might also check the topic in an encyclopedia. Encyclopedias often organize their articles around major categories or frame types of questions.

A frame matrix helps students organize information and see similarities and differences. It facilitates comparing and contrasting because categories being analyzed

■ **Frames** are categories of information that answer implied or stated questions.

■ A **frame matrix** has two intersecting parts: a frame, which provides essential categories of information, and the matrix, which allows the comparison of two or more elements in terms of the frames or categories.

FIGURE 5.10

Frame Matrix

Oceans of the World	Arctic	Atlantic	Indian	Pacific
Location	top of world	touches Europe, Africa, North America, & South America	touches Africa, Australia, East Indies, & Asia	touches North America, South America, Africa, & Asia
Size	5,440,000 square miles	31,530,000 square miles	28,356,000 square miles	63,000,380 square miles
Average Depth	5,010 feet	14,000 feet	13,000 feet	14,000 feet

are lined up side by side. Frame matrices are most effective when the text focuses on major categories of information.

Information Map

An adaptation of the frame matrix known as the **information map** restates categories as questions and is useful for studying and self-testing. In an information map, categories on the left (the frame items) are translated into questions, which makes them easier for students to respond to. Students can self-test themselves by covering the answers in the matrix cells and asking the questions on the left. After reciting the answers to themselves, they can verify their responses and review items that posed problems. Information maps can be constructed for a limited topic, such as comparing types of fog, or they can be created for topics studied over a full unit or semester (Heiman & Slomianko, 1986). An information map could be constructed comparing all fifty states, chemical elements, or the major systems in the body. An extended information map might be constructed over several months or even an entire semester and cover a portion of a wall.

> ■ An **information map** is an adaptation of a frame matrix that restates categories in question form.

Questions in an information map should seek essential information. The questions should also apply to all of the categories in the matrix. Questions should not be of the type that could be answered with a "yes" or a "no" (Heiman & Slomianko, 1986). A sample information map is presented in Figure 5.11.

Embedded Questions

One relatively easy way to provide guidance during reading is to use **embedded questions.** Most questions come at the end of a chapter. Questions at the end help the student summarize what was read but don't help with ongoing processing. Embedded questions are posed at key points in the text and help students process information in the text. Many students are passive readers and simply run their eyes over the text, hoping that they "get it." Embedded questions can provide guidance to help them "get it," to know when they have gotten it and when they haven't, and to know what to do if they haven't gotten it (Weir, 1998).

> ■ **Embedded questions** are questions that are placed within the text rather than before or after it. The checkup questions in this text are embedded.

The boldfaced checkup questions in this text are examples of embedded questions. Have you used them? Have you found them to be helpful? Why or why not?

When creating embedded questions, focus on the most essential information, provide guidance with elements that are most likely to cause difficulty, and prompt the kind of strategies that skilled readers would use. Create questions that will lead readers to predict, summarize, question, create images, evaluate, apply, or use context, glossary, or other word-analysis clues. After students have completed passages containing embedded questions, discuss their responses. As Salomon, Globerson, and Guterman (1989) note, talking about the responses to embedded questions may have as strong an impact as answering the embedded questions.

Some content area texts provide embedded questions. For instance, *Biology, the Living Science* (Miller & Levine, 1998) provides checkpoints that ask the reader to answer a question about the key information in a section that has just been read.

FIGURE 5.11

Information Map

Mesoamerican Civilizations

	Olmec	Maya	Toltec	Aztec
Where was this civilization?	Mexico's Gulf Coast	southern Mexico, Belize, Guatemala, Honduras, western El Salvador	central Mexican highlands	central and southern Mexico
When did it exist?	1200–400 B.C.	250–900 A.D.	900–1200 A.D.	1200–1600 A.D.
How was it ruled?	priests	no central government; ruler for each city and surrounding region	priest-king	emperor, nobles ruled cities
How did the people make a living?	farming	farming, trading	farming	farming, trading
What happened to it?	No one knows.	No one knows; could have been drought or disease.	No one knows.	defeated by Spanish
What were its main contributions?	first calendar; counting system; art: huge stone heads	calendar; paper; writing system; math with zero; astronomy; temples & pyramids	built greatest city of its time	roads & buildings

Checkpoint questions for the section on DNA include How does DNA replicate? How does RNA differ from DNA? What does RNA polymerase do? What are the three main forms of RNA? The text is difficult and complex. With subsequent sections building on previous ones, students will soon be overwhelmed if they don't grasp the key points. The embedded questions in the form of checkpoints give students the opportunity to see whether they have understood the key points so that they can go back over the material if they need to. Perhaps more important, it helps students review what they have learned before going on to a new topic. If students read the material without taking time to review, they will probably be overwhelmed by the sheer number of new ideas and facts.

✔ *CHECKUP*

1. What are some techniques that can be used to foster comprehension during reading?
2. How might these techniques be presented?

AFTER-READING TECHNIQUES

After completing reading, strategic readers may mentally summarize what they have read or ask themselves questions about the material. They may critically evaluate the new information and see how it fits in with what they already know. They may apply the information in some way, and they may seek clarifying information on confusing points or additional information on the topic. Techniques that can be used to foster after-reading activities include constructing analogies, creating graphic organizers, writing after reading, and extending and applying.

Constructing Analogies

Analogies can foster comprehension and are frequently used in the content areas, especially in science. Because electricity can't be seen, students better understand an explanation of the flow of electricity when it is compared to the flow of water in a pipe. However, when teaching with analogies, it is important to point out where the two items being compared differ. For instance, unlike water, electricity is not limited to flowing downhill (Baker & Piburn, 1997).

■ **Analogies** are full or partial comparisons between a concept to be learned and a familiar concept: for example, memory and file cabinet.

Recognizing and constructing analogies is one way of helping students bridge the gap between the new and the old. Point out analogies when they appear. Traditional analogies include the eye and a camera, the heart and a pump, the brain and a computer, cells and a factory, and memory and a file cabinet. The best analogies are those in which the items being compared share a number of features, which is why the analogy between the eye and a camera is especially effective. However, it is important that the item that is the basis for comparison (the camera) be familiar. If students don't know how a camera works, the analogy won't be very helpful (Glynn, 1994). Help students create their own analogies by comparing old information and new concepts. You might ask, for instance, "How is the eye like a camera? How is memory like a file cabinet?" Self-created analogies are generally more effective than those made up by others.

For best results in using analogies, discuss the analogy thoroughly. After introducing the target concept, explain the analogy and identify both similarities and differences between the target concept and the analog. Clarify any confusions that students might have (Glynn, 1994).

Constructing Graphic Organizers

Because they involve showing relationships visually, graphic organizers are one of the most effective devices for promoting understanding and retention of the kinds of complex concepts presented in content area material. Because graphic organizers involve encoding verbal material visually, they provide another route for storing and retrieving information and so aid recall (Robinson, 1998).

The content and structure of material and the teaching–learning purpose dictate the type of organizer used: structured overview, time line, or an organizer that highlights the steps in a process, contrasts elements, or identifies causes. Whatever form it takes, the visual display should focus on the most essential information and do so vividly. Key concepts should "jump out at the students as soon as their eyes meet the page" (Robinson, 1998, p. 100).

■ Simple Relationships

The simplest of the graphic organizers is the web or map, which is used to show a main idea and supporting details. The main idea is written in a circle or box, which is centered, and supporting details are written in circles or boxes surrounding the main circle or box. Lines are used to show that the surrounding circles or boxes are linked to the main circle or box, as in Figure 5.12.

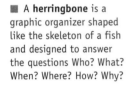

■ A **herringbone** is a graphic organizer shaped like the skeleton of a fish and designed to answer the questions Who? What? When? Where? How? Why?

An effective way to organize a variety of information about a topic is a **herringbone** ma**p.** Herringbone maps are used to present categories of information by answering the questions: Who did what? When? Where? How? Why? They are frequently used for fiction but also work well for summarizing historical events. Figure 5.13 shows a herringbone map summarizing the assassination of Archduke Francis Ferdinand.

For some elements, the best graphic organizer is a diagram. For example, a diagram is the best way to show the parts of the brain (see Figure 5.14). Although a blank diagram might be drawn or traced by the teacher and distributed to students, involving students in creating their own diagrams or drawings makes learning a more active process. When drawing the object, students have to note its parts. A va-

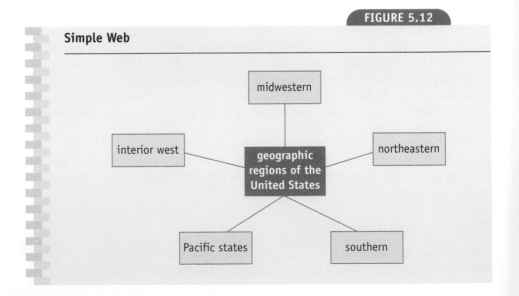

FIGURE 5.12

Simple Web

FIGURE 5.13

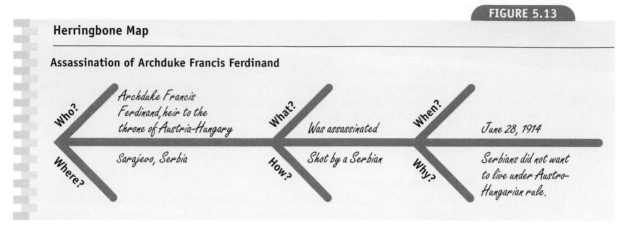

Herringbone Map

Assassination of Archduke Francis Ferdinand

Who? Archduke Francis Ferdinand, heir to the throne of Austria-Hungary

Where? Sarajevo, Serbia

What? Was assassinated

How? Shot by a Serbian

When? June 28, 1914

Why? Serbians did not want to live under Austro-Hungarian rule.

riety of diagrams are available as clip art. The drawing of the brain in Figure 5.14 was taken from a clip art collection.

■ Comparison/Contrast Relationships

To show similarities and differences, you can use Venn diagrams, as explained in Chapter 3, and a frame matrix. Venn diagrams can be expanded to include three items. Frame matrices or information maps can be expanded to include an unlimited number of items.

FIGURE 5.14

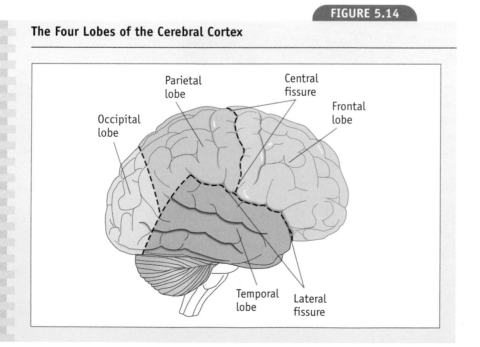

The Four Lobes of the Cerebral Cortex

Parietal lobe

Central fissure

Occipital lobe

Frontal lobe

Temporal lobe

Lateral fissure

■ Hierarchical Relationships

Because they show hierachial relationships, three of the most useful graphic organizers are the structured overview, Frayer's model, and concept maps. Frayer's model and concept maps were explained in Chapter 3. The structured overview and Frayer's model are frequently used as preparation for reading. However, they can also be used to review and extend concepts. For instance, if using the structured overview on diet shown in Figure 5.4, students can add specific examples of fats after reading the section on fats and specific examples of carbohydrates after reading that section. Once they have experience with structured overviews, they can create their own after reading a selection.

■ Showing Processes

Flow charts are especially useful for showing processes. A circular or cyclical flow chart can be used to show processes that are continuous and never-ending, such as the water cycle, as shown in Figure 5.15. Linear flow charts can be used to show processes that have a definite beginning and end point, as in the operation of a digital camera, shown in Figure 5.16.

An excellent teaching and learning tool, graphic organizers are used widely. To get the most out of graphic organizers, Egan (1999) recommends the following:

• Be prepared. Try out the graphic organizer before asking the class to use it. You may discover unexpected difficulties, problems, or needed adjustments.

FIGURE 5.15

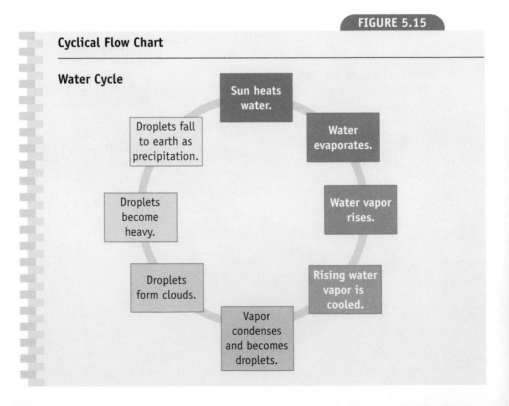

Cyclical Flow Chart

Water Cycle

Sun heats water.

Water evaporates.

Droplets fall to earth as precipitation.

Water vapor rises.

Droplets become heavy.

Rising water vapor is cooled.

Droplets form clouds.

Vapor condenses and becomes droplets.

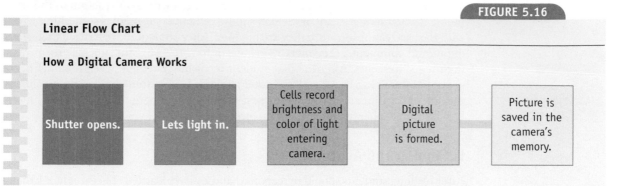

Linear Flow Chart

How a Digital Camera Works

| Shutter opens. | Lets light in. | Cells record brightness and color of light entering camera. | Digital picture is formed. | Picture is saved in the camera's memory. |

FIGURE 5.16

- Promote interaction among students. Graphic organizers lend themselves to group discussion and construction.
- Use graphic organizers with discrimination. If overused, graphic organizers can become tiresome. Graphic organizers should be used selectively, when they are the device that best fosters learning in a particular situation. The organizer selected should fit in with the learning objective and the nature of the material. Thus, a Venn diagram would be more appropriate than a semantic web when two ideas are being compared and contrasted.
- Expand the use of graphic organizers. Graphic organizers can be used with non-print material to organize information presented in lectures, simulations, experiments, or discussions.

Writing after Reading

After reading, students can summarize what they have learned in a quick write, or they can complete an entry in a learning log. In a quick write, students are given three minutes to tell what they have learned about a topic, raise questions, request additional explanations, or voice concerns. The quick writes can be discussed at that point in pairs, small groups, or the whole class. A more extensive reading–writing discussion activity is Save the Last Word for Me (Buehl, 2001). In Save the Last Word for Me, students are given five index cards and invited to record from their reading five statements that they found interesting or controversial or that they would just like to write about. The statements are marked with a check or sticky note. After they finish reading, students copy the statements onto their index cards. On the reverse side of the card, they write a reaction or comment that they would like to share with their group. For instance, Juan records the statement, "Historically, consumers purchasing used goods have had to follow the doctrine of *caveat emptor*, which is a

Writing brief summaries helps students check their understanding of what they have read.

Latin phrase that means 'buyer beware.'" Later, Juan writes his reaction to the statement. *"Caveat emptor* is unfair. Sellers should tell buyers if there is something wrong with the used car or furniture they are buying." After students have written their statements and comments, they meet in groups of four or five. Students take turns reading their statements. After the first student reads his statement, each member of the group comments on it. After all the other students have commented on the statement, the student who read the statement first reads his statement. A second group member then shares her statement and the process begins all over again.

Extending and Applying

After reading, students should reflect on what they have learned. They might ask themselves such questions as How does this fit in with what I already know? Is there anything confusing about this information? Is there anything else about this topic that I would like to know? How can I use this information? This reflection can be informal, or students can keep learning logs, as explained in Chapter 8. Students can also have a discussion about what they have learned and their reactions to their reading. Discussions can be whole-class, in pairs, or in small groups.

If students have unanswered questions or if their interest has been piqued, they might extend their knowledge by reading one of the books in the text's bibliography or by visiting a Web site on the topic or even creating one of their own. The additional reading could take the form of reading a book of historical fiction, a biography of a scientist, or a book of math puzzles. After reading about diet, students may want to take note of what they eat. After reading about recycling, they may want to plan a recycling program.

EXEMPLARY TEACHING

USING GRAPHIC ORGANIZERS

Teacher Gwen Hurt's 10th grade used graphic organizers to study the 1960s. In their organizers, they made comparisons between key elements in the 1960s and their generation. Categories included politics, entertainment, fashion, civil rights legislation, leaders, TV shows, and music. Students worked in small cooperative groups. They brainstormed topics and used many resources to obtain information, including interviews with relatives and neighbors who grew up in the 1960s.

Although students did much of their work in English class, the units was interdisciplinary and included twenty-five of the high school teachers. To investigate the music of the era, the students learned the songs and dances popular at that time. Their investigation of the tone and customs of the times were conducted in social studies classes. To obtain this information, they interviewed teachers. To learn more about the science of the times, they looked into the space program.

They use an enlarged frame to summarize information gathered. A Venn diagram was used to highlight commonalties and differences between the two eras. Despite the passage of time, a number of commonalties were found. In both eras, there were conflicts with foreign leaders and troops were sent to foreign lands. Civil rights was also a key concern in both eras (Ncrel, 1995).

✔ *CHECKUP*

1. What are some effective after-reading techniques?
2. What are the key elements in each technique?

SUMMARY

Conceptual understanding is a key factor in the comprehension of content area text. To develop conceptual understanding, content area reading lessons should specify content objectives and should take into consideration students' abilities, interests, and background knowledge. Lessons should prepare students to read, should offer guidance as they read, and should help them summarize and organize what they have read, relate it to what they already know, and apply it. Approaches that incorporate these elements include the instructional framework, the directed reading activity, and the directed reading-thinking activity. Along with these broad approaches, there are a number of specific techniques that can be used to foster conceptual understanding. Techniques designed to be used primarily before reading include the anticipation guide, PReP, structured overview, prereading survey, and drawing and writing

before reading. During-reading techniques feature study guides, including glosses, frame matrices, information maps, and embedded questions. After-reading techniques include constructing analogies, creating graphic organizers, writing, and extending and applying. A technique that encompasses before, during, and after reading is KWL Plus.

Reflection

Return to the Anticipation Guide at the beginning of this chapter. Respond once again to the items. Did your responses change? If so, how and why? Which teaching techniques discussed in this chapter do you think would be most effective in helping students better comprehend the text in your content area?

EXTENSION AND APPLICATION

1. Create an advanced organizer for a topic in your content area. If possible, try it out with students and evaluate its effectiveness.
2. Create a study guide for a topic in your content area. Select a topic that is important but that students find difficult to understand. If possible, try it out with students and evaluate its effectiveness. Note whether

the guide helped students grasp key points. Note, too, what might be done to make the guide more effective.

3. Try out a DRA or DR-TA with a group of students. What were the strengths of the technique? The weaknesses? New techniques take a while to learn. If possible, teach a series of lessons.

chapter 6

COLLABORATIVE AND COOPERATIVE APPROACHES FOR LEARNING

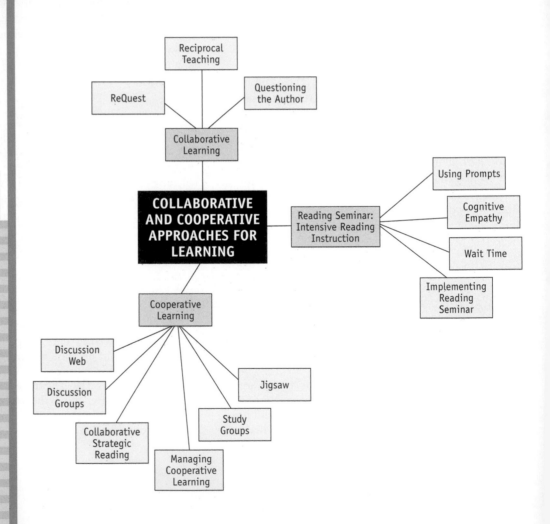

ANTICIPATION GUIDE

For each of the following statements related to the chapter you are about to read, put a check under "Agree" or "Disagree" to show how you feel. Discuss your responses with classmates before you read the chapter.

		Agree	Disagree
1	Learning through group discussions is superior to learning by lecture.	____	____
2	Student-led discussion groups are more effective than teacher-led groups.	____	____
3	In small group learning, the least able students are usually left out.	____	____
4	The main problem with student discussion groups is that they are difficult to manage.	____	____
5	Struggling learners do better with teacher-led instruction than they do with student-led groups.	____	____

USING WHAT YOU KNOW

Have you ever been a member of a cooperative learning group or studied with a friend? When you were in high school or elementary school, did your parents try to help you with your homework or a project, only to find out that they weren't quite sure what to do, but together you worked on the problem? Did you ever work with a classmate who knew more about the subject than you did, but you were able to make a limited contribution? If so, you have experienced collaborative/cooperative learning, which is what this chapter is about. As you reflect on your experiences, think how collaborative/cooperative learning might be used to foster learning in the content area that you teach.

COLLABORATIVE LEARNING

■ **Collaborative learning** is a form of learning in which students are active participants in the learning process and work with the teacher to construct meaning or solve problems.

Collaborative learning is an approach that sees students as active participants in the construction of meaning rather than as passive recipients of knowledge. In collaborative learning, teacher and student or students work as collaborators in order to build meaning. Conceptual learning is emphasized as students reflect on their learning, test out ideas, and learn to listen to other viewpoints through small-group and whole-class discussions. The atmosphere is cooperative rather than competitive. Students feel free to express ideas without being criticized and also learn to tolerate diverse viewpoints.

In some forms of collaborative learning, the teacher is very much a part of the group as an active participant or even discussion leader. In other forms, commonly referred to as cooperative learning or cooperative grouping, students complete tasks as members of a student-directed group.

There are two main approaches to teaching reading comprehension strategies: direct instruction/explanation and collaborative, which is also known as transactional. In the direct instruction/explanation approach, teachers introduce, explain, and provide guided and independent practice (National Reading Panel, 2000). Strategies presented in Chapter 5 represent a direct instructional/explanation approach. This chapter takes a collaborative approach. In a collaborative approach, students are taught strategies but the role of the teacher is different: the teacher facilitates discussions in which students "collaborate to form joint interpretations of text" and "discuss the mental processes and cognitive strategies that are involved in comprehension" (National Reading Panel, 2000, 4–122). Although strategies are explicitly taught, the emphasis is on the "interactive exchange among learners in the classroom" (National Reading Panel, 2000, 4–123).

*C*ollaborative learning is highly effective.

Reading a dense textbook may be an overwhelming experience for some students. Using collaborative approaches, such as ReQuest, Reciprocal Teaching, Questioning the Author, Collaborative Strategic Reading, or Reading Seminar, provides support from the teacher and peers and may be an excellent way to introduce students to effective content area reading. Reading takes on more meaning when students reflect on and discuss what they have read. This provides them with the opportunity to think about and reorganize the information they have derived from reading. It also gives them the opportunity to get the viewpoints of others and to hear information they have missed while reading.

ReQuest

An easy-to-implement but highly effective collaborative technique for fostering comprehension and student participation is ReQuest

(Manzo, 1969; Manzo & Manzo, 1993). **ReQuest** may be used with individual students, small groups of students, or whole classes. Using ReQuest, the teacher and student(s) alternate asking questions about the text until the students have built enough background to predict what the rest of the text might be about and then read the text on their own. ReQuest can be implemented by following the steps outlined below.

■ **ReQuest** is a procedure in which the teacher and student(s) take turns asking and answering questions.

Request Lesson
LESSON 6.1

Step 1: Explain the ReQuest procedure to students.

Tell them that they will be using a technique in which they get a chance to ask questions. Explain that you and they will take turns asking and answering questions about the first part of the selection. Tell them that asking and answering questions will help build comprehension and will also help prepare them for reading the rest of the selection on their own.

Step 2: Survey the text with the students.

Have them read the title, examine any illustrations that are part of the introduction, and discuss what the selection might be about.

Step 3: Have students read the first significant segment of text.

This could be the first sentence if the text is very dense. Or it could be the first paragraph. Explain that as they read, they are to think up questions to ask you. Students can make up as many questions as they wish. Tell them to ask the kinds of questions that a teacher might ask (Manzo & Manzo, 1993). Read the segment silently with the students.

Step 4: Students ask their questions.

The teacher's book is placed face down. Students keep their books open and may refer to their texts. If necessary, questions are restated or clarified. Answers can be checked by referring back to the text.

Step 5: After students have asked their questions, roles are switched and you ask your questions about the same segment of the test.

Beginning with the third or fourth sentence or paragraph, you might model higher-level questioning by asking for responses that require integrating several details in the text. Some of the questions might also focus on difficult concepts or vocabulary in such a way that these are clarified for students. At the end of your questioning, the next segment is read and students once again ask questions. When students ask especially appropriate or insightful questions, affirm their efforts with comments such as, "That's a good question," or, "That's the kind of question that really makes me think about what I've read."

Step 6:

The questioning proceeds in alternating fashion until the students know all the key words in the first section or paragraph and have acquired enough background information to set a purpose. That purpose could be to predict what the remainder of the text is about: "Now that we have read about the importance of oxygen, what do you think the rest of the article will tell us?" If the selection is complex, you can have students proceed through several paragraphs before turning it over to them. Manzo and Manzo (1993) recommended that the questioning be concluded as soon as a logical purpose or prediction can be established but no longer than ten minutes after beginning. Otherwise, students may begin to lose their focus.

Step 7:

After the rest of the selection has been read silently, discuss the prediction and any related questions.

Step 8: Follow-up.

Any one of a number of activities can be used to extend the learning. Students might summarize the selection in a graphic organizer, write a reflection in a learning log, continue reading, or read a related text.

Unless they have had experience creating questions, students may initially ask lower-level questions; but with coaching and modeling, they should soon begin asking higher-level ones. Whenever possible, call attention to especially effective questions asked by students so that these become models for other students to follow. Students should feel free to ask questions about words or ideas that are puzzling to them. For example, a students might ask, "How do you say the second word in the first sentence and what does it mean?" Presented below is an excerpt from a ReQuest lesson.

The Living Earth

Living things play a part in soil creation from the beginning. Lichens and mosses can colonize bare rock surfaces. They produce acids that eat into the rock surface, releasing the minerals that plants need to grow. The mosses and lichens also help to trap wind-blown particles in cracks and depressions in the rock surface. Over long periods, soil begins to form. (Snedden, 1999, p. 36)

Student: What plays a part in soil creation?
Teacher: Living things.
Student: When do the living things start playing a part in the creation of soil?
Teacher: From the very beginning.
Teacher: Do you have any more questions for me? Okay. It's my turn. My question is what does the sentence mean when it says "living things"?
Student: The sentence doesn't say. From the picture I would guess that *living things* means plants. But maybe it means earth creatures, too.
Teacher: Good thinking. That's my only question.
Student: What is the correct pronunciation for *l-i-c-h-e-n-s*?
Teacher: The *ch* has a *k* sound, so the word is pronounced "Ligh-kenz."

STRUGGLING READERS

ReQuest was originally devised as a technique for helping struggling readers improve their comprehension. It works well with all students but is also effective with students who have very serious comprehension difficulties.

Student: What are lichens?

Teacher: Lichens are plants.

Teacher: Where do lichens grow?

Student: It says that lichens colonize bare rocks, so I suppose that means that they grow on bare rocks.

Teacher: Good answer. Lichens are made up of lots of tiny plants known as algae and fungi. Because there are many of them growing together, they are said to colonize or set up colonies.

Student: What do lichens produce?

Teacher: Acids.

Student: What do the acids do?

Teacher: The acids eat into the rocks, and this begins to break them down.

Student: What is released?

Teacher: Minerals.

The discussion continues until concepts and vocabulary are clarified and a purpose for reading the rest of the article is set.

Reciprocal Teaching

A second technique that relies heavily on student questioning is Reciprocal Teaching. **Reciprocal Teaching,** which was created for use with small groups, is also a collaborative technique (Palincsar & Brown, 1986). Under the teacher's guidance, students take turns leading a discussion about segments of expository text. In a sense, students become cognitive apprentices as they use the teacher as a model but gradually take over increased responsibility for their learning and implementing Reciprocal Teaching's strategies. More complex than ReQuest, Reciprocal Teaching fosters four highly effective strategies: predicting, questioning, clarifying, and summarizing. Clarifying is a metacognitive strategy in which the reader recognizes that there is a problem and asks that a word, expression, or concept blocking comprehension be cleared up (Palincsar & Brown, 1986). Because Reciprocal Teaching is more complex than ReQuest, it will take longer to introduce. Steps for introducing Reciprocal Teaching are presented below.

■ **Reciprocal Teaching** is a form of collaborative learning in which students learn to use four key reading strategies in order to achieve improved comprehension: predicting, questioning, clarifying, and summarizing.

LESSON 6.2

Reciprocal Teaching Lesson

Step 1: Introduction

Tell students that they will be using a technique in which they take over the role of the teacher. Explain the purpose of the technique: to increase comprehension by using four of the best comprehension strategies and discussing a selection. Inform students that they will be taking turns leading the discussions.

Step 2: Teaching Key Strategies

Introduce and explain each of the four strategies: predicting, questioning, clarifying, and summarizing. If students are already familiar with these strategies, review them.

- *Predicting.* Explain to students that predicting helps them think about the key ideas in a selection and gives them a purpose for reading. Modeling the process, show students how you would use the title or heading, illustrations, and introductory paragraph, if there is one, to make predictions about the upcoming content. If the prediction is about a segment in the middle of the selection, you would use your knowledge of what had happened or the information given so far and headings to make a prediction. Provide opportunities for guided practice.

- *Questioning.* Show students how you create questions as you read. Also explain that you ask questions about the most important ideas in a selection. Provide sample questions and guided practice.

- *Clarifying.* Explain the need for clarifying and show what you do when you encounter a word, phrase, or passage that you find puzzling. Encourage students to locate words, expressions, or concepts in a sample selection that need clarifying. Discuss what might be done to provide clarification: rereading, using context or glossary to derive the meaning of a difficult word, using illustrations, etc.

- *Summarizing.* Explain to students that summarizing may be the most important reading strategy of all because it helps them concentrate on important points while reading. It also helps them review the main points and check on their understanding. Explain to students that if they can't summarize a passage, this is a sign that they may not have understood it and should go back and reread it. Provide guided practice.

In the beginning stages, you will play a major role in the implementation of Reciprocal Teaching. During the early sessions, you will provide prompts and probes and models strategies as necessary. Because creating questions is difficult for many students, you will model how you compose questions, use prompts to help students reword confusing questions, and supply model questions and possible question words. Over time, students take on added responsibility for leading discussions, answering questions, and implementing strategies.

The following is a sample Reciprocal Teaching lesson conducted with eighth-graders and is based on the reading of the first part of a chapter about Eleanor Roosevelt in the book *Profiles in American History, Volume* 7 (Moss & Wilson, 1998).

(Lead-in question)

Adam (student discussion leader): My question is, what was Eleanor Roosevelt's childhood like?

Carmen: She was rich. And her family was famous.

(Clarification request)

Reginald: The book says that her family was one of the original "400" aristocratic families in the United States. That needs to be clarified. I don't know who these 400 people were. And I'm not sure what *aristocratic* means.

Charles: Aristocratic means high class. I think maybe 400 is referring to the top 400 people in the United States. Maybe the richest 400.

Teacher: You are on the right track. I'm not sure myself how the 400 were chosen. That's something for us to research.

Adam: Eleanor Roosevelt did come from a wealthy family, but she had some problems. What were they?

Janine: Her mother was cold. She wasn't a very warm person. I mean she probably never hugged Eleanor.

Alicia: And she criticized her. Her mother told her she was awkward and too serious. She called her "Granny."

Charles: And her father was almost never home.

Carmen: Not even on Christmas.

Teacher: Good observation. What problem did Eleanor's father have?

Paula: He drank. He was an alcoholic. What a family. It just goes to show that money isn't everything.

Adam: But the family wasn't all bad. What good things did they teach Eleanor?

Carmen: They taught her to be kind. The father gave money to crippled kids. And Eleanor was sent to soup kitchens to help out.

Teacher: Good answers. Can you summarize this section of the chapter, Adam?

(Summary)

Adam: This section says that Eleanor Roosevelt's family was rich and famous, but they had problems. The mother was cold and critical, and the father drank too much and was hardly ever around. Still, he taught Eleanor to help others.

Teacher: That's an excellent summary, Adam. You've given us the highlights of this section.

(Prediction)

What do you predict will happen next?

Adam: I think the next section will tell us how Eleanor Roosevelt overcame some of the difficulties of her childhood and how she happened to meet and marry Franklin Roosevelt.

Teacher: Does anyone have a different prediction? Okay. Let's read the next section to see how our prediction works out. Who would like to be the leader for this section?

> **ENGLISH LANGUAGE LEARNERS**
>
> English language learners do especially well in cooperative learning situations because they are more willing to use their developing language skills in a small-group situation and they are more willing to ask for help.

Although designed for use with small groups, Reciprocal Teaching can be adapted for use with the whole class. First, students use the headings to make two predictions about the content of the text they are about to read. Second, after reading a segment, they write two questions and a summary and note any items that require clarification. The predictions, summaries, and clarification requests are discussed after the selection has been read. However, like other effective techniques, Reciprocal Teaching takes a commitment of time. High school students who received twelve to sixteen training sessions evidenced gains; those who participated in only six to eight sessions did not. In another study, junior high students' comprehension did not begin to improve until after seven lessons (Alfassi, 1998). Maximum gains weren't reached until after the fourteenth session. Then they began to stabilize.

Students should read fairly easy passages until they have a good grasp of Reciprocal Teaching strategies. It's difficult to learn to implement the strategies when the text is so difficult that it requires maximum effort to comprehend it (Mosenthal, 1990).

 **CHECKUP**

1. What are the key elements in ReQuest and Reciprocal Teaching?
2. Why would using ReQuest be good preparation for using Reciprocal Teaching?

■ **Questioning the Author** is a collaborative learning discussion technique in which the teacher uses prompts to help students construct the meaning of a text.

Questioning the Author

Concerned that students weren't learning very much from their American history texts, Beck, McKeown, Sinatra, and Loxterman (1991) revised the texts. Students' comprehension increased by 25 percent. Realizing that as they revised the texts, the researchers were using the kinds of strategies that would help students do a better job of constructing meaning, they planned a program in which students would read with a "reviser's eye." Because it is the reviser's task to make text more understandable, the program would show students how to read in such a way as to make the text understandable to themselves. A program was set up in which students read brief segments of text and then responded to teacher queries so that they were cooperatively constructing meaning as they processed the text instead of reading the entire text and then answering questions.

Students were told that sometimes the author's meaning wasn't clear, so they would have to ask themselves such questions as What is the author trying to say here? Having students ask the author questions made reading a more active process. Rather than simply extracting information from text, readers would have to build a genuine understanding of the text. Beck, McKeown, Hamilton, and Kucan (1997) compared it to the difference between building a model ship and being given one. The student who has assembled a model ship knows a great deal more about its parts than the one who has simply looked at the model.

The program used queries instead of questions. Questions assess students' comprehension after reading and promote teacher–student interaction. Queries assist students in their attempts to construct meaning and promote student-to-student interaction. Students construct meaning "on line" rather than after the entire section or chapter has been read. Initiating and follow-up queries are used. The teacher uses initiating queries to get the discussion started and to keep it moving. Initiating queries included: "What is the author trying to say here? What is the author's message? What is the author trying to tells us?" Follow-up queries help students construct meaning. If a passage is puzzling, the teacher might ask, "What did the author mean here? Did the author explain this clearly?" Queries that help students make connections are also posed: "Does this make sense with what the author told us before? How does this connect to what the author has told us here?" Other follow-up queries prompt students to seek reasons: "Does the author tell us why? Why do you think the author tells us this now?" Queries might also prompt students to see how what they are learning relates to their prior knowledge: "How does this fit in with what you know?"

To create discussions that foster the construction of meaning, the teacher uses six Question-the-Author moves: marking, turning back, revoicing, modeling, annotating, and recapping.

Marking. The teacher calls attention to a student's comment that is important to the meaning being built. The teacher might remark, "You are saying that the creation of highways was a good thing. It meant that people could get around more easily and could live farther from their jobs."

Turning back. The teacher turns students' attention back to the text so that they can get more information, fix up a misreading, or clarify their thinking: "Yes, I agree that highways helped the country to develop and changed the way that we live. But what does the author tell us about the effect of highways on cities?"

Revoicing. The teacher helps students express what they were attempting to say: "So what you're telling us is that although people found cleaner air, less noise, and more room when they moved to the suburbs, they lost a sense of neighborhood and community."

Modeling. The teacher demonstrates how she might go about creating meaning from text. She might show how she rereads a confusing passage, refers to a map or illustration to get additional information, visualizes a complex process, or uses the glossary to get the meaning of a key word. The teacher might say, "Here's what was going through my mind as I read that section," or, "Here's why I had to read that sentence twice," or, "Here are the kinds of questions I ask myself when I read about a controversial issue."

Annotating. The teacher fills in information that is missing from a discussion but that is important for understanding key ideas. It might be information that the author failed to include: "The author tells us that highways help people get to their jobs and see sights that they never would have seen and helps companies transport goods. What the author doesn't say is that highways are becoming more and more crowded and that each year drivers are wasting more time sitting in traffic jams."

Recapping. The teacher highlights key points and summarizes: "Now that we understand how highways have changed the country in some ways that are beneficial and some ways that are negative, do you think it was the best thing to spend all that money on roads, or should some have been spent on the railroads and other means of transportation?

Steps in a Questioning the Author lesson are listed in lesson 6.2.

Questioning the Author Lesson

Step 1:

Analyze the text and decide what you want students to know or understand as a result of reading the text. List two or three major understandings.

Step 2:

Note any potential difficulties in the text that might hinder students' comprehension. This could be difficult vocabulary or concepts, density of facts, lack of needed background knowledge, or explanations that are difficult to understand.

Step 3:

Segment the text into readable blocks. The segments depend on the major understandings that you believe students should acquire. A stopping point might coincide with the end of the presentation of a key understanding. A segment could be a single paragraph, if that incorporates a major idea, or a whole section.

Step 4:

In view of the understandings you wish students to acquire and the possible difficulties in the text, plan your queries. If a segment seems especially complex, you might plan a query such as "What is the author trying to say here?" that will help you assess what students got out of that segment and then use added queries to build on what they learned. Plan queries for each segment.

Step 5:

Introduce the selection. Discuss difficult vocabulary and build background necessary to understand a particular segment before that segment is read.

Step 6:

Students read the first segment silently.

Step 7:

Students and teacher discuss the first segment.

Step 8:

Students go on to the next segment.

Step 9:

At the conclusion, the class, with the teacher's help, sums up what they have read.

■ Implementing Questioning the Author

To implement Questioning the Author, arrange seating so that it is conducive to discussion. A U-shaped or circular arrangement is recommended. Explain to students that they will be reading and discussing what they read in a new way that is known as Questioning the Author. Explain that authors are real people and try hard to present information clearly but may leave out important facts, use unknown words, or write sentences that might be hard to understand. It is therefore the reader's job to try to figure out what the author meant and also to fill in details that the author might not have included. "The important message is that students hear the teacher say specifically why texts might be confusing and difficult. Such an explanation can reduce student defensiveness about not understanding" (Beck et al., 1997, p. 193).

To show students what you mean, read a text and think aloud as you do so. Note potentially confusing segments and demonstrate how you deal with them. Discuss with students portions that the author made clear and portions that were puzzling or misleading so that students realize that reading is a kind of conversation with an author in which the reader must ask questions in order to make meaning.

In addition to improving comprehension, Questioning the Author has changed the nature of classroom discussions. Teachers' Questioning the Author questions emphasize extending understanding rather than simply retrieving information. Students, in turn, spend more time integrating ideas rather than retrieving text information. The amount of student talk, student-to-student interactions, and student-initiated questions also increases (Beck et al., 1997). A sample Questioning the Author dialog follows:

The class just read a text segment about the presidency of James Buchanan, which stated that many people believed that he liked the South better than the North because he said that owning slaves should be a personal choice. The teacher began the discussion by posing a general query. After a student responded, the teacher asked a follow-up question.

Teacher: This paragraph that Tracy just read is really full of important information. What has the author told us in this important paragraph?

Laura: They think that Buchanan liked the South better because he said that it is a person's choice if they want to have slaves or not, so they thought that he liked the South better than the North.

Teacher: Okay. And what kind of problem then did this cause Buchanan when they thought that he liked the South? What kind of problem did that cause?

Janet: Well, maybe less people would vote for him because like in Pennsylvania we were against slavery and might have voted for him because he was from Pennsylvania. But now since we knew that he was for the South, we might not vote for him again.

Jamie: I have something to add on to Janet's 'cause I completely agree with her. We might have thought that since he was from Pennsylvania and Pennsylvania was an antislavery state, that he was against slavery. But it turns out he wasn't.

Teacher: Just like someone whom you think is your best friend, and then all of a sudden you find out, oh, they're not. (McKeown, Beck, & Sandora, 1996, pp. 112–113)

STRUGGLING READERS AND WRITERS

Questioning the Author works with all students but has been especially successful with struggling readers.

✔ CHECKUP

1. What are the main steps in Questioning the Author?
2. How would you go about implementing Questioning the Author?

READING SEMINAR: INTENSIVE READING INSTRUCTION

■ **Reading Seminar** is a collaborative learning technique in which prompted discussion and prompted strategy use are combined.

Based on other collaborative approaches, such as Questioning the Author, **Reading Seminar** is a holistic, interactive approach to reading content area text. Although similar to other collaborative approaches, Reading Seminar emphasizes strategy instruction in addition to collaborative discussion. Reading Seminar builds both background and strategy use.

The instruction is intensive because the teacher and students work with brief segments of text, but, through questioning and discussion, build a deep understanding of the text. Intensive reading instruction works best with text that is challenging.

Reading Seminar is an inclusive model. It includes the overlapping levels of reading discussed in earlier chapters: preparing, comprehending, organizing, elaborating, and monitoring. Not all levels are included in any one session. However, during the course of instruction, all levels are presented and practiced. In any one lesson or series of lessons, the teacher might guide instruction and discussion in such a way as to focus on a particular level or strategy.

*I*n Reading Seminar the text is read and discussed section by section.

Using Prompts

A key element in Reading Seminar is the use of prompts. Prompts guide the students' thinking and responding, provide structure and scaffolding, and also affirm and encourage. Rather than being used to test or find out whether students have read an assignment, prompts are used to instruct and scaffold. Suggested prompts are listed below. However, these should be adapted to fit your situation. Use only those prompts that are appropriate. For instance, if the selection does not lend itself to imaging, don't ask prompts such as, "What pictures, sounds, or smells came to mind as you read the selection?" Use a limited number of prompts so that your discussion has focus.

■ Preparational Prompts (before reading)

- Look at the title, illustrations, and subheads. Based on your survey, what do you think this selection might be about?

- What do you know about this topic?
- What would you like to find out?
- What strategies might you use to help us understand this section? (optional)
- How might you go about reading this? (optional)

■ Comprehension/Organizational Prompts (during/after reading) (choose two or three prompts)

As they read, students should have a question in mind. Usually, the question is based on the prereading survey. If headings are used, students can turn the heading into a question and read to answer the question. After a section has been read, use one or more of the following prompts:

- What is this part of the selection telling you?
- What seems to be the author's main point(s)?
- How does the author prove or explain his point(s)?
- What did you learn from this selection?
- How might you organize this information to help you understand it better?

■ Elaborational Prompts (choose one or two prompts)

- What important information did the author imply but not state?
- What questions came to mind as you read this selection?
- What word picture did the author create for you?
- What pictures, sounds, or smells came to mind as you read the selection?
- Based on the information in the selection, what conclusion might you reach?
- Was the information presented fairly? Was there any evidence of bias? Has the author provided both sides of the question?
- How does this information fit in with what you already know?
- How might you use this information?

■ Monitoring Prompts (choose one or two prompts)

(Students might be encouraged to put a sticky note on any passage that is not clear.)

- Was there anything in the article that was confusing?
- Were there any passages that weren't clear?
- Were there any words that weren't clear?
- Do you have any questions about anything that you read?

■ Strategy Prompts

- What helped you understand this section?
- What strategies did you use to help you get the meaning of this section? (Students or teacher might explain and model helpful strategies.)
- How did you go about reading parts that weren't clear to you at first?

■ Text Connecting Prompts (should be asked after reading more than one section)

To connect information from a previous section, ask the following questions:

- How does this fit in with what was said in the section (or sections) that we have already read?
- Putting together the information from all the sections that we have read, what have you learned so far?

■ Discussion Prompts

During discussions, use prompts to scaffold instruction, discover and clarify confusions, encourage students, and keep the discussion moving forward. Listed below are some suggested prompts. They should be used as needed.

- If a student does not provide sufficient information, ask, "Can you tell me more?"
- If a response is not clear, use a prompt in which you restate what you believe the student said and then ask if your restatement is correct: "You seem to be saying that Raphael should have told the truth, even though it would have gotten his best friend in trouble. Is that right?" The purpose of a clarifying prompt is to help the speaker clarify her thoughts. It can also be used to keep the speaker on track if she has gotten off the subject (Hyman, 1978).
- Reword the prompt if you believe the student may not understand it. Use simpler terms or simplify the question.

■ Scaffolding Prompts

Be aware of students' difficulties and pose questions that guide students' thinking. Instead of asking yourself, "Is this answer right or wrong?" ask, "What thought processes led the student to this response?" and, if the answer is wrong, "How can those thought processes be redirected?" Instead of calling on another student, telling where the answer might be found, or giving obvious hints, ask questions or make statements that help put students' thinking back on the right track. The key is asking yourself two questions: "What has gone wrong with the student's thinking?" and "What can I ask or state that would guide the student's thinking to the right thought processes and correct answer?"

The following is a scripted example of how a teacher might redirect a student who has inferred a main idea that is too narrow in scope:

Student (giving incorrect main idea): Getting new words from Indians.

Teacher: Well, let's test it. Is the first sentence talking about new words from the Indians?

Student: Yes.

Teacher: Is the next?

Student: Yes.

Teacher: How about the next?

Student: No.

Teacher: No. It says that Indians also learned new words from the settlers, right? Can you fit that into your main idea?

Student: The Indians taught the settlers words and the settlers taught the Indians words.

Teacher: Good. You see, you have to think about all the ideas in the paragraph to decide on the main idea. (Duffy & Roehler, 1987, p. 517)

Cognitive Empathy

As you help guide students' thought processes, show **cognitive empathy.** Cognitive empathy is an approach through which teachers work with students to help them use strategies to comprehend a puzzling passage or derive the meaning of a difficult word (Anderson & Roit, 1993). Students are encouraged to view reading as a problem-solving activity and to be open about any difficulties they are having so that the teacher and students can work collaboratively to solve them. Teachers look for signs that students are attempting to straighten out a confusing passage or to solve a similar literacy puzzle. Students indicate difficulty with comments but also with

> . . . furrowed brows, pauses, puzzled looks, and even short intakes of breath. Teachers use cognitive empathy to pick up on these reactions—to catch the moment when strategic thinking occurs—and to encourage students to make thoughts public by asking such questions as, "What's on your mind? You seem to thinking about something. How are you going about it? How can we help?" (Anderson & Roit, 1993, p. 2)

Teachers capitalize upon these teachable moments to show empathy and to encourage students to reveal their thinking as in the following exchange with a group of students who were having difficulty with the term *human aging:*

Teacher: I see a confused look here. Which part is confusing you?

Student 1: The part that says "human again."

Teacher: I guess it isn't really "again." Does anyone have a strategy to figure that one out? You usually have very good ones.

Student 2: "Agging."

Teacher: Do you know what "agging" means?

Student 2: To bother?

Teacher: I think that if I relate this word to the title, "Growing Old," that would help me to get an idea.

Student 1: Aging.

Teacher: Aging. What helped you get that?

Student 1: After you said growing old, I looked at the title and I just remembered that someone growing old is aging. (Anderson & Roit, 1993, p. 6)

Imitating the teacher's behavior, the students soon began to show cognitive empathy toward each other. Students begin giving suggestions to each other and discussing strategies that they use. Cognitive empathy is especially important when working with students who have a history of failure. "Having endured criticism from self and others, older low-achieving readers are naturally reluctant to talk about or even admit that they have problems with reading" (Anderson & Roit, 1993, p. 2).

■ **Cognitive empathy** is a collaborative approach through which teachers use reading problems faced by students to help students resolve difficulties in their reading.

STRUGGLING READERS
Cognitive empathy was highly successful with older struggling readers because it built on strategies that they were using and used peer as well as teacher collaboration so that students shared their thinking with each other as well as with the teacher.

Wait Time

Perhaps, the simplest way to improve students' responses is to use **wait time.** Wait time means that after calling on a student, you wait for a response. Maintain eye contact for five seconds after the student has responded to provide the opportunity for elaboration or explanation. Teachers often expect an immediate answer and, when none is forthcoming, call on another student. Because it gives students time to think, waiting five seconds results in longer, more elaborate, higher-level responses. There are also fewer no-responses and I-don't-knows. Teachers who use wait time actually grow in their ability to help students clarify and expand their responses (Dillon, 1983; Gambrell, 1980). Wait time after a response has been given also helps. Teachers tend to call on another pupil the second the respondent stops talking. Often, however, students have more to say if given a few seconds to collect their thoughts.

Implementing Reading Seminar

Intensive instruction follows a modified seminar model. Students meet to read and discuss a selection under the teacher's direction. Selections are read section by section so that students construct meaning for one section before going on to the next section. Listed below are steps for implementing Reading Seminar.

- To prepare a selection for intensive reading instruction, first decide what you want students to learn as a result of reading the selection. What ideas or understandings do you want them to come away with? List two or three of these. Then gear all instruction and activities toward helping students achieve those understandings. Also note any key words that might pose problems for them and which you judge they will not be able to get from context. Note, too, difficult concepts or unfamiliar background that may need to be introduced.

- In light of these target understandings, the nature of the text, and the students' abilities, segment the text. Segment the text into sections that you think students can handle. Difficult text that contains many key concepts should be read in shorter segments.

- Once you have segmented the text, decide on the question or questions that you will use to introduce each segment and the questions you will use after each segment has been read.

- Before students begin reading the first section, introduce the entire selection or conduct a preparatory discussion. Then introduce difficult vocabulary and concepts and provide needed background for the segment they are about to read. If you are working with older students, you might involve them in selecting difficult vocabulary. You might invite them to survey the selection quickly and note any words that are difficult (Anderson & Roit, 1993). Discuss these words beforehand.

- Read and discuss each segment.

- Summarize all segments. Because students have read the selection in parts, it is important that you help them see relationships between the parts and also with background knowledge that they have. Content area texts tend to be laden with facts, with little space devoted to how those facts are related to each other and to developing concepts or principles (Jitendra, Nolet, Xin, Gomez, Renmouf, & Iskold, 2001). In a study of geography texts, Jitendra, Nolet, Xin, Gomez, Renmouf, and Iskold (2001) found that students encountered a new fact every fourteen to twenty-four words. But relatively few concepts and almost no principles were developed. In addition, few of the questions or activities were designed to help students develop concepts or principles. If using texts of this nature, it is important that you decide which concepts and principles are important and develop these with students. It is especially important that students relate what they have learned to what they know and that they apply this knowledge. Students need a big picture framework within which to fit new information.

Reading Seminar Lesson

LESSON 6.4

Step 1: Explain the concept and purpose of reading seminar.

Tell students that they'll be reading short pieces of articles or parts of a chapter and then they'll be discussing them. Use a brief, but interesting article to demonstrate. Use the preparatory prompts and selected prompts from comprehending/organizing, found on p. 200–201. In the next lesson, add prompts from monitoring. Later, add prompts from elaboration. Also gradually add discussion prompts. Start using wait time and scaffolding responses. Adapt the prompts to fit your teaching style. Presented below is a sample lesson drawn from a sixth-grade world history text, *The World and Its People* (Garcia, Gelo, Greenow, Kracht, & White, 1997b).

Step 2: Key Student Learnings

- China is the oldest and largest civilization.
- The ancient Chinese had many remarkable achievements.
- The Chinese kept to themselves and believed they were better than others.
- The Chinese lived according to their beliefs in Confucianism, Daoism, and Buddhism.

Key Vocabulary: *vast territory, region, distinctive characteristics*

Step 3: Preparation

What is the title of this first chapter on China? Read the focus statement. Based on the focus statement, what do you think this chapter will tell us? Look at the headings and illustrations. What do they suggest about the content of this chapter? Based on a survey of the headings and illustrations, what are some of the topics that might be covered by this chapter? What do you already know about ancient China? What do you think we will learn about ancient China in the first section entitled "A Vast Land?" Another word for *land* is *territory*. What is *vast*? Because the territory is so vast, it is divided into regions, with each region having distinctive characteristics. What are distinctive characteristics? Let's read to find out what this section tells us about China's vast land.

Step 4: Discussion of First Segment

What did you learn about China's vast land? How might the map help you understand China's size?

What is the section telling us about China's regions? Why do you think the text tells us about China's rivers? What is the text hinting at when it says that the rivers run from west to east? What does this suggest about communication and transportation between north and south? Were there any parts in this section that weren't clear? Did you notice the words in blue? Did you find the glossary at the bottom of the page helpful? What are the important things that we have learned about China? How might we organize the information in this section?

Step 5: Preparation for Next Section

What is the heading for the next section? What does the author mean by a sense of superiority? When you feel superior, whether you are a person or a civilization, you tend to isolate yourself. What do you do when you isolate yourself? What does the author mean by a great civilization?

(Next segment is read and related to previous segment.)

As with any new approach, it is best to start out gradually. Once you and your students feel comfortable with the basic elements, move on to more advanced ones. Also feel free to adapt the approach to fit your situation.

 ***CHECKUP***

1. What are the key elements in Reading Seminar?
2. What are some of the prompts that might be used?
3. How might this technique be implemented?

COOPERATIVE LEARNING

Talking can be an effective way to learn. Although much of our learning is solitary, talking over concepts helps deepen our understanding of them. One of the best ways to foster understanding of a complex idea is to explain it to someone. Before we can explain it, we have to sort it out ourselves and translate it into understandable terms. Discussion as a way of learning is the basis of cooperative learning. **Cooperative learning** comes in many forms. It can be as simple as having a pair of students study or complete a project together. It can be as complex as having an entire class divided into four or five groups, with each group having a different segment of an overall task and each member of each group fulfilling a specific role to help complete the group's segment. It can be informal and temporary or highly structured and long-standing.

■ **Cooperative learning** is a format in which students work together to complete a learning task.

Cooperative learning has a dual payoff. Not only do students improve in their subject matter areas (Slavin, 1987), they also feel better about themselves and have the added satisfaction of working with and helping others (Johnson & Johnson, 1994). Although all students benefit from cooperative learning, struggling learners, members of minority groups, and English language learners benefit the most.

Jigsaw

Cooperative learning activities can take a variety of forms and serve a number of educational purposes. However, the major purpose of cooperative learning is to develop a deeper understanding of course content. Two of the most widely used types are jigsaw and study group. As its name suggests, **jigsaw** divides a project into four or five subtasks, with each member of the group having a separate portion of an overall topic (Aronson, 1978; Slavin, 1996). For a class studying ancient Egypt, the teacher might divide the overall topic into five parts: the nature of the Nile, trade and commerce, everyday life, major rulers, and accomplishments. Each member of a group is assigned one subtopic and given a series of questions to guide her reading. Each student is to become an "expert" on his topic. After getting their assignments, students do their reading and join an expert group. A sample expert sheet is presented in Figure 6.1. Each member of the expert group has the same assignment. For instance, all the students investigating Egypt's contributions join together in an expert group. Expert group members help each other with confusing concepts, difficult terms, and misunderstood details. If students are unable to resolve an issue or question, they may seek help from the teacher. The teacher, of course, actively mon-

■ A **jigsaw** cooperative group is one in which students divide up a task and then share what they have learned with the other members of their group.

FIGURE 6.1

Jigsaw Expert Sheet

United States History

Topic: *After the Great War*

Subtopic: *Wilson loses the peace.*

Read Chapter 2, Fourteen Points, pages 16–20, in the *Oxford History of Us,* by Joy Hakim.

1. What was the purpose of Wilson's Fourteen Points?

2. What was the League of Nations?

3. Why did Wilson want the United States to join the League of Nations?

4. Why were many Americans opposed to the League of Nations?

5. What happened as a result of Wilson's stroke?

Discussion: If you had been living in the time just after World War I, would you have been for or against the League of Nations? Why? Would you have voted for Wilson? Why or why not?

itors each group's progress. After students have mastered their subtopics, they meet with their teams. Each team member instructs the others in her subtopic. The members of the team make sure that everyone has a good grasp of all the subtopics. The goal is to have each team member pass a quiz prepared by the teacher.

Each team member is assessed on her performance. Teams may also be assessed as a group on total score, number of members receiving a passing score, and/or degree of improvement. Based on the students' performance, the teacher reteaches content if necessary. The teacher also evaluates group processes to see how well the members worked together.

Study Groups

■ In a **study group**, each member works on the whole task.

In a **study group,** students help each other learn information on a specific topic or from a section of the text (Hotchkiss, 1990). The teacher presents the information to be learned, provides practice, and then assigns students to heterogeneous groups to study or engage in additional practice. Team members work as a whole group or in pairs to complete the exercises. The goal is to help each student become knowledgeable in the topic being studied so that all can pass a test on the material.

Managing Cooperative Learning

One problem with cooperative learning is that students may spend time talking about nonacademic matters such as favorite TV shows or the latest fashions. However, if students find the tasks and discussions in which they are engaged interesting and valuable and if self-regulating behaviors have been emphasized, chances are they will stay on task (Herber & Herber, 1993). Based on extensive experience with cooperative learning, a group of content area teachers identified four key roles that teachers fulfill: directing, monitoring, probing, and supporting.

■ Directing

Directing means making sure that students understand and can carry out the cooperative learning tasks that have been assigned to them. Directing includes explaining, modeling, reviewing, and coaching.

■ Monitoring

Monitoring involves observing students and taking steps to improve performance as required. However, teachers are careful not to disrupt or take over discussions. Students are given the opportunity to discover and work on areas needing improvement for themselves.

■ Probing

Probing consists of using prompts and other devices to help students better understand content. Probes can be used to help students clarify confusions, evaluate responses, draw conclusions, perceive fallacies, obtain more information, or even apply what they have learned. Probes include prompts such as Can you clarify that statement? Can you tell me more? How might this be applied? Can you give me examples? However, think-alouds in which teachers show how they might analyze a problem or draw a conclusion can function as probes. Questioning whether other solutions might be posed or other conclusions drawn or whether all the evidence has been considered are other ways teachers can foster students' thinking (Herber & Herber, 1993).

■ Supporting

Supporting consists of using praise, affirming statements, and, in some instances, direct assistance. To be effective, praise must be genuine and specific. "You did a great job!" is too general. "You did a good job supporting your conclusions" is more effective. It lets students know what they did right so they know to do this again. And it is credible because it points to a specific instance. Otherwise, students, especially those who have a shaky sense of self-efficacy, may believe that you are just being nice to them. Statements that affirm students' efforts can also be helpful: "Keep at it. You're on the right track." Where possible, you want the students to find their own solutions and reach their own conclusions. However, when they are genuinely stuck, provide assistance that is needed. This is especially important when students need information in order to continue their efforts (Herber & Herber, 1993).

USING TECHNOLOGY

The Cooperative Learning Center at the University of Minnesota http://www.clcrc.com/index.html Has valuable additional information about cooperative learning.

✔ CHECKUP

1. What is cooperative learning?
2. How might cooperative learning using jigsaw groups be implemented?

Collaborative Strategic Reading

One form of cooperative learning has been specifically designed to help mainstreamed students learn in regular classrooms. With increasing diversity in the classroom, content area teachers are faced with the question How can I provide for the needs of all the students in each of my classes? One possible answer is **Collaborative Strategic Reading** (Vaughn, Klinger, & Schumm). Collaborative Strategic Reading combines cooperative learning with the use of high-payoff strategies and helps both mainstreamed and regular education students become more effective learners. These high-payoff strategies include previewing, developing key vocabulary thorough the use of click and clunk, getting the gist or main idea, and wrapping up by stating the most important information learned that day and composing questions that they think a teacher might ask on a test. Collaborative Strategic Reading has been specially designed to help struggling learners but may be used with all learners. Here's how it works.

Before assembling in cooperative groups, students are introduced to the topic they will be reading about. The teacher discusses the new topic and, if appropriate, ties it in with what was covered the previous day. The teacher introduces words that students would not be able to figure out on their own. The teacher also tells the class how much of the text is to be read. Students read the text section by section. Younger students might read a paragraph at a time. Older students might read longer portions.

■ **Collaborative Strategic Reading** is an approach to cooperative learning that incorporates effective learning strategies. It is designed for mainstreamed students.

■ Previewing

After the introduction, students begin working in cooperative groups. The first strategy they use is previewing. Previewing has two steps: brainstorming what is known about a topic and using the title and headings to predict what they will learn in this section. As they read the section, they can make new predictions. Students then read the text silently section by section.

■ Click and Clunk

■ **Click and clunk** is a procedure for monitoring for meaning and repairing comprehension.

A unique feature of Collaborative Strategic Reading, one that students elected as their favorite, is **click and clunk.** Clicks and clunks are compared with driving a car. When everything is going smoothly, the car is clicking along. When the car hits a pothole, there is a clunk. Clicks are portions of the text that are easy to understand. Clunks are problem portions. When students hit clunks, which are generally hard words or confusing sentences, they attempt to clarify them. If the clunk is a hard word, students might look for a familiar word part or use context, syllabic or morphemic analysis, or the glossary or dictionary. If unable to resolve a clunk, a student may request help from other members of the group. If no one in the group can help, students seek help from the teacher. Fix-up strategies also include those needed for removing comprehension clunks. Students are taught strategies for fixing clunks. A student who is especially adept at fixing clunks might be appointed the group's clunk expert.

■ Getting the Gist

■ The **gist** is the main idea of a selection or what the selection is all about.

Getting the **gist** entails getting the main idea of the section. After reading a section, students ask themselves, "What is this section mostly about (topic)?" or, "What is the most important idea about the topic?"

■ Wrap-Up

Wrap-up is a review of the day's reading. Students wrap up in two ways. They review or summarize the most important information they have learned. They can create a graphic organizer to highlight essential information. As part of the review, students also create questions of the type that might be found on a test. They create questions that involve the most important information in the selection. Students select their best questions and pose them to members of the group.

At the end of the lesson, the class meets as a whole and students discuss what they have learned. The teacher can ask groups to share the most important things they have learned, ask their best questions, or share their toughest clunk. The teacher makes sure that key concepts are understood and clarifies misunderstandings.

Before students work on their own, the teacher models strategies and has students try them out. Content area periodicals and brief news articles provide good materials for tryouts. Once students have grasped the reading strategies and also procedures for working in groups, they begin working in groups on their own. The teacher monitors their work and provides assistance as needed.

Each student fulfills a specific role. Roles may be assigned by the teacher, or the students might decide among themselves who will fulfill which role. Roles should be changed periodically. Students are given cue sheets to guide them as they fulfill their roles. Possible roles include the following:

- Leader: Gets the group started and leads discussions.
- Clunk expert: Provides assistance with clunks. Has a series of printed clunk cards that contain prompts that might be used to resolve clunks.
- Timekeeper: Times each section. For example, allows three minutes for preview, six minutes for reading a section and getting the gist. (Time may vary depending on length of selection.) Allows five minutes for wrap-up.
- Recorder: Records review, best questions, and unresolved clunks.
- Supervisor: Makes sure group stays on task and encourages everyone to participate.

 **CHECKUP**

1. What are the main elements in Collaborative Strategic Reading?
2. How might this approach to Collaborative learning be implemented?

Discussion Groups

Another popular form of cooperative learning is the discussion group. In a discussion group, the members all explore the same topic but have different roles. One popular type of discussion group is the **literature circle.** The circles are composed of four to six students who are reading the same book. The students may have chosen to read the same book or may have been assigned the book. Groups are formed in much the same way as other cooperative learning groups. Roles are assigned by the teacher, or the group decides who will fulfill which role. Key roles are the discussion leader, summarizer, literary reporter, illustrator, word chief, and connector (Bjorklund, Handler, Mitten, & Stockwell, 1998; Daniels, 1994).

All of the group members read the book. However, the discussion leader creates questions for the group and leads the discussion. The summarizer summarizes the selection. The literary reporter locates passages that contain key incidents, feature imaginative language, or create vivid pictures. The reporter might read the passages out loud, ask the group to read them silently and discuss them, or involve other members of the group in dramatizing them. An illustrator depicts a key part of the selection with a drawing or graphic organizer. The word chief identifies potentially difficult words or expressions in the selection, checks their meanings in the dictionary, and records their definitions. At the circle meeting, the word chief discusses the words with the group. The connector creates links between the book and other books the group has read or with events, problems, or situations in real life. The connector explains the connection and discusses it with the group. Although each student has a specific role, any member of the group may bring up a question for discussion, call attention to a passage that is memorable, ask about a confusing word, or note a personal or literary connection.

The roles reflect the kinds of strategies that expert readers apply as they read a text. They raise questions in their minds, make connections, create images, summarize, note key passages, decode difficult words and confusing passages, and appreciate expressive language and literary techniques. Students switch roles periodically so that each member of the circle has the opportunity to experience each of the roles.

■ **Literature circles** are cooperative learning groups set up for the purpose of reading and discussing a work of literature. They may be adapted to discuss content area trade books.

STRUGGLING READERS

Because it features teacher guidance and structured ways in which students can work together and help each other, Collaborative Strategic Reading is especially effective for helping struggling learners.

Job sheets are given students to provide them with directions for fulfilling roles. A sample job sheet for a discussion leader is shown in Figure 6.2. Although the job sheets are fairly specific, key tasks, such as creating questions, identifying imaginative language, deriving definitions of difficult words, and making connections are discussed and modeled. It is also helpful if the groups practice their jobs with a relatively easy selection first.

After a literature circle has been formed, the group meets and sets up a reading schedule. They might also decide on roles, unless the teacher has made that decision. After reading, students complete their job sheets and might also respond in a response journal. The teacher visits each group and might model asking questions or responding to a selection or simply be another participant. Whole class sessions are held each day so that groups can share with each other.

After the books have been read and discussed, students meet in groups according to the roles they fulfilled, just as students met in expert jigsaw groups. All the discussion leaders meet, as do all the summarizers, connectors, illustrators, word chiefs, and literary reporters. Students discuss the book they read from the point of view of their roles. Through this regrouping, the students get to know the books read in other groups. Literature circles can also be organized in a less formal way so that members meet to talk over their reading but don't have specific roles.

The type of organization used in literature circles can also be adapted to form discussion groups that talk about reading undertaken in social studies, science, and other content areas. The reading discussed might be drawn from trade books on key topics and could be teacher assigned or student selected.

STRUGGLING READERS

Discussion groups might be set up in such a way that students are reading and discussing texts that are on their level. For instance, if students are having difficulty with the text because it is above their reading level, they might read and discuss trade books that cover the same topics but are easier to read.

FIGURE 6.2

Discussion Leader Job Sheet

The discussion leader's job is to create and ask questions about the selection that the students in your group read. The questions should be of the kind that help readers better understand the selection. The questions should also help readers relate what happened in the selection to their own lives. Some kinds of questions that you might ask are:

• Were you surprised by anything that happened in this part of the selection?
• Was there anything in the selection that puzzled you?
• Who is your favorite character so far? Why?
• If the author were here, what would you say to her or him?
• What do you think will happen next?

Write your questions on the lines.

1. _____
2. _____
3. _____
4. _____

 **CHECKUP**

1. What are discussion groups?
2. What are some possible roles in a discussion group?

Discussion Web

One problem with discussion groups is the tendency for one or two individuals to dominate. A technique known as the Discussion Web alleviates this problem (Alvermann, 1991). Based in part on think-pair-share (McTighe & Lyman, 1988), the technique has each student thinking about the ideas that he wants to contribute. Students then pair up with a partner and share their ideas. This gives them a chance to clarify and extend their thinking. The partners then meet with another pair of partners. The four students discuss their conclusions and reasons, come to a consensus, and decide on reasons that best support their conclusion. Discussion Webs are incorporated within the framework of a lesson and are part of a six-step procedure.

 LESSON 6.5   **Steps in Discussion Web Lesson**

Step 1: Preparation

A selection is introduced in much the same way it would be in a directed reading activity. Background is activated, new concepts and vocabulary are introduced, interest is built, and a purpose for reading is set.

Step 2: Reading

The story is read silently.

Step 3: Initial Discussion

The selection is discussed and students, working in pairs, are asked to create a Discussion Web in response to a key question that has supporting reasons for and against it: Should the United States have dropped the atomic bomb in World War II? Should the United States have joined the League of Nations after World War I? Should coal-burning energy plants in the Midwest be required to eliminate pollution so that the air in the Northeast will be cleaner? Students jot down brief telegraphic phrases as reasons. However, they try to put an equal number of reasons in the yes and no columns.

Step 4: Second Discussion

Each pair meets with another pair to form a group of four. Members of the group compare and discuss their reasons and attempt to reach a consensus.

Step 5: Report of Conclusions

After each group has reached its conclusion, the group selects a spokesperson and also discusses and chooses the reason that they feel best supports their conclusion. Dissenting opinions are also noted. The spokesperson for each group is then called upon to report the group's conclusion, best reason, and dissenting opinions. Having groups choose a best reason reduces the possibility of duplication as the groups give their reports.

Step 6: Follow-Up

Students write individual essays in which they state and support their conclusions. Students should be encouraged to use the reasons that they composed on their own and also reasons that the group suggested.

The Discussion Web can be reworded to accommodate questions that do not lend themselves to a yes–no response. In science, students might create two or more hypotheses for a phenomenon and provide possible reasons for supporting each one. In social studies, the categories might be positions taken by key figures on important issues. Students might, for instance, write reasons to support Hamilton's views on democracy and Jefferson's views.

 CHECKUP

1. What is a Discussion Web?
2. What are the steps in implementing a Discussion Web?

SUMMARY

Collaborative learning is an approach that views students as active participants in the construction of learning rather than as passive recipients. In ReQuest, Reciprocal Teaching, Questioning the Author, Collaborative Strategic Reading, and Reading Seminar, teacher and students work together to construct meaning. These are examples of collaborative learning in which the teacher plays a very active role. All of these approaches can be used with both whole classes and small groups.

The simplest of the techniques is ReQuest, which consists of having teacher and students ask each other questions about text. Reciprocal Teaching stresses four highly effective strategies: predicting, questioning, clarifying, and summarizing. Using open-ended queries instead of questions, Questioning the Author is designed to help students, under the teacher's guidance, construct

meaning from a text by carefully examining brief segments of text and asking and discussing the question What is the author trying to say here? Reading Seminar, which is based on Questioning the Author, combines strategy instruction with open-ended questioning and discussion.

The term *cooperative learning* is typically used to refer to small groups of students working and learning together. Although cooperative learning can take many forms, two of the most widely used are the jigsaw and the study group. In jigsaw groups, each student is responsible for completing a piece of the report or project and teaching other group members. In study groups, students reflect on and discuss material in preparation for a test. They might subdivide the topic or have everyone contribute on the whole topic. In Collaborative Strategic

Reading, which was designed to help struggling learners in mainstreamed classes and in discussion groups, students help each other construct meaning from text. Although they all read the same text, each has a separate role in the group. In discussion groups, students also read the same material and have different roles. Discussion Webs incorporate think-pair-share.

Cooperative learning requires careful management. In fostering cooperative learning, the teacher fulfills four roles: directing, monitoring, probing, and supporting.

Reflection

Return to the Anticipation Guide at the beginning of this chapter. Respond once again to the items. Did your responses change? If so, how and why? How might cooperative or collaborative learning be used in content area classrooms? How might cooperative and collaborative learning be used to help struggling learners?

EXTENSION AND APPLICATION

1. Find out more about Questioning the Author by reading Beck, McKeown, Hamilton, & Kucan (1997). *Questioning the author: An approach for enhancing student engagement with text.* Newark, DE: International Reading Association.
2. Try out ReQuest or one of the other approaches described in the chapter. Assess its effectiveness. What seems to be its advantages and disadvantages?

3. With three or four other members of the class, set up a cooperative group for a particular learning task. It may be the reading of an article or a chapter in this text. Decide on the form your group will take and the role that each member will fulfill. Also evaluate the effectiveness of your group.

STUDY SKILLS AND STRATEGIES

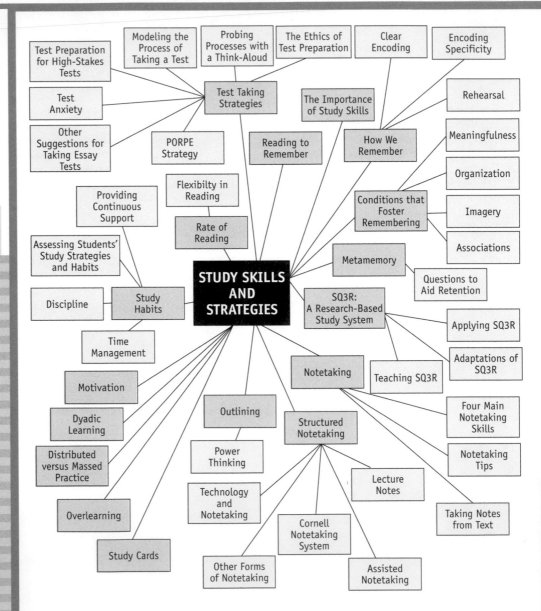

STUDY SKILLS AND STRATEGIES

- Test Preparation for High-Stakes Tests
- Modeling the Process of Taking a Test
- Probing Processes with a Think-Aloud
- The Ethics of Test Preparation
- Clear Encoding
- Encoding Specificity
- Test Anxiety
- Test Taking Strategies
- The Importance of Study Skills
- Rehearsal
- Other Suggestions for Taking Essay Tests
- PORPE Strategy
- Reading to Remember
- How We Remember
- Meaningfulness
- Organization
- Flexibilty in Reading
- Conditions that Foster Remembering
- Imagery
- Providing Continuous Support
- Rate of Reading
- Associations
- Assessing Students' Study Strategies and Habits
- Metamemory
- Questions to Aid Retention
- Discipline
- Study Habits
- SQ3R: A Research-Based Study System
- Applying SQ3R
- Time Management
- Adaptations of SQ3R
- Motivation
- Notetaking
- Teaching SQ3R
- Four Main Notetaking Skills
- Dyadic Learning
- Outlining
- Structured Notetaking
- Notetaking Tips
- Distributed versus Massed Practice
- Power Thinking
- Lecture Notes
- Overlearning
- Technology and Notetaking
- Taking Notes from Text
- Study Cards
- Cornell Notetaking System
- Other Forms of Notetaking
- Assisted Notetaking

ANTICIPATION GUIDE

For each of the following statements related to the chapter you are about to read, put a check under "Agree" or "Disagree" to show how you feel. Discuss your responses with classmates before you read the chapter.

		Agree	*Disagree*
1	Content area teachers should be responsible for teaching the study skills necessary to learn their subject matter.	____	____
2	One of the most effective study strategies is to reread material carefully.	____	____
3	Memory techniques such as making up rhymes are generally ineffective.	____	____
4	Poor study habits and poor self-discipline, rather than a lack of study strategies, is the main cause of poor preparation for content area tests.	____	____
5	Most students learn effective study techniques without any formal instruction.	____	____
6	Studying with a group is better than studying alone.	____	____

USING WHAT YOU KNOW

Previous chapters have presented a variety of suggestions for improving reading in the content areas. This chapter goes beyond reading to learn to explore strategies for reading to remember. Before reading this chapter, think about the way you study. What special techniques do you use? Do you use different techniques for different subjects? How effective do these techniques seem to be? What is your attitude toward studying? How would you rate your study habits? How might you help students improve their studying?

READING TO REMEMBER

Frank is discouraged. Although he had given up watching his favorite TV shows to read the chapter on plant life in his general science text, he had failed the quiz. Frank was determined to do better. In preparation for the next quiz, he read the chapter twice, even though it took up just about all his evening. However, he still failed the quiz. One question asked about the parts of a plant. He remembered reading about the parts of a plant, but except for petals, he couldn't remember what they were. "I guess I'm just stupid," Frank thought to himself.

The nature of Frank's reading has changed but Frank's strategies haven't. Even when reading expository text, Frank uses a narrative style. He plunges into the text without any preparation or purpose, except that of getting to the end of the chapter. He reads the concept-laden material as though it were a story. As he reads, he does nothing to organize the information or check his comprehension of it. And when he's finished reading, he closes his book. He does nothing to promote retention of the material.

Although he has learned to read, Frank must now learn how to learn through reading. He must acquire study strategies. In addition to learning how to comprehend complex materials, he must learn how to organize and retain that material.

*S*uccessful studying is a combination of a positive attitude, good habits, and effective strategies.

Frank is not alone. Many students lack suitable study strategies. When seeking fifth-grade students for an investigation of study techniques, researchers sought students who had adequate decoding skills but poor study strategies (Madden, 2000). They had no difficulty finding participants. Two-thirds of the students they screened met the criteria. High school students report use the following strategies: reading more slowly, rereading the text, and underlining the text (Schallert & Tierney, 1980). None of these strategies is particularly effective. They may work when the material is relatively easy and students have to remember it for only a short period of time. However, for heavy-duty studying, more effective strategies, such as outlining or taking notes or using a study system, work better. The good news is that students do benefit when instructed in the use of study strategies (Adams, Carnine, & Gerstn, 1982; Nist, Hogrebe, & Simpson, 1985). This instruction should include a metacognitive component that helps students decide which strategies are most appropriate for individual study conditions. In fact, metacognition is the foundation of effective study strategies. Metcacognition enables students to decide what to study, how to study, and how long they should study. As Eggen & Kauchak (2001) note, "The effectiveness of study strategies depends on the thought involved in making decisions about what is important enough to highlight, include in notes, or use in organizing ideas" (p. 339).

CHECKUP

1. How effective are student's study skills?
2. Why is metacognition the foundation of study skills?

THE IMPORTANCE OF STUDY SKILLS

Even students who have adequate comprehension may have difficulty preparing for tests or completing assignments. Students may read for understanding but fail to read to learn and remember. Students may lack study strategies, motivation, or confidence in themselves as learners. An effective program of study skills instruction will help them get to know themselves as learners and use this knowledge to set goals, plan study sessions, make use of a variety of study strategies, and monitor their studying.

HOW WE REMEMBER

We are in a better position to foster retention if we understand how memory works. Memory has three major theoretical parts: **encoding, storage,** and **retrieval.** Encoding is the process by which we convert sensory or other information into a form that can be stored in memory. Storage is the process of keeping information in memory. Retrieval is the process of getting information out of memory, or remembering. If memory is thought of as a filing system, encoding would be putting information into a file folder, storage would be putting the folder into a file cabinet, and retrieval would be similar to getting the file out of the file cabinet.

■ **Encoding** is the process through which sensory information is changed into a form, such as a phonological or visual form, that can be stored in the brain.
■ **Storage** is the process of placing and keeping information in memory.
■ **Retrieval** is the process of locating and using information stored in memory.

Clear Encoding

Generally, information is remembered better if it is clearly encoded. In order to remember a fact or idea, we need to have an accurate representation of it. We can't possibly remember a person's name if we didn't hear it clearly. We are more likely to remember a person's name if we listen attentively to it and also if we intend to remember it: by forming an intention to remember someone's name, we will take steps to remember it. We may rehearse the name—that is, we may say it over and over again. This is known as a maintenance rehearsal. It keeps the name from slipping out of our minds. It keeps it in short-term, or working, memory, but it may not place it in long-term memory. To make sure the name gets placed in long-term memory, we may use a more meaningful strategyWe may make an association. After meeting Joseph Snow, we may visualize him as a snowman. Or we may think that his name really fits because he seems to be a cold person, a kind of an emotional snowman. The more distinctive we can make our memory clues the better. Distinctive clues are more memorable.

What holds true for remembering names is also true of ideas. Fuzzy or confusing ideas are soon lost. We have nothing to hold on to. When getting a set of directions, it's a good idea to have them repeated to make sure that you understand each part of the direction. It's also a good idea to repeat the directions in your own words. That way, the person giving the directions can make sure that you got them right. And you can check your understanding. If you can't put a set of directions or an idea into your own words, chances are that you don't really understand it and won't remember it.

Encoding Specificity

How we encode information determines how we remember it. This is known as encoding specificity. For instance, name the days of the week as fast as you can. Now name the days of the week in alphabetical order. Naming the days of the week in alphabetical order is more difficult because when we encoded the names of the week into memory we organized them chronologically (Ashcraft, 1994). We tend to retrieve information in the same way that it was encoded or stored into memory. The lesson in all this is that the way we study should match the way we will be tested. The best way to prepare for an oral exam is to practice responding orally to possible questions. The best way to prepare for a practical exam, recognizing slides under a microscope, for instance, is to practice looking at slides under a microscope.

Information is not encoded into memory as isolated bits of data; rather, it is encoded into a "richer memory representation, one that includes any extra information about the item that was present during encoding" (Ashcraft, 1994, p. 228). The context in which you learn something serves as a retrieval cue or memory prompt. For instance, if you studied the foods that make up a balanced diet by visualizing key foods in a food pyramid, visualizing the pyramid will help you recall the names of the foods. If you paid particular attention to category names, such as fats, proteins, and carbohydrates, the category names should serve as retrieval cues.

Rehearsal

■ **Rehearsal** is the process of committing information to memory.

■ **Maintenance rehearsal** is the process of keeping information in memory by saying it over and over again or using some other low-level process.

■ **Elaborative rehearsal** is the use of meaningful processes, such as making meaningful associations or reflecting on the information, in order to keep information in memory.

Rehearsal is the process of committing information to memory. There are two kinds of rehearsal: maintenance and elaborative (Craik & Lockhart, 1972). **Maintenance rehearsal** is relatively simple. It's what you do when you look up a phone number and then punch in the phone number. To keep the number in memory, you might repeat it two or three times. Once you stop rehearsing the number, it fades away. This simple rehearsal was enough to keep the number in working, or short-term, memory but not strong enough to move it into long-term memory. In addition, there is the question of intentionality. Because you had no intention of retaining the number, you didn't rehearse it sufficiently or take steps to place it in long-term memory. **Elaborative rehearsal,** on the other hand, involves meaningful processes in which learners create connections between new information and information that is already known. When information is rehearsed in elaborative fashion, the information is stored more deeply in the memory system.

If you are learning a list of terms such as *circumference, diameter, radius, sector, arc,* and *chord* that are used to define the parts of a circle, you might organize the words to show how they are related to each other. You might also relate the words to experiences that you have had or create a visual image in which the words are placed as labels on the key parts of the image. You might also use roots and affixes to help you better understanding the meaning of each term and relate these new words to known words, relating *circumference* to *circle,* for instance. This elaborative processing creates connections with other concepts in memory and so results in more thorough storage.

Information can be processed in shallow or deep fashion. Shallow processing is similar to maintenance rehearsal. Deep processing corresponds to elaborative rehearsal. It means making meaningful connections so that the information is stored more deeply in the memory system and so is more readily retrieved. Although we sometimes remember pieces of information that were processed in shallow fashion, information that is deeply processed is usually better remembered (Ashcraft, 1994).

✔ CHECKUP

1. What are the main components of memory?
2. How does memory work?

CONDITIONS THAT FOSTER REMEMBERING

Based on what is known about the workings of memory, we can say that the following conditions foster remembering: meaningfulness, organization, imagery, associations, and metamemory.

Meaningfulness

As humans we strive to make sense of our world. For decades, psychologists used meaningless wordlike syllables to explore the workings of memory. They used nonsense words so that the participants would not be able to use the meaningfulness of materials as a memory aid. However, the psychologists discovered that cognition, including memory, is an active constructive process. Participants invested the nonsense syllables with meaning. For instance, participants might associate the nonsense syllable *yeg* with the name *Meg.* The more that students can build meaningfulness into their studying, the better they will be able to retain the material. For instance, a student may memorize the fact that water is denser than oil because although the oil molecules are larger, they are spread farther apart. From TV news stories about oil spills, the student knows that oil floats on water. Now she can apply that knowledge to help better understand and remember that oil is not as dense as water. She can hypothesize that the oil does not sink into the water because the denser molecules of the water hold it up. By integrating new knowledge with old knowledge, she achieves a better understanding and retention of both. Later, when she reads about methods of cleaning up oil spills, she is better able to understand and remember why it is possible to scoop up the oil for a time after a spill. The efficiency with which we learn new information depends not just on how much we have to learn but how easily the new information fits in with what we already know (Carlson & Buskist, 1997).

Organization

In addition to being meaning-makers, we are also organizers. Try this. Write down the names of as many birds as you can think of within a two-minute period. Now look at your list. Chances are it is organized in some way. You may, for instance, have placed all the song birds together and all the hunting birds together. When a researcher asked participants to learn a list of sixty items, the participants grouped the items into categories (Bousfield, 1953). The participants recalled the words the way they organized them. For instance, they recalled the animal names as a group and then the vegetable names as a group.

How effective is categorizing or clustering information? When it is presented in an organized fashion, students retain almost twice as much information (Bower, Clark, Lesgold, & Winzenz, 1969). When given 112 relatively unfamiliar terms, students learned all of them after just four presentations. When the same terms were presented in an unorganized display, the students, learned just 70 percent of the words. The organized display, by the way, was presented in much the same way as semantic maps are drawn (see Figure 3.1). If there is no logical organization, people tend to impose a subjective organization (Tulving, 1962).

Why is organization so important? Our concepts are stored in networks. We can understand and retain new information better if we relate it to already existing concepts. For instance, if students have a well-developed schema for the French and Indian War, they are better able to understand events that led up to the start of the Revolutionary War. By creating connections between the two wars, they can better understand why the British raised taxes on the colonies. They can also better understand why some tribes sided with the British and some sided with the colonists. Comprehension is also fostered if students use the organization of text to help them better understand and retain key ideas. Making connections not only makes text more understandable, it also reduces the load on memory because the ideas are remembered as part of a network rather than as isolated bits of information.

Imagery

Imagery has a unique, but apparently underused, potential to foster storage of information (National Reading Panel, 2000). Imagery can add encoding power to a word. According to Paivio's dual encoding hypothesis (1971), words that refer to concrete objects can be encoded in memory twice. The word *camel*, for instance, can be encoded verbally just as any other word can. But it can also be encoded visually as a mental picture of a camel. Because it is encoded twice, it can be retrieved from memory in two ways: verbally or visually. A word such as *truth*, since it lacks a visual counterpart, would be encoded verbally. It could be encoded visually, but it would take time to create a visual image.

 CHECKUP

1. How do meaningfulness, organization, and imagery foster remembering?

Associations

Associational devices are used when there are no basic principles underlying the information so meaningful connections can't be made. This occurs when relationships are arbitrary—for instance, when learning the names of presidents, formulas, or a similar type of material. Associational memory devices include rhymes, acronyms, acrostics, the keyword approach, and other mnemonic methods. They make use of information already stored in memory to help us remember new information.

Mnemonics consists of creating artificial connections between the known and the unknown. Mnemonic devices foster memory by adding elaborations such as a visualization, a rhyme, or a series of known words. Because more information is stored, it has more retrieval hooks and so is easier to remember. Mnemonic devices are structured in such a way that remembering a part leads to retrieval of the whole; for instance, the rhyme that tells how many days there are in the months of the year is a mnemonic device—the rhythm and rhymes it contains provoke memory. Mnemonic devices follow three principles of memory: (1) the material to be learned is practiced repeatedly, (2) the material is integrated into an existing memory framework, and (3) the practice provides an excellent means of retrieving information.

> ■ **Mnemonics** is a process to aid memory that makes use of artificial associations, such as rhymes. Mnemonics represents a deeper level of processing than simply saying an item over and over.

Naomi James (1979), the first woman to sail around the world alone, made her voyage both longer and more dangerous when she confused the words *latitude* and *longitude*. One runs north and south, the other east and west. Can you say for sure which is which? If students know the word *lateral*, they could relate *lateral* and *latitude*. Both refer to directions that are sideways, rather than up and down. In addition, a simple mnemonic will help distinguish the two words and would have saved Naomi James a lot of stress. The word *longitude* has an *n* (for *north*) in it, but *latitude* does not (Pauk, 1989). Other associational devices are reconstructive elaborations, acronyms, rhymes, acrostics, first-letter mnemonics, and narrative stories.

■ Reconstructive Elaborations

The key word strategy, which was introduced in Chapter 3 as a way of remembering the meanings of new words, has been adapted for use with content area information in a device known as **reconstructive elaborations.** The process is reconstructive because it involves modifying a word or other information so it will be more familiar or meaningful. It is elaborative because it involves linking or elaborating pieces of information. Elaborative reconstruction fosters better recall because it improves encoding by making it more meaningful and more familiar. Improved encoding fosters improved recall (Mastropieri & Scruggs, 1989).

> ■ A **reconstructive elaboration** is a memory device that involves modifying and elaborating a concept to be learned in order to make it more memorable.

To learn the fact that deciduous trees shed their leaves in the fall, students are taught a reconstructed key word for *deciduous*. The word chosen is *decided* because it is familiar, looks like *deciduous*, and partially sounds like *deciduous*. An interactive illustration is then created. It could be a picture of a tree which is clearly labeled as being deciduous, saying, "It's fall and I'm cold, so I have decided to let my leaves fall" (Mastropieri & Scruggs, 1989, p. 342). The statement becomes the elaboration: it links the word *deciduous* with the concept that leaves are dropped in the fall. Students can construct the interactive illustration or the teacher can supply it. The illustration is discussed so students make the connection between *decided* and *deciduous* and the concept that deciduous trees drop their leaves in the fall.

In a unit on the history of highways, for instance, key terms are listed and transformed into reconstructive elaborations. For the word *eroded*, the key word *road* is chosen. The interactive illustration shows a road and a hillside that are obviously eroded. A sign in the hillside warns, "Danger: Erosion," and a person nearby says, "The road has eroded" (Mastropieri & Scruggs, 1989, p. 394). Other important terms are presented in this same way. The authors of this adaptation report that through reconstructive elaboration, students have doubled their learning and retention.

STRUGGLING READERS
Reconstructive elaboration and other memory devices have been used successfully with struggling readers and students with learning disabilities. Achieving readers often devise their own strategies and so are not as reliant on teacher guidance as struggling readers and struggling learners are.

Acronyms

■ An **acronym** is a word made up of the first letter of each of a series of words.

An **acronym** is a word composed of the first letters of a series of words to be memorized. *HOMES* is an acronym for the names of the Great Lakes: Huron, Ontario, Michigan, Erie, and Superior. In recalling the names of the Great Lakes, the students uses *HOMES* as a mnemonic aid so that the letter *H* reminds them that the name of one of the Great Lakes begins with an *H*, the letter *O* reminds them that the name of another of the Great Lakes begins with an *O*, and so on. Students are not restricted to real words; they may use made-up words or even several made-up words. For instance, *ROY G. BIV* is a mnemonic for the colors of the spectrum: Red, Orange, Yellow, Green, Blue, Indigo, and Violet.

Rhymes

Rhymes are also used to assist memory.

Use *i* before *e* except after *c*.
Or when sounded as *a*
As in *neighbor* and *weigh*.

Acrostics

■ An **acrostic** is a device in which the first letters in a series of words spell out a word or phrase or correspond to the first letters in another series of words to be memorized.

An **acrostic** is a sentence or rhyme in which the first letter of each word stands for the first letter in a series of words to be memorized. The sentence My Very Exceptional Mother Just Served Us Nine Pizzas is a mnemonic to assist in the retrieval of the names of the planets: Mercury, Venus, Earth, Mars, Jupiter, Saturn, Uranus, Neptune, Pluto (Richardson & Morgan, 1997). The acrostic Please Excuse My Dear Aunt Sally helps in remembering the order of operations in algebra problems: Parentheses, Exponents, Multiplication, Division, Addition, and Subtraction. This can be combined with a mental image of your aunt doing something rude in an operating room to further aid retention (Applegate, 2001).

■ First-Letter Mnemonics

First-letter mnemonics uses both acronyms and acrostics to form mnemonic devices. *FIRST* is an acronym for the steps that students use to compose the devices:

Form a word
Insert a letter(s)
Rearrange the letters
Shape a sentence
Try combinations

To form a word, the student writes down the first letter of each word. From these letters, the student forms a word. For instance, if the student is trying to learn the three forms of matter, she might form the word *slag* for **s**olid, **l**iquid, **a**nd **g**as.

Because the list of words may not yield the letters necessary to form a word, the student can insert a letter to help create a word. For instance, in learning the names of the main kinds of rocks—metamorphic, igneous, and sedimentary—the student might create *mis* and add an *s* to it. If, even after adding a letter, the student is still unable to form a word, the student rearranges the letters. Rearranging letters is only feasible when the order of the items is not important. If nothing else is working, the student uses each of the letters as the first letters in words that are used to compose a mnemonic sentence. For instance, the mnemonic sentence Every Good Boy Does Fine was created as a memory aid for the major chords in music: E, G, B, D, F.

If students are still unable to form a mnemonic, they try combinations. They can rearrange and insert letters to make up a word or sentence. For instance, for the Romance languages, which include Italian, Spanish, French, Romanian, and Portuguese, you might make up the acrostic I See Five Red Porsches.

Creating mnemonics is an excellent group activity. Students report that the activity of creating mnemonics, since it involves a lot of planning and discussion, fosters retention of the material to be learned.

Creating a list of important information only works if the student knows which items to put on the list. In other words, the student must know which items are important enough that they need to be memorized. The teacher sometimes supplies a list, but often students must be able to determine a list on their own from information provided in a lesson or from the text.

How well did first-letter mnemonics work? Students using first-letter mnemonics improved their test averages by 30 percentage points (Bulgren & Lenz, 1996).

Students should be encouraged to be flexible and creative in their use of mnemonics. In some situations, mnemonics can be combined. The traditional device for the Great Lakes, *HOMES*, might be combined with the key word method so that students picture large homes on the Great Lakes. This adds visualization, a powerful mnemonic to verbal clues (Scruggs & Mastropieri, 1990). In another example, the acronym *TAG* can be used for the Central Powers in World War I: Turkey, Austria-Hungary, and Germany. Using key word visualization, students can imagine Turkey, Austria-Hungary, and Germany playing tag in Central Park (Mastropieri & Scruggs, 1991).

◼ Narrative Stories

Another way to learn a list of unrelated terms is to create a story using the words. Use the first item as a story starter. Then construct a narrative that includes the other items in the order in which they are to be memorized. Putting words to be memorized in a narrative results in a significant increase in recall (Bower & Clark, 1969).

Mnemonic devices aid memory in three main ways. They supply a structure for learning. The structure might be familiar events or a rhyme. By using visual images, rhyming words, or another device, they create a durable memory. Guidance through retrieval is also created. You are provided cues for recall. This characteristic is especially important because much of our forgetting is really a failure of recall. How many times have you had a fact or a person's name on the tip of your tongue while taking a test but couldn't retrieve it from memory until after the test (Ashcraft, 1994)? Although using already created mnemonic devices aids memory, creating one's own can be even more beneficial. To be most effective, use of mnemonic devices must be metacognitive. The student must know when and where to use them.

 CHECKUP

1. What are some associational techniques that can be used to aid memory?

METAMEMORY

◼ **Metamemory** is our awareness of our memory processes. It is knowing how to remember.

Memory is also aided by metamemory. **Metamemory** is our awareness of our memory processes. It is knowing how to remember. As we develop cognitively, we not only acquire information, we also learn *how* to acquire information and how to retain the information we have acquired. For instance, young children must be shown how to rehearse a series of numbers such as a phone number so as to memorize it. Lacking in metamemory, they don't see the need to rehearse. Even older students may have a limited metamemory. Middle school students had to be shown that an association method was more effective than a repetition strategy for learning new words (Pressley, Ross, Levin, & Ghatala, 1984). An essential component of studying is having enough metacognitive awareness or metamemory to know when you have learned something and when you haven't, and, of course, knowing what steps to take if your learning has not been successful. Strategic learners realize that special effort must be made to encode information into memory and keep it there.

What is the state of your metamemory and other metacognitive skills? On a conscious level, what do you do when you realize that you are facing a difficult studying task? Do you assess the task and think of steps you might take to better understand and retain the materials that you will be tested on? Do you consciously try to make the material more understandable? Do you use visualization or create a mnemonic? Do you make use of mnemonic devices to retrieve information? If you were to name the planets in order, would you use a mnemonic device (Ashcraft, 1994)?

CHECKUP

1. What is metamemory?
2. What role does it play in remembering?

Questions to Aid Retention

When attempting to commit information to memory, students should ask themselves the following questions, which attempt to help them form relationships between new and old learning and incorporate a variety of memory-fostering strategies:

1. How does this relate to what I already know?
2. What does it remind me of?
3. What can I associate it with?
4. Can I picture it in my mind?
5. What can I link this picture to?
6. How does it relate to the topic as a whole?
7. What crazy things pop up into my mind when I think of it?
8. How can I use this crazy association to help me remember?
9. How does this relate to what I learned before?
10. How does it relate to my life outside this class? (Devine, 1987, p. 302)

SQ3R: A RESEARCH-BASED STUDY SYSTEM

A five-step technique known as **SQ3R**—Survey, Question, Read, Recite, and Review—implements many of the principles presented in the previous section (Robinson, 1970). In use for more than half a century, it is the most thoroughly researched study technique in the English language (Caverly & Orlando, 1991; Caverly, Orlando, & Mullen, 2000). SQ3R is based on the following principles:

■ **SQ3R** is a five-step study technique: Survey, Question, Read, Recite, Review.

- Surveying headings and summaries increases speed of reading, helps students remember the text, and provides an overview of the text.
- Asking a question before reading each section improves comprehension.
- Reciting from memory immediately after reading fosters retention. If asked questions after having read a selection, students in one study were able to answer only about half of them (Robinson, 1970). After just one day, 50 percent of what was learned was forgotten. Students were then able to answer just 25 percent of questions asked about a text. However, those who recited after reading the material had a retention rate of more than 80 percent one day later. In another study, students who spent 20 percent of their time reading and 80 percent reciting were able to answer twice as many questions as those who simply read the material (Gates, 1917). The 20–80 rule works best with fact-laden material. For biographies and

similar materials, 60–40 would be sufficient. The denser the materials, the shorter the segment of text that should be read before reciting.

Recitation is probably the most important step in SQ3R. Recitation fulfills a number of functions. First of all, it is metacognitive. It lets you know how well you have understood the material. The more you can recite, the better you have understood the material. It also leads you to repair comprehension problems on the spot. If you can't recite, you know that you have to reread. It is also motivational. You will read each section a little more purposively because you know that you will be reciting at the end of the section. Being able to recite is a reward (Pauk, 1989).

- Comprehending major ideas and noting relationships among ideas aids comprehension and retention.
- Engaging in brief review sessions and relating information to personal needs and interests foster comprehension and retention.

SQ3R prepares students to read and helps them organize, elaborate, and rehearse information from text. In addition, SQ3R is metacognitive. It leads students to establish goals for studying, directs them to assess whether those goals are being met, and leads them to modify their processing if they haven't learned the material they set out to learn (Caverly, Orlando, & Mullen, 2000).

Applying SQ3R

1. *Survey.* Survey the chapter that you are about to read to get an overall picture of what it is about. Glance over the title and headings. Quickly read the overview and summary. Note the main ideas. (You might also want to predict what you think the chapter or section will be about.) This quick survey will give you a framework for organizing the information in the chapter as you read it.

2. *Question.* Turn each heading into a question. The heading Events Leading Up to World War I would become What events led up to World War I? Answering the question you created gives you a purpose for reading. (Textbook headings do not always lend themselves to questions or may even be misleading about the content that follows. If you find this to be so, change your question.)

3. *Read.* Read to answer the question you have created. Having a question to answer focuses your attention and makes you a more active reader. Read only the part covered by the heading. Reading a chapter in parts will help you to better understand and remember what you have read. Textbooks are loaded with ideas. If you try to learn everything in a chapter all at one time, chances are you will end up remembering very little of what you read. It's better to be sure you understand one section before going on to the next.

4. *Recite.* When you come to the end of the section, stop and test yourself. Try to answer your question. If you cannot, go back over the section and then try once again to answer the question. The answer may be oral or written. Note, however, that a written answer is preferable because it is more active and forces you to summarize what you have learned. In addition, the notes can be used for review later on. Use two-column notes. Put the question in the left column and the answer

in the right column. The answer should also be brief; otherwise, SQ3R takes up too much time. Do not take notes until you have read the entire section. Taking notes before completing the section interrupts your reading and could interfere with your understanding of the section. Repeat steps 2, 3, and 4 until the entire selection has been read.

   5. *Review.* When you have finished the assignment, spend a few minutes reviewing what you read. If you took notes, cover them up. Then, asking yourself the questions you created from the headings, try to recall the major points that support the headings. Check your responses by looking at your notes. The review helps you put information together and remember it longer.

   In general, special elements should be treated the same way as text. For graphs, tables, and maps, the title is turned into a question and the information in the graph, table, or map is then used to answer the question (Robinson, 1970). A diagram may be as important as the text and merits special effort. After examining the diagram carefully, students should try to draw it from memory and then compare their drawings with the diagram in the book (Robinson, 1970). Drawing becomes a form of recitation.

Adaptations of SQ3R

Over the years, numerous adaptations have been made to SQ3R. A step that several practitioners advocate adding is reflecting (Pauk, 1989; Thomas & Robinson, 1972; Vacca & Vacca, 1986). After reading, students are encouraged to think about the material and how they might use it. Vacca and Vacca (1986) also recommend that before reading, students reflect on what they already know about the topic.

Teaching SQ3R

To use SQ3R fully, students should be able to generate main ideas. It also helps if they have some knowledge of text structures (Caverly, Orlando, & Mullen, 2000; Walker, 1995). Teaching SQ3R requires a commitment of time and effort. Each step must be taught carefully, with ample opportunity provided for practice and application. Early and Sawyer (1984) recommended spending at least a semester when presenting it to older students. Even college students require extensive instruction in the application of SQ3R. They may need ten hours of instruction or more (Caverly, Orlando, & Mullen, 2000). Even after it has been taught carefully and practiced conscientiously, SQ3R requires periodic review and reteaching.

STRUGGLING READERS
Although all students can benefit from learning a study strategy such as SQ3R, struggling readers stand to benefit the most because they often do not have effective study strategies.

   When teaching SQ3R, build on what students already know about reading and studying. Chances are they have already been taught to survey and generate questions and to read to answer those questions. Also begin with easy, well-structured content selections. Although you can teach SQ3R in a few sessions, learning to apply the technique might take months.

   You might have conferences with students periodically to discuss their application of SQ3R. At that time, you might go over their SQ3R notes. Since studying is idiosyncratic, allow individual adaptations of SQ3R.

A key factor in the success of any study technique that students use is attitude. Using SQ3R or another study system requires hard work and active involvement. Passively reading and even rereading material is easier. Students need to see that the extra effort is paying off in their learning more material and earning higher grades. You also need to help students streamline the technique so there is no wasted effort.

Another key element is the attitude of the teacher. If the teacher believes that SQ3R will help students learn from text and conveys that message, students are more likely to use the strategy. For instance, Landy, a high school chemistry teacher, felt that SQ3R was an excellent aid for helping her students read their highly technical chemistry text (Moje, 1996). She carefully introduced SQ3R and also made its use part of students' homework assignments. They took SQ3R notes as they read and discussed them in class the next day. Since they were keeping three-column notes, they used the extra column to take class notes. Students used SQ3R regularly and believed that it helped them read a difficult text with understanding. Describing her use of SQ3R, one student commented:

> I think it reinforces what I know. . . . I think it's the actual steps that help, because what I do is I make up questions. . . . And I just make sure I answer the questions I made. That makes sure that I know what I read. (Moje, 1996, p. 184)

A second student commented:

> I use the SQ3R because it helps when I write things down. . . . The process helps because then I know exactly what I'm supposed to know or write down. It's the way you're supposed to do it for this class. I know this is the best way for this material. I trust Ms. Landy. (Moje, 1996, p. 187)

Note that part of the second student's motivation for using the strategy was that she trusted her teacher. She also implied that SQ3R worked for subjects like chemistry. A heavy-duty study system, SQ3R is probably most effective when students are reading very difficult fact-packed texts. Students who used SQ3R for chemistry did not use it when reading for English class. Students will not automatically transfer the use of a study strategy. Each content area teacher must show how a strategy can be used in a particular domain and must encourage its use.

If you are a content area teacher you might want to team up with the reading teacher. Perhaps the reading teacher will introduce the technique and you can show students how to apply the technique to your content area text.

 ✔ *CHECKUP*

1. What are the steps in SQ3R?
2. How might SQ3R be taught?

NOTETAKING

Pretend that you are back in high school or middle school. Picture this. An experienced notetaker comes into your class and takes careful, well-organized notes and posts them on the Web where they can be downloaded for free. The notes are neat and well organized. Sound like a fantasy? At some universities, students can obtain on the Web notes compiled by professional notetakers (Steinberg, 1999). Although the notes supplied might be somewhat better organized and neater than those taken by the average student, there is a problem. Notetaking serves two functions. First, it supplies students with a record of essential ideas that would otherwise be forgotten. And this the professional notes do quite well. However, notetaking leads students to select the most important information and organize it. This fosters comprehension and retention of material. Notetaking also makes students more active learners. Students who buy notes are cheating themselves of a learning opportunity. Not surprising, students who took their own notes did better than those who purchased notes.

Notetaking promotes selective attention. Through taking notes, students are more likely to focus on main ideas. Notetaking also fosters the integration of new information with old information, especially if students are taking notes from text in their own words and not simply copying (Cook & Mayer, 1988). Like any other learning strategy, the more students put into notetaking the more they get out of it. The most basic and least beneficial form of notetaking is simply copying from the text. More elaborated forms include putting the text ideas into one's own words, showing hierarchical and other relationships, and including one's own ideas. "The farther students move along the continuum from verbatim to elaborated notes, the greater the benefit they receive" (Smith & Tompkins, 1988, p. 46).

 *CHECKUP*

1. What are the characteristics of effective notetaking?
2. What are the benefits of effective notetaking?

The Four Main Notetaking Skills

Taking notes involves four skill areas: selectivity, organization, consolidation, and fluency. *Selectivity* means choosing the most important information. Students generally record only 50 percent to 70 percent of the main ideas given in a lecture, with most being closer to the 50 percent mark (Anderson & Armbruster, 1984). You can increase this percentage by signaling important details in your lectures.

Organization involves showing how ideas are related so supporting details and examples fall under the main idea. One method of improving organization is to encourage students to take two-column notes. Questions or cue words in the column on the left in effect organize the details on the right and can even be used to show cause–effect, opinion–proof, and other relationships.

Consolidation entails selecting the most important information and putting it in a telegraphic style so that only the most important and most necessary words are included. In general, when taking lecture notes, students should not attempt to put information in their own words because this will detract from their attempts to record the most important information (Pauk, 1989). Modeling notetaking and discussing finished products are effective ways to improve consolidation.

Fluency in taking notes is enhanced by all of the above, especially consolidation, and use of symbols and abbreviations. Some frequently used notetaking symbols and abbreviations include:

w = *with*   & = *and*   b = *but*

Notetaking Tips

Here are some tips that students can use to improve their notetaking.

- Write a dash and leave room for information that they didn't have time to write. This can be filled in later.
- Write question marks for anything they don't understand. Refer to the text or get help from the teacher to clear up any confusing information.
- Use an asterisk to signal information that is especially important—for instance, an item that the teacher announces will appear on the upcoming test.
- Use two columns for vocabulary. Put the new word in the left column and the definition in the right.
- Make sure to include sample problems, charts, diagrams, or other visuals.
- Make sure all notes have dates and headings.

Despite the importance of and universality of taking notes, even the best students vary greatly in the quantity and quality of their notes. An analysis of notes taken by tenth-graders in an advanced placement history class revealed that notes ranged from extensive near-verbatim notes to restatements of main ideas to sketchy telegraphic notes (Armbruster, 1996). If students are having difficulty taking notes, ask to see samples and analyze their performance. Note where they are having difficulty and provide help accordingly (Heiman & Slomianko, 1986).

 **CHECKUP**

1. What are the four main notetaking skills?
2. What are some tips for effective notetaking?

Taking Notes from Text

Taking notes from text is easier than taking lecture notes. Today's content area texts often have an overview and headings and subheads that help students organize information. And, of course, printed materials are easier to deal with because they don't disappear the way spoken words do.

 Notetaking Lesson: Steps in Teaching Students to Take Notes from Text

LESSON 7.1

Step 1:

Explain the purpose and value of notes. Draw from students experiences that they have had taking notes. Discuss with them ways in which taking notes has helped them. Also discuss some difficulties they have had taking notes. If students have just started taking notes and haven't had any experience taking notes for academic purposes, discuss everyday experiences that they may have had with taking notes, such as phone messages. Using a well-designed segment from a text that contains headings and subheads and which students are required to study, demonstrate how you would take notes.

Step 2:

Show students how you survey the whole chapter to get an overview, make predictions based on the overview, and activate prior knowledge. Also demonstrate how you establish a goal and set a purpose. (The goal is the reason for reading —for example, to prepare for a test or class discussion on the Constitution. The purpose is to find specific information or to answer a question: What led up to the creation of the Constitution?). Self-prompts that might be used include:

What is this all about? (survey)
What do I know about this? (prior knowledge)
Why am I reading this? (goal)
What do I want to find out? (overall purpose)

Step 3:

Explain that headings announce main topics. Turn each heading into a question just as was done with SQ3R. Explain how you read to answer that question. (Headings are sometimes misleading. The section following the heading might not develop the topic announced by the heading, or it may contain additional information. The reader must be flexible and create questions that are answered by the text. The reader might have to read the text first and then compose a question about the text content. For initial demonstrations, seek out text that has appropriate headings.)

Step 4:

Think aloud so students can see that as you read the section, you keep your question in mind but read flexibly. Show that you are prepared to change the question if necessary. Emphasize that you do not take any notes until you have finished reading the section. Taking notes while reading interrupts the process and results in including too many details in the notes.

Step 5:

Still thinking aloud, show students how you record your notes. Explain that at first you try to answer the question without looking back at the text, just as you did with SQ3R. After jotting down your notes, which is a form of recitation, you reread them to see if you have included all the important information. If not, you go back to the text to locate and record missing details. Stress the need to be selective. Only essential information should be recorded. Otherwise, you will be overwhelmed with details. Notes should be written in abbreviated form to save time. However, the notes should not be so abbreviated that they don't make any sense when you return to study them. Notes should be taken on illustrations as well as text, especially if important information is presented only visually. Key illustrations, such as the parts of a cell, should be included in the notes.

Step 6:

Review. Show students how you go over all the notes once you have finished so that you get a complete picture of the information. Explain that writing a brief summary of your notes for a section of text will help fix all the most important information in your mind and is also excellent preparation for an essay test. Demonstrate how you might quickly compose a summary.

Explain to students that it is best to master one section at a time. By mastering one section, students are better prepared to understand the next section. Demonstrations might be followed by opportunities for the class to take notes, under the teacher's guidance, on some sample sections of content area text.

 **CHECKUP**

1. What are the steps in teaching students to take notes for text?

STRUCTURED NOTETAKING

One way to ease into notetaking is to provide structure for students. For instance, if they are taking notes on a text assignment, you might set up the questions or topics in the left column and perhaps some of the details in the second column, as shown in Figure 7.1. As they become more proficient, you can gradually withdraw the support. Students might also use graphic organizers, such as webs or Venn diagrams, to take notes.

Lecture Notes

Because of the transitory nature of speech, taking notes from lectures is more difficult than taking notes from text. In addition, the organization of the information is not as apparent as it would be in an informational text containing heads and subheads. Notes are easier to take if the students have some knowledge of the subject. They can use that knowledge to help them determine how to organize their notes and to determine which ideas are most important. Students are in a better position to take notes if they have read the chapter for the day's topic the night before and therefore have some knowledge to bring to the class. Students should pay particular attention to any items that the instructor highlights. For instance, any items that the teacher puts on the board or shows on the overhead are probably of prime importance.

Students should also take particular note of technical vocabulary, formulas, and figures that the teacher highlights or displays.

Assisted Notetaking

If students are novice notetakers or have difficulty taking notes, provide practice. Present short, well-structured lectures and provide students a partial sketch of the lecture notes. You might provide the major topics of the lecture and two of the three subtopics for each and have them add the missing elements. Two-column notes, as explained below, are recommended. Topics would be written in the left column and supporting details in the right.

Using cueing techniques is also helpful. Tell students what the main idea of the lecture is. You might even write it on the board. Also use signal words to indicate the number of details: "There are three main kinds of rocks." "There are six kinds of nutrients." "Here are the four main effects of that law." Highlight important terminology and write it on the board. Also summarize your lectures and pause occasionally to give students time to catch up. Over time, have students take increased responsibility for taking notes. Requiring as it does the ability to distinguish important from unimportant information, independent notetaking should not be undertaken by students who are unable to identify main ideas (Santa, Abrams, & Santa, 1979). If students are unable to distinguish important from unimportant details, "they will tend to take verbatim notes of irrelevant concepts" (Caverly & Orlando, 1991, p. 121).

FIGURE 7.1

Structured Notetaking

Requirements for National Office

President	1. Must be 35 2. 3. 4.
Senate	1. Must be 30 2. 3 4.
House of Rep.	1. Must be 25 2. 3. 4.

CHECKUP

1. What are some techniques that might be used to help students learn to take lecture notes?

The Cornell Notetaking System

There are a number of systems for taking notes. In a typical system, students use indentations or outline format to show the relative importance of ideas. Other systems use two or three columns to record notes, with the extra columns being used to write names of topics or key words, comments, questions, or notes on the same topic from other sources. One of the best known of the multicolumn notetaking procedures is the Cornell system. Widely used for nearly half a century, the **Cornell notetaking system** is more than just a way of arranging notes in two or three columns (Pauk, 1989). It is a series of well-thought-out strategies for learning. It has six steps.

■ In the **Cornell notetaking** system, students record notes in one column and comments, questions, or key vocabulary in a second column.

*T*aking notes is easier if the material is well understood.

Step 1: Record

The student records notes in the second column of a sheet of paper that has been divided into two columns. The column on the left is two and one-half inches wide. The second column is six inches wide. Notes are taken in telegraphic style. Indentations might be used to show relative importance of information. Supporting details are indented under the main idea.

Step 2: Reduce or Question

As soon as possible after taking notes, the student should add missing information, clarify confused information, and rewrite portions that might be unclear. Once that has been done, the student rereads the notes, runs through the lecture in her mind, and reduces each major idea to key words or phrases, which are written in the lefthand two-and-one-half-inch column. The key words or phrases become cues to ideas and details in the wide column. As an alternative to recording key words, the student may elect to create questions that encompass major ideas in the notes.

Step 3: Recite

Using a blank sheet of paper, the student covers up the notes and uses the key words or questions to quiz herself on the material. She should state the questions and the answers out loud. Items that she has difficulty answering should be checked. She should

EXEMPLARY TEACHING

TAKING NOTES

Learning specialist Carol Josel (1997) was not surprised when her eighth-grade students at Arcola Intermediate School in Norristown, PA, asked her to repeat her lecture on Bunker Hill because they weren't able to get it all down, even though she had spoken at a slower-than-usual pace. Never having been taught how to take notes, the students attempted to write down every word and to spell out every word of the lecture, an impossible task. Josel's first step was to teach them how to use abbreviations. She gave another brief lecture and then showed them her notes, which contained only the essentials and had lots of abbreviations.

After discussing her notes, she shared with them her list of abbreviations, which includes a dollar sign for *money, w/* for *with,* and the % sign for *percent.* She also provided them with tips for abbreviating. Long names, for instance, need only be written once. After writing out *Tchaikovsky,* the students can thereafter refer to the composer as *T.* For most multisyllabic words, the word can be abbreviated by writing its first syllable. Thus *Congress* can be written as *Cong.* and *civilization* as *civ.* Josel also showed students how to eliminate unnecessary words. Encouraged to create their own shorthand system, students then practiced taking notes on dictated sentences.

Once students had created their own shorthand systems, they began taking notes on excerpts from their content area texts. With practice, they become confident, proficient notetakers.

also recite in her own words. Translating information into one's own words requires deeper processing and understanding and increases retention. Reciting increases retention of material fourfold (Pauk, 1989).

Step 4: Reflect

The student thinks about the information in her notes and tries to relate it to what she already knows about the topic. She might also think of ways in which she might apply the information. She asks such questions as: What are the main ideas and main facts? How does this information fit in with what I already know? How might I use this information? Through reflection, the student integrates new information with old and personalizes it.

Step 5: Review

The student periodically reviews her notes.

Step 6: Recapitulation

The student writes a brief summary of her notes. In addition to providing a review, this helps her highlight essential information.

A third column of notes might be used when students are combining lecture and text notes (Pauk, 1989). The notetaking page is set up with a two-and-one-half-inch column and two three-inch columns. Lecture notes are recorded in the center. Questions or cue words are written in the left-hand column. Notes from the text are written in the third column. The notes from the lecture and the text are aligned with the question or cue words in the first column, as in Figure 7.2. Summarizing three-column notes is especially important because it provides an opportunity for students to integrate information from the text with information from lectures. Instead of being used as a way of combining lecture and text notes, the third column can be used to record key vocabulary words, raise questions, or make comments.

✔ *CHECKUP*

1. What is the Cornell notetaking system and what are its advantages?
2. What are the steps in the Cornell notetaking system?

Other Forms of Notetaking

Graphic organizers and techniques such as KWLPlus, frame matrix, and information map, which were covered in Chapter 5, can also be used to record notes.

Technology and Notetaking

Many electronic references, such as encyclopedias, have built-in notetaking features. For instance, the electronic encyclopedia *Encarta* uses both Notemarks and Notecards to help students take notes from text. Notemarks serve the same purpose as Post-it notes. Students can mark a page or passage. Notecards function in the same way as traditional notecards. However, they reduce the amount of writing. Students can simply electronically copy key points and place them on Notecards or paste

---

STRUGGLING READERS

If students are having difficulty taking notes, ask to see samples and analyze their performance. Note where they are having difficulty and provide help as needed.

USING TECHNOLOGY

Most of the CD-ROM encyclopedia programs incorporate notetaking features, as does the Factfinders series. Because of the novelty and ease of use of notetaking in computer programs, they can be used to encourage notetaking.

USING TECHNOLOGY

NoteStar
http://notestar.4teachers.org/
Designed for students in grades 4 and up, NoteStar assists in taking notes from online sources. Source information (title, URL, etc.) is automatically recorded in order to assist in work citation. Less writing is involved because students may cut and paste from text. The teacher can use NoteStar to view students' work and e-mail comments.

FIGURE 7.2

Three-Column Notes

U. S. History, Panama Canal	Oct 23	
How did US get rights to build Pan Canal?	Polit Backgd. 　Pan. Part of Colum. 　Pan. wanted indep. 　T. Roos, helped Pan. 　Made deal with Pan.	Treaty with Pan favored US Gave US control of canal Canal returned to Pan. 12-14-99
What were the problems encountered in building the canal?	Build. of Canal 　1880s French group tried. 　Gave up.	Had heat, disease, & engin. problems Lost more than 20,000 men
What was the cost of building the canal?	US start can. in 1904 Fin. 1914 Lost 5,000 men Cost 380 mil.	US wiped out yel. fev. & red. malaria
What were the benefits of the canal?	US ships no longer had to sail around S. Amer. to get from east part of US to west & vice versa. Made trip from coast to coast shorter.	Before can., ship going from NY to SF had to go 18,000+ miles After can, 5,200 miles
	Trip from east US to Hawaii, China, & Japan shorter.	14,000+ ships use can. each yr.
	Navy ships could go from Atl to Pacif or Pacif to Atl more easily	too small for v lrg ships like sup carriers

them directly into their reports. Notes can be collected in a list form, edited, and printed out. The program automatically saves bibliographic information.

Even without electronic notetaking aids, students can electronically copy text from online references and Web sites unless it is in a form that does not allow copying. This makes taking notes easier. However, students must be careful to put copied material in quotes and also to copy the source of the material. One disadvantage of electronic notetaking is that students may put less of the material in their own words and so won't process it as deeply. Encourage students to paraphrase and summarize along with cutting and pasting. Also discuss when it is best to paraphrase and summarize and when it is best to cut and paste.

OUTLINING

Requiring that students note the relative importance and interrelationship of major and supporting details, outlining is a highly effective aid to comprehension, studying, and planning. As such, it is a skill that students should master. However, outlining is also a skill that is difficult to learn. As Anderson and Armbruster (1984) observed, "A potential problem with outlining as a study aid is that it is very time consuming to think through the logical relationships in text and represent the meaning in outline form" (p. 673).

As with other study skills, find out what students know about outlining. To assess their knowledge, you might ask them to outline a brief, well-organized selection. After analyzing the results, build on what they know. Emphasize the importance of determining the relative importance of ideas rather than the formatting of an outline. You might also take advantage of the outlining capacity of word processing programs. Using Microsoft Word, students can have their text displayed in outline form. They can rearrange headings and subheadings, and they can have an outline automatically formatted with the correct numbers and letters.

To introduce or review outlining, explain its value and show examples of various kinds of outlines. Discuss how the table of contents in a book is a kind of outline of main topics and sometimes encompasses three levels. Note that the headings in a book can be used to construct an outline. Demonstrate how you might create an outline for a brief, highly organized selection. Start with a three-level outline and gradually move to one that has more subdivisions. Guide the class as they construct group outlines for text that they have read.

After constructing group outlines, have students complete partially finished outlines, as in Figure 7.3. You might start with a three-level outline in which all the main ideas and most of the supporting details have been recorded. All the students need do is record the missing details. In future practice outlines, students should be responsible for adding a greater proportion of details, until they reach a point where they are adding all the details. Then have them complete outlines in which details are provided but some of the main ideas are missing.

FIGURE 7.3

Incomplete Outline

Parts of Plants Eaten as Vegetables

I. Roots	IV. Flowers	VII.
A. Carrots	A. Broccoli	A. Corn
B. Beets	B.	B. Peas
II. Stems	V. Fruits	C. Beans
A.	A. Tomatoes	VIII. Tubers
B. Rhubarb	B. Cucumbers	A. Potatoes
III. Leaves	C. Eggplants	B. Turnips
A. Spinach	VI. Bulbs	
B. Kale	A.	
C.	B. Garlic	

As an alternative to full outlining, have students create simple outlines in which they are given a proposition and asked to list supporting details, or are given some pros and cons asked to list additional pros and cons, or are given a cause and requested to list effects, as is shown in Figure 7.4.

 *CHECKUP*

1. What are the advantages and disadvantages of outlining?
2. How might outlining be presented?

■ **Power thinking** is a way of outlining that doesn't require knowledge of outlining format.

Power Thinking

Another alternative to the use of formal outlines is power thinking. **Power thinking** is a way of showing the relationship among central ideas and important details

FIGURE 7.4

Informal Outline

Convenience Foods

Pros	Save time
	Save work
	Need less work space and equipment to prepare
Cons	Cost more
	May not be as nutritious
	May have additives
	May not taste as good as homemade foods

The Mexican War

Causes of Mexican War	Mexico was against Texas becoming a part of US.
	After Texas was annexed, there was a boundary dispute.
	Mexico owed US citizens money.
	People in US were eager to expand.
	US cavalry was defeated by Mexican forces in disputed land. Polk used this as a reason to ask Congress to declare war.
Effects of Mexican War	Rio Grande became southern boundary of Texas.
	US paid 15 million for Calif., Utah, Nevada, & parts of Arizona, Colorado, & New Mexico.

(Santa, Havens, & Maycumber, 1996). All main ideas are preceded by a 1; second-level or supporting ideas by a 2; third-level details, which are those that support the second-level ideas, by a 3; and so on. For most texts, three levels will encompass all the essential information. Power thinking is outlining without the concern about format.

By eliminating the concern with whether the subhead should be preceded by an uppercase or lowercase *a*, the focus is placed on showing the hierarchy of ideas and the organization of the piece. It also provides a way of signaling the relative importance of ideas. A power 1 is a main idea. A power 2 supports the main idea. A power 3 supports a power 2 and so forth. If you tell students that you are talking about a power 1 idea, they know you are talking about a main idea. If you say that certain ideas are power 2 ideas, students know those ideas are supporting details. Recommended in CRISS, an exemplary program for teaching content area reading (Santa et al., 1996), power thinking has been used successfully by thousands of students across the land.

Power thinking has two major rules. The structure must be parallel; all 1s must be equal in power, as must all 2s and 3s and so forth. The powers must be arranged hierarchically in terms of their inclusiveness such that power 1s, include power 2s and power 2s include power 3s.

To demonstrate power thinking, start with readily definable categories from your subject matter area, such as transportation, types of food, or parts of the nervous system. Here is how the category of cats might be arranged. Note that, as in traditional outlining, subpowers are indented so that indentations are indicators of the relative importance of ideas.

1 Cats
  2 Wild
    3 Big cats
      4 Lions
      4 Tigers
      4 Cheetahs
      4 Leopards
    3 Small cats
      4 Bobcat
      4 Lynx
      4 Ocelot
      4 Wild cat
  2 Domestic
    3 Calico
    3 Tabby
    3 Manx
    3 Siamese
      4 Blue point
      4 Seal point

To introduce the concept of power thinking, place the power thinking analysis of cats on the board, but don't include all the 3s and 4s. Explain to students that power thinking is a way of organizing ideas that will help them better understand how main ideas and supporting details are related. Explain what a power 1 is, a power 2, and so on. If students are familiar with outlining, explain that this is a form of outlining. To involve them in the exercise, help them fill in some 3s and 4s. Stress the need to maintain parallel structure. After the power outline has been completed, do several outlines cooperatively until students have mastered the concept and format of power thinking.

Provide students with blueprints of increasingly complex power outlines. Easy exercises would contain a two-level power thinking outline. Provide lines indicating where the 1s and 2s should be placed, and fill in the 1s. Have students fill in the 2s from a list provided. Gradually work into more complex pieces in which students have to list 2s, 3s, and 4s, or, given 2s, 3s, and 4s, they have to list 1s.

Apply power thinking to text. Drawing well-constructed examples from materials students are reading, show how the 1s, 2s, and 3s might be used to show relationships among ideas. Using duplicated copies of the selection, have students put a 1 next to power 1 ideas, 2 next to power 2 ideas, and so on. Or have students complete a power thinking outline. Cut up well-structured paragraphs and ask students to arrange the cut-up details into power thinking outline form. This could be done as a group or individual activity.

Use naturally occurring opportunities to reinforce the concept of the hierarchical organization of details. After students have read a passage, ask them what the power 1 idea is and what the power 2 ideas that support it are. When students are writing a paragraph, ask them what power 2 ideas they will use to support their power 1 idea.

STRUGGLING READERS

Power thinking helps students focus on relationships among ideas, especially main ideas and supporting details.

✔ CHECKUP

1. What is power thinking?
2. Why might it be more effective than traditional outlining?

STUDY CARDS

One way of committing technical terms, dates, formulas, and other important information to memory is to use study cards. Students put the item to be learned—the word *monarch*, for instance—on one side and information about the item on the other (Moore, Moore, Cunningham, & Cunningham, 1992). The information could be a definition or the word used in a sentence or both. Or it could be a reconstructed, interactive image: Queen Elizabeth riding on a monorail, with a caption stating, "The monarch rode the monorail." The student might also note that *mono* means "one" and *arch* means "ruler," so that *monarch* means "one ruler."

Cards can be color coded to show similarities in information to be learned. For instance, in chemistry, the molecular formulas of ions are organized by charge: ions with one negative charge are recorded on one color of cards, ions with two negative charges are recorded on another color, and so on. So that students don't forget which color refers to which group of ions, they might use the color whose name comes first alphabetically (blue) to indicate one ion, the next color (green) two ions, the next color (orange) three ions and so on. By calling attention to the ion variable, color coding helps in encoding and retention of the information (Hurst, 2001).

Some biology tests require students to identify slides of cells, cell structures, or parts of the anatomy. The diagram or figure from the lab book or textbook can be photocopied in reduced form so that it fits on a flash card. Students can make two copies, one with the terms that identified the structures intact and one in which they have been blacked out. One copy is pasted on one side of the card; the other copy is pasted on the reverse side. To test themselves, students try to identify the structures whose labels have been blacked out. They check their responses by turning the card over to the side that contains the labels (Landsberger, 2001). Study cards for other kinds of diagrams can be created this same way.

Putting lists of words to be memorized in alphabetical order can be helpful. For instance, the major systems of the human body are: the circulatory, musculoskeletal, endocrine, reproductive, digestive, lymphatic, respiratory, excretory, and nervous systems. When put in alphabetical order, the list contains two series of consecutive letter combinations, *c–d–e* and *l–m–n*, plus *r* (Landsberger, 2001).

When presenting study cards, model and discuss how you would choose items to include and how you might decide what kinds of information to write on the other side of the card. Also model how you would study the cards. You might, for instance, attempt to identify the word on the card. Then check your response. If correct, put it on the pile on the right. If incorrect, see why it's wrong and put it on the pile on the left for further study. Also stress the need for review.

It's a good idea, too, to have sessions of guided practice with students studying with partners so that you can help them make the most of their efforts. You can post prompts on a poster to remind students of this and other study procedures. Moore, Moore, Cunningham, and Cunningham (1994) posted the following suggestions for using study cards:

1. Identify important terms.
2. Record one term on one side of a card and memory aids on the other.
3. Review the cards regularly. (p. 94)

Items to be learned can be put on a single sheet of paper instead of on cards. That way, lists of related items can be assembled. For instance, the student might put on one list all the words that have to do with maps. The paper might be folded in two, with the words to be learned in the left column and definitions or other identifying information on the right. The student could self-test by folding the paper and attempting to recite the definitions while looking just at the words and then unfolding the paper to check responses.

 **CHECKUP**

1. How might study cards or sheets be used?

OVERLEARNING

Students may not be aware of how much studying is required in order to learn a list of new words or several concepts thoroughly. They may lack a criterion for success. They may simply rehearse a series of words for ten minutes and stop. Instead, they should continue to study until they know the words. If they are aware of the principle of overlearning, they will continue to study even after they know the words. **Overlearning** entails continuing to study even after information can be recited. The purpose of overlearning is to reduce forgetting. In one experiment, participants had to repeat a list thirty-two times before they could recite it perfectly. However, when the group recited the list thirty-two more times for a total of sixty-four recitations, they remembered it twice as well (Ashcraft, 1994). In another experiment, participants who simply studied a list of words until they could say them perfectly remembered less than 25 percent of the list one day later and had forgotten almost all the words four days after that. In contrast, participants who overlearned the material remembered a significant proportion of the list two weeks later (Krueger, 1929).

■ **Overlearning** is the practice of continuing to study after the material has been learned in order to foster increased retention.

DISTRIBUTED VERSUS MASSED PRACTICE

In general, short, spaced study sessions are more effective than long ones, especially when students are memorizing information. Periodic reviews also lessen forgetting. Spacing studying over a number of sessions is known as **distributed practice** and works better than massed practice when the students are engaged in such rote learning tasks as learning chemical formulas or the names of the bones in the leg. It is easier to focus and concentrate for brief periods of time. **Massed practice,** or studying for extended periods of time, is more effective when the task has a wholeness, such as reading an essay or writing a report, in which the train of thought would be lost if it were segmented into several separate sessions. Massed practice is also known as cramming.

■ **Distributed practice** is studying or doing practice exercises at intervals.
■ **Massed practice** is studying or doing practice exercises all at one time.

 *CHECKUP*

1. What are the principles of overlearning and distributed versus massed practice?
2. What implications do the principles of overlearning and distributed versus massed practice have for studying?

DYADIC LEARNING

One way of improving students' studying is by arranging for them to help each other. Dyadic learning is a way of studying in which students check and bolster each other's learning (Larson & Dansereau, 1986). Both students read a passage. One then acts as recaller by summarizing the passage orally. The second is a listener/facilitator who corrects errors or supplies omitted information. Steps in the process are listed below.

Step 1: Both students read the passage.

Step 2: The recaller summarizes the passage without referring back to it. The recaller is encouraged to draw diagrams, if that is helpful. The listener may interrupt to make essential corrections.

Step 3: After the recaller has summarized the selection, the listener makes corrections and supplies missing details. The listener is encouraged to expand on the summary, relate important details to previously learned material, or evaluate the material. To make the text more understandable and more memorable, the listener is also encouraged to create mental images or drawings of the material. The listener may look back at the text.

Step 4: The recaller assists the listener in correcting or elaborating on the summary, relating it to known information, or evaluating it. At this point, the recaller may look back at the text.

Step 5: Students discuss what they learned from each other. Although originally used as a study technique, this method can be adapted for use in a variety of reading/writing situations. However, students need to be taught how to fulfill their roles, and their performance should be monitored. You also need to make sure that the students who work together are compatible and somewhat similar in achievement. Pairing a very low achiever with a very high achiever may create a difficult situation for both students. One advantage of dyadic learning is that as students are working together, you can visit pairs or diagnose difficulties and provide assistance as needed.

MOTIVATION

In addition to teaching students how to study, it is important to motivate them. The best motivator, of course, is success. Using ineffective study methods in the past, some students undoubtedly have put time into preparing for tests but did poorly. Discouraged or attributing their failure to lack of ability, they may not adequately prepare for tests because they don't think that studying will help them. Results are more convincing than the most impassioned exhortations, especially when we are asking students to make significant changes in their behavior. By the time they reach high school or even middle school, most students have firmly established study habits, which all too often are ineffective. One way of helping students adopt more effective techniques is to help them discover for themselves which techniques actually work best. High school teacher Jenny Watson Pearson (Pearson & Santa, 1995) involved students in a series of experiments in which they read articles, studied each in a different way, and then wrote down all the facts they could recall from each. Students then graphed the results, analyzed them, and reflected on them. It became clear that some approaches were better than others but that these could vary from student to student. However, most of the students concluded that they learned more when they organized the information in some way and when they talked over what they had learned with others. The experiments clearly demonstrated to the students the value of effective study techniques. As Watson commented (Pearson & Santa, 1995):

> As a high school teacher, I often thought about what is really important for my students to learn. I now think that it is most important to enable my students to make that decision for themselves. Through the investigation of their own learning styles and discovery of suitable study strategies, my students can become responsible and discriminating purveyors of their own knowledge. (p. 469)

STUDY HABITS

Study involves will as well as skill, although the two are related. The best study strategies are of little benefit if not applied. Students are most likely to study if the following conditions are met:

- Students know how to study. This knowledge could be subject specific. If students are not studying for a particular subject, it may be because they do not know how to study for that subject. Students may know how to study for history but not for geometry.
- Students are interested in the subject. If students are interested in a subject, they are motivated to learn and so put forth more effort.
- Students have a sense of their own self-efficacy. That is, they believe that studying will result in learning the materials and obtaining a higher grade. High-achieving students attribute their success to hard work. Low-achieving students may attribute their failure to a lack of ability. If students believe they aren't succeeding because they simply don't have the ability to learn the material, they have no motivation to study. Attributing success to hard work means that students believe that they will be successful if they study.

Some students may come to your class with a long history of failure and with a diminished sense of self-efficacy. To build students' sense of self-efficacy, help them see the connection between hard work and achievement. You might test some in-class assignments that are challenging but within the grasp of these students. Provide sufficient guidance so that students are virtually guaranteed a measure of success. Praise their effort so that they can see the connection between work and achievement. However, also praise their ability to learn. If you praise only their effort, they may believe that they are lacking in ability and so have to work harder than everyone else. This kind of thinking can weaken their sense of self-efficacy. Promote the idea that learning your subject area content is largely a matter of working hard and using one's abilities. Make sure that quizzes, tests, and assignments are structured in such a way that students who put forth effort will be at least partly successful. Success is fostered when:

- Students know what type of test they will be given and how to prepare for it. This follows the principle of task specificity. If you are giving an essay test, inform students of this. Demonstrate the kinds of preparation that might go into studying for an essay test.

- Students set goals for a course. The goals should be written and should state what students hope to learn or how they hope to change as a result of taking a course. Students should also note what steps they will take to reach their goals. Setting goals and creating a plan to attain them provide motivation for studying.

- Students build study routines. If possible, students should have a place to study that is quiet, is free from distractions, and contains the necessary equipment and supplies. Equipment and supplies should be organized so that they are readily accessible. Color coding might be used as an organizational device. For instance, each subject might have its own color. History materials might be placed in blue folders or notebooks, for instance. Students might also find it helpful to study at the same time each day. Studying should precede recreation. In fact, recreation such as watching a favorite show might be used as a reward for studying. Students should study in the same place. The study area should be well lit, cheerful, and quiet. Encouraging mottoes or a list of useful study strategies might be hung in the area. The study area should be used only for studying. That way when the student enters the area, he will get a this-is-the-place-where-I-study feeling. If the area is also used to play computer games, the student will also associate a feeling of recreation with the area. To help students get in the habit of studying, encourage them to keep a study log. The study log is a record of the date, time, place of studying, the study task, the amount of time spent studying, the study techniques used, comments and questions, and results of studying. Encourage students to reflect in their logs and have periodic conferences on them so that they can assess their progress and plan any needed changes in their study habits or techniques. A sample study log is presented in Figure 7.5.

> **ENGLISH LANGUAGE LEARNERS**
>
> Because they will probably be slower at processing English, English language learners should allocate more time for studying.

FIGURE 7.5

Study Log

Date	Study Task	Time Spent Studying	Study Method Used	Questions, Difficulties, Comments	Results (Test or Quiz Grades, Class Discussions)
3–5	Read chapter 6 in chemistry book.	7–7:45	SQ3R Mnemonic for kinds of reactions.	Not sure how to balance equations.	Named 5 kinds of reactions on quiz but was not able to balance equation.
	Read chapter 4 in history book.	8–8:50	SQ3R & information map.		

Time Management

With sports, clubs, recreation, and part-time jobs competing for students' time, time management is a crucial factor in an effective study program. One way of gaining more time is to manage it better. It is easy for students to dribble away countless minutes and hours of time. To assess your own use of time, keep track of the ways in which you use time for a week or so. Discuss your findings with students and have them do the same. Discuss ways in which time might be used more efficiently. Also encourage students to set schedules. Students might set up both a master schedule for the week, which shows their class time, work time, activities time, and time for eating and sleeping. They can then decide, based on the time available, when they will study and for how long. A semester schedule that includes major long-term assignments should also be drawn up. Most important of all, students should make the commitment to keep to the study portions of their schedules; however, they should be flexible.

Discipline

The hardest thing that students will have to master is themselves. Studying takes discipline and is especially challenging for underachieving students, because they don't have a history of success to encourage them and, in fact, might never have been rewarded for their efforts. Just as with physical exercise, the best way for a nonstudier to get started is to start out slowly. The nonstudier might begin by studying for just thirty minutes a day and gradually work up to an hour or two or whatever is required. Study assignments should be crystal clear, interesting, and doable. Successful completion should be affirmed with praise and encouragement. Students might also be encouraged to create a chart to track their progress.

Self-talk can be helpful in maintaining discipline. Students might use self-talk to help themselves get started. They might pretend to be cheerleaders; "Let's go, team. Let's hit those books." When energy and motivation begin to flag and they are tempted to quit, they might give themselves another cheer: "Defense! Defense!" They might call time out. Or they might tell themselves, "When the going gets tough, the tough get going." After a successful study session, they might give themselves a victory cheer.

Even disciplined students may find that they have a difficult time studying for subjects that aren't interesting to them or which are especially difficult. If the subject is boring, students should be encouraged to find some way to make it interesting. If this doesn't work, perhaps they can reward themselves for studying the subject by having a treat or watching a favorite TV show.

Social factors can be a powerful motivator for studying. Students who have difficulty studying alone might study with a buddy or a small study group. Talking with others will help clarify confusing points. And it also provides a more congenial way to study. Seeing a disciplined peer study might also inspire students who find studying to be a struggle. However, whether to study alone or in a group is a matter of personal preference. Some students do best when studying alone.

Students might find it easier to study if they attain an awareness of how and when they study best. Some students study best under conditions of absolute quiet. Other students prefer a little background noise. Some like to lie down when they study. Others prefer a straightback chair. And some may study best while pacing back and forth. Discuss your study strategies and habits and encourage students to do the same. Stress the strategies and habits that seem most effective. Discuss with students factors that promote studying and also obstacles to studying. As you discuss obstacles to studying, talk over some ways to overcome these obstacles. Note factors, such as a textbook that is too difficult, that might require intervention. Or students might be so hopelessly behind in a cumulative subject such as math or chemistry that they need help catching up.

 *CHECKUP*

1. What are the essential study habits?
2. What are some techniques that might be used to foster essential study habits, including discipline and time management?

Assessing Students' Study Strategies and Habits

To assess students' use of study strategies and their study habits, you might conduct an interview such as the one in Figure 7.6. You might also discuss with students how, when, and where they study. A good way to get some insight into their study skills and habits is to set aside some study time and observe them as they study. To make it realistic, you might assign a section of the text and explain that you are going to give them some time to study and that you will then be giving them a quiz. Note how rapidly students get down to business, how well they are able to concentrate, and what techniques they seem to be using. As part of the quiz, you might ask them to write a brief paragraph explaining how they studied the mate-

FIGURE 7.6

Study Strategies and Habits Interview

1. How often do you study?
2. When do you study?
3. About how much time do you spend studying?
4. Do you take breaks during your study sessions? If so, how many and for how long?
5. Where do you study?
6. What special things do you do to help you learn and remember information?
7. Which subject is easiest to study for? Why?
8. Which subject is most difficult to study for? Why? Pretend that you are studying for a quiz in

that subject. Show me how you would go about studying for it. [Note whether the text is on the appropriate level of difficulty. Note study strategies that the student uses. Also ask the student to describe the strategies he is using.]

9. What kinds of tests do your teachers give? How do you know what to study for those tests?
10. How do you go about studying for short-answer tests? For multiple-choice tests? For essay tests?

rial. The study logs described earlier might also shed some light on students' studying. They might, for instance, be asking a lot of questions that show that they are confused by their assignments.

 **CHECKUP**

1. How might students' study strategies and habits be assessed?

Providing Continuous Support

Learning a new habit, such as studying on a regular basis when one hasn't studied in the past, takes about three months or more (Prochaska, Norcross, & DiClemente, 1994). But change is difficult. As they go through the following stages of change, students need continued support and encouragement.

Precontemplation. Students don't see a need for change. They may blame their low grades on outside forces: poor teaching, a dull subject, or a difficult textbook. Or they may feel that they are in a hopeless situation. Having gotten poor marks all through their schooling, they may have given up. Students at this stage need to become aware of their problem. This might be done in general class discussions, through attending lectures about the importance of studying on a regular basis or in informal one-on-one talks or in counseling sessions.

Contemplation. Students note that their marks are low and that this is related to a lack of effective study. They are thinking about changing, but haven't made any attempts to do so. They may feel that they will fail if they try, so they put off trying. They focus on the problem rather than the solution. A sign that they are ready to change is that they shift their attention to possible solutions. They also begin to contemplate the future rather than regretting the past (Prochaska, Norcross, & DiClemente, 1994). To help students in this stage, continue to build their awareness, but also help them become aware of the benefits of changing. Discuss and have them visualize what will happen if they begin studying. Have them picture the excitement of learning new information, the praise they will get from their teachers and family, and how school will be much more pleasant because they won't dread being called on or failing tests. Help them to create an image of themselves as good students. Actual change is often preceded by imagined change.

Preparation. Students are getting ready to change but haven't started, or they have made a few minor changes, such as recording homework assignments and setting aside a quiet place to study. Students need encouragement to help them move into the action stage. They need to see the value of change. They specifically need to see that the benefits of change will outweigh the negative aspects, such as having less free time or giving up some favorite activities or having nonstudying friends become jealous because they are getting good marks. They also need to believe that they can change. Out of these beliefs is born commitment.

Action. Students have started to make changes. This is a critical, fragile period. They need intensive guidance and encouragement. Action, however, is not the same as change. Although students may have studied each night for a week or two, they haven't fully implemented the change and need support to help them to stabilize the change.

Maintenance. Students stabilize the changes so that they become a part of their lives. This step is also critical. Unfortunately, the teacher may have felt that she had expended enough effort to get students to change and that now they should be on their own. Students don't need the kind of intensive guidance and encouragement required in earlier stages. However, they do need continuous support. This stage may take two or three months or more.

Termination. This applies to changes such as giving up smoking. Changes such as adopting more effective learning habits probably never reach the termination stage. In addition, the learning tasks that students encounter change and grow more complex over the years. Booster sessions and continuous support are highly recommended.

It's important to know what stage students are in and to gear instruction and support accordingly. For instance, students in the precontemplation stage really don't see a need for change and probably would not respond to our exhortations. They need to be moved to the contemplation stage, where they see a need for change. On the other side of the coin, students who are in the action stage should not be held back from implementing their changes. They don't need encouraging messages telling them why they should change. They already know that. They need the kind of support that will help them to continue to change.

Although the stages have been presented in a list form, they are not linear. Students may move back and forth between stages and even relapse. They need to know that we slip, but we can pick ourselves up and start anew. In fact, most people who have changed successfully had to make several attempts. But even failed attempts moved them farther along the road to change, if they were able to learn from their failed attempts and try again.

 *CHECKUP*

1. What are the stages of change?
2. How might the teacher use knowledge of these stages to help students adopt more effective study habits?

RATE OF READING

An often overlooked factor in effective studying is rate of reading. Excessively slow reading will hurt the student in two ways: when the reading speed falls significantly below thinking speed, the mind tends to wander, and comprehension suffers. Slow reading is also time consuming. A student reading 100 words a minute will take twice as long to finish an assignment as one who reads 200 words a minute. As assignments grow heavier, the slow reader may simply not have enough time to complete them.

Flexibility in Reading

Slow reading is not necessarily bad reading. Contracts, math problems, and difficult, concept-laden material should be read slowly. It is only a problem when everything is read in low gear. Some students may be slow readers because they don't automatically recognize words. Their reading rate can be boosted by having them read many easy books so that their reading rate equals their thinking rate. On the other end of the continuum are students who are always in high gear. Often, they are superior readers who read everything in sight. Having honed their skills on narrative materials, which are designed to be read quickly, they race through chapters on rock formation or the founding of the thirteen colonies, and wonder why they do poorly in class discussions or on science and history quizzes.

Average reading rates are presented in Table 7.1. However, there is a considerable range in reading rate. For instance, the average reading rate in grade 7 is 191 wpm but may range from 96 to 282 words a minute (Carver, 1992). In high school the range is even greater. In one study rates ranged from 65 to 334 words a minute (Leslie & Caldwell, 2001).

According to Carver (1990, 1992), each of us has a rate of normal reading known as rauding. The word *rauding* was formed by combining the words *auding* and *reading*. Rauding refers to the rate at which we comprehend material that we are reading or listening to. Our reading and listening rates are apparently the same and are governed by our thinking speed or cognitive rate. Some students might be slow readers because they think in a slow, deliberative way. Rauding entails recognizing each word, encoding the meaning of each word, and integrating words and sentences into meaningful units. The rates provided in Table 7.1 are rauding rates. However, depending on our purpose for reading, we have a number of reading rates. From fastest to slowest, these are scanning, skimming, rauding, learning, and memorizing (see Table 7.2). In scanning we search printed materials to find a target word. If you were reading a section in a history text about the post–World War II era and you couldn't remember what countries belonged to NATO, you might quickly search the section for the acronym NATO. Skimming is a quick reading to get an overview of a passage. Rauding is the kind of reading we usually do. Learning is a slower form of reading in which we check to make sure the information is understood and remembered. The slowest form of reading is memorizing. The key to effective reading is to select an appropriate rate.

Flexibility is the key word. Rate of reading should match the nature of the material and the purpose for which it is being read. A light novel being read for entertainment could be read rapidly. A complex novel being read in preparation for a discus-

TABLE 7.1

AVERAGE SILENT READING RATES

Grade	Words per Minute
1	55
2	85
3	130
4	150
5	165
6	175
7	190
8	205
High School	250

TABLE 7.2		
MAJOR RATES OF READING		
Reading Process	Purpose	Rate for Average High School Student (words per minute)
Scanning	Recognizes target word.	550
Skimming	Gets quick overview of meaning of passage.	400
Rauding	Understands both main ideas of passage and details.	250
Learning	Checks to make sure material is remembered.	175
Memorizing	Says material over and over to bolster memory.	100

Extrapolated from *Reading Rate: A Review of Research and Theory* by R. O. Carver, San Diego, CA: Academic Press, 1990.

sion or a test should be read more slowly. Degree of familiarity with material will also help determine rate. The amateur herpetologist who is reading a selection on snakes can move through it much more quickly than someone who has only a passing familiarity with serpents. As part of preparation for reading, discuss the rate at which the material should be read. Ultimately, of course, students should be led to choose their own rates.

The SQ3R or other study technique acts as a natural check for those who speed through content area material. Knowing that they have to recite at the end of a section tends to slow down those who are inclined to read too rapidly. Conversely, the survey step tends to speed up reading for the slow or average reader since it gives an overview. This overview can also provide students with some clues as to how fast they can read the material. If it suggests the subject is familiar, the students may elect to read it fairly quickly (Bush & Huebner, 1979).

Often reading rate improves without being worked on directly. Students may be reading slowly because the material is too hard, their vocabularies limited, they don't know why they are reading, or they are easily distracted and so must reread. Building background and vocabulary, making sure that students have materials on appropriate levels, setting purposes for reading, emphasizing comprehension, and playing down oral reading often result in increased reading rate.

STRUGGLING READERS

An excessively slow rate of reading could be a symptom of an underlying difficulty. The material could be too hard, the student might be lacking in strategies, might be overly concerned about getting all the information in the text, or might not have much experience reading difficult text.

 *CHECKUP*

1. What are the major rates of reading?
2. What are some ways in which flexibility and appropriate rate of reading might be fostered?

TEST-TAKING STRATEGIES

In addition to teaching students how to study, also show them how to take a test. The best way to prepare for a test is to study consistently and strategically day in and day out. A well-organized way of teaching test-taking strategies is to implement **PLAE**: Preplanning, Listing, Activity, and Evaluating (Nist & Simpson, 1989).

■ **PLAE** is a procedure for studying that includes preplanning the nature and content of a test, listing steps to get ready for the test, activating a plan, and evaluating its effectiveness.

Preplanning. Students describe the study task, asking questions such as What will the test cover? What kind of questions will be asked? What will be the format of the questions? Model the process of preplanning for a test. Under your guidance, have the class as a whole group create a plan for studying for a test in your class or another class. Later, have students gather in small groups to create plans and ultimately to create individual plans. A sample preplan might be:

- The test will cover Chapter 3, Acceleration, Force, and Motion.
- I will need to know three laws of motion, keys terms, and formulas.
- The questions will be short answer and essay.

Listing. Based on preplanning information, students list the steps they will take to prepare for the test by answering the following questions: How will I get ready for the test? When will I study? How long will I study? Which study strategies will I use? A sample list might be:

- To get ready for the test, I will review the chapter and the notes that I have taken on it and class notes.
- I will put the three laws of motion, formulas, and key words on note cards.
- I will study half an hour each night for three nights and one hour the night before the test. I will study note cards on the bus and at odd times.

Activity. Students activate their plans and monitor them. They ask themselves, "Am I following my plan? If not, why not? Is my plan working? Am I learning what I need to learn? If not, what changes do I need to make in my plan? Am I using the best study strategies?"

Evaluating. Based on their performance on the test, students evaluate the effectiveness of their study plans. They might ask, "Which questions did I miss? Why? Did I study all the material that the questions were based on? Did I remember the material? How could I have studied to get more questions right?" After evaluating their study plan, students should make any necessary changes to improve it. They may decide to start a study group or work sample problems using the formulas covered in the chapter.

For tests in your subject area, provide students with the type of information that will allow them to show what they know. Let them know what the test will include. Will it cover just the book, or will it include information in the book and notes? Will it be essay, short answer, or multiple choice? Also show them how to study for the test. If students are to take a national standardized test or a standardized test in the content area that you teach, provide some preparation and practice sessions so that the format of the test doesn't become an obstacle and their scores aren't artificially lowered because they had inadequate test-taking skills.

To help students establish effective study strategies, arrange for practice study sessions and practice tests. Create a test that is similar in content and format to tests that you usually give in your subject matter area. Discuss the nature of the test and ways in which students might prepare for the test. After administering the test, discuss the results. Help students to determine how effective their studying was and what they might do to improve their studying. If students are preparing for essay tests, they might adapt a strategy such as PORPE.

PORPE Strategy

Searching over a period of four years for a writing strategy that students could use for planning, monitoring, and evaluating their learning in the content areas, Simpson (1986) devised a technique known as **PORPE: P**redict, **O**rganize, **R**ehearse, **P**ractice, and **E**valuate. While assisting students with their learning, PORPE also develops their ability to write more effective essay exams. Students who participated in a PORPE program were judged to have written better essays than those who did not. PORPE is modeled on the expert readers' ability to use strategies to identify key ideas, monitor for meaning, and take corrective action if comprehension is lacking. Here is how a PORPE lesson might be introduced:

■ **PORPE** is a procedure for preparing for essay tests that includes predicting the content of the test, organizing information for possible answers, rehearsing (studying) the material, taking a practice test, and evaluating the results.

LESSON 7.2 — A PORPE Lesson

Step 1: Predict

After explaining that PORPE is a strategy designed to help students prepare for essay tests, tell them that the first step is to predict what kinds of essay questions the teacher might ask. This step is subdivided into four phases.

Phase A. Introduction of Essay Terms. Introduce terms commonly used to compose essay questions: *describe, discuss, explain, compare, criticize, contrast, defend, support.* (Add the kinds of question words that you use if they aren't already there.) Discuss what each of the question words is asking students to do. For instance, explain that *discuss* means to give reasons and explanations in some detail; *criticize* means to judge but to give reasons for each judgment.

Phase B. Prediction of Possible Questions. Model and discuss with students what clues they might use to predict essay questions: points emphasized by the teacher, major points in texts, hints given by the teacher, past tests, notes, and ideas that were repeated. Tell students that the teacher may even give hints from time to time by noting that a certain topic or issue would make a good test question or that a certain idea is very important.

Phase C. Completion of Predicted Questions. Provide students with key words (*explain, compare, discuss*) and have them create sample essay items. They might do this in pairs or cooperative groups. Discuss whether their questions have covered all the most important topics. Also discuss which seem to be most likely to appear on the test.

Step 2: Organize

Using outlines, information maps, or other graphic organizers, students chart answers for the predicted questions. In the initial stages, you might model your own organizer, but students should eventually create their own. Display and discuss especially effective organizers. Guide students as they improve organizers that are not adequate. Help them, for instance, see the importance of including examples and reasons to support their positions.

Step 3: Rehearse

After reviewing steps for effective studying and modeling how you might study for a test, have students study their organizers. Emphasize the need to self-test oneself through reciting. Stress the need to restudy the material if the recitation isn't adequate. Also explain the value of overlearning and distributed practice. For an extended answer, students might do one section at a time, just as in SQ3R, but ultimately put the whole answer together. Rehearsal should also be continued over a period of several sessions.

Step 4: Practice

Students write a practice essay. Supply suggestions for students to follow: creating a semantic map or outline before starting, writing an opening sentence that clearly incorporates the essay question, or using a deliberate organizational pattern, such as "The Great Depression had five major causes." Then note the causes, using *first*, *second*, and so forth. Students supply examples, if appropriate, and end with a concluding sentence that restates the gist of the question or sums up the answer. Students also check the answer, asking, "Did I really answer the question as asked? Did I include all the main points? Is the answer as clear as I can make it in the time allowed?"

Step 5: Evaluate

Using a checklist or rubric that the teacher and the class compose, the students evaluate their responses and refine them as necessary. After three weeks of intensive training, PORPE students were able to use the technique on their own.

Other Suggestions for Taking Essay Tests

Students should be aware of how much time they have and allot it proportionately. They should not make the mistake of spending so much time on the first question that they have to rush through the second question and have no time for the last one. Should students misjudge their time, they should jot down a quick outline of the answer and a note saying they ran out of time.

ENGLISH LANGUAGE LEARNERS

Essay tests are especially difficult for English language learners because their English language development typically lags behind that of native speakers of English. Spend some time instructing students in some of the kinds of expressions that are commonly used to respond to essay questions in your subject matter. Also consider letting students respond in the language or combinations of language that will enable them to display their knowledge best.

EXEMPLARY TEACHING

TEST PREPARATION

As part of preparation for the PSAT, Laflamme (1997) had his tenth-graders compose testlike selections and multiple choice questions. Writing fostered both a deeper understanding of the structure of the selections and the nature of the questions. Composing the selections was preceded by a careful analysis of the kinds of selections contained on the PSAT, the types of questions asked,

and recommended steps for answering those questions. Students were provided with a flowchart that summarized the basic structure questions on the PSAT and also sample stems for the different types of questions asked. Students who wrote sample test selections and engaged in intensive vocabulary study outperformed those who took part in a traditional PSAT preparation course.

Students, especially those who are struggling, should be encouraged to use mnemonic devices, such as acronyms, rhymes, or reconstructive elaborations to help them retrieve essential information.

Students who have difficulty expressing themselves on an essay test may do better if they resist the temptation to dive right in and start answering the question. Instead, they might take a few minutes to organize their thoughts, construct a brief outline, and then begin answering the question.

 **CHECKUP**

1. What are some techniques that might be used to help students prepare for tests?

Test Anxiety

Taking tests is an affective as well as an academic activity. Being a little nervous before taking a test is natural. A little anxiety heightens performance. However, about one student out of every five becomes so anxious that his performance is harmed (Gaudrey & Spielberger, 1971). Test anxiety is a state of intense apprehension that may include physical symptoms, such as an upset stomach or a headache, and that is so severe that it interferes with students' functioning. Test anxiety is linked to fears of negative evaluation, a dislike of tests, and inadequate study skills. Students with high test anxiety have lowered self-esteem and feel less in control of outside events. They have more difficulty understanding and organizing material initially and have more difficulty concentrating.

Test anxiety requires a two-pronged approach: students need to have a good grasp of study strategies, and they need to have their confidence built so that they can overcome their unreasonable anxiety. School counselors might be called on to help with the confidence building, although content area teachers can help too. Some steps that can be taken to lessen test anxiety include:

- Instruction in comprehension and study skills. This might need to be subject specific. Some students may become anxious only before math or science tests.

- Instruction in test-taking skills.
- Instruction and counseling that builds self-efficacy and helps students learn to handle stress. This might include instruction in cognitive self-talk. Students are taught to overcome negative thoughts with positive self-assertions that provide them with specific actions that they can implement to reduce anxiety, such as taking a deep breath and relaxing and using specific test-taking strategies, such as doing the easy items first and then working on the difficult ones (Wark & Flippo, 1991).

Test Preparation for High-Stakes Tests

The teacher watched in amazement as his ninth-grade class completed the first section of a standardized reading test. Although the directions had clearly stated that there was a ten-minute time limit, most of the students were poking through the section. The vocabulary section of the test required that they choose from five alternatives the one that provided the best definition of the target word. There was no dense reading to be done. Test-wise students would have quickly answered all the items they were relatively sure of and then gone back to take a look at the more difficult, unanswered items. But these students plodded through. Many attempted only half the items. They did no better on the comprehension subtest. The teacher was not surprised that the scores were low. But because the students obviously lacked test-taking skills, he realized that the scores were probably lower than they should have been.

After a semester of intensive instruction in reading and writing strategies, the students' scores shot up. In just five months, some students were showing a gain of three or even four years. Wise to the ways of group assessment, the teacher realized that he couldn't take full credit for the students' improvement. Although some of their gains were most likely due to genuine improvement in reading vocabulary and comprehension, some of the gains were due to increased skill in taking tests. Because of inadequate test-taking skills, the students had not really demonstrated what they could do. After some instruction in test-taking skills that included pacing; active, focused reading; answering the easiest items first; informed guessing; and checking responses, the students were better able to handle group standardized tests. Their scores now provided a more realistic estimate of their abilities.

Taking tests is a life skill. Students take tests to get into special programs, to get admitted to certain high schools, and for admission to college. In some school systems, passing standardized tests is a prerequisite for being passed on to the next grade or receiving a high school diploma. In addition to these high-stakes tests, there are the numerous quizzes, tests, and exams that students are given in each of the subjects that they study.

Modeling the Process of Taking a Test

Discussing and modeling test-taking strategies is also helpful. Share some of the experiences you have had taking tests. Also show how you would go about taking a test of the type that your students are given. Explain your thinking processes as you read and follow directions. Think aloud as you go about eliminating distractors when you are not sure of an answer to a multiple choice question. Show, too, how you check answers and pace yourself. Encourage students who typically do well on tests to discuss their test-taking strategies. Provide extra help for those who work too rapidly and fail to check answers as well as those who work too slowly and are overly concerned with making a mistake. If the test has a number of challenging passages, provide students with strategies for reading difficult passages and answering tough questions. Also discuss the correction factor. On some tests, students lose a quarter of a point for wrong responses, and so are better off leaving an answer blank if they have no idea which of the options is correct. However, if they eliminate more than one of the options, the odds of getting the right answer are in their favor. Of course, if the test does not have a correction factor and there is no penalty for guessing, students should make a careful guess.

Probing Processes with a Think-Aloud

To find out whether students are applying effective test-taking strategies, use a think-aloud. While students are taking a practice test, have them tell you what's going on in their minds. Ask them what they are thinking about both as they read the passage and as they answer questions. Record their responses or take careful notes. You might also interview students after they have taken a test. First, have them read the test passage orally. Assess their performance to gauge whether or not the test is on their level of ability. They may be getting items wrong because the passage is too difficult. Or maybe they give up because the passage is a very challenging one. Scruggs, Bennion, and Lifson (1985a, 1985b) found that students who were able to describe specific strategies had higher scores. Two effective strategies were text referring ("I thought I had seen that in the story, so I checked back") and inferring strategies ("I figured this must be the correct answer because of what the story said"). Struggling students were far less strategic. A strategy, such as QAR (as explained in Chapter 4) adapted to test taking, should prove to be effective in helping students decide whether the answer is right there so that if they don't recall it, they can go back over the passage and find it, or whether it's author and me, so that students know they have to make an inference based on information contained in the passage.

Probe low-scoring students carefully to find out how they handle difficult passages, which they are sure to encounter. Do they give up? Do they take random guesses? Or do they try to make as much sense out of the passages as they can and, if all else fails, match up unknown words in the answer options with the same words in the selection? Students need to know that they can sometimes answer questions correctly even when they don't know every word in the passage. Also question students as to how sure they are of the correctness of their answers. Higher-scoring students are better able to predict their performance. This is an advantage because then they know which items to recheck (Scruggs & Mastropieri, 1992).

 **CHECKUP**

1. What are high-stakes tests?
2. What steps might be taken to prepare students for them?

The Ethics of Test Preparation

Test preparation must be ethical. There is no question that providing students with examples from the actual test is wrong. It is also unethical to raise students' scores without also increasing their underlying knowledge and skill. As one testing expert cautioned, "No test preparation practice should increase students' test scores without simultaneously increasing students' mastery of the assessment domain tested" (Popham, 2000, p. 82). The purpose of test preparation is to provide students with the test-taking skills that enable them to show with accuracy what they have learned. In fact, teachers would be negligent if they did not help students attain test-taking skills that make it possible for them to demonstrate what they truly know.

Keep test preparation to a minimum. The best preparation is a carefully taught course complemented by conscientious student participation and studying. In her study of high-performing versus low-performing secondary schools, Langer (1999) found that students in schools where teachers incorporated skills assessed on high-stakes tests into the curriculum did better than schools where teachers focused on test preparation.

Incorporating test preparation into the curriculum can be accomplished in a number of ways. You can ask the kinds of questions that demand the same type of cognitive processes as those posed on the high-stakes tests. For instance, many high-stakes tests ask students to back up responses with facts and reasons. You can do the same. In history, you might ask students to tell whether or not they think the Spanish-American War was justified and to give reasons for their opinions. In science, you might ask students to explain what scientists have learned about asteroids and what questions they still have. They might use their texts and a recent article on asteroids. If a rubric is used to assess students' work, you can use the same type of rubric to judge students' assignments. The rubric should be thoroughly discussed so that students understand what they are being required to do. In at least some of your quizzes and tests, use the same format, if applicable, that the high-stakes tests use.

 CHECKUP

1. How much and what kind of test preparation should students be given?

SUMMARY

Studying requires remembering in addition to understanding material. Retention of material depends on clear, active encoding, encoding material in the same way as it is to be tested, and adequate rehearsal or studying. Material that is meaningful and well organized aids memory storage. Retrieval is also improved by imagery and other forms of elaboration. Having an intention to learn and overlearning enhance retention. Associational or mnemonic devices are recommended for learning materials that lack meaningful connections.

A study strategy that has been effective with a variety of students is SQ3R (Study, Question, Read, Recite,

Review), which is based on a number of learning strategies that involve preparing, organizing, and elaborating, as well as metacognition.

Notetaking is a key technique and includes four skills: selectivity, organization, consolidation, and fluency. Two-column or three-column notes as implemented in the Cornell system are recommended. Formal outlining or informal systems such as power thinking are useful study strategies.

Because studying is affective as well as cognitive, students need to establish effective study habits. If students suffer from test anxiety, they may need confidence building and counseling along with instruction in studying and test-taking techniques.

If students read too slowly comprehension suffers and they have a difficult time keeping up with their reading assignments. There are five rates of reading: scanning, skimming, rauding, learning, and memorizing. Flexible readers choose the rate that matches the task.

An effective technique for taking tests is PLAE (Preplanning, Listing, Activity, and Evaluating). PORPE is an effective strategy for taking essay tests. The best preparation for high-stakes test is to incorporate content and skills being assessed into the regular curriculum. Test preparation that raises students' scores without also increasing their knowledge and skill is unethical.

Reflection

Return to the Anticipation Guide at the beginning of this chapter. Respond once again to the items. Did your responses change? If so, how and why? What is the role of the content area teacher in teaching study skills? How might effective study skills and habits be fostered in your content area?

EXTENSION AND APPLICATION

1. Assess your study strategies and study habits. How effective are they? What might you do to improve them?
2. Create a mnemonic device for learning some important facts in your content area. Using the device, memorize the facts. Then assess yourself a week later. How well did the mnemonic work?
3. Try out one of the study strategies described in this chapter for at least two weeks. How effective does to seem to be? What are its advantages and disadvantages?

chapter 8

WRITING TO LEARN

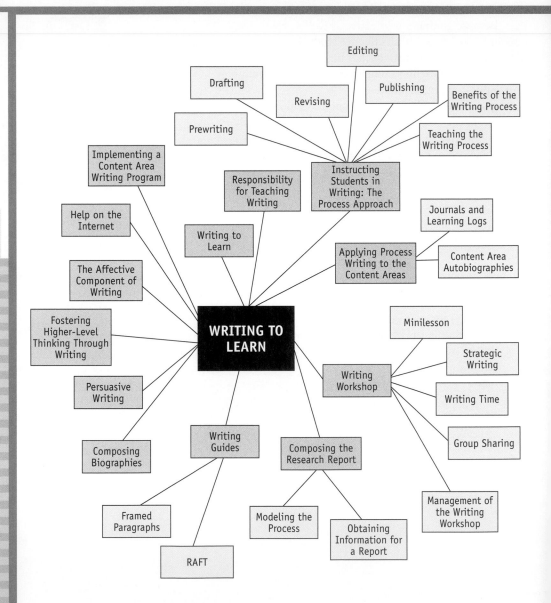

Editing

Drafting

Revising

Publishing

Benefits of the Writing Process

Prewriting

Teaching the Writing Process

Implementing a Content Area Writing Program

Responsibility for Teaching Writing

Instructing Students in Writing: The Process Approach

Help on the Internet

Journals and Learning Logs

Writing to Learn

Applying Process Writing to the Content Areas

Content Area Autobiographies

The Affective Component of Writing

WRITING TO LEARN

Minilesson

Fostering Higher-Level Thinking Through Writing

Strategic Writing

Writing Workshop

Writing Time

Persuasive Writing

Group Sharing

Composing Biographies

Writing Guides

Composing the Research Report

Management of the Writing Workshop

Framed Paragraphs

Modeling the Process

Obtaining Information for a Report

RAFT

ANTICIPATION GUIDE

Read each of the following statements. Put a check under "Agree" or "Disagree" to show how you feel about each one. If possible, discuss your responses with classmates.

		Agree	*Disagree*
1	Writing is an excellent way to learn content area material.	____	____
2	Responsibility for teaching writing skills belongs primarily to language arts teachers.	____	____
3	Content area teachers have a right to expect that students will have sufficient writing skills such that they will not need to instruct students in writing.	____	____
4	Content area teachers are responsible for teaching those writing skills that are specific to their content area.	____	____
5	The more direction students are given, the better they write.	____	____

USING WHAT YOU KNOW

When you were an elementary or secondary school student, what kinds of writing did you do in your content area classes? What were your favorite writing assignments? What kinds of writing did you find particularly difficult? What techniques did the teachers use to help you with your writing? Which of these techniques was most effective? Over the last two decades, writing instruction has changed dramatically and is believed to be more effective. This chapter provides an overview of the ways in which writing is taught today and has some suggestions for ways content area teachers might use writing to foster learning.

WRITING TO LEARN

Although we may write to inform others, writing is also a way to explore, discover, and synthesize. "The thinking that goes into careful writing can be used to develop, clarify, and refine students' understandings of concepts being studied" (Herber & Herber, 1993, p. 133). Although it is easy to see the value of writing in social studies, Zinsser (1988) notes that it also foster learning in science. "Writing . . . is one of the most powerful tools that science education possesses; a student can reason his way with words toward the solution of a problem and his teacher can watch him do it" (p. 203):

USING TECHNOLOGY

The National Writing Project
http://www.writingproject.org/ Research/NWP/nwp.html
Provides information about writing research and instruction.

> Writing organizes and clarifies our thoughts. Writing is how we think our way into a subject and make it our own. Writing enables us to find out what we know—and what we don't know—about what we're trying to learn. Putting an idea into written words is like defrosting the windshield: The idea so vague out there in the murk, slowly begins to gather itself into a sensible shape. (Zinsser, 1988, p. 16)

Langer and Applebee (1987) concluded that writing supports the learning of content in three different ways. It can be used as a preparation so that students use writing to access what they already know about a subject. Students might also write about related personal experiences so that they become motivated to study a topic. Writing is also used to review and consolidate what has been learned. And writing can be used to help students reformulate and extend ideas.

The Michigan Department of Education (Blakeslee, 1997) also concluded that writing in the content areas supports learning in a number of ways:

*C*ontent teachers teach the skills necessary to write in the content area they teach.

> Writing gives students a chance to think carefully about what they have observed and how they account for their observations. When held to high expectations for clarity in writing, students have to think deeply about the terms they choose to express their thoughts, as well as the logic of their arguments. Writing gives all students a chance to think about questions posed in class, rather than just listening to others' descriptions and explanations, providing a valuable forum for expression for those students who are reluctant to join into class discussions. . . .
>
> Students' written explanations, descriptions, and records of investigations are also important for teachers. They give teachers a window into each student's thinking that multiple choice questions do not, by allowing teachers to read the reasoning behind students' answers. Often this reasoning is surprising, sometimes naive, and sometimes shows that students can get the right answers to multiple choice questions for the wrong reasons. Knowing students' reasoning allows teachers to re-teach as necessary, to change their curriculum or instruction to improve students' reasoning.

✔CHECKUP

1. How does writing support learning?

RESPONSIBILITY FOR TEACHING WRITING

Just as content area teachers assume responsibility for teaching students the vocabulary and reading skills specific to their subjects, they should also teach students how to write lab reports, field notes, summaries of experiments and observations, a synthesis of the information contained in primary sources, and other kinds of writing that a scientist, geographer, or historian might be expected to do. Part of teaching a content area subject is teaching students the tools needed to learn more and to communicate more effectively in the content area. Writing in the content areas also expands students' writing skills, because it provides them with the opportunity to use a variety of forms and to write for a variety of purposes.

Although English teachers are often given the responsibility of developing writing skills, much of the writing that students do is assigned by content area teachers. On average, secondary school students complete about nine papers in social studies and seven in science (Applebee, 1984). However, as an outgrowth of the standards movement, there has been an increased emphasis on communication in many of the content areas. For instance, there is a call for all students to become scientifically literate (National Research Council, 1996). Part of being literate in science is being able to write about what has been learned or observed. The New Standards include the following performance communication standard in science:

> The student demonstrates effective scientific communication by clearly describing the natural world using accurate data, graphs, or other appropriate media to convey depth of conceptual understanding in science; that is, the student:
>
> a. Represents data and results in multiple ways, such as numbers, tables, and graphs; drawings, diagrams, and artwork; and technical and creative writing.
> b. Argues from evidence, such as data produced through his or her own experimentation or by others.
> c. Critiques published materials.
> d. Explains a scientific concept or procedure to other students.
> e. Communicates in a form suited to the purpose and the audience, such as by writing instructions that others can follow; critiquing written and oral explanations; and using data to resolve disagreements. (National Center on Education and the Economy and the University of Pittsburgh, 1997, p. 95)

In math the New Standards include the following performance communication standard:

> The student uses the language of mathematics, its symbols, notations, graphs, and expressions, to communicate through reading, writing, speaking, and listening, and communicates about mathematics by describing mathematical ideas and concepts and

explaining reasoning and results. (National Center on Education and the Economy and the University of Pittsburgh, 1997, p. 58)

In order to learn your subject matter and communicate what has been learned, what kinds of writing do your students need to be able to do? The answer to this question will depend on the content area that you are teaching. You may also be guided, in part, by considering the kinds of writing that students will be required to do once they have completed their schooling. Employer complaints about the writing abilities of recent graduates are universal.

 ✔CHECKUP

1. What is the content area teacher's responsibility for the teaching of writing?

INSTRUCTING STUDENTS IN WRITING: THE PROCESS APPROACH

■ The writing **process approach** is an approach to teaching writing that is based on the way students and professionals write.
■ **Extensive writing** is the kind of writing typically composed for school assignments.
■ **Reflexive writing** is writing that has been composed for a genuine audience, perhaps a friend or a group of peers.

Instruction should be based on the processes that successful writers use. The **process approach** has resulted in improved writing (Ballator, Farnum, & Kaplan, 1999). In a landmark study, Emig (1971) found that twelfth-graders generally wrote in one of two modes: extensive and reflexive. **Extensive writing** is the kind of writing typically composed for school assignments. The teacher is the ultimate audience. Little time is devoted to preparing for the writing or revising the writing. **Reflexive writing,** on the other hand, has a genuine audience, perhaps a friend or a group of peers. There is more planning and revising. In this and other studies, writing is seen as being a process that has five major parts: prewriting, composing or drafting, revising, editing, and publishing.

Prewriting

■ **Prewriting** is part of the writing process that includes all the things a writer does before composing, including selecting a topic and planning.

Prewriting includes the steps that a writer takes in preparation for writing. Depending on the nature of the writing and the age and experience of the writer, it may involve many hours of research or just a few minutes of contemplation before taking pen to paper. Included in preplanning are topic selection and revision, gathering material, and brainstorming or outlining one's topic or engaging in some other prewriting activity in preparation for writing.

Preplanning should take into consideration the nature of the writing task. When the writing task requires a summary of information or the explanation or elaboration of a single topic, activities designed to activate knowledge, such as brainstorming, work best. However, if the task requires analyzing or comparing and contrasting ideas, prewriting activities that help the student organize information, such as outlining or webbing, would be more effective. When students lack a solid grasp of information, they are more likely to write a summary piece even if an analytical piece is called for. Unable to analyze the information, they simply recite what they know. In this instance, teaching students how to write an analytical piece will not suffice.

They need to explore the topic until they have a sufficient understanding to analyze it. Writers also need sufficient information so that they can use details to flesh out a topic and make it interesting (Langer, 1984).

Teacher guidance during the preplanning stage can be especially effective. Secondary English teacher Jack Graves didn't want his students to feel lost when undertaking writing assignments (Langer & Applebee, 1987). In preparation for having them write an essay on Shakespeare's *Romeo and Juliet,* he had students meet in small groups to discuss alternative courses of action that Juliet might have taken when she learned that her parents had arranged a marriage for her. Using their notes from the discussion, the class discussed possible alternatives. Graves then discussed ways in which this information might be used in an essay. Included in the discussion were some possible topic sentences and some examples that might be used to support the topic sentences. The results of the preparation were well-developed essays and a better understanding of the play. Graves found that in providing guidance for students, he was walking a fine line. Without guidance, the students might founder. With too much guidance, they would be parroting his thoughts rather than making discoveries on their own.

STRUGGLING READERS

Struggling learners can create illustrations or graphic organizers to prepare for their writing. Illustrations sometimes act as a prompt to remind writers of details that they might not otherwise include in their writing.

Drafting

The core step in the writing process is composing, or **drafting.** The concept of drafting is emphasized so that students don't feel that they have to produce a finished product in one sitting. Students are urged to get their thoughts down on paper and then revise. With many students, the more preplanning that is done, the more productive the drafting. There are two schools of thought on the relationship between preplanning and drafting. Some writers like to have a fairly well-formed idea of what they want to say before they begin writing. Others see writing as a discovery process. Some fiction writers, for instance, say they can't wait to write each day so they can see what their characters are going to do. Many writers plan their writing in a general way so that there is plenty of room for discovery. Rehearsal can be an important part of the process. During rehearsal, writers compose stories, letters, or even informational pieces in their head so that when they sit down to write their ideas flow.

■ **Drafting** is that part of the writing process in which the writer composes a message. Drafting implies that the product is not finished and that the writer will engage in a revision process.

Students may approach writing from a top-down or a bottom-up approach. Students who take a top-down approach and see the big picture right from the start may jot down the theme or main idea and then generate supporting details. Students who focus on details may generate details and then build a main idea or theme from the details (Meltzer, Roditi, Haynes, & Biddle, 1996).

Audience has a major impact on students' writing. Often, the audience is teacher as examiner. When this is so, students focus on teacher expectations and stress surface features likely to result in a good grade. "When students had to shape their message constantly to fit the expectations of an examining audience, then whatever interest they had in the message eventually gave way to the details of its presentation" (Marshall, 1984b, p. 110). Students' writing has the potential to become more expressive when they have a genuine audience.

Revising

Revising goes beyond a concern for capitalization, spelling, and punctuation. It literally means to reenvision the piece and to take a close look at the content. It could entail adding a few details or completely rewriting the piece. Revising is aided by two factors. The first is the ability of the writer to step back and take a look at the writing from the audience's point of view and ask such questions as: Is the piece understandable? Is it complete? Is it well written? **Distancing** also helps. Writers let their pieces sit for a day or so. This puts a little distance between the labors of the writing and the written piece. It helps the writer take a more objective look at what she has written. Feedback from others is also invaluable, especially if it's constructive. To foster constructive criticism, discuss with students positive ways to respond to classmates' work. Model how you go about pointing out positive aspects of a piece and provide suggestions in an affirming fashion. Discuss and demonstrate how peer editors or the teacher might point out elements of the piece that they particularly liked and ask questions about parts that were not clear or that might be expanded: "Your beginning really grabbed me. I never realized how many lives seat belts save. I'm not sure though how the three-point seat belts work. You said that there are many other safety features that could be added to cars. Could you give some examples?" A constructive climate leads to constructive criticism.

Revising can be especially effective when needed guidance is supplied. Chemistry teacher Kathryn Moss was concerned that her students were having difficulty drawing conclusions about the experiments they conducted (Langer & Applebee, 1987). Instead of interpreting the data, they simply told what happened. In practice exercises, she showed them how drawing a conclusion was telling what one can believe as a result of conducting an experiment. As a group writing activity, students composed and revised statements about rates of chemical reactions. Then the class wrote conclusions about the rates of reactions. In the coming weeks, the class composed additional practice conclusions. Moss read the conclusions and provided feedback. Moss's focus was on helping students draw carefully considered, clearly expressed conclusions, an important goal in science.

It is sometimes easier to see the shortcomings in the writings of others than in one's own writing. Have students revise published pieces or anonymous pieces from past years. Select papers that can benefit from revision but are not so poorly written that students are overwhelmed. Do some pieces as a whole class or small group. Students might also work in pairs. They should discuss their reasons for revising (Spandel, 2001).

Students are also more likely to revise when the piece they are writing is intended for a wider audience than just the teacher. That wider audience might include classmates, peers, readers of the school or town newspaper, or visitors to the class's Web site. The more complex the writing task, the more extensive the revising is likely to be. In one study, papers that involved analysis or theorizing were much more likely to be revised than papers that required only summarizing (Butler-Nalin, 1984). Papers written for language arts were more likely to be revised than papers written for social studies or science. The extent and type of revisions were determined in part by the expertise of the writer. Struggling writers made more revisions, but often these were at the word or sentence level. The more accomplished writers made a greater number of higher-level changes and changes that affected more than one sentence (Butler-Nalin, 1984).

More accomplished writers are also more likely to produce multiple drafts. Multiple drafts provide students with the opportunity to obtain different views of their writing. Issues may pop up in a third draft that were not noticed in a second draft. Struggling writers need more guidance as they revise. They need to look beyond spelling and punctuation and consider the overall impact of the piece. They may not realize how much they have to say. Conferences designed to draw out their knowledge of a topic should help them see the potential for revision. Their past education may have placed too much focus on mechanics and not enough on content.

*P*eer editing helps students with their writing.

Editing

Editing involves correcting spelling and mechanical errors and may also include rewriting awkward sentences or confusing expressions. You might prepare a style sheet for your particular subject matter that guides students in the capitalization and spelling of key technical terms and in writing conventions specific to your content area. In chemistry, this will include the writing of abbreviations and formulas. In math, it might include such matters as when to write numbers as words or numerals and how to separate numerals with commas.

■ **Editing** is that part of the writing process in which the author searches for spelling, typographical, and other mechanical errors.

Publishing

Most school-type writing, such as assigned reports and critical essays, is composed for the teacher. Because the teacher already has expert knowledge of the subject, students do not have the experience of explaining a process or idea to someone who has little or no knowledge of the topic. **Publishing,** which entails writing assignments written for real audiences, has the potential to enrich students' creations. Publishing includes writing a children's book to describe an historical event or a scientific process, creating a video, writing an article for the school or local newspaper, and establishing a Web site.

USING TECHNOLOGY

Talking software can help students edit their writing. Hearing their pieces read on a talking word processor, students are better able to note dropped *ing*s and *ed*s, omitted words, and awkward expressions.

■ **Publishing** is that part of the writing process in which the author makes her writing public.

Benefits of the Writing Process

Although presented in step-by-step fashion, the writing process is recursive. The writer might plan and revise and even edit as he composes. As writers grow in expertise, the way they write changes, as does the relative amounts of time devoted to the processes they use. Less experienced writers use a knowledge-telling mode. They tell what they know about a topic and don't spend much time preplanning; this is

■ **Knowledge telling** is a process in which writers simply write down what they know without reflecting on it.

■ **Knowledge transformation** is a writing process in which writers reflect as they compose so that their thinking affects their writing and their writing affects their thinking.

similar to providing an oral explanation. It requires "no greater amount of planning or goal setting than ordinary conversation" (Bereiter & Scardamalia, 1987, p. 9). In **knowledge telling,** the writer simply records information without reflecting or putting much of himself into the process; students engaged in knowledge telling probably do not learn very much through their writing. In contrast, in **knowledge transformation,** students alter their ideas as they write. As they compose, their writing affects their thinking, and their thinking affects their writing. Instead of merely summarizing thoughts, they reconsider and draw conclusions, which are reflected in their writing. Knowledge transformation should lead to a deeper understanding of the topic being written about. Using a knowledge transformation process, writers learn as they write. "Thus it is that writing can play a role in the development of their knowledge" (Bereiter & Scardamalia, 1987, p. 11).

Langer and Applebee's (1987) research supports Bereiter and Scardamalia's conclusions. Working with twenty-three secondary science, home economics, English, and social studies teachers, they found that writing in the content areas has the following benefits: students gain new knowledge, review, reflect on, elaborate, and extend ideas. As might be expected, the benefits derived depended on the type of writing involved. Short-answer study questions in which students located answers and copied them resulted in recall of literal information and involved little reflection. Writing tasks that required comparing, contrasting, concluding, and evaluating and other processes in which students manipulated information led to deeper understandings.

The more reflective and analytical the writing, the more it fostered a deeper understanding. Students' writing also was more effective when the following conditions were met.

1. *Ownership.* Students knew why they were engaged in a particular writing task. They understood how completing the task would help them to better understand the content material. Students should go beyond simply summarizing information or following a rigid outline. "Effective instructional tasks must allow room for students to have something of their own to say in writing" (Langer & Applebee, 1987, p. 141).

2. *Appropriateness.* Students knew how to complete the tasks they were given. They had both the required knowledge and the required skill.

3. *Instructional support.* The teacher provided direct instruction, including modeling and feedback, in the types of writing that students were expected to do.

4. *Internalization.* Students internalized effective writing strategies.

As students move through the grades, they are called upon to write pieces that are more interpretive and analytical and that require higher levels of thinking and organization. They must move from writing pieces that summarize information and have a narrative or chronological organization to writing pieces that are interpretive and organized according to a variety of patterns of argumentation, such as the theses/support in English and social studies classes and the lab report in science classes. Both require students to construct a formal argument (Durst, 1984). In studies, students learned the new formats, but were sometimes overly constrained by them, especially the five-paragraph essay. In the five-paragraph essay, students write an opening paragraph that gives the essay's thesis, write three paragraphs that develop the thesis, and write a concluding paragraph. Although helpful in the beginning, students held on to the rigid formats too long or adhered to them too closely.

 **CHECKUP**

1. What is the process approach to writing?
2. What are the major parts of the process approach?

Teaching the Writing Process

Modeling the writing process is a highly effective way to teach it. You might model the entire process from topic selection through revising and editing. You might also have students who are accomplished writers discuss and/or model ways in which they write. As you model the process, it is important that you not only show students what you do but also make your thought processes known by thinking out loud so they get a deeper understanding of how topics are selected and pieces are revised.

Writing is learned, in part, through imitation. If you use accomplished writers as models, you must encourage students to find their own voices eventually. You might create models of the kinds of writing that you are asking students to do. Students might abstract the techniques that they feel are especially effective—starting a paper with an anecdote or a question, for instance. However, one problem with using models from published writers is that the level of writing is beyond that of most students. More realistic models can be obtained by saving samples of students' work from past years so that students can see what an excellent term paper or lab report looks like. You might also compose sample pieces for the class. Group compositions also help students understand how a piece is put together. As a group, and under your guidance, the class might compose a critical essay or a journal entry.

> **USING TECHNOLOGY**
>
> Real Kids, Real Adventures
> http://www.realkids.com/club.shtml
> This site for young writers features author information, writing guidelines and hints, and book reviews.

LESSON 8.1   ## Writing Lesson: Learning from a Model

Step 1: Introducing the Model Passage

Students examine a passage about Kublai Khan to see how the author developed the piece. They note the topic sentence: "Kublai Khan ran his empire well." They note the details that explain the main idea. They note, too, that the supporting details are frequently expanded or explained. The supporting detail "He saw to it that roads were good and trips were pleasant" is further developed by the explanation "There were stones to mark the way. And trees were planted to give shade to travelers." The class concludes that the piece follows a main idea/supporting details structure. You might also note some areas in which the piece could be improved. For instance, the piece doesn't end with a strong concluding sentence.

Step 2: Modeling the Writing Process

After analyzing and discussing the text, model how you might compose a similar piece. As you model the composition, include the steps of the writing process: prewriting, drafting, revising, editing, publishing. You might model how you go about selecting a topic, discussing, for instance, why you would choose Marco Polo, to write about. Discuss how you would obtain information, organize the information, and draft your piece. Also go through the revising and editing processes.

Step 3: Introducing Guide Sheets

Guide sheets, which are modeled on the think sheets created by Raphael and Englert (1990), provide a series of prompts designed to help students plan, organize, draft, revise, and edit their writing. There are separate sheets for the planning/organizing phase, the revising phase, and the editing phase. The planning sheets focus on main idea/detail organization, as in Figure 8.1. Planning sheets might also be created for other organizational patterns: compare/contrast; explanation/process; and problem/solution. (See Chapter 4 for a discussion of organizational patterns.)

A revision plan sheet (see Figure 8.2) poses a series of prompts designed to help students take a careful look at their papers and decide how they might strengthen them.

An editing guide sheet might be composed that would alert students to check the mechanics: sentence structure, usage, spelling, capitalization, punctuation, and any special format requirements. As students gain in skill, the guide sheets can be phased out.

Step 4: Providing Modeling, Guided Practice, and Application

Go through the guide sheets one by one. Discuss the planning guide sheet first. Model how you might fill out a planning guide. Next fill out a sample sheet as a whole class activity. Then have students fill theirs out on their own. Discuss the completed sheets. Discuss with students how they can use their planning sheets to compose a first draft. After the first drafts have been written, discuss them. At that point introduce and discuss revision sheets. Model the use of the revision sheet and fill one in cooperatively with the class. Have students complete their revision sheets and use them to revise their pieces. Discuss their revisions and introduce editing guide sheets.

Step 5: Publishing

After students have written, revised, and edited their pieces, have them shared in some way. Students' finished pieces might be posted, read aloud to classmates, placed on the class's Web site, placed in a class booklet, or made public some other way.

To help students remember the steps of the writing process, you might use a mnemonic such as SWEAT (Gunning, 2002). Good writing takes a little SWEAT.

FIGURE 8.1

Planning Sheet

Author's name _____   Date _____

Topic _____

Audience: Who am I writing for? _____

Details: What are some details that I need to include in my piece so that my audience will be convinced? What explanations of these details might I include?

_____

Detail 1: _____ Explanation _____

Detail 2: _____ Explanation _____

Detail 3: _____ Explanation _____

Organization: How might I organize my details?

In order of interest to the reader _____

In order of importance _____

In the order in which they happened _____

State the topic.

Write examples or details to develop the topic.

Explain the examples or details.

Add a strong ending.

Take a look at the piece and see if you have fully developed the topic sentence.

FIGURE 8.2

Revision Plan Sheet

Author's name _____   Date _____

Title _____

What do I like best about the paper? _____

Do I have a clear topic sentence? Is my topic sentence interesting? _____

Have I included all the important details? _____

Have I explained all or most of the details? _____

Do I have a strong closing? _____

Are there any parts that need changing? _____

How might I make the paper more informative, more interesting, or easier to understand? _____

CHECKUP

1. How might the process approach be taught?

APPLYING PROCESS WRITING TO THE CONTENT AREAS

Realizing the importance of students' ability to communicate, one chemistry teacher incorporated imaginative chemistry-based problems into her course (Zinsser, 1988). Students not only had to solve a chemistry problem, they also had to explain, discuss, or apply the results. Although students complained that they shouldn't be given such an assignment because this was chemistry, not English, they soon entered into the spirit of the assignment, and some became quite creative. After studying acids and bases, one student created an imaginary product that would keep the pH levels of a fish pond safe for the fish that lived there. She wrote a letter to a customer explaining how to use the product. Not wanting to take time away from chemistry, the teacher did not instruct the students in the mechanics of writing but did advise them that help was available at the school's writing center. The teacher found that incorporating writing into chemistry was a valuable activity for reasons that went beyond the learning of chemistry.

> I believe that writing is an effective means of improving thinking skills because a person must mentally process ideas in order to write an explanation. Writing also improves self-esteem because mentally processed ideas then belong to the writer and not just to the teacher or textbook author. (Zinsser, 1988, p. 208)

Writing can be used to help students rid themselves of misconceptions about a content area and gain new insights into its possibilities. As Countryman (1992), who has made extensive use of writing to teach math, states:

> Writing mathematics can free students of the assumption that math is just a collection of right answers to questions posed by someone else. Writing—and this includes writing notes, lists, observations, feelings, in addition to term papers, lab reports, and essay questions—will expand the narrow view of mathematics that many children carry around in their heads. (p. 11)

One of the benefits of writing is that it actively engages students. Instead of having just one student summarize a lesson or explain a procedure, you can have all students explain it in writing. "Once students are writing they are automatically taking an active role in the classroom. Instead of waiting for the teacher, or another student, to do, explain, discuss, summarize, or evaluate, each student is engaged in the learning process" (Countryman, 1992, p. 13).

The following writing activities can help clarify complex topics and deepen students' understanding of them.

- Comparing, contrasting, or evaluating key points in a chapter
- Writing critical reports on famous people or events, taking on the role of the famous person, or describing the key event as though one were there
- Interpreting the results of a science experiment conducted in class

- Writing an essay on a social studies or science topic: What does the Bill of Rights mean to me? What can we do to clean up our home, the earth?

Insofar as possible, help students relate what they are studying to their personal lives. For example, make the Bill of Rights provisions more concrete by having students write about how they exercise their rights every day or about an incident that made them appreciate their freedom to use their rights.

Students' writing in the content areas often consists of simply retelling information. One solution is to have them make firsthand investigations and report the results. They might undertake activities such as the following:

- Writing observations about a natural phenomenon (for example, changes in plants that are being grown from seed)
- Describing birds that visit a bird feeder, changes in a tree from season to season, or changes in a puppy or kitten as it develops over a period of months
- Summarizing and interpreting the results of a classroom poll
- Interviewing older family members about life when they were growing up

A writing activity that can be used in any content area class is having students explain a process to someone who has no knowledge of it. Processes include finding the area of a rectangle, how magnets work, how the president is elected, and how to find a particular state on a map. Students can also use graphics to help explain a process. Other kinds of writing-to-learn activities include the following (Noyce & Christie, 1989):

- Writing letters to convey personal reactions or request information on a topic
- Writing scripts to dramatize key events in history
- Writing historical fiction
- Writing a children's book on an interesting social studies or science topic
- Writing an editorial or commentary about a social issue
- Writing an illustrated glossary of key terms
- Creating captions for photos of a scientific experiment
- Creating a puzzle for key terms

Journals and Learning Logs

Journals and a type of journal known as a learning log can also foster understanding of content concepts and writing skills. **Journals** are a record of daily events and reflections. They vary in content and purpose from those that are highly private musings to those that function as travelogues or observations of nature or scientific experiments. Journals are often used for personal self-discovery. However, journals can also be a powerful tool for learning (Roe & Stallman, 1995).

■ A **journal** is a daily record of events, thoughts, ideas, or feelings.

■ Writers' Journals

Writers have long used journals to record observations, personal reflections, and story ideas and to try out new styles of writing. Student writers might be encouraged to do the same. Students might also record in their journals memorable passages from their reading. Journals provide the opportunity for students to collect possible writing topics and techniques and to try out techniques and styles. They can be used to help novice writers expand and hone their writing skills and to experiment. In their journals, novice writers might

- record interesting dialogue they have heard and use it as the basis for creating a story of their own.
- record favorite passages from their reading and note why they like the passage.
- imitate the style of an admired writer or piece of writing.
- create interesting settings.
- write from different points of view.
- reflect on how an event might look from someone else's point of view.
- note interesting words and expressions and then use them.
- note fascinating facts or interesting events and reflect on them.
- raise questions about intriguing, puzzling, or disturbing information.
- reflect on issues and topics.

Journals can be private or academic. Establish a set of ground rules with students. If you will be reading journals, inform students so that they don't include information or thoughts they wish to keep private. Reading students' writing journals makes the journals part of the writing program and encourages students to make entries. It also gives you insight into the students' writing and provides the opportunity for you to offer guidance and encouragement through your responses. Although students might be given credit for keeping a journal, journals are not graded or corrected. Otherwise, the flow of ideas will be hindered. However, knowing that the journals will be read and that you will be responding to them with comments will motivate students to put time and thought into their journal entries.

One of the disadvantages of journals is that they can become routine and lifeless. Provide thought-provoking prompts from time to time, and, as you respond to students' journals, encourage them to explore more deeply. You might also read from your journal or have volunteers read from theirs so that students see some of the many kinds of topics or formats that might be included in a journal entry. Another way to enliven journal writing is to have students share their entries with a partner or small group. Students can exchange journals or simply read excerpts from their journals. By reading excerpts, students may omit details that they would rather not share with classmates.

To get students started with journal writing, you may want to use a prompt. Here are some generic prompts.

- What was the highlight of the day?
- If I close my eyes and think about the day, what scene comes to mind?
- If I could change anything that happened today, what might it be?
- What did I learn today?
- If I were to write a post card to a friend about the day, what would I say?
- What are my plans for tomorrow?

If students can't think of a particular topic to explore, they can try freewriting. In freewriting, students write whatever comes to mind. They keep the pen moving for about ten minutes. If they can't think of anything to write, they may simply state that they can't think of anything to write about and perhaps reflect on why this might be so.

Writers' journals tend to be private and personal. Whereas the focus of writers' journals is on helping students develop topic ideas and writing skills and strategies, dialogue and double-entry journals and learning logs can be geared to help students learn and reflect on content area topics. These more subject-oriented formats are discussed in the following pages.

■ Dialogue Journals

Having just initiated a program in which students chose their own reading, Nancy Atwell soon realized that students needed opportunities to reflect on and discuss their reading. Because each of her classes had twenty-five students, individual conferences were impractical. She hit upon the idea of **dialogue journals.** She believed that "writing would give them time to consider their thinking and thoughts captured would spark new insights" (Atwell, 1987, p. 165). She also believed that an exchange between student and a knowledgeable adult would deepen students' understanding. Note the following exchange in which Jennifer reflects on her reading of the *Diary of Anne Frank* and compares it to the play by Hackett and Goodrich. Note, too, how Nancy Atwell's comment to Jennifer builds on and extends Jennifer's understanding.

> Ms. A.,
>
> Just to see what Anne Frank was going through was miserable. Her "growing up" with the same people every day. I think she got to know them a lot better than she would have if they weren't in hiding, her mother especially. That sudden change, going into hiding, must have been hard.
>
> It amazed me how much more they went downstairs in the book. It also told a lot more of her feelings, right up until the end. It must have come suddenly—to see police come in and arrest them.
>
> J. J.
>
> P. S. I think she could have been a writer.
>
> Dear J. J.,
>
> I don't have any doubt—if she'd survived, she would have been a writer all her life. Her prose style is so lively, and her insights are so deep. And she loved to write.
>
> We've talked about how movies alter (often for the worse) the books on which they're based. Plays can't help but do the same thing. All that inner stuff—reflections, dreams, thoughts, and feelings—doesn't easily translate into stage action, although Hackett and Goodrich tried with Anne's between-act voice-overs.
>
> If you're hungry for more information on Anne, please borrow my copy of Ernst Schnabels's *Anne Frank: Portrait in Courage* when Tom Apollonio returns it to me.
>
> Ms. A. (Atwell, 1987, pp. 165–166)

Dialogue journals are kept in spiral bound notebooks. At the beginning of the school year, the purpose of the dialog journals, which are written in the form of letters, is explained.

■ **Dialogue journals** are written exchanges in which students share thoughts with teachers or peers and are frequently used as a way of responding to and discussing literature.

In your letters talk . . . about what you've read. Tell what you noticed. Tell what you thought and felt and why. Tell what you liked and didn't and why. Tell how you read and why. Tell what these books said and meant to you. Ask questions or for help. And write back about your ideas, feelings, experiences, and questions. (Atwell, 1987, p. 193)

Students could submit their dialog journals as often as they wish. However, they were required to submit them at least once every two weeks.

Dialogue journals should be just that—a two-way conversation—between student and teacher. It is important that the teacher resist the temptation to evaluate and correct. "The teacher's role is to help expand and modify topics, not to direct or correct, although he or she may occasionally need to take the initiative in preventing or resolving communication breakdowns" (Dolly, 1990, p. 361). Because the focus is on expanding the meaning of the text, dialogue journals lead to a more active reading in which the dialoging readers construct meaning. Because readers are encouraged to voice their opinions, they are more likely to interact with the author. "Rather than passing over an author's comment with a vague sense of approval or disagreement, they will be motivated to think about why they agree or object" (Dolly, 1990, p. 362). Dolly found dialogue journals to be especially helpful when working with English language learners. Their dialogues often went beyond the reading to issues about language and culture that puzzled the students.

In a study comparing students' views about dialogue versus reflection journals, students felt that the dialogue journal was more valuable (Roe & Stallman, 1995). Although students agreed that both kinds of journals improved their writing, helped them to think critically, and provided a tool for them to reflect on what they were learning, they felt that the dialogue journal added an extra dimension. As one student explained, "To me the response journal was just part of my classwork, whereas in the dialogue journal somebody was answering and paying attention to what you said" (p. 9).

ENGLISH LANGUAGE LEARNERS

Using dialogue journals, you can model sentence structures which English language learners can then use on their own. For instance, you can model the use of different types of written questions so that the students can see and imitate these forms.

■ Double-entry Journals

■ **Double-entry journals** are journals in which the student makes an observation or other entry in one column or page and in the next column or page composes a reflection or other comment on the original entry.

In a DEJ (**Double-entry journal**), the left-hand page contains a stimulus for reflection or explanation. The right-hand page is used for the reflection. The left-hand page might contain notes, a science experiment, a math problem, a lab drawing, a drawing of a plant, or a prompt. In a sense, the left-hand page is the data. The right-hand page is an explanation of the data or reflection on it. For instance, in one DEJ entry, students drew diagrams of an experiment with batteries on the left-hand page. On the right-hand page, they explained what was happening in the experiment and its implications. The left-hand side might contain a new vocabulary word or concept. The right-hand side could then be used to explain the word or concept or give examples of its use or application. A description of the pH scale on the left might be complemented by a reflection on its use in swimming pool testing kits and soil testing kits. A math problem might be solved on one side and an explanation of the solution provided on the other side.

■ Nature Journals

One kind of journal that can be effective in science is the nature journal, in which students record their observations and thoughts about birds, animals, plants, trees, weather, sky, stars, landscapes, and the changing seasons. Verbal observations can be accompanied by drawings. In one project, students observed the moon for a month and recorded their observations with drawings that showed what they saw, verbal descriptions of their observations, and questions that they had (Project Base Technology Integrated Learning, 2002). A good source of suggestions is *Nature Journal: Discover a Whole New Way of Seeing the World around You* (Leslie & Roth, 1998).

■ Learning Logs

Another type of journal that fosters active involvement in the learning process is the **learning log.** Learning logs are journals, usually in spiral notebook form, in which students, on their own or in response to a teacher's prompts, "observe, speculate, list, chart, web, brainstorm, role play, ask questions, activate prior knowledge, collaborate, correspond, summarize, predict, or shift to a new perspective" (Atwell, 1990, p. xvii).

■ A **learning log** is a student's written account of his or her learning.

Learning log entries may be completed at home or in school. Entries should be brief and written in five or ten minutes. Although students should feel free to reflect on any aspect of their learning, prompts should be used in the beginning until students become familiar with the activity. Prompts can be generic. Some postreading or postlesson prompts include: What did I learn today? How does this fit in with what I already know? How might I use this knowledge now or in the future? What questions do I have about the topic? What else would I like to learn about the topic?

Prompts might be used to integrate affective and cognitive reactions: How did I feel after I read about the Holocaust? How did I feel when I read about the Great Famine in Ireland? How did I feel when I read about the slave ship?

Possible prompts for a unit on viruses and bacteria, only one of which would be provided for any one session, might include:

- What do I know about viruses and bacteria? What are some things that I don't know?
- What are some diseases caused by bacteria and viruses?
- Which of the diseases caused by bacteria have I had? Which sicknesses caused by viruses have I had? Which of these sicknesses was the worst?
- How are diseases caused by viruses treated?
- How are diseases caused by bacteria treated?
- What false ideas, if any, did I have about bacteria and viruses?

Prompts that promote reflection, manipulation of information, evaluation, and relating information to one's personal life lead to deeper understanding and longer retention of information. Learning logs also help a teacher keep in touch with her class. As she went over her students' logs, Countryman (1992) noted sources of confusion and frustration and used this information to help her students.

Some log entries may be composed before students read or at the beginning of a lesson or experiment. Before reading about Ancient Egypt, students might jot down what they know about the topic. Afterwards, they might note what they learned. Prelearning and postlearning entries help students activate prior knowledge and become more aware of what they already know and what they are learning (Santa, 1994).

Some log prompts might be used to elicit students' thoughts and feelings about key instructional activities: Which classroom activities do you find most helpful? Least helpful? Which classroom activities are easy for you? Which are difficult? What questions do you have about Ancient Egypt [or whatever the topic is] that we haven't covered? The best prompts are open-ended and personally involve writers by asking them "to discover their own opinions, draw on their prior experiences" (Atwell, 1990, p. 167).

One tenth-grade biology teacher used learning logs as a place where students could summarize a concept that they had recently learned. In their learning logs, they also interacted with text by recording a running commentary on their reading. They could summarize, raise issues, ask questions, or express opinions about what they had read. The purpose of these assignments was to provide students with the opportunity to relate new information to their background knowledge. The teacher checked the log entries but did not grade them so that students could write more freely. This informal writing was preparation for the later writing of essays (Marshall, 1984a).

Learning logs can be handled in a variety of ways. The class can discuss their learning logs, or the teacher can collect them and respond to them in writing. Although most teachers don't grade learning logs, they do check them and respond to them. The main purpose of logs is to have students think about their learning and ask questions about any elements that might not be clear (Atwell, 1990). Logs can also be used to record questions. Before reading a selection, students might record the questions they have about that topic. Later, they can evaluate how well their questions were answered. Whether students pose a question, jot down a reaction, or create a semantic map, the activity should help them reflect on their learning.

How effective are learning logs? According to one tenth-grade biology student, learning logs helped her to learn and forced her to think:

> If you write about it, you learn without wanting to. You don't have to sit there and study it. Phillips [the student's biology teacher] has you write down everything you know about a subject and that way you learn what you don't know . . . so you learn without trying. On multiple choice tests, you could guess. When you have to write, you have to think. (Marshall, 1984b, p. 168)

As noted earlier, personal journals such as the writer's journal should probably not be graded because that would tend to stifle creativity. However, logs and journals in which students record and reflect on their learning might be assessed. If assessing journals or logs, it's a good idea to create a rubric, and it's an even better idea to involve students in the rubric's creation. An informal survey of journal rubrics used by teachers revealed varied criteria. Some criteria judged journals on the basis of whether students made connections between class discussions and their reading, others counted neatness, whether students wrote in complete sentences, whether students drew illustrations for observations, or whether students spelled their entries correctly. Figure 8.3 shows a rubric for assessing a nature journal assignment.

FIGURE 8.3

Rubric for Assessing an Observational Nature Journal

	Beginning	Needs Some Additional Work	Satisfactory	Excellent
Number of observations	Five or fewer observations.	Missing several observations.	Missing no more than 1 or 2 observations.	All observations completed.
Visual description	No or few drawings.	Drawings for most observations. Drawings are lacking in detail or are not labeled.	Drawings for all observations. Lack of full detail in some drawings. Some captions lacking in full explanation.	Drawings for all observations. Drawings are detailed and have clear explanatory captions.
Verbal description	Little or no description.	Verbal description is lacking for some observations. Descriptions are lacking in detail.	Descriptions for all observations. Lack of full detail for some observations.	Descriptions for all observations. Descriptions are detailed.
Accuracy	Lack of data or many errors.	Some errors in drawings and descriptions.	A few minor errors in drawings or descriptions.	No errors.
Mechanics	Many errors in spelling, punctuation, etc.	Some errors in spelling, punctuation, etc.	A few errors in spelling, punctuation, etc.	No errors in spelling, punctuation, etc.

Note. Adapted from Project Base Technology Integrated Learning (2002). *Rubric for moon observation project.* Available online at: http://www.edutel.org/pbtil/cgs2/moon_journal/rubric.html

Content Area Autobiographies

Students who have weak backgrounds or who have negative experiences with a subject will be hindered in their quest to learn a subject. To find out what kinds of experiences students have had with your content area and also to provide them the opportunity to voice their feelings about the subject, you might have them write a content area autobiography (Countryman, 1992). In a content area autobiography, students describe their experiences with a subject from their earliest exposure to the present time. They are encouraged to describe failures as well as successes and how they feel about the subject. They should not, however, use the autobiography to criticize others. Autobiographies, such as the following, provide the teacher with valuable insight into students' attitudes and background in math and help her take steps to remove barriers to learning.

Up to about fifth grade I enjoyed and was quite good at math. After that, I often became confused, and, most of all, frustrated by it. A main problem that I have in math is that I will understand some of the material very well, but when I don't catch something right away or in a short amount of time, I have a problem ever understanding it. Sometimes I get so frustrated I think I hold myself back from learning it. This is strange because sometimes I find things which other people have trouble with quite easy, and vice versa. Either way, I always end up doing badly in math, and that's probably why I dislike it. (Countryman, 1992, p. 25)

 CHECKUP

1. What are some ways the process approach to writing can be applied to the content areas?

WRITING WORKSHOP

■ A **writing workshop** is a way of organizing writing instruction that includes a minilesson, strategic writing, time for students to write, individual and group conferences, and whole-class sharing.

One of the best ways to develop writing skills is through a **writing workshop** approach. In a workshop approach, both group and individual instruction are provided. Writing workshop consists of minilessons, strategic writing, writing time, conferences, and sharing. Workshops are most effective if held on a regular basis. Language arts and writing teachers may be able to hold writing workshops every day or every other day. Other subject matter teachers may be able to hold writing workshops on only a once-a-week basis. Even if you can't schedule writing workshops on a regular basis, you may still be able to implement some of the principles and techniques used in writing workshop.

Minilesson

■ The **minilesson** is a brief lesson on a needed writing or reading skill. The skill is usually applied in the following writing or reading workshop.

In the **minilesson,** which lasts for only about ten minutes, a needed writing skill is taught. Possible subjects are a review of the correct form for writing chemical formulas, selecting topics, correct e-mail format, or any one of a dozen fairly easy-to-teach skills. The minilesson is taught to the whole class or a small group.

Strategic Writing

■ **Strategic writing** is an approach to writing in which students are given direct instruction in writing strategies for which they have demonstrated a need.

Strategic writing is similar to the minilesson except that it embraces a more complex skill or strategy and so takes more time to develop. Developing a topic, summarizing, and other more complex skills and strategies are taught during strategic writing. A strategic writing lesson may take ten to twenty minutes or more and may be taught along with or instead of a minilesson. Strategic writing lessons might be geared to small groups of students who have specific needs. A group having difficulty supplying interesting examples to illustrate a point, for instance, might be assembled and presented with a lesson on composing examples. During the lesson, provide examples of the strategy as it appears in selections that students are reading and also in pieces written by students or you. Discuss the strategy and how it will help their writing. Model the use of the strategy, showing how you might include interesting examples in a piece that you are writing. Provide guided practice and have students apply the skill by using it in their own writing. Revision and evaluation should focus on providing interesting examples. The skill should be reviewed and reintroduced in conferences and follow-up lessons until it becomes part of the students' repertoire of writing strategies.

Writing Time

Writing time may vary but typically lasts for thirty minutes or longer. Students work on their individual pieces, have peer or teacher conferences, or meet in small groups to discuss their writing. Or they may meet in strategic writing groups for lessons geared to each group's needs. While students are writing, hold one or two small group strategic writing sessions, if you have grouped students according to common needs. After meeting with groups, and as time permits, move about the room and provide on-the-spot help and encouragement. You might explain to one student when a source needs to be quoted, help another narrow a topic, and encourage a third who is having trouble getting started. During this time you might hold individual **conferences** with several students, hold a conference with a group of students who are writing about a similar topic or who have similar concerns, or sit in on a peer conference that students have arranged.

■ A **conference** is a conversation between teacher and student(s) or among students designed to foster the development of one or more aspects of the writing process.

In peer conferences, students may meet in pairs or in small groups of four or five. During these conferences, one or more students may read their papers or portions of them and seek suggestions for improvement or reactions from the other members of the group. Because they provide individual focused assistance, conferences are probably the most valuable part of writing workshop.

Group Sharing

At the end of the workshop, students gather, and volunteers read their pieces. The atmosphere is positive and constructive. After a volunteer has read his piece, other students affirm the author by first telling what they liked about the piece. They also ask questions about any parts that might not be clear or in which they have a special interest. They also make constructive suggestions. By getting audience reaction, student writers get a sense of what's working and what's not and what they might do to add clarification and elaboration. Other class members get a sense of what their peers are writing about and learn about techniques that others are using that they might adapt.

Management of the Writing Workshop

Writing workshop works best when it is well organized. Before initiating the workshop, explain the setup of the room and note where supplies and materials are located. Involve the students in developing a series of routines. To prepare students for peer conferences or small sharing groups, discuss and model these activities.

Make sure, too, that students have specific plans for the workshop—for example, to revise a piece, confer with the teacher, or seek additional information about a topic. You may find it helpful to keep a record of students' activities in a workshop log.

As you move about the room, note students' progress and specific needs. If everyone seems to be having difficulty with the format of a report, discuss this in a minilesson. If a few students are writing pieces that have very little elaboration, schedule these students for a group conference or strategic writing lesson. Note the social dynamics of groups that are meeting. Note whether some students are dominating and others are being left out and whether the group is staying on task.

 CHECKUP

1. What is writing workshop?
2. How might it be conducted in my content area?

COMPOSING THE RESEARCH REPORT

According to National Assessment, more than half of the students in grades 4, 8, and 12 have some difficulty when asked to put their thoughts down on paper (Greenwald et al., 1999). They produce products that are uneven, insufficient, or unacceptable. Perhaps, because so many students have difficulty with writing, content area teachers may be reluctant to ask their students to write. Of course, this only makes the problem worse, because it denies students an opportunity to learn or apply skills.

One of the most complex tasks that students face is writing a research report, especially when they are asked to synthesize multiple sources (Many, Fyfe, Lewis, & Mitchell, 1996). Writing a report involves setting a goal, planning the content, locating sources, selecting information, understanding and synthesizing information, recording information, composing the report, and revising. Although expressed in linear fashion, these processes are recursive. For instance, students may revise their overall plan in light of unexpected information that they have located.

Obtaining Information for a Report

Students vary in their ability to obtain information for a report. As one secondary history teacher commented,

> Even older kids have a difficult time reading scholarly books and determining what's significant and what's not. Some of my eighth and ninth graders are adept at locating information. Those at the other end of the spectrum prefer to use the textbook. Their skills of accessing information are not that great, so they rely on one source.

In their study, Palmer and Stewart (1997) found some students who could not locate appropriate references, some who could locate appropriate references but were unable to find the information they needed, and some who could find the information but had difficulty interpreting or synthesizing it. Of course, there were a number of students who were able to complete their reports successfully.

Students vary in their understanding of what research involves. In a study of eleven- and twelve-year-olds assigned to research and write on a topic related to Word War

II, the students viewed research in one of three ways: accumulating information, transferring information, or transforming information (Many et al., 1996). How they viewed research directly affected the processes they used. Those who saw research as a matter of accumulating information or transferring information were most concerned with task completion. Their goal was to fill up the twelve-page booklets they had been given. There was little concern for audience or sticking to the topic.

The information accumulators paid little attention to the planning webs they had constructed at the beginning of the project. They included any information that was interesting, even though it did not support their specific topic; and they selected references because they were available, even if they weren't appropriate, instead of seeking out sources that addressed their topics. Information was recorded through a paraphrasing process.

Students who viewed research as a transferring process sought out relevant materials but did not go beyond recording that information in their own words. Although they may have used multiple sources, they did not synthesize information. Instead, they used one source for one subtopic and another source for a second subtopic, and so forth.

Those who viewed report writing as transforming information saw their task as providing information for a specific audience, in this case, students their own age. They engaged in careful planning, reviewed and revised their work in light of their planning, and considered their audience. They were also more likely to synthesize information from multiple sources and to reflect on the information they presented. Instead of focusing on filling up the pages, these students were concerned with conveying accurate information in an interesting way.

A key element in the research process was the availability of appropriate resources. When the references were difficult to read, even the most capable writers resorted to sentence-by-sentence paraphrasing or word-for-word copying.

The following steps can be implemented to turn information accumulators and information transferers to information transformers.

Step 1: Discuss the nature and purpose of the assignment. With the class's help, draw up a rubric so that students know exactly what is expected of them. (For more information about rubrics, see Chapter 13 and the sample rubric in Figure 8.3.) Rubrics are especially effective when students work in pairs or small groups and use the rubrics to make suggestions for the improvement of their own writing and that of their peers.

Step 2: Topics are selected or assigned. If possible, students should be given a choice of topics so that they have a sense of ownership and so are willing to invest the time and energy needed to compose an effective report. Students who have little knowledge of an area would have difficulty choosing an appropriate topic. Before students select a topic, encourage them to do some preliminary investigation so that they are better able to pick a topic of interest and have some idea how they might develop this topic. Also, help them pick a topic that is neither too broad nor too general. As part of the initial investigation, they can get some sense of whether or not there is adequate information available on the topic. The information should be on a suitable difficulty level so that students can use it.

USING TECHNOLOGY

For a list of sites that publish students' writing, see http://www.ala.org/parentspage/greatsites/amazing.html

USING TECHNOLOGY

The Staff Room http://www.odyssey.on.ca/~elaine.coxon/rubrics.htm Provides links to a variety of rubrics for content area writing assignments.

Step 3: Once students have chosen a topic, have them complete a preliminary planning guide. The planning guide can be an oral discussion or a written guide such as the one in Figure 8.4. The guide might include a brief description of the audience, the topic, key supporting subtopics, and a list of sources of information. The planning guide should be flexible so that as students make discoveries about their topic, they can revise the plan.

Step 4: Students select sources of information. Discuss possible sources. Also discuss ways in which students can determine whether or not the sources contain relevant information. Keeping their topic in mind, students should examine the index and table of contents of the text, in addition to looking at the title, to see whether it has relevant information (Dreher & Guthrie, 1990). Finding relevant information is deceptively difficult (Gans, 1940). Modeling, discussion, and guided practice can help. For guided practice, pose questions or topics and have students search through indices and tables of contents to locate what seem to be relevant passages. Then have the class read the passages and decide whether they are relevant. You might also distribute copies of selected passages and have the class decide whether they are relevant to a particular topic (Singer & Donlan, 1989). Students are asked to decide whether the passage helps answer their questions. If it does, students take notes from it. When passages fail to answer their questions, students sometimes mentally modify the question so that the passage seems relevant (Gans, 1940). Suggest that students write down the target questions so there is less chance that they will be modified. Also discuss and monitor students' research results to make sure that they are selecting relevant information.

Step 5: Once students have located relevant information, they extract it from the text. Because younger students and less expert writers have a tendency to copy, they need to be taught how to take notes. You can teach students a paraphrasing strategy in which they read a relevant passage, recall what they have read, and summarize

FIGURE 8.4

Planning Guide

Name _____ Class _____ Date _____

Audience _____

Topic _____

Key Supporting Subtopics

_____

_____

Sources of Information

_____

_____

what they have read in their own words. Once students have gathered the information, they can begin to organize their cards. Note cards, real or electronic, containing information on the same subtopic are grouped together. Groups of cards are arranged in sequential or some other kind of logical order and the report is ready to be written.

Step 6: Using information they have extracted and paraphrased, students compose their reports. When using multiple sources, students may use a cut-and-paste synthesis or a **discourse** synthesis. In a cut-and-paste synthesis, students jot down information from one source and then information from a second source. In discourse synthesis, students integrate the information from two or more sources. You should also teach students the importance of citing sources and how to do this.

> ■ **Discourse** is a form of speaking or writing that extends beyond a sentence.

Step 7: Students review their reports to make sure they are accurate and contain sufficient information (Many et al, 1996). They may check facts or decide that there are unanswered questions. They also check to see that sources have been cited.

Step 8: Revising/Editing. Although there is some overlap between this step and the previous one, the focus here is more on presentation. Students consider whether their reports are clear and interesting. They also check the mechanics.

Modeling the Process

One of the best ways to show students how to create a research report is to model the process. Show how you might go through the process of selecting and narrowing a topic, locating sources, extracting information, composing, reviewing, revis-

EXEMPLARY TEACHING

IMPACT OF WRITING ON ACHIEVEMENT

Reeves (2000) has studied a number of 90/90/90 schools. These are schools where 90% of the students are members of a minority group, 90% live in poverty, but 90% achieve at or above grade level. One of the characteristics of 90/90/90 schools is a focus on informational writing (Parker, 2002). Students are required to produce an acceptable piece of writing on a periodic basis. After being provided with thorough guidance and instruction, students write an informative piece and then are required to revise and edit as much as necessary in order to produce an acceptable product. For elementary schools, this is once a month. For secondary schools it is once a quarter. Writing is a whole school activity and is assessed using a common rubric. The rubric highlights key char-

acteristics of effective writing. The principal and teachers regularly discuss and share students' writing to maintain their focus on key characteristics of students' writing.

In their informational pieces students must include information that they do not already know so that the project becomes a genuine quest for new knowledge. The format can vary and might include a report, a persuasive editorial, a biography, or an explanation of a process in science. In writing their pieces, students not only increase content knowledge, they also develop thinking and writing skills.

Instruction is both whole group and small group. The whole class is instructed in procedures or skills that all need to learn. Small group instruction is used to teach groups of students who have common needs.

ing, and editing. Do a think-aloud in which you make known the cognitive processes involved in each of these steps. Also conduct lessons for key elements. For instance, provide direct instruction, guided practice, and application in the extraction and recording of information. Conduct these activities with material from your content area so that students are learning content as they learn writing skills.

Provide models of research reports. These might be exemplary reports turned in by past students. If possible, do a cooperative report with the class. In a cooperative report, the class selects a topic, narrows it, researches it, and goes through all the necessary steps as a group so that students have a better understanding of the process. Students might also do reports as part of a cooperative group before attempting to create reports on their own.

Because report writing is a complex, long-term undertaking, have the students complete it in parts. Part one might be topic selection and completion of a planning guide. Part two might be the first draft. Part three could be revising and editing. Part four might be the finished report.

Reports can be creative. Tenth-grade biology teacher Judith Stenroos asked her students to pretend that they were Gregor Mendel's lab assistant and that they were writing for a grant to further their research. In their applications, they had to write a clear explanation of their findings (Alvermann & Phelps, 2002). They were given a list of terms to include, such as *recessive*, *dominant*, *hybrid*, and *genes* and were reminded to explain the outcomes of the following gene combinations: two dominant genes, two recessive genes, and one dominant and one recessive gene. An eighth-grade teacher, Janyce Hepp, asked students to pretend that they were new immigrants. They were to write a letter to a relative back home telling about their experiences in this new country. Students were supplied with a list of possible topics that they might develop as part of the letter.

 CHECKUP

1. How can students be taught to write reports?

WRITING GUIDES

■ Writing guides are sets of questions, suggestions, and directions designed to assist students in the completion of a writing task.

Students may be unfamiliar with the kinds of writing required in the content areas. Just as study guides help students to understand content material better, guides can be used to help students write about content area topics. In a **writing guide,** the task is structured so that students are provided with prompts and suggestions that will help them write more effectively. Although somewhat similar to the guide sheets discussed earlier in the chapter, writing guides are more specific and are topic oriented. Initially, writing guides can be tightly structured so as to provide maximum help. As students become more confident, the guides can be less structured and more flexible. Writing assignments can be straightforward or creative, such as writing an editorial about the effects of the Industrial Revolution (Figure 8.5), or writing a diary of a young worker during the Industrial Revolution (Figure 8.6) .

FIGURE 8.5

Writing Guide: Industrial Revolution

Read the section on the Industrial Revolution (pp. 287–290). Notice how the Industrial Revolution changed the way people lived. Then take the role of an editorial writer. Write an editorial in which you are either for or against the Industrial Revolution. Write a topic sentence in which you give your opinion of the Industrial Revolution. Then give three to five reasons or examples to back up your opinion.

_____

_____

_____

RAFT

One way to provide guidance for students is to use **RAFT.** RAFT is a structured technique that helps students step out of themselves, focus on their audience, use their imaginations, explore a varied format, and write with conviction (Santa et al., 1996). RAFT is an acronym for the following elements: Role of the writer, Audience, Format, and Topic.

Role of the Writer. The writer can be a famous author, a scientist, a governor, a newspaper reporter, a detective, a creature from outer space, or even an animal or inanimate object.

Audience. The audience can be a judge of a writing contest, a district attorney, an ancestor, a legislative body, a favorite author, a talk show host, or whomever else the writer might want to address.

■ **RAFT** is a structured approach to writing that helps students focus on four key elements: Role of the writer, Audience, Format, and Topic.

FIGURE 8.6

Creative Writing Guide: Industrial Revolution

The year is 1790. You are a young person working in a textile mill in England during the Industrial Revolution. Although most workers can't read or write, you can. Write a diary entry telling what a day in the life of a young worker might have been like. In your diary, you might:

- Describe your home
- Tell where you work
- Tell what your job is
- Describe the long hours that you work there
- Talk about other young people who worked there

- Tell about your boss
- Remember what life was like before you moved from the family farm to the city

FIGURE 8.7

RAFT Planning Sheet

Role	Audience	Format	Topic
plant	*rain clouds*	*letter*	*drought*

Format. The piece could be a children's book, an editorial, a news story, a movie script, a journal entry, a speech, a memo, an infomercial, a play, a Web page, or whatever format seems to fit best.

Topic. The statement of the topic is accompanied by a strong verb so that it is an expression of the writer's purpose; for example *urge* everyone to block the new chemical plant, *demand* a refund for a faulty product, *persuade* a radio station to let the town's teens have an hour-long show each week, *convince* an investor to back your new invention.

FIGURE 8.8

Framed Paragraphs

Summarizing

After Columbus and other Europeans began exploring American, there was a two-way exchange of food. From the Americas foods such as _____.

From Europe, Asia, and Africa foods such as _____.

Because of the exchange, _____.

Explaining a Process

The process of _____ has _____ steps. In the first step, _____.

In the second step, _____.

In the next step, _____.

For the fourth and final step, _____.

If all the steps have been followed, _____.

Providing Support for a Judgment

_____ has my vote for being the best _____ for a number of reasons.

First, _____.Second, _____.

Most important of all, _____.

You won't find a better _____ than _____.

To introduce RAFT, explain its purpose and components and model writing a RAFT piece. Brainstorm possible topics. The topics might fall under a general theme. For instance, if you are studying the colonial period, have students suggest possible RAFT pieces, such as a teen writing a letter to his cousin in England, a merchant writing a letter of protest about the new taxes, or an editorial writer urging independence. A plan for a RAFT piece is shown in Figure 8.7.

Framed Paragraphs

Of all the techniques for supporting writing, **framed paragraphs** are the most structured. They are particularly useful when introducing new types of writing and when working with struggling writers. In a framed paragraph, the main idea of the piece is supplied. The frame indicates how many supporting details the piece might contain and it may also supply transition words and a conclusion. The amount of support and structure supplied can be varied. You might start out supplying maximum support and gradually fade the support until students are writing without the assistance of the frames. See Figure 8.8 for a sample frame.

 CHECKUP

1. What are writing guides?
2. How might they be used in the content area that I teach?

COMPOSING BIOGRAPHIES

Biographies put a human face on inventions, scientific discoveries, and important historical events. Until I read a biography of Mendel, to me he was just an obscure monk who grew a lot of peas. A biography made him and his ideas come alive. Each content area has its key people. Composing a biography about a famous inventor, leading scientist, president, or explorer is an excellent complement to material in the textbook. Written as they are for a general audience, biographies typically take special pains to explain their subjects' contributions clearly and to put these contributions in context.

Because every person's life has interesting aspects, biographies are an engaging kind of writing, if the biographer goes beyond the bare details of the subject's life and seeks out key incidents that define the subject. Patricia and Fredrick McKissack (2001), who have collaborated on more than fifty biographies, offer the following suggestions for student biographers.

1. Choose a person that you care about. This doesn't mean that you have to like the person. You just have to be interested in her or him.
2. Read an encyclopedia or other article about your subject. This will give you an overview of the person's life.
3. Research your subject thoroughly. Check books, newspaper and magazine articles, and Internet sources.

■ **Framed paragraphs** provide support for students who are having difficulty organizing their thoughts. The frames can also prompt students to add needed details.

STRUGGLING READERS
See "New Directions in Writing," which can be found in the *Teacher's Resource Book for New Directions in Reading,* Levels 5–10 (Houghton Mifflin, 1986), for a variety of suggestions for using framed compositions and letters.

USING TECHNOLOGY
Biography Maker http://www.bham.wednet.edu/bio/biomak2.htm Provides step-by-step directions for composing biographies.

4. Be objective about your subject. Don't leave out the person's failures or bad points because you like the person. And don't emphasize bad points because you dislike the person. Let the person's life speak for itself.
5. Be accurate. Check all your facts.
6. Tell a good story. Highlight interesting incidents in the person's life. Emphasize events that show what kind of a person your subject is. If you were writing a biographical sketch of Franklin D. Roosevelt, you might start off your biography with an account of his battle with polio. In a biography of Frederick Douglass, the McKissacks highlighted Douglass's use of a sailor's protection papers to escape to New York.

PERSUASIVE WRITING

Tests or assignments often call on students to compose persuasive pieces. However, persuasive pieces may well be the most difficult writing assignment (Gleason, 1999). The heart of writing persuasive pieces is understanding how to back up claims with logical, carefully reasoned arguments that contain convincing evidence or reasons. All too often, students' persuasive pieces contain more heat than light and engage in circular reasoning and unsupported statements such as "The space program should be supported because it's good for the country."

In a series of experiments, a curriculum designed to foster improved persuasion resulted in dramatically improved persuasive writing (Gleason, 1999). The curriculum included the following features.

- Discussion of a model of persuasive pieces
- Direct instruction in writing an opinion statement, offering supporting reasons/facts, and elaborating on these supporting reasons/facts
- Direct instruction in writing a conclusion
- Planning sheets that guided students through the process
- Checklists that helped students note whether or not key elements had been included
- Direct instruction on how to locate support for an argument in periodicals, textbooks, or other sources.

In addition to being taught the process of composing a persuasive piece, students were directly taught how to locate supporting information and take notes on it so they might use it in their pieces.

The teacher's role was an active one. The teacher modeled the process, broke the task down into manageable chunks, and provided feedback. However, students also engaged in small-group discussions and reviewed each other's work. Students also engaged in minidebates so that they could apply the reasoning skills they were learning.

Logical argumentation is a high-level cognitive skill. Students' ability to write persuasive pieces depends in large measure on their ability to argue in logical, convincing fashion. Their writing reflects their thinking. Learning how to debate orally prepared students to write persuasive essays.

FOSTERING HIGHER-LEVEL THINKING THROUGH WRITING

In addition to being taught to read like an historian, students need to be taught how to write like an historian. In addition to composing reports that summarize events, issues, or the lives of key historical figures, they need to be able to write opinion pieces in which they take a stand on issues and, most important of all, offer support for their stand. In their study of tenth-graders in advanced placement history classes, Stahl and colleagues (1996) found that when asked to form an opinion based on their reading of multiple texts on a controversial issue, students tended to make unsupported statements even though an examination of their notes showed that they contained details that would have buttressed their opinions. They apparently didn't realize that they were supposed to support their opinions.

In science classes, a typical writing assignment consists of completing lab reports. The report may have a highly structured format and offer little opportunity for students to reflect on their observations or explore their thoughts. To foster reflection and exploration, the science writing heuristic is designed to help students conduct experiments and write in such a way that they are engaging in knowledge transformation (Keys, 2000). As compared with traditional lab reports, the intent of the science writing heuristic is threefold: (1) to show students that writing is generated through the experimental process and is not just a summary of the experiment; (2) to stress the collaborative nature of science as students discuss experiments in small groups; and (3) to help students make connections among their observations, claims, and evidence. Students are asked to describe a pattern, make a generalization, state a relationship, or construct an explanation. They are then asked to support their claim, compare their claim with other sources of information, and reflect on what they have learned. This is designed to help students "bridge the gap between raw data and scientific meaning" (Keys, 2000, p. 680).

When given instruction in the writing of a thoughtful report, most students draw inferences, create and support hypotheses, and explain observations. For instance, after completing an experiment on erosion, one student produced the following segment, which contains thoughtful observations, several inferences, and explanations and hypotheses about the causes and effects of erosion.

> The grass is worn down where people have walked, water has run down the hill, where gravity and wind have moved soil. The erosion is bad enough that rocks once under the surface have been exposed and gullies have formed. I measured the gullies. They seem to vary in their depth due to their width. The more narrow gullies were deeper and had more rocks exposed.
>
> This is probably because of the concentration of the water and how hard it must have been raining at the time. The wider gullies seem to be more shallow because the water spread out over a larger area. (Keys, 2000, p. 687)

Once students have a clear sense of the purpose of their lab experiments, they are better able to write reports. As secondary science teacher Christina Hart reports, "Having a clear purpose for writing . . . greatly enhanced the quality of their descriptions of the experimental procedure" (Hart, Mulhall, Berry, Loughran, & Gunstone, 2000, p. 664).

CHECKUP

1. How can students be helped to write effective biographies? Persuasive pieces?
2. How might writing be used to foster higher-level thinking skills?

THE AFFECTIVE COMPONENT OF WRITING

Writing is affective as well as cognitive. Just as students who have had bad experiences with numbers may develop math anxiety, students who have had negative experiences with writing may develop writing apprehension. Students have writing apprehension when their anxiety about writing is so intense that they resist writing or avoid it (Singer & Donlan, 1989). Instructional situations that contribute to writing apprehension include unclear or vague assignments; writing tasks that are new and complex, such as writing a research report or term paper for the first time; having work assessed, especially if the assessment is a stringent one; and, of course, having had papers or exams assessed as unsatisfactory (Daly & Hailey, 1984). To combat writing apprehension, provide needed guidance; establish a constructive, positive atmosphere; and give students choice whenever possible. You can also plan some kinds of writing in which success is virtually guaranteed. Students can free write, compose group stories, or write cooperative pieces—pieces for which students suggest ideas and you write them on an overhead transparency or on the chalkboard. A discussion of past experiences with writing might alert you to negative attitudes.

HELP ON THE INTERNET

Scholastic (scholastic.com) sponsors writing workshops. Recently, Scholastic sponsored a workshop on writing biographical sketches. Workshop directors were Pat and Fred McKissack. In their workshop, they explain why and how they write and have useful tips for collecting information, checking facts, creating a biographical sketch, and revising.

One source of electronic help for student writers are OWLs, which are Online Writing Labs. OWLs are extensions of campus writing labs set up by colleges and universities to help their students. But many have an open-door policy and will help anyone who contacts them (Anderson-Inman, 1997). Many of the sites strictly designed for college students have handouts that address basic problems of usage and mechanics that would be appropriate for secondary school students. For a directory of OWLs, see the Writing Online Resource Directory (http://darkwing.uoregon.edu/~uocomp/cwc/wwwlinks.html).

IMPLEMENTING A CONTENT AREA WRITING PROGRAM

Based on extensive studies of students' writing, Langer and Applebee (1987) suggest using the following questions as guidelines for writing-to-learn programs. Although written nearly two decades ago, the guidelines are just as valid now as they were then.

1. Does the task permit students to develop their own meanings rather than simply follow the dictates of the teacher or text? Do they have room to take ownership of what they are doing?
2. Is the task sufficiently difficult to permit new learnings to occur, but not so difficult as to preclude new learnings? Students being given their first research or library paper may feel overwhelmed unless provided with lots of guidance and support.
3. Is the instructional support structured in a manner that models appropriate approaches to the task and leads to a natural sequence of thought and language?
4. Is the teacher's role collaborative rather than evaluative? In collaborative writing, "the teacher's role is one of helping students toward new learning rather than of testing the adequacy of new learning" (p. 143).
5. Is the external scaffolding removed as the student internalizes the patterns and approaches needed? (pp. 180–181).

SUMMARY

Writing is a powerful way to foster learning in the content areas. Students who use a process approach outperform those who don't. The five elements in the writing process are prewriting, drafting, revising, editing, and publishing. Although the English teacher may play a major role in teaching general writing skills, content area teachers are responsible for teaching those skills that are specific to their content area. Current nationwide standards include a call for writing proficiency in the content areas. Techniques for teaching writing include modeling and direct and guided instruction.

Types of writing in content area programs include writers' journals, dialogue journals, double-entry journals, nature journals, learning logs, content area autobiographies, biographies, reports, persuasive writing, structured types of writing, and the types of writing normally demanded in the content areas. The benefit students obtain from writing depends on the type of writing they do. Completing short-answer questions helped students learn details. Taking notes led to a concentration on information but little integration of that information. Writing essays resulted in generating, evaluating, and integrating information. Although teachers should offer students support as they write, there should be a balance so that students receive the guidance they need but maintain a sense of ownership of their writing.

Reflection

Return to the Anticipation Guide at the beginning of this chapter. Respond once again to the items. Did your responses change? If so, how and why? What are your current views on teaching writing in your content area?

EXTENSION AND APPLICATION

1. To experience the benefits of a journal or learning log, keep one for this course or another course that you are taking.
2. Plan and try out, if possible, a guided writing lesson in your content area.
3. Write a content area autobiography for the content area you teach and also for writing. Reflect on the positive and negative experiences you have had and how these might have shaped your learning.

chapter 9

TEACHING CONTENT AREA LITERACY TO DIVERSE LEARNERS

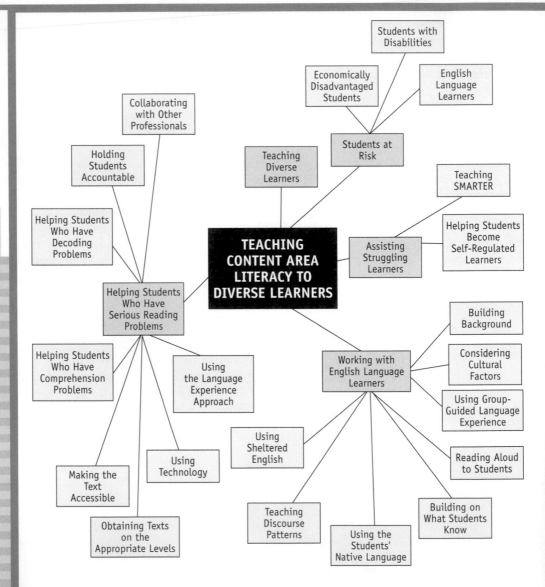

ANTICIPATION GUIDE

For each of the following statements related to the chapter you are about to read, put a check under "Agree" or "Disagree" to show how you feel. Discuss your responses with classmates before you read the chapter.

		Agree	*Disagree*
1	Instead of being asked to read their texts, struggling readers should be provided content information through lectures, audiovisual aids, and hands-on activities.	____	____
2	English language learners should be taught content area material in their native language.	____	____
3	In the interest of equity, all students should have the opportunity to learn the most challenging content.	____	____
4	Using easy-to-read textbooks shortchanges students because the content is watered down.	____	____
5	When teaching English language learners and struggling learners, content teachers should teach the language of their discipline as well as the concepts of the discipline.	____	____

USING WHAT YOU KNOW

Most of us have struggled with one or more content areas. Maybe it was advanced algebra, physics, or history. Or maybe it was learning a skill such as using a complicated computer program or playing a new sport. How did you feel when you were struggling to learn? How did you cope with the situation? What help were you given? How effective was it? What else might the teacher have done to help you? Thinking back on your school days, can you recall any teachers who were especially effective at helping struggling learners? What did they do? What steps might be taken to help struggling learners who are studying your discipline?

TEACHING DIVERSE LEARNERS

In the past, some content area teachers geared their instruction for the B students so that the presentation wasn't too simplified for the A students and was challenging but not overwhelming for C students. The D and F students were left to fend for themselves and were expected to "get what they can" (Bulgren & Lenz, 1996).

In general, content teachers expected that students would arrive with prerequisite background knowledge and learning skills. While content teachers agreed that students should acquire and use learning strategies, they didn't feel it was their responsibility to teach the strategies. However, that attitude has changed.

Given the greater diversity in today's content area classes and the **inclusion** of students who were previously taught in special education settings, today's content area teachers benefit, more than ever, from finding ways to teach struggling learners. They are finding that the weaker a student's preparation, the greater the need for using techniques and devices that help the student learn.

■ **Inclusion** is the practice of educating within the classroom all students, including those with special needs. In full inclusion, all support services are provided within the classroom setting. In partial inclusion, the student may be pulled out of the classroom for special instruction.

■ The term **at risk** refers to students who have been judged likely to have difficulty at school because of poverty, low grades, retention in a grade, excessive absence, or other potentially limiting factors.

STUDENTS AT RISK

Not all students who come from diverse backgrounds have difficulty learning in the content areas. Many do exceptionally well. However, a fairly large proportion of diverse learners experience some difficulty learning and are said to be at risk. **At-risk** students have been identified as those who are likely to experience difficulty in school (Frymier & Gansneder, 1989; Strickland, 1998). This includes 25 percent to 35 percent of the nation's students. Students are designated as being at risk if they have any six of some forty-five factors. The list includes such factors as parents or peers who use drugs and alcohol, retention in a grade, low marks, low scores on standardized tests, IQ below 90, membership in a special education class, negative self-image, illness, excessive absence from school, frequent changes of schools, and a home where English is not the principal language. Students who come from homes in which English is not spoken have significantly lower scores in reading, math, and science (Lemke et al., 2001). Poverty and attending a substandard school are also major risk factors (Snow, Burns, & Griffin, 1998). It should also be noted that an estimated 25 percent to 40 percent of U.S. students do not read well enough to cope with the texts in their content courses in middle and secondary schools. A disproportionate number of students who live in poverty or have other risk factors are also struggling readers.

Although widely used, the term *at risk* is avoided by some because it has a negative connotation. Ironically, if educators fault the victims or their backgrounds or begin making excuses because of adverse conditions, they may lower their expectations for these students. Slavin (1997–1998) recommends that we start looking at these students as being "at promise" and give them the kinds of high-quality programs that build success. Whatever term is used, it is clear that large numbers of students will need additional help if they are going to become successful learners of content area material.

Economically Disadvantaged Students

Although the percentage of children living below the poverty level has fallen recently, 16 percent of the nation's children aged seventeen and under live below the official poverty level (U.S. Bureau of the Census, 2001). Poverty is usually associated with lowered achievement. By age seventeen, **economically disadvantaged** children lag about four years behind more affluent students (Langer, Applebee, Mullis, & Foertsch, 1990). Even so, many students do achieve success despite poverty, especially if their homes are achievement oriented (Dave, 1964) and they are given effective instruction (Snow et al., 1998).

Students with Disabilities

Approximately 13 percent of all students are in programs for the disabled (U.S. Department of Education, 2000). Nearly half of these, or 6 percent of the total school population, are classified as **learning disabled,** with about 85 percent of those classified as learning disabled evidencing a serious reading difficulty. Approximately 43 percent of all students classified as disabled receive most of their instruction within the regular classroom.

English Language Learners

There are currently more than 3.5 million students in the United States who are classified as being limited English proficient. These are students whose native language is not English but whose lack of English may pose problems for them in classes where the instruction is in English (Kindler, 2002). This text uses the term English language learners rather than limited English proficient.

The number of ELLs is increasing rapidly. The largest proportion of **English language learners** (ELLs) are Latinos. Latino students comprise 15 percent of K-through-12 students, a proportion projected to increase to 25 percent by 2025 (ERIC Clearinghouse on Urban Education, 2001). Statistically, Latino students have lower-than-average achievement in school and high dropout rates; only a little more than half complete high school. Latino students also read significantly below average as a group (Donahue et al., 1999). Achievement is hindered by poverty and limited English proficiency (ERIC Clearinghouse on Urban Education, 2001). About 75 percent of ELL students attend high-poverty schools.

Bilingual instruction is now being de-emphasized in favor of programs that foster the acquisition of English. ELLs in grades 3 through 8 are required to take tests in English reading and language arts after completing three consecutive years of instruction (U.S. Department of Education, 2002). California now has a one-year English immersion program, unless parents object and request a bilingual program. According to bilingual experts, oral proficiency in conversational English may take two or more years to develop. However, it may take five or more years for students to reach the same level of proficiency in academic English obtained by their English-speaking peers. Catching up is difficult because while ELLs are acquiring more advanced English

■ **Economically disadvantaged** people are those whose lives and opportunities are limited or put at risk by having insufficient economic resources.

USING TECHNOLOGY

For information about urban education, contact Urban Education Web: http://eric-web.tc. columbia.edu/

■ **Learning disability** is a general term used to refer to a group of disorders which are evidenced by difficulty learning to read, write, speak, listen, or do math. Speaking and listening difficulties are not caused by articulation disorders or impaired hearing.

■ **English language learners** (ELLs) are students whose native language is not English but who are in various stages of learning English.

USING TECHNOLOGY

National Clearinghouse for English Language Acquisition http://www.ncbe.gwu.edu/ Provides an overview of bilingual education and English language acquisition

ENGLISH LANGUAGE LEARNERS

When working with ELLs, focus on their understanding of what they read. Because of limited English, second language readers may have difficulty fully explaining what they know about a selection they have read. They may mispronounce words whose meanings they know. The key element is whether students are getting meaning from these words, not whether they are pronouncing them correctly.

USING TECHNOLOGY

For more information on learning disabilities contact:
Learning Disabilities Association of America:
http://www.Ldanatl.org
International Dyslexia Association:
http://www. interdys.org
Council for Exceptional Children:
http://www.cec.sped.org

language skills, so are the native speakers of English (Cummins, 2001). Proficiency with conversational English may hide deficiencies in the kinds of higher-level language skills needed to learn content area material (Sutton, 1989). Although ELLs may be able to exchange ideas with friends, they may have difficulty with the abstract, formal language used to convey content area concepts. As a content area teacher, you may therefore find that you need to assist some of your students with learning the language of your content area and the language of instruction in general.

 *CHECKUP*

1. Who are the students at risk?
2. What factors cause them to be at risk?

ASSISTING STRUGGLING LEARNERS

A first step in helping struggling learners is to find out who they are and what their difficulties might be. Bulgren and Lenz (1996) note that "many teachers lack information about which students in a class have learning disabilities and which instructional techniques, activities, and materials have proven effective with these students" (p. 418). In addition to students who have been labeled as having a learning disability or reading problem, there may be a number of students who are struggling to learn but have not been identified. Plan a conference with the learning disabilities specialist and the reading specialist. Seek out information on the students' difficulties and ways to help them learn the material in your content area. The specialists may provide demonstrations or even work with the students in your classroom. However, simply observing one or two high-achieving and one or two low-achieving students and their responses to instruction has helped teachers revise their planning so as to accommodate students at both ends of the spectrum (Bulgren & Lenz, 1996).

Teaching SMARTER

One approach that content area teachers can take in order to cope with both the overstuffed curriculum and the increased academic variability of today's classes is to teach SMARTER (Bulgren & Lenz, 1996). SMARTER is an acronym for a guide for planning for classes that include struggling learners. However, SMARTER is designed to benefit all students. The seven steps are Select, Map, Analyze, Reach, Teach, Evaluate, Reevaluate.

1. Select the key content that you wish students to learn. State the content in terms of questions that students will be expected to answer: What has Roman civilization contributed to our way of life? What has Greek civilization contributed to our way of life? How does understanding how people lived in early times help us to understand ourselves? Students can use the questions to assess their grasp of key con-

cepts. Creating the questions helps the teacher link planning, instruction, and assessment. Questions are a concrete way of restating course objectives or standards. As Bulgren and Lenz (1996) note, "Questions require the teacher to think about how he or she would like the student to think about or talk through the content or task" (p. 46). Students can ask themselves key questions and see if they can answer them.

2.   Map the organization of the content to show how key concepts are related to each other and to student's current knowledge. Maps can be created for the whole course, a unit, or individual lessons. For units and lessons, it is recommended that the map include no more than seven elements.

3.   Analyze why the content may be difficult to master. Consider such factors as density and complexity of concepts and student background and interest.

4.   Reach decisions about how to teach the content. Consider especially what might be done to enhance learning. Instructional enhancements include advanced organizers, such as structured overviews, graphic organizers, charts, graphs, tables, and demonstrations. Many of the techniques covered in previous chapters qualify as enhancements.

5.   Teach the content and also teach the enhancements. Students may not realize that you are using special devices or techniques to foster learning. Students make better use of enhancements when these are pointed out and their purpose and application is explained. You might explain, for example, that the enhancement known as the structured overview will help the class understand what kinds of animals are reptiles and how reptiles are grouped in comparison to other animals.

6.   Evaluate students' learning. Evaluation can take many forms. It may be observation of students' discussions, lab work, or assignments, or it may take the form of quizzes and tests.

EXEMPLARY TEACHING

BUILDING ON STUDENTS' INTERESTS

Struggling readers are often reluctant readers. Not being proficient readers, they read less. Reading less, they fall further and further behind. To break the cycle, it is essential that they read, read, read. Chris Tovani broke that cycle with her ninth-grade reluctant readers by bringing in newspaper articles that touched students' lives. One editorial blasted her high school for allowing smoking on campus even though smoking was prohibited in virtually every other place and it was illegal for students under eighteen to purchase cigarettes.

Students became highly defensive. One student claimed that smoking was no big deal and that 95 per-cent of adults smoked. Tovani suggested that the class research the issue. For the next week, using the Internet and other sources, students intensively researched the topic. One student found from an authoritative source that only 28 percent of adults smoked. Another learned that smoking was indeed a big deal. She had located a long list of smoking-related health risks.

Having learned the truth about smoking, students felt a sense of accomplishment and self-efficacy. They were also in a better position to make an informed decision about smoking. And they had learned the value of sustained expository reading. As the year progressed, they investigated other topics of interest (Harvey, 1998).

7.   Reevaluate the effectiveness of the instruction and revise as necessary. Review concepts and skills that students had difficulty with, especially if they form the foundation of future learning.

Helping Students Become Self-Regulated Learners

Although students at the Benchmark School, a school for struggling readers, responded well to carefully programmed instruction—99 percent returned to a mainstream class reading at or above grade level—the staff realized that the students needed more than a command of academic strategies (Gaskins & Elliot, 1991). Many of the students had to overcome maladaptive learning habits and styles that either caused or were a result of their earlier struggles with school. All too often, their performance was marred by impulsivity, rigidity, and lack of persistence or follow-through.

A first step in working with struggling learners is to help them set goals. Goals should be challenging but realistic. Three sets of goals should be drawn up: long-term goals, mid-term or in-between goals, and short-term goals (Eisenberger, Conti-D'Antonio, & Bertrando, 2000). Long-term goals provide focus but lack immediacy. Mid-term goals provide a convenient place for pausing to see how things are going and making some needed adjustment before it is too late. Short-term goals help the student to focus on daily tasks.

The beginning of a school year or semester or the beginning of a unit or project is a good time to set goals. Students should be involved in the goal-setting process so that they have a sense of ownership. A long-term goal might be to create a PowerPoint presentation of the life of Teddy Roosevelt for American history class. Short-term goals might be to gather material on Roosevelt, write up the material, revise the material, learn how to use PowerPoint, set up a presentation, try out the presentation, and give the presentation. Part of goal setting might be having students assess their academic strengths and weaknesses: What do they do that helps them learn history? What could they do to improve in history? Responses could be used to set learning goals: reading the text, taking notes in class, or handing in assignments on time, for instance.

Once they have set their goals, students should draw up a plan for achieving them. They might list all the steps they will take and deadlines for finishing each of the steps. To help in both their goal setting and their planning, students might visualize the finished product and each of the steps. They might imagine themselves gathering the material, putting the material together, revising their write-up, and transferring their write-up to PowerPoint.

After drawing up a plan, students put it into action. As students put their plan into action, they are constantly assessing their progress and making adaptations when necessary. Reflection helps students to judge the effectiveness of their actions and to grow in independence as they take responsibility for their learning. Teachers should model the process of reflecting on one's learning so that students see that this is something that even experts need to do. Frequent reflection also keeps students on task. Some students find it helpful to complete a written reflection and discuss it with their teachers. Possible areas to be reflected on and discussed include progress being made toward reaching the goal, aids to reaching the goal, obstacles, plans for over-coming obstacles, and next steps.

Self-talk might be used to overcome fears and worries and sudden attacks of neg-ativity. Students might tell themselves that they can take the test and do well on it. Or, yes, they can stand in front of the class and give an oral report. To help them overcome negative thoughts, students might write a series of "I can't" statements, such as "I can't spell. I can't do math;" they then list the negative associations that they have with each statement. They might then think of ways in which they can turn the "I can't" situations into "I can" ones (Eisenberger et al., 2000).

■ **Self-talk** is the recita-tion of self-positive beliefs such as "I can do it" in order to overcome negative feelings and attitudes or self-defeating behaviors.

CHECKUP

1. What are some steps that might be taken to assist struggling learners?

WORKING WITH ENGLISH LANGUAGE LEARNERS

Based on their research and observation, Gersten and Baker (2000) identified five spe-cific instructional components in a program for English language learners:

1. vocabulary as a curricular anchor, 2. visuals to reinforce concepts and vocabulary, 3. cooperative learning and peer tutoring strategies, 4. strategic use of the native lan-guage, and 5. modulation of cognitive and language demands.

Vocabulary as a Curricular Anchor. A major barrier for English language learners is having a limited English vocabulary. Vocabulary instruction should be intensive and should focus on key words, which are those words most needed to grasp major con-cepts in a discipline. Typical high school students can recognize up to an estimated 50,000 to 100,000 words when they meet them in print (Nagy & Herman, 1987). For second language learners, vocabulary is a major obstacle to comprehension. They may recognize only 5,000 to 7,000 English words. Students need not know all the words in a selection in order to grasp it. However, ELLs often have a tendency to read each word slowly and deliberately (Johnson & Steele, 1996). Instruction should focus on those key terms essential for an understanding of the selection's major points. Instruction for ELLs should include guidance in the selection of which words to focus on and which to skip.

Visuals to Reinforce Concepts and Vocabulary. Visuals, dramatizations, and gestures should be freely used. In fact, visuals including illustrations and graphic organizers should be used whenever possible when instructing English language learners.

Cooperative Learning and Peer Tutoring Strategies. Working with peers provides excellent opportunities for English language learners to apply language skills. In a small group, they are less reluctant to speak. In addition, they are better able to make themselves understood and better able to understand others.

Strategic Use of the Native Language. Teachers should use that level of English that students are familiar with. However, for developing complex concepts, they should

USING TECHNOLOGY

Dr. Mora's Website is an excellent source of information about bilingual education: http://coe.sdsu.edu/people/jmora/

use the students' native language, if possible, or ask another student to provide a translation. That way the student doesn't have the burden of trying to understand difficult content expressed in terms that may be hard to understand.

Modulation of Cognitive and Language Demands. When cognitive demands are high, language expectations are simplified. Teachers may accept brief or partial responses in English. When cognitive demands are low, the teacher might demand more extensive use of English. For instance, for the literal-level question from a U.S. history text, "What contributions did Eads and the Roeblings make to bridge construction?" (Boorstin & Kelley, 2002, p. 453), ELLs might be able to respond primarily in English. Words needed to respond are directly stated in the text. However, for a related question, "How did bridge building contribute to the growth of cities?" (p. 453), which requires constructing a generalization, students might need to be allowed to make use of their native language.

Because reading is such an essential skill, it used to be said that every teacher is a teacher of reading. Now, with so many ELL students in schools, it is being said that every teacher is a teacher of English. This doesn't mean teaching English skills from the ground up. It does mean teaching those language skills that students are lacking but need to learn key concepts in the content area you teach. As Echevarria, Vogt, and Short (2000) note:

> Because of the large numbers of English language learners in schools today, all teachers are teachers of English, even if their content specialization is science, math, or social studies. For students learning English, teachers must create ample opportunities to practice using academic language, not simply social uses of language. (p. 92)

Building Background

ENGLISH LANGUAGE LEARNERS

Before students read a piece, activate their prior knowledge. Because of cultural and linguistic differences, students might not realize that they have background to bring to a story or article. Also, emphasize comprehension over pronunciation (Chamot & O'Malley, 1994).

Because of gaps in their schooling, when they may have missed topics because of transferring from one school to another or moving from one country to another, ELLs may lack background for key content area concepts. One solution is to teach lower-level concepts. However, if possible, grade-appropriate content should be taught. The better solution is to build students' background so that they will be prepared to learn the concepts being taught. If the whole class needs the background, this can be done as a whole-class activity. If just one or two students need help, this can be done in a small-group session. If tutors are available, they might do the background building. Vogt (Echevarria et al., 2000) uses a jumpstart technique in which she previews material for underprepared ELLs before it is introduced in the regular class. These jumpstart minilessons include reviewing key concepts, introducing new vocabulary, going through the chapter or section to be read and providing an overview of it, conducting or observing experiments, and taking part in simulations and role playing.

Considering Cultural Factors

ELL students are faced with more than just learning English. They must also learn the customs and culture of the classroom. Students from some countries may see their role as memorizing what they have been taught. Thinking for themselves is not encouraged. Questioning the teacher might be interpreted as a sign of disrespect. Students need to be guided to see that it is not only okay to think for oneself, it is desirable. However, this is a gradual process, especially for older students who may have spent years in a school culture that discouraged independent thought.

Deng, a fifth-grade student who is a native of Laos and speaks Hmong, found both the language and culture of his U.S. school confusing (Brock, 2000). In his fifth-grade language arts classroom, the teacher wanted to contrast the words *home* and *homelessness.* Deng was not aware of the meaning of *contrast.* He confused it with the word *contest.* He wondered if it referred to some sort of race. But Deng did not ask the teacher to clarify the meaning of the word. And he never responded to questions by the teacher. In Laos, students were not expected to ask questions and were punished if they gave wrong answers.

As a result of language confusions and cultural constraints, Deng did not do well in whole-group lessons. However, he performed much better in small groups. Other students helped him with difficult words and confusing procedures. They also provided prompts so that Deng was able to take part in their discussions.

Using Group-Guided Language Experience

Use **language experience** with English language learners. A language experience selection is one in which students dictate the content of a written piece and the teacher functions as a facilitator and scribe. Because students dictate the story, the language is theirs. This works well for younger students and students who are less proficient in English and also in situations in which the textbook is too difficult for students. As students gain in proficiency, use a collaborative approach. In a collaborative approach, you and students work together to create a selection. As an active participant, you can scaffold the language to a higher level. Here is how one teacher helped his secondary students create a story. They first read Maupassant's classic tale, "The Necklace," in which a poor but socially ambitious woman borrows what she thinks is an expensive necklace from a wealthy friend so that she can make an impression at a party (Schifini, 1999). Having lost the necklace and too embarrassed to admit it, she slaves at menial jobs for years in order to replace it. Later, prematurely aged by her efforts, she encounters the owner of the necklace and learns that the necklace was just an inexpensive piece of costume jewelry. She had sacrificed her youth and beauty in vain. After reading and discussing the selection, the students discussed times when they had borrowed items. Then they decided to write their own story involving borrowing as a general theme. Cooperative groups were set up. Each group created an element of the story. One group created characters, another the setting, a third, the plot. The groups then met as a whole class and, through discussion and negotiation, created their story.

As the class, with the teacher's help, created their story, the teacher emphasized one or two teaching points. For this selection, he suggested that students incorporate dialogue and review ways of writing dialogue. After creating the story, reading it, and revising it, the students used a word processing program to create a book, complete with illustrations. They then read their books to younger students.

■ **Language experience** is a teaching technique in which the teacher writes down an experience or ideas dictated by students which students, with the teacher's guidance, then read.

Reading Aloud to Students

One way to build background and language is to read aloud to students. Reading to students helps to familiarize them with the more formal language of print. For younger students, select well-organized, predictable books that are heavily illustrated. Books that present one or two key concepts are especially helpful. A book such as *Tools* or *Shoes*, by Ann Morris, will help students learn new labels for familiar objects (Schifini, 1996). Choose books that have a straightforward style and don't use figurative language or idioms, which pose special problems for English language learners.

For older students who are more proficient in English, select books that are more detailed and complex but also focused and well illustrated. Choose books that have a favorable print-to-illustration ratio and illustrations that do an especially effective job at depicting key concepts.

Preparation for the oral reading should take into account students' language ability, proficiency, and needs. Before reading the text, provide an overview so that students have a sense of the plot or the main ideas. This will help them get ready for a higher level of language comprehension. As you read the selection, make use of illustrations to help convey its meaning. Also demonstrate and act out key words. After reading a section of the selection, discuss it with students so they can reflect on and use the information it conveyed as well as some of the terms used to convey those concepts.

Building on What Students Know

Cognitive and academic skills learned in one language transfer to a second language (Cummins, 1994). If I know the water cycle or understand the functioning of the cell in Spanish, I will know it in English once I acquire the proper labels. If I learn to read and write Spanish, I can transfer these skills and strategies into English once I learn the language.

A group of English language learners taking a state mastery test in English were puzzled by the selection presented. The selection was about ostriches, but *ostrich* was unfamiliar to them. Since they didn't know the word, the selection made little sense to them. They knew what ostriches were. But they didn't know the label. Comprehension was hampered, not by a lack of background knowledge, but because they didn't have the English label for the creatures. Another group of students had difficulty reading a selection about a farm because, although some of them had been raised on farms, they didn't know the English label *farm*.

English language learners can be stymied by words such as *farm* and *ostrich*, which you might assume they know. If the unknown words are key words, they may lose the whole sense of the selection. Before students read a selection or listen to a lecture, go over the key terms with them. If they speak one of the romance languages, such as French or Spanish, have them seek out cognates, words that are descended from the same language or form. The word for electricity in Spanish is *electricidad*. Seeing the word *electricity*, the Spanish-speaking reader often realizes that it means the same thing as *electricidad*. Native speakers of Spanish may not realize how many Spanish words have English cognates.

■ Spanish–English Cognates

Although pronunciation may differ, many words are spelled the same in Spanish and English: *abdomen, base, capital, canal, film, larva, superior, usual, variable.* In hundreds of others there are slight changes in spelling as in the following:

Added *a:* artista, dentista, forma, secreta

Added *o:* acto, barbero, globo, infinito, objecto

Added *e:* abundante, accidente, heroe, importante, residente

Omitted *e:* aptitud, gratitud, latitud

Presence of *cia* instead of *ce:* abundancia, distancia, competencia

Suffix *cion* instead of *tion:* conversacion, educacion, nacion

In some cognates there are several changes in spelling so that students might need to examine these carefully before recognizing them as familiar elements as in *hidrosfera* for *hydrosphere* or *actitud* for *attitude.* Students need to be cautioned that there are false cognates. The word *exito* looks like the English "exit" but it means "success." Likewise *largura* does not mean "large"; it is the Spanish word for *length.* Students need to be taught to use context to check to see if the word that seems to be a cognate makes sense in the sentence or overall context in which it appears (Thonis, 1983). Model the process of using cognates by demonstrating how you use cognates to read Spanish words.

Using the Students' Native Language

On occasion, depending on their language proficiency and the nature of the material being learned, English language learners can benefit from having concepts explained in their native language. Clarification can be provided by the teacher, a bilingual aid, or another bilingual student. It can occur on a one-to-one basis. If there are no other resources available, the teacher can turn to content area texts written in the students' native language (Echevarria et al., 2000). Or the teacher or students might use an electronic translator such as the one found on Altavista Babel Fish (http://babelfish.altavista.com/), which translates text up to 150 words long and even Web sites. You can type in key words or phrases and get the equivalent in the students' language. You could also type in summaries of key concepts and have them translated into the students' native language. Students can also use these tools to translate difficult English passages into their native language. The guiding principle in whether to use English or the students' native language is to do whatever it takes to foster understanding.

Teaching Discourse Patterns

School language has a linear discourse pattern. Explanations follow a definite sequence. Events are explained in the order in which they occurred. The speaker sticks with the topic and does not include information that is not directly related to the topic. However, there is some evidence that many native speakers of Spanish, Native Americans,

USING TECHNOLOGY

More than 3,000 books in Spanish, ranging from beginning reading, to secondary reading can be found at Rennaissance Learning: http://www.renlearn.com/store/quiz_home.asp. Click on Advanced Search and search by Spanish language. Readability levels are supplied.

and African Americans use a nonlinear discourse pattern (Escamilla & Cody, 2001). When writing about an event, students from these cultures may include a number of details that happened at the time of the event but which were not directly related to the event. Their discourse style may be more associative: they include details that they associate with the main idea but which do not directly support it. Their descriptions and explanations might be quite accurate, but they seem more roundabout because they bring in what seem to be extraneous or nonessential details. Teachers may give them lower grades for their responses, even though the information they are supplying is accurate.

These students need to be exposed to academic discourse, both spoken and written. They need to be shown how to write in linear fashion and to exclude extraneous details. They also need to be taught linear logic. Escamilla & Cody (2001) note,

> When Spanish-speaking students are learning to write in English they must be explicitly taught English linear logic and the rhetorical and discourse patterns used in English writing. It is not enough to simply learn the mechanics of writing in English as a second language. Students must also learn how to "think" in English. (p. 55)

Unit or thematic organization also works particularly well for English language learners. Seeing the overall topic being explored or question being asked, students are better able to make sense of instruction. Since concepts are developed in more detail in thematic units and vocabulary is naturally repeated, thematic organization is more meaningful to English language learners, and vocabulary is more fully developed because words are repeated more often (Freeman & Freeman, 2002).

 CHECKUP

1. What are some techniques that might be used to help English language learners learn content material?

Using Sheltered English

■ **Sheltered English** is the practice of teaching subject matter content in English to English language learners who have learned conversational English but not academic language. The purpose of sheltered instruction is to build both language skills and content knowledge.

In **sheltered English,** teachers make a special effort to make content instruction understandable to all students, including those who are still acquiring academic English. This is something that conscientious teachers have always done. However, sheltered instruction has a second component. While presenting content, the teacher also takes steps to foster language development. Colburn and Echevarria (1999) comment that sheltered classes are "distinguished by careful attention to students' needs related to learning another language" (p. 36). In a sense, content and language objectives are combined.

A good place to begin sheltered instruction is building on what has worked in the past and adapting these techniques to ELLs. Schifini (1994) suggests that you ask yourself, "How does any youngster come to comprehend and glean new information from text? What has worked well for students I have taught in the past?" (p. 162). Make a list of the effective techniques. Then ask yourself a third question,

"How can I adapt or modify these techniques so that they will help ELLs learn?" Some adaptations that may help include the following:

- Make your presentation as understandable as possible. Speak slowly and distinctly. Use simple, direct language. Avoid jargon, figurative language, idioms, and cultural references that students may not be familiar with.

- Use the visual to support the verbal. Use audiovisual aids, gestures, facial expressions, demonstrations, and skits to make the language as meaningful as possible.

- Make directions as clear as possible. Show students what to do in addition to telling them. If possible, model the process for them. Have students attempt to carry out directions or apply a concept under your guidance. Provide feedback as needed.

- Emphasize hands-on activities, drawings, webs, and maps so that students can use techniques that are less language dependent to deepen and express their knowledge.

Illustrations and models help English language learners develop concepts and vocabulary.

- Use brainstorming, quick write, and similar techniques to tap prior knowledge. In a quick write, students are given two or three minutes to sum up what they know.

- Modify the use of text. You might use Questioning the Author or Reading Seminar to help students collaboratively construct meaning.

- Obtain texts that use a simpler language.

- Encourage students to discuss content in their native language as well as in English.

- Provide prompts that encourage students to clarify or expand responses: That's interesting. I'd like to hear more about that. Can you explain that? Can you tell us more? So what happened next?

- Scaffold instruction. Provide prompts and other assistance as needed.

- Provide opportunities for students to talk over ideas. This could be in whole-class discussions, pairs, or small groups. This gives English language learners the opportunity to use academic language as they engage in activities and discuss procedures and findings.

- Pantomime actions and demonstrate processes.

- Use time lines, graphs, videos, and filmclips on CD-ROM. Use manipulatives such as globes and Cuisinaire rods.

- Use realia such as recycling and nutrition labels, menus, job applications, and bank deposit slips.

- Provide generous amounts of wait time. Instead of expecting students to answer as soon as you ask a question, wait a few seconds. This benefits all students (Lake, 1973; Rowe, 1969) but is especially helpful to ELLs because, being less familiar with the language, they need extra time to formulate their responses.

- When assessing, allow students to demonstrate their knowledge in multiple ways. Where possible, include ways that don't rely so heavily on language. They might conduct an experiment, draw a diagram, or complete a project.

Here is how one secondary teacher sheltered the content in her social studies class (Schifini, 1999). As part of a unit on indigenous cultures, the class was studying the Mayan people. To introduce the lesson, the teacher provided each group with an artifact from the culture and asked them to discuss the nature of the artifact and how the Mayan people may have used it. After discussing the artifacts, students then read about them in the easy-to-read, heavily illustrated *New True Book about the Maya* (McKissack & McKissack, 1986).

As part of this discussion of the Maya, students wrote one thing that they liked about the Maya. Students also looked at pictures of the Mayans and wrote things that they knew or thought they knew based on the illustrations. Students then participated in a KWL, as explained in Chapter 5, and read a portion of the book. Generally, brainstorming is the first step of a KWL and there is no prior preparation. The discussion of the artifacts had built a solid foundation for KWL. As a result of the preparation, students were able to read the text with enhanced comprehension. They had little difficulty filling out their KWL charts and noting what they had learned. Because of their well-prepared reading, they engaged in a lively discussion of the topic.

Summarized below is a well-planned science lesson designed to introduce students to the concepts of density and buoyancy (Colburn & Echevarria, 1999). How might this lesson be adapted to meet the needs of ELLs?

Into a tank of water, the teacher placed two oranges, one that had been peeled and one that hadn't. The class discussed why the peeled orange sank. Students then created boats and charted in graph form how much they could load onto their boats before they sank. As the students worked, the teacher circulated around the room and asked students, "Tell me what you're thinking," to get insight into their thought processes. The teacher also discussed the relationship between density and buoyancy. The teacher then assigned the section of the textbook that explains density and buoyancy.

With its hands-on activities, demonstration, and emphasis on inquiry, the lesson was highly effective and helped the students not just to talk or read about the concepts of density and buoyancy but to experience them as well. However, there are several steps that could be taken to shelter this same content.

- In addition to giving students oral directions, the teacher could demonstrate what she wants them to do. Instead of just telling them to make boats, she could make one as an example and load it up until it sinks. This helps ensure that students who miss a word here or there know exactly what to do because they have seen a demonstration.

- To foster language development, the teacher could highlight key vocabulary words and discuss them and, if possible, show illustrations of them or demonstrate them. This way, there would be an increased probability that students will have used them in their discussions.

- The teacher in this case walked around the room as the students worked and asked what they were thinking. In addition, it would be helpful to observe the graphs students create. If a student's academic language is limited, her graph may reveal an aspect of her thinking that she can't put into words.
- The teacher could provide more preparation for reading the textbook assignment. He could give the students an overview of the content or read portions of it to them. Or, he could prepare a gloss or study guide. Or, he could do all these preparations.

 **CHECKUP**

1. What is sheltered instruction?
2. How is it implemented?

HELPING STUDENTS WHO HAVE SERIOUS READING PROBLEMS

In Hartford, Connecticut, a typical urban school system, 25 percent of ninth-graders were reading on a fourth-grade level or below, with some students reading on a first-grade level. This is not a new phenomenon. There have always been older students who are not able to read despite being in a school system for nine years or more. With increased accountability occasioned by the standards movement and high-stakes testing, this shortcoming has become more visible. If students have serious reading problems, they should be provided with expert assistance by well-trained professionals.

Many content area classes will contain students who have serious reading difficulties. This textbook has made a number of suggestions for making information accessible to students who can't read it for themselves. However, you may find that you are the only source of help for a student, or you may like to offer assistance to students who have serious reading problems, or you may like to help your school's tutoring program for these students. Or you may simply want to gain a better understanding of how older struggling readers can be instructed. Discussed below are several suggestions for working with older students who have serious reading problems.

*S*tudents who have difficulty reading can read along with taped versions of texts.

- Find out what level the student is reading on. One way to do this is to have the student read a series of passages that gradually become more difficult. You can use the benchmark passages in Chapter 2 for this purpose. Have the student read the passages orally. On a copy of the passages, note errors that the student makes while reading orally. Errors include misreading words, inserting words, or omitting words. Students' instructional level is the point where

EXEMPLARY TEACHING

MATCHING INSTRUCTION TO STUDENTS' NEEDS

In an urban high school, students' reading levels will vary, with most being significantly below grade level. In Hartford, Connecticut, for instance, the average reading level for ninth-graders in the system's three high schools is 6.9, with nearly one of every four students reading at a fourth-grade level or below. Concerned by its high dropout rate, the school system created a school within a school for its ninth-graders. The ninth-grade academies were given their own administrators, teachers, and counselors. Emphasis was placed on matching instruction to the students' individual needs. Both the reading and the content area programs were transformed. In the reading program, students were carefully placed according to their level of achievement and were provided with a carefully monitored structured program designed for older students. Many of the students jumped several levels. In science class, a hands-on program was adopted which emphasized inquiry-oriented instruction so that the students would also be minds-on. As their reading skills improved, students began feeling good about themselves and their attitude toward school began to change. Instead of nodding off during science lectures, they became deeply involved as they constructed DNA models and built robots. Two ninth-graders who were being suspended asked if they could come back for science class. As a result of a changed attitude toward school, the drop-out rate decreased by 30 percent (Gottlieb, 2001).

they can read 95 percent to 98 percent of the words. The frustration level is 90 percent word recognition or below. In other words, students are misreading 10 or more words out of 100. To assess students' comprehension, ask questions about the passages or ask students to tell you what they read. The instructional level for comprehension is found at 70 percent to 75 percent correct answers.

- If students are reading on a first- or second-grade level, they will need instruction in basic phonics and syllabication skills. The Word Pattern Survey, a quick test of phonics, can be found on the author's Building Literacy Web site, at http://Thomasgunning.org. The Survey will indicate students' level of phonics knowledge and which patterns they need to be taught. Also, analyze the results of the benchmark passages. Note the kinds of errors the student made. The Building Literacy Web site has suggestions for teaching phonics. Suggested materials are listed for both older and younger students. You may choose to use a commercial program. Some commercials programs are listed in Table 9.1.
- If students are reading on a third-grade level or above, they have mastered basic phonics but may need some help with multisyllabic words or morphemic elements.
- Students may do well reading the words but have difficulty understanding or remembering what they have read. Techniques such as ReQuest and Reading Seminar, which were discussed in Chapter 6, should work well with these students.

Using the Language Experience Approach

It is sometimes not possible to obtain texts that are on the students' level. One way to provide even the poorest readers with content area selections that they can read is

TABLE 9.1

PROGRAMS FOR OLDER STRUGGLING READERS

Title	Publisher	Interest Level	Grade Level	Overview
Breaking the Code	SRA	4–12	1–3	Intensive program for older students who lack basic decoding skills.
Contemporary Reader	Jamestown	7–12	2.5–5	Features informational selections and comprehension exercises.
Fast Track Reading	Wright Group	4–8	1–6+	High interest selections. Has word work, comprehension, and fluency strands. Has phonics program for students who need it.
Core Reading	Glavach	5–12	3–10	Develops vocabulary, syllabic analysis, and fluency in key content areas.
Focus on Reading	SRA	5–12	2.5–6	Fictional and informational selections, some by well-known writers. Comprehension and vocabulary exercises.
Great Series	Steck-Vaughn	6–12	2–4	Each text features great escapes, great rescues, or other events. Comprehension and vocabulary exercises.
High Noon Reading	High Noon	3–12	1–4+	Features systematic instruction in decoding and comprehension. Best bet for most severely disabled readers.
New Directions in Reading	Houghton Mifflin	5–12	2–7	Anthologies of fiction, nonfiction, real-world reading, and poetry. Skills books with exercises on comprehension, vocabulary, and word analysis. Writing component at upper levels.
Reading Skills for Life	American Guidance Service	6–12	1–6	Includes worktexts, easy readers, and extra practice on CD-ROM.
Reading XL	Scholastic	6–8	4–7	Includes reading of trade books and anthologies.
Soar to Success	Houghton Mifflin	3–8	2–8	Features cooperative groups, reading of trade books, and teaching of comprehension strategies.

to compose experience text. Language experience text can be used to create a readable content area information text for struggling readers. An experience text is a selection that has been dictated by a single student or a group and recorded by the teacher. The text, once it has been recorded, is then read by the students who dictated it. Because it was dictated by the students, the language is familiar to them. If the selection is brief and simply written, it can be used as the students' reading material. This technique is a tried-and-true method for working with adult illiterates as well as school-age students who have serious reading problems. However, it can also be highly effective in a content area class. Here is how it works.

Composing Experience Text

Step 1: Obtaining Information

Information for the experience can be obtained in a number of ways. The text might be written about an actual experience. For instance, students may have taken a trip to an historical site, they may have observed or conducted an experiment, they may have had a discussion about a segment in a text, they may have viewed a video on eating disorders, or you may have read a segment of a textbook to them.

Step 2: Discussing the Information

The field trip, experiment, video, or other source of information is discussed and summarized.

Step 3: Recording of Experience Text

Record the information on the chalkboard, overhead transparency, or computer projector. Prior to recording the information, help students organize it. They can put events in sequential order, describe a process step by step, or note the main points in a history chapter. Record the information in the students' own words. If this is a selection to be read by a group, you can do some light editing. However, don't rewrite the selection because students will lose their sense of ownership. An experience story is presented in Figure 9.1.

Step 4: Reading of Experience Text

Read the text to students. Discuss with them whether or not the text says what they want it to say. Ask if there are any details that they would like to add, take out, or change. After changes have been made, read it a second time. Ask students if they are satisfied with the changes. These multiple readings will familiarize students with the text so that they will be better able to read it on their own. Through these multiple readings you are also reviewing the key points covered.

Step 5: Student Reading of Experience Text

The experience text is duplicated and becomes the students' text. If the experience text has been composed on a transparency, the transparency can be copied, as long as the writing is readable. If composed on a computer that projects on a screen large enough for everyone to see, copies can be printed for everyone. After being given printed copies, students read the selection for any of the same reasons they may read a textbook. They may read it that night to review information covered in class or to prepare for a quiz. They can also provide illustrations, such as a map or diagram, to go along with written information. Experience text selections can be saved and put into a folder or binder. They can serve as a source of review so students can study the selections in preparation for a test.

STRUGGLING READERS

Hands-on experiences help make abstract concepts more understandable and more concrete. For instance, students achieve a deeper understanding of kinetic energy when they calculate the kinetic energy of a cart running down a ramp.

FIGURE 9.1

Experience Story

Antarctica

Antarctica is at the bottom of the world. It is where the South Pole is. Antarctica is the coldest place on earth. One time the temperature hit 100 degrees below zero. It is the only place on Earth where no people live all the time. Scientists come there and stay for a few months, but no one lives there all year round.

People think that Antarctica has lots of snow and ice. There is plenty of ice there. In some places the ice is 5,000 feet thick. But it hardly ever snows there. Antarctica only gets about two inches of snow a year. The reason is that air gets drier as it gets colder. The air is so cold that it is very dry.

Antarctica is very large. It is larger than the United States and Canada put together. There is also one very surprising thing about Antarctica. It has a volcano. Most people don't know that. It is hard to believe that the coldest place on earth has a volcano.

Providing students with printed copies of key topics gives them materials that they can study. It also builds content area literacy, so that in time students may be able to read content area texts on their own. This technique can also be used with literary selections that students may not be able to read on their own. One way of structuring an experience text is to read a literary selection to students and then have them retell it (Crawford, 1993). Record the retelling.

The experience text approach can be used with all students but is especially valuable for English language learners because it uses their language. If the group is composed entirely of English language learners who speak the same native language, students may include in the recorded text words and expressions from their native language.

Using Technology

Technology can be used in a number of ways to make material accessible to struggling readers. A number of encyclopedias have a speech feature. For instance, *Encarta* has a Speak command under Options that allows the student to have a whole article or highlighted portions, which could be a single word or a sentence, read. *Grolier* has a similar feature, which is activated by clicking on the sound icon. In addition, multimedia such as illustrations, filmclips, and tape recordings help make the text more understandable. One word of caution. The readability in some electronic texts is quite high. Articles may include complex syntactic structures and difficult vocabulary. An article on rock and roll in one electronic encyclopedia was a on a twelfth-grade readability level according to the Flesch-Kincaid. Articles may contain so many hard words or difficult concepts that students will not understand them even if they are read to them.

■ Screen Readers

■ A **screen reader** is a program that will read aloud whatever appears on a computer screen.

Many computers are equipped with **screen readers.** They will read whatever appears on your screen. CAST eReader, formerly known as Ultimate Reader, reads text but also offers visual highlighting, which means that what is being read is highlighted so that the student is better able to follow along. Speed of reading can be regulated. Students can also take notes and receive speech feedback while typing. CAST eReader also has a spell checker.

Obtaining Texts on the Appropriate Level

In an average class, the textbook is too difficult for nearly one student in every three. One solution is to eliminate the text and conduct learning through hands-on activities, lectures, and discussions. The problem with this approach is that students are denied the opportunity to learn to read content area material. Another solution is to obtain texts that are easy to read. A list of easy-to-read texts is presented in Table 9.2. Presented below is a passage from an easy-to-read world history text. Although designed for use by high school students, the text is written on a fourth-grade level. The text presents difficult vocabulary at the beginning of each chapter and has a summary and chapter checkup at the end of each chapter. Also listed below is a passage on the same topic from an on-grade text. What are the differences between the two texts? What are the advantages and disadvantages of using easy-to-read texts?

Passage from Easy-to-Read Text

Sometimes the rivers flooded and washed rich bottom-soil up on the land. This made the land good for farming. People settled on this rich land. They grew their crops and raised animals. In the south, in a land called Sumer, a great civilization grew.

The people of Sumer are called Sumerians. Although the land they settled was fertile, it was not a perfect place to live. (Suter, 1994, p. 29)

Passage from Grade-Level Text

In Sumer, as in Egypt, the fertile land of a river valley attracted Stone Age farmers from neighboring regions. In time their descendants produced the surplus food needed to support growing populations.

Just as control of the Nile was vital to Egypt, control of the Tigris and Euphrates was key to developments in Mesopotamia. The rivers rose in terrifying floods that washed away topsoil and destroyed mud-brick villages. (Ellis & Esler, 2001)

The obvious problem with easy-to-read texts is that the characteristics that make them accessible may limit what students learn. They may be ex-

TABLE 9.2

CONTENT AREA TEXTS FOR STRUGGLING READERS

Text	Publisher	Grade Level	Reading Level
Language Arts			
American Literature	AGS	6–12	3.5–4
Basic English	AGS	6–12	3.8
Basic English Composition	AGS	6–12	3.8
Basic English Grammar	AGS	6–12	3.2
English for the World of Work	AGS	6–12	3.6
English to Use	AGS	6–12	3.3
Exploring Literature	AGS	6–12	3.5–4
Pacemaker Curriculum American Literature	Globe Fearon	6–12	3–4
Pacemaker Curriculum English Composition	Globe Fearon	6–12	3–4
Pacemaker Curriculum World Literature	Globe Fearon	6–12	3–4
World Literature	AGS	6–12	3.5–4
Science			
Biology	AGS	6–12	3.5
Concepts and Challenges in Earth Science	Globe Fearon	6–12	5–6
Discover Health	AGS	6–9	3.5–4
Earth Science	AGS	6–12	3.5
General Science	AGS	6–12	3.8
Life Skills Health	AGS	9–12	3.6
Wonders of Science	Steck–Vaughn	7–12	2–3
Social Studies			
America's History: Land of Liberty	Steck–Vaughn	8–11	5–6
America's Story	Steck–Vaughn	7–12	2–3
Pacemaker Curriculum World History	Globe Fearon	6–12	3–4
United States History	AGS	9–12	3.6
World Geography	AGS	9–12	3.9
World Geography and You	Steck–Vaughn	6–12	3–4
World History	AGS	6–12	3.8
World History and You	Steck–Vaughn	6–12	4
Math			
Algebra	AGS	9–12	3.5
Basic Math Skills	AGS	6–12	3.5
Consumer Mathematics	AGS	6–12	3.3
Earning Money	Phoenix	7–12	5–6
Essential Math Skills	Phoenix	7–12	5–6
Life Skills Math	AGS	6–12	3.9
Math for the World of Work	AGS	6–12	3.9
Pre-Algebra	AGS	6–12	3.5
Using Money	Phoenix	7–12	5–6

posed to fewer vocabulary words and less information. If you do use easy texts, make sure that you present through discussion, experiments, simulations, audio-visual aids, or other means important information that was omitted.

Making the Text Accessible

It is sometimes not possible to obtain easy-to-read texts for students who need them. There are a number of steps that can be taken to make a text more accessible.

- Audiotape summaries of chapters (Vogt, 2001) or obtain audiotaped versions of texts. Audiotaped versions of texts are available from some publishers and also from Recordings for the Blind and Dyslexic.

- Mark key text to be learned with highlighter. A few copies of a text or even a whole set might be highlighted to reduce the demands of reading the text. Highlight key segments and those that you think the students will be able to handle on their own. Most texts have extraneous material that can readily be deleted.

- Provide written summaries. One way to provide students with ongoing readable text is to use a language experience approach to summarize key concepts. After a discussion or demonstration, have students orally summarize key points. As they dictate their summaries, write them on the board or on chart paper. Students can copy these summaries and then read them over as an assignment and use them as a basis for studying.

- Accumulate a library of easy-to-read explanations of key concepts. These could be excerpts from easy-to-read texts, easy-to-read trade books, magazine articles, materials from the Internet, or materials that you have constructed. The library could also include taped books, CD-ROMs, and videos. See Appendix A for easy-to-read trade books that cover key concepts.

- Oral reading. Read portions of the text out loud to students. The most difficult vocabulary and concepts often come at the beginning of the chapter. You might read an initial section to provide an overview and build background so students can read the rest of the chapter on their own.

- Adapt the text. Rewrite portions of the text to make it more readable. Rewriting a whole text would be a monumental task, so rewrite segments that present key ideas. If you rewrite one segment a week or even every two weeks, you will soon have a substantial amount of rewritten material. The major aim of rewriting is to make the text more accessible to students. Rewriting should result in easier vocabulary and simpler syntax. However, it should go beyond merely substituting easier words and simpler sentences. Before rewriting, take a look at the main concepts being explained. Perhaps they demand background that hasn't been supplied. In your rewrite, fill in the needed background. Also look at the presentation of the material. Is it clear? If not, clarify it. Also, relate key concepts to students' background. Authors sometimes include interesting details that actually interrupt the flow of information. If so, delete these. On the other hand, the authors may be trying to cover too much material. Decide which are the essential ideas and develop these fully. To rewrite a text, do the following:

STRUGGLING READERS

For students who have severe reading difficulties, obtain tape versions of their texts and review ways of studying information from an oral source. Recordings for the Blind and Dyslexic (20 Roszel Road, Princeton, NJ, 08540) provides taped versions of school textbooks for students with reading problems. Taped periodicals and children's books are available from Talking Books, National Library Service for the Blind and Physically Handicapped (includes dyslexia), Library of Congress, Washington, DC, 20542.

- Decide what is important for the learners to know. Add essential information if it is missing.
- Delete unnecessary details. Eliminate details that are interesting but off the topic.
- Explicitly explain essential information or supporting details that are only implied.
- Explicitly state the main idea or topic.
- Make clear the relationship between the main idea and supporting details.
- Make sure that antecedents and their referents are clearly marked. If there is some distance or the possibility of confusion between a pronoun and its antecedent, repeat the antecedent.
- Define words in context. Use simpler terms when possible. Limit the number of technical terms.
- Break up or rewrite lengthy confusing sentences, especially those that have embedded clauses. However, don't break up sentences that are lengthy because they are showing relationships. Breaking up the sentence "The colonists were angry because they were being taxed but had no say in the government" into the sentences "The colonists were angry. They were being taxed. But they had no say in the government" forces the reader to establish relationships. The three short sentences are harder than the one long sentence in this instance.
- Provide background or an orientation to the topic if necessary. Explain how this topic ties in with a previously studied topic.
- Use concrete examples and analogies.

Helping Students Who Have Comprehension Problems

Nothing is more frustrating to students than reading a chapter and then not knowing what they have read. Most students have the necessary decoding skills to read content area texts but, for one reason or another, fail to comprehend what they have read. Possible reasons for having comprehension difficulties despite possessing adequate decoding skills include the following:

- *Lack of adequate background.* Students without some knowledge of algebra and some general background in science, for instance, will have difficulty with a physics text.
- *Lack of comprehension strategies.* Students who are passive readers, who don't know how to read for main ideas, make inferences, summarize as they read, or monitor as they read will have difficulty comprehending challenging text.
- *Lack of purpose or goal in reading.* Students simply read to fulfill the assignment but do not have any particular questions in mind that they are seeking to answer and do not have a specific reason for reading.

For some students, the problem may be some of all three: poor background and lack of strategies, purpose, and goals. To help students become better comprehenders, it is not necessary for you to become an expert in teaching reading. You are an expert in reading in your subject matter area. You are better at reading your content area than the school's reading specialist. In a sense, you are the person best qualified to help your students. All you need do is share with your students the strategies you use to comprehend written materials in your area. As an expert in your area, you probably do not think much about what it is that you do to understand text. To get a feel for what it is that you do as a reader, slow down your reading and try to become deliberately conscious of the strategies that you use. You might try reading a text that is particularly challenging and note what you do to construct meaning. Once you become familiar with your processes, demonstrate them to students. Model the process of reading the textbook. Note how you survey the text, activate background, make predictions, and read for specific purposes or questions to be answered. Also show how you reread when you have not fully understood a passage.

Because struggling readers lack metacognitive awareness, help them to become aware of their thought processes as they read. Once they are aware of their thought processes, they can take steps to control them better. To foster metacognitive awareness, encourage students to place a sticky note next to any sentence or passage that is confusing to them. Students should also take steps to resolve their confusions. In class, discuss confusing passages and steps that were taken to resolve them. Through discussing confusions and how they were resolved, students learn strategies from each other.

Provide help with unresolved confusions. Also note whether there is a pattern present—whether students have problems making inferences or imaging scenes, for instance. These can form the basis for future modeling.

High school English teacher/reading specialist Chris Tovani (2000), who had herself been a noncomprehender, recommends the following steps for implementing a demonstration think-aloud:

1. *Select a short piece of text.* It could be an especially difficult section from your class's text. It should contain material that would lend itself to the demonstration of the particular strategy you have chosen to demonstrate. If you are demonstrating imaging, for instance, select a high-imagery passage. Place the text on a transparency and/or give students a copy.

2. *Foresee difficulty.* Analyze the passage and note elements that might pose problems for your students—figurative language or long, involved explanations, for instance. Do not overwhelm students with a passage that contains too many difficulties. If you want to demonstrate how you use your background knowledge to comprehend text, tell what you know about the topic and explain how this relates to the topic and helps you to understand it. For instance, when reading about limbs atrophying because of disuse, you might relate how you know from personal experience about this because your arm lost almost all of its strength when it was in a cast after you broke it. Explain also how relating what you are reading to a personal experience or something that you have read or heard about helps you make connections and improves your understanding of what you are reading.

3. *Read the text out loud and stop often to share your thinking.* When you are reading the text, point to the sentence you are reading. When you share your thinking, look at the students so they know you are talking about your thoughts.

4.   *Point out the words in the text that trigger your thinking.* "When I read the words *oil spill cleanup*, I picture people cleaning seabirds who are coated in gooey oil. I picture people shoveling up chunks of tar on sandy beaches. And I picture ships putting large floats around oil spills to keep them from spreading. This helps me to understand some ways in which oil spills are cleaned up. It also helps me to understand how difficult it is to clean up an oil spill."

Focus on key strategies. High-payoff strategies include the following:

- surveying
- activating background knowledge and predicting
- setting a purpose for reading
- asking questions as one reads
- distinguishing important information
- summarizing
- making inferences
- imaging
- monitoring for meaning and using fix-up strategies

■ Providing Help during Reading

To provide assistance as students read, provide a gloss or study guide that highlights both essential information and strategies that might be used to comprehend that information (see Chapter 5). In the beginning, focus on brief segments of text. As students build background and learn to apply strategies, increase the amount of reading.

Helping Students Who Have Decoding Problems

Although students may have mastered single-syllable phonics, they frequently experience difficulty with multisyllabic words. Unfortunately, many programs for older struggling readers focus on building comprehension but neglect this vital skill. In a program that included ten minutes a day working with multisyllabic words in combination with instruction in vocabulary development, comprehension, and daily independent reading, struggling seventh- and eighth-graders gained an average of four years of growth in both word identification and comprehension (Shearer, Ruddell, & Vogt, 2001). To help students who have difficulty with multisyllabic words, review key mutlisyllabic words from the text that students are about to read. Say each syllable in the words and say the syllables as you underline them.

Holding Students Accountable

Realizing that their students are not getting much out of their reading, many content teachers discuss the reading assignment the next day or provide the information in lecture form. Students quickly catch on that it is not necessary to read the material. All they need do is listen in class. Students should be held responsible for reading the text; otherwise, the process is short-circuited. When the time comes that students run into a situation where the teacher does not explain the text, they are lost. They find that the skills they need failed to develop because they never had to read challenging text.

If reading a chapter is an overwhelming burden because students are underprepared, have them read brief segments and provide a great deal of preparation and encouragement so that they can read the text with a measure of success. Make sure that they are held accountable for the reading, however. Have them respond in logs or journals, in study guides, or in small or large discussion groups. Students may need sustained support in the beginning, but gradually lead them to the point where they are becoming increasingly independent.

Collaborating with Other Professionals

Although you can implement a program of assistance on your own, enlist the help of specialists. They may be able to provide help with students who have more serious reading problems and may render technical assistance. If at all possible, get the entire staff or as much of the staff as possible involved. Although each content area has its own special demands, there are basic strategies that are common to all disciplines. If all the teachers are saying basically the same thing about reading and writing in the content area, students are far more likely to get the message and the help they need. If surveying, summarizing, monitoring for meaning, and so on are emphasized in each class, students are far more likely to learn these skills faster and better. Just as you may get help with students who have reading problems, you might seek assistance with English language learners.

A dedicated teacher, Dan was concerned with his inability to reach the second language learners who were showing up in increasing numbers in his language arts classes (Coppola, 2002). He was also frustrated because the ELL students missed many of his classes to attend pull-out ESL sessions. Meanwhile, Leah, the ESL teacher, was feeling somewhat overwhelmed by the demands of colleagues. Often colleagues would give her an overview of a unit and ask her to help students learn the major concepts of the unit.

Fortunately, Leah and Dan decided to collaborate. All of Dan's ELL students were placed in one class. Instead of attending pull-out ESL sessions, students stayed in Dan's class but were assisted by Leah, who began co-teaching with Dan. Leah taught the reader response part of the lesson in which students discussed the selections they had read, while Dan took responsibility for comprehension skills and correlated reading.

Leah was able to demonstrate effective techniques for supporting ELL students and engaging them in reading and discussion. Dan became better acquainted with effective techniques that a classroom teacher might adopt for helping ELL students. Leah learned more about the curriculum and some of the obstacles to working with ELL students in a regular classroom.

Over time, the class was transformed into one in which English language learners were integrated into the regular classroom. For the first time, they became active participants in discussion groups and had access to grade-level curriculum. They were also able to read related materials on their instructional levels. These materials had been housed in Leah's office, but she had never had time to use them. Both Dan and Leah felt more satisfied with their roles in working with ELL students, especially since the students were making excellent progress.

Although programs work best when the administration supports them, Dan and Leah constructed their collaboration on their own. They met before and after school. The lesson is clear. Lack of administrative support is no excuse for a lack of professional collaboration.

In a more extensive collaboration, one that might become a model for other school districts, curriculum leaders and teachers in language arts, special education, and bilingual/English as a second language classes in Arlington, Virginia, began collaborating (Zolman & Wagner, 2002). The three departments found that they were facing the same issues: struggling readers, struggling teachers, and high frustration. When creating curriculum, representatives from all three areas met. Thus, when the language arts teachers designed programs, the special education and ESL specialists made suggestions for ways in which their students might be served, including making modifications in approaches and acquiring easier-to-read materials. New materials and approaches were modeled by the special education and ESL teachers who then reported back to the other special education and ESL teachers. The curriculum was differentiated in such a way that provisions were made for all students.

For a unit on Mark Twain, regular education teachers, special ed teachers, and ESL teachers met and discussed the need for the unit, the skills incorporated in the unit, and possible activities. Later, a small collaborative group selected materials, including adaptations, and created activities and lesson plans. These were introduced to the entire staff. In a related project, book lists were created that included titles on a variety of difficulty levels.

Collaboration is a highly effective approach for working with at-risk learners. Although your school or district might not have the same type of carefully planned collaboration that is implemented in Arlington, Virginia, you can seek out other professionals in your school and plan ways in which you can work together to provide better instruction for at-risk learners.

 **CHECKUP**

1. What are some techniques and approaches that can be used to help struggling readers?
2. What are some techniques and approaches that can be used to help all students who are at risk?

SUMMARY

In the past, content area teachers typically geared their instruction for average students and expected that students would arrive with prerequisite background knowledge. Given the greater diversity in today's content area classes and the inclusion of students who were previously taught in special education settings, today's content area teachers benefit, more than ever, from finding ways to teach struggling learners. The weaker the students' preparation, the greater the need for using techniques and devices that help the student learn.

About 25 percent to 35 percent of the nation's students are at risk for failing for a variety of academic and nonacademic reasons. It is also estimated that 25 percent to 40 percent of American students do not read well enough to cope with the texts in their content courses in middle and secondary schools. Students at risk include economically disadvantaged students, students with learning and other disabilities, and English language learners. Identifying struggling learners, adjusting content to fit the needs of diverse learners, and teaching SMARTER are some of the approaches that can be taken to help at-risk students.

Instructional components for an effective program for English language learners feature (1) focus on vocabulary, (2) use of visuals, (3) cooperative learning and peer tutoring, (4) strategic use of the native language, and (5) adjustment of cognitive and language demands. Programs should also build content area background and consider cultural factors. Sheltered instruction is recommended. In sheltered instruction, teachers make a special effort to make content instruction understandable to all students, including those who are still acquiring academic English. The language experience approach in which the teacher scribes key content area concepts dictated by students can be an effective learning tool for both ELL students and disabled readers.

Struggling learners benefit when they are helped to become self-regulated learners. With increased accountability occasioned by the standards movement and high-stakes testing, students with serious reading disabilities have become more visible. It is important to provide these students with materials on their level. Materials can be made more accessible through the use of talking software, screen readers, rewritten texts, and added preparation for reading.

Students who have decoding problems may need specialized assistance but would benefit by being provided with help for reading complex technical terms. Students who have adequate decoding skills but are poor comprehenders can be taught a series of strategies for becoming active, metacognitively aware, meaning-seeking readers. A program for helping at-risk learners will be more effective if professionals collaborate.

Reflection

Return to the Anticipation Guide at the beginning of this chapter. Respond once again to the items. Did your responses change? If so, how and why? What would be your approach to working with at-risk learners in your classroom?

EXTENSION AND APPLICATION

1. Read the following account of a secondary teacher who worked with adolescents who had difficulty reading their texts: Tovani, C. (2000). *I read it, but I don't get it.* Portland, ME: Stenhouse. How might you use the techniques advocated by the author?

2. Investigate the availability of easy-to-read textbooks in your discipline. Evaluate the coverage provided. Is it adequate, or would it have to be supplemented?

3. If possible, observe a sheltered English class. Even though you are not a trained bilingual or ESL teacher, how might you adapt the techniques used in sheltered English?

4. Try using a language experience approach for one or more lessons with struggling readers or English language learners. What are its advantages? Disadvantages? How might you adapt it to make it more effective?
5. Rewrite a segment of a textbook so that it is easier to read. If possible, try it out with disabled readers.

What difference do you notice between their ability to handle rewritten text and their ability to handle regular text?
6. Explore talking software or screen readers. How might you use these with struggling learners?

READING AND WRITING IN LANGUAGE ARTS AND SOCIAL STUDIES

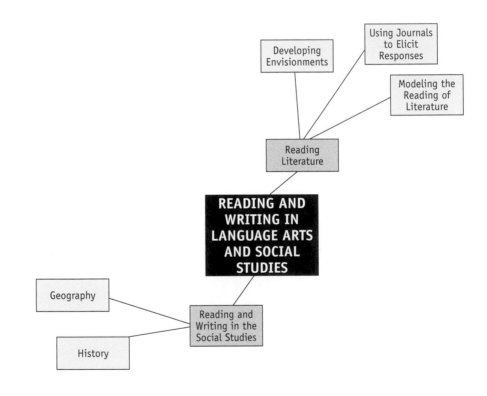

ANTICIPATION GUIDE

For each of the following statements related to the chapter you are about to read, put a check under "Agree" or "Disagree" to show how you feel. Discuss your responses with classmates before you read the chapter.

		Agree	*Disagree*
1	The key to developing an understanding of literature is being aware of the historical context in which the piece was written.	____	____
2	Students need to be taught the correct interpretation of difficult pieces of literature.	____	____
3	Most primary documents are too difficult for students to read.	____	____
4	Students need to be taught to read history texts critically because history texts are subjective.	____	____
5	Social studies texts are more difficult to read than literature texts because social studies texts are more abstract.	____	____
6	Students have a fairly good knowledge of history and geography facts, but have difficulty interpreting that knowledge.	____	____

USING WHAT YOU KNOW

What kinds of reading do you do in your spare time? How is your approach to reading a piece of literature different from your approach to reading a popular novel? How do you go about reading a history or geography text? How is reading a history or geography book different from reading a work of literature or a popular novel? Although there are some common processes used when students read a work of literature, a popular novel, or a history text, each of these makes different demands on the reader. Reading literature requires a deeper level of involvement than does reading a popular novel. Reading a history or geography text generally places greater demands on organizational skills and memory.

READING LITERATURE

The study of literature has a number of jumping-off points. Literature may be seen as a product of the times and so viewed in an historical context. Or, literature may be seen as autobiographical and interpreted in terms of the author's life. Literature may also be seen in humanistic terms as a source of inspiration and guidance. However else it may be viewed, literature is regarded as a work of art that blends elements of style and substance in an original way. Given its originality and creativity, literature has the power to evoke a deep emotional and aesthetic response.

■ **Aesthetic reading** is the experience of emotions evoked by a piece of writing.

■ **Efferent reading** is reading to comprehend the information conveyed by a piece of writing.

■ **Reader response theory** is a view of reading in which the reader plays a central role in constructing the meaning of a text. The meaning is not found in the text or in the reader but rather in the relationship or transaction between the two.

*S*tudents enjoy sharing their responses to books they have read.

Literature makes demands that go beyond those made by science or social studies texts or popular fiction. Social studies and science texts may inform, and popular fiction may entertain, but only literature has the power to evoke the feeling of wholeness or wonder at being lifted out of oneself that is the hallmark of the aesthetic response. As Rosenblatt (1978) notes, in **aesthetic reading** the reader is carried away by feelings evoked by the text: "In aesthetic reading, the reader's attention is centered directly on what he is living through during his relationship with that particular text" (p. 25). In contrast, **efferent reading** involves reading for information; the reader's attention is directed to "concepts to be refined, ideas to be tested, actions to be performed after the reading" (Rosenblatt, 1978, p. 24). In efferent reading, the reader "carries away" meaning. In aesthetic reading, the reader is "carried away" by feelings evoked by the text. The same text can be read efferently or aesthetically. For example, we could read an essay efferently for ideas, but if we respond to its irony or the author's graceful style and humor, our stance becomes aesthetic. As Rosenblatt (1991) explains, "We read for information, but we are conscious of emotions about it and feel pleasure when the words we call up arouse vivid images and are rhythmic to the inner ear" (p. 445).

Growing out of the aesthetic view of literature is **reader response theory.** In reader response theory, reading is seen as a transaction between reader and writer. In a transaction, the reader is changed by the text and the text is changed by the reader. Because the transaction grows in part out of the reader's experience and consciousness, the response is personal. The poem that stirs deep emotion in one reader may leave another reader unmoved. Teaching literature is largely a matter of creating an environment in which students respond to a selection in terms of their personal experiences and sensibilities and then clarify the impact of the selection in terms of itself and its meaning in their lives. Although students' initial responses may be personal and concrete and exist primarily on a gut level, over time, through discussion and guidance, their responses become more refined and more evaluative. Personal response becomes the basis for "growth toward more and more balanced, self-critical, knowledgeable interpretation" (Rosenblatt, 1990, p. 100).

All too often, students have the sense that a poem or other work of literature has a certain interpretation. Failing to engage with the work, they wait for the teacher to tell them what the work means. In a way, works of literature have as many interpretations as there are readers. Although there is no one correct interpretation, interpretations should be based on a careful reading of the text. Students should be prepared to discuss and clarify their responses; a response that is based on a misreading of the text should be revised. Students who have misread the text should be encouraged to go back over the text, get the correct information from the text, and modify their response accordingly.

 *CHECKUP*

1. What are the aesthetic and efferent stances?
2. Which of these is more appropriate for the reading of literature? Why?

Developing Envisionments

Langer (1990, 1995) calls the development of aesthetic responses envisionments. An **envisionment** is "the understanding a reader has about a text—what the reader understands at a particular point in time, the questions she has, as well as her hunches about how the piece will unfold" (p. 812). Envisionment changes as new ideas come to mind. As students create an envisionment, they go through a series of stances, or changing relationships with the text:

■ **Envisionment** is the understanding that a reader has of a text. The understanding may change with reflection, additional reading, or discussion.

1. being out and stepping in
2. being in and moving through
3. being in and stepping out
4. stepping out and objectifying the experience

Phase 1: Being Out and Stepping In
Students use their background knowledge and knowledge of the unfolding story to make "initial acquaintance with the characters, plot, setting—and how they interrelate" (Langer, 1990, p. 813). In a sense, students are beginning a conversation with themselves about the world that they have entered (Langer, 1995). They are trying to "step into" the world of the story.

Phase 2: Being In and Moving Through
Having entered the text world, students are building a more elaborated meaning. "We take new information and immediately use it to go beyond what we already understand, asking questions about motives, feelings, causes, interrelationships, and implications. We make connections among our thoughts, move our understandings along, and fill out our shifting sense of what the piece is about" (Langer, 1995, p. 17).

Phase 3: Being In and Stepping Out
Readers step away from the story, stand back, and think about their own lives in terms of the story. "They use what they read in the text to reflect on their own lives, on the lives of others, or on the human condition in general" (Langer, 1990, p. 813). This stance does not occur as often as the others because every piece we read does

not personally affect us and it also may take a cumulative experience with literature before we begin to experience its effect on us (Langer, 1995).

Phase 4: Stepping Out and Objectifying the Experience

"We distance ourselves from the envisionment we have developed and reflect back on it" (Langer, 1995, p. 18). We analyze and judge the piece and compare it to other works that we have read.

The concept of envisionments provides a basis for instruction. Because responses depend on students' background knowledge, experience, and predictions, they need to feel free to offer responses and have them accepted. Discussions are patterned on the kinds of conversations that a group of adults might have about a book they have all read or a movie they have seen. The students have "a real conversation in which they interact with and build from one another's ideas" (Langer, 1995, p. 44). In such an environment, the teacher assumes that each student can and does make sense of literature. The assumption is also made that any "misreadings, misinterpretations, or weakly founded views can and will be noticed and rethought by the individual, using ideas from the group to stimulate but not direct thinking" (Langer, 1995, p. 75). To foster a developing response to literature, the teacher listens intently so as to understand the student's growing envisionment and works to help the student more fully develop that envisionment. Students are encouraged to pursue their own ideas while accepting and considering the ideas of others. Considering the ideas of others helps students to enrich their own interpretations as they reflect on ideas that they had not considered and also assess their own interpretations. Considering a selection from the viewpoint of others opens the students up to other interpretations. Students are encouraged to explore possibilities of meaning. Langer suggests that teachers engage in four types of questions.

STRUGGLING READERS

For struggling readers, read aloud portions of a novel that they are required to read to help them form an overall picture of the text and to introduce characters and the setting and some difficult terms that might occur throughout the book.

1.   *Initial understandings.* Ask open-ended questions that invite students to share their reactions to the piece. What comes to mind as you think about the piece? Which part of the work stands out in your mind? Was there anything in the work that bothered you or surprised you or that didn't seem to fit? Do you have any questions about the work? One teacher asks her students to jot down "questions that you think we need to talk about" (Langer, 1995, p. 64).

2.   *Developing interpretations.* Pose questions that encourage students to explore their envisionments. These questions can help students think more deeply about motivations, character development, theme, or setting: Why were the main character's actions surprising? What do you think made the man give all his money away? Could this story have taken place in today's times? What is the author trying to say here? Students might also be encouraged to look at the events in the selection from the viewpoint of other characters or to look at the story from someone else's viewpoint.

3.   *Reflecting on personal experience.* Ask questions that help students relate what they have read to personal knowledge or experience. This might be people they know, experiences they have had, or events they have witnessed: Does the main character remind you of anyone you know? Have you ever been in a situation similar to the one she was in? How would you have handled it? Does this story make you think of anything that has happened in your life?

4. *Evaluating.* Once students have responded personally to the piece and have developed their interpretations more fully, encourage them to step out of the piece and consider issues raised with a critical eye. What do you think the author is trying to say in this piece? Do you agree with the author's interpretations? What are some other interpretations that might be just as valid? Does the author reveal any biases? Whose side does the author seem to be on? How does the author describe the good guys? The bad guys? Students also view the work from an aesthetic point of view in which they take a careful look at the author's craft. They might compare it with other pieces they have read and critique its character development, originality, development of plot and theme, and overall impact: What was the best part of the piece? Did the characters seem real? What made them seem real? What special techniques did the author use? How did the author keep you guessing up until the very end? What original expressions or figurative language did the author use? Which of these did you like best? If you were the author's editor, what would you say to the author? What changes might you ask the author to make? Why? How would you compare this piece to other similar pieces that you have read? One teacher has his students read critical reviews after they have critiqued a piece and compare their views from those of the critic (Langer, 1995).

An integral part of the process of building envisionments is learning the concepts and language needed to discuss literature, such as *metaphor, theme, symbolism,* and *omniscient point of view.* Noting that her students lacked the concept of *characterization,* one teacher had the students assume the roles of the characters in the short story "Charles," by Shirley Jackson, at various points in the story. They discussed the way they believed the characters might think and behave and then role-played the characters (Langer 1995).

> **STRUGGLING READERS**
> Consider using easy classics with struggling readers. Hemingway's short stories are written in relatively easy-to-read language.

■ Role of Small-Group Discussions

Small-group discussion is an excellent way to foster the building of envisionments. In small groups, each student has a better opportunity to express her response to the piece and compare it with that of others. Discussion is essential because it leads to deeper exploration of a piece.

For short pieces, students might read and jot down their response to it. Writing provides the opportunity for thoughtful and personal reflection and provides a foundation for discussion. In order to evoke a personal, aesthetic response, Rosenblatt (1982) suggests asking questions similar to the following: "Did anything especially interest (annoy, puzzle, frighten, please) you? Did anything seem familiar (weird)?" (p. 276).

Probst (1992) recommends similar questions: "What feelings did this text evoke in you as you read? Did this text awaken any memories, recall for you any memories, recall for you any people, or places, or experiences?" (p. 64).

After the small groups have discussed the piece for about ten minutes, invite the whole class to discuss it. Each group might summarize the responses of its members. The group might then discuss commonalities and differences in the responses and any issues that are especially evocative or puzzling. No attempt should be made to come to a consensus interpretation or response. However, the teacher should help students see commonalities in responses or viewpoints despite varied interpretations. Students may agree that the ending was powerful even though they may not agree on its suitability. With longer selections, students might compose their responses as reflections in journals.

1. What are envisionments?
2. How might they be implemented?

Using Journals to Elicit Responses

> ■ **Response journals** are notebooks in which students write their responses to literary selections, compose observations, or pose questions.

Response journals, or literary logs, provide an excellent opportunity for students to reflect on their reading. In their response journals, students might pose questions about puzzling passages, note particularly powerful language, identify symbols, note the theme, note conflicts, comment on characters, note feelings evoked, comment on the plot, predict forthcoming events, warn or scold characters, note similarities between this and other works, or note weaknesses in the plot. Responses need not be strictly verbal. Students might also illustrate a scene, draw a character, create a character web, create a storyboard, compose a plot outline, map a journey, create a time line, or compose a family tree.

Not all response formats are equal. Some yield higher-level and deeper responses than others. Ollmann (1996) tried out seven different response formats. Vague invitations to respond often resulted in plot summaries. One of the most successful prompts was one that asked the readers to record specific quotes from the text in their double-entry journals and then analyze them. This required them to think about aspects of the story such as key plot events and character development and motivation. In double-entry journals, students tell what is happening in one column and reflect on it in a second column (Probst, 1992).

Another format that worked well was the character journal. In a character journal, students take on the role of the main character and respond in the journal the way they think the character may have responded. This response was especially effective in helping students better understand the main character. Students' responses tended to be formal and stilted when they were directed to the teacher; however, their tone was much livelier and more natural when they wrote to each other in book buddy journals. In book buddy journals, pairs of students discuss their responses. Students gather in pairs, small groups, or as a whole class to discuss the work and their envisionment. The discussion is based on their journal entries. The discussion might be initiated with the following comments by the teacher:

> Now that you've read the chapter (novel, essay, play) and recorded what happened as you read, read back over your notes and think back over the experience. What is your own sense of the text or of the experience it offered you—does it have any significance for you; does it recall memories, associations; does it affirm or contradict any of your own attitudes or perceptions? (Probst, 1992, p. 65)

Once students have personally responded to a piece, they are better able and more willing to look at the construction and literary significance of it. They are better

> **ENGLISH LANGUAGE LEARNERS**
>
> Response journals can be effective devices for English language learners to learn how to respond. Because responses are written, students have time to compose their thoughts. If encouraged to use drawings and graphic organizers, students will be able to respond more fully. They should respond in their native language when they are unable to express their thoughts or feelings in English. Because students are still learning the language, some awkwardness of expression is to be expected.

able to see how the author's choice of words, original images, symbolism, or development of plot or theme evoked the response that it did.

Modeling the Reading of Literature

Although they have the power to evoke deep feelings, works of literature can be difficult to read. Model how you go about reading a difficult piece of literature. You might read a challenging poem and discuss the thoughts and feelings that come to mind. You might note language that is particularly appealing to you. You might note how you respond to the author's allusions or create an interpretation of figurative language or deal with a theme that is only hinted at. Stress, however, that response is very personal. The poem that is your favorite might be someone else's least-liked poem.

 CHECKUP

1. How might journals and modeling be used to foster response to literature?

READING AND WRITING IN THE SOCIAL STUDIES

Drawing from a variety of disciplines, social studies includes the study of history, geography, political science, anthropology, sociology, and psychology. Complex vocabulary, unfamiliar writing styles and organization, topics with which students have had little experience, and abstract concepts can make social studies challenging to read, especially for students who have little experience with expository text. For instance, a student may have little difficulty reading a narrative about a teenager living during the Revolutionary War. Students are aided by an interesting story line, familiar story structures, and familiar words. However, students may have difficulty with a section in the textbook that discusses the topic "democracy, not monarchy." This is a complex, abstract idea. Moreover, the section may include terms such as *separation of powers, civil rights, limited government,* and *representative government.* The student has little experience that obviously relates to these concepts. However, the overall concept is one of the most important in social studies (Parker, 2001).

*U*sing a globe can help students better understand social studies texts.

History

History is, above all, a story, and that is how it is learned and understood by students. Students weave together a chain of temporal-causal events in order to create a reconstruction of what happened. The initial understanding is rapid (Perfetti, Britt, & Georgi, 1995). Students read in order to find out

USING TECHNOLOGY

History/Social Studies Web
Site
http://www.execpc.
com/~dboals/boals.html
Provides help for using the
Web as a resource for
teaching history and geography.

what happened in much the same way that they might read a piece of fiction. However, history is more than a story. It also involves reasoning and interpretation; understanding the story seems to be a prerequisite for reasoning about events and issues. Students' ability to reason about history improves as their knowledge increases. As students learn more, their understanding becomes more complex.

Learning history, however, is gradual. Although the story may be reconstructed fairly rapidly, learning essential details takes somewhat longer. Details are most readily learned if they are connected to the story. In their study of students' comprehension of historical topics, Perfetti, and colleagues (1995) found that rereading multiple texts added to students' knowledge of details and led to increased reasoning about events.

What students learn is also determined in part by their learning styles. Some readers depend more on the text; others rely more heavily on personal knowledge. Some read for the big picture; others take in details such as dates and names. And some do both.

 CHECKUP

1. What do history standards require?
2. What are the main characteristics of the study of history?

■ Comprehending History Texts

History texts often combine narrative and expository writing. Narrative text tells a story. Because it is telling a story, narrative text is concrete and, generally speaking, easier to follow and understand than expository text. Expository text is more analytical and requires more cognitive effort. The reader is called on to compare and contrast, note causes and effects, draw conclusions, interpret, and evaluate. At the lowest levels, history texts are primarily narrative but may be a mixture of narrative and expository. At the higher levels, history texts become more abstract and require greater depth of reasoning. Technical vocabulary also increases and can become quite extensive (Chall, Bissex, Conard, and Harris-Sharples, 1996).

A chapter on the Industrial Revolution tells the story of the switch from goods made in homes to goods made in factories. However, it also discusses the causes and effects of the Industrial Revolution and introduces abstract concepts such as *imperialism, investors, raw materials, natural resources,* and, of course, *industrial revolution.* The chapter has two major structures: a time sequence structure and cause and effect. Creating a time line of key events would help the reader comprehend and remember key events leading up to and extending the Industrial Revolution. A graphic organizer, such as a web, would help readers organize the causes and effects of the Industrial Revolution. Reflecting on ways it formed the foundation of modern life would help students achieve a deeper understanding of the Industrial Revolution. Students might relate the Industrial Revolution to other sweeping changes that have taken place, in particular the technology revolution and the changes it is producing. By comparing and contrasting the two movements, students will achieve a deeper level of understanding of the causes and effects of broad changes on society.

Understanding history requires having a grasp of the basic facts and events. But it also means understanding the causes and effects of events and theories, such as mercantilism and imperialism, that motivated key movements. Understanding key theories and movements puts events within a conceptual framework and makes them more memorable.

At times, texts attempt to cover too many theories in too few pages. One eighth-grade text introduces imperialism, mercantilism, and balance of trade in just two columns of text. Balance of trade is explained in just two lines. In situations of this type, the text needs to be supplemented with discussions, explanations, and/or additional readings.

At other times, extraneous material is introduced. For instance, the text that devoted just two lines to explaining balance of trade presents a three-page description of the Great Exhibition of 1851. If time is a deciding factor, this segment could be condensed or omitted.

 **CHECKUP**

1. What are some factors that make history texts difficult to understand?

■ Making History Come Alive

Although it tells the story of our past, history is one of the least-liked subjects. It is often seen as a series of events, dates, and people's names and accomplishments to be memorized. Students fail to see that history has relevance to their lives and has the potential to offer discovery and insight. As professional historian Tom Holt (1990) observes, "We are all historians. . . . Moreover in the process of doing history, one can be changed, transformed by what one learns. Stories have power. The power to change things" (p. 11).

One way to make history come alive is to make the work of history visible and open to students. History texts chronicle events and facts. They tell who did what. However, they also interpret and draw conclusions. Students get caught up in the facts and see history as something to be memorized. They don't realize that although the facts are valid, the interpretation is open to question. By reading and analyzing primary documents, students can draw their own conclusions. Primary materials are "'live' that is, they allow the students direct access to see and hear for themselves and thus to formulate their own questions and answers" (Holt, 1990, p. 23). However, interpretations are not always objective. "The act of interpretation cannot be value neutral or entirely objective. The discipline we aspire to brings the values and subjective influences out into the open. In other words, we must ask questions of ourselves as well as of the documents" (Holt, 1990, p. 360).

In order to achieve a fair and balanced understanding of the past, students need to learn to understand how history is constructed. Using primary sources helps them to achieve this understanding. In reading primary sources, students must

USING TECHNOLOGY

Internet Resources for Children
http://www.ericit.org/ weblinks/weblinks.shtml
Provides a list of resources for history and other subjects.

USING TECHNOLOGY

Mount Vernon
http://www. mountvernon.org/ education/biography/gwbio1.asp
Features easy-to-read biography of Washington.

EXEMPLARY TEACHING

READING PRIMARY SOURCES

Zev was a typical high school history student. When asked to read and discuss an actual letter in which ex-slaves pleaded to be allowed to retain land that had been given to them but was now about to be taken back, Zev expressed reluctance. He saw history as facts carved in stone, not something that could be imagined or thought about or interpreted: "You can't just read into a document like it's some kind of story that ends any way you want it to" (Holt, 1995, p.41). Zev's teacher was complementing the course textbook with primary sources. Zev read the letter and other primary sources. The letter was an eye-opener. Zev had believed that the slaves were illiterate. Yet the letter was an eloquent plea. Zev shifted his thinking. He began to see the freedpeople in a new light. He changed his view of the problem facing the freedpeople. Illiteracy was not their problem.

Their problem was getting the people in power to listen to them. Zev imagined how the three signers of the letter must have felt. He imagined them sitting around a table drafting and redrafting the letter until it said exactly what they wanted it to say.

Zev then made a connection between the letter writers and more current figures in the Civil Rights Movement. He related their breaking of the literacy barrier to barriers broken by Malcolm X, Martin Luther King, and others. Thinking of the letter writers, Zev was also better able to reflect on one of the overall messages of the unit, which was the concept of *freedom:* Is freedom just freedom from slavery, or is it also the freedom to develop one's abilities and quality of life to the fullest? Zev had learned that to do history is to "pursue an idea, to fit it out with facts, to test it, and to ask what it means" (Holt, 1995, p. 48).

not only ask what the documents have to tell them, they must also ask whether the documents can be trusted. Context is also needed. Interpretation requires knowledge of the times and the circumstances under which the document was produced and also information about the person or group who created the document. One of the goals of using primary documents is to help students become more analytical readers of history. Realizing how history is created, they will be better able to read with a critical eye.

History becomes more understandable if students learn to see similarities in events and draw conclusions about these similarities. In order to learn to form generalizations about historical events, students should ask such questions as these:

- What was the long-term significance of these events?
- What impact did these events have on people living then? Living today?
- What can we who are living today learn from the past?
- And taken together—as a whole—what do these events tell us about the way the world of people works? (Hennings, 1993, p. 368)

Students might create organizers that show how generalizations they have formed are supported, as in the sample organizer shown in Figure 10.1.

Comprehending history also requires understanding historical figures in the context of the times in which they lived. When reading about famous people, students should ask themselves the following questions in order to develop their own hypotheses about historical cause-and-effect relationships.

FIGURE 10.1

Generalization/Support Organizer

Generalization	Support

- What were the influences on this person that made him or her do what he or she did?
- What were the influences that made him or her become the kind of person he or she was?
- What effect did this person have on people and events of that time and of today? (Hennings, 1993, p. 366)

For instance, in older, traditional history texts, Columbus is portrayed as a courageous explorer. In revisionist texts, Columbus is described as being greedy and the chief cause of the downfall of a peaceful people. In a postrevisionist text, Columbus is portrayed as a product of the times and as neither better nor worse than other explorers (Hynd, 1999).

■ Providing a Personal Perspective

One way to activate students' schemata and to help them understand themes and key concepts in history is by having them relate historical events to happenings in their lives. For instance, in preparation for reading about the Pilgrims' voyage to America, students might gather in small groups and discuss moves that they have made: how far they moved, why they moved, how they moved, the adjustments they had to make to their new home, and how they felt about the whole experience. Students who have never moved might tell where they would like to move to and why. As they read, students can compare their experiences to those of the Pilgrims.

 *CHECK.UP*

1. What might be done to make history more interesting and more understandable?

Geography

Learning geography requires the ability to use a variety of specialized tools and resources. Major tools in geography are maps and atlases. Charts, graphs, tables, and time lines are also widely used. Students have a basic understanding of how to use these tools as long as they are fairly simple. However, students have difficulty with the graphs, charts, and tables that have a degree of complexity. Students have an especially difficult time explaining graphically displayed data in terms of outside factors. Students can tell what happened but not why. For instance, twelfth-grade students using a bar graph could correctly determine during what years hydrocarbon production increased and decreased but had difficulty using background knowledge to explain how environmental, economic, or other factors might account for a rise and fall in pollution levels. In fact, only one student in a hundred successfully completed the task by providing two possible reasons for a rise and fall in hydrocarbon levels (Hawkins et al., 1998). Students at all grade levels had difficulty using higher-order thinking skills and formulating written responses.

■ Survey Technique

Relying heavily on maps, charts, graphs, tables, and photos, geography makes special demands on students' ability and willingness to make use of visual information. In many disciplines, visuals are helpful adjuncts. In geography, visuals convey critical information. One technique that helps students make effective use of visuals is the **survey** technique.

Using the Survey Technique

LESSON 10.1

Step 1: Modeling the Process

Discuss the importance of visuals in geography. To show students how important visuals are, select a chart or map and put the information conveyed by the visual into words. Note that the information is detailed and also harder to understand when it is in a verbal rather than a visual form. Using a think-aloud procedure, model how you use both visual and verbal means to survey a chapter or section before reading it.

Step 2: Guiding the Process

Guide students as they survey a chapter in their geography books. In a chapter on natural resources, guide students as they read the title, read a brief chapter preview, read the headings, and look at the visuals and read the captions. After the survey, discuss what they believe the chapter will cover. If students fail to use the visuals, guide them through a survey in which they use just the visuals and see how much information they can garner.

Step 3: Practice and Application

Guide students through additional practice sessions. Once they have caught onto the idea of surveying, encourage them to use it on their own. However, review the process from time to time and ask questions that require students to analyze the visuals in a selection.

✓CHECKUP

1. What are the steps in the survey technique?
2. How does the survey technique help make geography more understandable?

SUMMARY

Literature has the power to evoke the feeling of wholeness or wonder at being lifted out of oneself that is the hallmark of the aesthetic response. In aesthetic reading, the reader is carried away by feelings evoked by the text. In contrast, efferent reading involves reading for information. Growing out of the aesthetic view of literature is reader response theory. In reader response theory, reading is seen as a transaction between reader and writer. Personal response is seen as a basis for growth in understanding and appreciating literature.

The development of aesthetic responses is labeled *envisionments.* An envisionment is the understanding a reader has about a text. Envisionments change as new ideas come to mind. Large- and small-group discussions and writing in journals and logs can be used to develop responses to literature. Key elements include accepting students' responses and using responses to build deeper, more critical responses and aesthetic appreciation.

Complex vocabulary, abstract concepts, unfamiliar writing styles and organization, and topics with which students have had little experience can make social studies challenging to read. Students are better at identifying facts than they are at interpreting them. History standards encompass two broad areas: historical knowledge and perspective and historical analysis and interpretation. History texts often combine narrative and expository writing. Because it is telling a story, narrative text is concrete and easier to follow and understand than expository text. Expository text is more analytical and requires more cognitive effort.

Students often fail to see that history has relevance to their lives. Reading and analyzing primary documents can help history come alive and help students learn to understand how history is constructed. Because of difficult vocabulary, complexity of concepts, and archaic language, the documents can be hard to read. But the reading becomes manageable if preparation is provided.

As they read history, students need to grasp the basic facts and also go beyond the facts to interpret their significance. History becomes more understandable if students learn to see similarities in events and draw conclusions about these similarities. Comprehending history also requires understanding historical figures in the context of the times in which they lived. One way to activate students' schemata and help them understand themes and key concepts is by having them relate historical events to happenings in their lives.

Learning geography requires the ability to use maps, atlases, charts, graphs, tables, and time lines. Students have a basic understanding of how to use these tools but have difficulty interpreting graphically displayed data. The survey technique helps students make effective use of visual and verbal information.

Reflection

Return to the Anticipation Guide at the beginning of this chapter. Respond once again to the items. Did your responses change? If so, how and why? Which content areas seem most difficult to read? Why? Why might a student with good general reading skills still have difficulty reading in the social studies?

EXTENSION AND APPLICATION

1. Examine a social studies text. What reading skills does the text require? Does the text have any suggestions for reading it effectively? If so, what are they?
2. From the Library of Congress (http://lcweb.loc.gov) or another source, locate some primary source material. How might you use this material with students reading social studies or language arts?
3. With a small group of students, select a piece of literature to read. Try the reader response approach in your discussion. What are the strengths of the approach? Its weaknesses?

chapter 11

READING AND WRITING IN SCIENCE AND MATH

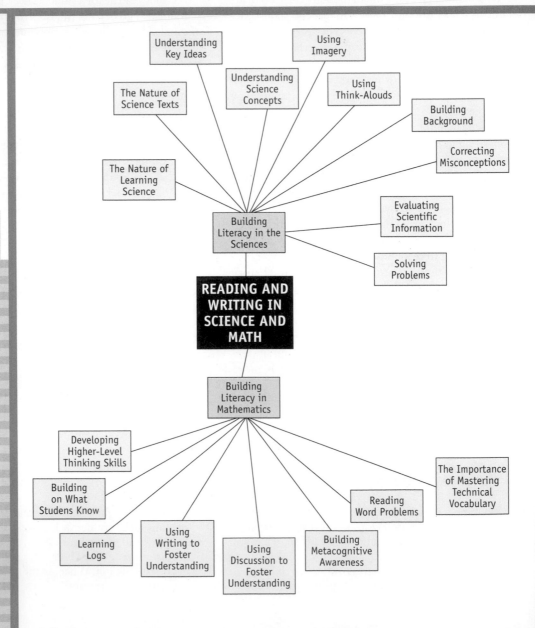

Understanding Key Ideas

Using Imagery

The Nature of Science Texts

Understanding Science Concepts

Using Think-Alouds

Building Background

Correcting Misconceptions

The Nature of Learning Science

Building Literacy in the Sciences

Evaluating Scientific Information

Solving Problems

READING AND WRITING IN SCIENCE AND MATH

Building Literacy in Mathematics

Developing Higher-Level Thinking Skills

Building on What Students Know

The Importance of Mastering Technical Vocabulary

Reading Word Problems

Learning Logs

Using Writing to Foster Understanding

Using Discussion to Foster Understanding

Building Metacognitive Awareness

ANTICIPATION GUIDE

For each of the following statements related to the chapter you are about to read, put a check under "Agree" or "Disagree" to show how you feel. Discuss your responses with classmates before you read the chapter.

		Agree	*Disagree*
1	Reading in the sciences is easier than reading in the social studies because the sciences are less abstract and better organized.	____	____
2	Students who have adequate general reading skills should have little difficulty reading math and science texts.	____	____
3	The biggest obstacle to understanding reading in science is the large number of technical terms that students encounter.	____	____
4	Of all the content areas, physics is the most difficult to read.	____	____
5	Struggling readers do well in math because they are dealing mostly with numbers rather than words.	____	____

USING WHAT YOU KNOW

Which of the sciences did you find most difficult? How would you compare the difficulty of reading a biology text with that of reading a general science or chemistry text? What were the main obstacles to reading each text? How did you overcome these obstacles? What special strategies did you use? What steps did your science teachers take to help you read the texts more effectively? How would you compare reading in math with reading in the sciences? What makes reading math problems difficult? Did your math teachers suggest strategies for reading problems? If so, what were they and how well did they work?

BUILDING LITERACY IN THE SCIENCES

The Nature of Learning Science

■ In the **inquiry approach,** a question is posed and students gather information through reading, experimentation, observation, or other means and compose an answer or come to a conclusion based on the information gathered. In a scientific inquiry, students ask questions, plan and conduct experiments, observe and quantify, reflect and reason, draw conclusions, and solve problems.

Just as in reading comprehension, scientific knowledge is constructed (Baker & Piburn, 1997); it is built on students' personal knowledge, or schemata. It is built using an **inquiry approach** in which students ask questions, plan and conduct experiments, observe and quantify, reflect and reason, draw conclusions, and solve problems. Standards call for "scientific inquiry in which students come to understand, through guided inquiry and problem solving, doing science as being about posing questions, justifying and critiquing findings, drawing conclusions and reflecting upon the limits and consequences of these conclusions" (Spillane & Callahan, 2000, p. 404). Students don't replace old knowledge with new knowledge; rather they develop "new understandings of a scientific idea by reconstructing their existing knowledge of that idea. Prior knowledge and experience are crucial resources that the individuals use to make sense of new information and construct new understandings" (pp. 404–405). For instance, students may understand that the moon is a heavenly body but may believe that the moon is stationary. Through observation and discussion, students can be led to see that the moon rises and sets and moves across the sky.

Many schools overemphasize textbooks, which tend to stress facts and vocabulary. Feeling pressured to cover the text, teachers accept a low level of understanding. Students read about science instead of doing science. Reading about concepts such as *work* and *energy*, which are abstract, students get little meaning from the text; they need real experiences. Today's students, in contrast to farm children of yesteryear, have few direct experiences with nature. They have plenty of images from TV and computers but few direct experiences. They need to grow plants, raise classroom animals, examine rock collections, and experiment with batteries and magnets. By doing science, students acquire a store of experiences that they can reflect on and use to build concepts. In inquiry science, students are actively engaged with the real world. Teamwork and collaboration are promoted, and different learning styles are accommodated.

 *CHECKUP*

1. How is science learned?

The Nature of Science Texts

One reason science is difficult is because of the number of new concepts introduced. In fact, according to one study, secondary school science texts introduce more new vocabulary words per page than foreign language texts do (Carey, 1986). An examination of a current chemistry and a current physics text reveals that each contains more than 400 technical terms. Moreover, it isn't enough just to know the meanings of words in science. For measurement terms, students must go beyond being able to define *gram* or *kilogram* and be able to manipulate the measurement. Words such as *density* and *velocity* require knowing and being able to apply a formula.

Science texts are also written in complex, precise language. However, the difficulty of science texts differs from discipline to discipline. When researchers Chall, Bissex, Conard, and Harris-Sharples (1996) set out to create a scale for measuring the difficulty of science texts, they soon found that they needed two scales, one for the life sciences and another for the physical sciences. Both the patterns of writing and the reasoning processes involved in comprehending the two branches of science were different. The **life sciences** are primarily descriptive/technical and are more concrete. They describe creatures that can be directly observed, sometimes with the help of a microscope, or depicted. Texts are devoted to describing the makeup and characteristics of various species. At the easiest levels, life science texts are concrete and devoted primarily to describing familiar creatures and phenomena. As the texts become more advanced, they become more technical and more detailed and deal with the unknown.

■ The **life sciences** include biology and ecology.

The **physical sciences** are more conceptual and theoretical. At the easiest levels they, too, are concrete and deal mainly with familiar topics. But as the texts become more advanced, they become more abstract and deal with concepts such as *space* and *relativity* that can not be seen and may require an understanding of math in order to be comprehended. There is, of course, overlap between the two kinds of science reading. The life sciences also deal with abstractions and theories, and understanding the physical sciences frequently requires a grasp of technical details. However, in general, reading in the life sciences places a heavy burden on memory while reading in the physical sciences places a greater demand on reasoning, especially as students move into higher levels.

■ The **physical sciences** include physics, astronomy, geology, chemistry, and space science.

Both the life and physical sciences demand a precise kind of reading in which students construct an exact rather than an interpretive meaning, identify and organize key ideas, note cause and effect and other relationships, use graphic information, and understand scientific formulas and symbols. Reading directions in order to carry out lab experiments is also a key skill.

■ Demands on the Reader in the Life Sciences

Because they deal with different types of topics and require different kinds of reasoning, texts in the life and physical sciences have different ways of presenting their ideas and require different kinds of reading and study strategies. The life sciences frequently follow a list structure in which a main idea is stated and supporting details follow. Often there are a number of details that must be understood and remembered. The details are not difficult to understand. Most are concrete and may be depicted by illustrations in the text. The difficult part is remembering all the details. For instance, a chapter in a tenth-grade biology texts explains what a cell is and then describes in words and illustrations the parts of a cell. In fewer than 500 words of text, the following terms are introduced: *cell membrane, cytoplasm, nucleus, nuclear envelope, cell organelles, mitochondria, ribosomes, endoplasmic reticulum, golgi bodies*, and *vacuoles*. These terms are carefully explained. However, to remember the details, readers need some way of organizing them and also some solid study strategies.

The best way to foster retention is to build understanding. In other words, students will remember the parts of a cell better if they understand why the cell needs each of its parts to sustain life: the nucleus can be seen as the control center; the nuclear envelope its covering; the vacuoles are storage containers for food and water; and so on. Knowing the morphemic structures of the terms will also aid understanding. For instance, the term *cytoplasm* is easier to remember if one knows that *cyto* means "cell" and *plasma* means "living substance." Knowing that *endo* means "within" and *reticulum* means "little net" will help the student understand that the endoplasmic reticulum is a netlike structure within the cell's plasma.

Other strategies that may help are visualizing the cell and its parts, constructing and labeling a diagram of the cell, and, of course, viewing a cell under a microscope. Creating an analogy also helps students understand and remember the parts of the cell and their functions. In one text, the operation of a cell was compared to the operation of a factory. Diffusion was compared to having a group of people pass through a crowded room.

In the sciences, knowledge is often cumulative. Future chapters will build on the students' knowledge of the cell. In fact, the next section describes plant cells and contrasts these with animal cells. When layer after layer of information is presented in this way, plan activities in which students achieve understanding of one topic before moving on. For instance, after reading the section on animal cells, ask students to summarize what they know and complete a diagram before moving on to the section on plant cells. A second biology text has a checkpoint that asks readers to respond to summary questions such as "What is diffusion? What is osmosis?" (Miller & Levine, 1998, pp. 56–57).

Although the chapter on cells follows a basic list structure, it also requires comparing and contrasting as students are asked to note how plant cells are similar to but different from animal cells. The chapter also gets into higher reasoning skills as it concludes with an explanation of cell theory and how this developed.

As students' knowledge becomes more advanced, the explanations of process becomes more detailed. For instance, in the tenth-grade biology text by Miller and Levine (1998), a much more detailed, more complex description of cells is provided. The amount of technical terminology is nearly tripled and the explanations of processes include more steps and more technical details. The explanations become so complex that students will have a difficult time remembering them if they don't understand why Step A leads to Step B and Step B leads to Step C. Cause-and-effect reasoning is involved. Creating process diagrams should help students better understand and retain explanations of these processes.

■ Demands on the Reader in the Physical Sciences

A chapter in a high school physics text discusses waves. The chapter begins with a general description of waves. Following a list structure, it discusses types of waves and properties of waves. Technical vocabulary is introduced: *crest, trough, transverse, longitudinal, compressions, refraction, amplitude, wavelength, frequency*, and *speed*. The speed of a wave is expressed in mathematical terms with a formula: $v = f \times \lambda$ (Greek letter lambda) where wave speed (v) = frequency $(f) \times$ wavelength (λ). Within the chapter, cause/effect and comparison/contrast structures are used to show what causes waves and to compare different types of waves. Both the language and the concepts are abstract. The basic idea being conveyed that a wave is a disturbance that travels through matter or space is difficult to picture. The concept that the transfer of energy causes a wave is also abstract. It is also counterintuitive. Watching an ocean wave, one thinks water moving toward the shore causes it and might be surprised to learn that energy causes waves.

As in the life sciences, the material is cumulative. Concepts build on each other. Reading in small doses and checking one's comprehension through summarizing and self-questioning are recommended. It is essential that students understand key concepts before moving on. Using graphics and visualizing aid comprehension. Making a chart of the characteristics of different types of waves helps make the information more concrete and more memorable.

The vocabulary load is heavy and abstract. Common words take on exact, specific meanings. *Speed* and *velocity* are used interchangeably in ordinary conversation but have different meanings in physics. Morphemic analysis should help. It also helps if students try out the mathematical formulas used to define terms. Calculating the velocity and wavelength of a wave will help students better understand all three terms involved: *velocity*, *wavelength*, and *wave*. Students might also discuss technical terms, such as *hertz* and *high frequency*, that are used in everyday life so they can relate what they know to what they are learning.

 CHECKUP

1. What are the key characteristics of science texts?
2. How do the demands made by physical science texts differ from the demands made by life science texts?

Understanding Key Ideas

To understand science, students must get the big picture or the main ideas that the science explores. For instance, a key idea in chemistry is that all matter consists of very tiny, characteristic particles called atoms (Dickson, 1995). This key idea helps students to understand such key concepts as the states of matter, elements and compounds, the periodic table, the structure of atoms, and the formation of compounds. Keeping this key idea in mind will help students organize and better understand key concepts.

Understanding Science Concepts

Students cannot simply memorize concepts. They must construct their own understandings. "They must be guided to actively construct their own mental models of the basic concepts. Passive acceptance of the teacher's own mental model will not suffice" (LeMay, Beall, Robblee, & Brower, 2000, p. T7).

Science concepts are learned in spiral fashion. Most concepts are not learned once and for all and for good. Many concepts are changed or refined as we gain new knowledge or have additional experiences. As we encounter and reencounter a concept over the years, our understanding becomes deeper and richer.

The Learning Cycle

In keeping with the way knowledge is constructed, concepts are presented through a learning cycle. Emphasizing the importance of experience, the **learning cycle** has three phases: student exploration or discovery, teacher explanation, and student application. This cycle reverses the typical sequence of presenting a new concept. In the past, the concept was explained and was followed by a demonstration or experiment. In the learning cycle approach, instruction begins with the experiment or demonstration and progresses to explanation and application.

Exploration

The exploratory phase is designed to create new understandings or refine old ones. It is also designed to spark students' interest. Students are provided with a set of materials to explore. They may be given a set of magnets or a series of objects with various buoyancies and a container of water. They work with the materials and make predictions about them. After conducting experiments with the materials, they discuss their findings in small groups.

Explanation or Concept Development

In the explanation phase, the teacher helps students discover target concepts as they focus on the findings of their experiments. This might be done through a discussion of the experiments—why some objects sank and others floated, for instance. Scientific terminology is used at this point. The teacher might introduce the words *buoyancy* and *density*, for instance. Concepts are also developed through reading, lectures, and demonstrations.

The use of analogy can be an aid to understanding because it uses familiar objects or situations as a way of explaining unfamiliar concepts. For instance, in one high school chemistry text, atoms were compared to letters in the alphabet to explain how 100 atoms can be combined in a variety of ways to form hundreds of substances:

> There are about 100 elements, which means that there are about 100 different kinds of atoms. These atoms combine to form each of the vast number of substances that make up the world around us. In a sense, atoms are like the 26 letters of the alphabet, which in different combinations form the immense number of words in the English language. And just as the rules of spelling and phonics define how letters can combine to form a word, so do certain scientific laws govern how atoms combine to form matter. (LeMay et al., 2000, p. 93)

Completing lab experiments helps make the text more understandable.

Application

Students apply their newly learned concept or expand it. They can, for instance, investigate methods of measuring buoyancy (Marian, Sexton, & Gerlovich, 2001). They can also apply newly learned concepts through lab work, problem solving, or discussion of environmental, consumer, or other issues.

Some of the best applications are those that can be applied to everyday life. In a chapter in a chemistry text in which the authors have introduced the concept of atoms, the authors explain that the phrase "100 percent natural" often used by advertisers is a bit misleading from a chemical point of view. Because all atoms in each molecule of a given chemical compound are identical to the atoms in every other molecule, the combination of atoms found in that compound in nature will be identical to those found in that same compound assembled in a lab. "A compound's properties come from the identity and arrangement of its atoms, not the place where those atoms were assembled" (LeMay et al., 2000, p. 93).

To foster full development of concepts, use the learning cycle and the following techniques.

1. Focus on fewer concepts, but in greater depth.
2. Use a variety of teaching strategies.
3. Present concepts from several different viewpoints.
4. Elicit students' misconceptions and directly address them in class.
5. Encourage students to discuss concepts with one another.
6. Include concept mastery questions on tests. (LeMay et al., 2000, p. T7)

> **STRUGGLING READERS**
> Holding demonstrations before students read in their textbooks about the principles they illustrate provides preparation for reading. Students acquire the vocabulary and background knowledge needed to read the text and so get more out of it.

Using Imagery

Imagery is an excellent aid to fostering science understanding. For instance, to help them understand the chemical molecular theory, students may visualize molecules as bouncing off each other the way pool balls do, except that they keep on moving. Chlorine gas might be envisioned as greenish particles in constant motion. We can imagine the gas particles being heated within a balloon. Heat causes the particles to move faster. Moving faster, they push against the surface of the balloon and so expand it (Dickson, 1995).

 **CHECKUP**

1. What is the learning cycle?
2. How does this foster the learning of science concepts?
3. What are some of the other ways to foster an understanding of science concepts?

Using Think-Alouds

One way to help students understand their text is to show how you, an expert reader, go about constructing the meaning of a science text. Think-alouds provide students with insight into the thinking processes and strategies that readers use to comprehend text. Here is a sample think-aloud for an excerpt from a text on astronomy.

The **meridian** is the line that bisects the sky by running from the due north point on the horizon up to the zenith and then down to the due south point on the horizon. (Schaff, 1998, p. 7)

Meridian is boldfaced, so it must be important. This word bisects. I've never seen it before. But bi *means two, as in* bicycle *for two wheels and* binomial *for two numbers. So I think it means divides something in two. And that's what the drawing shows, the sky divided into an eastern part and a western part.*

If you don't know where due north and due south are at the place where you're now standing, just look back toward the setting sun. And once you know which way west is, you can figure where north and south are and where the meridian runs. (Schaff, 1998, p. 7)

Let's see. The sentence says, "And once you know which way west is, you can figure where north and south are and where the meridian runs." But I can't. I'll look at the illustration. It shows a man looking west toward where the sun is setting. Well, I do know that the sun rises in the east and sets in the west. But how does that help me figure out which way north is? Let's see; the drawing shows that north is to the right of the man as he stands facing west. Now I get it. But how will I remember that north is to the right and south is to the left when you are facing west? Hey, they call lefthanders southpaws, *so I'll just remember it that way. South is to your left when you're facing west.*

But why is the meridian, dividing the sky into eastern and western halves, more important than a line dividing the sky into northern and southern halves?. (Schaff, 1998, p. 7)

That's a good question. I wonder why.

The answer is that the sun and almost all heavenly objects—the moon, planets, and most stars—appear to ascend in the eastern half of the sky and descend in the western half of the sky. (Schaff, 1998, p. 7)

Ah ha! Now I get it.

Discuss with the class strategies that you used as you read. Talk over, for instance, how you monitored for reading as you read, how you used an illustration to help you, and how you responded to the author in an interactive way. When the author asked questions, you attempted to answer them.

After modeling the process of thinking your way through a difficult segment of text, provide students with opportunities to do the same. You can have them work in pairs and take turns thinking out loud as they read to a partner. Discuss any difficulties that they may have encountered as they read. Discuss strategies that they use. In their journals, they can reflect on reading strategies that they used as well as on the content that they read. As their reading requires the use of specialized strategies, demonstrate with think-alouds and provide guided practice. For instance, you might demonstrate imaging and summarizing as strategies that might be effective when reading about processes involving a number of steps.

Building Background

When examining a text, note in particular the background required to read the text. For instance, many upper-level science texts assume the ability to apply algebraic formulas. Some biology texts may assume a knowledge of chemistry or physics. Also note the depth of coverage and the rate at which new concepts are introduced. Texts vary greatly in the number and depth of concepts and amount of technical vocabulary they introduce. It is better that students learn the basic concepts well than to become overwhelmed by being introduced to more concepts than they can handle.

■ Using Questioning to Build Background

Although a challenging subject, science begins on the most concrete of levels: observation. Students begin to learn science as they observe plants grow, the sun rise and set, the tides move in and out, the body respond to medicines, steam rising from boiling water, and other phenomena. From the observation of several events, concepts are formed as commonalities of the events are abstracted. Abstracting relationships among concepts leads to generalizations. Abstracting relationships among generalizations leads to laws and theories. Because science begins on a concrete level, it is accessible to all students (Singer & Donlan, 1989).

Through using a technique for teaching known as **Quest (Question Sequence for Teaching Thinking)** (Taba, 1965), students can be led from an observational level to a generalization level (Singer & Donlan, 1989). Quest starts with the stating of the lesson objective, which might be to develop the generalization that sound passes faster through media in which molecules are closer together. The teacher then decides what kind of observations students would need to make in order to come to this conclusion. What experiences, either direct or indirect, might be set up in order to provide the foundation for this conclusion? The teacher decides to drop a felt blackboard eraser and a pen on a long table and have a student tell how the sound waves traveled to her ears (Cuevas & Lamb, 1994). The student would note that she didn't hear the eraser hit the table but she heard the sound waves from the pen as they traveled through the air. Then repeat the experiment. This time the student puts one ear to the table and covers the other one with her hand. The student notes that this time she heard the waves from both the felt eraser and the pen traveling through the table. The teacher discusses the experiment and other related experiences that students have had. The teacher uses a series of questions known as FELS, for Focusing, Extending, Lifting, and Substantiating as shown in Table 11.1.

Although many texts first explain scientific principles or generalizations and then have students conduct experiments or observations, the reverse is a more effective procedure for building a foundation of knowledge and understanding upon which to base the generalization (Baker & Piburn, 1997). After students have experience with the Quest procedure, they can be given Quest guides and use them in a cooperative learning group or an individual effort to formulate generalizations.

■ **Quest (Question Sequence for Teaching Thinking)** uses observations and carefully planned questions to lead students to construct generalizations.

TABLE 11.1

FELS QUESTIONING DURING A QUEST SCIENCE LESSON

Type of FELS Question	Purpose	Question
Focusing	Focus on topic.	How did the student hear the sound waves before she put her ear to the table? How did she hear the waves after she put her ear to the table?
Extending	Gather more information on the same level.	How do whales communicate with each other? How does the sound travel? What did we learn about sound on the moon?
Lifting	Raises level of students' responses.	What can we say about sound? What kinds of things carry sound?
Substantiating	Requires students to provide support for their responses.	How do we know that sound travels faster along solid objects? Why did Native Americans put their ears to the ground when they were searching for buffalo? In what two ways was the sound traveling? Which was the faster way?
Lifting		Why do you think sound travels faster on a hot day than on a cold one? What did we learn in the last unit about the molecules in the air on cold and hot days? How might the closeness of the molecules affect the speed of sound? What can we say about the relationship between the speed of sound and the closeness of the molecules in the medium through which sound is traveling?

CHECKUP

1. How might think-alouds and background-building techniques be used to develop an understanding of science texts?

Correcting Misconceptions

Science is sometimes made more difficult because of the way our minds work. We are constantly trying to make sense of the world around us. We create theories about why the sun rises and sets and why it is warmer in summer than in winter. According to our observations, we would probably attribute summer warmth to the theory that the sun is closer to the Earth during the summer months. Once we have constructed theories, they become part of our schemata. Changing a **misconception** may mean changing a whole network of ideas. Our thinking in that area has to be reorganized. Even when we understand the new idea, we may not want to let go of our misconception. Changing a misconception is hard work. Students find it difficult to accept the idea that the sun is actually closer to Earth in the winter time and it isn't the distance of the sun from the Earth that causes seasons to change but the angle of the sun's rays (they are less direct in the wintertime).

Students' misconceptions may not be addressed because teachers may not realize that students have them. Whenever a new concept is being introduced, the teacher should first assess students' understanding of the concept—a recommended prac-

■ **Misconceptions** are erroneous ideas that people have about scientific and other phenomena. These misconceptions may be formed through observation, reasoning, erroneous information from others, or misinterpretation of correct information. Some science educators refer to misconceptions as preconceptions (Baker & Piburn, 1997).

tice in every subject. For instance, the teacher might ask, "Why is it hot in the summer and cold in the winter?" Responses should reveal students' conceptions and thinking. The teacher can then confront misconceptions and also build on accurate ideas students might have.

Beliefs that are deeply entrenched are especially hard to change (Chinn & Brewer, 1993). An entrenched belief is one for which the believer has a significant amount of evidence, especially if that evidence comes from several sources. The young child's flat earth belief is deeply entrenched because it is supported by frequent observations. Some beliefs are firmly held because they reflect the believer's concept about the fundamental characteristics of matter. For instance, students may believe that force, heat, light, and current are material substances and may continue to believe that the electrical current making a circuit is weaker at the end of its circuit than it is at the beginning (Dupin & Joshua, 1987).

Students are more likely to change beliefs when the source of new information is credible. For instance, students are more likely to believe that plants make their food through photosynthesis when they see that plants placed in a closet wither. They are also more likely to replace erroneous concepts when all possible explanations for them are shown to be false. For instance, if students believe that plants placed in a closet don't grow because of lack of fresh air, and not because of lack of sunlight, it would be necessary to place the plants in a room in which there was fresh air but no sunlight. Care must be taken to find out what the students' objections are and to answer each of them. Students should also be encouraged to think carefully about the information that contradicts an erroneous concept. They are more likely to alter concepts if they engage in deep processing. For instance, if students are asked to explain a concept to others, they are more likely to confront and rethink their erroneous information. It also helps if they have a personal involvement in the issue (Chinn & Brewer, 1993). For instance, students are more likely to change their misconceptions that plants get their food from the soil if they are asked to explain photosynthesis to their cooperative group and if they are in charge of the class's plants.

 *CHECKUP*

1. What are some steps that might be undertaken to correct misconceptions in science?
2. Why are some science misconceptions difficult to correct?

Evaluating Scientific Information

One of the marks of scientific literacy is being able to interpret scientific information that appears in the media, which is a key source of ongoing scientific information, especially after students have completed their formal schooling. Indeed, scientific information is pervasive and can be found in most newspapers and magazines. Many of our personal decisions, such as seeking medical treatment and caring for the environment, as well as civic decisions, such as deciding on where to place landfills and how to deal with toxic wastes and pollution, are influenced by these sources of information (Phillips, Norris, & Korpan, 2000). Unfortunately, students, even those who have a fairly rich scientific background, are not very good at interpreting scientific information. They tend to overestimate the validity of information and frequently accept tentative conclusions as proven. In one study of older students who had a relatively rich background in science, only one student in three was able to interpret cause–effect statements correctly. They also had difficulty making predictions based on scientific information and interpreting explanations. Even scientifically literate students need to learn to apply critical reading/thinking skills to scientific information.

Solving Problems

Science texts frequently present activities that ask students to apply principles or concepts that they have learned by solving problems. Before being asked to solve problems, students should have achieved a conceptual understanding of the topic. The process of solving problems should be modeled. Students should also be encouraged to think of the method of solving a problem rather than jumping in and mechanically applying a formula. Students should also be taught to be flexible so that if one method of solving a problem fails to work, they can try another. Encourage students to discuss how they go about solving problems. Students' think-alouds can reveal their thinking and help you provide needed guidance.

Working sample problems in the textbook will also foster problem-solving ability. Each problem usually has some feature that is not present in previous ones, so students gradually build up the ability to solve a wider range of problem types (Krause, 2001). To aid students in solving problems, Singer and Donlan (1989) suggest demonstrating the solution of similar problems, using the following steps.

Step 1. List the formula.
Density = mass/volume or d = m/v

Step 2. Show how the formula may be manipulated so that given any two variables, the third can be calculated.
A. Given mass and volume, find density: d = m/v
B. Given density and volume, find mass: m = dv
C. Given density and mass, find volume: v = m/d

Step 3. Show how a problem that is stated in various ways can be reworded so that the student knows which formula to apply.
Aluminum has a density of 2.70 g/cm³. Gold has a density of 19.32 g/cm³. Which object contains more matter, a block of aluminum that has a volume of 500 cm³ or a block of gold that has a volume of 50 cm³?
(Student must recognize that "amount of matter" means the same as *mass* and so apply the formula: m = dv.)

Step 4. Apply the scientific principle that is necessary for solving the problem.
You are given two small metal bars. Both have the same mass: 1500 g. But Bar A

EXEMPLARY TEACHING

INTEGRATING KEY INSTRUCTIONAL FACTORS

Three major determinants affect what is learned in science class: language, experiments and experiences, and social factors (Griesel, Anders, & Maxfield, 2000). To make science learning come alive in her class, Shelley Ann Maxfield carefully planned experiments for her students at a desert site set aside for her class. Students worked in groups to plan and carry out experiments. However, the use of language was a strong component. In one activity, students studied a desert plant and then described it in such careful detail that someone would be able to go to the site and find the plant strictly on the basis of the description. Recognizing that not all students learn in the same way, Maxfield planned multiple learning activities. Students found hands-on activities to be helpful and also responded positively to group activities. As one student explained, "I like it when we work together on the same thing. . . . The actual hands on, . . . You actually get to do the things and research yourself. . . . [T]hat gives me my best understanding of science when I actually get to do it" (Griesel et al., 2000). Students also found having multiple resources, including the Internet, helpful.

needs a box that is 133 cm^3 to contain it, while Bar B fits in a box that is 142 cm^3. Which one is lead? Which one is silver? The student would apply the following principle. The more dense a substance, the less space it takes up. Matter varies in its density. Density is often used to determine what an object is made of.

Step 5: Assess the solutions or answers to see whether they make sense. Because you can see on a density chart that lead has a higher density than silver, you know that an equal volume of it would take up less space.

 CHECKUP

1. What can be done in science labs to foster improved problem-solving ability and increased literacy?

BUILDING LITERACY IN MATHEMATICS

The Importance of Mastering Technical Vocabulary

Although we may conjure up images of numbers when we think of math, this content area also introduces a number of technical terms. In a unit on geometry, for instance, students need to know such words as *angle, protractor, polygon, quadrilateral, pentagon, hexagon, octagon, perimeter, area, parallelogram, circumference, radius, volume, space,* and *figure.* Learning and being able to apply in automatic fashion key technical terms is an essential skill in math. For instance, to understand what a ray is, students need to know how it differs from a line and a line segment. They also need to have had enough exposure to the terms so that when they hear them or see them they will immediately know how to apply them. If students have to stop and think about the meanings of key terms, this hesitation may hinder their understanding of a new concept or problem that uses the terms. Unless students have a firm grasp of the meaning of the term *ray*, they will have difficulty with the following definition: "An angle is formed by two rays with the same endpoint. The endpoint is called the vertex of the angle" (Globe Fearon, 2000, p. 340). Without automatic knowl-edge of the term *ray*, students will be hindered as they follow directions for using a protractor: "Read the number of degrees where the second ray crosses the protractor. Use the scale that reads 0 degrees" (Globe Fearon, 2000, p. 342).

 **CHECKUP**

1. What can be done to foster the development of technical vocabulary in math?

Reading Word Problems

Word problems pose special difficulties for students. In addition to requiring careful reading and the ability to translate a series of written directions into mathematical operations, math problems also require knowledge of specialized symbols and the tech-nical vocabulary of math. In one study, about one third of the errors made by low-achieving math students were, in fact, reading problems. Students were simply unable to decode or understand critical words or phrases (O'Mara, 1981). From a reading point of view, the student may misinterpret individual words or have difficulty with the relationships expressed by the words. For instance, one disabled reader had dif-ficulty with the following problem: "There are seven bike racks. If each bike rack has eight bikes, how many bikes in all?" (Nelson, 1999). Despite having read each word of the problem without hesitation, the student's response was "seven." To find out where the student's thinking had gone wrong, the teacher asked her to sketch out the problem. The student drew seven racks, but when asked to show how many bikes were in each rack, she drew only one for each. A simple rereading of the prob-lem helped her correct her error.

■ Solving Problems

What literacy skills are involved in reading the following explanation for solving equa-tions with more than one operation?

    To solve equations involving more than one operation, do the follow-ing steps.

1. First undo any addition and subtraction.
2. Then undo any multiplication or division.

Solve for x. $2x + 5 = 15$

Step 1   First undo the addition with subtraction. $2x + 5 - 5 = 15 - 5$
          Subtract 5 from both sides. $2x = 10$

Step 2   Then undo the multiplication with division. $2x/2 = 10/2$
          Divide both sides by 2. $x = 5$

Step 3   To check, replace the variable in the equa- $2x + 5 = 15$
          tion with your answer. $(2 \times 5) + 5 = 15$
                                                                $10 + 5 = 15$
                                                                    $15 = 15$

The solution to the equation $2x + 5 = 15$ is $x = 5$. (Globe Fearon, 2000, p. 406)

Because each word is essential, students must be able to read the directions with 100-percent accuracy. They must be able to read and know the meaning of *undo, operation, equation, variable,* and *replace.* They must be able to follow a series of directions. They must also be able to monitor for meaning. They need to know when they are not able to follow directions because they have forgotten a part of the directions or skipped a step. Monitoring for meaning also means that they have to check the math as well as the reading to make sure that the results of their operations make sense from a math point of view. Students must be able to use repair strategies if comprehension fails. Repair strategies involve rereading or using the example to check on the meaning of the directions. Retention is also involved; students must understand and remember the steps so that they can apply them to new problems.

Solving two-step word problems is a more complex reading process. What literacy processes might a student use to solve the following word problem?

The cost to rent a car is $35 per day plus a fee of $20. Mr. Hillwig rented a car for $195. For how many days did he rent the car?

Students need to know what information is given and what they are asked to solve for. Because reading is difficult for them, poor readers may just abstract the numbers from the problem without carefully reading the problem. Students need to read to focus on cost per day as the rate and realize that this is the figure that is divided and that a fee is referring to an initial payment. They also need to be able to translate the word problem into a series of steps. There are a number of systems for solving word problems. One such system is Read, Reread, Plan, Do, Check (Globe Fearon, 2000).

Read first to get an overview.

Reread more carefully to see what you need to find out.

For how many days did Mr. Hillwig rent the car?

Plan what you need to do.

Write an equation to solve the problem.

STRUGGLING READERS

Analyze problems students are expected to solve and note at what point they might have difficulties. For instance, ask, "Will they be able to read all the words and understand what is being asked?"

Cost = rate per day × number of days rented + fee

Put in the numbers from the problem.

Solve for cost.

Do the plan.

Cost = (35 × d) + 20

195 = (35 × d) + 20

195 − 20 = (35 × d) + 20 − 20

175 = 35 × d

175/35 = (35 × d)/35

5 = d

Check to see whether your answer makes sense.

From a literacy standpoint, students should also reread the problem to make sure that they were solving for the variable that the problem was asking for and that they followed the necessary steps and made all the correct substitutions.

Building Metacognitive Awareness

Based on her work with students who had difficulty with both math and reading, Kresse (1984) recommends helping students become metacognitively aware of the processes that they use to solve word problems. This involves modeling the reasoning processes in think-alouds and gradually having students take over more and more of the procedure. The key is to have students become aware of their thought processes so that they are better prepared to select the correct procedures.

Another procedure that helps students understand math problems is to have them create their own. Having students compose their own problems helps them to see how problems are constructed. In the beginning, students might simply change textbook problems. With increased understanding and confidence, they can begin to compose their own. In one study, the teacher gave the students, who were underachievers in math, the equation and the students created problems to fit the equation (Ferguson & Fairburn, 1985). The students then solved each other's problems and made significant progress in their ability to solve math problems.

 CHECKUP

1. What techniques can be used to develop the ability to solve word problems?

Using Discussion to Foster Understanding

Just as discussion fosters learning in history, language arts, and other highly verbal subject matter areas, discussion also promotes learning in math. To foster increased understanding of the math text and also to help students learn the skills and vocabulary needed to comprehend math texts, discuss portions of the text with them. Types of questions you might pose include those that probe understanding of the concepts or operations being discovered, those that help students make connections between current concepts and past concepts, those that probe students' ability to apply the concepts or operations to other situations, and metacognitive questions that probe students' awareness of their understanding of what they are reading and steps they might take to promote increased understanding. Questions used by Leah Casados (Tanner & Casados, 1998), a high school math teacher, included the following:

- What possible applications can you see for the law of sines and cosines?
- What are some different methods you can use to rotate a point 180 degrees and find the coordinates of the image?
- Are there any new ideas in this section? Is there anything in this section you have seen before?
- What steps/procedures did the author recommend following?
- What steps did you actually use? (p. 345)

The discussions helped. As Casados commented, discussion "showed me that my students can become insightful, logical mathematical problem solvers by talking through ideas and taking ownership of them" (Tanner & Casados, 1998, p. 396). Through discussion, students began articulating math concepts, started using the vocabulary of math, and shared strategies that they used to solve problems.

Teacher think-alouds and demonstrations help students understand what is involved in solving math problems.

Using Writing to Foster Understanding

Writing can also be a valuable learning tool in mathematics. Through writing, students can reflect on and organize their thoughts and even simplify problems. Some types of writing that have been used to foster understanding include restatement and brief summaries. Restatement writing can be used to restate a problem in simpler terms, as in the following example.

> Original: Find three positive, even, consecutive integers such that the product of the two smallest integers is equal to two-thirds the product of the two largest integers.

> Rewrite: Find three even whole numbers. They must be in a row, like 2, 4, 6 or 10, 12, 14. If you multiply the two smallest and get your answer, it should be the same number as when you multiply the two largest and then take ⅔ times that answer. (Havens, 2001)

The rewrite could be a whole-class, group, or individual project. Through rewriting, students must achieve and demonstrate a concrete understanding of the technical vocabulary and also the math processes needed to solve the problem.

One-sentence summaries have also been shown to be helpful. Before turning in an assignment, students compose a one-sentence summary of a key concept, process, or term. If students are writing about a process that involves a series of steps, they can use a frame that contains the words *begins with*, *continues with*, and *ends with*:

> Adding a series of decimal numbers *begins with* your writing the numbers one right under the other with the decimal points in each number lined up, *continues with* your adding the numbers in columns as if they were whole numbers, and *ends with* your bringing the decimal point straight down from the numbers above into the answer. (Havens, 2001)

As they read, students can use sticky notes to rewrite procedures or problems in their own words, devise their own examples, note where they are having difficulty and why, draw a comparison with materials read previously or in another source, or use pictures to illustrate concepts (Havens, 2001).

Learning Logs

Learning logs can be used to provide students an opportunity to reflect on their understanding of math. Students can explain processes they used to solve problems, reflect on what they have learned, or raise questions about puzzling concepts or procedures. Learning logs help students to become more thoughtful in math and to become more aware of their cognitive processes. Being more aware of cognitive processes, they are better able to make full and effective use of them. Learning logs can be read by the teacher to gain insight into the students' understanding of math.

Building on What Students Know

Through analyzing class discussions and students' writing, teachers can discover what students know about a topic and plan accordingly. Students are required to learn a variety of strategies for solving math problems and also when and where to use those strategies and which strategies seem to work best for them. When assessing students, note not only their grasp of math processes, but also the cognitive and language strategies they use to solve problems. Are they able to sift through the information to see what the major question being asked is? Are they able to apply problem-solving skills? Are they able to monitor their work from both a math and a reading point of view?

 **CHECKUP**

1. How might discussion and writing be used to develop understanding in math?

Developing Higher-Level Thinking Skills

One way to help students develop higher-level thinking skills is to provide them with opportunities to solve problems that have more one way of being solved and to ask them to explain their reasoning processes. Students reflect on their thinking and teachers gain insight into students' reasoning processes. Note in the Exemplary Teaching feature how one teacher used problems with multiple solutions to foster higher-level thinking skills.

SUMMARY

Reading in the sciences is inquiry based and constructive. Students construct their understandings based on what they know. Written in complex, precise language, science texts make demanding reading. Life science texts are primarily descriptive/technical. Physical sciences are more conceptual and theoretical. Both life and physical science texts contain a large number of technical terms. Science material is cumulative. Concepts build on each other. Reading in small doses, using visual aids, and checking one's comprehension through summarizing and self-questioning are recommended. Teachers can foster conceptual understanding by using think-alouds, building on what students know, using well-planned questioning techniques, and developing strategies such as using imagery.

Having created their own intuitive understanding of the way the world works, students often construct misconceptions. Teachers need to be aware of students' misconceptions, address them directly, and replace them with accurate concepts that students find acceptable because they see the logic of them and the concepts are credible. Students also need to be taught higher-level thinking skills so that they can evaluate scientific information.

Science texts frequently require students to solve problems. Before being asked to solve problems, students should have conceptual understanding of the topic. Strategies for solving problems should be modeled, discussed, and practiced.

Learning math is also a constructive process in which students build understanding based on their prior knowledge and personal perspective. Word problems pose special difficulties for students. In addition to requiring careful reading and the ability to translate a series of written directions into mathematical operations, math problems also require knowledge of specialized symbols and the technical vocabulary of math. Students should be taught strategies for solving problems. Instruction should

foster metacognitive awareness so students can better control their cognitive processes and also create problems of their own.

Both discussion and writing can be used to help students become more aware of their thought processes and of effective problem-solving strategies. In restatement writing, students restate a problem in simpler terms. Students can use sticky notes to rewrite procedures or problems in their own words, devise their own examples, note where they are having difficulty and why, draw a comparison with materials read previously or in another source, or use pictures to illustrate concepts Learning logs can be used to provide students with an opportunity to reflect on their understanding of math.

Through analyzing class discussions and students' writing, teachers can discover what students know about a topic and plan accordingly. To help students attain conceptual knowledge, it is essential to find out what students know about a topic and then build on that knowledge. Metacognition is also an essential element in conceptual understanding. Students need to be aware of what they know and what is puzzling.

Reflection

Return to the Anticipation Guide at the beginning of this chapter. Respond once again to the items. Did your responses change? If so, how and why? Which content areas seem most difficult to read? Why? Why might a student with good general reading skills still have difficulty reading in the sciences or in math?

EXTENSION AND APPLICATION

1. Examine a text from one of the sciences. What reading skills does the text require? Does the text have any suggestions for reading it effectively? If so, what are they?
2. Examine a math text. What reading skills does the text require? Does the text have any suggestions for reading it effectively? If so, what are they? What suggestions does the text have for reading and solv-

ing word problems? Try out the suggestions. How easy to use and effective are they?
3. Every day for a week, read a portion of a challenging math or science text. In a journal or learning log, note the strategies that you use, the difficulties that you encounter, and how you deal with these difficulties.

USING TECHNOLOGY, TRADE BOOKS, AND PERIODICALS IN THE CONTENT AREAS

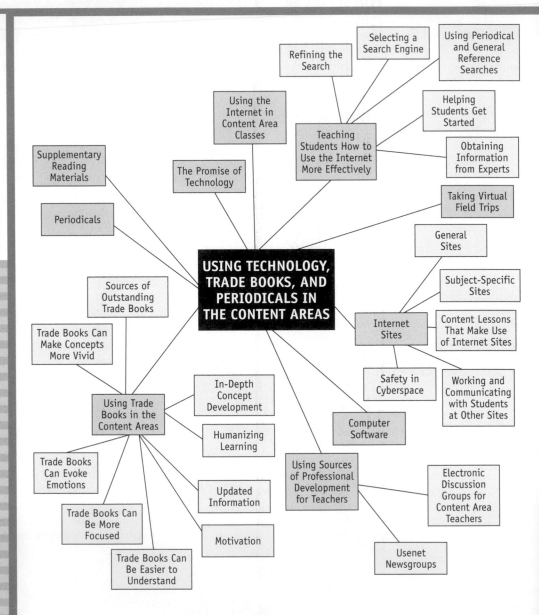

- Selecting a Search Engine
- Refining the Search
- Using Periodical and General Reference Searches
- Using the Internet in Content Area Classes
- The Promise of Technology
- Teaching Students How to Use the Internet More Effectively
- Helping Students Get Started
- Obtaining Information from Experts
- Supplementary Reading Materials
- Periodicals
- Taking Virtual Field Trips
- General Sites
- Subject-Specific Sites
- Sources of Outstanding Trade Books
- **USING TECHNOLOGY, TRADE BOOKS, AND PERIODICALS IN THE CONTENT AREAS**
- Internet Sites
- Content Lessons That Make Use of Internet Sites
- Trade Books Can Make Concepts More Vivid
- Safety in Cyberspace
- Working and Communicating with Students at Other Sites
- Using Trade Books in the Content Areas
- In-Depth Concept Development
- Humanizing Learning
- Computer Software
- Trade Books Can Evoke Emotions
- Using Sources of Professional Development for Teachers
- Electronic Discussion Groups for Content Area Teachers
- Updated Information
- Trade Books Can Be More Focused
- Motivation
- Trade Books Can Be Easier to Understand
- Usenet Newsgroups

For each of the following statements related to the chapter you are about to read, put a check under "Agree" or "Disagree" to show how you feel. Discuss your responses with classmates before you read the chapter.

		Agree	*Disagree*
1	Trade books do a better job of presenting information than most textbooks do.	_____	_____
2	Most students are unable to use the Internet well to explore topics.	_____	_____
3	The Internet should be used sparingly in content classes.	_____	_____
4	The Internet should be used only under close supervision.	_____	_____
5	Periodicals are underused and undervalued in most content area classes.	_____	_____

USING WHAT YOU KNOW

How do you know what you know? All of us have learned from textbooks and lectures, but what are some other sources of information that have been valuable to you? How has the Internet added to your store of knowledge? How have you used the Internet to explore a topic or acquire information? How about periodicals and trade books? Did any of your teachers use periodicals in the classroom? Did any use textbooks? How might these sources of information—technology, trade books, and periodicals—be used to foster increased knowledge in your content area?

THE PROMISE OF TECHNOLOGY

Without leaving their desks, today's students can watch President Kennedy give his inaugural address, listen to songs of a whale, check up on the space station, view photos of the Civil War, read diaries of children heading west, talk to an expert on DNA, take a virtual tour of a rain forest, communicate with a friend across the street or across the continent, or read and print out any one of 2 million magazine articles. Through the Internet, today's students have access to a vast, rapidly expanding storehouse of information. They also have at their fingertips an array of tools for communicating. Through the Internet, they can present reports not just to classmates but to other students around the world. Depending on their ability to use today's tools, they can complement their words with film clips, photos, songs, speeches, and art work. As Bransford et al. (2001) note,

> The new technologies provide opportunities for creating learning environments that extend the possibilities of "old"—but still useful—technologies—books; blackboards; and linear, one-way communication media, such as radio and television shows—as well as offering new possibilities. Technologies do not guarantee effective learning, however. Inappropriate uses of technology can hinder learning—for example, if students spend most of their time picking fonts and colors for multimedia reports instead of planning, writing, and revising their ideas. And everyone knows how much time students can waste surfing the Internet. (p. 206)

USING THE INTERNET IN CONTENT CLASSES

Web sites can be used to supplement and amplify textbook information. A middle school science text contains two pages of information on acid rain. The Acid Rain Program sponsored by the EPA presents more than a dozen pages of information and describes nine easy-to-conduct experiments. Related Web sites are also noted.

■ The **Internet** is a network of interlinked but independent computer networks that allows the exchange of vast amounts of information.

Although the **Internet** has the potential to enrich learning in previously unimaginable ways, it demands a higher level of literacy. With vast sources of information available, much of it written on sophisticated levels, students must be able to decide what is important and what isn't, what is useful information and what isn't. Students must also be able to synthesize large amounts of information and judge the reliability of information.

E-mail and interactive sites require that students be able to communicate in writing and also to combine the visual and the verbal. Students also need to be adaptable and able to learn new skills as today's technological wonders are soon replaced by tomorrow's.

Just as students need to learn to read and write in the content areas, they also need to be able to use technology to help them learn content and communicate what they have learned. Being able to use technology has become an essential skill. According to a report by Dwyer (1995), there is

> a new set of basic core competencies that take their place alongside reading, writing and arithmetic: organizing resources; working with others; locating, evaluating and using

*C*arefully chosen Web sites can be used to amplify information contained in texts.

information; understanding complex work systems; and working with a variety of technologies. These are the skills of the information age.

 *CHECKUP*

1. What role is technology, and especially the Internet, playing in content area instruction?

TEACHING STUDENTS HOW TO USE THE INTERNET MORE EFFECTIVELY

The Internet has been described as the greatest library in the world, but one in which all the books have been tossed onto the floor. The information is there but it can be hard to find and overwhelming. Typing in key words such as *Martin Luther King* or *diabetes* can turn up thousands of sites. Mixed in with excellent sites are sites of limited value or sites that are too advanced for students.

Although most students may be familiar with the Web, they may not understand how to conduct an efficient search. An efficient search starts with a careful delineation of the topic and the questions that the student hopes to answer and then a determination of whether the information is relevant and reliable. The topic might be assigned or selected. Whether assigned or selected, the student writer must formulate a thesis statement or question to be answered. With novice writers, a key skill is narrowing the topic so that it has reasonable limits. A student interested in the development of the automobile, for instance, might limit her topic to concept or prototype cars. On reflection, she might decide to focus on current concept cars as a

USING TECHNOLOGY

The American School Directory http://www.asd.com/asd/ Has free Web sites for 108,000 elementary and secondary schools. Web sites contain information about the school, daily announcements, a creative corner to display student work, and a bulletin board. ASD also provides free e-mail for any teacher or student who wants it. In addition, ASD has a list of sites recommended by the faculty at Vanderbilt University.

USING TECHNOLOGY

A thorough but easy-to-understand explanation of techniques for searching on the Web is Worlds of Searching at http://www. worldsofsearching.org/

way of predicting what the cars of the future might look like. Her question might be: What are the main features of current concept cars? The Web can be searched through a search engine.

Refining the Search

■ **Boolean operators** are words such as OR, AND, NOT, and NEAR that are used to combine or exclude items in computer logic.

Internet key word searches can be refined by using the **Boolean operators:** AND (+), OR, NOT , (–), and NEAR. OR broadens a search by signaling the engine to pick items that have at least one of the search terms. Using OR to link *cars* OR *autos* will pick up more references than using either term by itself. The term AND limits the search. It signals that the reference must contain both items. If I wanted to find references for concept cars, I would limit the search by typing in *cars* AND *concept.* A plus sign (+) can be used instead of an AND. However, the plus sign must be placed next to the term to be included with no spaces between the two: *cars +foreign.* NOT limits the search by excluding items. If I wanted to exclude foreign cars, I would type in NOT *foreign.* Using the NOT operator, however, can exclude some items that might be appropriate. For instance, it would exclude an article entitled U.S. and Foreign Concept Cars. A minus (–) sign can be used instead of NOT but must be placed next to the term to be excluded with no space between the two: *vehicles –trucks.* Quotation marks can be used to find an exact phrase: "concept cars." The term NEAR can be used to show that you will accept an item if the two terms specified are close to each other, usually within about 10 to 100 words. For instance, *cars* NEAR *concept* tells the engine to pick up the item if the word *cars* appears and the word *concept* is close to it. Some search engines also use an asterisk or question mark to pick up variations of a word. For instance: futur* would search for *future, future's, futuristic, futurity,* and *futurology.* The most important search words should be placed first. When possible, select the word or phrase that uniquely describes what you are looking for. However, also be aware of other terms that might be used to name the concept you are seeking. Avoid the use of articles and other function words.

Students should click on the help or information portion of a search engine to get additional information about search techniques. Many of the engines also have a menu for advanced searches with which students can limit their searches. In its advanced search, AltaVista will list references by category. Northern Light's power search seems to have the most extensive devices for limiting the search. Northern Light returned 2,458 hits for *concept cars.* These hits were organized into twelve categories. The category *sports utility vehicle* yielded just seventy-two hits. Based on this search, the student could limit her investigation to *sports utility vehicles of the future* or select one of the other categories. The searcher can also elect to have sources listed by date and limit the search by selecting only the most recent postings.

An excellent way to introduce students to the concept of a Boolean search is to have them find information about inventions on the U.S. Patent Office's Web site: http://www.uspto.gov/go/kids/kidsearch.html. Explaining that finding a patent is like being a detective, the site walks them through searches in which they use the patent number to find an invention, the inventor's name, and various descriptions of the article they wish to find. The descriptions use the Boolean operators.

Selecting a Search Engine

■ Using Indexes

To locate information on the Web, it is necessary to use a **search engine.** Search engines come in two forms: indexes and directories. After establishing a topic and search question, the next step is to decide which search tool to use. Most search engines compile information in the form of indexes of key words arranged in alphabetical order. The compilation, in most instances, is mechanical. Electronic **Web crawlers** scan the Web and simply extract key words from names or descriptions of Web sites. Directories, on the other hand, arrange information by categories. **Indexes** are more complete and up-to-date and so are used more frequently. Four of the most effective index search engines are

Google: http://www.google.com

AltaVista Advanced: http://www.av.com

Northern Light: http://www.northernlight.com

All the Web All the Time: http://www.alltheweb.com

> Google, AltaVista, and All the Web have optional filtering devices designed to screen out objectionable content. Another popular search engine is Ask Jeeves (http://www.ask.com/). Ask Jeeves is a search engine that uses questions rather than key words to conduct a search. The reader types in a question and the engine responds by listing the writer's question and/or similar questions and sites that provide possible answers to the questions

■ Using Directories

Because they are compiled by humans, **directories** are better organized and less cluttered than indexes but don't normally contain as many items. Directories are searched by examining and clicking on category names. Directories are arranged in hierarchical fashion. For instance, in Yahoo, the topic *Auroras* is listed under *Astronomy*, which is listed under *Science*. Directories are most useful when a student wants to explore an area but isn't sure what the area contains. A student who is planning a paper on insects but isn't sure which one might click on *Insects* and see which ones are listed.

> There is some overlap between directories and indexes. Yahoo, for instance, allows searching by category or key word. Five of the most effective directories are

About.com: http://www.about.com

Librarians' Index: http://www.lii.org

Open Directory Project: //http://dmoz.org/

WWW Virtual Library: http://www.vlib.org/

Yahoo!: http://www.yahoo.com

■ Search Engines for Young People

Search engines specifically designed for young people include the following (Bennett, 2000). Most are directories.

■ A **search engine** is a program used to search the Web.

■ **Web crawlers** are robot-like devices that move through the Web and pick up the names of new sites or note sites that have been taken off the Web.

■ **Indexes** are search engines that list Web sites alphabetically by key word. Searches are conducted by electronic devices.

■ **Directories** are search engines that organize Web sites by category. Directories are generally put together by humans.

- Ask Jeeves for Kids: Responds to questions posed by young people.
  http://www.ajkids.com/
- CyberDewey: Hotlist of Internet sites organized using Dewey Decimal Classification codes.
  http://ivory.lm.com/~mundie/CyberDewey/CyberDewey.html
- KidsClick! Web search for kids by librarians.
  http://sunsite.berkeley.edu/KidsClick!/
- Yahooligans! The Web Guide for Kids: Web guide for kids from Yahoo!
  http://www.yahooligans.com/
- Web Sources for Information on New Sites for Kids: Multimedia Schools "CyberBee" by Linda Joseph.
  http://www.infotoday.com/MMSchools/MMStocs/MMScybertoc.html
- School Library Journal "Surf For: A Thematic Guide to Internet Sites" by Gail Junion-Metz.
  http://www.slj.com/articles/surffor/surfforarchive.asp

Using Periodical and General Reference Searches

Also available are computerized searches of periodicals and general references that include the text so that students can view the references and obtain the articles. One such service is Infotrac, which has several versions designed specifically for students. The general student edition contains nearly 2 million articles. Libraries subscribe to the service and then offer it to patrons. Patrons use their library bar codes or some sort of password to access the services from their home or school computer. For the topic *concept cars*, I obtained twenty-four references.

Helping Students Get Started

Before students start their searches, discuss their topics and the key questions that they will be asking. After students have established their questions, they decide what key or concept words will enable them to obtain answers to their questions. For instance, a student interested in the cars of the future might frame her questions as What will tomorrow's cars be like? Possible key words include *cars, autos, concept, dream, experimental, prototype,* and *future.* A sample worksheet for searching the Internet is presented in Figure 12.1.

Once students have located sources of information, they need to decide which sources are useful and which are not. Living in the information age, this is one of the most important literacy skills in all content areas and in life. Without it, we are in danger of drowning in trivia. Discuss with students, the importance of selecting material that provides answers to their questions. Show how you might use titles or brief annotations or quickly skim articles to decide whether or not a source is appropriate. If you have narrowed your *concept cars* topic down to include only U.S. cars, show how you quickly reject sites that are devoted to foreign concept cars or sites that merely describe auto shows. If you are investigating current concept cars, show how you reject sources that talk about concept cars of the past, or how, when you

FIGURE 12.1

Internet Search Plans

What question do you want answered?

What will cars of the future look like?

What are the key words for your concept? What are synonyms for your key words?

Key Word	Synonym
car	*auto, vehicle*
concept	*experimental, prototype, dream, futuristic*

How will you word your question for the Internet?

(car* OR auto) AND (concept OR dream OR experimental OR futuristic OR prototype)

Hints: Put parentheses around synonyms and join them with OR. Put AND between key words. Use an asterisk to signal a search for different forms of the words.

Adapted from Creighton University (2001). *Conducting an Internet Search.* Available online at http://www.creighton.edu.

are reading an article, you skip descriptions of past cars and home in on current concept cars. Narrowing the topic and the search makes this stage of the process easier because students do not have as much material to wade through.

In addition to assessing the source to see whether it contains pertinent information, students must also evaluate the source to see whether the information is trustworthy. Students should evaluate sources for authority, objectivity, reliability, timeliness, and coverage (Kentucky Virtual Library, 2002). To assess authority, students must ask, "Who is the author?" On some Web sites, the author is not identified. The site may have been put up by an organization, and the author's name may not be provided. The student must also ask, "What are the author's credentials?" Students should look to see what the author's education and experience are. Some authors may be experienced writers but may not have experience in the field they are writing about. People who are experts in one field sometimes speak out in a field in which they have little or no expertise. To assess objectivity, the student must ask, "Is the author unbiased? Does the author have anything to gain by taking a particular standpoint?" One way to assess the objectivity of a site is to see whether it is a commercial site. Commercial sites tend to favor a point of view that profits their interests. The students might also look at the language used and note whether it seems to be fair. Are all sides of the issue presented? The student should also note the author's purpose. Is it to inform, entertain, or persuade? Advertisement, editorials, and political addresses are designed to persuade.

Students should also assess the accuracy of information. For instance, one Web source describes John Boole, the famous mathematician, as English. Another says he was Irish. One way to verify information is to use more than one source or to use a highly reliable source to check facts contained in Web sites or other sources of unknown reliability.

Depending on the nature of the topic, timeliness is a concern. The information in a just-published book may be two or more years old. Information in a newspaper or on-line sources may be just hours old.

 CHECKUP

1. How can students use the Internet more effectively?

Obtaining Information from Experts

One advantage of the Internet is that students and teachers can contact experts for information. Some general locations for contacting experts in science include:

- Ask A+ Locator: The Ask A+ Locator is a database of high-quality "Ask A" services designed to link students, teachers, parents, and other K through 12 community members with experts on the Internet. Profiles of each Ask A service include identification information (e.g., publisher, e-mail address, contact person, links to service's home page), scope, target audience, and a general description of the service. The Ask A+ Locator is searchable by subject, key word, grade level, or alphabetical list. Ask A+ Locator is part of the Virtual Reference Desk. http://www.vrd.org/locator/index.html
- Ask an Expert: This is a general site with links to a wide range of experts. http://www.askanexpert.com/askanexpert.html
- Ask a Mad Scientist: This resource will put you in touch with a wide range of scientists around the world. http://128.252.223.239/~ysp/MSN/

TAKING VIRTUAL FIELD TRIPS

Because the new technologies are interactive, they can foster a greater intensity of participation and a greater depth of understanding. Through the new technologies, students can have virtual experiences, conduct virtual experiments, and take virtual field trips that were not possible in the past. Here are some of the best sites.

- GOALS: Global Online Adventure Site: Features a series of ongoing adventures such as a trip around the world. With words and illustrations the explorers describe their adventure. Students can track their progress. http://www.goals.com/
- Virtual Space Station Tour: Students can tour a mock-up of the space station or engage in a number of other activities. http://quest.arc.nasa.gov/common/events/index.html
- Global Warming Lab: Students find out about global warming on a worldwide level and also analyze local conditions.

http://www.riverdeep.net/earthpulse/data/globalwarming/globalwarming_intro.html

- GLOBE: Global Learning and Observations to Benefit the Environment: Students can work in their own classroom or can collaborate with students in other schools. http://www.globe.gov/

   Help in planning an Internet collaboration is available from a number of sources, such as NickNacks at http://home.talkcity.com/academydr/nicknacks/. NickNacks helps with the planning of projects, including helping you find possible projects and collaborators. It also lists completed projects.

INTERNET SITES

General Sites

One approach to making use of the Internet's vast resources is to use central sites rather than key word searches (Leu & Leu, 2000). In the best central sites, the links have been screened so that they are of high quality and appropriate for students. Here are some recommended general sites.

- Berit's Best Sites for Children: One of the oldest and most reliable lists of sites for children in primary grades. Compiled by a librarian.
  http://www.cochran.com/theodore/beritsbest/
- BJ Pinchbeck's Homework Helper: Compiled by a middle school student who understands the reference needs of his fellow students.
  http://www.bjpinchbeck.com/
- Education World: Features news for educators and links to thousands of useful sites for students.
  http://www.education-world.com/
- Kathy Schrock's Guide for Educators: Home Page: A popular site for teachers. Compiled by a school librarian who has also created a collection for students.
  http://school.discovery.com/schrockguide/
- Kid Info/School Subjects: Another student-created site. Arranged by subject area and linked to many of the best educational sites online.
  http://www.kidinfo.com/School_Subjects.html
- PBS Teachersource: Sites selected for curriculum content, arranged by subject areas.
  http://www.pbs.org/teachersource/recommended/rec_links.shtm
- 700+ Great Sites from ALA: Compiled by members of the American Library Association. For students, teachers, librarians, and parents.
  http://www.ala.org/parentspage/greatsites/

Subject-Specific Sites

Although many sites have a general utility, some are more subject specific. In history, for instance, sites that contain primary documents are especially helpful. However,

STRUGGLING READERS

A piece of software known as *Cast eReader* (http://www.cast.org) reads aloud and highlights text from the Internet or word processing programs. Provides access to materials poor readers might not be able to read on their own.

students need instruction in both locating primary documents and interpreting them in the context of the times in which they were written. In science students need to learn to become more critical readers. With some sites making doubtful claims, especially in the fields of health and medicine, students need to be able to tell the difference between reliable and questionable information. With the increase in the wealth of knowledge available comes the responsibility of using that wealth wisely.

 CHECKUP

1. What are some of the resources on the Internet that are of potential help to the content area teacher?

Content Lessons That Make Use of Internet Sites

Math and science lessons that make use of materials contained in the Internet are listed on the Illuminations sections of the National Council of Teachers of Math site (http://www.NCTM.org). For instance, in one block of lessons created by Habits of Mind (Lessons: 9–12, Adolescent Sleep), students integrate science, math, and technology to examine the arguments for and against changing the school start time for high school students based on the findings of several scientific research studies on sleep and school achievement. The teacher can download and print out studies, or students are directed to the sites so that they can read and analyze the studies.

As students read summaries of the studies, they ask themselves the following questions.

1. What was the purpose of the study?
2. Who were the subjects of the study?
3. Describe the methods used.
4. Summarize the findings of the study.
5. What evidence is presented to support the findings?
6. How would you assess the logic of the argument presented? Explain your reasoning.

After reflection and discussion, students apply language arts skills by composing an editorial in which they express their opinions regarding high school start times. In keeping with the requirement for writing an effective persuasive piece, they present what they believe is the strongest evidence to support their opinion as well as arguments to refute what they perceive to be the strongest evidence against their position. As an extension and application of statistical math skills, students survey others in their school and community to find out how they would feel about a later school start time for high school. Opinions of the various groups are compared by age, gender, and occupation.

The Web can also be used to foster a better appreciation of literature. Possible projects include using Web sites to gather historical, social, and cultural information about a literary movement or period. For instance, as part of a unit in which students are reading about Harlem Renaissance writers, they might gather additional information about artists and photographers or jazz and blues singers and musicians of that period. Students might also research the history of Harlem and gather photos of the time period. They might begin their search with the Web site Harlem 1900–1940 at http://www.siumich.edu/CHICO/Harlem/index.html (Claxton & Cooper, 2000). Students might work in small groups to investigate aspects of the topic. An end product might be a Web site displaying the results of their efforts. The Harlem project could be a joint venture for a history and an English teacher.

With its riches of information and opportunity for collaboration, the Internet lends itself to inquiry projects (Bruce & Bishop, 2002). Inquiry begins with asking questions, and includes investigating solutions, gathering information, discussing discoveries, and reflecting on our new-found knowledge. On the Inquiry Page (http://inquiry.uiuc.edu/), teachers and other professionals work together to create inquiry units. These units can be used as they are or revised. Many of the units are still being created. Visitors to the site are invited to add their expertise.

 CHECKUP

1. What are some of the kinds of lessons offered on the Internet?

Working and Communicating with Students at Other Sites

Through the Internet, students are able to communicate school to school, class to class, or student to student with virtually anyone who has an Internet connection. Global SchoolNet (GSN) (http://www.gsn.org/) is a leader in collaborative Internet learning. GSN maintains an Internet Projects Registry that contains information on more than 700 projects. Projects listed include their own as well as projects under the direction of various other organizations, such as NASA and TERC (a nonprofit organization devoted to improving instruction in science, math, and technology). Projects are varied and span all curriculum and age levels. Projects may involve a contest, putting on a show for hospitalized children, studying air or noise pollution and exchanging data, and sharing rock collections. Technologies used also vary. Some use only e-mail. Others use video CU-SeeMe video conferencing, IRC (Internet Relay Chat), or other technologies to enable students to discuss topics in **real time.** Technology exists for a variety of ways of collaborating, ranging from exchanging e-mail to holding a real-time video conference.

■ **Real time** refers to an activity that occurs as soon as it is initiated rather than at a later time. In a real-time discussion, participants' messages are read as soon as they are sent.

 CHECKUP

1. What are some of the ways students can work with others on the Internet?

Safety in Cyberspace

In addition to providing valuable, worthwhile information, the Internet unfortunately also allows access to information and sites that are inappropriate and even harmful to students. The Internet can also be used to threaten or insult others and interfere with their work and privacy. Because of these factors, it is essential to put safeguards

USING TECHNOLOGY

Teachers in 94 percent of public schools monitor Internet use, and 74 percent of schools have blocking or filtering software. Nearly two thirds of schools also have an honor code relating to Internet use. Virtually all schools have an acceptable-use policy (Cattagni & Wesstat, 2001).

in place. Most schools now have acceptable-use policies and ask students and their parents to sign agreements by which they promise to abide by the school's policies. In addition, students should always be supervised when using the Internet. And some schools have taken the precaution of installing software that blocks objectionable sites. Guidelines for protecting students are available at Global School Network (http://www.gsn.org/web/tutorial/issues/index.htm#begin). A sample acceptable-use policy can be obtained at: ftp://ftp.classroom.net/wentworth/Classroom-Connect/aup-faq.txt.

COMPUTER SOFTWARE

USING TECHNOLOGY

For more information about filtering or blocking devices, see: http://www.neosoft. com/ parental-control/

In addition to providing a portal to the Internet, computers are also widely used to run software. One of the most effective uses of software is as a learning or communication tool. Outstanding general tool software includes

- word processing software, such as Microsoft Word, which allows students to type up and design reports.
- graphic organizer software, such as *Inspiration*, that allows students to create a variety of visual displays of data.
- presentation software, such as PowerPoint, that allows students to prepare a variety of visual or audiovisual aids.
- database and spread-sheet software that allows students to collect, organize, and manipulate data and prepare charts and graphs.

In addition, there are hundreds of pieces of software that allow students to organize and manipulate data in specialized ways or provide simulations or carefully thought-out drill and practice. (The Internet is also a rich source of tools, reference, and drill-and-practice programs.) Up-to-date content texts generally recommend

EXEMPLARY TEACHING

USING TECHNOLOGY

One teacher used a variety of media and technology to help students develop a deeper understanding of the office of the president and some of the men who led the United States during the twentieth century. After watching the Discovery Channel School series *The Modern Presidency*, students in Michael Hutchinson's high school history classes researched one of the presidents who held office during the past century. They used both Internet sites and texts. In many instances, they were able to view film clips and examine primary documents. Students in senior classes used the presentation software PowerPoint to compose reports on the presidents they had studied. They also created a Web page to report their research. The reports were of such high quality that they have been used by other students who are studying the presidency. Presentations can be viewed at: http://www.vcsc.k12.in.us/staff/mhutch/modpres/mainpage.htm.

effective software. In addition, descriptions and reviews of software are available from the following sources.

- Children's Software Revue: Provides reviews of more than 3,000 software programs. Has links to software publishers and related sites.
  http://www.childrenssoftware.com
- Software Reviews by the Northeast Regional Technology in Education Consortium
  http://ra.terc.edu/SoftwareEval/SoftwareEvalHome.cfm

Forms for reviewing software are available at the following sites.

- Children's Software Revue
  http://www.childrenssoftware.com
- PEP Registry of Educational Software Publishers
  http://www.microweb.com/pepsite

 *CHECKUP*

1. What are some ways to use software in a content area class?

USING SOURCES OF PROFESSIONAL DEVELOPMENT FOR TEACHERS

One benefit of using technology is that teachers and students become learners together. Because the teacher is learning the new technology along with the students, the teacher can model how an experienced learner goes about obtaining and applying new skills. It also changes the nature of the teacher–student relationship from one in which the teacher is the dispenser of knowledge to one in which teacher and student are involved in a collaboration. This new relationship is often a self-esteem builder for students. Intrigued by the technology, some students may spend so much time with a topic or one aspect of technology that they learn more about it than anyone else, even the teacher, and so they are in the position of being able to share their exclusive knowledge, sometimes for the first time (Bransford et al., 2001).

The Internet also provides teachers with a range of opportunities for professional development. Each major professional organization has a Web site, and these are excellent sources of information and encouragement. Many professional sites even have sample units and lesson plans, some of which are portrayed in film clips so that teachers can view segments of lessons.

Electronic Discussion Groups for Content Area Teachers

There are a number of electronic discussion groups, known as **listservs,** for professionals. Members of these groups communicate by sending e-mail to teach other; an e-mail sent to the listserv goes to everyone. A good example of a listserv is Readpro. Sponsored by the ERIC Clearinghouse for Reading, English, and Communication,

■ A **listserv** is a program that manages mailing lists by distributing messages that have been posted and adding and deleting members.

it is devoted to the analysis of issues facing reading professionals, with emphasis on practical applications and problem solving. Typical topics include collaborative learning activities, phonics instruction, children's literature, Web resources for the language arts, reading assessment, and conferences and meetings on reading-related subjects. Because it is a popular mailing list, members may receive ten to twenty e-mail messages a day. To subscribe to Readpro, send an e-mail to readpro-subscribe@topica.com. The message can be blank. You will soon receive a confirmation of your request for enrollment in the group, which you will need to respond to in order to activate your subscription. You will receive an acknowledgment via e-mail of your request for enrollment in the list. After replying to the message, you should send a brief introductory message to the group to give other members some sense of your background and experience in the reading and language arts professions. Readpro also has a Web site at: http://www.indiana.edu/~eric_rec/gninf/readpro.html. Lists of electronic discussion groups can be found at the following sites.

- EdWeb E-Mail Discussion Lists and Electronic Journals
  http://www2.h-net.msu.edu/lists/
- Liszt Select
  http://www.liszt.com/
- TileNet
  http://tile.net/search.php?table=&search_text=

Usenet Newsgroups

■ **Usenet** is a system of thousands of newsgroups. Messages sent by members are read with a newsreader. A newsgroup is a topic area. Chatrooms are similar to newsgroups except that messages are exchanged immediately as in a conversation.

Usenet newsgroups, are an electronic bulletin board system, accessible via the Internet, that consists of discussion forums. In this format, messages are left for others to read. They are not delivered as in a listserv. A message might be a question or an answer to a question raised. Some groups are moderated; the message is sent to a moderator for approval before being posted. Users should contact their system operator for instructions. To access a newsgroup, you need a newsreader. Many Internet providers and browsers have built-in newsreaders. Free and subscription newsreaders are available on the Internet. Google (http://groups.google.com/) has an extensive listing of newsgroups, an archive of millions of messages, and easy access to newsgroups. Here are some of the Usenet newsgroups that content area teachers might be interested in (Sprague, 2000).

news: k12.chat.teacher: General discussion between K through 12 teachers.

news: k12.ed.art: Arts and crafts education.

news: k12.ed.business: Business education.

news: k12.ed.comp.literacy: Teaching computer literacy in grades K through 12.

news: k12.ed.life-skills: Life skills education.

news: k12.ed.math: Mathematics education.

news: k12.ed.music: Music and performing arts.

news: k12.ed.science: Science education.

news: k12.ed.soc-studies: Social studies education.

news: k12.ed.special: Educating students with special needs.

news: k12.library: Implementing information technologies in school libraries.

In addition, the National Council of Teachers (http://www.NCTE.org) sponsors several discussion groups. Members are encouraged to start their own groups.

✔ CHECKUP

1. How can the Internet be used for professional development?

USING TRADE BOOKS IN THE CONTENT AREAS

In one U.S. history text, the Great Depression is covered in less than a page. Ireland's Great Famine and its impact on the United States is not covered at all. In a science text, Marie Curie is mentioned in passing. Madame Curie remains a name to be remembered rather than a brilliant, courageous scientist to be admired. One is told of her important contributions, but there is little information on the person. With the information explosion, today's content area texts are more fact-packed than ever. There simply isn't enough room to explore topics in detail or to get a feel for what is was like to be jobless and have family support in the 1930s or to leave one's homeland for the promise of a better life in the United States, only to encounter signs that say, "No Irish Need Apply."

One solution to this problem is to use **trade books.** Trade books can provide the depth of coverage missing in the text. They can also bring ideas and people to life. Having more leeway than textbook writers, the authors of trade books can bring a richness of background, originality of style, and creativity that is often missing in textbooks. They can hook readers with interesting anecdotes and fascinating facts.

Trade books also offer another point of view. In fact, some trade books, such as a set of texts entitled *Perspectives*, are designed to portray a series of multicultural events and topics in U.S. history. In the *Perspectives* series, American history is told from the perspective of people of color, ethnic minorities, poor whites, and women and, as such, provides a fuller description of key events in our history. History varies according to who's doing the telling. Immigration told from the immigrants' point of view will differ from immigration told from the point of view of those who faced the loss of jobs due to the influx of immigrants, which will differ from the point of view of factory owners and railroad builders who used this fresh supply of labor. Of course, the careful historian balances these points of view. From a comprehension point of view, contrasting perspectives leads to greater understanding and retention because it forces students to process information more deeply as they make comparisons and contrasts and attempt to synthesize information that is sometimes conflicting. From a social studies point of view, multiple perspectives bring students face to face with the work of the historian. Students are called upon to reconcile conflicting ac-

■ **Trade books** are books that are written for and sold to the general public and distributed through book stores and libraries.

USING TECHNOLOGY

Making Multicultural Connections through Trade Books http://www.mcps.k12.md .us/curriculum/socialstd MBDBooks_Begin.html Offers many resources for using multicultural books. It provides an extensive list of multicultural books and suggestions for content and technology connections.

counts. This introduces them to historical inquiry so that they "begin to understand and appreciate differences in historical perspectives, recognizing that interpretations are influenced by individual experiences, societal values, and cultural traditions" (National Council for the Social Studies, 1994, p. 22). As Palmer and Stewart (1997) note, "By using a variety of nonfiction trade books, students can explore a broad range of topics or examine a single topic in depth, while synthesizing information and applying critical reading/thinking skills" (p. 631).

In-Depth Concept Development

Trade books can also offer a greater depth of explanation. In textbooks, complex science concepts are often covered in a page or two. For instance, one high school biology text gave symbiosis less than a page of text. Trade books devoted to single concepts can develop them in depth and also explain the concept in a more interesting and understandable fashion. In the *Science Concepts* series, the highly respected science writers Alvin and Virginia Silverstein have written sixty-four-page books, each designed to develop one key concept—for instance, evolution, food chains, photosynthesis, and symbiosis. Woven into the explanation of each concept are interesting examples and little-known facts designed to maintain readers' interest. In the book on symbiosis, for example, notice how the authors entice readers into the text with intriguing questions and an interesting example of symbiotic behavior:

> Imagine a world where hungry sharks and tiny fish can live a peaceful existence together. How about man-eating crocodiles and tiny birds? These animal relationships may be hard to believe, but they actually occur. Some plants even have ants as bodyguards to attack intruders. In nature, there are many strange relationships where different kinds of animals, plants, and other organisms in the five kingdoms of life come together for the benefit of at least one partner.
>
> Animal partnerships are very important to many species because their survival depends on the association. But other partnerships occur because of a coincidental meeting that may be helpful for one or both of the partners. (Silverstein, 1998, p. 5)

USING TECHNOLOGY

HELP Read™ freeware is a program developed by the Hawaii Education Literacy Project (HELP) and distributed freely over the Internet at http://www. dyslexia.com/helpread. htm. This program uses a text-to-speech synthesizer and can read text files, Web pages, e-books, and text in the Windows clipboard.

The authors then explain how the honey guide, a small, delicate bird who likes honey but is unable to take honey from a beehive, finds honey and signals to the ratel, a member of the weasel family, who breaks open the nest and eats the bee grubs. The honey guide then eats the honey. The authors also explain how the honey guide is involved in two other relationships, one in which it uses bacteria in its intestine to help it digest food and the other in which it tricks other birds into hatching their eggs and rearing their young.

After creating reader interest and giving concrete examples of three kinds of symbiosis, the authors explain what symbiosis is and define the three major types. At this point, students are able to build the concept on the concrete example that the authors provided so that their understanding goes from the concrete to the abstract. With the help of many examples and interesting information, the rest of the text expands on the concept of symbiosis. Because of space limitations, textbook authors are unable to present such a carefully developed concept.

Trade books can even make a complex, abstract topic such as the periodic table both interesting and comprehensible. *The Elements: Gold* (Angliss, 2000), along with explaining how gold is mined and some of the many interesting ways in which gold is used, also discusses its special properties, including its location on the periodic table. The author also supplies an informative, easy-to-understand explanation of the periodic table. Other books in the *Elements* series investigate calcium, hydrogen, and magnesium.

Trade books that place concepts within the framework of a story have the power to make concepts both more understandable and more memorable. Based on carefully designed studies of how students learn content, Nuthall (1999) concluded that

> Our studies suggest that narratives provide powerful structures for the organization and storage of curriculum content in memory. Stories often contain a rich variety of supplementary information and connect to personal experiences, as well as being integrated and held together by a familiar structure. (p. 337)

Humanizing Learning

One of the goals of content area instruction is to lead students to think like a scientist, a mathematician, or an historian. Reading biographies of scientists can provide students with insight into the methods that scientists use. They also come to understand the social and historical context in which the discoveries were being made and the obstacles the discoverers had to overcome. For instance, *Fish Watching with Eugenie Clark* (Ross, 2000) is a fascinating account of the obstacles that Eugenie Clark overcame on her way to fame and accomplishment as one of the nation's best-known scientists. Readers are also introduced to methods of scientific experimentation and information about sharks and other fascinating sea creatures.

> Reading about the different experiments of scientists and their individual struggles with revolutionary ideas provides students with insights into the tentative nature of discovery. . . . Autobiographies, biographies, and fictionalized histories of scientists can serve to draw students into the personal world of the scientist and allow them to vicariously share the experience of exploration. (VanSledright & Frankes, 2000, p. 119)

An excellent source of biographies is *Profiles in American History. Profiles* is an eight-volume series that provides an overview of key eras and events in American history and also portrays in-depth major historical figures. Each chapter focuses on one event, places it in historical context, and profiles two to seven figures who were major participants in the event. The series gives a human face to history.

Updated Information

Trade books can also offer information that is more up-to-date. Because of their expense, textbooks are often used for five or even ten years before being replaced. Trade books can be used to update textbooks. Students who use trade books have the opportunity to learn more content than students restricted to a text (Guzzetti, Kowalinski, & McGowan, 1992).

Motivation

Trade books can also be motivating. They can be used to launch a unit of study. As one social studies teacher comments, "Literature is a way to entice and engage students initially so they are motivated to discover the substance and the facts" (Lindquist, 1995, p. 89). Tarry Lindquist initiates a study of colonial life and the American Revolution by having her students read Scott O'Dell's (1980) *Sarah Bishop:*

> I like this book because both boys and girls find it engaging. It does a good job of bringing out multiple perspectives about the Revolutionary War and provides a setting for the more historically driven information the students will need to understand the Constitution and the Bill of Rights. (Lindquist, 1995, p. 88)

STRUGGLING READERS
See Appendix A for titles of easy-to-read trade books in a variety of content areas.

An excellent series for expanding on modern U.S. history is *A Cultural History of the United States: Through the Decades.* Each text tackles a decade in the twentieth century. Chapters are theme-based. The text devoted to the 1990s provides an overview of the 1980s and highlights key topics from the 1990s, such as changes in Washington, the end of the Cold War, violence in America, trends in family and education, gender and race conflict, pop culture, and technology, medicine, and the environment. An epilogue makes predictions for life in the twenty-first century.

Trade Books Can Be Easier to Understand

Written on a variety of levels, trade books can also be easier than textbooks. Recently, when I was taking a course in brain development, an area in which I had limited background and so found the text tough going, I read a children's book on the subject. The book provided me with an overview of the subject, some basic vocabulary, and key concepts so that I was better able to cope with the text. I have also used children's books to learn about the Internet, DNA, and other technical topics. I discovered that I was not the only adult relying on children's books for information, especially in unfamiliar areas. Science writer Eugene Garfield refers to children's books when he encounters concepts or processes that are difficult to understand.

Trade Books Can Be More Focused

Today's social studies textbooks attempt to convey not only the political history of the time but also the social and cultural history. As a result, students may lose sight of the essential events and movements. *The Drama of American History* series focuses on the political and institutional aspects so that students have a better sense of what happened and why. As the authors state, "The difference between this series and many standard texts lies in what has been left out. We are convinced that students will better remember the important themes if they are not buried under a heap of names, dates, and places" (Collier & Collier, 1998, p. 7). The texts are especially effective in establishing why events took place and what their impact was. This should make the information both more understandable and more memorable.

Trade Books Can Evoke Emotions

Using literature adds another dimension to the study of content area concepts. Most content areas involve the learning of information and concepts from a cognitive-logical point of view. Literature offers the possibility of complementing logic with emotion. Through literature, students can experience the feeling side of learning. Fred and Patricia McKissack, a husband-and-wife writing team, have created dozens of highly regarded books for young people in order to put some feeling into the events of the past. Fred McKissack (2001b) explains,

> One of the reasons we write for children is to introduce them to African and African-American history and historical figures and to get them to internalize the information not just academically, but also emotionally. We want them to feel the tremendous amount of hurt and sadness that racism and discrimination cause all people, regardless of race.

Trade Books Can Make Concepts More Vivid

The writing in carefully chosen trade books is more vivid and can foster a deeper, more complete understanding. Helen Roney Sattler's (1995) figurative language creates a memorable picture of plate tectonics:

> The understanding of plate tectonics has helped scientists solve many of Earth's puzzling mysteries. Continents and oceans ride on the plates like passengers on a raft and move about Earth's surface. This explains how the Antarctic region could have had a warm climate at one time. It also explains why evidence of past glaciers is found in the Sahara Desert and why a coral reef lies under the topsoil of my backyard, five hundred miles from the nearest seashore. (p. 10)

DK (Dorling Kindersley) books such as Stephen Biesty's (1998) *Incredible Body* provide highly visual descriptions of the body's key systems. In *Stinkbugs, Stick Insects, and Stag Beetles and 18 More of the Strangest Insects on Earth* (Kneidel, 2001), the author uses the strange appearance and antics of twenty-one arthropods to con-

vey key concepts about insects. *Grolier's New Book of Popular Science Series* (Grolier Educational, 2000) consists of six separate volumes that emphasize the basic information needed for scientific literacy. Although advertised for students in grades 5 and up, the books could provide a useful reference for older students who may have missed or forgotten key concepts.

✔ *CHECKUP*

1. What are some of the ways in which trade books can be used in content area classes?

Sources of Outstanding Trade Books

An excellent source of information about trade books that can be used in the social studies is the annotated bibliography *Notable Social Studies Trade Books for Young People*, published each spring in the National Council for Social Studies journal, *Social Education*. Annotated listings for current and some past years are also available at http://www.ncss.org/resources/notable/. Books selected for this bibliography were published in the previous year and written primarily for students in grades pre-K through 8.

The National Science Teachers Association (NSTA) publishes an annotated list of high-quality science books in the March issue of *Science and Children*. Books selected for this bibliography were published in the previous year and written primarily for students in grades pre-K through 8. Lists for the past five years are available at http://www.nsta.org/pubs/sc/ostb00.asp or by fax at (888) 400-NSTA. The NSTA also has an extensive list of books reviewed in its periodicals.

Periodicals and trade books provide updated information and information in-depth.

PERIODICALS

Periodicals enable students to read about the latest space probe, new medicines, new inventions, national elections, and major events and issues in the nation and the world. They offer an excellent means for updating and complementing textbook content. Periodicals created to foster learning in the content areas are cited in Tables 12.1, 12.2, and 12.3.

In addition, there are a number of online magazines of note.

- *Scholastic:* Provides stories from current and past issues Scholastic News 3, 4, and 5–6, a number of interesting activities, and links to other sites. http://www.scholastic.com/scholasticnews/
- *Weekly Reader:* Provides a number of articles from their elementary and secondary periodicals including updates and breaking news. http://www.weeklyreader.com/teennewsweek/index.html

USING TECHNOLOGY

Center for the Study of Books in Spanish for Children and Adolescents http://www.csusm.edu/cgi-bin/portal/www.book.book_home?lang=SPFeatures a recommended list of more than 3,000 books in Spanish. Books are listed by age, grade level, and country. Also includes new additions.

TABLE 12.1

SOCIAL STUDIES PERIODICALS

Periodical	Appropriate Grades	Content
Cobblestone	4–9	American history.
Current Events	6–10	Current events.
Junior Scholastic	6–8	Current events and general social studies topics.
Know Your World Extra	6+	Current events and general interest. For students in grades 6 or above reading on a 2.0–3.9 level.
Living History on Line http://www.livinghistoryonline.com/	9–12	History and historical reenactments.
News for You	High school & adult.	News and general interest. Easy to read. At least one article on a 2–3 level.
New York Times Upfront	7–12	Current events, trends, and entertainment.
Scholastic News	1–6	Current events and general interest.
Scholastic News en Español	1–3	Translation of early levels of *Scholastic News*.
Teen Newsweek	6–10	Current events and general interest.
Time for Kids	4–6	Current events and general interest.
Weekly Reader	K–6	Current events and general interest.
Zillions Online at http://www.zillions.org/	3–6	Consumer issues.

SUPPLEMENTARY READING MATERIALS

A number of sites contain magazine articles and other materials related to topics covered in the content areas. These include the following sources.

- EBSCOlearn Science Series: Includes articles from *Scientific American* (high school and advanced placement), *National Wildlife* (grades 7 through 12), and *Ranger Rick* (grades 4 through 7). Articles are accompanied by comprehension questions and lexile readability scores so students can be matched with material on the appropriate level.

- EBSCOlearn Social Studies Series: Includes articles form *U.S. News and World Report* (grades 7 through 12) and *Biography* (grades 7 through 12). Articles are accompanied by comprehension questions and lexile readability scores so students can be matched with material on the appropriate level.

TABLE 12.2

SCIENCE PERIODICALS

Periodical	Appropriate Grades	Content
Current Health 1	4–7	Health.
Current Health 2	7–12	Health.
Current Science	6–10	Various science.
Dragonfly http://miavx1.acs.muohio.edu/ ~dragonfly/	1–6	Features a number of intriguing activities.
National Geographic World	3–6	General interest with an emphasis on ecology, animals, and nature.
Odyssey	3–8	Science with an emphasis on astronomy and space.
Owl	4–7	General science with an emphasis on nature.
Ranger Rick	1–6	Wildlife and ecology.
Scholastic Math	7–9	Math.
ScienceDynaMath	3–6	Science and math.
Science Week http://www.scienceweek.com/	10–12	Advanced general science. Free archive of reports from back issues.
Science World	7–10	General science.
Super Science	3–6	Emphasis on high-interest science topics.

TABLE 12.3

LITERATURE/READING/ FINE ARTS PERIODICALS

Periodical	Appropriate Grades	Content
Action	7–12	Literature, current biographies. High-interest features. Easy to read: 3–5 reading level.
Literary Cavalcade	9–12	Classic and current literature and writing workshop.
Read	6–10	Literature selections, current issues, writing.
Scholastic Art	7–12	Art techniques, biography, and student art.
Scholastic Scope	6–8	Fiction, nonfiction, and poetry. Easy to read.
Stone Soup	3–8	Stories, poems, and book reviews by and for young writers.
Storyworks	3–5	Variety of literary selections.

 CHECKUP

1. What role might periodicals and supplementary materials play in content area classrooms?

SUMMARY

With virtually all schools having an Internet connection, today's teachers and students have access to rich resources. However, these rich resources demand a higher level of literacy. Today's students must be better able to search for, select, assess, and synthesize large amounts of information and be able to combine the visual and the verbal in communication. To search the vast amounts of available information effectively, students must carefully formulate search questions and strategy.

Both general and specific Web sites feature useful information and activities for a wide variety of topics. In addition to getting information from Web sites, students can also obtain information from experts. Other educational uses of the Internet include virtual field trips and working and communicating with students at other sites. Also available are content lessons specifically designed to make use of Internet sites.

Unfortunately, the Internet also allows access to information and sites that could be harmful to students. Safeguards need to be put into place.

Computers are also widely used to run software. One of the most effective uses of software is as a learning or communication tool. Outstanding general tools include word processing software, graphic organizer creators, presentation software, Web site creation software, and database software.

The Internet provides teachers with a range of opportunities for professional development. Each major professional organization has a Web site. Many professional sites even have sample units and lesson plans. In addition, there are a number of electronic discussion groups for professionals.

Trade books have a number of potential uses in the content areas. They offer another point of view, offer a greater depth of development, humanize learning, provide updated information, and can also be motivating. In addition, trade books can be easier to understand, be more focused, add an emotional component to learning, and make science and other content areas more vivid.

Periodicals also offer an excellent means for updating and complementing textbook content. Online magazines offer the most current news and information. Databases of thousands of periodical articles are also available.

Reflection

Return to the Anticipation Guide at the beginning of this chapter. Respond once again to the items. Did your responses change? If so, how and why? What role might technology, trade books, and periodicals play in the teaching and learning of content area concepts? What new literacy skills must students learn in order to take full advantage of technology to help them learn content area material?

EXTENSION AND APPLICATION

1. Explore some of the Internet sites mentioned in this chapter. Maintain a file of useful Internet sites.
2. Start a database of titles of trade books that might be useful in the teaching of your content area.
3. Check out the site maintained by the professional organization for your subject matter area. What kinds of resources are available? How might you use these?

EVALUATING PROGRESS IN THE CONTENT AREAS

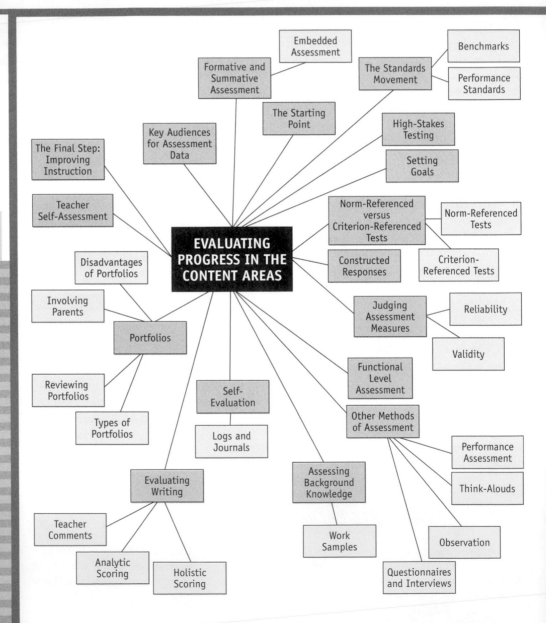

Embedded Assessment

Formative and Summative Assessment

The Standards Movement

Benchmarks

Performance Standards

The Starting Point

High-Stakes Testing

Setting Goals

Key Audiences for Assessment Data

The Final Step: Improving Instruction

Teacher Self-Assessment

Norm-Referenced versus Criterion-Referenced Tests

Norm-Referenced Tests

Disadvantages of Portfolios

Constructed Responses

Criterion-Referenced Tests

Involving Parents

EVALUATING PROGRESS IN THE CONTENT AREAS

Portfolios

Judging Assessment Measures

Reliability

Validity

Reviewing Portfolios

Self-Evaluation

Functional Level Assessment

Types of Portfolios

Logs and Journals

Other Methods of Assessment

Performance Assessment

Evaluating Writing

Assessing Background Knowledge

Think-Alouds

Teacher Comments

Observation

Analytic Scoring

Holistic Scoring

Work Samples

Questionnaires and Interviews

For each of the following statements related to the chapter you are about to read, put a check under "Agree" or "Disagree" to show how you feel. Discuss your responses with classmates before you read the chapter.

		Agree	Disagree
1	Nationwide tests are essential for the assessment of academic performance.	____	____
2	High standards lead to high achievement.	____	____
3	Teaching to tests is educationally unsound.	____	____
4	For important educational decisions, such as passing and graduation, teachers should rely on at least three sources of information.	____	____
5	Informal assessment yields more information about a student's progress and achievement than formal tests do.	____	____

USING WHAT YOU KNOW

Evaluation is an integral part of content area learning. Evaluation is a judgment by teachers, students, parents, administrators, and the public as to whether instructional goals or standards have been met. It provides teachers with data so they can judge how well programs and individual students are doing and make changes as necessary. Self-evaluation gives students guidance so they can become more involved in their learning.

What experiences have you had with evaluation? How was your school work assessed in the content areas? Which assessments seemed to be the most effective? What role did assessment play in your learning?

KEY AUDIENCES FOR ASSESSMENT DATA

The basic purpose of assessment is to provide feedback. Feedback is an essential component for learning. Students need feedback to see whether they are on the right track and to help clarify misunderstood information or procedures. Teachers need feedback so they can implement instruction based on students' current level of understanding. School boards and administrators need feedback to see how well programs are working. The public needs feedback to see how well its schools are doing.

FORMATIVE AND SUMMATIVE ASSESSMENT

■ **Assessment** is the process of gathering data about an area of learning through tests, observations, work samples, or other means.

■ **Formative assessment** is ongoing with the results of the assessment being used to make needed improvements.

■ **Summative assessment** is the final measure of progress towards meeting a goal.

Assessment can be thought of as being formative and summative. **Formative assessment** is ongoing assessment which can be used to plan instruction and offer additional instruction if needed. Formative assessment is often informal and may take the form of observation, discussions, quizzes, or examination of lab reports and other assignments. Both individuals and groups are assessed. Frequent formative assessment fosters learning and transfer and teaches students the value of review (Bransford et al., 2001).

Summative assessment occurs at the conclusion of a semester or unit of study. Its main purpose is to evaluate whether goals were reached. Coming at the end of a period of instruction, summative instruction cannot be used to improve ongoing instruction but might be used to rethink or replan future instruction. Summative evaluation can also be used by administrators and school boards to evaluate achievement over long periods of time. It can be used on a state and national level to assess the achievement of the nation's school children and to compare one state with another or even one nation with another.

Embedded Assessment

■ **Embedded assessment** is a type of formative assessment in which assessment is a part of instruction.

Embedded assessment, which is a type of formative assessment, is built into instruction. For example, after being introduced to a concept, students discuss it. The teacher observes how well students grasp concepts and notes areas that need clarifying or expansion. As students are conducting lab experiments, the teacher observes how well they plan and implement their experiments and how familiar they are with lab procedures. Based on observations, the teacher provides on-the-spot help. After looking at rough drafts for an essay, the teacher notes common needs for the whole class and individuals and provides needed instruction. Learning logs, journals, exit slips, and portfolios—the latter two are discussed later in the chapter—also offer opportunities for ongoing assessment.

✔ *CHECKUP*

1. What is formative, summative, and embedded assessment?
2. What are some examples of formative and summative assessment?

THE STARTING POINT

Evaluation starts with a set of goals. You cannot tell whether students are performing satisfactorily if you aren't quite sure what it is that you want them to learn. Calkins, Montgomery, and Santman (1998) recall observing a language arts teacher whose students were conducting an author study. The students were engaged in a number of interactive activities, but something seemed to be missing. The activities seemed to lack a focus. The teacher was asked, "Why did you choose this author to study?" At first, the teacher seemed to be confused by the question. She seemed to feel that an author study was inherently beneficial. "It was something to do. And we had the books," the teacher responded. Further questioning revealed that she had no plans for assessing the effectiveness of the author study. Except for wanting to see her students engage in a variety of reading and writing activities, the teacher had no clear goal. Lacking a goal, she had no way to assess the effectiveness of the author study. Goals need to be translated into objectives that are clear and observable. Some possible goals in this case could have been to study an author's development, to compare an author's earlier works with later works, to analyze an author's style, or to increase reading fluency by reading several books by the author.

Once goals have been established, you then need to decide how you will tell whether students have reached that goal. For instance, the goal that students will conduct an author study might be translated into the more specific objective that students will compare two of Mark Twain's books and create a diagram showing similarities and differences in theme, style, plot, and characterization. It's important, of course, that students have a role in setting goals or are, at least, aware of them and how they will be assessed.

> ■ **Evaluation** is the process of using the results of tests, observations, work samples, or other devices to judge the effectiveness of a program or students' learning.

THE STANDARDS MOVEMENT

Goals for all major content areas now exist in lists of **standards.** Standards are statements of what students should know or be able to do. They are listings of the content and skills students are expected to acquire. Sometimes referred to as *objectives*, content standards form a foundation for a subject's curriculum. Content standards for grades 9 through 12 in physical science include the following:

> ■ **Standards** are statements of what students should know and be able to do.

All students should develop an understanding of

- Structure of atoms
- Structure and properties of matter
- Chemical reactions
- Motions and forces
- Conservation of energy and increase in disorder
- Interactions of energy and matter. (National Research Council, 1996, p. 176)

A related content standard sets forth a set of inquiry skills that students should acquire:

- Design and conduct scientific investigations.
- Use technology and mathematics to improve investigations and communications. (National Research Council, 1996, p. 175)

Benchmarks

■ **Benchmarks** are more specific statements of general standards. They translate broad statements of standards into specific objectives.

Broad content standards are typically translated into more specific objectives, which are sometimes known as **benchmarks.** Benchmarks articulate standards. For instance, the health standard "All students will practice health- enhancing behaviors and reduce health risks" is translated into more specific benchmarks, such as "Demonstrate strategies to positively manage stress" and "Demonstrate ways to avoid threatening situations and reduce conflict" (Michigan Department of Education, 1998, p. 5).

Performance Standards

■ **Performance standards** state how much students should know or to what degree they should be able to perform a task.

In addition to content standards, there are **performance standards.** Whereas content standards tell what a student should know or be able to do, performance standards tell "how good is good enough" (National Center on Education and the Economy & The University of Pittsburgh, 1997). A content standard might state that students will read a variety of both fiction and nonfiction books. A performance standard would tell how many books they are to read and how they will demonstrate that they have read the book, as in this excerpt from the National Standards (National Center on Education and the Economy & The University of Pittsburgh, 1997):

> The student reads at least twenty-five books or book equivalents each year. The quality and complexity of the materials to be read are illustrated in the sample reading list. The materials should include traditional and contemporary literature (both fiction and non-fiction) as well as magazines, newspapers, textbooks, and online materials. Such reading should represent a diverse collection of materials from at least five different writers.
>
> Examples of activities through which students might produce evidence of reading twenty-five books include:
> • Maintain an annotated list of works read.
> • Generate a reading log or journal.
> • Participate in formal and informal book talks. (p. 22)

Performance standards often incorporate rubrics or are accompanied by them so that student performance can be more effectively assessed.

In addition to standards recommended by national organizations, states and local school districts have issued standards or curriculum frameworks. National standards are available for the professional organization that teachers in your discipline have formed. (All states are required to have standards in math and reading and will be required to have standards in science by the 2005–2006 school year.) Because some disciplines have more than one set of standards or have circulated standards that have been judged to be unsatisfactory, the Mid-continent Research for Education and Learning has collated and summarized standards for each discipline. These are available in book form (Kendall & Marzano, 2000) and on the Web (http://www.mcrel. org/standards/index.asp). State standards are available at state departments of education. Ultimately, these national and state standards have to be translated, adapted, and revised so that they fit the needs of your students.

HIGH-STAKES TESTING

As its name suggests, the outcome of a **high-stakes test** determines the answer to an important question. The question might be whether the student passes or fails, is placed in a special program, or is awarded a diploma. In a position paper, the International Reading Association (IRA) announced its opposition to high-stakes testing. The IRA is not opposed to assessment. It is opposed to making critical decisions based on a single test. In addition, because of their importance in students', teachers', and administrators' lives, high-stakes tests have had an undue influence on what is taught in the schools. As the Board of Directors of the International Reading Association (1999) commented, "Our central concern is that testing has become a means of controlling instruction as opposed to a way of gathering information to help students become better readers" (p. 257).

In other words, high-stakes tests have in some instances become the tail that wags the dog. Instead of being used to assess how well students are doing and providing information for program improvement, high-stakes tests dictate curriculum. Instead of teaching what their community has judged to be important, educators teach what is tested. This has the impact of narrowing the curriculum. If reading, writing, and math are emphasized on a high-stakes test, then there is a temptation to drop art and music and even instruction in the content areas in the elementary school in order to spend more time teaching to the test. Ironically, because content area material is challenging, fostering reading and writing in the content areas extends students' abilities. One unfortunate effect of neglecting content area instruction in the lower grades is that students will be less prepared for subject matter instruction in the upper grades.

Despite the controversy, high-stakes testing is intensifying. According to recently passed legislation, all public school students in grades 3 through 8 will be tested in math and reading beginning in the 2005–2006 school year (U.S. Department of Education, 2002). Although the testing is nationwide, each state will be allowed to choose the tests it wishes to use. Schools, especially those who have large numbers of underperforming students, are expected to show improvement and will be penalized if they fail to do so.

In addition, tests have become more inclusive. Federal legislation requires that states adopt challenging content and performance standards in math and reading and, by the 2005–2006 school year, in science and develop or adopt assessment measures aligned with those standards (U.S. Department of Education, 2002). States are also required to assess all students, including special education and ELL students. ELL students are to be tested in reading using tests writ-

■ A **high-stakes test** is one in which the results are used to make important decisions such as passing students, graduating students, or rating a school.

*H*igh-stakes tests provide just one source of information about students' performance.

ten in English after students have had three consecutive years of education in the United States (excluding Puerto Rico). However, students may also be tested in their primary language for a period of five years.

Insofar as possible, all students are required to take the same tests. However, there can be some modifications and adaptations. Some special education students might take an easier form of the test or be given an alternative assessment. In content areas, ELL students are to be assessed in the language and form most likely to yield the most valid and reliable results. If the state has content and performance standards in academic subjects, then students are to be assessed in those areas. This means that many students previously excluded from tests will be assessed. It also means that more students will be provided with challenging academic subject matter because virtually all students will be tested in those areas.

CHECKUP

1. What are standards and high-stakes assessment?
2. What impact do they have on assessment?

SETTING GOALS

Assessment is conducted in terms of the goals that you set. National, state, and local standards will have an impact on your goals, as will assessments used to measure students' progress. However, your goals should also reflect the basic principles of learning presented in Chapter 1. Students need an in-depth understanding of key concepts. A basic goal of learning is that students should be able to transfer knowledge and skill to other topics in the domain, to other domains, and to the world outside school. Before knowledge or skills can be transferred, they must be mastered. Information that is thoroughly understood is far more likely to be transferred than information that has simply been memorized or skimmed. Focus on broad themes and seeing how facts are interrelated fosters the necessary understanding. If your goals include a depth of knowledge and understanding, your assessment should reflect those goals. The assessment devices that you use need to reveal how well students can integrate or apply key concepts. Questions that require students to state the causes of the Great Depression should be complemented by items that require the student to apply such concepts as supply and demand, business cycles, and the role of government in a market economy to today's world. In other words, if you teach for understanding, you need to assess to see how well students have achieved understanding. Not surprisingly, students tend to focus on the kinds of skills and knowledge that are being assessed.

A wide variety of measures is available to assess whether goals have been met, whether programs are effective, or how well students do when compared with national or international samples of students. Widely used assessment measures include norm- and criterion-referenced tests, book tests, teacher-created tests and quizzes, observation, rubrics, think-alouds, anecdotal records, questionnaires and interviews, and portfolios.

1. What are some factors that should be considered when setting goals?

NORM-REFERENCED VERSUS CRITERION-REFERENCED TESTS

Norm-Referenced Tests

Tests are either norm-referenced or criterion- or standards-referenced. In a **norm-referenced test,** students are compared with a representative sample of others who are the same age or in the same grade. The scores indicate whether students did as well as the average, better than the average, or below the average. The norm group typically includes students from all sections of the country, from urban and nonurban areas, and from a variety of racial or ethnic and socioeconomic groups and is chosen to be representative of the nation's total school population.

■ With **norm-referenced tests,** students are compared with a representative sample of students who are the same age or are in the same grade.

■ Norm-Referenced Reporting

Norm-referenced scores offer a variety of comparisons.

- *Raw score.* A **raw score** represents the total number of correct answers. It has no meaning until it is changed into a percentile rank or other score. However, it is important to check the raw score to see how many possible questions there were and how many the student got correct. If the student got all or almost all the answers correct, the test did not have enough ceiling room. The student may have done even better if the test had contained additional items at higher levels. If the student answered only a few items correctly, the test did not have an adequate floor and may simply have been too difficult for the student. If the test has a multiple choice format, the student may have a chance score. A chance score is one that can be achieved strictly by guessing. For instance, if the test has four answer options, the test taker has a one-in-four chance of getting an answer correct through sheer guessing. If the student did not get more than one out of four items correct out of those that were attempted, the score can be attributed to chance and is invalid.

■ A **raw score** is the number of correct answers or points earned on a test.

- *Percentile rank.* A **percentile rank** tells where a student's raw score falls on a scale of 1 to 99. A score at the first percentile means that the student did better than 1 percent of those who took the test. A score at the fiftieth percentile indicates that the student did better than half of those who took the test and is an average score. A top score is the ninety-ninth percentile. Most norm-referenced test results are now reported in percentiles; however, the ranks are not equal units and should not be added, subtracted, divided, or used for subtest comparison. As you can see by looking at the normal curve in Figure 13.1, percentile ranks in the middle are closer together than they are at ends of the curve. This means that getting one or two more answers correct will move an average percentile score more than it will move a very low or very high score. Getting two more an-

■ The **percentile rank** is the point on a scale of 1 to 99 that shows what percentage of students obtained an equal or lower score. A percentile rank of 75 means that 75 percent of those who took the test received an equal or lower score.

FIGURE 13.1

Normal Curve and Comparison of Norm-Referenced Scores

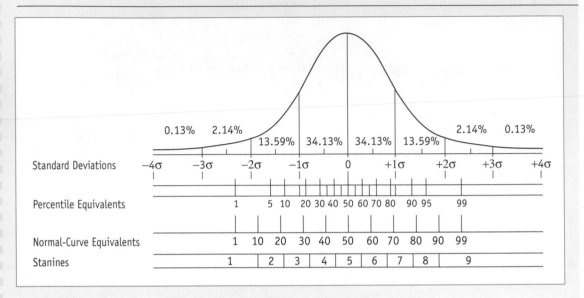

swers correct might move a student from the fiftieth to fifty-fifth percentile but move a student only from the ninety-fifth to the ninety-sixth percentile. Percentiles should not be confused with percentages. One mother complained that her son had done poorly because he had scored only in the eightieth percentile. She believed that he had gotten 20 percent of the answers wrong. Actually, he had done better than 80 percent of the norm group who had taken the test.

■ A **grade equivalent score** indicates the score that the average student at that grade level achieved. Grade equivalent scores have been sanctioned by the International Reading Association and are relatively valid when pupils are tested on their instructional level and when extrapolations are limited to a year or two beyond the target grade level.

■ A **normal curve equivalent** is the rank on a scale of 1 through 99 that a score is equal to.

- *Grade equivalent score.* The **grade equivalent score** characterizes a student's performance as being equivalent to that of other students in a particular grade. A grade equivalent score of 8.2 indicates that the student correctly answered the same number of items as the average eighth-grader in the second month of that grade. Note that the grade equivalent score does not tell on what level the student is operating; that is, a score of 8.2 on a reading test does not mean that a student is reading on an eighth-grade level. Grade equivalent scores are more meaningful when the test students have taken is at the right level and when the score is not more than a year above or a year below average. Grade equivalent scores are also more meaningful at the lower grades. It takes quite a bit of reading ability to move from a 3.2 to a 4.2. However, scores tend to flatten out as students move up through the grades. It doesn't take as much reading ability to move from a 9.2 to a 10.2. Because grade equivalent scores are misleading and easily misunderstood, they should be used with great care or not at all.

- *Normal curve equivalents.* **Normal curve equivalents** (NCEs) rank students on a scale of 1 through 99. The main difference between NCEs and percentile ranks is that NCEs represent equal units and so can be added and subtracted and used for comparing performance on subtests.

- *Stanine.* **Stanine** is a combination of the words *standard* and *nine.* The stanines 4, 5, and 6 are average points, with 1, 2, and 3 being below average, and 7, 8, and 9 above average. Stanines are useful when making comparisons among the subtests of a norm-referenced test.

■ A **stanine** is a point on a nine-point scale, with 5 being average.

- *Scaled scores.* **Scaled scores** are a continuous ranking of scores from the lowest levels of a series of norm-referenced tests—first grade, for example—through the highest levels—high school. They start at 000 and end at 999. They are useful for tracking long-term reading development through the grades. They are also useful for out-of-level testing. For instance, a ninth-grade student reading on a fourth-grade level should be given a fourth-grade test. However, a percentile score would be meaningless, as would a stanine or NCE because they would compare the ninth-grader with fourth-graders. However, the scaled score could be checked against ninth-grade norms and yield a valid score, even though the student had taken a fourth-grade test.

■ A **scaled score** is a continuous ranking from 000 to 999 of a series of norm-referenced tests from the easiest- to the highest-level test.

Scores reported on norm-referenced tests are not particularly helpful to teachers. Of what value is it to know that a student scored in the thirtieth percentile or fourth stanine? It indicates that the student is performing below average when compared to the norm group but does not yield any information about what the student knows or is having difficulty with.

For additional information about tests, especially norm-referenced instruments, see the *Fifteenth Mental Measurements Yearbook* (Plake, Impara & Spies, 2003), which contains reviews of recent tests and suggestions for choosing and using tests.

Norm-referenced tests are available for virtually all subject matter areas. However, norm-referenced tests are most frequently given in reading and math. In checking norm-referenced scores in your subject matter area, take a look at the students' reading scores. These will give you an estimate of the students' reading ability. However, a low score on the reading test may indicate that the results of the subject matter test are invalid. Unless students are reading close to grade level, they may have difficulty reading the subject matter portion of the test. A low score may reflect below-level reading ability rather than a lack of knowledge of science or history.

Norm-referenced tests are not particularly useful for gauging achievement. Their purpose is to sort students: to show who is average, who is above average, and who is below average. Test items are selected on the basis of the ability to discriminate. Thus, a question that assesses a key concept in a subject matter area might not be included because most students would be able to answer it and so it would have a low discriminatory value (Popham, 2000). A well-constructed criterion-referenced test will emphasize items that assess key concepts.

Two major types of norm-referenced tests are survey and diagnostic. Survey tests may cover two or three areas. Reading survey tests, for instance, typically assess general comprehension and vocabulary. Diagnostic tests assess more areas and in greater depth. One of the best-known diagnostic tests, the Stanford Diagnostic, for instance, assesses decoding, comprehension, vocabulary, and scanning. It also contains a greater number of easier items, so that it does a better job of assessing below-level readers. Diagnostic tests can indicate general areas of strength and weakness and may be used as a screening device to identify students who have special needs. Complete survey batteries contain tests in reading, language arts, math, social studies, and science. However, they may attempt to assess each area with just forty or so items. This is not enough to provide an in-depth look at any area but might be used as a screening device to identify students who need additional assessment because their scores are very low. It can also be used to identify students who might benefit from added challenge because their scores are very high. The results can also identify areas of strength and weakness. Comparatively speaking, for instance, students might not be doing as well in science as they are in social studies. Or a careful analysis of students' responses might indicate weaknesses in specific areas, such as difficulty with spelling items in the language arts area or difficulty interpreting maps in the social studies area.

Norm-referenced tests may also be used to measure overall gains. But because they typically use a multiple choice format, guessing becomes a factor and skills and knowledge are not tested in the way in which they are used in and out of the classroom. In addition, group norm-referenced tests tend to be general in content and may have just a few items for key areas or skills, so they will probably not provide an adequate assessment of your subject.

Despite their disadvantages, norm-referenced tests are used extensively. For instance, in 61 percent of schools, norm-referenced tests are the primary tool for determining placement in secondary programs for below-level readers (Barry, 1997). In 58 percent of schools, norm-referenced tests are also used to determine progress made in these programs. Often, another form of the test used to place students is used as a posttest to measure gains. However, there is an encouraging trend toward using teacher observation, portfolios, and teacher-made tests to place students in intervention programs and to gauge progress. In pre-1950 programs, 90 percent of the schools relied on norm-referenced tests to place students, as opposed to today's figure of 61 percent.

CHECKUP

1. What are norm-referenced tests?
2. How are they used in content area programs?
3. In what ways are scores on norm-referenced tests reported?

Criterion-Referenced Tests

■ In a **criterion-referenced test**, the student's performance is compared to a criterion or standard.

For content area teachers, criterion-referenced measures are more helpful than norm-referenced ones. In contrast to a norm-referenced test, a **criterion-referenced test** compares students' performance with some standard, or criterion. For instance, the criterion on a comprehension or a science test might be answering 80 percent of the questions correctly. The informal reading inventory is criterion referenced; a student must have at least 95-percent word recognition and 75-percent comprehension to be on the instructional level. Tests that accompany content area texts are generally criterion referenced. Many have a passing score, which is the criterion. The quizzes and tests that you construct for your students are also criterion referenced; you set the criterion for a passing score.

Performance on criterion-referenced tests is not reported in the same way as it is on norm-referenced tests. In norm-referenced reporting, a student's performance is compared with that of other students. In criterion-referenced reporting, a student's performance might be described in terms of a standard or expected performance or in terms of the student's goals. One of the best known criterion-referenced tests in the content areas is the Advanced Placement Test. Students must meet certain criteria or get a certain number of items correct in order to pass the test. Standards-based tests are also criterion referenced; the criterion is meeting a certain standard. Many of the state tests are criterion referenced; students must achieve a certain score in order to pass. One problem with criterion-referenced tests is that the criterion may be set arbitrarily or unrealistically. For instance, someone might set a criterion for reading comprehension of material at 90 percent. While a high level of comprehension is desirable, it may be unrealistic. Before setting a criterion, the test constructors should find out how students actually perform on the measure. In some states, for instance, the criterion was set so high that more than half the students failed to meet the standard. In Connecticut, only 38 percent of the students achieve a proficient score on the science test. This suggests that the standard has been set at an unrealistic level. The same is probably true of the NAEP tests since only about a third of students reach proficiency on most of them.

Although no one would argue with setting challenging standards, setting standards that are unrealistically high is demoralizing to both students and educators and creates a false impression among the general public that schools are not doing very well. Standards also create a pass/fail mentality. Scores are reported in terms of those who met the standard. Those who failed to meet the standard—even if by just a point or two—are regarded as having failed. Performance should also be reported in terms of how well students did overall, perhaps by including a score showing percentage of items answered correctly. Federal legislation now requires that scores be reported in three categories: advanced, proficient, and partly proficient. The third level allows states to track the progress of low-achieving students toward meeting state standards.

■ Rubrics

One type of standard or criterion is the **rubric.** A rubric is a written description of what is expected in order to meet a certain level of performance. As such, it functions as a scoring guide so that the assessor can differentiate between below-average, average, and superior performance. Rubrics can be used to assess science experiments, social studies projects, art work, musical performances, pieces of writing, and other products produced by students. They are becoming increasingly popular because they can be constructed to fit in with many of the content area standards. The sample rubric in Table 13.1 is designed to help with the creation of a Web site. Note the concrete description of four levels of achievement.

■ A **rubric** is a description of the traits or characteristics of standards used to judge a process or product.

TABLE 13.1

RUBRIC FOR WEB SITE CREATION

	Novice	Apprentice	Proficient	Advanced
Content	Very little information.	Limited information. Main ideas not fully developed.	Adequate information. Main ideas well developed.	Very informative. Goes beyond giving basic details.
Style	Text is difficult to understand. Poorly written.	Text is not clear in some spots. Some portions are awkwardly written.	Text is clear and easy to follow.	Text is appealing and has voice.
Layout/ Design	Little or no evidence of design.	Not all elements fit into the overall design.	Design is functional.	Design is eye-catching and highly effective.
Navigation/ Links	Has no links or links fail to operate.	Has insufficient links. Some links do not seem relevant.	Has a sufficient number of key links.	Has more than enough links. Some links to hard-to-find sources.
Mechanics	A number of spelling, punctuation, capitalization, or usage errors.	A few mechanical errors.	No errors.	No errors.

Rubrics have a number of advantages. First, they help objectify subjective judgment. They also lead the evaluator to decide what characterizes different levels of performance, and, when shared with students, provide them with a clear idea of what they must do in order to perform adequately. If students help develop the rubrics, they acquire a sense of ownership and a better understanding of the task's requirements. Students who participated in the creation of rubrics for a writing assignment turned in better writing pieces than those who didn't (Boyle, 1996).

Rubrics vary in complexity. (Some of the most detailed rubrics are used in the assessment of writing.) They may be holistic or analytic. In holistic scoring, instead of noting specific strengths and weaknesses, a teacher evaluates a composition or other piece of work in terms of a limited number of general criteria. The teacher does not stop to check the activity to see if it meets each of the criteria but simply forms a general impression. Analytic scoring involves analyzing pieces and noting specific strengths and weaknesses. It requires the teacher to create a set of specific scoring criteria. A sample analytic writing rubric is presented in Figure 8.3. The teacher should also use anchor pieces along with the rubric to assess compositions. Anchor pieces, which may be drawn from the work of past classes or from the compositions that are currently being assessed, are writing samples that provide examples of poor, fair, good, and superior pieces. The teacher decides which of the anchor pieces a student's composition most closely resembles.

Constructing a Rubric.   To construct a rubric, first analyze the standard or objective to be met. Then ask yourself, "How will I be able to tell when this standard has been

USING TECHNOLOGY

Rubrics from The Staff Room for Ontario Teachers http://www.odyssey.on.ca/ ~elaine.coxon/rubrics.htm Contains links to an impressive variety of rubrics covering virtually every subject. Provides excellent links for information about portfolios, including electronic ones.

meet? What criteria might I use to judge it?" For writing, the criteria would include some combination of content and form. For a persuasive piece, the criteria might include how convincing the piece is, the strength of the writer's argument, the quality of the writing, and the correctness of expression. For an analytic rubric, the four categories would then be further broken down into key elements. The next step would be to decide how many levels of competence would be included and to write descriptions for each level. Ideally, these descriptions should be grounded in students' performance. If possible, use papers previously written, perhaps by last year's class, and divide them into as many groups as you have levels. Then note the characteristics of the top group and each of the other groups. You might number each of the categories or choose names for them: novice, apprentice, proficient, and advanced or beginning, developing, proficient, and distinguished. Construct a frame that includes the descriptions you have chosen. For each description or criterion, include possible indicators that the criterion have been met. The criterion is the general description of what the student needs to do: The piece persuades the reader to take an action. The indicator is a specific example of how the criterion might be met: The paragraph recommends a specific course of action that is supported by at least three reasons. Discuss the rubric with students, or, better yet, involve them in the construction process. Try out the rubric with a set of papers and revise as necessary. For a sampling of rubrics, see Rubrics Download at http://www.classnj.org/IDEA/. Also consult WWW 4 Teachers at http://www.uni.edu/profdev/rubrics.html. WWW 4 Teachers features a host of teacher tools, including RubiStar. RubiStar allows teachers to customize any one of several dozen rubrics.

 *CHECKUP*

1. What are criterion-referenced assessment measures?
2. What role do they play in content area programs?

CONSTRUCTED RESPONSES

Increasingly, achievement tests are requiring students to answer questions in writing, rather than simply to select the correct response in multiple choice items. In Michigan (Blakeslee, 1997), which uses **constructed responses** in its content area tests, many teachers complained that the constructed response items were not fair because their students don't know how to write well. As it turned out, students scored as well on constructed response items as they did on multiple choice items. Apparently, constructed response items allow students to express their knowledge of science as well as or better than multiple choice items do. As students learn what constitutes a good written explanation and learn to compose their explanations according to these criteria, their performance on the constructed response items may even be superior to that on multiple choice items. In the meantime, they are learning a valuable writing skill.

USING TECHNOLOGY

RubiStar
http://rubistar.4teachers.org/ RubiStar provides generic rubrics in a format that can be customized and printed out. For each rubric, teachers can select from a variety of categories or add their own and change almost all suggested text in the rubric to make it fit their project. A number of the rubrics are in Spanish.

■ **Constructed responses** are answers that have been composed by students, such as an essay or written explanation.

JUDGING ASSESSMENT MEASURES

Reliability

■ **Reliability** is the degree to which a test yields consistent results. In other words, if you took the test again, your score would be approximately the same.

To be useful, tests and other assessment instruments, whether criterion- or norm-referenced, must be both reliable and valid. **Reliability** is a measure of consistency, which means that if the same test were given to the same students a number of times, the results would be approximately the same. Reliability is usually reported as a coefficient of correlation and ranges from 0.00 to 0.99 or –0.01 to –0.99. The higher the positive correlation, the more reliable the test. Reliability is tested in two major ways: through a mathematical calculation of internal consistency and through test-retest—that is, giving the same test a second time to see if relative performance stays approximately the same. Group tests should have an internal consistency of 0.85 and a test-retest of 0.70 or higher. For tests on which individual decisions are being based, reliability should be in the 0.90s. A test that is not reliable is of no value. The results of measurement could be different each time.

Validity

■ **Validity** is the degree to which a test measures what it is supposed to measure, or the extent to which a test will provide information needed to make a decision. Validity should be considered in terms of the consequences of the test results and the use to which the test results will be put.

In general, **validity** means that a test measures what it says it measures: vocabulary knowledge or science knowledge, for instance. For content area teachers, the key validity is curricular or content validity, which means that the test measures the content that has been presented and assesses it in the way it has been taught or is typically used. To be valid, the assessment must also present useful information. Ultimately, it means that a particular test will provide the information needed to make a decision, such as whether to review misunderstood concepts or go on to the next level or whether to give a passing grade (Farr & Carey, 1986). To check for content validity, list the objectives or standards of the program and note how closely a particular test's objectives match them. The test's specific content should be examined, too, to see whether it reflects the type of material that the students have covered. Also, determine how knowledge or skills are tested. If a test assesses skills or content that you do not cover or assesses them in a way that is not suitable, the test is not valid for your class.

Closely tied to validity are the uses to which the assessment will be put. For instance, a statewide assessment that is tied to graduation will almost surely be used by teachers as a kind of curriculum guide. If the test assesses only a narrow part of the curriculum, it will be detrimental and thus invalid (Joint Task Force on Assessment, 1994). If a state's high-stakes test assesses persuasive writing, this area may be overemphasized and other kinds of writing neglected.

Assessment measures should also be fair to all who take them. There should be no biased items, and the content should be such that all students have had an equal opportunity to learn it.

1. How are assessment measures judged?

FUNCTIONAL LEVEL ASSESSMENT

The typical class will exhibit a wide range of reading ability. Just as students need appropriate levels of materials for instruction, they should have appropriate levels of materials for testing. Unfortunately, many of the high-stakes tests may lack sufficient bottom. That is they fail to include content appropriate for struggling learners. Approximately one student out of four is reading significantly below grade level. That means that if these students are given tests that are written on grade level, they will not be able to read most of the items. The poorest readers may not be able to read any of the items. In addition to being inhumane, such a test is also invalid for struggling learners. It yields no useful information except to indicate that the student is operating below grade level. This type of test is also potentially damaging. If students are unable to demonstrate what they have learned, a prime source of external motivation is taken away. One solution is **functional level testing.** In functional level testing, which is also known as out-of-level testing, students are given tests that are on their reading level rather than on their grade level. To ascertain students' reading level, you can use your professional judgment. Or you can use a test such as the GRADE Locator Test (American Guidance Services), a brief test designed to estimate the reading levels of students in grades 4 through 12. Although designed for students in grade 4 and above, the GRADE Locator Test has items on beginning reading levels as well as advanced reading levels.

■ **Functional level testing** is the practice of assigning students to a test level on the basis of their reading ability rather than their grade level.

Another possible way to assess struggling readers is to read items to the students so that the below-level readers are not penalized. This works for content areas but not reading. The only solution for reading is to give students tests that are on their level.

Federal regulations require that states include as many students as possible in their assessments. This includes students in Title I, special education programs, and programs for English language learners. However, accommodations are permissible. These accommodations should be made not just for students who are in a special program but for all students who have the need for them.

Assessing English language learners is a complex issue. Testing ELLs in their native language seems to be a logical approach. This works best for students who are new arrivals. If students have been exposed to English for a period of time, then they will know some of the new terms they have learned in English but not in their native language. On the other hand, there are students who have extensive experience with English; these students should be tested in English. However, there may be terms and concepts that they know in their native language but not in English. One solution to this dilemma is to test students in both languages (Cummins, 2001). The Bilingual Verbal Abilities Test (BVAT) is one instrument that accomplishes this task. The BVAT (Riverside) consists of three verbal tests derived from the Woodcock-Johnson-Revised: picture vocabulary, oral vocabulary, and verbal analogies. These tests have been translated into fifteen languages. Students take the tests in both languages so they are given credit for responses in English and items that they failed to respond to in English but were able to answer in their native language. When used with nonverbal tests, the BVAT offers a reasonably valid estimate of students' aca-

ENGLISH LANGUAGE LEARNERS
ELL students should be tested in the languages most likely to result in the most valid assessment of their knowledge. However, recently passed legislation requires that all ELLs in grades 3 through 8 be assessed in English reading and English language arts after three consecutive years of instruction in English (except in Puerto Rico).

demic ability. Applying this principle to the content areas, the most effective assessment would allow students to be assessed in both English and their native language.

 *CHECKUP*

1. What is functional level assesssment?
2. How might functional level assessment be implemented in a content area program?
3. How should ELLs be assessed?

OTHER METHODS OF ASSESSMENT

Performance Assessment

■ **Performance assessment** involves employing tasks in which knowledge, skills, or strategies are assessed in the way they are typically used.

Performance assessment is just what its name suggests. Instead of showing what they know by answering multiple choice questions or composing an essay, students demonstrate knowledge through their performance (Popham, 2000). They might write and put on a one-act play or plan a balanced diet. They might be given materials and asked to design an experiment—for instance, one designed to assess whether a sample of water is acidic. Or the teacher might set up stations in which students have to perform a variety of basic lab tasks or identify rock specimens.

Performance tasks potentially assess knowledge and skills in a more realistic way and assess them at the application level. In the sciences, performance assessments can be set up to show whether students can use scientific equipment and conduct measurements and other lab procedures. It's one thing to be able to answer questions about starches, sugars, protein, and oils in foods. It's quite another to measure the starches, sugars, protein, and oils in foods and plan a balanced diet based on these measurements. Students who will be assessed on a performance measure need to be more active learners and to be able to apply knowledge rather than merely recite it. Despite its obvious value, performance assessment does have some limitations. Performance assessment can be more expensive and more time-consuming. The assessments are also narrower in scope than paper-and-pencil tests, which are better at assessing a wide range of knowledge.

Think-Alouds

■ **Think-alouds** are procedures in which students are asked to describe the processes they are using as they engage in reading or another cognitive activity.

Think-alouds have been presented in previous chapters as a device for instructing students. Think-alouds can also be used to gain insight into the thought processes students use as they deal with difficult words, study, write reports, or attempt to understand a chapter in a content area text. During a think-aloud, the reader explains her thought processes while reading a text or writing. These explanations can come after each sentence, at the end of each paragraph, or at the end of the whole selection or while engaging in a particular task, such as deriving the meaning of an unknown word. Think-alouds reveal whether the reader is focused on individual words, phrases, sentences, or the integration of sentences. It tells what kinds of inferences the reader is making and what kinds of memory processes they are using (Trabasso & Magliano, 1996).

According to data from think-alouds, readers engage in a variety of processes as they read. They summarize, paraphrase, make inferences, highlight essential details, integrate portions of the text, monitor for meaning, and react personally (Pressley & Afflerbach, 1995). Skilled readers and those who have more prior knowledge generally apply a greater variety of strategies as they read. As a result, they remember more (Goldman, 1997). Because think-alouds have the power to provide insight into students' use of strategies and cognitive processes, they are a valuable assessment tool. They have the potential to reveal why students are having difficulty comprehending their content area texts. Because they reveal comprehension processes, think-alouds can be used to plan instruction for students in strategies that they are neglecting or may not be using effectively.

Because think-alouds are unfamiliar devices for most students, they should become accustomed to the technique before you use it to assess them. Before asking students to engage in think-alouds, model the process. A variety of coding systems can be used to classify students' comments, or you can simply take informal notes.

An excellent example of the use of think-alouds with content area texts can be found in the Qualitative Reading Inventory-3 (Leslie & Caldwell, 2001). In their procedures, they first have a student read a segment of text in the regular way. The student then reads the second section but stops when the word *stop* appears. At that point, the teacher explains that she is going to demonstrate a think-aloud. After reading the section, she tells what she is thinking and invites the student to do the same. In the third section, the student reads, stops when the word *stop* appears, and then thinks aloud. The students' responses are recorded and coded. The following think-aloud responses indicate understanding:

- Paraphrasing or summarizing
- Making new meaning. This includes drawing an inference or conclusion or reasoning about what has been read.
- Questioning that indicates understanding. The questioning generally indicates that a student is seeking to find out how a particular piece of information fits in with what has already been read or what its significance might be.
- Noting understanding. The student verbalizes that he understands what he has read.
- Reporting prior knowledge. The student explains how a passage agrees with what he already knows or explains how this passage has caused him to alter his thinking.
- Identifying personally. The student comments on how the text affects him personally or makes a personal judgment about text.

Some comments indicate a lack of understanding. They include:

- Questions that indicate lack of understanding. The student might ask a question about the meaning of a word or phrase or ask a question about the content of the passage, which indicates that he has not understood the passage.

- Noting lack of understanding. The student comments that he doesn't understand a word or phrase or does not understand the passage (Leslie & Caldwell, 2001).

In one study, the type of responses made by students in think-alouds varied in type and quality. Students who engaged in summarizing or paraphrasing and making inferences had the highest level of comprehension. Some students showed a preference for one type of strategy, such as summarizing, whereas others used a variety of strategies. A number of students offered no comments at all (Leslie & Caldwell, 2001). Think-alouds are affected by the difficulty level, familiarity, and nature of the text being read. Students who are reading about an unfamiliar topic would probably use summarizing or paraphrasing. They would be attempting to simply retell what the author said. They would have more difficulty drawing inferences or conclusions. Students also are more likely to respond personally to literary selections than they are to science or social studies passages (Leslie & Caldwell, 2001).

As students think aloud, record and then analyze their responses. Note the behaviors listed below. Then come to conclusions about the effectiveness of the strategies that the student is using and the extent to which the student is monitoring for meaning.

- Made predictions or created hypotheses
- Revised prediction or conclusion based on new information
- Considered information previously read
- Made inferences
- Drew conclusions
- Made judgments
- Visualized or created images
- Paraphrased
- Summarized
- Constructed questions
- Reasoned about reading
- Made connections
- Monitored for meaning
- Noted difficult words
- Noted confusing passages
- Used fix-up strategies
- Reread section
- Used illustrations as an aid
- Used context or other decoding skills
- Used glossary
- Skipped difficult words. (Gunning, 2002)

A sample think-aloud is presented in Figure 13.2.

Think-alouds can be used to examine specific processes as well as general reading ability. In the think-aloud protocol quoted below, students were asked to locate

FIGURE 13.2

Sample Think-Aloud

Teacher explanation: I would like you to read this section and then tell me what you were thinking as you read it. If I know what students are thinking as they read, it will help me better understand how they are reading their textbooks. Once I know how they are reading their textbooks, I can show them ways to get more out of their reading. Read the section silently as you normally would. Stop reading when you come to the word *stop*. Then I will ask you to tell me what you were thinking about as you read. I will show you what I mean. Then you can give it a try. [Teacher demonstrates.]

> Volcanic belts form along the boundaries of Earth's plates. At plate boundaries, huge pieces of the lithosphere diverge (pull apart) and reconverge (push together). Here, the lithosphere is weak and fractured, allowing magma to reach the surface. Most volcanoes occur along diverging plate boundaries, such as the mid-ocean ridge, or in subduction zones around the edges of ocean. But some volcanoes form at "hot spots" far from the boundaries of continental or oceanic plates. (Exline et al., 2001, p. 179) STOP

Teacher: What were you thinking as you read?

Student: It says that volcanoes form along the plate boundaries. It says that here is where pieces of lithosphere pull together and push apart. What is lithosphere? It says volcanoes occur where plates diverge or in subduction zones. Diverging plates are plates that pull apart. But I don't know what a subduction zone is. Sub means "under." Could it mean "under the ocean"? Part of this is in heavy black print. That means it's important. I better read that again.

[Additional helpful probing questions include Did you look at the map? If so, did the map help? How? What might you do to get the meanings of *lithosphere* and *subduction*? Do you ever use the glossary? What did you do before you started reading?]

Volcanoes at Diverging Plate Boundaries

Volcanoes form along the mid-ocean ridge, which marks a diverging plate boundary. Recall from Chapter 4 that the ridge is a long, underwater rift valley that winds through the oceans. Along the ridge, lava pours out of cracks in the ocean floor. Only in a few places, as in Iceland and the Azores Islands in the Atlantic Ocean, do the volcanoes of the mid-ocean ridge rise above the ocean's surface. (Exline et al., 2001, p. 179) STOP.

Teacher: What were you thinking as you read?

Student: It looks like volcanoes in the ocean pour lava out of cracks in the ocean floor. But some volcanoes actually come up from beneath the sea. Does that mean that volcanoes form islands?

difficult words in books that they were reading and discuss their thought processes as they tried to analyze the words. What does the brief interchange between researcher and student tell you about the student's strategies? How might you use the information to plan a program for the student?

The whole system could suddenly collapse. And that was what he said about Jurassic Park. That it had *inherent instability*. (Crichton, 1990, p. 243)

Researcher: What do you think this means?

Brady: Instant. You inherit it instantly.

Researcher: What gives you that idea?

Brady: Well, because the first word—instant, it looks like . . . uh . . . something.

Researcher: Does that make sense with the story?

Brady: Well, the sentence doesn't sound right to me though. That it had *inherent* . . . it sounds like it needs an *ed* at the end of *inherent*.

Researcher: What else?

Brady: I don't know.

Researcher: Does it bother you to keep on reading?

Brady: No. (Harmon, 1998, p. 583)

In confusing the word *inherent* with *inherited* and *instability* with *instant*, Brady uses word analysis, rather than contextual clues, to derive a possible meaning for the word. The meaning doesn't fit the context, but Brady moves ahead anyhow. Brady obviously needs instruction in context clues, especially clues that might be found in other sentences. He also needs to keep on working at the word until he achieves a definition that makes sense. And he needs to use the dictionary or glossary when other strategies don't work. The think-aloud provides invaluable information about Brady's use of word analysis skills and needs.

■ Informal Think-Alouds

Think-alouds can be brief and informal. For instance, during a discussion of a selection, you might ask questions similar to the following:

- How did you figure out that difficult word?
- What do you do when you encounter a difficult word?
- What were you thinking about as you read the selection?
- What was going through your mind as you read the selection?
- Were there any parts of the selection that were confusing? How did you handle those parts?
- If you were going to be given a test on this selection, show me how you would go about studying for it.

■ Group Assessment of Text Processing

Obtaining think-alouds from large numbers of students would be prohibitively time-consuming. However, it is essential that you obtain information about the way students process their texts, especially if they are having difficulty with them. In most content area classes, the text is a major source of information. To save time, think-alouds may be expressed in writing. Students can be asked to provide a written description of their thoughts as they read a selection in a content area text. In their learning logs, students can note the difficulties they encountered in confusing passages and describe the processes they used to comprehend the selections. In follow-up class discussions, they can compare their thought processes and strategies with those of other students (Brown & Lytle, 1988). Students can also be asked to attach sticky notes to passages that they find confusing. The class might discuss which passages were confusing and why and what steps they took to resolve the confusion. If a number of students found the same passages to be confusing, you might analyze the reason for this and take steps to help students sort through the passages. The passage might be poorly written, or the students might not be using effective comprehension strategies.

Another way to obtain insight into the ways students process information in the text is to administer a group text processing assessment. The text processing assessment seeks two types of information: what the students understood and how they went about constructing meaning. Students read brief segments of text, generally a paragraph at a time. Text for the assessment could be segments from the textbook students are using with notations telling students where to stop reading and respond by thinking aloud. On a sheet of paper divided into two columns, they are asked, "Tell what the text was about in your own words. Summarize the main points." In a second column, students are asked, "Tell what was going on in your mind as you read the section. Tell what you were thinking or seeing in your mind. Tell about anything in the paragraph that was confusing to you." Model the process and work through a sample selection with students. As they work through the inventory, note how they go about reading it and responding to it. After students have completed the inventory, discuss it with them. This provides them with the opportunity to expand on their responses.

Observation

One of the best ways to assess students is through observation. Through observation, you can verify information gleaned from tests. You can also assess behaviors that could not readily be assessed in any other way. Through observation, you can assess how well a student works with others and how well students participate in class and hands-on activities such as experiments and presentations to others.

Observation can be supplemented by asking questions. For instance, by asking questions as students work, you can gain insight into their reasoning processes. Analyzing the kinds of questions that students ask is also a good source of information about their understanding.

Observation is an invaluable tool. However, observations can be subjective and unreliable. Planning observations and keeping records adds to their reliability, validity, and overall usefulness. For instance, if you wish to assess students' work habits in a cooperative group, it would be more reliable if you observed several meetings. Otherwise, you might catch the students on a bad day or a good day and so form an erroneous impression. It would also help if you have a checklist to guide your observations (see Table 13.2). A checklist notes essential behaviors of a task and is a way of keeping a record of your observations.

To find out how students read their textbooks, provide them with some class time to read them. Note how they go about this task: What do they do before they read? Do they survey the chapter, for instance? As they read, do they take notes? Do

USING TECHNOLOGY

Handheld computers can be used to take observational notes. Software such as *ThoughtManager for Education* (Hands High Software) can be used to organize these notes.

TABLE 13.2				

CHECKLIST FOR PERFORMANCE IN A COOPERATIVE GROUP

Name _____ Date _____

	Never	Occasionally	Usually	Always
Completes assignments	____	____	____	____
Has needed materials	____	____	____	____
Helps others	____	____	____	____
Attends meetings	____	____	____	____
Joins in discussion	____	____	____	____
Respects opinions of others	____	____	____	____
Gets along well with other group members	____	____	____	____

they use graphic aids? After observing their reading, administer a questionnaire or interview that inquires about the way they read their texts (see Figure 13.3). After students have completed their questionnaires, discuss with them how they go about reading their texts. Based on the information obtained, provide instruction for efficient use of texts.

FIGURE 13.3

Text Usage Interview

Before Reading
What do you do before you read?
Do you read the title and headings?
Do you look at the illustrations, charts, graphs, and maps?
Do you predict what the selection might be about?
Do you ask yourself what you know about the topic?
Do you plan how you are going to read the selection—fast, medium, or slow?
Do you have questions in mind that you plan to answer through your reading?

During Reading
What do you do while you're reading?
Do you think about what you're reading?
Do you stop every once in a while and ask yourself what you've read so far?
Do you picture in your mind the people, events, and places that you are reading about?
Do you make up questions in your mind as you read?
Do you try to answer those questions?

Do you imagine that you are talking to the author as you read?

What do you do if the passage is confusing?
Do you read it again?
Do you just keep on reading?
Do you try to get help from photos, charts, graphs, or maps?

What do you do if you run into a hard word?
Do you use context to try to figure it out?
Do you look for word parts that you know?
Do you use a dictionary or a glossary?

After Reading
After reading the selection, what do you do?
Do you think about what you've read?
Do you do something with the information that you've learned?
Do you compare what you've just learned from your reading with what you already know?

To gain some insight into students' study habits, give them a brief selection to read and announce that you will be giving them a quiz after they have read the material. Note how they go about studying for the quiz. After administering the quiz, discuss their study strategies. Also administer a study habits questionnaire (see Figure 13.4).

■ **Anecdotal Records**

Another way of collecting observational data is to keep anecdotal records or take field notes. An **anecdotal record** is the recording of an event that sheds some light on the student's learning behavior. It may be very brief but should contain a summary portrayal of the event, including time, date, names of persons involved, and a description of the setting.

> ■ An **anecdotal record** is the recording of the description of a significant incident in which the description and interpretation are kept separate.

Anecdotal records may be used to obtain data about students' learning processes, interests, attitudes, work habits, interaction with others, or other elements of the program. Records might be kept daily, weekly, or monthly. When making anecdotal records, include a number of observations so conclusions are based on representative data. Also, take note of positive factors as well as negative ones. There is a tendency to stress the negative (Bush & Huebner, 1979).

An anecdotal record should be a neutral recording, not an evaluation of behavior. You tell what the student did, not how you evaluate the behavior. For instance, the statement "Alexia was defiant today" is an evaluative statement, whereas the statement "Alexia refused to follow directions" is a neutral description of her behavior. Anecdotal records are most helpful when they shed light on a key behavior. In order for anecdotal records to be useful, they should be reviewed periodically and summarized. Teachers should look for patterns of behavior. In going over anecdotal records, the teacher should ask what this information reveals about the student and how it

FIGURE 13.4

Study Habits Questionnaire

Name_____ Grade_____ Date _____

Study Habits Questionnaire

Answer each of the following questions.

1. Which of your subjects is the hardest to study for?
2. What makes that subject hard to study?
3. Which of your subjects is the easiest to study for?
4. What makes that subject easy to study?
5. What do you do when something is hard to understand?
6. What do you do to try to help you remember facts or ideas that you are studying?
7. Where do you usually study?
8. When do you usually study?
9. About how long do you usually study?
10. What things might you do to help you study better?

FIGURE 13.5

Anecdotal Record

Student _Anya_   Date _11-2_

During lab, Anya let her partner do much of the work. She observed as her partner dissected the sheep's brain. Anya's role was to hand her partner the dissecting tools and to check in the lab manual to make sure that procedures were being followed.

Student _Anya_   Date _11-3_

While completing the drawing of the dissected sheep's brain, Anya copied the illustration from the text rather than from the actual sheep's brain that her partner had disssected. Anya was focused on the drawing. She didn't even look when two students in the back of the room got into a brief argument.

can be used to plan her or his instructional program. See the sample anecdotal record in Figure 13.5.

Observations can be recorded in notebooks, on sticky notes, or on hand-held computer devices. Software is available for collating student assessment data.

Questionnaires and Interviews

■ A **questionnaire** is an instrument in which a subject is asked to respond to a series of questions on some topic.

■ An **interview** is the oral process of asking a subject a series of questions on a topic.

Questionnaires are useful devices for obtaining information about work and study habits, reading interests, and attitudes (see Figures 13.3 & 13.4). **Interviews** are simply oral questionnaires. The advantage of an interview is that the teacher can probe a student's replies, rephrase questions, and encourage extended answers and so obtain a wide range of information. An interview can focus on such topics as a student's favorite activities in a class, favorite authors, or work habits. One kind of interview, the process interview, provides insight about the learning strategies students use. Because it helps students become aware of their processes, they can gain more control over them and so use them more effectively (Jett-Simpson, 1990). The process interview can be conducted informally on a one-to-one basis, but if time is limited, you can hold sessions with small groups or seek written responses instead of oral ones. Possible process interview questions include the following, which are adapted from Jett-Simpson (1990). Only one or two of these questions should be asked at one sitting.

1. How do you choose something to read?
2. How do you get ready for reading?
3. How do you go about studying for tests?
4. When you come to a word you don't know, what do you do?
5. When a paragraph is confusing, what do you do?
6. How do you go about reading your science [history; geography] text?
7. What do you do to help you remember what you've read?
8. How do you go about reading and solving a math word problem?

Unfortunately, questionnaires, interviews, and ratings have a common weakness. Their validity depends on students' ability and willingness to supply accurate, honest information. Students may supply answers that they think the teacher wants to hear. Information gathered from these sources, therefore, should be verified with other data.

CHECKUP

1. What are some informal ways of assessing students' performance?
2. How can these approaches be used in a content area program?

ASSESSING BACKGROUND KNOWLEDGE

More than almost any other factor, background knowledge will determine what students learn and, indeed, how well they understand their texts. In one study, conceptual knowledge was a better predictor of reading comprehension than reading ability (Leslie & Caldwell, 2001). The more students know, the more they are prepared to learn. In some instances, students' background knowledge is a potential barrier to learning because they have formed erroneous concepts. This is especially true in science. Students will be unable to form accurate concepts until their misconceptions have been corrected.

Background knowledge may be assessed in a number of ways: free recall, word association, structured questions, unstructured questions, and recognition. A quick and easy way to assess background knowledge is through free association or brainstorming. For instance, if you are a science teacher about to begin a unit on cells and are unsure of the extent of students' knowledge, place the word *cells* on the board and ask students to brainstorm it. Ask, "What comes to mind when you think of the word *cells*?" Jot down students' responses on the chalkboard. After jotting down responses, you might ask them to tell which words go together and explain why. This will help you determine both the extent and the depth of their knowledge and also its accuracy. If students are English language learners, note the extent of their academic English. They may have a relatively good command of everyday English but be less familiar with the more formal academic language.

A fairly straightforward way to assess background is to have students survey a chapter and predict what the chapter will be about. For instance, before students read a brief history of conflict in the Balkans, ask them to look at the title (The Balkan Powder Keg) and the subheads (A Region of Divided Loyalty, The East-West Tug-of-War, An Ethnic Patchwork, and Nations Emerge in the Balkans). Also have them examine the accompanying illustrations. Based on a survey of these items, students predict what information the section will contain. Some students may make very general predictions: the section will describe difficulties in that part of the world. Others may be able to make a series of predictions: the section will tell that there was trouble in the region, it will tell about different ethnic groups, it will tell about the many countries in the Balkans. Other students will be able to integrate the information garnered from the survey and complemented by their background knowledge. They may be able to predict that the section will explain that the region has had many conflicts because the people have different ethnic identities, different religions and languages, and have been split by a number of wars. Through students' responses, you can gauge the quality and quantity of their background knowledge. Another way to assess background knowledge is through PReP, which was explained in Chapter 5.

Work Samples

Samples of student work are an excellent source of assessment information, especially if they shed light on the students' thought processes; this helps the teacher understand how students are conceptualizing information and ways in which misconceptions might be clarified. For instance, concept maps have an excellent potential for revealing students' grasp of ways in which ideas are related. Semantic maps can also be used to assess grasp of content and relationships. If students compose maps before and after a learning unit, concept maps can be used as a pre- and postassessment. Essays, lab reports, projects, and completed math problems which show students' work also have high potential for yielding useful information about students' thought processes and grasp of content.

SELF-EVALUATION

The most important evaluation is self-evaluation. Unless students assess their own progress toward meeting goals, they are hampered in taking the steps necessary to reach those goals. The first step in self-evaluation is the setting of goals. At the beginning of the semester and periodically during the semester, students should be encouraged to set learning goals. They should then use their sense of how they are doing, quizzes, tests, assignments, work samples, and portfolios—if they have them—to assess their progress and make improvements in their work habits and effort as needed. Students need to ask themselves how they are doing so they can do better. Teachers might hold conferences in which they discuss content learned or skills mastered, as well as goals for the future and how those goals might be met. Portfolios, which are described later in this chapter, also offer opportunities for self-assessment.

Logs and Journals

Learning logs and response journals, as explained in Chapter 8, can be a part of students' self-evaluation, as well as a source of information for the teacher. Learning logs or journals provide a record of topics covered, key concepts learned, and students' reflections on their learning. Response journals provide a record of students' responses to their reading. Logs and journals offer opportunities for self-evaluation, especially if the teacher confers with students about them or encourages students to set learning goals and reflect on what the journals and logs show about their progress towards reaching their learning goals.

CHECKUP

1. What role can self-evaluation play in a content area program?

EVALUATING WRITING

Because it is probably the most complex cognitive task in which students engage, writing is also one of the most difficult to assess. Two major approaches to assessing writing are holistic and analytic scoring.

Holistic Scoring

In **holistic scoring,** instead of noting specific strengths and weaknesses, a teacher evaluates a composition in terms of a limited number of general criteria. The criteria are used "only as a general guide . . . in reaching a holistic judgment" (Cooper & Odell, 1977, p. 4).

The teacher does not stop to check the piece to see whether it meets each of the criteria but simply forms a general impression. The teacher can score a piece according to the presence or absence of key elements. There may be a scoring guide, which can be a checklist or a rubric. (A holistic scoring guide in the form of a rubric is shown in Table 13.3.)

■ **Holistic scoring** is a process for sorting or ranking written pieces on the basis of an overall impression of the piece. Sample pieces (anchors) or a description of standards (rubric) for rating the pieces might be used as guides.

TABLE 13.3

HOLISTIC SCORING GUIDE

	Beginning	Developing	Accomplished	Exemplary
Topic	Not relevant or appropriate.	Too broad or too narrow.	Appropriate.	Interesting and original.
Content	Little or no development.	Limited development.	Adequate development.	Fully developed; includes convincing details or examples.
Organization	Little or no organization.	Some evidence of organization but irrelevant details are included and some details are in the wrong place.	Has an obvious organization; details are relevant and appropriately placed.	Well organized.
Style	Lack of style.	Some parts are not clear.	Clearly written.	Appealing, convincing style.
Mechanics	Many errors in spelling, punctuation, usage, and sentence structure.	Some errors in mechanics.	Very few errors in mechanics.	Flawlessly written.

TABLE 13.4

ANALYTIC SCORING GUIDE

	Beginning	Developing	Accomplished	Exemplary
Topic	Not relevant or appropriate.	Too broad or too narrow.	Appropriate.	Interesting and origina.l
Content	States an idea but fails to develop it.	Develops an idea with one or two details. Details are not fully explained.	Develops an idea with three or more details. Details are explained but not elaborated on. Details are fairly ordinary.	Develops an idea with three or more details. Details are elaborated but not overly so. Details are interesting and convincing and include one or more that are original.
Organization	Little or no organization.	Main idea is stated in a topic sentence. Some of the details support the main idea, but some do not. Main idea does not stand out. Important and unimportant details might be mixed in so it is difficult to tell which are the key details.	Main idea is stated in a topic sentence that clearly explains that this is the main idea. Supporting details follow. Concluding sentence sums up or restates main idea. Uses connecting words such as *next, so,* and, *however* to show that ideas are related. Announces concluding sentence. Structure of the piece is apparent.	Main idea is emphasized through placement in beginning of report and is supported by details that follow. Uses placement of ideas rather than formal connecting words to show that ideas are related. Uses placement and flow of language to indicate main idea, supporting details, and conclusion. Has subtle but strong structure.
Style	Lack of style.	Some ideas are not clearly expressed.	Ideas are expressed in language that is plain and easy to understand. Limited use of varied vocabulary or varied sentence structure.	Ideas are expressed in language that is both clear and appealing. First sentence piques reader's interest. Intriguing details and examples keep reader interested. Varied vocabulary, and varied sentence patterns make the writing flow.
Mechanics	Many errors in spelling. First word in the sentence and names of people and places are not capitalized. Failure to use end punctuation.	Some errors in spelling. Failure to capitalize some proper names. Some sentence fragments and run-on sentences.	Few errors in mechanics. No more than one or two misspelled words. May have an error or two in use of commas, colons, or semicolons.	Virtually flawless. Uses semicolons, colons, dashes appropriately. Varied vocabulary is spelled correctly.

■ Applying Holistic Scoring

Before scoring the pieces, the teacher should quickly read them all to get a sense of how well the class did overall. This prevents setting criteria that are too high or too low. After sorting the papers into four groups—poor, fair, good, and superior—the teacher rereads each work more carefully before confirming its placement. If possible, a second teacher should also evaluate the papers. This is especially important if the works are to be graded.

Analytic Scoring

Analytic scoring involves analyzing pieces and noting specific strengths and weaknesses. It requires the teacher to create a set of specific scoring criteria. Instead of overwhelming students with corrections, it is best to decide on a limited number of key features, such as those that have been emphasized for a particular writing activity. Key factors generally include content, organization, style, and conventions. Although more time-consuming than holistic scoring, analytic scoring allows the teacher to make constructive suggestions about students' writing. An analytic scoring guide is presented in Table 13.4.

■ **Analytic scoring** is a type of scoring that uses a description of specific features to be considered when assessing the piece.

It is important that students understand the rubric or criteria for assessing their written pieces. As Dahl and Farnan (1998) note,

> When writers lack specific standards and intentions, their ability to reflect on and evaluate their writing is severely compromised. It is not surprising that if writers do not know what they want to accomplish with a particular writing, it will be difficult for them to judge whether they have created an effective composition. (p. 121)

Teacher Comments

When checking students' papers, resist the temptation to mark all errors. Focus your corrections and comments. Students do their best when comments are positive and when there is emphasis on one or two areas, such as providing a fuller explanation or combining choppy sentences. This is especially effective when instruction is geared to the areas highlighted and students revise targeted areas in their compositions (Dahl & Farnan, 1998).

 ✔ *CHECKUP*

1. How can writing be assessed?

PORTFOLIOS

Although once the domain of artists, photographers, actors, and designers, **portfolios** are now used widely in education. Portfolios provide a broader sampling of work for assessment and do a better job of showing growth over time. More important, they actively involve students in the assessment process and have the potential

■ A **portfolio** is a collection of work samples, test results, checklists, or other data used to assess a student's performance.

to help them become more reflective and more engaged learners. As science educators Baker and Piburn (1997) note:

> The process of putting together a portfolio results in a number of positive outcomes besides learning and the development of positive attitudes toward science and scientific dispositions. It builds a feeling of self-efficacy because students are participating in the assessment of their own progress and they are *not* being compared to others. It fosters motivation because it is not being used as a way to control behavior. It also fosters reflection and the development of metacognitive strategies as students evaluate their own progress. (p. 383)

The foundation of the portfolio is a statement of objectives or standards. The purpose of the portfolio is to show the extent to which these key objectives have been met. Work samples are included to document to what degree each objective has been reached. The portfolio should contain a statement of key objectives, a listing of work samples or other items that show that objectives have been met, and an overall reflection in which students discuss the progress they have made and discuss future plans. The core of the portfolio should be the documentation. Each item should have a caption that briefly explains why it documents a particular objective.

Documentation varies depending on the subject area and objectives. Items might include field notes of observations, a recording or write-up of an interview with the town manager, photos of insects, a labelled rock collection, models, charts, an annotated listing of books read, a video of a skit on acid rain, the results of a questionnaire, lab reports, logs, journal entries, and so on.

In math, students might include a write-up of a statistical investigation, a reflection on processes used to solve a complex problem, and graphs and charts. A writing portfolio might include samples of the student's best work or selections that the teacher and student agree are representative of the student's work. If process is being emphasized, samples from the beginning, middle, and end of the year might be included along with samples that show the whole process from preplanning notes through drafts to final copy.

Types of Portfolios

Portfolios vary according to purpose (Valencia & Place, 1994). The four major kinds of portfolios are the showcase, evaluation, documentation, and process portfolios. Showcase portfolios are composed of works that students have selected as their best. Students in work-study programs or in the graphic arts program might assemble showcase portfolios in order to document their abilities as they apply for additional schooling or work. The emphasis in the evaluation portfolio is on obtaining representative pieces of work from key areas. The samples included might be standardized; that is, they have to embrace a certain topic or task and must conform to a standard set of directions. A documentation portfolio contains elements of the showcase and evaluation portfolios. It is designed to provide evidence of students' growth. As such, the documentation portfolio is more open-ended and allows for more student choice in the selection of items to be included. The purpose of the process portfolio is to show the learning processes that students use, so it includes documentation from various stages of a project. For writing, rough drafts as well as final copies would be included.

Each artifact or document should have a brief caption that identifies the item and notes which goal it documents. Students might also explain why they chose a particular item—it shows their ability to draw logical conclusions from an experiment, for example. Through classroom discussions and in conferences, help students explore criteria for including items in their portfolios.

Portfolios are most effective when a rubric is created for assessing them. The rubric is most effective when students have a role in creating it so that they have a deeper understanding of the rubric as well as a sense of ownership (see Table 13.1). Students should write a cover letter or complete a statement in which they reflect on their portfolios. The reflection might include a description of goals they feel they have met, areas that need added work, and plans for the future.

*H*olding conferences with students helps them to evaluate their own progress and set goals.

The value of portfolios extends well beyond providing assessment data. When Liza, a teen enrolled in an alternative high school, was asked how portfolio conferences helped her, she replied, "By letting me know what I should work on more, and makes me and Ms. Young be more closer—like friends. Not just student and teacher" (Young, Matthews, Kietzmann, & Westerfield, 1997, p. 348).

In portfolio assessment, students become active participants in the learning process and get to know themselves as learners. Through assembling a portfolio, they become part of the evaluation process. However, in order to play an active role in the portfolio process, students should assess their work before placing it in a portfolio. Using the rubric created for a particular essay, project, or other product, students should note its strengths and weaknesses and plans for improvement (Popham, 2000). They should also assess the overall portfolio periodically. Through periodic assessment, students might note that they are writing only narratives and should branch out to dramatic or poetic pieces or that they are doing a lot of reading in science but very few hands-on projects. Through examining and reflecting on the materials contained in the portfolio, they gain insights into their strengths and weaknesses and see what they need to work on to improve their skills. In addition to helping students set goals, portfolios help students track their progress towards meeting those goals A form for student evaluation of a portfolio is presented in Figure 13.6.

Reviewing Portfolios

To check on students' progress, periodically review their portfolios. Portfolio conferences might be held at the end of each unit of instruction or before the end of each marking period. Young (Young et al., 1997) held conferences every six weeks. As a result of those conferences and related classroom activities, students built a relationship with the teacher, began taking more responsibility for their learning, began setting more specific goals, and began to gain insight into what they needed to do to meet their goals.

FIGURE 13.6

Portfolio Self-Evaluation

Name_____ Date _____

Portfolio Self-Evaluation

What were my goals in writing for this period?

What progress toward meeting these goals does my portfolio show?

What are my strengths as a writer?

What are my weaknesses?

What are my goals for improving as a writer?

How do I plan to meet these goals?

What questions do I have about my progress as a writer?

(Gunning, 2003)

Before you start to review a portfolio, decide what you want to focus on. It could be number of books read, changes in writing, or effort put into revisions. Your evaluation should, of course, consider the student's stated goals; it is also important to emphasize the student's strengths. As you assess the portfolio, consider a variety of pieces and look at the work in terms of its changes over time. Ask yourself, "What does the student's work show about his progress over the time span covered? What might he do to make continued progress?"

To save time and help organize your assessment of the portfolio, you may want to use a checklist that is supplemented with personal comments. A sample portfolio review checklist is presented in Figure 13.7. Because the objective of evaluation is to improve instruction, students should be active partners in the process. "It follows that . . . assessment activities in which students are engaged in evaluating their own learning help them reflect on and understand their own strengths and needs, and it instills responsibility for their own learning" (Tierney, Carter, & Desai, 1991, p. 7).

Involving Parents

Used to letter or numerical grades on tests, quizzes, and writing assignments, parents may need an introduction to the concept of portfolios. A meeting with parents early in the school year and a written explanation sent home should help them understand the nature and benefits of portfolio assessment. The written explanation should include the rubric used to assess the portfolio. During parent-teacher conferences, go over the portfolio with parents. Stress the range of work it contains and the evidence showing that their child is learning. Students should also be encouraged to take their portfolios home and share them with their parents.

Disadvantages of Portfolios

Portfolios are not without their shortcomings. Being subjective, portfolios are difficult to evaluate fairly and consistently. Although using a rubric helps, effective

FIGURE 13.7

Sample Portfolio Review Checklist

	Not adequate	Adequate	Proficient	Advanced
Amount of writing				
Variety of writing				
Planning				
Revising				
Self-editing				
Content				
Organization				
Style				
Mechanics				

Strengths:_____

Needs:_____

Comments:_____

rubrics are difficult and time-consuming to compose. In addition, assessing portfolios is time-consuming (Popham, 2000). Unless the purpose and nature of the portfolio is clearly stated and unless students understand what kinds of things should be included in the portfolio and are selective in their choices, portfolios might become unwieldy collections of miscellaneous items.

 CHECKUP

1. What are the advantages and disadvantages of portfolio assessment?
2. How might portfolio assessment be used in a content area program?

TEACHER SELF-ASSESSMENT

Virtually all of the assessment measures used to evaluate students can be used by teachers to evaluate the effectiveness of their programs. However, the best assessment measures are those that are most fully aligned with the teacher's goals and curriculum. Teacher-created quizzes and unit tests provide a measure of the content students have learned. Portfolios provide a measure of content learned but also provide insight into the effectiveness of assignments. In some classes, students complete exit slips on which they talk about what they have learned that day or raise questions that they did not have time to raise in class or were reluctant to raise. Exit slips are composed in the last five or ten minutes of class. Students might read their slips and discuss them, or the teacher can read them over to get a sense of what students learned and what they might need help with. During the next class period, the teacher can answer questions that have been raised or clarify confusions. Entrance slips, in which students reflect on the previous day's class and/or home assignments, might be used instead of exit slips. Learning logs and journals might perform a similar function (see Chapter 8). As an alternative, the teacher and the class might design a form on which students tell what they learned in a certain class and list questions that they still have. Exit slips and log and journal entries provide information about the quality and clarity of daily instruction. They might also provide insight into the quality of the classroom atmosphere. External tests, such as those mandated by the district or state, also provide a measure of student learning. But the validity of the data depends on the extent to which the tests measure what was taught. Through reflection on these measures, the teacher can judge the effectiveness and quality of instruction and, based on these reflections, decide what changes need to made in the program and in instruction.

THE FINAL STEP: IMPROVING INSTRUCTION

Evaluation begins with the setting of goals and ends with action. An essential component is improvement of instruction. Once strengths and weaknesses are noted, steps should be taken to build on the strengths and repair the weak spots. For example, if you find that students' ability to interpret graphs is weak, you should make plans to improve that area. If students are unable to synthesize data from two sources of information or solve word problems, you should work on those skills. As the Board of Directors of the International Reading Association (1999) commented, "Assessment involves the systematic and purposeful collection of data to inform actions. From the viewpoint of educators, the primary purpose of assessment is to help students by providing information about how instruction can be improved" (p. 258). The final step in evaluation is to improve the program and the achievement of each of your students.

SUMMARY

The basic purpose of assessment is to provide feedback so that improvements can be made. Formative assessment is ongoing assessment which can be used to plan instruction. Summative assessment is designed to evaluate achievement over long periods of time. Evaluation starts with a set of goals. Goals now exist in lists of standards for each major content area. In addition to standards recommended by national organizations, states and local school districts have issued standards or curriculum frameworks. Goals should reflect basic principles of learning.

Standards are often assessed with high-stakes tests. A high-stakes test is one in which an important decision will be based on the outcome of a single test. Important decisions should be based on more than one source of assessment. High-stakes testing has the potential for narrowing the curriculum if educators allow tests to dictate what is taught. Despite being controversial, high-stakes testing is intensifying. In addition, tests have become more inclusive. Insofar as possible and with modifications and accommodations if necessary, English language learners and students in special education programs are required to take part in state and national assessments.

Tests are either norm-referenced or criterion-referenced. In norm-referenced tests, test takers are compared to a representative sample of children who are the same age or in the same grade. Scores are reported in a variety of ways: raw scores, percentile ranks, grade equivalent scores, stanines, normal curve equivalents, and scaled scores. In criterion-referenced tests, students' performance is assessed in terms of a criterion or standard. Because they indicate whether students have mastered a particular skill or strategy, these tests tend to be more valuable than norm-referenced tests for planning programs. Rubrics are a form of criterion-referenced reporting. Rubrics provide descriptions of expected or desirable performances as well as of unsatisfactory performances.

Tests should be reliable, valid, and fair. Students should also be given tests designed for the level on which they are reading. Tests that are too easy or too difficult are invalid and yield erroneous information.

Informal means of assessment include think-alouds, which are designed to gain insight into the thought processes students use, observation, checklists, ratings, questionnaires, and interviews. Observation may include composing anecdotal records or field notes. An anecdotal record is the recording of an event that sheds some light on the student's learning behavior.

Because background knowledge is such an important element in learning, it should be carefully assessed. Background knowledge may be assessed through free recall, word association, structured questions, unstructured questions, recognition, brainstorming, and predictions.

The most important evaluation is self-evaluation. Unless students assess their own progress toward meeting goals, they are hampered in taking the steps necessary to reach those goals. Tests and quizzes, exit and entrance slips, learning logs, and response journals can be a part of students' self-evaluation, as well as a source of information for the teacher. Portfolios also offer opportunities for self-assessment.

Writing can be assessed holistically or analytically. In holistic scoring, a composition is evaluated in terms of a limited number of general criteria. Analytic scoring involves analyzing pieces and noting specific strengths and weaknesses.

Portfolios provide a broad sampling of work for assessment and are effective in showing growth over time. They also actively involve the student in the assessment process.

The final step in evaluation is to improve the programs and student achievement.

Reflection

Return to the Anticipation Guide at the beginning of this chapter. Respond once again to the items. Did your responses change? If so, how and why? Why is assessment such an important part of instruction? Which practices seem to lead to the most effective assessment? Why is high-stakes testing controversial?

EXTENSION AND APPLICATION

1. Maintain a file of rubrics, observation guides, checklists, sample tests, think-aloud protocols, questionnaires, and other assessment devices that might be useful.
2. Examine the assessment devices in texts in your content area. Which kinds of devices are available? Is there provision for observation and portfolios? Which devices would seem to be most useful? Are standards or goals clearly stated? Is assessment aligned with standards?
3. Construct a checklist for an important area in your subject: lab reports, study strategies, participation in class or cooperative learning groups, work habits, or a similar area. If possible, try out the checklist. Revise it, if necessary.
4. Try out the think-aloud technique with a classmate. What does the think-aloud reveal about your reading process? How might you use this assessment technique in your content area?

CREATING AN EFFECTIVE CONTENT AREA PROGRAM

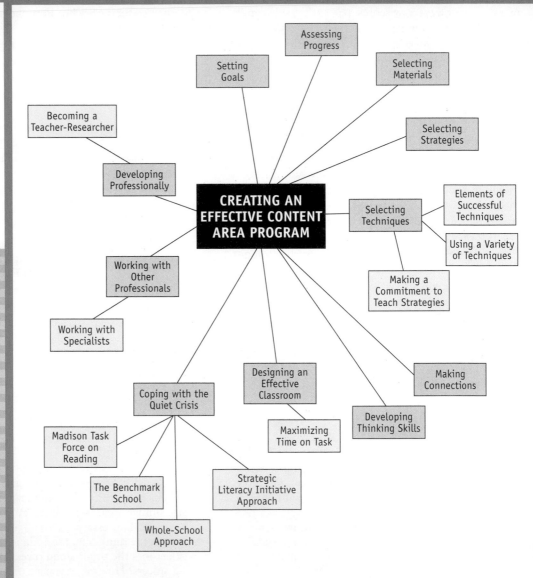

For each of the following statements related to the chapter you are about to read, put a check under "Agree" or "Disagree" to show how you feel. Discuss your responses with classmates before you read the chapter.

		Agree	*Disagree*
1	Instruction in literacy skills should pay off in increased content area learning.	____	____
2	Students who have superior background knowledge will learn more than students who have superior learning strategies.	____	____
3	Because of differences in subject matter that they teach and in approaches, it would not be advisable for content area teachers to agree to teach a core of strategies.	____	____
4	It's best to master one or two effective teaching techniques rather than to try to use six or more techniques.	____	____
5	Content area teachers must take extra steps to help struggling learners.	____	____

USING WHAT YOU KNOW

The previous thriteen chapters have discussed methods, materials, and assessment measures that you might use in a content area program. Think back on content area teachers who taught you who were particularly effective. What made them effective? What techniques did they use? How did they make the material understandable and interesting? How did they organize their classes? What kinds of materials did they use? Based on the highly effective teachers that you have known, what you have read, and your own experiences, how would you set up the literacy dimension of the content area that you teach? As you read this last chapter, be prepared to add, delete, or modify elements.

The overall intent of this text was to explore techniques, strategies, approaches, methods, materials, and organizational patterns that would build literacy in the content areas—and that would result in students learning more content area material and how to learn and communicate in the content areas. Special attention was paid to students who have traditionally had a difficult time learning content area material. This final chapter is designed to look at ways to set up a content area program that will result in maximum learning for all students. In a sense, this chapter will summarize the key points of all the previous chapters so that you can see practical ways of implementing key practices and principles.

SETTING GOALS

Organizing an effective content area program starts with a statement of goals. You need to decide what it is that you want your students to know and be able to do. According to research, setting goals and providing feedback has a powerful impact on student learning. In one study, students gained an average of six months and 23 percentile points when their teachers set goals and provided feedback as to whether goals were being met (Marzano, Gaddy, & Dean, 2000). To set goals, consider the standards set by your national professional organization. Also look at standards set by the state in which you teach or plan to teach and the district. The state and/or district may have a curriculum guide. Also take a look at the kinds of tests that your students will be asked to take. In Connecticut, for instance, students are asked to construct essay-type responses to interdisciplinary questions. Goals should then be adapted to fit the needs of the community in which you will be teaching and the needs of your students. In most subject matter areas, goals include a statement of content to be taught.

*C*ontent area teachers decide which key concepts they want students to learn.

You could, of course, simply accept the district's or state's goals. By adapting them to fit your situation, you are reflecting on what is important from your professional point of view. You are making the goals your own and so you will have greater commitment to reaching them. In addition, in some instances, goals are vaguely stated or stated in such general terms that they fail to provide adequate guidance. In other instances, the goals might be adequately stated but you may wish to add to them. Once goals have been set, you have a foundation for selecting materials and deciding on instructional approaches and techniques.

The next step is to build students' awareness of the goals, so they know what they are going to learn and why. Also, help students set personal goals based on overall goals. For instance, the content goal in health might be to learn how to plan a balanced diet. A student who is member of the cross-country team might be interested in learning what kind of diet is best to build endurance and also what kind of meal would be best to eat on the day of a race. Students are more motivated when they can personalize goals. A student who is very thin may want to set a goal of planning meals that will foster weight gain. A budget-conscious student might want to determine which foods are both nutritious and inexpensive. Having students set personal goals is a way of having them buy into the overall content goal or standard. Both long-term and short-term goals should be set. And there should be some way of monitoring progress toward reaching those goals.

A key element in setting goals and indeed in all instruction is feedback. On the basis of an analysis of hundreds of studies, one researcher concluded that "the most powerful single modification that enhances achievement is feedback " (Hattie, 1992, p. 9). Tutoring is such an effective way of learning because students get immediate, personal feedback (Bloom, 1976). However, not all feedback is created equal. The best feedback lets the students know what was right, what was wrong, and what can be done to improve. Feedback should also be timely. Feedback given long after the test or project was completed is less effective than feedback given immediately or the next day. The best feedback tells students whether they are on the right track or not, and if they are not, it helps them to make needed corrections (Marzano et al., 2000).

 **CHECKUP**

1. What role do goal setting and feedback play in a content area program?

ASSESSING PROGRESS

In order to provide students the feedback they need, it is essential that their work be assessed on an ongoing basis. Assessment should be embedded in instruction so the teacher knows when review, reteaching, or a change in approaches is required. It is also important that needed background skills and knowledge be assessed. Planning and implementing a content area literacy program requires the following information:

- Students' instructional reading level
- Students' grasp and use of reading strategies in the target content area
- Students' grasp and use of study skills and strategies
- Students' background knowledge in the target content area
- Students' ability to do the kind of writing typically expected in the content area
- Students' interests and attitudes
- Difficulty level and reading demands of the texts that will be read. (Farr & Pritchard, 1996)

Quizzes, unit tests, logs and journals, rubrics, observation, checklists, students' self-assessment, think-alouds, and portfolios can be used to obtain formative information and also summative information on students' progress. In addition, information can be obtained from assessments mandated by the district, state, and nation. To make major decisions, such as whether to pass or fail a student, several

USING TECHNOLOGY

Sharing Success: Effective Practices and Strategies http://www. sharingsuccess.org/code/ strategies.htm Provides information on various aspects of organizing programs to foster increased learning.

sources of information should be used. Recommended assessment measures include the following:

Placement: Informal or group inventory, and cloze inventory, verified by students' actual performance in assigned materials.

Background knowledge: Quizzes, questionnaires, PReP or other brainstorming technique, and learning logs. Students might be given a list of key terms from an upcoming unit and asked to check those that they are familiar with. Class discussions also provide insights into student background knowledge.

Knowledge of comprehension strategies: Group or individual think-alouds, placement inventory, quizzes, and observation of discussion of responses after a selection has been read.

Knowledge and use of study strategies: Questionnaire, discussion, observing students as they study, learning or study logs, and discussion of study approaches and habits.

Content area writing ability: Writing samples, observing students as they write, and portfolios.

Difficulty level and demands of text: Readability formula, subjective analysis, results of cloze or other group inventory, and discussion with students after they have read a portion of text.

Students' interests and attitudes: Discussions, questionnaires, observation, journals, and conversations with students.

 CHECKUP

1. What elements should be assessed in a content area literacy program?
2. How might these elements be assessed?

SELECTING MATERIALS

Once goals have been set and you have some idea about the level of materials students can handle, materials can be selected. In most content area classes, the textbook is the basic source of printed information. In some instances, the textbook will be selected by a committee or a department. In other instances, you may have the freedom to choose your own text. When choosing a text, consider the match between your goals and the content of the text. Also note the kinds of learning aids that the text offers and supplementary resources such as the availability of a Web site or audiovisual aids. Some texts are available in taped versions so that if students are unable to read the words, they can read along with the tape. If some of your students will be unable to read the text, consider using an easy-to-read text or trade books written on an easier level with those students. Consider the text to be just one source of information. Also have available as resources a library of trade books, periodicals, computer software, video tapes, CD-ROMs, and DVDs. You might also create a list of bookmarked Web sites as a resource.

SELECTING STRATEGIES

Recently, a number of learning experts (Marzano et al., 2000; National Reading Panel, 2000; Rosenshine et al., 1996) identified strategies that research has demonstrated work particularly well. These highly effective strategies are listed in Table 14.1. Some of the most effective strategies are remarkably simple and easy to implement. For instance, the most effective practice was encouraging students to see similarities and differences in concepts. Each of the strategies was then tried out in a number of studies with experimental and control groups. The National Reading Panel concluded that seven of the sixteen strategies it studied were highly effective. These are also noted in Table 14.1. Other learning experts calculated the **effect size** of the strategies. The effect size is the degree to which the experimental group did better than a matched group of students. Effect sizes are typically expressed in standard deviations. A **standard deviation** is a measure of the variability of performance. It can be translated into percentiles or months of growth. One standard deviation is roughly equivalent to a year's growth. For instance, summarizing and notetaking have an effect size of 1. This is equal to a year's growth above and beyond what the control group achieved. It is also equal to a percentile gain of thirty-four points. If students were at the fiftieth percentile (an average rank) before the treatment, they would be at the eighty-fourth percentile after the treatment. In other words, instead of doing better than 50 percent of students, they would be doing better than 84 percent.

■ **Effect size** is a statistical technique used to determine how well an experimental group performed when compared to a control group. Effect sizes provided in this chapter are based on tests made up by the experimenter. Effect sizes yielded by standardized tests were much smaller.
■ **Standard deviation** is a statistical measure of how much scores vary from the average. In a normal distribution, ⅔ of the scores would fall above or below the standard deviation of the average score. Approximately 98 percent would fall within two standard deviations.

TABLE 14.1

HIGHLY EFFECTIVE STRATEGIES

Strategy	Average Effect Size	Percentile Gain
Identifying similarities and differences	1.61	45
Summarizing and notetaking	1.00 NRP top 7	34
Generating questions	.86	31
Combined predicting, questioning, summarizing, and monitoring	.85 NRP top 7	30
Creating graphic organizers and other nonlinguistic representations	.75 NRP top 7	27
Story grammar	NRP top 7	
Combined strategies used in cooperative learning	.73 NRP top 7	27
Generating and testing hypotheses	.61 NRP top 7	23
Activating prior knowledge	.59	22
Monitoring comprehension	NRP top 7	

Of course, this doesn't mean that if you teach one of these strategies your students will achieve exactly the same gains. The authors of the study warn:

> The effectiveness of a strategy depends in part on the current achievement level of a student, in part on the skill and thoroughness with which a teacher applies the strategy, and in part on contextual strategies such as grade level and class size. (Marzano et al., 2000, p. 5)

An examination of the research indicates that the most effective strategies are those that have been highlighted in previous chapters. (Table 14.2 lists key comprehension strategies presented in this text.) Strategies are especially effective if they activate prior knowledge, highlight, organize, summarize, involve students in generating hypotheses or questions, and involve students in monitoring their reading. Using graphic organizers is also highly effective. Although most strategies are taught individually, this doesn't mean that they're applied in that way. Note that two of the highly effective listings (in Table 14.1) are multiple (combined) strategies. As they read a selection, students apply a number of strategies. It makes sense to teach strategies one at a time, so that students don't become confused or overwhelmed. However, after students

---

TABLE 14.2

RECOMMENDED COMPREHENSION STRATEGIES

Preparational
    Activating prior knowledge
    Previewing/Surveying
    Predicting
    Setting goal/purpose

Selecting/Organizing
    Using text structures to organize information
    Determining main ideas/essential information
    Summarizing
    Using graphic organizers

Elaborational
    Making connections
    Connecting new information with background knowledge
    Inferring
    Imaging
    Creating analogies
    Generating questions

Monitoring for Meaning (Metacognition)
    Monitoring
    Regulating
    Checking

Repairing/Reading difficult material
    Looking back
    Rereading
    Using graphics
    Reading intensively step by step
    Reading out loud
    Paraphrasing

Study
    Rehearsing
    Organizing information
    Seeking understanding
    Creating images
    Making associations/Using mnemonics
    Using narratives to organize information
    Using SQ3R
    Taking notes
    Outlining
    Using metamemory
    Setting and keeping study schedules
    Managing time
    Using self-talk
    Using test-taking strategies
    Adjusting rate of reading to purpose

Writing
    Brainstorming
    Freewriting
    Rehearsing
    Distancing
    Drawing

Word Recognition
    Using context
    Using morphemic analysis
    Using the dictionary/glossary

have learned a new strategy, they should be taught to integrate it with other strategies. Monitoring for meaning should be integrated with summarizing and other strategies. Not being able to summarize is a sign that one hasn't understood a passage.

Not all of the strategies explored in this text made the effective strategy list in Table 14.1. Imaging is missing, as is inferring. These are still highly effective strategies. They have been studied enough so that they can be recommended with confidence, but have not been sufficiently studied so that they can be listed as exemplary strategies.

 **CHECKUP**

1. Which strategies seem to be most effective?
2. What do effective strategies have in common?

SELECTING TECHNIQUES

Ed Fry (1995), the creator of the Fry Readability Graph discussed in Chapter 2, tells the story of observing a teacher in Africa teaching reading to a group of students. The students were outside under a tree. They had no computers, no chalkboard, no books. The teacher was writing a story in the dirt with a stick. The students then read the stick-written story. Despite the lack of materials, the children were learning and learning well. Although materials are helpful, it is the teacher who is the key to what students learn. As the teacher, you will decide which approach to use with your students and which techniques, how to adapt approaches and techniques, and when to switch them because a technique isn't working or the students are tired of it. A number of techniques were covered in this text. They are listed in Table 14.3 along with some of their advantages and disavantages.

In addition to being taught strategies, students need to be provided with preparation in background and vocabulary. Instruction in strategies, background, and vocabulary are often combined in techniques that foster improved comprehension of content area knowledge. Reading assistance can be provided through a variety of techniques. For instance, a segment to be read might be presented through a DRA, DR-TA, KWL Plus, ReQuest, Reciprocal Teaching, Questioning the Author, Reading Seminar, or even a cooperative learning group. If students are reading on their own, they might use SQ3R. All of these approaches are designed to provide preparation before reading, guidance during reading, and discussion of or reflection on material read. Which approach is best? All are best under some circumstances. Table 14.3 lists the key features, advantages, and disadvantages of each technique. The Directed Reading Activity works best when maximum preparation is needed. Reading Seminar and Questioning the Author are effective ways to help students work their way through dense text.

Elements of Successful Techniques

Based on a careful analysis of instructional studies, Rosenshine, Meister, and Chapman (1996) identified a number of key elements that fostered success. These included:

TABLE 14.3

TECHNIQUES FOR BUILDING LITERACY

Comprehension	Advantages	Disadvantages
Before-During-After Reading		
Instructional Framework	Carefully structured.	Mostly teacher directed.
Directed Reading Activity	Structured. Works well with students who need maximum preparation before reading.	Students may be passive participants.
Directed Reading-Thinking Activity	Involves students in making predictions.	Requires some background knowledge and ability to make predictions.
KWL-Plus	Builds background. Involves students in creating questions and finding answers to questions.	Requires some background knowledge.
ReQuest	Students involved in both asking and answering questions. Is especially effective with students who have difficulty comprehending.	Students may have difficulty composing higher-level questions.
Reciprocal Teaching	Fosters four effective strategies: predicting, questioning, summarizing, and clarifying as students and teacher discuss selections.	Students may experience difficulty applying some of the strategies.
Questioning the Author	Students and teacher collaboratively build meaning of selection section by section. Works well with material that is difficult and contains many new ideas.	Can be time-consuming.
Reading Seminar	Similar to Questioning the Author but places added emphasis on strategies.	Can be time-consuming.
Cooperative Learning/ Discussion Groups	Students work together on a project. Students are more fully involved and learn to work as members of a group.	Some students may not be accepted by the group. Students may be off task.
Collaborative Strategic Reading	Adds the structure of learning strategies to cooperative learning. Designed to help struggling learners.	Students may have difficulty coping with puzzling passages.
Before Reading		
Anticipation Guide	Involves students by having them agree or disagree with statements. Good for correcting erroneous concepts and considering controversial issues.	Requires background knowledge.
PReP	Uses brainstorming and discussion to assess and build background.	May provide just a rough idea of students' background knowledge.
Structured Overview	Displays key concepts so students can see how they are interrelated.	Mostly teacher directed. Can be adapted to obtain added student input.
Prereading Survey	Involves students in surveying, selecting, and obtaining an overview.	Texts do not always lend themselves to a survey.
Drawing Before Reading	Works well with ELL students and students who are better at representing what they know graphically rather than verbally. Involves everyone in responding.	Requires background knowledge. Students who are not visually oriented may have difficulty.
Writing Before Reading	Gives students time to organize their ideas.	Requires background knowledge.
During Reading		
Study Guides/Glosses	Students are provided with questions and explanations to help them comprehend material as they read.	Students may become overly focused on answering questions.

(continued)

TABLE 14.3

TECHNIQUES FOR BUILDING LITERACY *(continued)*

Comprehension	Advantages	Disadvantages
Frame Matrix/Information Map	Students compare and contrast ideas.	Doesn't work with all kinds of writing.
Embedded Questions	Students respond to questions as they read.	Students may focus on sections covered by questions and fail to integrate information across sections.

After Reading

Constructing Analogies	Helps students see how new ideas or processes are similar to familiar ideas or processes.	Analogies may be misleading. No two items are exactly alike. Students may fail to see how items being compared are different.
Constructing Graphic Organizers	Helps students organize ideas.	May oversimplify information.
Writing After Reading	Helps students summarize and reflect on new ideas.	Writing may become humdrum.
Extending and Applying	Students build on new knowledge and put it to use.	Not all new knowledge can be put to immediate use.
Modeling/Think-Alouds	Reveals thinking processes.	Students may have difficulty relating to teacher's thinking processes.
Using Prompts	Develops students' thinking. Provides scaffolding.	Questions can become oral quizzes rather than invitations to discuss.
Direct Instruction	Builds background and skill and provides practice and application.	Students may be too passive.
Reading Aloud	Builds background and appreciation of language.	Selections may not be equally interesting to all students.
Sheltered English	Provides support for ELLs as they learn content and build language skills.	Requires much preparation.
Language Experience	Uses language of students to summarize content selections or compose stories or essays. Works well with struggling learners and ELLs.	Language may be too restricted.

Writing

Modeling/Think-Alouds	Provides insight into processes writers use.	Models might be too advanced.
Using Models	Provides insight into craft of writing	Models can be so advanced that students can't relate to them.
Brainstorming/Discussing	Builds topics for writing.	Students may become overly reliant on anothers' ideas.
Freewriting	Fosters fluency.	Students may get idea that writing without planning beforehand is an effective practice.
Minilessons/Strategic Writing Lessons	Direct instruction in needed skills.	Application may be neglected.
Writing Workshop	Opportunities for instruction, feedback, practice, and application.	May not provide enough guidance.
Conferences	Provides instruction, guidance, and encouragement.	Tendency for teachers to be overly directive.
Dialogue Journals	Can be used to model good writing and prompt extended responses.	Over time, journals may become routine.

- Providing prompts
- Providing models
- Anticipating potential difficulties
- Regulating the difficulty of the material
- Guiding student practice
- Providing feedback and corrections
- Assessing student mastery

As the researchers noted, most of these elements involved scaffolding. The purpose of scaffolding is to provide temporary support to students so that they are able to accomplish a task with assistance that they couldn't complete on their own (Bruner, 1986). Prompting and providing models are two examples of scaffolding. Prompting, providing models, and other elements used to foster improved comprehension are discussed in the following paragraphs.

■ Providing Prompts

STRUGGLING READERS

Ironically, struggling readers are often provided fewer prompts than more able students. Provide prompts that will help struggling learners build on what they know and that will also encourage them to respond.

Prompts can be used in all content areas but have been widely used in reading instruction. Prompts for reading comprehension include such questions as What is the author trying to say here? What is the main point of this passage? What are the key details that back up the main point? How does what I just read relate to what I know about this subject? Prompts that are concrete and provide guidance are most effective (Rosenshine et al., 1996). In a study in which students with learning disabilities made dramatic progress learning to summarize, the following prompts were used:

1. What's the most important sentence in this paragraph? Let me underline it.
2. Let me summarize the paragraph. To summarize, I rewrite the main idea sentence and add important details.
3. Let me review my summary statements for the whole subsection.
4. Do my summary statements link up with one another? (Wong, 1986)

Questioning the Author and Reading Seminar make extensive use of prompts. For a list of possible prompts, see pages 196 to 206. Cue cards and checklists similar to the list of summarizing prompts above have also been a part of many successful comprehension programs.

Just as with any other procedure, prompts can be overused or used inappropriately. If the teacher overprompts, students may do little cognitive processing and so may not internalize the necessary procedures or achieve the understanding necessary to complete the task. Students may also come to overrely on prompts. Prompts should be faded so that students internalize the operations initiated by the prompts and begin to operate independently.

■ Modeling

Strategies being taught should be modeled and accompanied by think-alouds so that students gain insight into the cognitive processes required to apply a strategy. Students might also be shown printed copies of successful performance. Students who are learning to generate questions or summaries should be presented with models of well-constructed questions or summaries. Models and think-alouds might be presented in the introductory stage, during guided practice so students can get help completing the task, and after completing the task so students can compare their performance with that of the model.

■ Anticipating Potential Difficulties

For many strategies, potential difficulties can be anticipated and dealt with before students experience them. For instance, students can be taught not to include too many details when summarizing. Students can be taught to avoid composing main idea statements that are too narrow when generating main ideas. In question generation, students can be taught to avoid questions that focus on unimportant details or are not clear.

■ Regulating the Difficulty of the Material

Successful programs start out with brief, well-structured passages and move into longer, more complex ones. Prompts might also be reduced. The practice selections should be relatively easy so that students don't have to grapple with difficult vocabulary at the same time they are trying to apply a new strategy. Ultimately, students apply their skills to the kind of reading that they will be expected to do in their content area subjects.

■ Guided Practice

Guided practice is an essential element in all successful programs. Most often, guided practice is teacher directed. In some instances, guided practice is provided in reciprocal teaching groups. And in some instances it is provided in learning pairs or cooperative groups.

■ Providing Feedback and Corrections

Feedback and accompanying corrections are powerful factors in improving performance. Feedback and corrections can be provided in a variety of ways. In can be provided to the whole class or to small groups, orally or in written form. It can be provided by self-checking materials, as in some computer software programs. Students might also use checklists or other devices to obtain feedback and make corrections. Davey and McBride (1986) used the following checklist to help students assess and correct the kinds of questions they had generated:

- How well did I identify important information?
- How well did I link information together?
- How well could I answer my questions?
- Did my "think" questions use different language from the text?
- Did I use good signal words? (p. 260)

■ Assessing Student Mastery

The most effective programs assessed students' performance and provided added instruction until students had achieved **mastery** of the strategy. In the summarizing program involving students with learning disabilities (Wong et al., 1986), students kept working on the learning activities until they achieved 90 percent accuracy for three

STRUGGLING READERS
Struggling learners often end up with materials that are well beyond their reading ability. Make sure that steps are taken to make the content area reading material accessible. See Chapter 9 for suggestions.

■ **Mastery learning** is based on the principle that just about all students will learn if given appropriate instruction and enough time.

EXEMPLARY TEACHING

PROVIDING PREPARATION FOR READING

Dissatisfied with her traditional introduction of Faulkner's "The Bear," in which she gave students a brief introduction to the rather difficult short story, Patton (1993), a high school teacher, decided to try an approach in which she increased students' preparation for reading the story. She began her introduction by asking students how many had ever gone hunting. Several had. A discussion ensued in which students voiced a variety of reactions, some positive, some negative, to hunting. There was talk of gaining confidence, showing courage, and of getting to know family members better as well as comments about the ethics of killing defenseless creatures. It was a period of "emotional activation of prior knowledge" (p. 131). Students had discussed some key issues before

reading the story. Other classes discussed these same issues only after reading the story. To see whether before-story discussion worked better than after-story discussions, Patton compared the performance of two classes on a quiz. The before-story group outperformed the after-story group and also had a more productive discussion after reading the selection. They were better able to respond to the higher-level questions that were asked. More important, they seemed to be more deeply involved in the story. The results had profound implications for Patton's approach to teaching. She realized that setting the stage for students' construction of meaning worked better than directing the interpretation of the story. She realized that she should be more a guide than the expert interpreter who was the only one who really knew what the story meant.

---

days in a row. Some students needed two months before they could compose a summary correctly. However, the progress of the group was significant, especially when one considers that summarizing is one of the most difficult of the comprehension strategies to learn.

Using a Variety of Techniques

Students benefit from a variety of techniques and activities. Memory is both semantic and episodic. Semantic memory is our recall of facts and ideas. Episodic memory is our recall of events. One way of recalling an idea is to remember the setting in which it was learned. For instance, we may remember how mold forms by recalling an experiment in which slices of bread were exposed to different degrees of dampness. When students perform the same kinds of activities over and over again, the activities take on a sameness and so it is difficult to distinguish one from the other. Their value as episodic cues to help students recall the content continued within the activities is lost.

If the same content was presented within a variety of contexts and activities, it would be learned more completely and effectively. Different ways of representing content also leads to different connections. Even the most effective techniques lose their value if repeated too often (Nuthall, 1999).

Making a Commitment to Teach Strategies

Although evidence has been presented that instruction in strategies pays off in increased learning, you may still feel hesitant to try out the content area strategies presented in this text. If so, you are not alone. Several studies suggest that content area teachers fail to implement strategies that they have been taught. A primary reason is that we tend to teach the way we were taught. If we were taught by a one-book-fits-all lecture method, there is a good chance that we will teach that way. Another hindrance has to do with the way we learned about strategies. If we know them primarily through hearing and reading about them but have never actually tried them out, we may not feel familiar enough with them to try them. An effective way to learn strategies is to try them out with our own reading, see how they work, and then try them out with students (Keene & Zimmerman, 1997). This tryout should be more than a one-shot attempt. You may find that the strategy doesn't work too well at first. Like any other new learning, you might be awkward with it at first. Give yourself and your students time to work out the kinks and become familiar with the strategy or approach.

You may also believe that teaching literacy strategies eats into the limited time you have to teach your content area. As discussed earlier in the text, this may be true at first. But as students catch onto the strategies, you should be able to cover more content in greater depth because students will be able to take more responsibility for their learning and will also remember more of what they have read. At any rate, keep in mind that you are not being asked to be a reading and writing teacher. You are only asked to teach those reading and writing strategies that are essential to understanding your content area, to continuing to learn in that content area, and to communicating with others.

You may also feel pressured by district, state, or even national tests to teach in such a way that students are well prepared to take those tests. Teaching strategies and teaching in depth provide the best preparation for just about any test that students will take.

 *CHECKUP*

1. What are the major instructional techniques?
2. What are the key elements of effective techniques?

MAKING CONNECTIONS

Making connections and developing key concepts foster learning. As noted earlier, learning to see similarities and differences is a powerful strategy, as in the ability to derive generalizations. One organizational pattern that helps students see similarities and differences and construct generalizations is a **thematic approach.** In a thematic approach, content is studied in terms of broad ideas or questions. Themes help students build connections to other disciplines. For instance, although there are many topics in chemistry, they are related to nine overarching themes: energy, stability, patterns of change, systems and interactions, unity and diversity, scale and structure, form and function, models and organization, and evolution and adaptation (LeMay, Roblee, Beall, & Brower, 2000). The concept of *energy* is developed in a number of chapters in a popular chemistry text, as are the other major themes. The theme of energy can be related to physics, earth science, history, and geography. By seeing relationships, students form more connections among ideas and activities that might

USING TECHNOLOGY

The Knowledge Loom Adolescent Literacy in the Content Areas http://knowledgeloom.org/ adlit/media/ meltzer_media.html Discusses the need for content area literacy instruction in the secondary school.

■ The **thematic approach** is the organization of instruction around themes or central ideas rather than around subject matter topics.

otherwise be isolated. The more connections that are formed, the deeper and broader the understanding.

In a series of carefully conducted studies, Nuthall (1999) and his colleagues concluded that it takes four significant encounters with a concept before it is learned and passed into long-term memory. Encounters with concepts are multiplied when a thematic approach is taken. Observing a unit in which Antarctica was studied from both a science and a social studies perspective, Nuthall noted that the teacher introduced human interest materials from the social studies along with scientific information. Students were able to establish links between geological information about Antarctica to the hardships scientists endured collecting that information.

Subject matter can be presented through single disciplines, through **coordination** between or among disciplines, or through **integration** (Allan & Miller, 2000). Many schools follow a single discipline model in which chemistry is taught by one teacher, English by a second teacher, and history by a third teacher. However, in many instances, teachers point out connections between their subjects and other subjects. While discussing the makeup of the atom, the chemistry teacher might discuss the history of its exploration and the consequences of using nuclear energy. Coordination comes about when teachers work together to explore the same topics or themes. The math teacher might review problem-solving techniques while students balance atomic equations in chemistry. The physics teacher might discuss the particle and wave theories of the internal structure of the atom. These are all examples of coordination. Integration occurs when students use two or more of the disciplines to explore broad themes or topics. The theme of change, for instance, might be viewed through science, social studies, and the humanities.

At Rogers High School in Spokane, Washington, Peter Perkins, the social studies teacher and English teacher Jeri Giachetti teamed up to teach a full-year interdisciplinary course called "It's My American History." In this two-period course, students related their personal family history to the literature and history of twentieth-century America. Students also took part in a service learning project at a local community center in which they each interviewed and composed the personal history of a senior citizen for a multimedia CD-ROM presentation (Perkins, 2001). Students also related the history of their families to the history of the twentieth century and created a personalized portfolio. Students used electronic technology, library resources, and human resources from the community to complete their studies.

Students used journal entries to compose a biography and a compare/contrast piece in which they compared the life of someone living between 1950 and 1970 with someone living today. Students also created a news show on the impact of immigration on Spokane and the nation.

■ **Coordination** is the process of introducing the same concept or topic from different subject matter areas so that they are covered at the same time and reinforce each other or using skills or topics in one subject to support the skills or topics in another content area.

■ **Integration** is an approach in which varied subject matter areas are drawn upon to solve problems, answer broad questions, or explore topics or themes.

USING TECHNOLOGY

Theme Pages for Elementary School Students and Teachers http://www.stemnet.nf.ca/ CITE/themes.html Provides links to 150 topics.

DEVELOPING THINKING SKILLS

In one way or another, standards for all of the disciplines call for developing higher-level thinking skills. Making connections is an excellent device for developing a variety of thinking skills: comparing and contrasting, classifying, constructing generalizations, drawing conclusions, and so on. Based on extensive research into how students learn content area concepts, Nuthall (1999) concluded that

> Tasks need to be set up that model and give students practice in activities that involve making connections between related pieces of information and identifying implications and potential differences and contradictions. As students practice these activities and become expert in the habits of mind involved in the activities, these habits become internalized and an unconscious but automatic part of the way their minds deal with new experiences. (p. 337)

Nuthall warns against restricting the opportunities for struggling learners to apply higher-level thinking skills:

> Restricting the intellectual complexity of tasks (as is usual for students in low-track classes) results in a progressive lowering of scores on tests of academic aptitude (Oakes, 1992). The success of activities designed to increase students' facility with "habits of mind" such as questioning, explaining, and evaluating evidence has been demonstrated in studies such as those by King and Rosenshine (King, 1994; King & Rosenshine, 1993). (p. 337)

 **✓ CHECKUP**

1. Why is making connections important?
2. What are some ways connections can be made?

DESIGNING AN EFFECTIVE CLASSROOM

Effective content area classrooms come in a variety of shapes and sizes. However, they share a number of characteristics. In a series of studies on effective instruction, Pressley and his colleagues discovered that motivation had a significant impact on students' learning (Pressley, Wharton-McDonald, Mistretta-Hampston, & Echevarria, 1998; Boothroyd, 2001). Motivation, the researchers discovered, is mainly a matter of creating a positive and encouraging but challenging environment. Students get the feeling that they are valued and competent and that they are engaged in interesting, worthwhile learning activities. The following characteristics are also featured:

- Cooperation rather than competition is emphasized.
- Hands-on activities are prominent. However, the activities are minds-on and have legitimate learning goals.
- A variety of techniques is used. Techniques are matched to students' needs.
- Routines and procedures are well established. The classroom is orderly.
- Effort is emphasized. Praise and reinforcement are used as appropriate.
- The teacher builds a sense of excitement and enthusiasm.

In his decade-long study, Ruddell (1995) concluded that **influential teachers**

■ **Influential teachers** are teachers who stand out in students' memories because they had a lasting, significant, positive impact on their learning.

- use highly motivating and effective teaching strategies,
- help students with their personal problems,
- create a feeling of excitement about the subject matter or skill areas they teach,
- exhibit a strong sense of personal caring about the students, and
- demonstrate the ability to adjust instruction to the individual needs of the student. (p. 455)

Ruddell also found that influential teachers had in-depth knowledge of their content areas and methods of teaching it, had well-formulated instructional plans, and appealed to intrinsic motivation rather than extrinsic motivation. In other words, students were motivated to learn because their curiosity was aroused, learning gave them a sense of personal control, and they were interested in the subject. Extrinsic motivation, such as learning in order to please the teacher or get high grades, played a relatively minor role. Influential teachers also fostered higher-level thinking skills and used probes and prompts to draw out students' responses in discussions. Their class discussions were instructional conversations rather than oral quizzes. Influential teachers helped students construct meaning and make discoveries.

Maximizing Time on Task

■ **Time on task** is a component of effective instruction. The term refers to the amount of class time that students actually spend on an activity.

Effective teachers use their time well. One of the best predictors of academic achievement is the amount of **time** spent **on task,** assuming, of course, that the task is one that results in learning. Worksheets completed during class time, for instance, don't usually result in much learning. The key to learning, especially for students who are struggling, is active instruction. Observe students' responses to activities. Eliminate or revise those activities during which students have difficulty staying on task (Baker & Piburn, 1997). Also look for wasted time. In one study, content area teachers wasted as much as 30 percent of class time (Mitman, Mergendoller, Packer, & Marchman, 1984). Time is most likely to be lost at the beginning of the period, at the end, and during transitions between activities. Careful planning and establishing effective management techniques, including having a useful activity as soon as students enter the room, should reduce lost time.

✔ CHECKUP

1. What steps can be taken to design an effective content area literacy program?

COPING WITH THE QUIET CRISIS

In today's middle schools and high schools, there is a quiet crisis. The quiet crisis is the inability of many students to deal with their academic texts (Schoenbach et al., 1999). Although most of these students can read at a basic level, they can't currently achieve the higher-level comprehension demanded by many of their subject matter texts. They have hit a "literacy ceiling":

We have come to refer to students' difficulty with reading and understanding subject area texts as the literacy ceiling—a ceiling that limits what students can hope to achieve both in the classroom and in their lives outside of school. (p. 5)

One reaction to the literacy crisis has been to assume that little can be done for these students, an idea that Schoenbach and colleagues termed "incorrect and de-structive" (p. 7). In a carefully planned program implemented in a number of schools, they have shown that it is possible to help older students obtain the skills and atti-tude required to be strong, independent readers.

Strategic Literacy Initiative Approach

To help students caught in the quiet crisis, the Strategic Literacy Initiative (SLI) was created. Based on research and tryouts, the SLI adapted a reading apprenticeship model in which the classroom teacher functions as the master reader to the student apprentice readers. The program can be implemented in two ways: (1) as a supplementary liter-acy program or (2) as a program integrated within an academic subject. The Strategic Literacy Initiative featured four dimensions:

1. *Social.* Class became a community of learners in which students helped each other and felt free to express their ideas. Students felt free to be open about their reading and writing difficulties.
2. *Personal.* Students' sense of self and academic self-confidence were built.
3. *Cognitive.* Students' learning strategies and thinking processes were fostered.
4. *Knowledge building.* Students' backgrounds were built so that they had more to bring to the text and would get more out of it.

> **USING TECHNOLOGY**
>
> For more information about the Strategic Literacy Initiative, see the WestEd Web site.
> http://www.wested.org/stratlit/

To build the social dimension, students read biographical selections that demon-strated the power of literacy and the role it played in the lives of famous people. Through discussions, they shared interpretations of texts, and also the strategies they used to construct meaning and the difficulties they encountered and how they dealt with them.

To develop the personal dimension, students looked as themselves as readers. They wrote and discussed their reading experiences and reading likes and dislikes. They also explored the processes they used when reading and discovered ways to persist when the reading was difficult. One of the activities that helped them gain insight into themselves as readers was to keep metacognitive logs of their reading. They were asked to think of themselves as scientists and to record what was going on in their heads as they read. In addition to teaching them more about themselves as readers, this activity gave students the opportunity to discover the problems they came upon as they read and to explore possible solutions.

To develop the cognitive dimension, students explored key strategies, such as mon-itoring for meaning, setting purposes, adjusting reading processes, and reading for main ideas and details. They also engaged in scaffolded practice and application.

To build knowledge, students shared information about key topics, developed essential vocabulary, and noted the kinds of writing and thinking used in major aca-demic areas. They also looked at the kinds of questions that content areas explored and the kinds of language that each discipline used. Specially created units led them to think, read, and write as historians and scientists.

Whole-School Approach

ENGLISH LANGUAGE LEARNERS

See the section on sheltered content in Chapter 9 for suggestions for helping students who are still learning English.

When middle school principal Alice Quiocho (1997) noticed that the list of students failing in the major subject areas was growing, she began asking why. The teachers reported that the students weren't meeting standards. Not satisfied with that circular response, she began asking students what was wrong. While visiting classes, she talked to students about their work: "What are you doing to complete this task? How did you decide what you had to do to complete this task?"(p. 450). In many instances, their responses conveyed a sense of helplessness and lack of direction. Some confessed that they didn't understand what they read. Classroom observations revealed that many students lacked strategies. Students were asked to tell what helped them learn and what got in their way. Working in groups, dividing up the assignment into sections, and seeing and hearing information at the same time were helpful to students. Big words, hard words, too many ideas on a page, not knowing how things are related, and forgetting what was just read were some of the things that got in the students' way.

Based on the students' responses and a review of the research on strategy instruction, ongoing staff training was implemented. After discussing the students' needs and possible strategies, content area teachers began incorporating strategy instruction as part of their content area instruction. Teachers began this implementation by presenting the strategy that they felt most comfortable with. Follow-up observations and reports indicated that the students did best when they worked in groups and when they engaged in active, meaning-constructing strategies such as SQ3R. The program worked because it was built on the concerns of both teachers and students. In addition, the principal went to the students for answers. As she explains, "If we wonder *why* so many students fail, ask students. Once included in the teaching and learning processes, middle school students can tell us what works best for them" (p. 454).

The Benchmark School

The Benchmark School was established to help students who were bright but had difficulty learning to read and write. Having failed in the past, many students had adopted styles that were impulsive, rigid, and nonpersistent. They gave up in the face of difficulty. The staff felt that students should become aware of their cognitive processes so they could better exercise control over them. However, the staff did not agree on the role of the content teacher. Some content teachers felt that it was not the content area teacher's role to teach strategies. Others felt that strategies would be best taught as a stand-alone course. It was decided, after much debate, to have a dual program: a stand-alone course in learning strategies and the integration of strategy instruction with content teaching (Gaskins & Elliot, 1991).

The staff then constructed a curriculum that included which strategies were to be taught, when they were to be taught, and how they were to be taught. The curriculum was tentative. Based on teacher and student feedback, many revisions and adaptations were made. Teachers soon realized that some strategies were more effective than others and that teaching strategies was a long-term commitment. It might be many weeks or even months before students actually began applying strategies independently. Particular emphasis was placed on motivating students and helping them to overcome personal obstacles that got in the way of their success. Strategy instruction included teaching students ways to overcome these obstacles.

Madison Task Force on Reading

In Madison, Wisconsin, a task force was established to look into the issue of struggling readers in the secondary schools. It found that "Struggling readers typically receive reading instruction in remedial programs that are isolated from the learning demands expected of them the rest of the day in their content classes. Struggling readers are frequently expected to perform independently in their content classrooms without the benefit of teaching strategies" (Buehl & Stumpf, 1999; Buehl & Stumpf, 2000). The task force recommended a school- and districtwide commitment to reading in which reading specialists worked closely with content area teachers. The task force also recommended

> Classroom interventions: which emphasize teaching strategies which assist struggling readers, both in the effective learning of content as well as reinforcing their growth as readers.
>   Support for learning: in content classes, such as tutoring assistance and skill development, which is offered within a class, during study periods, or outside the school day. (Buehl & Stumpf, 2000)

Ability plays a limited role in what students learn. Students classified as slow learners learn just as much as students classified as average or above average if the material is well taught (Nuthall, 1996). "If the appropriate number of learning experiences occur, without significant gaps between them, learning occurs regardless of the learning ability of the students" (Nuthall, 1996, p. 33). One factor that does limit learning is students' knowledge of the culture of the school. Understanding and being able to carry out academic tasks has an influence on what students learn (Nuthall, 1996). This means understanding the language of instruction: *paraphrasing, quality, quantity, essay,* and so on.

> Those who fail to acquire the implicit understandings that characterize the language of a classroom are those who do not share the cultural understanding and background of the majority of the students. They may end up working hard . . . but the work is not valued by the teacher, or it results in critical learning experiences being missed. (Nuthall, 1996,. p. 28)

Explaining the purpose of assignments and providing thorough, clear instructions help students who lack the knowledge of how academic tasks should be completed. Students also need to feel valued and competent.

CHECKUP

1. What are some approaches to helping struggling learners?
2. What do the approaches have in common?

USING TECHNOLOGY

Middle School Reading Task Force Report
http://www.madison.k12.wi.us/tnl/langarts/msread.htm
Contains information about how struggling readers may be helped to learn content area literacy skills.

WORKING WITH OTHER PROFESSIONALS

The most effective programs are those in which a whole department, or better yet, a whole school participates. The school agrees on overall goals, including strategies that students should know, assessment measures, and techniques. For instance, all teachers might agree to use SQ3R, KWL-Plus, or graphic organizers. In one urban high school in San Diego, the school's staff development committee agreed to focus on six instructional techniques: concept mapping, vocabulary instruction, KWL-Plus, writing to learn, structured notetaking, and reciprocal teaching, which include four powerful student strategies: predicting, questioning, summarizing, and clarifying or monitoring for meaning. In addition to learning more content material, the students achieved significant gains in reading (Fisher, 2001). Having a whole school agree to focus on a common set of strategies is highly effective because students then apply the same strategies in each class and so become better strategy users. Teachers save time because they can build on what other teachers in the school have already done and also have their efforts reinforced by other teachers.

In some instances, teachers weren't aware of techniques they could use to enhance students' performance. As one English teacher explained:

> We used to think that they [the students] knew all the words in the book, but that they were lazy. Now we know that they have a lot of vocabulary to learn and that we better make that part of our teaching. Now I can't imagine asking students to read something at home without previewing the vocabulary. Can you imagine what it must have been like to start reading your homework and not knowing a whole bunch of the words on the page? (Fisher, 2001, p. 96)

Teachers multiply their effectiveness by collaborating with other professionals.

Programs work best when teachers buy into them—participation in the San Diego program was voluntary—and when there is strong administrative support. It also helps if teachers have input. Although pleased with their success, the teachers at the high school saw two major needs: writing across curriculum and providing literacy instruction in after-school programs. The teachers also wanted a writing rubric that could be used in all classes. As one science teacher explained:

> I wasn't trained to teach and evaluate student writing. I know it's important, but I need to know what the English teachers want me to look for. If we all use the same format to give students feedback about their writing, the consistency will have a positive impact. (Fisher, 2001, p. 99)

Perhaps the most important factor in the school's success was that teachers were working together to achieve common goals. Having become aware that students needed help reading content area materials and writing about content area topics, they were willing to try out new approaches. At the beginning of the program a student teacher at the school asked, "Why do we have to teach them to take notes? Can't they figure it out on their own? It seems like we're babying them with all this" (p. 96). Two months later she commented:

> If we want them to understand the content of our class, we have to make sure that they know how to record information from the textbook, their research, and our lectures. How did I think they would learn this? Notetaking is really different in each class and grade. (p. 96)

Even if your school lacks an all-department or all-school approach, you can team up with others. Perhaps you can work with the teachers who teach other sections of the same grade or who teach the same students that you teach. Or, you can seek out likeminded colleagues and work with them. You might start a study group in which you discuss common concerns and seek solutions. Since you have a certain amount of expertise in this area after taking a course in content area reading, you might agree to share your knowledge with others.

Working with Specialists

Take full advantage of the expertise of the school's specialists. Seek the advice of the learning disabilities specialist when working with struggling learners, of the bilingual or ESL teacher when working with English language learners, and of the reading specialist when working with struggling readers or writers. The reading specialist can suggest materials and techniques that might be used with struggling readers and might also assess the literacy capabilities of struggling readers in your class. One underused resource is the school's guidance counselor. The guidance counselor can provide advice on handling controversial issues, information about what to do when students reveal information that suggests that they are in some sort of danger from drugs or abuse, or some steps that might be taken to help a student who is undergoing a difficult time at home or at school.

 *CHECKUP*

1. What are some of the benefits of working with other professionals?

DEVELOPING PROFESSIONALLY

Much of the information in this textbook is based on research. There is a wealth of research, for instance, to show that strategies work, especially when they are combined with each other and integrated with content knowledge. Research has also shed light on how students go about constructing meaning from text, and there is research that shows that cooperative learning has a variety of positive payoffs. Much of the information in this textbook was derived from personal research of an informal nature. For instance, suggestions for using morphemic analysis and context clues and cognates are based on my personal experience and informal tryouts with stu-

TABLE 14.4

CHECKLIST FOR AN EFFECTIVE CONTENT AREA LITERACY PROGRAM

	Never	Seldom	Often	Regularly
Teaching Practices: General				
Provide in-depth exploration of key concepts.	___	___	___	___
Stress overall themes.	___	___	___	___
Help students relate new information to old and apply it to their lives.	___	___	___	___
Develop the vocabulary needed to understand my subject matter.	___	___	___	___
Foster intrinsic motivation and sense of self-efficacy.	___	___	___	___
Teaching Practices: Reading				
Teach preparatory strategies such as surveying and predicting.	___	___	___	___
Teach during-reading strategies such as questioning, inferring, and monitoring.	___	___	___	___
Teach after-reading strategies such as summarizing, comparing, applying, and extending.	___	___	___	___
Teach morphemic analysis skills especially helpful in my subject area.	___	___	___	___
Make use of graphic organizers and encourage students to do the same.	___	___	___	___
Teaching Practices: Speaking				
Foster higher-level discussions with active student involvement.	___	___	___	___
Provide opportunities for student-to-student discussions.	___	___	___	___
Provide opportunities for students to communicate their knowledge about the content area.	___	___	___	___
Provide opportunities to use technology and presentation software.	___	___	___	___
Teaching Practices: Studying				
Directly instruct students in study techniques especially effective for my content area.	___	___	___	___
Foster helpful study habits. Teach notetaking techniques especially useful in my content area.	___	___	___	___
Teach how to use research techniques and materials, including the Internet.	___	___	___	___
Teaching Practices: Writing				
Use process and strategic instruction approach.	___	___	___	___
Teach skills necessary to communicate in my content area.	___	___	___	___
Assign essays, library papers, and other tasks that develop higher-level thinking skills.	___	___	___	___
Plan a variety of writing activities.	___	___	___	___
Give students choices of topics and tasks when possible.	___	___	___	___
Teaching Practices: Selecting and Using Materials				
Use high-quality materials that provide in-depth, accurate coverage.	___	___	___	___

(continued)

TABLE 14.4

CHECKLIST FOR AN EFFECTIVE CONTENT AREA LITERACY PROGRAM *(continued)*

	Never	Seldom	Often	Regularly
Supplement texts with trade books, periodicals, Web sites, and other sources of information.	____	____	____	____
Provide materials that are user friendly and accessible.	____	____	____	____
Provide materials that are accessible to struggling readers by adapting them, acquiring easy-to-read materials, or providing added guidance.	____	____	____	____
Present skills and strategies needed to make use of materials.	____	____	____	____

Evaluating

	Never	Seldom	Often	Regularly
Set goals and objectives based on accepted standards.	____	____	____	____
Align assessment with goals.	____	____	____	____
Continually monitor progress with embedded, formative assessment.	____	____	____	____
Use informal as well as formal assessment measures.	____	____	____	____
Involve students in the assessment process. Encourage self-assessment.	____	____	____	____
Use rubrics.	____	____	____	____
Use portfolios.	____	____	____	____
Use formative and summative assessment data to improve the program.	____	____	____	____

Organizing/Managing

	Never	Seldom	Often	Regularly
Provide for individual differences.	____	____	____	____
Use varied ways to present information so that it is accessible to all.	____	____	____	____
Provide sheltered instruction for English language learners.	____	____	____	____
Make needed modifications and accommodations for students with special needs.	____	____	____	____
Challenge the gifted.	____	____	____	____
Help the undereducated catch up.	____	____	____	____
Maximize time on task and emphasize high-payoff activities.	____	____	____	____
Involve students in decisions.	____	____	____	____
Provide opportunities for various kinds of grouping, including cooperative learning.	____	____	____	____

Professional

	Never	Seldom	Often	Regularly
Set up short- and long-term objectives for professional development.	____	____	____	____
Keep abreast of latest developments in my content area.	____	____	____	____
Keep abreast of latest developments in teaching techniques and technology.	____	____	____	____
Play an active role in professional organizations.	____	____	____	____
Attend professional conferences and meetings.	____	____	____	____
Try out new methods and materials.	____	____	____	____
Engage in teacher research.	____	____	____	____
Assess the effectiveness of my teaching and make necessary changes.	____	____	____	____

dents. Formal research will never answer all the questions that teachers have about the best way to present a particular topic or to handle a particular learning problem or organizational issue. Instructional or action research should be an essential part of the content area teacher's professional development.

Becoming a Teacher-Researcher

Teachers have always tried out new techniques, materials, and organizational plans on their own. Instructional research makes this process more reflective, more formal, and more intrinsic to teaching so that it becomes more beneficial both to the teacher and to the students. As Atwell (1993) comments, "Educators who learn in their classrooms become the best possible teachers, thoughtful about how students learn and how they can help" (p. vii).

■ **Teacher research** is a form of action research in which teachers conduct studies to seek answers to questions they have about ways to improve instruction in their classroom.

The steps in **teacher research** include identifying a problem or issue, composing questions that can be answered through research, determining the method and procedure for investigating the issue, carrying out the research and collecting the data, analyzing the data, drawing conclusions, and making decisions or changes based on the data (Vacca & Vacca, 2002). Dissatisfaction with her students' responses and hearing about other ways of teaching literature and writing led Nancy Atwell (1993) to become a teacher-researcher. She reports having hundreds of questions: "Are there patterns of growth in the writing of adolescents? What conventions or skills will these writers need, and how do I best teach them? Will their reading affect their writing?" (p. ix). Her teaching and research went "hand in hand." She took notes on students' performance, tape-recorded discussions, and collected writing samples. But the magic was in the analysis of the data and the reflection. Writing about her findings helped her to understand them better and also provided a means of sharing with others. Her action research resulted in readers' workshop, a highly effective approach to teaching adolescents, which is described in her classic book, *In the Middle* (Atwell, 1987).

Joining professional organizations, taking courses, attending conferences, reading professional journals and texts, obtaining professional information from the Internet, and joining a professional study group or a school committee are some of the many other ways to develop professionally. You may find it helpful to compose a professional development plan. Fill out the Checklist for an Effective Content Area Literacy Program, found in Table 14.4. This will help you assess your strengths and weaknesses as a content area teacher. List steps that you can take to build on your strengths and reduce or eliminate weak areas.

 CHECKUP

1. What are some ways content area teachers can develop professionally?

SUMMARY

Organizing an effective content area program starts with a statement of goals. It includes assessing progress toward reaching those goals, selecting appropriate materials, student strategies to be taught, and techniques to be used. Although strategies can be taught singly, students should learn how to use them in integrated fashion. Effective instructional techniques include providing prompts, providing models, anticipating potential difficulties, regulating the difficulty of the material, guiding student practice, providing feedback and corrections, and assessing student mastery. Although strategies have been shown to increase student learning, content area teachers may be reluctant to present them because they feel insecure teaching the strategies, don't feel it is their responsibility, or believe teaching strategies will take time away from teaching content area material. Because it helps students make connections, developing themes also fosters students' learning.

In an effective classroom, cooperation is emphasized, hands-on activities are prominent, varied techniques matched to students' needs are employed, routines are established, effort is emphasized, and a sense of excitement and enthusiasm are built by the teacher. Effective teachers also exhibit a strong sense of personal caring about the student, and demonstrate the ability to adjust instruction to their individual needs. Effective teachers have in-depth knowledge of their content areas and appeal to intrinsic motivation. In effective classrooms, time on task is maximized and activities that have limited instructional value are minimized.

The quiet crisis facing many content area teachers is the large number of students who struggle to learn. Programs to help these students are varied but stress the teaching of strategies, building background, and building a sense of self-knowledge and competence. Finding out what obstacles stood in the way of students' learning and helping students overcome them was also effective. Having professional staff work together to help students was also a factor in effective teaching.

Reflection

Return to the Anticipation Guide at the beginning of this chapter. Respond once again to the items. Did your responses change? If so, how and why? What role do you think the content area teacher should play in the teaching of learning strategies? What is your attitude toward teaching learning strategies? What do you think is the content area teacher's role in helping struggling learners? Who was the most effective teacher that you have ever had? What made that teacher effective?

EXTENSION AND APPLICATION

1. Create a five-year plan for professional development. Include both short-term goals and long-terms goals.
2. Select two or three key strategies and use them until you feel you have thoroughly mastered them. Then devise a plan for teaching them to your students.
3. Think of the characteristics of effective teachers. Which of these characteristics do you possess? In which areas do you feel you are lacking? What can you do to strengthen those areas?

APPENDIX A

GRADED LISTING OF CONTENT AREA TRADE BOOKS

First-Grade Books

Easy First

Morris, Ann. *Tools.* Lothrop, Lee & Shepard, 1992, 32 pp.

Noll, Sally. *Surprise!* Greenwillow, 1997, 24 pp.

Perkins, Al. *The Ear Book.* Random House, 1968, 28 pp.

Siddals, Mary McKenna. *Tell Me a Season.* Houghton Mifflin, 1997, 26 pp.

Middle First

Barton, Byron. *Bones, Bones, Dinosaur Bones.* Crowell, 1990, 30 pp.

Brown, Craig. *In the Spring.* Greenwillow, 1994, 24 pp.

Donnelly, Liza. *Dinosaur Days.* Scholastic, 1987, 30 pp.

Miller, Margaret. *My Five Senses.* Simon & Schuster, 1994, 22 pp.

Morris, Ann. *Work.* Lothrop, Lee & Shepard, 1998, 29 pp.

Ending First

Arnosky, Jim. *Come Out, Muskrats.* Lothrop, Lee & Shepard, 1989, 22 pp.

Barton, Byron. *Dinosaurs, Dinosaurs.* Crowell, 1989, 36 pp.

Greene, Carol. *Truck Drivers Deliver Goods.* The Child's World, 1999, 32 pp.

Parish, Peggy. *Dinosaur Time.* HarperCollins, 1974, 32 pp.

Williams, Sherley Anne. *Working Cotton.* Harcourt, 1992, 26 pp.

Second-Grade Books

Beginning Second

Bancroft, Henrietta, & Van Gelder, Richard G. *Animals in Winter.* HarperCollins, 1997, 32 pp.

Cole, Joanna. *Hungry, Hungry Sharks.* Random House, 1986, 48 pp.

Demuth, Patrick. *Johnny Appleseed.* Grossett & Dunlap, 1996, 32 pp.

Jordan, Helene J. *How a Seed Grows.* HarperCollins, 1960, 1992, 30 pp.

Ling, Mary. *See How They Grow, Butterfly.* Dorling Kindersley, 1992, 21 pp.

Penner, Lucille. *Dinosaur Babies.* Random House, 1991, 32 pp.

Rotner, Shelley, & Kreisler, Ken. *Nature Spy.* Simon & Schuster, 1992, 26 pp.

Second

Arnosky, Jim. *Otters Under Water.* Putnam, 1992, 24 pp.

Arnosky, Jim. *Every Autumn Comes the Bear.* Putnam, 1993, 28 pp.

Branley, Franklyn M. *Day Light, Night Light.* HarperCollins, 1998, 32 pp.

Brenner, Barbara. *Wagon Wheels.* HarperCollins, 1978, 64 pp.

Chermayeff, Ivan. *Fishy Facts.* Harcourt Brace, 1994, 29 pp.

Demuth, Patricia Brennan. *Achoo!* Grossett & Dunlap, 1997, 30 pp.

Fowler, Allan. *Frogs and Toads and Tadpoles, Too.* Children's Press, 1992, 32 pp.

Hopkins, Lee Bennett (Ed.). *Surprises.* HarperCollins, 1986, 64 pp.

Hopkins, Lee Bennett. *Questions: Poems Selected by Lee Bennett Hopkins.* HarperCollins, 1992, 64 pp.

Kramer, Sydelle. *Wagon Train.* Grossett & Dunlap, 1997, 48 pp.

Kuskin, Karla. *Something Sleeping in the Hall.* HarperCollins, 1985, 64 pp.

Kuskin, Karla. *Soap Soup and Other Verses.* HarperCollins, 1992, 64 pp.

Levy, Elizabeth. *Schoolyard Mystery.* Scholastic, 1994, 45 pp.

Murphy, Stuart J. *Jump, Kangaroo, Jump.* HarperCollins, 1999, 32 pp.

Penner, Lucille Recht. *The True Story of Pocahontas.* Random House, 1994, 48 pp.

Rabe, Tish. *On Beyond Bugs! All about Insects.* Random, 1999, 44 pp.

Ryden, Hope. *Joey, the Story of a Baby Kangaroo.* Tamborine, 1994, 38 pp.

Wallace, Karen. *Duckling Days.* Dorling Kindersley, 1999, 32 pp.

Zoehfeld, Kathleen Weidner. *What Lives in a Shell?* HarperCollins, 1994, 26 pp.

Third-Grade Books

Easy Reading Level: Grade 2 (Interest Level: Grade 3)

Dorros, Arthur. *Ant Cities.* HarperCollins, 1987, 32 pp.

Hopkins, L. B. (Ed.) *Questions: Poems of Wonder.* HarperCollins, 1992, 64 pp.

Lundell, Margo. *A Girl Named Helen Keller.* Scholastic, 1995, 48 pp.

Penner, Lucille Recht. *Sitting Bull.* Grossett & Dunlap, 1995, 48 pp.

Dr. Seuss. *The Cat's Quizzer.* Random House, 1976, 62 pp.

Smith, Christine. *How to Draw Cartoons.* Gareth Stevens, 1997, 24 pp.

Average Reading Level: Grade 3 (Interest Level: Grade 3)

Adler, David A. *A Picture Book of Benjamin Franklin.* Holiday, 1990, 32 pp.

Adler, David A. *A Picture Book of Harriett Tubman.* Holiday, 1992, 32 pp.

Adler, David A. *A Picture Book of Rosa Parks.* Holiday, 1993, 32 pp.

Arnosky, Jim. *Crinkleroot's Guide to Knowing Butterflies and Moths.* Simon & Schuster, 1996, 32 pp.

Ball, Jacqueline. *Do Fish Drink? First Questions and Answers about Water.* Time Life, 1993, 48 pp.

Branley, Franklyn M. *The Planets in Our Solar System* (Rev.). HarperCollins, 1987, 32 pp.

Cole, Joanna. *The Magic School Bus and the Electric Field Trip*. Scholastic, 1997, 48 pp.

Cromwell, Sharon. *How Do I Know It's Yucky?* Rigby Interactive Library, 1998, 24 pp.

Darling, Kathy. *Rain Forest Babies*. Walker, 1996, 32 pp.

George, Jean Craighead. *Arctic Son*. Hyperion, 1997, 30 pp.

Gibbons, Gail. *Weather Words and What They Mean*. Holday, 1990, 30 pp.

Gibbons, Gail. *Marshes and Swamps*. Holday, 1998, 30 pp.

Glaser, Linda. *Spectacular Spiders*. Millbrook Press, 1998, 27 pp.

Guthrie, Donna, Bentley, Nancy, & Arnsteen, Katy Keck. *Young Author's Do-It-Yourself Book: How to Write, Illustrate, and Produce Your Own Book*. Millbrook Press, 1994, 64 pp.

Hodge, Deborah. *Whales, Killer Whales, Blue Whales and More*. Kids Can Press, 1997, 32 pp.

Lafferty, Peter. *Why Do Balls Bounce? First Questions and Answers about How Things Work*. Time Life, 1995, 48 pp.

Leedy, Loreen. *Mapping Penny's World*. Holt, 2000, 30 pp.

Malam, John. *Leonardo DaVinci*. Carolrhoda, 1998, 24 pp.

Markle, Sandra. *Outside and Inside Bats*. Atheneum, 1997, 40 pp.

Middleton, Don. *Big Cats: Tigers*. Rosen, 1999, 24 pp.

Riggio, Anita. *Secret Signs along the Underground Railroad*. Boyds Mill Press, 1997, 28 pp.

Ripley, Catherine. *Why Does Popcorn Pop? And Other Kitchen Questions*. Firefly Books, 1997, 32 pp.

Zoehfeld, Kathleen Weidner. *How Mountains Are Made*. HarperCollins, 1995, 32 pp.

Challenging Reading Level: Grade 4 (Interest Level: Grade 3)

Adler, David A. *A Picture Book of Thurgood Marshall*. Holiday, 1997, 32 pp.

Bulloch, Ivan, & James, Diane. *Watch It Grow*. Two-Can Publishing, 2001, 32 pp.

Gibbons, Gail. *Recycle! A Handbook for Kids*. Little, Brown, 1992, 28 pp.

Gibbons, Gail. *Planet Earth/Inside Out*. Morrow, 1995, 26 pp.

Harrison, Michael, & Stuart-Clark, Christopher. *The New Oxford Treasury of Children's Poems*. Oxford University Press, 1995, 174 pp.

Penner, Lucille Recht. *Monster Bugs*. Random House, 1996, 48 pp.

Zoehfeld, Kathleen Weidner. *Terrible Tyrannosaurus*. HarperCollins, 2001, 30 pp.

Fourth-Grade Books

Easy Reading Level: Grade 3 (Interest Level: Grade 4)

Adler, David A. *Lou Gehrig, The Luckiest Man*. Harcourt Brace, 1997, 30 pp.

Ballard, Robert. *Finding the Titanic*. Scholastic, 1993, 48 pp.

Donnelly, Judy. *Tut's Mummy Lost . . . and Found*. Random House, 1988, 48 pp.

Little, Emily. *The Trojan Horse: How Greeks Won the War*. Random House, 1992, 48 pp.

Penner, Lucille Recht. *Twisters*. Random House, 1996, 46 pp.

Prelutsky, Jack. *The Beauty of the Beast*. Knopf, 1997, 100 pp.

Rogers, Daniel. *Earthquakes*. Raintree Steck Vaughn, 2000, 32 pp.

Shuter, Jane. *The Ancient Egyptians*. Heinemann, 1997, 32 pp.

Wells, Robert E. *What's Faster than a Speeding Cheetah?* Whitman, 1997, 29 pp.

Average Reading Level: Grade 4 (Interest Level: Grade 4)

Arnold, Eric. *Volcanoes! Mountains of Fire*. Random House, 1997, 64 pp.

Brown, Don. *Alice Ramsey's Grand Adventure*. Houghton Mifflin, 1997, 32 pp.

Cooper, Floyd. *Coming Home: From the Life of Langston Hughes*. Philomel, 1994, 30 pp.

Coote, Roger. *The Earth*. Zigzag Multimedia (Smithmark), 1997, 32 pp.

Donati, Annabelle. *Animal Record Holders*. Western, 1993, 32 pp.

Earle, Sylvia. *Hello, Fish*. National Geographic Society, 1999, 30 pp.

Earth Works Group. *50 Simple Things Kids Can Do to Save the Earth*. Andrew and McMeel, 1990, 156 pp.

Engel, Trudie. *We'll Never Forget You, Roberto Clemente*. Scholastic, 1996, 106 pp.

Facklam, Margery. *Creepy, Crawly Caterpillars*. Little, Brown, 1996, 32 pp.

Fritz, Jean. *And Then What Happened, Paul Revere?* Coward, McCann & Geoghegan, 1973, 48 pp.

Graham, Ian. *The Best Book of the Moon*. Kingfisher, 1999, 32 pp.

Gregory, Christiana. *The Winter of the Red Snow: The Revolutionary War Diary of Abigail Jane Stewart*. Scholastic, 1996, 167 pp.

Hanly, Sheila. *The Big Book of Animals*. Dorling Kindersley, 1997, 48 pp.

Hermes, Patricia. *The Starving Time: Elizabeth's Diary, Book Two*. Scholastic, 2001, 110 pp.

Kerr, Daisy. *Knights & Armor*. Franklin Watts, 1997, 39 pp.

Kerr, Daisy. *Medieval Town*. Franklin Watts, 1997, 39 pp.

Lauber, Patricia. *You're Aboard Spaceship Earth*. HarperCollins, 1996, 32 pp.

Lewellyn, Claire. *Scholastic First Encyclopedia: Our Planet Earth*. Scholastic, 1997, 77 pp.

Miller, Geoff. *Nature's Children: Komodo Dragons*. Grolier, 1999, 48 pp.

Moss, Cynthia. *Elephant Woman: Cynthia Moss Explores the World of Elephants*. Atheneum, 1997, 42 pp.

Murphy, Jim. *West to a Land of Plenty: The Diary of Teresa Angelino Viscardi*. Scholastic, 1998, 204 pp.

Nathan, Emma, *What Do You Call a Group of Hippos? And Other Animal Groups?* Blackbirch, 2000, 24 pp.

O'Connor, Jim. *Jackie Robinson and the Story of All-Black Baseball*. Random House, 1989, 48 pp.

Peterson, David. *Asia*. Children's Press, 1998, 48 pp.

Petty, Kate. *I Didn't Know that the Sun Is a Star and Other Amazing Facts about the Universe*. Copper Beech Books, 1997, 32 pp.

Press, Judy. *The Kids' Natural History Book*. Williamson, 2000, 144 pp.

Seabrooke, Brenda. *The Care and Feeding of Dragons*. Dutton, 1998, 120 pp.

Simon, Seymour. *Seymour Simon's Book of Trucks*. HarperCollins, 2000, 32 pp.

Walker, Jane. *Fascinating Facts about Volcanoes*. Millbrook Press, 1994, 32 pp.

Walker, Niki. *The Moon*. Crabtree, 1998, 32 pp.

Wilkinson, Philip. *Spacebusters: The Race to the Moon*. Dorling Kindersley, 1998, 48 pp.

Challenging Reading Level: Grade 5 (Interest Level: Grade 4)

Bernhard, Emery, & Bernhard, Durga. *Prairie Dogs*. Harcourt, 1997, 29 pp.

Bishop, Nic. *Animal Flight*. Houghton Mifflin, 1997, 32 pp.

Facklam, Margery. *The Big Bug Book*. Little, Brown, 1994, 32 pp.

Fritz, Jean. *Why Don't You Get a Horse, Sam Adams?* Coward, McCann & Geoghegan, 1974, 48 pp.

Henry, Marguerite. *Benjamin West and His Cat Grimalkin*. Macmillan, 1947, 147 pp.

Israel, Elaine (Ed.). *The World Almanac for Kids*. World Almanac Books, 2002, 336 pp.

McCully, Emily Arnold. *The Bobbin Girl*. Dial, 1996, 30 pp.

Fifth-Grade Books

Easy Reading Level: Grade 3 (Interest Level: Grade 5)

Giovanni, Nikki. *Spin a Soft Song, Revised Edition*. Farrar, Strauss & Giroux, 1985, 57 pp.

Hamilton, Virginia. *The People Could Fly*. Knopf, 1985, 173 pp.

Easy Reading Level: Grade 4 (Interest Level: Grade 5)

Banim, Lisa. *A Spy in the King's Colony*. Silver Moon Press, 1994, 76 pp.

Marschall, Ken. *Inside the Titanic*. Little, Brown, 1997, 31 pp.

McSwigan, Marie. *Snow Treasure*. Scholastic, 1942, 156 pp.

Average Reading Level: Grade 5 (Interest Level: Grade 5)

Arnold, Caroline. *Did You Hear That?* Charlesbridge, 2001, 30 pp.

Arnosky, Jim. *Watching Water Birds*. National Geographic, 1997, 28 pp.

Ballard, Carol. *The Lungs and Respiratory System*. Raintree Steck Vaughn, 1997, 48 pp.

Barrett, Tracy. *Growing Up in Colonial America*. Millbrook Press, 1995, 96 pp.

Bender, Lionel. *Heat and Drought*. Raintree Steck Vaughn, 1998, 48 pp.

Brill, Marlene Targ. *Diary of a Drummer Boy*. Millbrook Press, 1998, 48 pp.

DiSpezio, Michael. *Awesome Experiments in Electricity & Magnetism*. Sterling, 1998, 160 pp.

Elliott, Leslee. *Mind Blowing Mammals*. Sterling, 1994, 64 pp.

Ford, Harry, & Barnham, Kay. *Outer Space*. Zigzag Multimedia (Smithmark Publishers), 1997, 32 pp.

Giff, Patricia Reilly. *Lily's Crossing*. Delacorte, 1997, 180 pp.

Greenberg, Keith. *Risky Business, Storm Chaser: Into the Eye of a Hurricane*. Blackbirch Press, 1998, 32 pp.

Kent, Peter. *Quest for the West: In Search of Gold*. Millbrook Press, 1997, 32 pp.

Lasky, Kathryn. *Hercules, the Man, the Myth, the Hero*. Hyperion, 1997, 30 pp.

Lauber, Patricia. *What Do You See and How Do You See It?* Crown, 1994, 48 pp.

Lobosco, Michael L. *Mental Math Challenges*. Sterling, 1999, 80 pp.

Lord, Betty Bao. *In the Year of the Boar and Jackie Robinson*. HarperCollins, 1984, 169 pp.

Loves, June. *Airplanes*. Chelsea House, 2001, 32 pp.

Lowry, Lois. *Number the Stars*. Houghton Mifflin, 1989, 137 pp.

Macdonald, Fiona. *The World in the Time of Marco Polo*. Chelsea House, 2001, 48 pp.

Markle, Sandra. *Outside and Inside Sharks*. Atheneum, 1996, 40 pp.

McEvey, Shane F. *Beetles*. Chelsea House, 2001, 32 pp.

O'Brien, Patrick. *Megatooth*. Holt, 2001, 30 pp.

San Souci, Robert D. *Young Arthur*. Doubleday, 1996, 28 pp.

Steele, Philip. *Aztec News*. Candlewick Press, 1997, 32 pp.

Williams, Nick. *How Birds Fly*. Benchmark Books, 1997, 32 pp.

Challenging Reading Level: Grade 6 (Interest Level: Grade 5)

Bray, Rosemary. *Martin Luther King*. Greenwillow, 1995, 40 pp.

Erickson, Paul. *Daily Life in the Pilgrim Colony*. Clarion, 2001, 48 pp.

Richards, Jon. *What If . . . Sharks?* Copper Beech Books, 1996, 44732 pp.

Silverstein, Alvin, Silverstein, Virginia, & Nunn, Laura Silverstein. *Photosynthesis*. Millbrook Press, 1998, 64 pp.

Silverstein, Alvin, Silverstein, Virginia, & Nunn, Laura Silverstein. *Symbiosis*. Millbrook Press, 1998, 64 pp.

Taylor, Barbara. *Animal Homes*. Dorling Kindersley, 1996, 44 pp.

Williams, Brian. *Ancient China*. Viking, 1996, 48 pp.

Zeman, Anne, & Kelly, Kate. (1994). *Everything You Need to Know about Science Homework*. Scholastic, 1994.

Sixth-Grade Books

Easy Reading Level: Grade 5 (Interest Level: Grade 6)

Bridges, Ruby. *Through My Eyes*. Scholastic, 1999, 61 pp.

Martell, Hazel Mary. *Looking Back: Imperial China, 221 B.C. to A.D. 1294*. Raintree Steck Vaughn, 1999, 64 pp.

Silcox-Jarrett, Diane. *Heroines of the American Revolution: America's Founding Mothers*. Green Angel Press, 1998, 92 pp.

Average Reading Level: Grade 6 (Interest Level: Grade 6)

Burton, John A. *The Changing World: Jungles and Rainforests*. Thunder Bay Press, 1996, 73 pp.

Clay, Rebecca. *Ukraine: A New Independence*. Benchmark Books, 1997, 64 pp.

Dolan, Edward T. *The American Revolution: How We Fought the War of Independence*. Millbrook Press, 1995, 110 pp.

Erickson, Paul. *Daily Life on a Southern Plantation 1853*. Penguin Putnam, 1998, 48 pp.

Fitzgerald, Karen. *Story of Oxygen*. Franklin Watts, 1996, 63 pp.

Forbes, Esther. *Johnny Tremain*. Houghton Mifflin, 1943, 256 pp.

Ford, Harry. *The Young Astronomer*. Dorling Kindersley, 1998, 38 pp.

Finlayson, Reggie. *Colin Powell*. Lerner Publications, 1997, 64 pp.

Freedman, Russell. *Out of Darkness*. Houghton Mifflin, 1997, 81 pp.

Jeffrey, Laura S. *Guion Bluford. A Space Biography*. Enslow, 1998, 48 pp.

Jones, Charlotte Foltz. *Accidents May Happen: Fifty Inventions Discovered by Mistake*. Delacorte, 1996, 86 pp.

Kelley, Brent. *James Madison*. Chelsea House, 2001, 90 pp.

Kerrod, Robin. *Weather*. Gareth Stevens, 1998, 68 pp.

King, David C. *First Facts about American Heroes*. Blackbirch Press, 1996, 112 pp.

Klise, Kate. *Trial by Jury Journal*. HarperCollins, 2001, 238 pp.

Macdonald, Fiona. *Step into the Celtic World*. Annes, 1999, 64 pp.

Macdonald, Fiona. *The World in the Time of Abraham Lincoln*. Chelsea House, 2001, 48 pp.

McCullough, L. E. *Plays of America*. Smith & Kraus, 1996, 160 pp.

Morey, Janet, & Dunn, Wendy. *Famous Hispanic Americans*. Dutton, 1996, 190 pp.

Morley, Jacqueline, & Antram, David. *Exploring North America*. Peter Bedrick, 1996, 48 pp.

Rootes, David. *Exploration into the Polar Regions*. Chelsea House, 2001, 48 pp.

St. George, Judith. *Sacagawea*. Putnam, 1997, 115 pp.

Sauvain, Philip. *Oceans*. Marshall Cavendish, 1996, 32 pp.

Simon, Seymour. *Now You See It, Now You Don't: The Amazing World of Optical Illusions*. Morrow, 1998, 64 pp.

Simon, Seymour. *Tornadoes*. Morrow, 1999, 29 pp.

Smith, Linda Wasmer. *Louis Pasteur, Disease Fighter*. Enslow, 1997, 128 pp.

Snyder, Zilpha Keatley. *Gib Rides Home*. Delacorte, 1998, 246 pp.

Stein, R. Conrad. *The Underground Railroad*. Children's Press, 1997, 32 pp.

Streissguth, Thomas. *Raoul Wallenberg*. Rosen, 2001, 112 pp.

Tank, Shelly. *The Buried City of Pompeii*. Heparin/Madison, 1997, 48 pp.

Taylor, Leighton. *Creeps from the Deep*. Chronicle Books, 1997, 45 pp.

Challenging Reading Level: Grade 7 (Interest Level: Grade 6)

Aaseng, Nathan. *Meat-Eating Plants*. Enslow, 1996, 48 pp.

Ash, Russell. *Incredible Comparisons*. Dorling Kindersley, 1996, 63 pp.

Blos, Joan W. *A Gathering of Days*. Aladdin, 1979, 144 pp.

Brook, Donna. *The Journey of English*. Clarion, 1998, 47 pp.

Christian, Spencer, & Felix, Antonia. *Can It Really Rain Frogs? The World's Strangest Weather Events*. Wiley, 1997, 121 pp.

Cole, Michael D. *Living on Mars: Mission to the Red Planet*. Enslow, 1999, 48 pp.

Curtis, Patricia. *Animals You Never Even Heard Of*. Sierra Club Books, 1997, 32 pp.

Darling, Kathy. *There's a Zoo on You*. Millbrook Press, 2000, 48 pp.

Dickinson, Joan D. *Bill Gates: Billionaire Computer Genius*. Enslow, 1997, 104 pp.

Dingle, Derek T. *First in the Field: Baseball Hero Jackie Robinson*. Hyperion, 1998, 48 pp.

Fox, Mary Virginia. *Lasers*. Benchmark Books, 1996, 63 pp.

Mann, Elizabeth. *The Great Wall*. Mikya Press, 1997, 48 pp.

Parker, Steve. *20th Century Inventions: Satellites*. Steck-Vaughn, 1997, 48 pp.

Potter, Joan, & Claytor, Constance. *African Americans Who Were First*. Dutton, 1997, 116 pp.

Putnam, James, & Hart, George. *Ancient Egyptians*. Dorling Kindersley, 1996, 128 pp.

Simon, Seymour. *They Swim the Seas: The Mystery of Animal Migration*. Harcourt, 1998, 34 pp.

Seventh/Eighth-Grade Books

Easy Reading Level: Grade 5 (Interest Level: Grade 7–8)

Ayers, Katherine. *North by Night: A Story of the Underground Railroad*. Delacorte, 1998, 176 pp.

Easy Reading Level: Grade 6 (Interest Level: Grade 7–8)

Atkin, S. Beth. *Voices from the Fields: Children of Migrant Farm Workers Tell Their Stories*. Little, Brown, 1993, 96 pp.

Collier, James L. *My Brother Sam Is Dead*. Scholastic, 1974, 216 pp.

Crist-Evans, Craig. *Moon over Tennessee: A Boy's Civil War Journal*. Houghton Mifflin, 1999, 60 pp.

Fleischman, Paul. *Bull Run*. HarperCollins, 1993, 104 pp.

Fleischman, Paul. *A Joyful Noise: Poems for Two Voices*. HarperCollins, 1993, 102 pp.

Jube, A., & Jones, Thomas D. *Scholastic Encyclopedia of the United States*. Scholastic, 1998, 188 pp.

Average Reading Level: Grade 7–8 (Interest Level: Grade 7–8)

Aaseng, Nathan. *You Are the President II*. Oliver Press, 1994, 160 pp.

Armstrong, Jennifer. *Shipwreck at the Bottom of the World: The Extraordinary True Story of Shackleton and the Endurance*. Crown, 1998, 131 pp.

Armstrong, Jennifer. *In My Hands: Memories of a Holocaust Rescuer*. Knopf, 1999, 276 pp.

Bartoletti, Susan Campbell. *Growing Up in Coal Country*. Houghton Mifflin, 1996, 127 pp.

Batten, Mary. *Anthropologist, Scientist of the People*. Houghton Mifflin, 2001, 64 pp.

Bonnet, Bob, & Keen, Dan. *Science Fair Projects: Physics*. Sterling, 2000, 96 pp.

Bonvillain, Nancy. *The Sac and Fox*. Chelsea House, 1995, 110 pp.

Buller, Laura. *Native Americans: An Inside Look at the Tribes and Traditions*. Dorling Kindersley, 2001, 96 pp.

Calvert, Patricia. *Great Lives: The American Frontier*. Atheneum, 1998, 388 pp.

Collier, Christopher, & Collier, James Lincoln. *Pilgrims and Puritans*. Benchmark Books, 1998, 94 pp.

Collier, Christopher, & Collier, James Lincoln. *The United States Enters the World Stage, 1867–1919*. Benchmark Books, 2000, 94 pp.

Corrick, James A. *Life of a Medieval Knight.* Lucent Books, 2001, 95 pp.

DeAngelis, Gina. *Francisco Pizzaro and the Conquest of the Inca.* Chelsea House, 2001, 64 pp.

De Angelis, Gina. *Jackie Robinson.* Chelsea House, 2001, 104 pp.

Dingle, Derek T. *First in the Field: Baseball Hero Jackie Robinson.* Hyperion, 1998, 48 pp.

Frank, Anne. *The Diary of a Young Girl.* Random House, 1952, 285 pp.

Freedman, Russell. *Kids at Work: Lewis Hine and the Crusade Against Child Labor.* Clarion, 1994, 97 pp.

Goodman, Joan. A *Long and Uncertain Journey: The 27,000-Mile Voyage of Vasco da Gama.* Mikya Press, 2001, 42 pp.

Hansen, Joyce. *Women of Hope: African Americans Who Made a Difference.* Scholastic, 1998, 31 pp.

Herriot, James. *All Creatures Great and Small.* Bantam, 1989, 499 pp.

Johnson, Rebecca L. *Science on the Ice: An Antarctic Journal.* Lerner Publications, 1995, 126 pp.

Kallen, Stuart A. *The Mayans.* Lucent Books, 2001, 112 pp.

Kipling, Rudyard. *Captains Courageous.* Doubleday, (1896) 1964, 210 pp.

Marcovitz, Hal. *John C. Fremont: Pathfinder of the West.* Chelsea House, 2002, 64 pp.

Mazer, Harry. *A Boy at War: A Novel of Pearl Harbor.* Simon & Schuster, 2001, 104 pp.

Miller, Marilyn. *Words that Built a Nation.* Scholastic, 1999, 172 pp.

Pinkney, Andrea Davis. *Let It Shine: Stories of Black Women Freedom Fighters.* Harcourt, 2000, 30 pp.

Platt, Richard. *Stephen Biesty's Incredible Body.* Dorling Kindersley, 1998, 32 pp.

Rice, Terence M. G. *Russia.* Gareth Stevens, 1999, 96 pp.

St. George, Judith. *John & Abigail Adams.* Holday, 2001, 147 pp.

Sayre, April Pulley. *Antarctica.* Millbrook Press, 1998, 64 pp.

Soto, Gary. *Jessie De La Cruz: A Portrait of a United Farm Worker.* Persea Books, 2000, 116 pp.

Steffens, B., & Weaver, R. M. *Cartoonists.* Lucent Books, 2000, 112 pp.

Wulffson, Don L. *The Kid Who Invented the Trampoline.* Dutton, 2001, 120 pp.

Average Reading Level: Grade 9–10 (Interest Level: Grade 9–12)

Aaseng, Nathan. *The Crash of 1929.* Lucent Books, 2001, 128 pp.

Ambrose, Stephen E. *Citizen Soldiers.* Simon & Schuster, 1998, 528 pp.

Ambrose, Stephen E. *Nothing Like It in the World.* Simon & Schuster, 2000, 431 pp.

Ambrose, Stephen E. *Band of Brothers.* Simon & Schuster, 2001, 333 pp.

Burchard, Peter. *Lincoln and Slavery.* Atheneum, 1999, 196 pp.

Challoner, Jack. *The Visual Dictionary of Chemistry.* Dorling Kindersley, 1996, 64 pp.

DuTemple, Lesley A. *Coral Reefs.* Lucent Books, 2000, 96 pp.

Farrington, Karen. *Historical Atlas of Expeditions.* Checkmark Books/Facts on File, 2000, 192 pp.

Fox, Mary Virginia. *Edwin Hubble, American Astronomer.* Franklin Watts, 1997, 112 pp.

Hardy, P. Stephen, & Hardy, Sheila. *Extraordinary People of the Harlem Renaissance.* Children's Press, 2000, 288 pp.

Kallen, Stuart A. *Cultural History of the United States.* Lucent Books, 1999, 127 pp.

Kowalski, Kathiann M. *Hazardous Waste Sites.* Lerner Publications, 1996, 92 pp.

Little, Marjorie. *The Endocrine System.* Chelsea House, 2001, 112 pp.

London, Jack *The Call of the Wild.* Viking, 1996, 126 pp.

Macquity, Miranda, & Papastavrou, Vassili. *Sharks, Whales & Dolphins.* Dorling Kindersley, 1997, 128 pp.

McKissack, Patricia C. *Black Hands, White Sails: The Story of African-American Whalers.* Scholastic, 1999, 152 pp.

Morgan, Sally. *Superfoods: Genetic Modification of Foods.* Heinemann, 2002, 64 pp.

Nishi, Dennis. *The Inca Empire.* Lucent Books, 2000, 96 pp.

Rodriguez, Consuelo. *Cesar Chavez.* Chelsea House, 1991, 106 pp.

Sandburg, Carl. *Abe Lincoln Grows Up.* Harcourt, 1928, 222 pp.

Yount, Lisa. *Disease Detectives.* Lucent Books, 2001, 112 pp.

Average Reading Level: Grade 11–12 (Interest Level: Grade 9–12)

Bjornlund, Lydia. *The Constitution and the Founding of America.* Lucent Books, 2000, 128 pp.

Hall, Eleanor J. *Ancient Chinese Dynasties.* Lucent Books, 2000, 128 pp.

Matthews, John R. *The Rise and Fall of the Soviet Union.* Lucent Books, 2000, 112 pp.

Stwertka, Albert. *A Guide to the Elements.* Oxford, 1996, 238 pp.

Swisher, Clarice. *Victorian England.* Lucent Books, 2001, 128 pp.

APPENDIX B

MORPHEMIC ELEMENTS FOR THE CONTENT AREAS

Prefixes

ab: from; away; off
abnormal, abdicate, abduction, abstain, abstract, absurd

ambi: both
ambidexterous, ambiguous, ambilateral

amphi: around; on both sides; both
amphibious, amphibian, amphipod, amphitheater

ante: before; earlier; in front of
anterior, antebellum, antecedents, antedated, anteroom

anti: against; opposite
anti-American, antibacterial, antibiotics, antibodies, anticlimax, anticoagulants, anticommunist, antidote, antifederalists, antigens, antinuclear, antioxidants, antipollution, antipoverty, antiseptics, antislavery, antisocial, antitoxin, antitrust, antiwar

bi: two; twice
bicameral, biceps, bicuspids, bicycle, bilateral, bilingual, binary, bipedal

co: with
coanchor, coarticulation, codiscoverer, coeducation, coeditor, coexistence, copilot

com: with
commingle, commensurate, community, communication

contra: against; opposite
contra-angles, contraband, contradict, contradistinction, contrariwise

counter: opposite counteract, counter-arguments, counterattack, counterbalance, counterclockwise, counterculture, countermeasures, counteroffensive, counteroffer, counterproductive, counterrevolutionary, counterweight

di: two; twice; double
diagonal, diatoms, diodes, dioxide, diploid, divide

dia: passing through; opposed; thoroughly
diabetes, diathermy, dialysis, dialect, diaphragm, diagram, dialects, diameter

em: form of en generally used before b, m, p
embankment, embark, embitter, emboldened, embrace, empowered

en: in; cause to
be enable, enact, enacted, encased, encircled, enclosed, enclosure, encompasses, encounter, encouragement, endanger, engrossed, engulfed, enlarged, enlightened, enlist, enraged, enrich, enrolled, enslaved, entangled, entitled, entrenched, entropy, entrusted

epi: over; outer; near; beside
epicardium, epicenter, epicuticle, epidemic, epidemiologist, epidermis, epiglottis, epimetheus, epiphytes

extra: outside; beyond
extracellular, extract, extradition, extramarital, extraneous, extraordinary, extrapolate, extrasensory, extraterrestrial, extraterritorial, extravagance, extraverted

fore: before; front; superior
forearm, forebode, forebrain, forecast, foredeck, forefather, forefinger, foregone, forehand, foreknowledge, foreman, foremast, forenoon, foreperson, forerunner, foreshadow, forewoman, foreword

hemi: half
hemisphere, hemialgia, hemiparesis, hemiplegia

hemo, hemato: blood
hematology, hematocycst, hematoma, hemoglobin, hemophilia, hemorrage

hyper: above; beyond
hyperactive, hyperbole, hyperextension, hyperglycemia, hyperkinetic, hypersensitive, hypersonic, hyperspace, hyperstimulation, hypertension, hyperthyroidism, hypertonic, hyperventilation

hypo: under; beneath; below; below normal
hypoactive, hypoallergenic, hypochondria, hypocritical, hypodermis, hypogastric, hypoglycemia, hypokinetic, hypotension, hypothalamus, hypothermia, hypothyroid, hypoventilation

il: not; variant of in used before words beginning with l
illegal, illegimate; illlegible, illicit, illititerate

im: not
imbalance, immature, immeasurably, immobile, immoral, immortal, immovable, impartial, impassable, impatient, impenetrable, imperfect, impersonal, impolite, impossible, impractical, improbable, improper

in: not
incredible, indefinite, independence, indifferent, indirect, inefficient, inexpensive, informal, inorganic, insignificant, insoluble, insufficient, invariably, invertebrates, involuntary

inter: between; among
interalliance, interbank, interchangeable, intercirculation, intercorrelation intercortical, interfamily, intergeneration, interlibrary, interlinear, intermediate, intermission, international

intra: within
intracellular, intramural, intrastate, intraveneous, intramuscular

meta: beyond; after; along with; in chemistry: the least hydrated of a series
meta-antimonic, metamorphic, metabolic, metaphor, metacognitive, metaphysics, metaphysical,

metamorphosis, metacomet, metacarpal

para: beyond; outside of; similar to
paralanguage, paramagnetic, paraphrase, paraprofessionals, parapsychology, parasympathetic

peri: around; about; surrounding
periscope, pericardium, perigee, perimeter, periphery, peripheral

post: after; later than
postcranial, postdated, posterior, postgraduate, posthumously, post-industrial, postmortem, postnatal, postoperative, postpartum, post-school, postscript, post-season, postsecondary, postwar

pre: before; in front of
preamble, precambrian, precaution, preceded, precedent, preconceived, predetermined, prediction, predisposition, preface, prehistory, prejudice, premature, prenatal, prepaid, prerequisite, preschool, preset, preview

re: again; back
react, rebirth, rebuild, recall, recover, recycle, renaissance, renewable, repay, replace, rewrite

sub: under, below; not perfect
subarctic, subatomic, subcategories, subcommittee, subcommittees, subconscious, subcontinent, subculture, subdivided, subdivision, subfloor, subgroups, subheadings, submarine, submerged, subordinate, subphyla, subregion, subspecies, substrate, subsystems, subterranean, subtitle, subtropical

syn: with; together
asynchronous, idiosyncracies, idiosyncrasy, idiosyncratic, synapse, synchronized, synchrotron, syncopated, syndicated, syndrome, synergy, synonym, synthesis, synthesize, synthetic

trans: across
transaction, transatlantic, transcend, transcontinental, transcribe, transcript,

transducer, transfer, transform, transfusion, transgression, transience, transient, transistor, transition, translate, translucent, transmission, transmit, transmutation, transparent, transpiration, transplant, transponder, transport, transportation, transverse

un: not; opposite
unaided, unavoidable, unconscious, unconstitutional, uncontrolled, undigested, unemployment, unequal, unexplored, unfavorable, unfortunate, unhealthy, uninhabited, unlikely, unlimited, unnatural, unofficial, unpopular, unprecedented, unpredictable, unreliable, unrest, unsafe, unsaturated

uni: one
unicameral, unicellular, unicorn, unicycle, unidirectional, uniform, uniformity, unilateral, union, unique, unison, unitary, unitized, univalves, universe, university

Suffixes

able: capable of; able to; tending to
affordable, arable, biodegradable, disposable, distinguishable, durable, equitable, fashionable, favorable, flammable, habitable, honorable, impassable, impenetrable, impermeable, implacable, impregnable, inalienable, incurable, indescribable, indispensable, inflammable, inhospitable, insurmountable, malleable, measurable, memorable, navigable, negotiable, notable, objectionable, perishable, permeable, profitable, taxable, variable, venerable

age: collection; process; rate of; place of; charge
acreage, amperage, anchorage, assemblage, bandage, blockage, bondage, brokerage, coinage, hemorrhage, heritage, mileage, mortgage, orphanage, parsonage, patronage, percentage, plumage, postage, sewage, steerage, suffrage, voltage

al: pertaining to; often makes adjectives of nouns
abdominal, aerial, agricultural,

anatomical, ancestral, annual, architectural, asexual, astronomical, bilateral, biochemical, biographical, biological, bronchial, celestial, centrifugal, cerebral, chronological, classical, clinical, coastal, colonial, congressional, constitutional, continental, cylindrical, diagonal, dictatorial, digital, directional, dorsal, ecclesiastical, ecological, economical, editorial, electoral, electrical, electrochemical, elliptical, environmental, equatorial, experimental, fetal, fiscal, fractional, gastrointestinal, geographical, geological, geothermal, glacial, global, governmental, grammatical, gravitational, historical, horizontal, hormonal, hypothetical, international, intestinal, judicial, lateral, legal, liberal, mathematical, mechanical, nasal, naval, neural, numerical, nutritional, optical, orbital, physical, physiological, political, provincial, psychological, racial, radial, regional, skeletal, societal, spatial, spherical, spinal, statistical, subtropical, symmetrical, technical, tidal, tropical, transcontinental, tribal,

umbilical, universal, vertical, viral, visual

an: forms adjectives from nouns
American, Russian, Puritan, Republican

ance: forms nouns from adjectives or verbs
abundance, appearance, assistance, brillance, distance, elegance, entrance, ignorance, importance

ant: (forms nouns and adjectives from verbs): having or acting as; thing that carries out a certain action
abundant, buoyant, coolant, defendant, defiant, descendant, disinfectant, dominant, dormant, immigrant, inhabitant, malignant, migrant, militant, mutant, pollutant, predominant, radiant, reactant, recombinant, resistant, significant, stimulant, triumphant, tyrant, valiant

ar: forms adjectives
angular, circular, familiar, globular, lunar, muscular, popular, similar, singular, solar, stellar, triangular

ate: forms adjectives or verbs
advocate, ajudicate, approximate, dedicate, deviate, domesticate, educate,

emancipate, evaporate, extricate, hesitate, illustrate, liquidate, locate, permeate

eer: one associated with
auctioneer, buccaneer, cannoneer, charioteer, engineer, harpooneer, mountaineer, musketeer, pamphleteer, pioneer, privateer, profiteer, puppeteer, volunteer

en: forms adjectives
ashen, brazen, frozen, golden

ence:
absence, abstinence, competence, conference, dependence, difference, incontinence, independence, influence, insistence, intelligence, residence, persistence

ent: forms nouns or adjectives from verbs
absent, accident, belligerent, confident, competent, dependent, different, independent, insistent, intelligent, persistent, resident

er: one who; one who has
astronomer, banker, builder, commander, commissioner, consumer, customer, designer, employer, explorer, laborer, lawyer, leader, manager, manufacturer, mariner, minister, observer, officer, owner, philosopher, photographer, pitcher, researcher, retailer, trader, voter, weaver, worker

ess: female
actress, countess, duchess, empress, governess, princess, waitress

etic: forms an adjective and occurs in some nouns
aesthetic, anesthetic, apathetic, cybernetic, diabetic, diuretic, eidetic, electromagnetic, esthetic, genetic, kinesthetic, kinetic, magnetic, onomatopoetic, parasympathetic, photosynthetic, poetic, prophetic, prosthetic, synthetic

ful: full of; having; characterized by
boastful, bountiful, distrustful, doleful, dutiful, grateful, healthful, lawful, merciful, mournful, plentiful, powerful, resourceful, respectful, scornful, successful, thoughtful, truthful, uneventful, vengeful, wasteful

fy (–ify): make; cause to be: beautify, deify, dignify, glorify, horrify, liquefy, magnify, notify, signify, terrify

ian: variant of *an*
plebian, Bostonian

itis: inflammation of
bronchitis, gastritis, hepatitis, neuritis

ial: variant of –al: filial, imperial, facial, fictional, financial, industrial, influential, marital, martial, official, pictorial, presidential, terrestrial, territorial, trivial, tropical

ible: variant of *able*
audible, combustible, contemptible, credible, deductible, illegible, incomprehensible, incredible, indelible, indivisible, inflexible, intelligible, invincible, permissible, plausible, visible

ic: forms adjectives; used in some nouns; when used with chemical terms is used to show the one that has a high valence: ferric oxide
acidic, allergic, anesthetic, antibiotic, aquatic, aristocratic, atmospheric, atomic, autocratic, carcinogenic, climatic, cosmic, cubic, democratic, domestic, economic, electrolytic, electronic, electrostatic, endothermic, exothermic, galactic, gastric, genetic, geographic, geologic, geometric, Germanic, hydraulic, hydrochloric, inorganic, isometric, kinetic, linguistic, magnetic, metabolic, metallic, microscopic, nucleic, numeric, olympic, organic, Paleozoic, parasitic, periodic, photoelectric, pneumatic, poetic, prehistoric, republic, scientific, seismic, sulfuric, symbolic, synthetic, systematic, thermodynamic, toxic, tragic, ultrasonic, volcanic

ician: forms a noun indicating occupation
beautician, mortician, physician

ide: used in the names of chemical compounds bromide, carbide, chloride, cyanide, dioxide, disaccharide, disulfide, hydrochloride, hydroxide, iodide, monosaccharide, monoxide, nucleotide, oxide, peptide, peroxide, polypeptide, polysaccharide, sulfide, tetrachloride, triglyceride

ish: forms adjectives from nouns and other adjectives; belonging to; like; having the characteristics of
babyish, bookish, foolish, fourtyish, Swedish, youngish

ism: state of; way of behaving; belief
authoritarianism, behaviorism, botulism, capitalism, colonialism, communism, Confucianism,

constitutionalism, consumerism, despotism, fascism, federalism, humanism, humanitarianism, imperialism, impressionism, industrialism, isolationism, liberalism, Marxism, mercantilism, metabolism, mutualism, nationalism, patriotism, pluralism, progressivism, puritanism, racism, romanticism, sectionalism, socialism, symbolism, terrorism, totalitarianism

ist: one who; one that
abolitionist, anthropologist, archaeologist, archeologist, audiologist, biochemist, biologist, capitalist, chemist, colonist, communist, conservationist, ecologist, economist, entomologist, fascist, federalist, feminist, geneticist, geologist, humanist, hygienist, imperialist, lobbyist, loyalist, meteorologist, nationalist, naturalist, neurologist, paleontologist, pathologist, physicist, populist, protagonist, racist, scientist, socialist, sociologist, terrorist

ite: native; follower of; part of
anthracite, bauxite, graphite, hematite, meteorite, nitrite, pyrite, satellite, sulfite, trilobite

ity: state or condition
ability, adversity, captivity, charity, civility, dignity, eternity, jollity, majority, reality, sensitivity, severity, sincerity, uniformity, university

ive: tending toward a certain action
active, corrective, supportive

ization: action; state
authorization, centralization, characterization, civilization, colonization, crystallization, decentralization, fertilization, hospitalization, immunization, industrialization, ionization, mechanization, mobilization, modernization, nationalization, naturalization, neutralization, pasteurization, rationalization, socialization, specialization, stabilization, sterilization, urbanization, vaporization

ize: make; cause to
actualize, agonize, anesthetize, anodize, categorize, characterize, civilize, colonize, crystalize, energize, popularize

less: without; not having
bloodless, boundless, cloudless, colorless, countless, heartless, heedless, jobless, landless, lawless, limitless, motionless, nameless, needless, numberless, odorless, penniless, stainless, timeless, weightless, wireless

ment (forms a noun): result; action; state
amendment, announcement, bombardment, commandment, commitment, confinement, department, deployment, detachment, disarmament, discouragement, displacement, endorsement, enforcement, enlightenment, enlistment, environment, equipment, experiment, government, impeachment, imprisonment, improvement, indictment, installment, measurement, nourishment, replacement, requirement, resentment, retirement, sediment, settlement, shipment

ness: state of; having
aggressiveness, awareness, bitterness, consciousness, greatness, hardness, heaviness, numbness, seriousness, unconsciousness, uniqueness, vastness, weakness, weariness, wilderness

oid: looking; having the form of
amoeboid, arachnoid, asteroid, celluloid, haploid, hominoid, meteoroid, paranoid, sphenoid, steroid, tabloid, thyroid, trapezoid, typhoid

or: one that does; thing that does
accelerator, aggressor, ambassador, ancestor, compressor, conductor, connector, conqueror, depositor, detector, dictator, generator, governor, incinerator, incubator, indicator, insulator, inventor, investor, legislator, liberator, mediator, microprocessor, monitor, navigator, proprietor,

prospector, regulator, resistor, surveyor, translator, warrior

ose: having or being
bellicose, comatose, fructose, glucose, lactose, morose, sucrose, varicose

osis: actions; disorders; states
hypnosis, osmosis, multiple sclerosis, tuberculosis

ous: having; full of
amorphous, analogous, aqueous, autonomous, carnivorous, coniferous, contagious, deciduous, dubious, fibrous, gaseous, hazardous, heterogeneous, homogeneous, igneous, industrious, infectious, intravenous, melodious, mountainous, nervous, nonferrous, noxious, nutritious, poisonous, populous, porous, precious, thunderous, unanimous, victorious

sion: forms a noun
admission, aggression, commission, concussion, convulsion, corrosion, dimension, dispersion, division, emission, emulsion, erosion, exclusion, excursion, expansion, extension, fission, fusion, hypertension, illusion, intermission, inversion, percussion, permission, propulsion, recession, revision, secession, subdivision, submission, succession, suppression, suspension, tension, transfusion, transmission, vision

some: forms adjectives
burdensome, irksome, quarrelsome

ster: forms nouns
gangster, huckster, mobster, roadster, songster, trickster

tion: forms nouns
absorption, acceleration, application, assassination, association, assumption, characterization, circulation, civilization, classification, colonization, combustion, communication,

compensation, computation, condensation, confederation, conservation, constitution, declaration, digestion, distillation, elevation, equation, eruption, evaluation, evaporation, evolution, expedition, experimentation, extinction, fertilization, formulation, foundation, friction, function, immigration, industrialization, infection, inflation, injection, insulation, integration, invention, investigation, ionization, irrigation, isolation, legislation, location, migration, moderation, modernization, multiplication, nation, navigation, nomination, notation, nutrition, occupation, operation, opposition, oxidation, pollination, pollution, population, precipitation, proclamation, proportion, radiation, reaction, respiration, revolution, rotation, sanitation, segregation, solution, starvation, taxation, transaction, transition, translation, transportation, urbanization, vaccination, variation, vegetation

ty: quality or state of
Christianity, clarity, complexity, creativity, density, dynasty, equality, equity, fertility, gravity, heredity, humanity, humidity, minority, mobility, nobility, polarity, popularity, probability, productivity, prosperity, quantity, radioactivity, relativity, reliability, sovereignty, stability, superiority, utility, validity, velocity

ure: action; result of
adventure, capture, creature, culture, departure, feature, fixture, fracture, furniture, future, legislature, literature, manufacture, mixture, nature, overture, pasture, pressure, puncture, signature, temperature, torture

Roots and Combining Forms

aero: air
aerobic, aeronautics, aerospace, anaerobic, aerobics, aeronautical, aeronaut, aerosols, aerodynamic, anaerobes, aerobes, aeromedics, aeronautical, aerosol-sprayed

anthrop, anthropo: human being
anthropoids, anthropological, anthropologist, anthropology,

anthropomorphism, misanthropy, paleoanthropologists, philanthropic, philanthropists, philanthropy

aqua: water
aquarium, aquaculture, aquafarm, auanaut, aqueducts

arthr, arthro: joint
arthritis, arthroplasty, arthropod, arthroscope

aud (i): hearing; sound
audience, audiences, auditory, auditorium, audio, audit, audible, audiologist, audition, auditor, audiovisual, audibly, audiometer, auditions

auto: self; same
autonomy, autobiography, autonomic, autocratic, autograph, autoimmune,

autonomous, autocracy, autosome, autotroph, autotrophic, autobiographical, autopsy, autoharp, semiautonomous

bene: well
benefit, beneficial, benevolent, beneficiary, benevolence, beneficiaries, benediction, benefactor, benefiting

bi: two; twice
biannual, biceps, bicultural, bicuspid, bilabial, bilateral, bimetalism, bimonthly, binary, binomial, binocular, biped, biplane, bicycle, bipolar

bio: life
antibiotics, biochemical, biodiversity, biodegradable, biofeedback, biography, biological, biologist, biology, bioluminescence, biomass, biome, biomedical, biomolecules, biotic, biopsy, biorhythms, biosphere, biosynthesis, biotic, microbiologist, symbiosis

card(i): heart
cardiac, cardiologist, cardiopulmonary, cardiorespiratory, cardiovascular, electrocardiograms, electrocardiograph, endocarditis, myocardial, pericardium

centi: hundredth part
bicentennial, centauri, centennial, centigrade, centimeters, centipede, percentile

cephal, cephalo: head
cephalopod, cephalothorax, encephalitis, hydroencephalic

cerebro: forebrain and midbrain
cerebellum, cerebral cortex, cerebrospinal, cerebrum

chlor: green
chlorate, chloride, chlorides, chlorinated, chlorine, chlorophyll, chloroplast, hydrochloric, tetrachloride

chrom: color
chromatic, chromotism, chromoplast, chromosome

chron, chrono: time
chronic, chronically, chronicle, chronicler, chronological, chronology, chronometer, synchronized, synchrony

cide: kill
biocide, fungicides, herbicides, homicides, infanticide, insecticides, pesticides

corpus: body

corporal, corporate, corporation, corps, corpse, corpulent, corpus, corpuscles, incorporate

cred: believe
accreditaion, credible, credence, credential, credit, creditor, credulous, incredible, incredulous

deca: ten
decade, decapod, decathlon, decimal

derm: skin
dermatology, dermatologist, dermatosis, epidermis

di: two; twice; double
diatomic, digraph, dialogue, dichotomy, diode, dioxide, dipolar

dict: to say
abdicate, benediction, contradict, contradiction, diction, dictation, dictator, dictionary, dictum, edict, indictment, jurisdiction, malediction, predict, predictive, valedictorian, verdict

dys: bad; difficult
dysentery, dysfluency, dysfunction, dysfunctional, dyslexia, dystrophy

eco: ecology; environment; nature
ecohazard, ecological, ecology, ecosystem

ecto: outer; outside; external
ectoblast, ectoderm, ectogenous, ectomorph, ectopia, ectotherm, ectoplasm

ectomy: surgical removal of
appendectomy, tonsillectomy

endo: within
endocrine, endoderm, endogeneous, endomorphism, endoskeleton, endosperm, endospore, endotherm

fidelis: faithful
affidavits, confidence, confident, confidential, fidelity

gastro: stomach
gastritis, gastropod, gastrointestinal, gastrovascular cavity

ge(o): earth; ground
geography, geographic, geologists, geometry, geometric, geology, geologic, geothermal, geophysical

gen: that which produces
antigen, carcinogen, hydrogen, endogen

gram: drawing, writing, record
monongram, telegram

giga: billion
gigabyte, gigacycle, gigahertz, gigawatt

graph: something written
autograph, climatograph, digraph, electrocardiograph, electroencephalograph, electromyograph, heliograph, histograph, micrograph, monograph, paragraph, phonograph, photograph, pictograph, polygraph, seismograph, sonograph, spectrograph, telegraph, thermograph

hepta: seven
heptachlor, heptagon, heptahedron

heter, hetero: other
heterogeneity, heterogeneous, heterosporous, heterotroph, heterozygote, heterozygous

hexa: six
hexachloride, hexafloride, hexagon, hexameter

hom, homo: same; similar
homogeneity, homogeneous, homogenized, homographs, homologous, homonyms, homophones, homozygous

hydr, hydro: water
carbohydrate, dehydrated, dehydration, hydrant, hydrated, hydration, hydraulic, hydrocarbon, hydrochloric, hydroelectric, hydrofoil, hydrogen, hydrogenated, hydrogens, hydrolysis, hydrometer, hydrophilic, hydrophobia, hydroplane, hydroponics, hydrosphere, hydroxide, hydroxyl

iso: equal
isobars, isobath, isochromatic, isodynamic, isometric, isotherm

jec(t): throw
conject, conjecture, deject, dejected, eject, ejection, inject, injection, interject, interjection, object, objection, project, projectile, projection, projector, reject, rejection, trajectory

jur: law
jurisdiction, jurisprudence, jury, perjury

kilo: thousand
kilocalories, kilogram, kilohertz, kilometer, kilowatt

leg: law
illegal, legal, legacy, legality, legitimate, legislate, legislation, legislature

lith(o): stone
lithium, lithography, lithosphere, megalith, mesolithic, monolith, monolithic, neolithic, paleolithic

logy: study of; science of

anthology, anthropology, archaeology, archeology, astrology, bacteriology, biology, chronology, cosmology, criminology, cytology, ecology, epidemiology, etymology, geology, gerontology, high-technology, ideology, immunology, meteorology, methodology, microbiology, mythology, paleontology, pathology, phonology, physiology, psychology, psychopathology, sociology, technology, terminology, theology, zoology

lumen: light
bioluminescence, illuminated, illumination, luminance, luminary, luminosity, luminous

macr(o): large
macroanalysis, macrocosmic, macroeconomic, macrominerals, macromolecules, macronucleus, macronutrients, macro-organization, macroscopic

magna: great
magnification, magnificences, magnificent, magnificently, magnify, magnitude

mal: bad; abnormal
maladaptive, malady, malaise, malaria, malevolent, malfunction, malice, malicious, malignant, malnourished, malnutrition, malocclusion, malpractice

mania: great enthusiasm; madness
bibliomania, kleptomania, megalomania, pyromania

mar: sea
marina, marine, mariner, marines, maritime, submarine

mega: great; large, multiplied by a million
megacycles, megahertz, megalith, megalodon, megalomania, megalopolis, megalosaurus, mega-malls, megaphone, mega-predator, megaton, megatrends, megavitamin, megawatt

meso: middle
mesoblast, mesocephalic, mesoderm, Mesolithic, mesosome, mesosphere

meter: 39.37 inches; means of measuring
altimeter, ammeter, anemometer, audiometer, barometer, calorimeter, centimeter, chronometer, diameter, galvanometer, hydrometer, hygrometer, kilometer, micrometer,

micrometers, millimeter, odometer, ohmmeter, perimeter, photometer, radiometer, spectrometer, speedometer, tachometer, thermometer, voltmeter

metry: process of measuring
allometry, asymmetry, audiometry, calorimetry, geometry, optometry, photogrammetry, spectrometry, symmetry, trigonometry

micro: very small; one millionth
microbes, microbiology, microclimate, microcomputer, microelectronics, microfilm, microfossils, micrometer, micronesia, microphones, microprocessor, microscope, microseconds, microsurgery, microwave

mon(o): one
monochromatic, monochrome, monocots, monocular, monograph, monolithic, mononucleosis, monoplane, monopod, monopolize, monopoly, monorail, monosaccharide, monosyllables, monotheistic, monotone, monotonous, monotony, monoxide

ne(o): new
neoclassical, neocolonialism, neoliberal, neolithic, neonates, neophyte

neur(o): nerve
neural, neuralgia, neurasthenic, neuroanatomy, neurological, neurologist, neuromuscula, neuron, neuroses, neurosis, neurosurgeon, neurotic, neurotransmitter

nona: nine
nonagon, nonagenerain, novena

octa, octo: eight
octachord, octagon, octameter, octave, octogenerian

omni: all
omnibus, omnibuses, omnidirectional, omnipotence, omnipotent, omnipresence, omnipresent, omniscience, omniscient, omnivores, omnivorous

ortho: straight; right; correct
orthodox, orthopedic, orthodontics, orthography

ovi: egg
oviduct, oviferous, oviparous, ovipositor

pale(o): very old

paleoanthropologists, paleocene, paleo-Iindians, Paleolithic, paleontologist, paleontology, Paleozoic

pan: all
panacea, pan-American, pandemic, pandemonium, pandora, Pangaea, panorama

path(o): suffering, disease
pathetic, pathology, pathogen, psychopath, sympathy

ped, pod: foot
arthropod, cephalopd, centipede, impede, milliped, pedal, pedestal, pedestrian, pedomoter, podiatrist, podium, podiatry

pel, pul: drive, push
compel, compulsory, dispel, expel, expulsion, impel, impulse, impulsive, propel, propeller, propulsion, repel

pent(a): five
pentagon, pentameter, pentathlon, pentecost, penthouse, pentoxide

phil(o): love of
philanthropic, philanthropy, philharmonic, philosophy

phobia: fear
agoraphobia, claustrophobia, gerontophobia, hydrophobia, photophobia

phon(o): sound; voice
homophones, hydrophone, megaphone, microphone, phonemes, phonics, phonograph, saxophone, symphony, telephone, Xenophon, xylophone

phot(o): light
photocell, photochemical, photocopy, photoelectric, photograph, photometer, photons, photosensitive, photosynthesis, photosynthetic, photovoltaic, telephoto

poly: many; much
monopoly, polychrome, polyester, polyglot, polygon, polygraph, polymers, Polynesia, polynomial, polypeptide, Polyphemus, polysaccharides, polystyrene, polytechnic, polytheistic, polyunsaturated, polyvinyl

port: carry
deport, import, export, portable, porter, support, transport

proto: first; earliest form

protoceratops, protococcus, proton,
protoplasm, prototype, protozoa

pseud(o): false pseudo-event,
pseudomonas, pseudonym,
pseudopods, pseudoscience

psych(o): mind; spirit; soul
psyche, psychobiography, psychology,
psychiatry, psychic, psychomotor,
psychotic

quad: four
quadrangle, quadrant, quadraphonic,
quadratic, quadrennial, quadrilateral,
quadriplegic, quadruped, quadruple

quasi: resembling
quasi-academic, quasi-favorable, quais-
official, quasi-scientific

quint: five
quintet, quintile, quintillion, qintuplets

scrib, script: write
ascribe,circumscribe, conscript,
describe, description, inscribe,
inscription, prescribe, prescription,
proscribe, proscription, scribble,
Scripture, subscribe, subscript,
subscription, superscript, transcribe,
transcription

sect: cut; part of
bisected, dissecting, intersection,
resection, section, sectioned, sector,
sects

sept, septi: seven
septuagenerian, septet, septillion

sex: six
sextet, sextant, sextillion

some: body
autosome, chromosome

spec, spect: see
aspect, inspect, inspector, perspective,
retrospect, retrospective, speculate,
spectacle, spectacles, spectacular,
spectator, spectroscope, spectrum

sphere: round body; surrounding layer of
gas
biosphere, hemisphere, ionosphere;
spherical, stratosphere

spira, spire: to breathe
aspirants, aspiration, aspire,
cardiorespiratory, conspiracy,
conspirators, conspire, inspiration,
inspirational, inspire, perspire,
respiration, respirator, spirited,
spiritually, transpiration, transpired

stella: star
constellation, interstellar, stellar

terra: earth; land
extraterrestrial, terrace, terrain,
terrarium, terrestrial, terrier, territories

tetra: four
tetrachloride, tetragon, tetrahedron,
tetrameter, tetraoxide, tetrapod

therm(o): heat
ectothermal, endothermal,
endothermic, exothermic, geothermal,
hypothermia, isotherm, thermal,
thermochemical, thermodynamic,
thermograms, thermograph,
thermometer, thermonuclear,
thermoplastic, thermos, thermosetting,
thermostat

tri: three
triacid, triad, triangle, triathlon,
triceratops, trichromatic, tricycle,

trifold, triple, tripod, triumvirate, trivet

ultra: beyond
ultrahigh-frequency, ultrahigh-speed,
ultralow, ultramarine, ultramicroscope,
ultramodern, ultranationalist,
ultra-new, ultrapure, ultrasauraus,
ultrasensitive, ultrasonic, ultrasound,
ultra-suspicious, ultrasweet, ultrathin,
ultraviolet

uni: one
unicolor, unicorn, unicycle, uniform,
unilateral, unipod, unison, unitary,
universe

vert, vers: turn
avert, aversion, convert, convertible,
controversy, conversion, diversify,
divert, diversion, invert, inversion,
reverse, revert, reversion, subversion,
subvert, universe, versatile, versus,
vertigo

vide, vis: see
evident, evidence, invisible, provide,
provision, revise, supervise,
supervision, video, videocassette,
videotape, visa, visible, vision, visionary,
visitation, vista

viv, vit: live
revive, revival, survive, survival, vital,
vitality, vitalize, vitamin, viviparous,
vivid, vivisection

voc: call
avocation, advocate, convocation,
equivocal, evoke, evocative, invocation,
invoke, irrevocable, provoke, revoke,
revocation, vocabulary, vocal, vocalize,
vocation, vociferous

REFERENCES

Professional

Adams, A., Carnine, D., & Gersten, R. (1982). Instructional strategies for study reading content area texts in the intermediate grades. *Reading Research Quarterly, 17,* 27–55.

Afflerbach, P., & VanSledright, B. (2001). Hath! Doth! What? Middle graders reading innovative history text. *Journal of Adolescent & Adult Literacy, 44,* 696–707.

Alexander, P. A., & Jetton, T. L. (2000). Learning from text: A multdimensional and developmental perspective. In M. L. Kamil, P. B. Mosenthal, P. D. Pearson, & R. Barr (Eds.), *Handbook of reading research: Volume III* (pp. 285–310). Mahwah, NJ: Erlbaum.

Alfassi, M. (1998). Reading for meaning: The efficacy of reciprocal teaching in fostering reading comprehension in high school students in remedial reading classes. *American Educational Research Journal, 35,* 309–332.

Allan, K. K., & Miller, M. S. (2000). *Literacy and learning: Strategies for middle and secondary school teachers.* Boston: Houghton Mifflin.

Alley, G., & Deshler, D. (1979). *Teaching the learning disabled adolescent: Strategies and methods.* Denver: Love.

Alvermann, D. E. (1991). The discussion web: A graphic aid for learning across the curriculum. *The Reading Teacher, 45,* 92–99.

Alvermann, D. E., &, Moore, D. W. (1991). Secondary school reading. In R. Barr, M. L. Kamil, P. Mosenthal, & P. D. Pearson (Eds.), *Handbook of reading research* (Vol. II, pp. 951–983). New York: Longman.

Alvermann, D. E., & Phelps, S. F. (2002). *Content area reading and literacy: Succeeding in today's diverse classrooms* (3rd ed). Boston: Allyn & Bacon.

American Association for the Advancement of Science. (2001). *Designs for science literacy.* New York: Oxford.

American Federation of Teachers. (1999). *Making standards matter.* Available online at http://www.aft.org/edissues/standards99/Toc.htm.

American Guidance Service. (2002). *Reading-level indicator: Description and sample items.* Available online at http://www.agsnet.com/curr/rd/2.asp.

Anderson, R. C., Reynolds, R. E., Schallert, D. L., & Goetz, E. T. (1977). Frameworks for comprehending discourse. *American Educational Research Journal, 14,* 367–381.

Anderson, T. H. (1980). Study strategies and adjunct aids. In R. J. Spiro, B. C. Bruce, & W. F. Brewer (Eds.), *Theoretical issues in reading comprehension: Perspectives from cognitive psychology, artificial intelligence, linguistics, and education* (pp. 483–502). Hillsdale, NJ: Erlbaum.

Anderson, T. H., & Armbruster, B. (1984). Studying. In P. D. Pearson, R. Barr, M. L. Kamil, & P. Mosenthal (Eds.), *Handbook of reading research* (pp. 657–679). New York: Longman.

Anderson, V., & Roit, M. (1993). Planning and implementing collaborative strategy instruction for delayed readers in grades 6–10. *The Elementary School Journal, 94,* 121–137.

Anderson-Inman, L. (1997). OWLs: Online writing labs. *Journal of Adolescent & Adult Literacy, 40,* 650–654.

Anderson-Inman, L. (1998). Electronic text: Literacy medium of the future. *Journal of Adolescent & Adult Literacy, 41,* 678–682.

Andrews, S. (1997). Admit/exit slips. *Journal of Adolescent & Adult Literacy, 41,* 141–142.

Applebee, A. N. (1984). *Contexts for learning to write: Studies of secondary school instruction.* Norwood, NJ: Ablex.

Applebee, A.N. (1984). Background to the study. In A. N. Applebee (Ed.), *Contexts for learning to write: Studies of secondary school instruction* (pp. 1–5). Norwood, NJ: Ablex.

Applebee, A. N. (2000). Alternative models of writing development. In R. Indrisano & J. R. Squire (Eds.), *Perspectives on writing, research, theory, and practice* (pp. 90–110). Newark, DE: International Reading Association.

Applebee, A.N., Durst, R.K., & Newell, G. E. (1984). The demands of school writing. In A. N. Applebee (Ed.), *Contexts for learning to write: Studies of secondary school instruction* (pp. 55–77). Norwood, NJ: Ablex.

Applegate, D. (2001). Information organization. *Learning strategies database.* Muskingum College Center for Advancement of Learning. Available online at http://www.muskingum.edu/~cal/database/organization.html.

Armbruster, B. (1996). Considerate texts. In D. Lapp, J. Flood, & N. Farnan (Eds.), *Content area reading and learning instructional strategies* (2nd ed.) (pp. 47–57). Boston: Allyn & Bacon.

Armbruster, B. B., & Anderson, T. H. (1981). *Content area textbooks* (Tech. Rep. No. 23). Champaign: University of Illinois, Center for the Study of Reading.

Aronson, E. (1978). *The jigsaw classroom.* Beverly Hills: Sage.

Ashcraft, M. H. (1994). *Human memory and cognition*. New York: HarperCollins.

Atwell, N. (1987). *In the middle*. Portsmouth, NH: Boynton/Cook.

Atwell, N. (1990). *Coming to know: Writing to learn in the intermediate grades*. Portsmouth, NH: Heinemann.

Atwell, N. (1993). Foreword. In L. Patterson, C. M. Santa, K. G. Short, & K. Smith (Eds.), *Teachers are researchers: Reflection and action* (pp. vii–x). Newark, DE: International Reading Association.

Bahrick, H. P., Bahrick, P. C., & Wittlinger, R. P. (1975). Fifty years of memories for names and faces: A cross-sectional approach. *Journal of Experimental Psychology: General, 104,* 54–75.

Baker, D. R., & Piburn, M. D. (1997). *Constructing science in middle and secondary school classrooms*. Boston: Allyn & Bacon.

Baker, L., & Brown, A. L. (1984). Metacognitive skills and reading. In P. D. Pearson, R. Barr, M. L. Kamil, & P. Mosenthal (Eds.), *Handbook of reading research* (pp. 353–394). New York: Longman.

Ballator, N., Farnum, M., & Kaplan, B. (1999). *NAEP 1996 trends in writing: Fluency and writing conventions*. Washington, DC: National Center for Education Statistics.

Barron, R. F. (1979). Research for classroom teachers: Recent developments on the use of the structured overview as an advanced organizer. In H. L. Herber & J. D. Riley (Eds.), *Research in reading in the content areas: Fourth report* (pp. 171–176). Syracuse, NY: Syracuse University, Reading and Language Arts Center.

Barron, R. F. (1969). Research for the classroom teacher: The use of vocabulary as an advanced organizer. In H. L. Herber & P. Senders (Eds.), *Research in reading in the content areas: The first report* (pp. 28–47). Syracuse, NY: Syracuse University, Reading and Language Arts Center.

Barry, A. L. (1997). High school reading programs revisited. *Journal of Adolescent & Adult Literacy, 40,* 524–531.

Bartlett, F. C. (1932). *Remembering: A study in experimental and social psychology*. London: Cambridge University Press.

Baskin, B. H. & Harris, K. (1995). Heard any good books lately? The case for audiobooks in the secondary classroom. *Journal of Adolescent & Adult Literacy, 40,* 450–455.

Bean, T. W., Bean, S. K., & Bean, K. F. (1999). Intergenerational conversations and two adolescents' multiple literacies: Implications for redefining content area literacy. *Journal of Adolescent & Adult Literacy, 42,* 438–448.

Beck, I. L., & McKeown, M. G. (1983). Learning words well—a program to enhance vocabulary and comprehension. *The Reading Teacher, 36,* 622–625.

Beck, I. L., McKeown, M. G., Hamilton, R. L., & Kucan, L. (1997). *Questioning the author: An approach for enhancing student engagement with text*. Newark, DE: International Reading Association.

Beck, I. L., McKeown, M. G., Sinatra, G. M., & Loxterman, J. A. (1991). Revising social studies text from a text-processing perspective: Evidence of improved comprehensibility. *Reading Research Quarterly, 26,* 251–276.

Bennett, B. (2000). Internet resources for K–8 students: Update 2000. *ERIC Digest*. Syracuse, NY: ERIC Clearinghouse on Information and Technology. Available online at: http://ericit.org/digests/EDO-IR-2000-04.shtml.

Bereiter, C., & Scardamalia, M. (1987). *The psychology of written composition*. Hillsdale, NJ: Erlbaum.

Bereiter, C., & Scardamalia, M. (1989). Intentional learning as a goal of instruction. In L. B. Resnick (Ed.), *Knowing, learning, and instruction: Essays in honor of Robert Glaser* (pp. 361–392). Hillsdale, NJ: Erlbaum.

Berkowitz, S. J. (1986). Effects of instruction in text organization on sixth-grade students' memory for expository text. *Reading Research Quarterly, 21,* 161–178.

Bjorklund, B., Handler, N., Mitten, J., & Stockwell, G. (1998, October). *Literature circles: A tool for developing students as critical readers, writers, and thinkers*. Paper presented at the 47th annual conference of the Connecticut Reading Association, Waterbury.

Blachowicz, C. L. Z. (1986). Making connections: Alternatives to the vocabulary notebook. *Journal of Reading, 29,* 643–649.

Blakeslee, T. (1997). *Helping students with constructed response items on the HSPT and MEAP's*. Available online at http://cdp.mde.state.mi.us/science/constructedresponseitems.html.

Bloom, B. (1976). *Human characteristics and school learning*. New York: McGraw-Hill.

Bloom, B. (Ed.). (1957). *Taxonomy of educational objectives*. New York: McKay.

Board of Directors of the International Reading Association (1999). High-stakes assessments in reading. *The Reading Teacher, 53,* 257–264.

Boothroyd, K. (2001, December). *Being literate in urban third-grade classrooms*. Paper presented at the annual meeting of the National Reading Conference, San Antonio, TX.

Bormuth, J. R. (1971). *Development of standards of readability: Report of development* (Project No. 9–0237). Chicago: University of Chicago. (ERIC Document Reproduction Service No. ED 054–233).

Bousfield, W. A. (1953). The occurrence of clustering in the recall of randomly arranged associates. *Journal of General Psychology, 30,* 149–165.

Bower, G. H. (1970). Analysis of a mnemonic device. *American Scientist, 58,* 496–510.

Bower, G. H., Clark, M. C., Lesgold, A. M., & Winzenz, D. (1969). Hierarchical retrieval schemes in recall of categorical word lists. *Journal of Verbal Learning and Verbal Behavior, 8,* 323–343.

Boyle, C. (1996). *Efficacy of peer evaluation and effects of peer evaluation on persuasive writing*. Unpublished master's thesis, San Diego State University, San Diego, CA.

Bransford, J. D., Brown, A. L., & Cocking, R. R. (2001). *How people learn: Brain, mind, experience, and school*. Washington, DC: National Academy Press.

Bristow, P. S., Pikulski, J. J., & Pelosi, P. L. (1983). A comparison of five estimates of reading instructional level. *The Reading Teacher, 37,* 273–279.

Brock, C. (2000, May). *Serving English language learners in English dominant classroom: Important issues and considerations*.

Paper presented at the annual conference of the International Reading Association, Indianapolis, IN.

Brophy, J. E., & Good, T. L. (1986). Teacher behavior and student achievement. In M. E. Wittrock (Ed.), *Handbook of research on teaching* (pp. 328–375). New York: Macmillan.

Brown, A. L. (1985). *Reciprocal teaching of comprehension strategies: A natural history of one program for enhancing learning* (Tech. Rep. No. 334). Champaign: University of Illinois, Center for the Study of Reading.

Brown, A. L. & Day, J. D. (1983). Macrorules for summarizing text: The development of expertise. *Journal of Verbal Learning and Verbal Behavior, 22*(1), 1–14.

Brown, C. S., & Lytle, S. L. (1988). Merging assessment and instruction: Protocols in the classroom. In S. M. Glazer, L. W. Searfoss, & L. M. Gentile (Eds.), *Reexamining reading diagnosis: New trends and procedures* (pp. 94–102). Newark, DE: International Reading Association.

Bruce, B. C., & Bishop, A. P. (2002). Using the Web to support inquiry-based literacy development. *Journal of Adolescent & Adult Literacy, 45*, 706–714.

Bruner, J. (1963). *The process of education.* New York: Vintage.

Bruner, J. (1986). *Actual minds, possible worlds.* Cambridge, MA: Harvard University Press.

Buehl, D. (2001). *Classroom strategies for interactive learning* (2nd ed.). Newark, DE: International Reading Association.

Buehl, D., & Stumpf, S. (1999). *High school reading task force report.* Madison, WI: Madison Metropolitan School District.

Buehl, D., & Stumpf, S. (2000). *Developing middle school and high school programs for struggling readers.* Paper presented at the annual meeting of the International Reading Association, Indianapolis, IN.

Bulgren, J., & Lenz, K. (1996). Strategic instruction in the content areas. In D. D. Deshler, E. S. Ellis, & B. K. Lenz (Eds.), *Teaching adolescents with learning disabilities* (pp. 409–473). Denver: Love.

Bulgren, J., & Scanlon, D. (1997–1998). Instructional routines and learning strategies that promote understanding of content area concepts. *Journal of Adolescent & Adult Literacy, 38*, 372–376.

Bush, C., & Huebner, M. (1979). *Strategies for reading in the elementary school* (2nd ed.). New York: Macmillan.

Butler-Nalin, P. (1984). In A. N. Applebee & J. N. Langer (Eds.), *Contexts for learning to write: Studies of secondary school instruction.* Norwood, NJ: Ablex.

Calkins, L., Montgomery, K., & Santman, D. (1998). *A teacher's guide to standardized reading tests.* Portsmouth, NH; Heinemann.

Campbell, J. R., Hombro, C. M., Mazzeo, J. (1999). Trends in academic progress: Three decades of student performance. *Education Statistics Quarterly; 2,* 31–36. Available online at http://nces.ed.gov/ssbr/pages/trends.asp

Cantrell, R. J. (1997). KWL learning journals: A way to encourage reflection. *Journal of Adolescent & Adult Literacy, 40,* 392–393.

Carey, S. Cognitive science and science education. *American Psychologist, 10,* 1123–1130.

Carlson, N. R., & Buskist, W. (1997). *Psychology: The science of behavior* (5th ed.). Boston: Allyn & Bacon.

Carver, R. P. (1975–76). Measuring prose difficulty using the rauding scale *Reading Research Quarterly, 11,* 660–685.

Carver, R. (1990). *Reading rate: A review of research and theory.* New York: Academic Press.

Carver, R. (1992). What do standardized reading comprehension tests measure in terms of efficiency, rate, and accuracy? *Reading Research Quarterly, 27,* 346–359.

Cattagni, A. & Wesstat, E. F. (2001). *Internet access in U.S. public schools and classrooms: 1994–2000.* Washington, DC: U.S. Department of Education, National Center for Education Statistics. Available online at http://nces.ed.gov/pubsearch/pubsinfo.asp?pubid=2001071.

Caverly, D. C., & Orlando, V. P. (1991). Textbook study strategies. In D. C. Caverly & V. P. Orlando (Eds.), *Teaching reading and study strategies at the college level* (pp. 86–165). Newark, DE: International Reading Association.

Caverly, D. C., Orlando, V. P., & Mullen, J. L. (2000). *Textbook study reading.* In R. F. Flippo & D. C. Caverly (Eds.), *Handbook of college reading and study strategy research* (pp. 105–147). Mahwah, NJ: Erlbaum.

Chall, J. S., & Dale, E. (1995). *Readability revisited: The new Dale-Chall readability formula.* Cambridge, MA: Brookline.

Chall, J. S., Bissex, G. L., Conard, S. S., & Harris-Sharples, S. H. (1996). *Holistic assessment of texts: Scales for estimating the difficulty of literature, social studies, and science materials.* Cambridge, MA: Brookline.

Chamot, A. U., & O'Malley, J. M. (1994). Instructional approaches and teaching procedures. In K. Spangenberg-Urbschat & R. Pritchard (Eds.), *Kids come in all languages: Reading instruction for ESL students* (pp. 82–107). Newark, DE: International Reading Association.

Chinn, C. A., & Brewer, W. F. (1993). The role of anomalous data in knowledge acquisition: A theoretical framework and implications for science instruction. *Review of Educational Research, 63,* 1–49.

Christenbury, L., & Kelly, P. (1983). *Questioning: A path to critical thinking.* Urbana, IL: National Council of Teachers of English.

Ciardello, A.V. (1998). Did you ask a good question today? *Journal of Adolescent & Adult Literacy, 42,* 210–220.

Claxton, M. M., & Cooper, C. C. (2000). Teaching tools: American literature and the World Wide Web. *English Journal, 90,* 97–103.

Colburn, A., & Echevarria, J. (1999). Meaningful lessons. *The Science Teacher, 66*(2), 36–39.

Coleman, E. B. (1971). Developing a technology of written instruction: Some determiners of the complexity of prose. In E. Z. Rothkopf & P. E. Johnson (Eds.), *Verbal learning research and the technology of written instruction* (pp. 155–204). New York: Teachers College Press.

Collins, A., & Smith, E. (1980). *Teaching the process of reading comprehension* (Tech. Rep. No. 182). Urbana: University of Illinois, Center for the Study of Reading.

Coppola, J. (2002, May). *Creating opportunities to learn: Literacy instruction for English language learners in a fifth-grade, all-English classroom.* Paper presented at the annual meeting of the International Reading Association, San Francisco.

Conard, S. S. (1990, May). *Change and challenge in content text-*

books. Paper presented at the annual conference of the International Reading Association, New Orleans.

Conley, M. R. (1997). *Content reading instruction* (2nd ed.). New York: McGraw-Hill.

Cook, L. K., & Mayer, R. E. (1988). Teaching readers about the structure of scientific text. *Journal of Educational Psychology, 80*, 448–456.

Cooper, C. R., & Odell, L. (1977). *Evaluating writing: Describing, measuring, judging*. Urbana, IL: National Council of Teachers of English.

Countryman, J. (1992). *Writing to learn mathematics: Strategies that work*. Portsmouth, NH: Heinemann.

Crago, M. B. (1992). Communicative interaction and second language acquisition: An Inuit example. *TESOL Quarterly, 26*, 487–505.

Craik, F. I. M., & Lockhart, R. S. (1972). Levels of processing. *Journal of Verbal Learning and Verbal Behavior, 11*, 671–684.

Crawford, A. N. (1993). Literature, integrated language arts, and the language minority child: A focus on meaning. In A. Carrasquillo (Ed.), *Whole language and the bilingual learner* (pp. 61–75). Norwood, NJ: Ablex.

Cummins, J. (1994). The acquisition of English as a second language. In K. Spangenberg-Urbschat & R. Pritchard (Eds.), *Kids come in all languages: Reading instruction for all ESL students* (pp. 36–62). Newark, DE: International Reading Association.

Cummins, J. (2001). Assessment and intervention with culturally and linguistically diverse learners. In S. R. Hurley & J. V. Tinajero (Eds.), *Literacy assessment of second language learners* (pp. 115–129). Boston: Allyn & Bacon.

Curtis, M. E. R., & Longo, A. M. (1999). *When adolescents can't read: Methods and materials that work*. Boston: Brookline.

Dahl, K., & Farnan, N. (1998). *Children's writing: Perspectives from research*. Newark, DE: International Reading Association & National Reading Conference.

Dale, E., & O'Rourke, J. (1971). *Techniques of teaching vocabulary*. Chicago: Field.

Daly, J. A., & Hailey, J. L. (1984). Putting the situation into tate and disposition as parameters of writing apprehension. In R. Beach & L. Bridwell (Eds.), *New directions in composition research*. New York: Guilford Press.

Daniels, H. (1994). *Literature circles: Voice and choice in the student-centered classroom*. York, ME: Stenhouse.

Dave, R. H. (1964). *The identification and measurement of environmental process variables that are related to educational achievement*. Unpublished doctoral dissertation, University of Chicago.

Davey, B., & McBride, S. (1986). Effects of question-generation training on reading comprehension. *Journal of Educational Psychology, 78*, 256–262.

Devine, T. G. (1987). *Teaching study skills: A guide for teachers* (2nd ed.). Boston: Allyn & Bacon.

Dillon, J. T. (1983). *Teaching and the art of questioning*. Bloomington, IN: Phi Delta Kappa.

Dole, J. A., Sloan, C., & Trathen, W. (1995). Teaching vocabulary within the context of literature. *Journal of Reading, 38*, 452–460.

Dolly, M. R. (1990). Integrating ESL reading and writing through authentic discourse. *Journal of Reading, 33*, 360–365.

Donahue, P. A., Voelk, K. E., Campbell, J. R., & Mazzeo, J. (1999). *NAEP 1998 report card for the nation and the states*. Washington, DC: U.S. Department of Education.

Dreher, M. J., &Guthrie, J. T. (1990). Cognitive processes in textbook chapter search tasks. *Reading Research Quarterly, 25*, 323–339.

Duffelmeyer, F. A., Daum, D. D., & Merkley, D. J. (1987). Maximizing reader-text confrontation with an extended anticipation guide. *Journal of Reading, 31*, 146–150.

Duffy, G. G., & Roehler, L. R. (1987). Improving reading instruction through the use of responsive elaboration. *The Reading Teacher, 40*, 514–520.

Duffy, T., Higgins, L. Mehlenbacher, B., Cochran, C., Wallace, D., Hill, C., Haugen, D., McCaffrey, M., Burnett, R., Sloane, S., & Smith, S. (1989). Models for the design of instructional text. *Reading Research Quarterly, 24*, 434–457.

Dupin, J. J., & Johsua, S. (1987). Conceptions of French pupils concerning electric circuits: Structure and evolution. *Journal of Research in Science Teaching, 24*, 791–806.

Durst, R. K. (1984). The development of analytical writing. In A. N. Applebee (Ed.), *Contexts for learning to write: Studies of secondary school instruction* (pp. 79–102). Norwood, NJ: Ablex.

Dwyer, D. C. (1995, July). *Finding the future in the past: Readying schools for the 21st century*. Proceedings of the Australian Computers in Education Conference, Perth, Australia. Available online at http://www.tdd.nsw.edu.au/resources/papers/info_skills.htm.

Early, M., & Sawyer, D. J. (1984). *Reading to learn in grades 5 to 12*. New York: Harcourt Brace Jovanovich.

Eccles, J. S., & Midgley, C. (1989). Stage/environment fit: Developmentally appropriate classrooms for early adolescents. In R. E. Aames & C. Ames (Eds.), *Research on motivation in education* (Vol. 3, pp. 139–186). New York: Academic Press.

Echevarria, J., Vogt, M., & Short, D. J. (2000). *Making content comprehensible for English language learners: The SIOP model*. Boston: Allyn & Bacon.

Education Week on the Web. (2001, January 11) *Quality counts 2001: A better balance*. Available online at: http://www.edweek.org/sreports/qc01/.

Edugreen. (2001).What you can do t reduce *air pollution*. Available online at http://edugreen.teri.res.in/explore/air/ucan.htm.

Eeds, M., & Cockrum, W. A. (1985). Teaching word meanings by expanding schemata vs. dictionary work vs. reading in context. *Journal of Reading, 28*, 492–497.

Egan, M. (1999). Reflections on effective use of graphic organizers. *Journal of Adolescent & Adult Literacy, 42*, 641–645.

Eggen, P., & Kauchak, D. (2001). *Educational psychology: Windows on classrooms* (5th ed.). Upper Saddle River, NJ: Merrill Prentice Hall.

Eisenberger, J., Conti-D'Antonio, M., & Bertrando, R. (2000). *Self-efficacy: Raising the bar for students with learning needs*. Larchmont, NY: Eye on Education.

Electronic Journal of Combinatorics. (2001). *Who was John*

Venn? Available on line at: http://www.combinatorics.org/Surveys/ds5/VennJohnEJC.html.

Elkins, J., & Luke, A. (1999). Editorial: Redefining adolescent literacies. *Journal of Adolescent & Adult Literacy,, 43,* 212–215.

Elley, W. B. (1992). *How in the world do students read?* The Netherlands: IEA.

Emig, J. (1971). *The composing processes of twelfth-graders.* Urbana, IL: National Council of Teachers of English.

ERIC Clearinghouse on Urban Education. (2001). *Latinos in school: Some facts and findings.* Available online at: http://eric-web.tc.columbia.edu/digests/dig162.html.

Escamilla, K., & Cody, M. (2001). Assessing the writing of Spanish-speaking students: Issues and suggestions. In S. R. Hurley & J. V. Tinajero (Eds.), *Literacy assessment of second language learners* (pp. 43–63). Boston: Allyn & Bacon.

Estes, T., & Vaughn, J. (1985). *Reading and learning in the content classroom* (2nd ed.). Boston: Allyn & Bacon.

Farr, R., & Carey, R. F. (1986). *Reading: What can be measured?* Newark, DE: International Reading Association.

Farr, R., & Pritchard, R. (1996). In D. Lapp, J. Flood, & N. Farnan (Eds.), *Content area reading and learning instructional strategies* (2nd ed.) (pp. 383–402). Boston: Allyn & Bacon.

Ferguson, A. M., & Fairburn, J. (1985). Language experience for problem solving in mathematics. *The Reading Teacher, 38,* 504–507.

Fisher, D. (2001). "We're moving on up": Creating a schoolwide literacy effort in an urban high school. *Journal of Adolescent & Adult Literacy, 45,* 92–101.

Flexner, S. B., & Hauck, L. C. (1994). *The Random House dictionary of the English language* (2nd ed., rev.). New York: Random House.

Freeman, Y, & Freeman, D. (2002, May). *Teaching language through content themes and literature.* Paper presented at the annual meeting of the International Reading Association, San Francisco.

Fry, E. (1995). African reading stories (Reading around the World). *The Reading Teacher, 48,* 444–445.

Frymier, J., & Gansneder, B. (1989). The Phi Delta Kappa study of students at risk. *Phi Delta Kappan, 71,* 142–146.

Fusaro, J. (1988). Applying statistical rigor to a validation study of the Fry Readability Graph. *Reading Research and Instruction, 28,* 44–48.

Gallas, K. (1994). *Talking their way into science: Hearing children's questions and theories, responding with curricula.* New York: Teachers College Press.

Gambrell, L. B. (1980). Think time: Implications for reading instruction. *The Reading Teacher, 34,* 143–146.

Gambrell, L. B., & Bales, R. J. (1986). Mental imagery and the comprehension monitoring performance of fourth- and fifth-grade poor readers. *Reading Research Quarterly, 21,* 454–464.

Gambrell, L. B., Kapinus, B. A., & Wilson, R. M. (1987). Using mental imagery and summarization to achieve independence in comprehension. *Journal of Reading, 30,* 638–642.

Gambrell, L. B., Wilson, R. M., & Gantt, W. N. (1981). Classroom observations of good and poor readers. *Journal of Educational Research, 24,* 400–404.

Gans, R. (1940). *Study of critical reading comprehension in interme-diate grades: Teachers College contributions to education, No. 811.* New York: Bureau of Publications, Teachers College, Columbia University.

Gardner, H. (1983). *Frames of mind: The theory of multiple intelligences.* New York: Basic Books.

Garner, R. (1994). Metacognition and executive control. In R. B. Ruddell, M. R. Ruddell, & H. Singer (Eds.), *Theoretical models and processes of reading* (4th ed.) (pp. 715–732). Newark, DE: International Reading Association.

Gaskins, I., & Elliot, T. (1991). *Implementing cognitive strategy instruction across the school.* Cambridge, MA: Brookline.

Gates, A. I. (1917). Recitation as a factor in memorizing. *Archives of Psychology, 40,* 65–104.

Gaudrey, E., & Spielberger, C. D. (1971). *Anxiety and educational achievement.* Sydney, Australia: John Wiley & Sons.

Gelman, R., and Greeno, J. G. (1989). On the nature of competence: Principles for understanding in a domain. In L. B. Resnick (Ed.), *Knowing and learning: Essays in honor of Robert Glaser,* (pp. 125–186). Hillsdale, NJ: Erlbaum Associates.

Gersten, R., & Baker, S. (2000). What we know about effective instructional practices for English-language learners. *Exceptional Children, 66,* 454–470.

Gleason, M. M. (1999). The role of evidence in argumentative writing. *Reading and Writing Quarterly, 15,* 81–106.

Glynn, S. M. (1994). *Teaching science with analogies: A strategy for teachers and textbook authors* (Reading Research Report No. 15). Athens, GA: National Reading Research Center.

Goldman, S. (1997). Learning from text: Reflections on 20 years of research and suggestions for new directions of inquiry. *Discourse Processes, 23,* 357–398.

Gonzales, O. (1999). Building Vocabulary: Dictionary consultation and the ESL student. *Journal of Adolescent & Adult Literacy, 43,* 264–270.

Gottlieb, R. (2001, January 8). Dropout rate falls in city. *Hartford Courant,* pp. A1, A8.

Graham, K. G., & Robinson, H. A. *Study skills handbook: A guide for all teachers.* Newark, DE: International Reading Association.

Grant, R., Guthrie, J. T., Bennett, L., Rice, M. E., & McGough, K. (1994). Developing engaged readers through concept-oriented instruction. *The Reading Teacher, 47,* 338–340.

Graves, M. F. (1987). Roles of instruction in fostering vocabulary development. In M. G. McKeown & M. E. Curtis (Eds.), *The nature of vocabulary acquisition* (pp. 165–184). Hillsdale, NJ: Lawrence Erlbaum.

Greenwald, E. A., Persky, H. R., Campbell, J. R., & Mazzeo, J. (1999). NAEP 1998 writing report card for the nation and the states. *Education Statistics Quarterly, 1*(4) 23–28.

Griesel, P., Anders, P. L., & Maxfield, S. A. (2000, December). *Teacher and student actions to construct biology literacy at a community college: A bounded case study.* Paper presented at the National Reading Conference, Scottsdale, AZ.

Groff-Palmero, S. (2001, July 2). New York tells drivers to hang up. *Scholastic News Zone.* Available online at http://teacher.scholastic.com/newszone/index.asp.

Grunwald Associates. (2001). *Children, families and the Internet.* Available online at http://www.grunwald.com/survey/survey_content.html.

Guerra, C. (1998). SQRC: A strategy for guiding reading and higher level thinking. *Journal of Adolescent & Adult Literacy, 42*(4), 265–270.

Gunning, T. (1987, May). *A comparison of the Wide Range with the Spache and Dale-Chall readability formulas.* Paper presented at the annual meeting of the International Reading Association, New Orleans.

Gunning, T. (1999, May). *Objective/subjective leveling system.* Paper presented at the annual meeting of the International Reading Association, San Diego.

Gunning, T. (2002). *Assessing and correcting reading and writing difficulties* (2nd ed.). Boston: Allyn & Bacon.

Gunning, T. (2003). *Creating literacy instruction for all children* (4th ed.). Boston: Allyn & Bacon.

Guthrie, J. T., & Wigfield, A. (1997). Reading engagement: A rationale for theory and teaching. In J. Guthrie & A. Wigfield (Eds.), *Motivating readers through integrated instruction* (pp. 14–33). Newark, DE: International Reading Association.

Guthrie, J. T., Alao, S., & Rinehart, J. M. (1997). Engagement in reading for young adolescents. *Journal of Adolescent & Adult Literacy, 40,* 438–446.

Guthrie, J. T., Bennett, L., McGough, K., & Rice, M. E. (1996). Concept-oriented reading instruction: An integrated curriculum to develop motivations and strategies for reading. In L. Baker, P. Afflerbach, & D. Reinking (Eds.), *Developing engaged readers in school and home communities* (pp. 165–190). Hillsdale, NJ: Erlbaum.

Guthrie, J. T., Van Meter, P., McCann, A. D., Wigfield, A., Bennett, L., Poundstone, C. C., Rice, M. E., Faibisch, F. M., Hunt, B., & Mitchell, A. M. (1996). Growth of literacy engagement: Changes in motivations and strategies during concept-oriented reading instruction. *Reading Research Quarterly, 31,* 306–332.

Guzzetti, B. J., Kowalinski, B. J., & McGowan, T. (1992). Using a literature-based approach to teaching social studies. *Journal of Reading, 36,* 114–122.

Haggard, M. R. (1982). The vocabulary self-collection strategy: An active approach to word learning. *Journal of Reading, 27,* pp. 203–207.

Hague, S. (1987). Vocabulary instruction: What L2 can learn from L1. *Foreign Language Annals, 20,* 217–225.

Halliday, M. A. K. (1994). *An introduction to functional grammar* (2nd ed.). London: Edward Arnold.

Hansen, J., & Pearson, P. D. (1982). *Improving the inferential comprehension of good and poor fourth-grade readers* (Report No. CSR-TR-235). Urbana: University of Illinois, Center for the Study of Reading (ERIC Document Reproduction No. ED 215–312).

Harmon, J. M. (1998a). Constructing word meanings: Strategies and perceptions of four middle school learners. *Journal of Literacy Research, 30,* 561–599.

Harmon, J. W. (1998b). Vocabulary teaching and learning in a seventh-grade literature-based classroom. *Journal of Adolescent & Adult Literacy, 41,* 518–529.

Harris, A. J., & Jacobson, M. D. (1982). *Basic reading vocabularies.* New York: Macmillan.

Harris, A. J., & Sipay, E. R. (1990). *How to increase reading ability* (9th ed.). New York: Longman.

Hart, C., Mulhall, P., Berry, A., Loughran, J., & Gunstone, R. (2000). What is the purpose of this experiment? Or can students learn something from doing experiments? *Journal of Research in Science Teaching, 37,* 655–675.

Harvey, S. (1998). *Nonfiction matters: Reading, writing, and research in grades 3–8.* York, ME: Stenhouse.

Hatano, G., & Inagaki, K. (1996). *Young children's thinking about the biological world.* New York: Psychology Press.

Hattie, J. A. (1992). Measuring the effects of schooling. *Australian Journal of Education, 36*(1), 5–13.

Havens, L. (2001). *Daily writing in mathematics and science helps students become metacognitive and improves their problem solving skills.* Paper presented at the annual conference of the International Reading Association, New Orleans.

Hawkins, E., Stancavage, F., Mitchell, J., Goodman, M., & Lazer, S. (1998). *Learning about our world and our past: Using the tools and resources of geography and U.S. history—a report of the 1994 NAEP assessment.* Washington, DC: National Center for Education Statistics.

Head, M. H., & Readence, J. E. (1986). Anticipation guides: Meaning through prediction. In E. K. Dishner, T. W. Bean, J. E. Readence, & D. W. Moore (Eds.), *Reading in the content areas* (2nd ed.) (pp. 229–234). Dubuque, IA: Kendall/Hunt.

Heiman, M., & Slomianko, J. (1986). *Methods of inquiry.* Cambridge, MA: Learning Associates.

Heller, M. F. (1997). Reading and writing about the environment: Visions of the year 2000. *Journal of Adolescent & Adult Literacy, 40,* 332–341.

Hennings, D. G. (1993). On knowing and reading history. *Journal of Reading, 36,* 362–370.

Hennings, D. G. (2000). Contextually relevant word study: Adolescent vocabulary development across the curriculum. *Journal of Adolescent & Adult Literacy, 44,* 268–279.

Herber, H. L. (1970). *Teaching reading in content areas.* Englewood Cliffs, NJ: Prentice-Hall.

Herber, H. L., & Herber, J. N. (1993). *Teaching in content areas with reading, writing, and reasoning.* Boston: Allyn & Bacon.

Hill, C. (2002). *Developing educational standards.* Available online at http://edStandards.org/Standards.html.

Hodgson, A. R., & Bohning, G. (1997). A five-step guide for developing a writing checklist. *Journal of Adolescent & Adult Literacy, 41,* 138–141.

Holt, T. (1990). *Thinking historically.* New York: College Entrance Examination Board.

Hopkins, G., & Bean, T. W. (1998–1999). Vocabulary learning with verbal-visual word association strategy in a Native American community. *Journal of Adolescent & Adult Literacy, 21,* 274–281.

Hotchkiss, P. (1990). Cooperative learning models: Improving student achievement using small groups. In M. A. Gunter, T. H. Estes, & J. H. Schwab (Eds.), *Instruction: A models approach* (pp. 167–184). Boston: Allyn & Bacon.

Huffman, L. E. (1996). What's in it for you? A student-directed text preview. *Journal of Adolescent & Adult Literacy, 40,* 56–57.

Huffman, L. E. (1998). Spotlighting specifics by combining focus questions with K-W-L. *Journal of Adolescent & Adult Literacy, 41,* 470–472.

Hurst, D. (2001). Notetaking. *Learning strategies database.*

Muskingum College Center for Advancement of Learning. Available online at http://www.muskingum.edu/~cal/database/notetaking.

Hyman, R. T. (1978). *Strategic questioning*. Englewood Cliffs, NJ: Prentice-Hall.

Hynd, C. R. (1999). Teaching students to think critically using multiple texts in history. *Journal of Adolescent & Adult Literacy, 42,* 428–436.

International Reading Association. (1999). *High stakes assessments in reading: A position statement of the International Reading Association*. Newark, DE: International Reading Association.

International Reading Association & National Council of Teachers of English. (1996). *Standards for the English language arts*. Newark, DE.

Internet Surveys. (2001). *How many online?* Available online at http://www.nua.ie/surveys/how_many_online/index.html.

Jensen, S. J., & Duffelmeyer, F. A. (1996). Enhancing possible sentences through cooperative learning. *Journal of Adolescent & Adult Literacy, 39,* 658–659.

Jett-Simpson, M. (Ed.). (1990). *Toward an ecological assessment of reading progress*. Schofield: Wisconsin State Reading Association.

Jiménez, R. T. (1997). The strategic reading abilities and potential of five low literacy Latina/o readers in middle school. *Reading Research Quarterly, 32,* 224–243.

Jitendra, A. K., Nolet, V., Yan, P. X., Gomez, O., Renmouf, K, & Iskold, L. I. (2001). An analysis of middle school geography textbooks: Implications for students with learning problems. *Reading and Writing Quarterly, 17,* 151–173.

Johnson, A. P., & Rasmussen, J. B. (1998). *Journal of Adolescent & Adult Literacy, 42,* 204–207.

Johnson, D., & Steele, V. (1996). So many words, so little time: Helping college ESL learners acquire vocabulary-building strategies. *Journal of Adolescent & Adult Literacy, 39,* 348–357.

Johnson, D. D., & Pearson, P. D. (1984). *Teaching reading vocabulary* (2nd ed.). New York: Holt, Rinehart & Winston.

Johnson, D. W., & Johnson, R. T. (1994). *Learning together and alone: Cooperative, competitive, and individualistic learning* (4th ed.). Boston: Allyn & Bacon.

Joint Task Force on Assessment. (1994). *Standards for the assessment of reading and writing*. Newark, DE: International Reading Association and Urbana, IL: National Council of Teachers of English.

Jones, M. S., Levin, M. E., Levin, J. R., & Beitzel, B. D. (2000). Can vocabulary-learning strategies and pair-learning formats be profitably combined? *Journal of Educational Psychology, 92,* 256–262.

Jorgenson, G. W. (1975). An analysis of teacher judgments of reading levels. *American Educational Research Journal, 12,* 67–75.

Josel, C. A. (1997). Abbreviations for notetaking. *Journal of Adolescent & Adult Literacy, 40,* 393–394.

Joshua, S., & Dupin, J. J. (1987). Conceptions of French pupils concerning electric circuits: Structure and evolution. *Journal of Research in Science Teaching, 24,* 791–806.

Kastberg, D., Arafeh, S., Williams, T., & Tsen, W. (2000). *Pursuing excellence: Comparisons of international eighth-grade mathematics and science achievement from a U.S. perspective, 1995 and 1999*. Washington, DC: National Center for Education Statistics.

Katims, D. S., & Harris, S. (1997). Improving the reading comprehension of middle school students in inclusive classrooms. *Journal of Adolescent & Adult Literacy, 41,* 116–123.

Keene, E. O., & Zimmermann, S. (1997). *Mosaic of thought: Teaching reading comprehension in a reader's workshop*. Portsmouth, NH: Heinemann.

Kendall, J. S., & Marzano, R. J. (2000). *Content knowledge: A compendium of standards and benchmarks for K–12 education* (3rd ed.). Aurora, CO: McREL (Mid-continent Research for Education and Learning).

Kentucky Virtual Library. (2002). *Why evaluate information sources?* Available online at http://www.kyvl.org/html/tutorial/research/whyeval.shtml

Keys, C. W. (2000). Investigating the thinking processes of eighth grade writers during the composition of a scientific laboratory report. *Journal of Research in Science Teaching, 37,* 676–690.

Kieran, C. (1981). Concepts associated with the equality symbol. *Educational Studies in Mathematics, 12,* 317–326.

Kindler, A. L. (2002). *Survey of the states' limited English proficient students and available educational programs and services, 1999–2000*. Washington, DC: National Clearinghouse for English Language Acquisition and Language Instruction Educational Programs.

King, A. (1994). Autonomy and question asking: The role of personal control in guided student-generated questioning. *Learning and Individual Differences, 6,* 163–185.

King, A., & Rosenshine, B. (1993). Effects of guided cooperative-questioning on children's knowledge construction. *Journal of Experimental Education, 6,* 127–148.

Kintsch, W. (1994). The role of knowledge in discourse comprehension: A construction-integration model. In R. B. Ruddell, M. R. Ruddell, & H. Singer (Eds.), *Theoretical models and processes of reading* (4th ed.) (pp. 951–995). Newark, DE: International Reading Association.

Kintsch, W., Kozminisky, E., Streby, W. J., McKoon, G., & Keenan, J. M. (1975). Comprehension and recall of text as a function of content variables. *Journal of Verbal Learning and Verbal Behavior, 14,* 196–214.

Kletzien, S. B. (1991). Strategy use by good and poor comprehenders reading expository text of differing levels. *Reading Research Quarterly, 26,* 67–86.

Krause, C. (2001). Information organization. *Learning strategies database*. Muskingum College Center for Advancement of Learning. Available online at http://www.muskingum.edu/~cal/database/organization.html.

Kresse, E. C. (1984). Using reading as a thinking process to solve math story problems. *Journal of Reading, 27,* 598–601.

Krueger, W. C. F. (1929). The effect of overlearning on retention. *Journal of Experimental Psychology, 12,* 71–78.

Laflamme, J. G. (1997). The effect of the multiple exposure vocabulary method and the target reading writing strategy on test scores. *Journal of Adolescent & Adult Literacy, 40,* 372–381.

Lake, J. H. (1973). The influence of wait time on the verbal dimensions of student inquiry behavior. *Dissertations Abstracts*

International, 34, 6476A (University Microfilms No. 74–08866).

Landsberger, J. (2001). *Study guides and strategies.* University of St. Thomas' ISS-Learning Center. Available online at http://www.iss.stthomas.edu/studyguides.

Langer, J., & Applebee, A. N. (1987). *How writing shapes thinking.* Urbana, IL: National Council of Teachers of English.

Langer, J. A. (1981). From theory to practice: A prereading plan. *Journal of Reading, 25,* 152–156.

Langer, J. A. (1990). Understanding literature. *Language Arts, 67,* 812–816.

Langer, J. A. (1995). *Envisioning literature: Literary understanding and literature instruction.* New York: Teachers College Press.

Langer, J. A. (1999). *Beating the odds: Teaching middle and high school students to read and write well.* Albany, NY: National Research Center on English Learning and Achievement. (ERIC Document Reproduction Service No. ED-435-993.)

Langer, J. A., Applebee, A. N., Mullis, I. V. S., & Foertsch, M. A. (1990). *Learning to read in our nation's schools: Instruction and achievement in 1988 at grades 4, 8, and 12.* Princeton, NJ: Educational Testing Service.

Langer, J. N. (1984). Where problems start: The effects of available information on responses to school writing tasks. In A. N. Applebee (Ed.), *Contexts for learning to write: Studies of secondary school instruction* (pp. 135–148). Norwood, NJ: Ablex.

Langer, J. N. (1986). *Children reading and writing: Structures and strategies.* Norwood, NJ: Ablex.

Lapp, D., Flood, J., & Hoffman, R. P. (1996). Using concept mapping as an effective strategy in content area instruction. In D. Lapp, J. Flood, & N. Farnan (Eds.), *Content area reading and learning instructional strategies* (2nd ed.) (pp. 291–305). Boston: Allyn & Bacon.

LaPray, M., & Ross, R. (1969), The graded word list: Quick gauge of reading ability. *Journal of Reading, 12,* 305–307.

Larson, C. O., & Dansereau, D. F. (1986). Cooperative learning in dyads. *Journal of Reading, 29,* 516–520.

Leavell, A. G., Maher, S. B., White, A., & Oxford, R. (2000). *Content literacy in the high school: Students' and teachers' perceptions of the benefits and obstacles to systematic strategy usage in social studies and science.* Paper presented at the National Reading Conference, Scottsdale, AZ.

Lemke, M., Calsyn, C., Lippman, L., Jocelyn, L., Kastberg, D., Liu, Y., Roey, S., Williams, T., Kruger, T., &, Bairu, G. (2001). *Highlights From the 2000 Program for International Student Assessment (PISA).* Washington, DC: U.S. Department of Education, National Center for Educational Statistics. Available online at http://nces.ed.gov/pubs2002/2002116.pdf.

Leslie, C. W., & Roth, C. (1998). *Nature journal: Discover a whole new way of seeing the world around you.* Pownal, VT: Storey Books.

Leslie, L., & Caldwell, J. (2001). *Qualitative reading inventory-3.* New York: Addison Wesley Longman.

Lester, J. H. & Cheek, E. H. (1997–1998). The "real" experts address textbook issues. *Journal of Adolescent & Adult Literacy, 41,* 282–291.

Leu, D. (2001). *Developing new literacies: Using the Internet in content area instruction.* Available online at http://web.syr.edu/~djleu/content.html.

Leu, D. J., & Leu, D. D. (2000). *Teaching with the Internet: Lessons from the classroom* (3rd ed.). Norwood, MA: Christopher-Gordon.

Levin, J. R., Johnson, D. D., Pittelman, S. D., Hayes, B. L., Levin, K. M., Shriberg, L. K., & Toms-Bronowski, S. (1984). A comparison of semantic and mnemonic-based vocabulary-learning strategies. *Reading Psychology, 5*(2), 1–15.

Linden, M., & Wittrock, M. C. (1981). The teaching of reading comprehension according to the model of generative learning. *Reading Research Quarterly, 17,* 44–57.

Lindquist, T. (1995). Why and how I use historical fiction. *Instructor, 105*(3), 46–50, 52, 80.

Madden, N. (2000, February) Meeting the expository challenge with SFA. *Success Story,* p. 6. Available online at http://www.successforall.net/current/successstories_2_00.pdf.

Many, J., Fyfe, R., Lewis, G., & Mitchell, E. (1996). Traversing the topical landscape: Exploring students' self-directed reading-writing research processes. *Reading Research Quarterly, 31,* 122–135.

Manzo, A. V. (1969). The ReQuest procedure. *Journal of Reading, 13,* 123–126.

Manzo, A. V., & Manzo, U. C. (1993). *Literacy disorders: Holistic diagnosis and remediation.* Fort Worth, TX: Harcourt Brace Jovanovich.

Maria, K. (1990). *Reading comprehension instruction: Issues and strategies.* Parkton, MD: York Press.

Marian, R., Sexton, C., & Gerlovich, J. (2001). *Teaching science for all children* (3rd ed.). Boston: Allyn & Bacon.

Marshall, J. D. (1984a). Process and product: Case studies of writing in two content areas. In A. N. Applebee (Ed.), *Contexts for learning to write: Studies of secondary school instruction* (pp. 149–168). Norwood, NJ: Ablex.

Marshall, J. D. (1984b). Schooling and the composing process. In A. N. Applebee (Ed*.),* *Contexts for learning to write: Studies of secondary school instruction.* Norwood, NJ: Ablex.

Marzano, R. J., Gaddy, B. B., & Dean, C. (2000). *What works in classroom instruction.* Aurora, CO: Mid-continent Research for Education and Learning.

Mastropieri, M. A., & Scruggs, T. E. (1989). Reconstructive elaborations: Strategies for adapting content area information. *Academic Therapy, 24,* 391–406.

Mastropieri, M. A., & Scruggs, T. E. (1991). *Teaching students ways to remember: Strategies for learning mnemonically.* Cambridge, MA: Brookline.

McConnell, S. (1992–1993). Talking drawings: A strategy for assisting learners. *Journal of Reading, 36,* 260–269.

McKenna, M. C., & Robinson, R. D. (1990). Content literacy: A definition and implications. *Journal of Reading, 34,* 184–186.

McKenna, M. C., & Robinson, R. D. (1995). *Teaching through text: A content literacy approach to content area reading* (2nd ed.). New York: Longman.

McKeown, M. G., Beck, I. L., & Sandora, C. A. (1996). Questioning the author: An approach to developing meaningful classroom discourse. In M. F. Graves, P. Van den Broek, & B. M. Taylor, (Eds.), *The first R: Every child's right to read* (pp. 97–119). New York: Teachers College Press.

McKissack, P., & McKissack, F. (2001a). A biographical sketch of Frederick Douglass. *Biography writing with Patricia and Fredrick McKissack*. Available online at http://teacher. scholastic.com/writewit/biograph/biography_sketch.htm.

McKissack, P., & McKissack, F. (2001b). Brainstorming. *Biography writing with Patricia and Fredrick McKissack*. Available online at http://teacher.scholastic.com/writewit/ biograph/biography_brainstorming.htm.

McNamara, T. P., Miller, D. L., & Bransford, J. D. (1991). Mental models and reading comprehension. In R. Barr, M. L. Kamil, P. Mosenthal, & P. D. Pearson (Eds.), *Handbook of reading research* (Vol. II, pp. 490–511). New York: Longman.

McREL. (2001). *Standards*. Available online at http://www. mcrel.org/standards/index.asp.

McTighe, J., Lyman, F. T., Jr. (1988). Cueing thinking in the classroom: The promise of theory-embedded tools. *Educational Leadership, 45*(7), 18–24.

Meltzer, L. J., Roditi, B. N., Haynes, D. P., & Biddle, K. (1996). *Strategies for success: Classroom teaching techniques for students with learning problems*. Austin, TX: ProEd.

Meyer, B. J. F., & Rice, G. E. (1984). The structure of text. In P. D. Pearson, R. Barr, M. L. Kamil, & P. Mosenthal (Eds.), *Handbook of reading research* (pp. 319–351). New York: Longman.

Michigan Department of Education. (1998). *Health education standards and benchmarks*. Available online at http://www. state.mi.us/mde/off/health/healthedsb.pdf.

Mitman, A., Mergendoller, J., Packer, M., & Marchman, V. (1984). *Scientific literacy in seventh grade life science*. San Francisco: Far West Laboratory.

Moje, E. (1996). "I teach students, not subjects": Teacher-student relationships as contexts for secondary literacy. *Reading Research Quarterly, 31*, 172–195.

Moore, D. W., & Moore, S. A. (1986). Possible sentences. In E. K. Dishner, T. W. Bean, J. E. Readence, & D. W. Moore (Eds.), *Reading in the content areas: Improving classroom instruction* (2nd ed.) (pp. 174–179). Dubuque, IA: Kendall/Hunt.

Moore, D. W., Moore, S. A., Cunningham, P. M., & Cunningham, J. W. (1992). *Developing readers and writers in the content areas* (2nd ed.). New York: Longman.

Moore, D. W., Readence, J. E., & Rickelman, R. J. (1989). *Prereading activities for content area reading and learning* (2nd ed.). Newark, DE: International Reading Association.

Mosenthal, J. H. (1990). Developing low-performing, fourth-grade, inner-city students' ability to comprehend narrative. In J. Zutell & S. McCormick (Eds.), *Literacy theory and research: Analyses from multiple paradigms* (Thirty-ninth Yearbook of the National Reading Conference) (pp. 275–286). Chicago: National Reading Conference.

Mosenthal, P., & Kirsch, I. S. (1998). A new measure for assessing document complexity: The PMOSE/IKIRSCH document readability formula. *Journal of Adolescent & Adult Literacy, 41*, 638–657.

Moyer, R. S. (1973). Comparing objects in memory: Evidence suggesting an internal psychophysics. *Perception and Psychophysics, 13*, 180–184.

Muskingum College. (2001). Center for Advancement of Learning. Available online at http://www.muskingum.edu/ ~cal/database/organization.html.

Muth, K. D. (1987). Teachers' connection questions: Prompting students to organize text ideas. *Journal of Reading, 31*, 254–259.

Nagy, W. E. (1988). *Teaching vocabulary to improve reading comprehension*. Newark, DE: International Reading Association.

Nagy, W. E., & Anderson, R. C. (1984). How many words are there in printed English? *Reading Research Quarterly, 19*, 304–330.

Nagy, W. E., & Herman, P. A. (1987). Breadth and depth of vocabulary knowledge: Implications for acquisition and instruction. In M. G. McKeown & M. E. Curtis (Eds.), *The nature of vocabulary acquisition* (pp. 19–35). Hillsdale, NJ: Lawrence Erlbaum.

National Academy of Sciences. (1996). *Science for all children*. Washington, DC: National Academy Press.

National Center for Educational Statistics. (2002). *The nation's report card: 2001 U.S. history results*. Available online at http://nces.ed.gov/nationsreportcard.

National Center on Education and the Economy and The University of Pittsburgh (1997). *Performance standards: Vol. 1. Elementary school*. Washington, DC: New Standards.

National Council for Geographic Education (2002). *The eighteen national geography standards*. Available online at http://www.ncge.org/publications/tutorial/standards/

National Council for the Social Studies (NCSS). (1994). *Expectations of excellence: Curriculum standards for social studies*. Available online at http://www.ncss.org/standards/stitle.html.

National Council of Teachers of Mathematics. (1989). *Curriculum and evaluation standards for school mathematics*. Reston, VA: Author.

National Council of Teachers of Mathematics. (2000). *Principles and standards for school mathematics*. Reston, VA: Author. Available online at http://standards.nctm.org/document/ index.htm.

National Institute of Child Health and Human Development (2000). *Report of the National Reading Panel: Teaching children to read: An evidence-based assessment of the scientific research literature on reading and its implications for reading instruction: Reports of the subgroups* (NIH Publication No. 00–4754). Washington, DC: U.S. Government Printing Office.

National Research Council. (1996). *National science education standards*. Washington, DC: National Academy Press.

National Science Board. (2001). *Science and engineering indicators 2001*. Arlington, VA: National Science Foundation.

Nelson, G. D. (1999). Science literacy for all in the 21st century. *Educational Leadership, 57*(2) 14–17.

NCTE (2001, May) On the Net: Teaching reading at the high school level. *The Council Chronicle, 10*(4), pp. 10–11.

Nelson-Herber, J. (1986). Expanding and refining vocabulary in content areas. *Journal of Reading, 29*, 626–633.

Newmann, F. M., & Wehlege, G. G. (2000). *Successful school restructuring*. Madison, WI: Center on Organization and Restructuring of Schools.

Nichols, W. D, Jones, J., Wood, K., & Hancock, D. (2000, November). *Exploring the relationship between teacher reported instructional design and students' perceptions of how they learned: Why are students task oriented learners?* Paper presented at the National Reading Conference, Scottsdale, AZ.

Nist, S, L., Hogrebe, M. C., & Simpson, M. L. (1985). The relationship between the use of study strategies and test performance. *Journal of Reading Behavior, 7*, 15–28.

Nist, S. L., & Simpson, M. L. (1989). PLAE, a validated study strategy. *Journal of Reading, 33*, 182–186.

Noble, C. E. (1952). The role of stimulus meaning in serial verbal learning. *Journal of Experimental Psychology, 43*, 437–446.

Novak, J. (1991). Clarifying with concept maps. *The Science Teacher, 58*(7), 44–49.

Noyce, R., & Christie, J. F. (1989). *Integrating reading and writing instruction in grades K–8.* Boston: Allyn & Bacon.

Nuthall, G. (1996, December). *What role does ability play in classroom learning?* Paper presented at the meeting of the New Zealand Association for Research in Education. Nelson, New Zealand (ERIC Document Reproduction Service No. ED 414 042).

Nuthall, G. (1999). The way students learn: Acquiring knowledge from an integrated science and social studies unit. *The Elementary School Journal, 99*, 303–335.

Oakes, J. (1992). Can tracking research inform practice? Technical, normative, and political considerations. *Educational Researcher, 21*, 12–21.

Ogle, D. M. (1989). The know, want to know, learn strategy. In K. D. Muth (Ed.), *Children's comprehension of text* (pp. 205–223). Newark, DE: International Reading Association.

Ogle, D. M. (1996). Study techniques that ensure content area reading success. In D. Lapp, J. Flood, & N. Farnan (Eds.), *Content area reading and learning instructional strategies* (pp. 277–290).

Ollmann, H. E. (1996). Creating higher level thinking with reader response. *Journal of Adolescent & Adult Literacy, 39*, 576–581.

O'Mara, D A. (1981). The process of reading mathematics. *Journal of Reading, 25*, 22–30.

Paivio, A. (1971). *Imagery and verbal process.* New York: Holt.

Palincsar, A. S., & Brown, A. L. (1986). Interactive teaching to promote independent learning from text. *The Reading Teacher, 39*, 771–777.

Palincsar, A. S., Winn, J., David, Y., Snyder, B., & Stevens, D. (1993). Approaches to strategic reading instruction reflecting different assumptions regarding teaching and learning. In L. J. Meltzer (Ed.), *Strategy assessment and instruction for students with learning disabilities: From theory to practice* (pp. 247–292). Austin, TX: Pro-Ed.

Palmer, R. G., & Stewart, R. A. (1997). Nonfiction trade books in content area instruction: Realities and potential. *Journal of Adolescent & Adult Literacy, 40*, 630–641.

Paris, S. G., & Myers, M. (1981). Comprehension strategies of good and poor readers. *Journal of Reading Behavior, 13*, 5–22.

Parker, D. (2002, May). *Accelerated literacy for English language learners (ELLS): A field-tested, research-based model of training and teaching.* Paper presented at the annual meeting of the International Reading Association, San Francisco.

Parker, W. C. (2001). *Social studies in elementary education* (11th ed.). Upper Saddle River, NJ: Merrill Prentice Hall.

Parker, W. C., & Jarolimek, J. (Eds.). (2001). *A sampler of curriculum standards for social studies: Expectations of excellence.* Upper Saddle River, NJ: Merrill Prentice Hall.

Patton, L. (1993). *In the woods: The impact of prereading activities.* In L. Patterson, C. M. Santa, K. G. Short, & K. Smith (Eds.), *Teachers are researchers: Reflection and action* (pp. 130–136). Newark, DE: International Reading Association.

Pauk, W. (1989). *How to study in college* (4th ed.). Boston: Houghton Mifflin.

Pearson, J. W., & Santa, C. M. (1995). Students as researchers of their own learning. *Journal of Adolescent & Adult Literacy, 38*, 462–469.

Pearson, P. D. (1986, November). *What research has to say about comprehension.* Paper presented at the quarterly meeting of the Connecticut Association for Reading Research, New Britain, CT.

Pearson, P. D., & Camperell, K. (1994). Comprehension of text structures. In R. B. Ruddell, M. R. Ruddell, & H. Singer (Eds.), *Theoretical models and processes of reading* (4th ed.) (pp. 448–568). Newark, DE: International Reading Association.

Penner, D. E. (2000). Explaining systems: Investigating middle school students' understanding of emergent phenomena. *Journal of Research in Science Teaching, 37*, 784–806.

Perfetti, C. A., Britt, M. A., & Georgi, M. C. (1995). *Text-based learning and reasoning.* Hillsdale, NJ: Erlbaum.

Perkins, P. (2001). *It's my American history: Compendium of practices: Models of contextual teaching and learning in K–12 classrooms and preservice teacher preparation programs.* Washington State Consortium for Contextual Teaching and Learning Compendia. Available online at http://depts.washington.edu/wctl/itsmyamhist.htm.

Peters, C. (1979). The effect of systematic restructuring of material upon the comprehension process. *Reading Research Quarterly, 11*, 87–110.

Phillips, L. M., Norris, S. P., & Korpan, C. A. (2000). *Texture and structure of media reports of science: University students' interpretations and their need to understand the metadiscourse of science.* Paper presented at the National Reading Conference, Scottsdale, AZ.

Plake, B. S., Impara, J. C., & Spies, R. A. (Eds.), (2003). *The fifteenth mental measurements yearbook.* Lincoln, NE: University of Nebraska Press.

Popham, W. J. (2000). *Modern educational measurement: Practical guidelines for educational leaders.* Boston: Allyn & Bacon.

Pressley, M., & Afflerbach, P. (1995). *Verbal protocols of reading: The nature of constructively responsive reading.* Hillsdale, NJ: Erlbaum.

Pressley, M., Ross, K. A., Levin, J. R., & Ghatala, E. S. (1984). The role of strategy utility knowledge in children's strategy decision making. *Journal of Experimental Child Psychology, 38*, 491–504.

Pressley, M., Wharton-McDonald, R. Mistretta-Hampston, J., & Echevarria, M. (1998). Literacy instruction in 10 fourth- and fifth-grade classrooms in upstate New York. *Scientific Studies of Reading, 2*, 159–194.

Probst, R. (1992). Five kinds of literary knowing. In J. A. Langer (Ed.), *Literature instruction: A focus on student response* (pp. 54–77). Urbana, IL: National Council of Teachers of English.

Prochaska, J. O., Norcross, J. C., & DiClemente, D. C. (1994). *Changing for the good.* New York: Avon.

Quiocho, A. (1997). The quest to comprehend expository text: Applied classroom research. *Journal of Adolescent & Adult Literacy, 40,* 450–455.

Rakes, G. C., Rakes, T. A., & Smith, L. J. (1995). Using visuals to enhance secondary students' reading comprehension of expository texts. *Journal of Adolescent & Adult Literacy, 39,* 46–54.

Raphael, T. E. (1984). Teaching learners about sources of information for answering questions. *The Reading Teacher, 28,* 303–311.

Raphael, T. E. (1986). Teaching question/answer relationships, revisited. *The Reading Teacher, 39,* 516–522.

Raphael, T. E., & Englert, C. S. (1990). Writing and reading: Partners in constructing meaning. *The Reading Teacher, 43,* 388–400.

Ravitch, D. (1993). Launching a revolution in standards and assessments. *Phi Delta Kappan, 74,* 767–772.

Readence, J. E., Moore, D. W., Rickelman, R. J. (2000). *Prereading activities for content area reading and learning* (3rd ed.). Newark, DE: International Reading Association.

Reese, C. M., Miller, K. E., Mazzeo, J., & Dossey, J. A. (1997). NAEP 1996 mathematics report card for the nation and the states: Findings from the National Assessment of Educational Progress. Washington, DC: U.S. Department of Education.

Reeuwijk, M. van (2001), *From informal to formal, progressive formalization: An example on "solving systems of equations."* Freudenthal Institute. Available online at http://www.fi.ruu.nl/publicaties/literatuur/4465.pdf.

Reeves, D. (2000). *The 90/90/90 schools: A case study.* Available online at http://www.makingstandardswork.com/Downloads/AinA%20Ch19.pdf.

Reid, L. (2001). On the Net: Teaching reading at the high school level. *The Council Chronicle, 10*(4), 10–11.

Richardson, J. S., & Morgan, R. F. (1997). *Reading to learn in the content areas* (3rd ed.). Belmont, CA: Wadsworth.

Richgels, D. J., & Hansen, R. (1984). Gloss: Helping students apply both skills and strategies in reading content texts. *Journal of Reading, 27,* 312–317.

Rinehart, S. D., Stahl, S. A., & Erickson, L. G. (1986). Some effects of summarization training on reading and studying. *Reading Research Quarterly, 21,* 422–438.

Robinson, D. H. (1998). Graphic organizers as aids to text learning. *Reading Research and Instruction, 37,* 85–105.

Robinson, F. P. (1970). *Effective study* (4th ed.). New York: Harper & Row.

Roe, M. F., & Stallman, A. C. (1995). *A comparative study of dialogue and response journals* (Tech. Report No. 612). Champaign: University of Illinois, Center for the Study of Reading.

Roehler, L. (1996). The content area teacher's instructional role: A mediational view. In D. Lapp, J. Flood, & N. Farnan (Eds.), *Content area reading and learning instructional strategies* (2nd ed.) (pp. 141–152). Boston: Allyn & Bacon.

Rosenblatt, L. (1978). *The reader, the text, the poem.* Carbondale: Southern Illinois University Press.

Rosenblatt, L. (1991). Literature—S. O. S.! *Language Arts, 68,* 444–448.

Rosenblatt, L. M. (1982). The literary transaction: Evocation and response. *Theory into Practice, 21,* 268–277.

Rosenblatt, L. M. (1990). Retrospect. In E. S. Farrell & J. R. Squire (Eds.), *Transactions with literature: A fifty-year perspective* (pp. 97–107). Urbana, IL: National Council of Teachers of English.

Rosenblatt, L. M. (1994). The traditional theory of reading and writing. In R. B. Ruddell, M. R. Ruddell, & H. Singer (Eds.), *Theoretical models and processes of reading* (4th ed.) (pp. 1057–1092). Newark, DE: International Reading Association.

Rosenshine, B., & Meister, C. (1994). Reciprocal teaching: A review of the research. *Review of Educational Research, 64,* 479–530.

Rosenshine, B., Meister, C., & Chapman, S. (1996). Teaching students to generate questions: A review of the intervention studies. *Review of Educational Research, 66,* 181–221.

Ross, J., & Lawrence, K. A. (1968). Some observations on memory artifice. *Psychonomic Science, 13,* 107–108.

Rothenberg, S. S., & Watts, S. M. (1997). Students with learning difficulties meet Shakespeare: Using a scaffolded reading experience. *Journal of Adolescent & Adult Literacy, 40,* 532–539.

Rowand, C. (2000). U.S. Department of Education, National Center for Education Statistics (2000). *Teacher use of computers and the Internet in public schools.* Available online at http://nces.ed.gov/pubs2000/quarterly/summer/3elem/q3-2.html.

Rowe, M. B. (1969). Science, silence, and sanctions. *Science for Children, 6*(6), 11–13.

Rubenstein, M. C., & Wodatch, J. K. (2000). *Stepping up to the challenge: Case studies of educational improvement and Title 1 in secondary schools.* Washington, DC: U. S. Department of Education.

Rubenstein, R. N. (2000). Word origins: Building communication connections. *Mathematics in the Middle School, 5,* 493–498.

Ruddell, M. R. (1992). Integrated content and long-term vocabulary learning with the vocabulary self-collection strategy. In E. K. Dishner, T. W. Bean, J. E. Readence, & D. W. Moore (Eds.), *Reading in the content areas: Improving classroom instruction* (3rd ed.) (pp. 190–196). Dubuque, IA: Kendall/Hunt.

Ruddell, R. B. (1995). Those influential literacy teachers: Meaning negotiators and motivation builders. *The Reading Teacher, 48,* 454–463.

Rumelhart, D. (1984). Understanding understanding. In J. Flood (Ed.), *Understanding reading comprehension* (pp. 1–20). Newark, DE: International Reading Association.

Sadowski, M., & Paivio, A. (1994). A dual coding view of imagery and verbal processes in reading comprehension. In R. B. Ruddell, M. R. Ruddell, & H. Singer (Eds.), *Theoretical models and processes of reading* (4th ed.) (pp. 582–601). Newark, DE: International Reading Association.

Salomon, G., Globerson, T., & Guterman, E. (1989). The computer as a zone of proximal development: Internalizing reading-related metacognitions from a reading partner. *Journal of Educational Psychology, 81*, 620–627.

Santa, C. (1994, October). *Teaching reading in the content areas.* Paper presented at the International Reading Association's Southwest Regional Conference, Little Rock, AR.

Santa, C., Havens, L., & Maycumber, E. M. (1996). *Creating independence through student-owned strategies* (2nd ed.). Dubuque, IA: Kendall/Hunt.

Santa, C. M., Abrams, J., & Santa, J. (1979). Effects of notetaking and studying on the retention of prose. *Journal of Reading Behavior, 11*, 247–260.

Schallert, D. L., & Tierney, R. J. (1980). *Learning from expository text: The interaction of text structures with reader characteristics.* Washington, DC: U.S. Department of Education. National Institute of Education. (ERIC Document Reproduction Service No. ED221833.)

Schifini, A. (1994). Language, literacy, and content instruction. In K. Spangenberg-Urbschat & R. Pritchard (Eds.), *Kids come in all languages: Reading instruction for all ESL students* (pp. 36–62). Newark, DE: International Reading Association.

Schifini, A. (1996). Discussion in multilingual, multicultural classrooms. In L. Gambrell & J. F. Almasi (Eds.), *Lively discussions! Fostering engaged reading.* Newark, DE: International Reading Association.

Schifini, A. (1999). *Successful strategies for your older struggling readers.* Torrance, CA: Staff Development Resources.

Schnorr, J. A., & Atkinson, R. C. (1969). Repetition versus imagery instructions in the short- and long-term retention of paired associates. *Psychonomic Science, 15*, 183–184.

Schoenbach, R., Greenleaf, C., Cziko, C., & Hurwitz, L. (1999). *Reading for understanding: A guide to improving reading in middle and high school classrooms.* San Francisco: Jossey-Bass.

Schwartz, R. M. (1988). Learning to learn vocabulary in content area textbooks. *Journal of Reading, 32*, 108–118.

Schwartzman, S. (1994). *Words of mathematics: An etymological dictionary of mathematical terms used in English.* Washington, DC: Mathematical Association of America.

Scott, T. (1998, May). *Using content area text to teach decoding and comprehension strategies.* Paper presented at the annual meeting of the International Reading Association, Orlando, FL.

Scruggs, T. E., & Mastropieri, M. A. (1990). The case for mnemonic instruction: From laboratory investigations to classroom applications. *Journal of Special Education, 24*, 7–32.

Scruggs, T. E., & Mastropieri, M. A. (1992). *Teaching test-taking skills: Helping students show what they know.* Cambridge, MA: Brookline.

Scruggs, T. E., Bennion, K., & Lifson, S. (1985a). An analysis of children's strategy use on reading achievement tests. *Elementary School Journal, 85*, 479–484.

Scruggs, T. E., Bennion, K., & Lifson, S. (1985b). Learning disabled students' spontaneous use of test-taking skills on reading achievement tests. *Learning Disability Quarterly, 8*, 205–210.

Shearer, B. (1999). *The vocabulary self-collection strategy (VSS) in a middle school.* Paper presented at the 49th Annual Meeting of the National Reading Conference, Orlando, FL.

Shearer, B. A., Ruddell, M. R., & Vogt, M. E. (2001). Successful middle school reading intervention: Negotiated strategies and individual choice. In J. V. Hoffman, D. L. Schallert, C. M. Fairbanks, J. Worthy, & B. G. Maloch (Eds.), *Fiftieth yearbook of the National Reading Conference, 50* (pp. 558–571). Chicago: National Reading Conference.

Silver, E. A., Kilpatrick, J., & Schlesinger, B. (1990). *Thinking through mathematics: Fostering inquiry and communication in mathematics classrooms: The thinking series.* New York: College Entrance Examination Board.

Simonsen, S. (1996). Identifying and teaching text structures in content area classrooms. In D. Lapp, J. Flood, & N. Farnan (Eds.), *Content area reading and learning instructional strategies* (2nd ed.) (pp. 59–75). Boston: Allyn & Bacon.

Simpson, M. L. (1986). PORPE: A writing strategy for studying and learning in the content areas. *Journal of Reading, 29*, 407–414.

Sims, R. S. (Ed.). (1994). *Kaleidoscope: A multicultural booklist for grades K–8.* Urbana, IL: National Council of Teachers of English.

Singer, H. (1975). The SEER technique: A non-computational procedure for quickly estimating readability levels. *Journal of Reading Behavior, 3*, 255–267.

Singer, H., & Donlan, D. (1989). *Reading and learning from text* (2nd ed.). Hillsdale, NJ: Lawrence Erlbaum.

Slater, W. H., & Graves, M. F. (1989). Research on expository text: Implications for teachers. In K. D. Muth (Ed.), *Children's comprehension of text* (pp. 140–166). Newark, DE: International Reading Association.

Sippola, A. E. (1995). K-w-l-s. *The Reading Teacher, 48*, 542–543.

Slavin, R. E. (1987). Cooperative learning and the cooperative school. *Educational Leadership, 45*(3), 7–13.

Slavin, R. E. (1996). A cooperative learning approach to content area reading. In D. Lapp, J. Flood, & N. Farnan (Eds.), *Content area reading and learning instructional strategies* (2nd ed.) (pp. 369–382). Boston: Allyn & Bacon.

Slavin, R. E. (1997–1998). Can education reduce societal inequity? *Educational Leadership, 55*(4), 6–10.

Smith, P. L., & Tompkins, G. E. (1988). Structured notetaking: A new strategy for content area readers. *Journal of Reading, 32*, 46–53.

Smith, W. L. (1978). Cloze procedure as applied to reading. In O. K. Buros (Ed.), *Eighth mental measurements yearbook, Vol. II* (pp. 1176–1178). Highland Park, NJ: Gryphon Pres.

Snow, C. E., Burns, M. S., & Griffin, P. (1998). *Preventing reading difficulties in young children.* Washington, DC: National Academy Press.

Spandel, V. (2001). *Creating writers through 6–trait writing assessment and instruction.* New York: Longman.

Spillane, J. P., & Callahan, K. A. (2000). Implementing state standards for science education: What district policy makers make of the hoopla. *Journal of Research in Science Teaching, 37*, 401–425.

Sprague, C. (2000). An introduction to Internet resources for K–12 educators. Part II: Question answering, electronic discussion groups, newsgroups, Update 2000. *ERIC Digest.* Syracuse, NY: ERIC Clearinghouse on Information and Technology. Available online at http://ericit.org.

Stahl, S. A. (1986). Three principles of effective vocabulary instruction. *Journal of Reading, 29*, 662–668.

Stahl, S. A., Hynd, C. R., Britton, B. K., McNish, M. M., & Bosquet, D. (1996). What happens when students read multiple source documents in history? *Reading Research Quarterly, 31*, 430–456.

Stahl, S. A., & Kapinus, B. A. (1991). Possible sentences: Predicting word meanings to teach content area vocabulary. *The Reading Teacher, 45*, 36–43.

Stauffer, R. G. (1969). *Directing reading maturity as a cognitive process.* New York: Harper & Row.

Stauffer, R. G. (1970, January). *Reading-thinking skills.* Paper presented at the annual reading conference at Temple University, Philadelphia.

Steinberg, J. (1999, Sept. 9). Free college notes on the Web: Aid to learning, or laziness. *The New York Times*, p. A1.

Sternberg, R. J. (1987). Most vocabulary is learned from context. In M. G. McKeown & M. E. Curtis (Eds.), *The nature of vocabulary acquisition* (pp. 89–105). Hillsdale, NJ: Lawrence Erlbaum.

Sternberg, R. J., & Powell, J. S. (1983). Comprehending verbal comprehension. *American Psychologist, 38*, 878–893.

Stewart, R. A., & Cross, T. L. (1993). A field test of five forms of marginal gloss study guide: An ecological study. *Reading Psychology, 14*, 113–139.

Stotsky, S. (1984). Commentary: A proposal for improving high school students' ability to read and write expository prose. *Journal of Reading, 28*, 4–7.

Strickland, D. S. (1998). Educating African-American learners at risk: Finding a better way. In C. Weaver (Ed.), *Practicing what we know: Informed reading instruction* (pp. 394–408). Urbana, IL: National Council of Teachers of English.

Sturtevant, E. G., Ivey, G., & Anders, P. (2000). *What educators say about the needs of adolescent literacy learners.* Paper presented at the National Reading Conference, Scottsdale, AZ.

Sunal, C. S., & Haas, R. (1993). *Social studies for the elementary / middle school student.* Fort Worth, TX: Harcourt Brace Jovanovich.

Sutton, C. (1989). Helping the nonnative English speaker with reading. *The Reading Teacher, 42*, 684–688.

Taba, H. (1965). The teaching of thinking. *Elementary English, 42*, 534–542.

Tanner, M. L., & Casados, L. (1998). Promoting and studying discussions in math classes. *Journal of Adolescent & Adult Literacy, 41*, 342–350.

Thomas, E. L., & Robinson, H. A. (1972). *Improving reading in every class: A sourcebook for teachers.* Boston: Allyn & Bacon.

Thonis, E. (1983). *The English-Spanish connection.* Compton, CA: Santillara.

Tierney, R. J., & Readence, J. E. (2000). *Reading strategies and practices: A compendium* (5th ed.). Boston: Allyn & Bacon.

Tierney, R. J., Carter, M. A., & Desai, L. E. (1991). *Portfolio assessment in the reading-writing classroom.* Norwood, MA: Christopher-Gordon.

Tonjes, M. J. (1991). *Secondary reading, writing, and learning.* Boston: Allyn & Bacon.

Touchstone Applied Science Associates (1994). *DRP handbook.* Brewster, NY: Author.

Tovani, C. (2000). *I read it but I don't get it: Comprehension strategies for adolescent readers.* Portland, ME: Stenhouse.

Trabasso, T., & Magliano, J. P. (1996). How do children understand what they read and what can we do to help them? In M. F. Graves, P. Van den Broek, & B. M. Taylor, (Eds.), *The first R: Every child's right to read* (pp. 160–188). New York: Teachers College Press & International Reading Association.

Tulving, E. (1962). Subjective organization in free recall of "unrelated" words. *Psychological Review, 69*, 344–354.

U.S. Bureau of the Census. (2001). *Nation's household income stable in 2000, poverty rate virtually equals record low, Census Bureau reports.* Press release cb98–175. Available online at http://www.census.gov/Press-Release/www/2001/cb01-158.html.

U.S. Department of Education. (2001). *No child left behind: Moving limited English proficient students to English fluency* (Title III). Available online at http://www.ed.gov/offices/DESE/esca/nclb/part7.html.

U.S. Department of Education. (2002). *The No Child Left Behind Act of 2001.* Available online at http://www.ed.gov/legislation/ESEA02/.

U.S. Department of Education (Office of Special Education and Rehabilitative Services). (2000). *Twenty-second annual report to Congress on the implementation of the Individuals with Disabilities Education Act.* Washington, DC: Government Printing Office.

Unsworth, L. (1999). Developing critical understanding of the specialized language of school science and history texts: A functional grammatical perspective. *Journal of Adolescent & Adult Literacy, 42*, 508–521.

Vacca, R. T., & Vacca, J. L. (1986). *Content area reading* (2nd ed.). Boston: Little, Brown.

Vacca, R. T., & Vacca, J. L. (2002). *Content area reading: Literacy and learning across the curriculum* (7th ed.). Boston: Allyn & Bacon.

Valencia, S. W., & Place, N. A. (1994). Literacy portfolios for teaching, learning, and accountability: The Bellevue literacy assessment project. In S. W. Valencia, E. H. Hiebert, & P. P. Afflerbach (Eds.), *Authentic reading assessment: Practices and possibilities* (pp. 134–156). Newark, DE: International Reading Association.

van den Broek, P., & Kremer, K. E. (2000). The mind in action: What it means to comprehend during reading. In B. Taylor, M. F. Graves, & P. van den Broek (Eds.), *Reading for meaning: Fostering comprehension in the middle grades* (pp. 1–31). New York: Teachers College Press.

Van der Meij, H., & Dillon, J. T. (1994). Adaptive student questioning and students' verbal ability. *Journal of Experimental Education, 62*, 277–290.

VanSledright, B. A., & Frankes, L. (2000). Concept- and strategic-knowledge development in historical study: A comparative exploration in two fourth-grade classrooms. *Cognition and Instruction, 18*, 239–283.

Vardell, S. (1991). A "new picture of the world": The NCTE Orbis Pictus award for outstanding nonfiction for children. *Language Arts, 68*, 265–269.

Vaughn, S., Klinger, J., & Schumm, J. (N.D.). *Collaborative strategy instruction: A manual to assist with staff development.* Miami: University of Miami.

Vogt, M. E. (2001, May). *Strategic approaches to engage struggling readers.* Paper presented at the annual conference of the International Reading Association, New Orleans.

Walker, M. L. (1995). Help for the "fourth-grade slump": SRQ2R plus instruction in text structure or main idea. *Reading Horizons, 36,* 38–58.

Walpole, S. (1998–1999). Changing texts, changing thinking: Comprehension demands of new science textbooks. *The Reading Teacher, 52,* 358–369.

Wark, D. M. & Flippo, R. F. (1991). Preparing for and taking tests. In R. F. Flippo & D. C. Caverly (Eds.), *Teaching reading and study strategies at the college level* (pp. 294–338). Newark, DE: International Reading Association.

Warner, L. A, Bierer, L. K., Lawson, S. A., Cohen, T. L. (1991). *Life science: The challenge of discovery.* Lexington, MA: Heath.

Watson, B., & Konicke, R. (1990). Teaching for conceptual change: Confronting children's experience. *Phi Delta Kappan, 72,* 683–685.

Weinstein, C., & Mayer, R. (1986). The teaching of learning strategies. In M. C. Wittrock (Ed.), *Handbook of research on teaching* (pp. 315–327). New York: Macmillan.

Weir, C. (1998). Using embedded questions to jump-start metacognition in middle school remedial readers. *Journal of Adolescent & Adult Literacy, 41,* 458–467.

Weisberg, R., & Balajthy, E. (1990). Development of disabled readers' metacomprehension ability through summarization training using expository text: Results of three studies. *Journal of Reading, Writing, and Learning Disabilities International, 6,* 117–136.

Wixson, K. K., & Dutro, E. (1998). *Standards for primary-grade reading: An analysis of state frameworks.* (CIERA Report #3–001). Available online at http://www.ciera.org/library/reports/inquiry-3/3-001/3-001.html.

Wong, B. Y. L. (1986). The efficacy of a self-questioning summarization strategy for use by underachievers and learning disabled adolescents in social studies. *Learning Disabilities Focus, 2*(1), 20–35.

Wood, E., Willoughby, T., McDermott, C., Motz, M., Kaspar, V., & Ducharme, M. (1999). Developmental differences in study behavior. *Journal of Educational Psychology, 91,* 527–536.

Young, J. P., Mathews, S. R., Kietzman, A. M., & Westerfield, T. (1997). Getting disenchanted adolescents to participate in school literacy activities: Portfolio conferences. *Journal of Adolescent & Adult Literacy, 40,* 348–360.

Zakaluk, B. L., & Samuels, S. J. (1988). Toward a new approach to predicting comprehensibility. In B. L. Zakaluk & S. J. Samuels (Eds.), *Readability: Its past, present, and future* (pp. 121–144). Newark, DE: International Reading Association.

Zhao, Y. (2001, July 3). One-third of public school students enroll for summer school. *The New York Times,* p. B2.

Zolman, M. F., & Wagner, H. (2002, May). *Professional development plan for secondary teachers on strategies for struggling readers.* Paper presented at the annual meeting of the International Reading Association, San Francisco.

Zinsser, W. (1988). *Writing to learn.* New York: Harper & Row.

Trade Books and Textbooks

Angliss, S. (2000). *Gold (The Elements).* New York:Benchmark Books.

Badders, W., Bethel, L. J., Fu, V., Peck, D., Sumners, C., & Valentino, C. (1999a). *Discovery works 2.* Parsippany, NJ: Silver Burdett Ginn.

Badders, W., Bethel, L. J., Fu, V., Peck, D., Sumners, C., Valentino, C. (1999b). *Discovery works 4.* Parsippany, NJ: Silver Burdett Ginn.

Badders, W., Bethel, L. J., Fu, V., Peck, D., Sumners, C., Valentino, C. (1999c). *Discovery works 6.* Parsippany, NJ: Silver Burdett Ginn.

Berkin, P. (1984). *History of the American nation.* New York: Macmillan.

Biesty, S. (1998). *Incredible body.* New York: Platt.

Bledsoe, L. J. (1994). *Fearon's biology* (2nd ed.). Paramus, NJ: Globe Fearon.

Boorstin, D. J., & Kelley, B. M. (2002). *A history of the United States.* Upper Saddle River, NJ: Prentice Hall.

Bridges, R. (2000). *Through my eyes.* New York: Scholastic.

Brimblecombe, S., Gallannaugh, D., & Thompson, C. (1998). *QPB science encyclopedia.* New York: Helicon.

Brown, G. W., Syukys, P. A., Anderson, L. H. (1993). *Understanding business and personal law* (9th ed.). Lake Forest, IL: Glencoe.

Cather, W. (1900). The sentimentality of William Tavener. In V. Faulkner (Ed.) (1970), *Willa Cather's collected short fiction, 1892–1912.* (pp. 353–357).

Clay, R. (1997). *Ukraine, A new independence.* New York: Benchmark Books.

Cleary, B. (1983). *Dear Mr. Henshaw.* New York: Morrow.

Collier, C., & Collier, J. L. (1998). *The American Revolution.* New York: Marshall Cavendish Benchmark Books.

Collier, C., & Collier, J. L. (1999). *The Jeffersonian Republicans: The Louisiana Purchase and the War of 1812.* New York: Marshall Cavendish Benchmark Books.

Crane, S. (1985). The red badge of courage. In A. Mellors & F. Robertson (Eds.) (1998), *The red badge of courage and other stories.* New York: Oxford.

Crichton, M. (1990). *Jurassic Park.* New York: Random House.

Cuevas, M. M., & Lamb, W. G. (1994). *Holt physical science.* New York: Holt, Rinehart, and Winston.

Dickson, T. R. (1995). *Introduction to chemistry* (7th ed.). New York: Wiley.

Dixon, D. (1992). *The practical geologist.* New York: Simon & Schuster.

Dolan, E. (1995). *The American Revolution: How we fought the War of Independence.*

Duncan, L. (1977). *Summer of fear.* Boston: Little, Brown.

Ellis, E. G., & Esler, A. (2001). *World history: Connections to today.* Upper Saddle River, NJ: Prentice Hall.

Ellison, R. (1952). *The invisible man.* New York: Random House.

Exline, J. D., Pasachoff, J. M., Simons, B. B., Vogel, C. G., & Wellnitz, T. R. (2001). *Earth science.* Upper Saddle River, NJ: Prentice Hall.

Garcia, J. R., Gelo, D. J., Greenow, L. L., Kracht, J. B., & White, D. G. (1997a). *Our United States.* Parsippany, NY: Silver Burdett Ginn.

Garcia, J. R., Gelo, D. J., Greenow, L. L., Kracht, J. B., White, D. G. (1997b). *The world and its people.* Parsippany, NY: Silver Burdett Ginn.

Globe Fearon. (1994). *Basic mathematics* (3rd ed.). Paramus, NJ: Author.

Globe Fearon. (1994). *The Latino experience in U.S. history.* Paramus, NJ: Author.

Globe Fearon. (2000). *Basic mathematics* (4th ed.). Paramus, NJ: Author.

Goldstein, M. (1999). *Weather guide for complete idiots.* New York: Alpha Books.

Grolier. (1997). *Grolier multimedia encyclopedia.* Novato, CA: Mindscape.

Grolier Educational. (2000). *Grolier's new book of popular science series.* Danbury, CT: Grolier.

Hakim, J. (1993). *Oxford history of US: Making thirteen colonies.* New York: Oxford.

Hakim, J. (1994). *Oxford history of US: An age of extremism.* New York: Oxford.

Heiserman, D. L. (1992). *Exploring chemical elements and their compounds.* New York: McGraw Hill.

James, N. (1979). *Alone around the world.* New York: Coward, McCann & Geoghegan.

Kallen, S. A. (1999). *The 1950s.* San Diego, CA: Lucent.

King, D. C. (1996). *First facts about American heroes.* Woodbridge, CT: Blackbirch.

King, W. & Napp, J. (1998). *Our nation's history.* Circle Pines, MN: American Guidance Service, p. 524.

Klag, M. J. (1999). *Johns Hopkins family health book.* New York: HarperCollins.

Kneidel, S. (2001). *Stinkbugs, stick insects, and stag beetles and 18 more of the strangest insects on earth.* Boston: John Wiley.

LeMay, H. E., Beall, H., Robblee, K. M., & Brower, D. C. (2000). *Chemistry: Connections to our changing world.* Upper Saddle River, NJ: Prentice Hall.

LeVasseur, M.L., Schaleman, Jr., H. J., Sheldon, S., & Gleason, H.M. (2002). *World geography.* Upper Saddle River, NJ: Prentice-Hall, Inc.

Litwin, L. B. (1999). *Benjamin Bannneker, astronomer and mathematician.* Springfield, NJ: Enslow.

Malam, J. (1999). *Mesopotamia and the fertile crescent, 10,000 to 539 B.C.* Austin, TX: Raintree Steck Vaughn.

Massa, R., (1998). *Ocean environments.* Austin, TX: Steck Vaughn.

McKeever, S., & Foote, M. (1998). *The DK science encyclopedia.* New York: DK Publishing.

McKissack, P., & McKissack, P. (1986). *The new true book of the Maya.* Chicago: Children's Press.

Milani, J. P., Erk, S., McInerney, F. C., McIver, P. D., Mayer, W. V., Slowiczek, F., Stone, C. L., & Uno, B. E. (1987). *Biological science: An ecological approach* (6th ed.). Dubuque, IA: Kendall/Hunt. p. 18.

Miller, K. R., & Levine, J. (1998). *Biology, the living science.* Upper Saddle River, NJ: Prentice Hall.

Morgan, S. (1996). *Weather.* Syndney, AUS: Allen & Unwin.

Moss, J., & Wilson, G. (1998). *Profiles in American History: Civil Rights movement to the present.* Detroit, MI: UXL.

Neff, M. M. (1990). Legends: How Gordie Howe was a hockey star in his youth and also when he was a grandpa. *Sports Illustrated for Kids, 2*(2), p. 48.

Nicolson, C. P. *The planets.* Tornonto, ONT: Kids Can Press.

Nishi, D. (1998). *Life during the Great Depression.* San Diego, CA: Lucent Books.

O'Dell, S. (1980). *Sarah Bishop.* New York: Scholastic.

Parker, S. (1999). *An ant's life by Ant, With help from Steve Parker.* Pleasantville, NY: Readers Digest.

Press, P. (1999). *The 1930s.* San Diego, CA: Lucent

Roberts, P. C. (1997). *Ancient Rome.* New York: Time Life.

Ross, M. E. (2000). *Fish watching with Eugenie Clark.* Minneapolis, MN: Carolrhoda.

Sager, R. J., & Helgren, D. M. (1997). *World geography today.* New York: Holt, Rinehart & Winston.

Sattler, H. R. (1995). *Our patchwork planet: The story of plate tectonics.* New York: Lothrop, Lee & Shepherd.

Sauvain, P. (1996). *Oceans.* Minneapolis: Carolrhoda.

Schaaf, F. (1998). *40 nights to knowing the sky.* New York: Holt.

Silverstein, A., & Silverstein, V. (1998). *Symbiosis.* Brookfield, CT: Millbrook Press.

Simon, S. (1993). *Weather.* New York: Morrow.

Simon, S. (1998). *Now you see it, now you don't: The amazing world of optical illusions.* New York: Morrow.

Smith, M. (1996). *Living earth.* New York: Dorling Kindersley.

Snedden, R. (1999). *Earth and beyond.* Des Plaines, IL: Heinemann.

Speare, E. (1958). *The witch of Blackbird Pond.* Boston: Houghton Mifflin.

St. George, J. (2001). *John & Abigail Adams.* New York: Holiday.

Suter, J. (1994). *World history.* Paramus, NJ: Globe Fearon.

Uschan, M. V. (1999). *The 1950s: Cultural history of the United States through the decades.* San Diego, CA: Lucent Books.

William, K. (1986). *Sweet Valley High: Winter carnival.* New York: Bantam.

Wilson, J. H., & Clark, J. R. (1993). *South-western economics.* Cincinnati, OH: South-western.

Yolen, J. (1992). *Encounter.* Orlando, FL: Harcourt.

Zell, F. (1996). *A multicultural portrait of the American Revolution.* New York: Marshall Cavendish Benchmark Books.

Zeman, A., & Kelly, K. (1994). *Everything you need to know about science homework.* New York: Scholastic.

INDEX

Note: Page numbers followed by *f* and *t* indicate figures and tables, respectively.

Photo Credits

Pages 7, 139, 218, 236, © Michael Newman/PhotoEdit; pp. 11, 35, 422, © David-Young Wolff/PhotoEdit; pp. 52, 200, © Michelle Bridwell/PhotoEdit; pp. 75, 95, 124, © Will Faller; pp. 176–177, from *World Geography Today*, Revised Edition, Pupil's Edition. Copyright © 1997 by Holt Rinehart and Winston. Reprinted by permission of the publisher; pp. 178, 380, © Myrleen F. Cate/PhotoEdit; p. 185, © Jeff Greenberg/PhotoEdit; pp. 198, 269, 328, 415, 440, © Will Hart; p. 264, © Spencer Grant/PhotoEdit; p. 309, © Paul Conklin/PhotoEdit; pp. 311, 357, © Steve Skjold/PhotoEdit; pp. 333, 363, © Will Hart/PhotoEdit; p. 346, © Tony Freeman/PhotoEdit; p. 389, © Mary Kate Denny/PhotoEdit